ALSO BY ALEXANDRA RICHIE

Faust's Metropolis: A History of Berlin

WARSAW
1944

WARSAW 1944

1944

HITLER, HIMMLER, AND THE WARSAW UPRISING

ALEXANDRA RICHIE

PICADOR   FARRAR, STRAUS AND GIROUX   NEW YORK

Picador
120 Broadway, New York 10271

Originally published in 2013 by William Collins, an imprint of HarperCollins
Publishers, Great Britain, as *Warsaw 1944: The Fateful Uprising*
Published in the United States in 2013 by Farrar, Straus and Giroux
First Picador edition, 2019

The epigraphs at the beginning of each chapter are from *Appian Roman History*,
Volume I, Book VIII, I, *The Punic Wars*, ed. Jeffrey Henderson, trans. Horace White,
Harvard University Press, London, 1912.

Library of Congress Control Number: 2013950010
Picador Paperback ISBN: 978-0-374-53891-0

Our books may be purchased in bulk for promotional, educational, or business
use. Please contact your local bookseller or the Macmillan Corporate and
Premium Sales Department at 1-800-221-7945, extension 5442, or by e-mail
at MacmillanSpecialMarkets@macmillan.com.

Picador® is a U.S. registered trademark and is used by Macmillan Publishing Group,
LLC, under license from Pan Books Limited.

picadorusa.com • instagram.com/picador
twitter.com/picadorusa • facebook.com/picadorusa

For book club information, please visit facebook.com/picadorbookclub
or e-mail marketing@picadorusa.com.

1 3 5 7 9 10 8 6 4 2

For Antonia and Caroline

Contents

A photographic section follows page 370.

Illustrations

Hitler in Warsaw, 5 October 1939. *(Topfoto)*

Soviet troops advance on Warsaw in the summer of 1944. *(AKG)*

'Agaton' leads his troops to battle on 1 August 1944. *(Zygmunt Walkowski)*

A Warsawian attempts to cross a street to safety on the first day of the uprising. *(Zygmunt Walkowski)*

Barricade at Marszaticorska and Zlota streets. *(Zygmunt Walkowski)*

German troops in Wola. *(Zygmunt Walkowski)*

Heinz Reinefarth, who ordered the first wave of massacres in Wola. *(Zygmunt Walkowski)*

An Azeri unit sharing sausages with their German colleagues. *(Zygmunt Walkowski)*

Men, women and children killed on 5 August 1944.

Wanda Lurie and her son Mścisław. *(Courtesy Mścisław Lurie)*

Dirlewanger troops advancing. *(Zygmunt Walkowski)*

Hala Mirowska, one of the sites of mass murder by the Dirlewanger Brigade. *(Zygmunt Walkowski)*

A Polish flag raised over Starynkiewicza Square in the first days of the uprising. *(Zygmunt Walkowski)*

A Junkers landing at Okęcie airfield. *(Zygmunt Walkowski)*

A 'Karl' mortar, the largest self-propelled siege gun ever built. *(Zygmunt Walkowski)*

Aerial view of Warsaw during the uprising. *(National Archives and Records Administration (NARA), College Park Annex, microfilm and documents collections)*

Women being taken from Ochota to Zieleniak camp. *(Zygmunt Walkowski)*

Women and children on their way to Pruszków transit camp. *(Zygmunt Walkowski)*

Civilians and a German tank in Żelazna Brama Square. *(Zygmunt Walkowski)*

Krowas hurtling towards an AK-held area of Warsaw. *(Zygmunt Walkowski)*

Krowas being unloaded. *(Zygmunt Walkowski)*

A victim of a *Krowa* attack. *(Warsaw Rising Museum, http://www.1944. pl/en/)*

A 'Goliath' remote-controlled miniature tank. *(Zygmunt Walkowski)*

The Panzer train that bombarded the Old Town. *(Zygmunt Walkowski)*

German troops attack the Stone Steps in the Old Town. *(Zygmunt Walkowski)*

German soldiers clamber over rubble in the ruins of the Old Town. *(Zygmunt Walkowski)*

Germans remove their dead using stretchers provided by the AK. *(Zygmunt Walkowski)*

A mass grave in Długa Street. *(Warsaw Rising Museum, http://www.1944. pl/en/)*

Swastikas and red crosses painted on the roofs of buildings in Ochota to prevent German planes from bombing their own positions. *(National Archives and Records Administration (NARA), College Park Annex, microfilm and documents collections)*

Supplies dropped on Warsaw by the Western Allies. *(akg-images/East News)*

An AK soldier emerging from the sewers into German hands on Dworkowa Street. *(Mondadori via Getty Images)*

German soldiers drop leaflets informing Warsawians of the city's surrender. *(Zygmunt Walkowski)*

A German soldier guarding members of the resistance after the end of the uprising. *(Getty Images)*

Warsawians emerging from their hiding places. *(Zygmunt Walkowski)*

Two AK nurses leave the city as prisoners of war in October 1944. *(Zygmunt Walkowski)*

Von dem Bach presents a box containing Chopin's heart to the Archbishop of Warsaw.

Bór meets von dem Bach after the surrender. *(Topfoto)*

German troops setting fire to buildings around Warsaw Castle after the surrender. *(Zygmunt Walkowski)*

Maps

Poland, 1939

Baltic Sea

LITHUANIA

Memel

Kovno

Gdynia
Königsberg
Vilnius

Gdańsk

EAST
PRUSSIA

Minsk

GERMANY

Berlin

Bromberg

Annexed by Germany

Białystok

Brest-
Litovsk

Pinsk

Warsaw

Breslau

Łódź

P O L A N D

Annexed by USSR

Lublin

Prague

General
Government

USSR

Occupied
Czechoslovakia

Kraków

Lwów

Rovno

SLOVAKIA

0   50   100 miles
0   50   100   150 kms

HUNGARY

ROMANIA

WARSAW
1944

INTRODUCTION

—=•◦•=—

It was decreed that if anything was still left of Carthage, Scipio should raze it to the ground, and that nobody should be allowed to live there. (Chapter XX)

On 1 August 1944 Adolf Hitler was at his headquarters, the Wolfsschanze (Wolf's Lair) at Rastenburg, deep in East Prussia, and he was busy. Army Chief of Staff General Heinz Guderian and Field Marshal Walter Model had just launched a massive counter-offensive against the Red Army only a few kilometres north-east of Warsaw, and the Führer was waiting anxiously for progress reports. He was annoyed rather than angry when news about some skirmishes in the Polish capital began trickling in. Apparently some 'bandits' with red-and-white armbands had been shooting at the police. Hitler was not worried. The day before, he had sent his trusted 'fireman' General Reiner Stahel to take charge of Warsaw, and was convinced that the city was in good hands. Himmler, too, had assured him that there would be no uprising in the hated capital. 'My Poles will not revolt,' the German Governor in occupied Poland, Hans Frank, had chimed in.

But the problem did not go away, and by evening the Germans were starting to get worried. As time went on it became clear that these were not isolated incidents, but that the Poles had managed to stage a simultaneous, well-coordinated attack throughout the whole of Warsaw. By evening the 'unbeatable' Stahel was trapped in the Brühl Palace along with his staff, and could do nothing. 'Himmler wants answers!' SS Obergruppenführer Wilhelm Koppe, SS and police leader in Kraków, yelled at Brigadeführer Paul Otto Geibel in Warsaw. Geibel was cowering in the basement of his headquarters, which was also under fire, and his troops were pinned down. As news poured in about entire districts being overrun by Polish 'bandits', Himmler raced to see Hitler in Rastenburg. He found the Führer purple with rage.

Hitler had good reason to be angry. He had wanted Model's counter-offensive to be the great set piece of the summer of 1944: 'If the Eastern Front is stabilized,' he had told General Walter Warlimont the night before, 'it would show the Romanians, the Bulgarians, the Hungarians and also the Turks' that Germany was strong. The last thing he wanted was some 'Schweinerei' in Warsaw, which would make him look weak, and possibly even give other insurgents an excuse to start their own uprisings.

By this point in the war Hitler was quite deranged. He was more bothered by the injuries he had recently sustained in the 20 July assassination attempt than was commonly known, and was addicted to a cocktail of drugs, including cocaine, administered by his trusted doctor Theodor Morell. He had by now completely lost faith in his generals, whom he blamed for all past failures on the Eastern Front. He was in no mood for leniency. Himmler's first act upon hearing of the seriousness of the Warsaw Uprising was to send word to Berlin to have the captured Polish resistance leader General Stefan 'Grot' Rowecki murdered. Then he tried to calm Hitler down. This uprising was a blessing in disguise, he said. It would give them the excuse to do what they had wanted to do for years – to erase Warsaw from the map.

'*Mein Führer*,' Himmler said, 'the timing is unfortunate. But from a historical point of view it is a blessing that the Poles are doing this. We will get through the four or five weeks [it will take] and then Warsaw, the capital city, the brain, the intelligence of this sixteen-to-seventeen-million-strong Polish nation will have been obliterated. This nation, which has blocked our path to the east for seven hundred years and since the first battle of Tannenberg, has always been in the way. Then the historic problem will no longer be a major one for our children, for all those who come after us, or for us either.' Hitler, ever the opportunist, agreed. He and Himmler drafted the Order for Warsaw that evening. It stands as one of the most chilling documents of the war.

Warsaw was to be razed to the ground – '*Glattraziert*' – so as to provide a terrifying example for the rest of Europe. Himmler passed the order on to General Heinz Reinefarth personally. It read: '1. Captured insurgents ought to be killed regardless of whether they are fighting in accordance with the Hague Convention or not. 2. The part of the population not fighting, women and children, should likewise be killed. 3. The whole town must be levelled to the ground, i.e. houses, streets, offices – everything that is in the town.'

In one evening Himmler and Hitler had decided that the entire population remaining in one of Europe's great capital cities was to be murdered in cold blood. Then the city – which Himmler referred to as 'that great abscess' – was to be completely destroyed. Hitler had often talked before about the utter destruction of cities – Moscow, Leningrad, Minsk – but this was the first and only time he was actually able to put his insane ideas into practice. Tragically, this order was largely fulfilled. That is the story of this book.

Before the ravages of the Second World War, Warsaw was one of Europe's great capital cities. It had grown quickly in its seven-hundred-year history, reaching dizzying heights during the late-sixteenth- and early-seventeenth-century Polish-Lithuanian Commonwealth. In the nineteenth century its star had waned as it languished under hated Russian rule, but all that changed in 1918.

11 November might be a day of sombre commemoration in much of the world, but not in Poland: for the end of the First World War marked the rebirth of the Polish nation. The generation that came of age there in the 1920s and 1930s loved their capital and their country, and relished their newfound freedom. The city of Warsaw flourished once again.

The interwar Poles became known as the 'Columbus Generation', always on the lookout for something new and different. Warsaw was their spiritual home. The city had its political, economic and social problems, to be sure, but everything from theatre to newspapers, from cabaret to painting, took off. All government and military institutions had to be re-created from scratch, and new national institutions were founded by the dozen. Despite competition from Kraków and Lwów, Warsaw was fast becoming the political, finan-cial, cultural and intellectual centre of the Polish nation, and acted as a magnet for the most ambitious and creative people in the land. New social housing projects were built by innovative architects; hospitals, schools – indeed entire new districts like Żoliborz – were built for journalists, generals and civil servants. The university was a celebrated centre of learning, and its chemistry and mathematics faculties – under Wacław Sierpiński, who in turn was influenced by the great school in Lwów – led the world. Music, painting and experimental theatre were everywhere. Warsawians watched the first of Pola Negri's films, read Isaac Bashevis Singer's subtle depictions of Jewish life in the city, listened to new music by the likes of Karol Szymanowski and read the poetry of 'Young Picadors' including Jan Lechoń and Julian Tuwim. After 1933 Warsaw became temporary home to many refugees fleeing Hitler's Germany; for a brief time they added immeasurably to the life of the city.

This optimistic and vibrant world ended on 1 September 1939. Warsawians awoke that morning to the sound of bombs being dropped on their city. The world had never seen anything like it. It was as if Guernica, in which 1,650 people were killed, was a terrible rehearsal for Warsaw, which was pounded over the course of twenty-seven days in the first air terror attack of the war. On 25 September alone Major General Wolfram von Richthofen's bombers dropped five hundred tonnes of high explosives and seventy-two tonnes of incendiaries in 1,150 sorties. When the city capitulated on 27 September 25,000 people lay dead in the ruins. Hitler had made it clear – he wanted Warsaw destroyed.

The destruction of the Polish capital was more than mere metaphor; on the contrary, actual plans had been drawn up for the purpose. The 'Pabst Plan' of 1939, which Hitler approved just before his invasion of Poland, called for the removal of all but 80,000 of Warsaw's 1.3 million inhabitants; those who remained would be allowed to live only in the east-bank suburb of Praga. One hundred and thirty thousand Aryan Germans were to be brought from the Reich to live in the new, ideal German town which was to be built in place of the old Polish capital. The ideological justification for the erasure of Warsaw was simple. Warsaw had 'at one time been German', but had been 'corrupted' by the Poles and the Jews. In a 1942 edition of *Das Vorfeld* ('The Approach' – a periodical for Germans living in occupied Poland), the Nazi historian Dr Hans Hof wrote: 'In 1420, 85 per cent of the names of burghers in Warsaw were German, and they were the only ones who brought any cultural and economic life, administration and justice to the city.' 'Polish immigrants' changed the city for the worse, 'as they did in other such places founded by the Germans'.[1] The Germans had decided that only the Old Town was worth saving, along with a few palaces that might be used by Hans Frank and Hitler as official residences. The rest of the city was slated for destruction long before the Warsaw Uprising of 1944 broke out.

The first inhabitants to be targeted were the Polish elite; some 10,000 members of Warsaw's intelligentsia were murdered before the uprising. They included one in six of the staff of pre-war academic institutions and one in eight priests. Politicians and lawyers, architects and doctors, writers and businessmen – indeed anyone who might be a threat to the new Nazi order – could also expect to be taken away and killed.[2]

The next phase of repression marked the beginning of the most dreadful crime ever to take place on Polish soil – the extermination of the country's Jews. Beginning on 16 October 1939 the Germans began the systematic forced round-up of 400,000 Jews from the city and surrounding area into a newly created ghetto. From 1 April 1940 a wall was constructed around the district, effectively turning it into a gigantic prison. Food rations were deliberately cut to less than subsistence levels, with the result that by 1942 82,000 people had died of starvation, disease and maltreatment. Those who remained continued to be taken to Treblinka, where they were murdered.

On 19 April 1943 a small group of Jews decided to fight back. The Warsaw Ghetto Uprising happened not because the trapped fighters had any hope of defeating the Germans, but because they knew with certainty the fate that awaited them if they got on the trains. The Germans had left them a simple choice: either to die passively, or to die fighting. They chose the latter. The uprising was crushed, and carefully documented in the official SS report written by Jürgen Stroop. The ghetto was razed to the ground, and a concentration camp, populated largely by foreign Jews who had been sent there to clear the ruins of the ghetto, was set up in its place. Miraculously, a handful of the insurgents survived; some went into hiding under the ghetto's rubble, while others like Marek Edelman would later join in the Warsaw Uprising of 1944.

The German invasion came as a terrible shock to most Poles, and they resisted Nazi rule from the very beginning. The terror was so immediate and unrelenting that collaboration was rare. That, along with the bitterness and anger at the fact that their beloved country had been invaded by both Nazi Germany and Soviet Russia in 1939 meant that there was little serious cooperation with the enemy. There were no Polish quislings or Polish SS divisions during the Second World War; on the contrary, from the first day of the war Poles began to organize resistance movements throughout the country. By 1942 these had been consolidated under the AK – the Armia Krajowa, or Polish Home Army, which was under the auspices of the Polish government-in-exile in London. 'Grot' Rowecki, and following his arrest by the Gestapo his successor General Bór-Komorowski and others, eventually created a force of 300,000 volunteers, both men and women, which became the largest underground army in Europe. The AK was extremely well organized, with a military command structure based on the regular Polish army, but in which only pseudonyms were used, and members were only permitted to know those in their own 'cell', in case of interrogation. Weapons were gathered and recruits taught how to use them in secret training sessions; arsenals of equipment were hidden around the country; bombs were manufactured and plans drawn up for the eventual liberation of Poland.

As the Germans rounded up and imprisoned ever more

Warsawians the AK engaged in operations of its own. Intelligence-gathering was a priority, and the Poles were responsible for great coups like providing Britain and France with a reconstructed Enigma machine and a V-2 rocket; they also brought proof of the extermination of Polish Jews to the Western Allies. The AK was engaged in more practical matters, too, including the assassination of Nazi officials and collaborators on the streets of Warsaw, primarily carried out by the elite Directorate of Diversion, or 'Kedyw' unit.

Nor did the terror stop the Poles from carrying on their cultural life. The Nazis had banned schools, universities and all Polish cultural organizations, but Warsawians set up new clandestine ones – underground university degrees were awarded throughout the occupation, and concerts, poetry readings and secret cabarets which mocked the German rulers were features of underground life. The secret life of Warsaw was testament to the spirit of the city, and offers a glimpse into the reason so many young men and women were willing to fight and to lay down their lives for the city and the country they loved when the call came in 1944.

The AK had been planning an uprising from the beginning of the war. In the early years they had hoped that liberation might come from the west, from Allied forces, but by 1944 it was clear that it would be left to the Soviets to clear the Nazis from Eastern and Central Europe. Relations between the Poles and the Soviets had declined after Stalin's seizure of 'his' part of Poland in 1939; they reached rock bottom with the discovery of thousands of murdered Polish army officers in the mass graves of Katyń. The Poles knew that the Soviets were responsible for this crime, but when they called for an official Red Cross investigation Stalin feigned outrage, and used it as an excuse to break off relations with the 'London Poles' altogether, making it impossible for the Poles to cooperate with the Soviets in any meaningful way in the months to come. The Western Allies also knew that the Soviets were responsible for Katyń, but persisted in the charade that Hitler had committed the crime, so as not to annoy Stalin. It was an ominous foretaste of things to come.

Up until the summer of 1944 the AK's plans for an uprising, code-named 'Burza' (Tempest), had called for operations aimed mainly at harassing the Germans as they were retreating, and assisting the Red Army when and where possible. Warsaw had deliberately been left out of the plans because, as Bór put it, he wanted to protect the city and the civilian population from the ravages of war. Carefully laid plans saw weapons being stored throughout Poland; indeed, crucial caches were taken from Warsaw only days before the uprising began. But in July 1944 a series of events took place which changed everything. Years of careful work were thrown out in the heat of the moment. The consequences would be tragic for the city of Warsaw.

The Warsaw Uprising is very often treated as if it were an isolated event, somehow removed from the war going on around it. On the contrary, the uprising was critically linked to three crucial events which determined its future course: the Soviet Operation 'Bagration', the 20 July attempt to assassinate Hitler, and Walter Model's unexpected counter-offensive at the very gates of Warsaw on 29 July.

Bagration was the single greatest Nazi defeat of the Second World War. It began on 22 June 1944 – the third anniversary of Operation 'Barbarossa', the German invasion of the Soviet Union – and saw the Red Army sweep through Byelorussia at breakneck speed, taking Vitebsk and Orsha, Mogilev and Mińsk. Soviet soldiers surrounded hapless German troops in gigantic pockets and finished them off at their leisure. Three hundred thousand

German soldiers were killed; twenty-eight divisions lost. The scale of the disaster echoes that of Napoleon's Grande Armée in 1812, and ranks as one of the greatest military defeats of all time. In order to prove the scale of his victory to a disbelieving world, Stalin had 50,000 German prisoners of war marched through Moscow's Red Square on 17 July on their way to captivity.

The speed and force of the Soviet advance into Byelorussia shocked even Stalin. It had been planned that the Red Army would take a maximum of two hundred kilometres in the entire offensive; they covered that in a few days. The Poles watched as the Soviets raced towards Vilnius, Lwów and Lublin. The AK helped the Red Army soldiers as they entered Polish territory, and relations were cordial at first, but then the NKVD arrived, and began arresting anyone suspected of being involved in the Polish resistance. At the same time, Stalin announced the creation of a Soviet-backed Polish puppet government, known as the 'Lublin Poles'. It was soon abundantly clear that he was fighting a political as well as a military war, and that he wished to bring Poland under the Soviet yoke. The AK was powerless against the might of the Red Army, but its leaders believed that they could still make a political statement by protesting against Stalin's plans. They had fought in order to see the restoration of a free, liberal, democratic state led by the men who made up the government-in-exile in London; the vast majority of Poles longed for the same thing. They did not want to live under the Soviet oppression which Stalin was trying to impose on them. With the Red Army moving inexorably towards Warsaw, the decision was made to take a stand in the capital city, for the Poles to push the Germans out themselves, and to greet the Soviets as equals. Surely then the rest of the world would heed their call for independence, and put pressure on Stalin. The plan seemed so simple in those heady summer days.

The notion that the Germans were about to collapse was

widespread in Warsaw in the final days of July 1944. For weeks Warsawians had watched as bedraggled German soldiers made their way through the city, wounded, filthy and dejected. When news of the plot to kill Hitler reached Warsaw it really did seem as if the Third Reich was about to implode. The AK believed that the time was right to rise up against the departing Germans and seize the capital just before the Soviets arrived. They could welcome the Red Army into their city as the rightful 'hosts', and score an enormous political victory over Stalin. That, at least, was the plan.

The second important event of that summer in relation to the uprising was the 20 July attempt to assassinate Hitler at the Wolfsschanze, because it elevated Himmler at the expense of the Wehrmacht, with terrible consequences for Warsaw. The Führer survived the attack, only to become increasingly paranoid and suspicious of his generals. Himmler took advantage of their fall from grace, and worked to increase his own power. After the beginning of the Warsaw Uprising Guderian requested that Warsaw be put under the jurisdiction of the 9th Army, but Himmler wanted the prize for himself. Hitler deferred to the Reichsführer SS. As Guderian put it, 'Himmler had won'. The uprising would be put down not by regular troops, but by some of the most notorious of Himmler's SS thugs, who had honed their skills in the killing fields of Byelorussia – Erich von dem Bach-Zelewski, Oskar Dirlewanger, Bronisław Kaminski and members of Einsatzgruppe B, who had been unceremoniously ejected from their comfortable fiefdoms in the east. As a result of this decision, the crushing of the Warsaw Uprising would become the only major German ground combat operation of the Second World War to be run almost entirely by the SS.[3]

The third decisive event was Field Marshal Walter Model's counter-offensive, which began only hours before the start of the uprising. It was the only major offensive launched by the Germans against the Soviets in the summer of 1944, and it too would have far-reaching consequences.

On 31 July the people in the countryside around the pretty town of Radzymin, thirty-five kilometres east of Warsaw, felt the earth shaking underfoot as if in an earthquake. Smoke and dust filled the air as countless tanks rumbled across the sandy fields and into position. The battle against the Soviets was about to begin.

Model and Guderian had amassed some of their best troops for the attack: the Waffen SS Viking Panzer and Totenkopf Divisions, the Luftwaffe's Hermann Göring Division, General von Saucken's 39th Panzer Korps and the 4th and 19th Panzer Divisions. It was a formidable force, and it slammed into the unsuspecting Red Army as it made its way towards Warsaw, changing the course of the war.

Like Bagration itself, these battles are now largely forgotten, but they were titanic clashes, with the loss of hundreds of tanks. The Battle of Wolomin was the largest tank battle fought on Polish soil in the entire war, and it saw the German Panzer divisions crush the Soviet 3rd Tank Corps and maul the 8th Guards Tank Corps. Fierce fighting raged for weeks throughout the area; indeed, the Soviets would succeed in finally pushing all of the German forces over the Vistula only in January 1945. One consequence was that even if Hitler had wanted to send regular troops in to retake Warsaw there were simply none available; all were needed at the front.

Tragically, the Poles waiting in Warsaw mistook the distant sounds of battle for the triumph of the Red Army. With no direct contact with the Soviets, they could only guess at what was happening, and they miscalculated badly. The AK's Warsaw commander Colonel 'Monter' rushed into a meeting at 5 o'clock on 31 July with the incorrect information that the Soviets 'are in

Praga, and urged that to delay the uprising would be a disaster. General Bór – who was in many ways unsuited for the role thrust upon him by history – did not wait for verification, but gave the order to commence the uprising. Neither Bór nor Monter had understood the significance of Model's counter-offensive. There was now no way that the Red Army could have reached Warsaw in the first week of August, but the Poles did not know that. Mobilization for the uprising had already begun. It would commence at 5 p.m. on 1 August, and it would ultimately bring utter destruction to the city of Warsaw.

When ancient Carthage began to rebuild itself in the second century BC, after the Second Punic War, the Romans were worried. The city was seen as a threat to Roman domination of North Africa; and after some deliberation Rome's senators decided that it had to be attacked, conquered, and erased from history.

They knew that the task would not be easy. Carthage was strongly fortified, and it contained a desperate population who were determined to fight rather than be crushed into submission by the Romans.

The attack began in 149 BC; Carthage fought back, and the Romans set up a siege. The Carthaginians defended their city like lions, fighting from house to house and street to street, but eventually the Romans proved too powerful, and Carthage capitulated in 146 BC. Fifty thousand of its inhabitants were sold into slavery, the city walls were torn down and the city razed to the ground. It is said that the Romans even sowed salt in the ruins so that nothing would grow there. Carthage had ceased to exist.

Hitler might well have modelled his treatment of Warsaw on that ancient city. In his play *The Fall of Carthage* the Nazi writer Eberhard Wolfgang Möller championed the great Roman republic – the bearer of all civilization – and applauded it for grinding 'corrupt' and 'venal' Carthage into the dust. The Berlin audiences clapped and cheered. For Hitler, the symbolism was clear.

If Carthage is the epitome of the wanton destruction of a great city in the ancient world, the sacking of Warsaw was its unique counterpart in modern history. No European capital has undergone such trauma at the hands of an invader. After the merciless bombing raids that began on 1 September 1939 its population was terrorized by the Gestapo, and almost its entire Jewish community was murdered. During the uprising of the summer of 1944 its people were massacred, besieged, pulverized and burned. In the end the entire population, which before the war had numbered over 1.3 million people, was gone. More than 400,000 of Warsaw's Jews were dead. Over 150,000 of its remaining citizens died during the uprising and lay buried under the rubble; 18,000 members of the AK also lay dead. The remaining citizens might still have found shelter in the city, but Hitler would not permit anyone to remain; hapless civilians were hauled from their shelters and sent to Pruszków transit camp on the outskirts of the city, from where 60,000 innocent men, women and a substantial number of children were despatched to concentration camps including Auschwitz, Ravensbrück and Dachau, where many of them perished. Nearly 100,000 people were sent as forced labourers to the Reich, the last source of cheap labour for Albert Speer and Fritz Sauckel.[4] Ernst Kaltenbrunner, chief of the RSHA, the Reich's Security Office, warned of the security risk of so many young men being brought to German towns; as a result more children and women were used instead. Families were deliberately split up at Pruszków; many were never reunited.

The rest – those too old or too sick to be of any use to the Reich – were sent off to find somewhere to live in occupied Poland. This too was fraught with problems. The poor people in the countryside had no place for them, and many refugees were forced to eke out an existence by tending animals or cooking. One group, above all, remained in grave danger throughout.

For a brief moment in August 1944, when the city was 'free', Warsaw's Jews had been rid of Nazi tyranny, but as the Germans retook district after district the terror returned with them. The Poles suffered terribly during the uprising, but the danger for the Jews was infinitely worse – even at the very end the Germans showed no mercy, and killed any they could find. SS specialists under Alfred Spilker scoured the crowds of refugees trudging to Pruszków for anyone who looked Jewish; they were taken aside and shot. Some, like Stanisław Aronson and Yehuda Nir, miraculously survived by mingling in the crowds; others, like Władysław Szpilman and other so-called 'Robinsons', took their chances by hiding in the stricken city until Soviet liberation in January 1945.

The fate of those Warsawians who decided to stay after the capitulation to the Germans is one of the little-known stories of tenacity and human courage to come out of the uprising. These men and women were sometimes literally buried alive in bunkers for weeks or months at a time, facing not only desperate shortages of food and water, but also the fear of discovery as Hitler's squads looted and ravaged the city. The Germans found many of the secret hiding places during this orgy of destruction; untold numbers were killed. This was made worse when in October General Smilo Freiherr von Lüttwitz of the 9th Army heard that there were still 'sneaky Poles' hiding in the ruins, and sent out special teams to search the city for them.

With the people gone, Hitler began to loot and destroy in earnest. Hundreds of trains laden with goods left Warsaw for the Reich; over 45,000 wagons loaded with everything from dismantled factories to works of art were sent from Warsaw between August 1944 and January 1945; lorry-loads of goods followed, until there was nothing of value left. Then the demolition began.

Special 'destruction kommandos' armed with flamethrowers, mines and bombs were sent in to level everything – churches and synagogues, museums and archives, hospitals and factories. It was an atrocious act of sheer spite, done despite the fact that at the time the Germans were desperately short of manpower and matériel. Hitler insisted on carrying on, and 30 per cent of the destruction of Warsaw happened after capitulation. When the Soviets finally entered on 17 January 1945 they found a silent ruin of a city. The destruction of Warsaw was one of the great tragedies of the Second World War. And yet, after 1945, the Polish capital's terrible ordeal virtually disappeared from history.

The Poles who had fought so hard for their freedom did not regain it. Instead, one monstrous dictatorship was replaced by another, and Stalin ensured that mention of the uprising was suppressed. Those who tried to comment on it were silenced; tens of thousands of AK members were arrested, deported and killed.

The Poles may not have been permitted to mention the uprising; the Germans simply did not want to. If one reads the self-serving memoirs that appeared in East and West Germany after the war, one would be forgiven for thinking that the uprising had not happened at all. Even serious histories of the Second World War seem to gloss over the summer and autumn of 1944 on the Eastern Front as if nothing in particular was happening in Poland, and none of the main criminals of the uprising was ever brought to justice. The Germans, of course, had every reason not to want to discuss one of the most terrible crimes of the Second World War, and whereas there are thousands of memoirs of Stalingrad or Kursk, the library shelves are sparse when it comes to Warsaw. At Nuremberg the Nazi defendants fell over themselves to deny and cover up their involvement in the crushing of the uprising. Guderian was one of the most creative. When asked about the order to destroy the city, he said that at times it was 'very difficult to recognize if an order which we got was against international law . . . it is also difficult for generals because they didn't study international law'. Von dem Bach claimed that he had arrived in Warsaw in 'mid-August'; even in his diary (which was not available during the trial) he admitted that he was already there on 6 August. Reinefarth, too, lied about the date of his arrival so as not to be linked to the massacres he had ordered on 5 August. On 23 September 1946 he testified at Nuremberg: 'Around 6 August 1944 I met Himmler in Posen . . . Around 8 August I reported to von Vormann in Warsaw.' He claimed that not until the 9th did he first set foot on Wolska Street – over a week after his actual arrival.[5]

The Soviets, too, glossed over their involvement – or lack thereof. Red Army commanders Zhukov and Rokossovsky briefly mention Warsaw in their memoirs, but Zhukov is careful to chide Bór for not having contacted the Soviets before calling for the uprising, and Rokossovsky claims that the Soviet forces were too exhausted to carry on the fight in the summer of 1944. Both almost ignore the uprising itself, hastening on to the conquest of Berlin. Official Soviet histories of the war are no better, maintaining the line that the Red Army had to stop at the Vistula to be re-supplied; even today official histories claim that the uprising was a 'reckless adventure' inspired by the British and the irresponsible AK. After the war Stalin imposed a ban on any but approved accounts of the uprising; even the famous author and journalist Vasily Grossman was discouraged from writing about it.

The uprising was not particularly well known in the West during the war, and any memory of it quickly faded after 1945. Things were hard enough, and people set about rebuilding their lives with little thought to the fate of those now trapped behind the Iron Curtain. Émigré Poles tried to keep the memories of the uprising alive, but their accounts were read largely within Polish circles. The Poles did not participate in the official celebrations of VE-Day in London, despite their valiant contribution to the war. It was easier to forget.

In Poland the artificial vow of silence imposed on the uprising changed dramatically with the collapse of Communism in 1990. It was as if, having been forced to be silent for so long, a great geyser of memory was unleashed, and the history of the uprising became a focal point of Warsaw life. Statues, monuments and street names commemorating every battalion and leader of the AK sprang up like mushrooms; histories and memoirs abounded; the Museum of the Warsaw Uprising was opened on the sixtieth anniversary of the conflict; re-enactments of famous battles became commonplace on the streets; and there was even a board game to teach children as they played. It was right that the people of the battered city should finally be able to commemorate the history of this terrible period; the annual wreath-laying to the dead of Warsaw on 1 August, and the ensuing minute of silence, during which the whole city stops, is very moving. But the pendulum swung so far that many accounts of the uprising read like hagiographies, in which the AK and its soldiers could do no wrong, and the only things that failed in the uprising were the Western Allies and Stalin. Strangely, in all these accounts there is very little information about the suffering of Warsaw's civilians, and even less about the activities of the occupying Germans. This book is an attempt to redress the balance.

It is not intended to be a complete history of the Warsaw Uprising. The fundamental questions which inform the whole are why, at the end of July 1944, when the Germans had virtually abandoned the city, did they suddenly decide to return to it; and why, when the uprising began, did they crush it with such viciousness? This is not a book about what 'should' have happened, or what 'might' have happened, or what Stalin or the Western Allies 'could' have done – it is a story of what actually did happen in the summer of 1944, in particular between the Germans and the Poles. My aim has been to synthesize many different elements of the uprising into a single narrative. I begin with a framework of military and political history in order to put the uprising in context, not only of the relationships between Churchill, Roosevelt and Stalin, but also in relation to the war on the Eastern Front, including the Soviet summer offensive Operation 'Bagration', to Hitler's racial war of extermination, and to the coming Cold War. It is impossible to avoid 'top-down' history when writing about an event so dominated by Hitler and Himmler. These men wielded such enormous power that any order they issued was followed unquestioningly by every level of the Nazi hierarchy; when the order went out in early August to destroy Warsaw and kill all its inhabitants, everyone from Guderian to von Vormann, Reinefarth and von dem Bach fell into line, despite the fact that the policy made no military sense. The behaviour, likewise, of Stalin, Churchill and Roosevelt is also crucial to understanding the uprising in a broader context.

But such conventional political and military history alone contains almost no information on the ordinary people whose lives were so affected by these men and their policies. The solution was to weave 'grassroots' history into the narrative, adding dozens of personal testimonies and accounts by combatants and civilians alike to show what it was actually like to live through this ordeal. The Nazis practised the deliberate dehumanization of their victims, referring to them as 'pieces' and burning their bodies on pyres on the streets of Warsaw to remove the evidence of their violent deaths. I have tried to pay homage to at least some of these people by attempting to bring their stories to life. Because I ask why Hitler and Himmler decided to crush the Polish capital with such irrational brutality, I have also concentrated on the 'interface' between Germans and Poles in Warsaw: as a result I looked for testimonies not just from the Poles themselves, but also from others who found themselves in Warsaw that summer, from foreign journalists to SS men guarding the prisoners of the 'Cremation Commando', and from Wehrmacht soldiers who longed to get out of the 'second Stalingrad' to the troops of the Soviet-led Berling's Army, who crossed the Vistula only to die in their hundreds under German fire.

Traditionally, the destruction of the Warsaw ghetto and the Warsaw Uprising have been treated as two entirely separate events. This is understandable, as the liquidation of the ghetto and the murder of its inhabitants is a unique and terrible crime in history. Even so, the story of Warsaw's Jewish population did not begin or entirely end with the destruction of the ghetto. It is often forgotten that many Jews were also killed in the bombing of 1939, and that many of those who survived the horrors of the ghetto would die in the 1944 uprising or its aftermath. Throughout, I have tried to trace the fate of some who did manage to survive – Władysław Szpilman and Stanisław Aronson amongst others – in an attempt to show the uniquely perilous existence they led in the wartorn city. I have also tried to show that the Jewish tragedy was also a tragedy for the city of Warsaw in its entirety, and also affected the uprising of 1944. As Gunnar Paulsson put it, 'Ninety-eight per cent of the Jewish population of Warsaw perished in the Second World War, together with one-quarter of the Polish population: in all, some 720,000 souls . . . undoubtedly the greatest slaughter perpetrated within a single city in human history'.[6] My references to Carthage are a deliberate attempt to emphasize the epic scale of the tragedy of this city.

I

BYELORUSSIAN PRELUDE

Scipio finding no sort of discipline or order in the army, which Piso had habituated to idleness, avarice, and rapine, and a multitude of hucksters mingled with them, who followed the camp for the sake of booty, and accompanied the bolder ones when they made expeditions for plunder without permission. (Chapter XVII)

The Bandit Wars

'Before battle,' the Soviet journalist Ilya Ehrenburg wrote, 'there is a period of great stillness – nowhere is there such a stillness as in war.' In the spring of 1944 Germany waited, knowing that the Western Allies and the Soviet Union were both planning their summer offensives, but not knowing when or where they would come. The tension was palpable.

In Warsaw, too, people were waiting. Life under Nazi occupation, with the constant fear of an early-morning knock at the door by the Gestapo or the SD (the Sicherheitsdienst – the intelligence service), had led to the Armia Krajowa, the Polish Underground Army, becoming the largest of its kind in occupied Europe. Sheer Nazi brutality and racially motivated crimes

– against the Polish Jews above all, but also the hated Slavs – had ruled out the kind of cooperation between occupier and occupied experienced by other peoples deemed 'racially acceptable' by the Germans. The AK had spent much of the war attacking and sabotaging the German war effort and planning for further action, and as the tide turned against the Germans after Stalingrad the number of assassinations of German officials on the streets of Warsaw rose steadily. One of the AK's plans, the most ambitious of all, was code-named 'Burza', or Tempest. It called for an uprising to be held when the Red Army entered pre-war Polish territory. It was to be a military uprising, in that Polish soldiers would help the Soviets push the Nazi occupiers out of their country, but it was also to have a political element. By participating in the fight to liberate their own country, the insurgents hoped to establish the right to the restoration of a free independent state when the hostilities were over. The Poles watched and waited in the spring of 1944, ready to act as soon as the Red Army moved in.

Despite the impending downfall of Nazi Germany, Adolf Hitler was in a surprisingly buoyant mood that spring, not least because of the injections of glucose and, soon, cocaine administered by his trusted but utterly incompetent doctor, Theodor Morell. The Führer was increasingly losing touch with reality. When the Luftwaffe ace Günter Rall saw him in early 1944 he said, 'This was a very different Hitler. He was no longer talking about tangible facts. He was talking about: "I see the deep valley. I see the strip on the horizon," and it was all nonsense . . . It was clear to me that this man was a little out of his mind. He did not have a truly clear, serious concept of the situation.'[1]

Hitler was enjoying cosy domestic life 'at home' in the Berghof in the Bavarian mountains, far from the desperate privations of the Eastern Front, and his gloomy Prussian headquarters, the Wolfsschanze (Wolf's Lair) at Rastenburg, where the forced labourers of Organization Todt were pouring seven metres of concrete as a protective layer against Soviet bombs. Bunkers had been dug on 'The Mountain' too, and camouflage netting shrouded the buildings, but Hitler lived as if the war was no more than a distant, irrelevant skirmish. He spent mornings in bed, rising late for his vegetarian Bircher-Benner breakfast prepared in the cavernous kitchen by his dietician Constanze Manziarly. Then he would relax in the company of the Berghof 'regulars' – SS General Sepp Dietrich, Armaments Minister Albert Speer, the grossly obese Dr Morell, his close friend Walther Hewel, and his personal secretary, Martin Bormann. Other guests came and went, joining in the customary afternoon stroll to the 'little tea house' on the Mooslahner Kopf, where Hitler had his customary cocoa and apple pie. Eva Braun and the other 'girls', Margaret Speer, Anni Brandt and Eva's sisters Ilse and Gretl, would lounge on the terrace, play in the bowling alley or watch the latest films in the projection room, commenting on fashion trends and the hairstyles of the stars.

As the clouds of the Allied invasion of Europe loomed, Hitler, perversely, seemed to grow more confident. On 3 June he threw a lavish party to celebrate the wedding of Eva Braun's sister Gretl. The groom was Hermann Fegelein, who would play a key role in the Warsaw Uprising.

Fegelein was a suave playboy, a charmer and a mass murderer rolled into one. He had risen to power thanks to Reichsführer Heinrich Himmler, who treated the witty and sleek young man almost like a son. It was Himmler who had plucked the young Hermann out of obscurity to make him Commander of the new SS Main Riding School in Munich, before promoting him through the ranks to become SS Gruppenführer with the 8th SS Cavalry Division Florian Geyer, a unit which was particularly ruthless in the fight against partisans in the east under Erich von dem Bach-Zelewski. When Fegelein was wounded on the Russian Front for the third time, Himmler brought his favourite home and appointed him Waffen SS Liaison Officer at Führer headquarters. This not only got Fegelein away from the front, but also gave Himmler even more access to and power over Hitler. It was an inspired choice.

Fegelein's influence on the uprising came about in part because of his skill as a horseman. Before the war he had competed in a number of events on the international circuit, and had even created the equestrian facilities for the 1936 Berlin Olympic Games. One of his long-time competitors, and a man he admired, was a Polish cavalry officer named Count Tadeusz Komorowski, who trained the Polish eventing team which won a silver medal at the Olympics. What Fegelein did not know was that Brigadier-General Bór-Komorowski, as he was now known ('Bór' being his wartime code-name), had, a few months before the lavish wedding party, been appointed commander of the Polish Home Army based in Warsaw. Even as the SS cavalry officer was quaffing champagne and flirting with Eva Braun, General Bór was planning the uprising that would link the two men once again.

The day after the wedding, on 4 June 1944, Field Marshal Erwin Rommel, on his way to his holiday home, talked to Hitler about the expected Allied invasion of France. Rommel agreed with Hitler that the Allies were most likely to strike at the Pas de Calais, and reminded him that the most important thing was that they must not be allowed to establish a bridgehead on the coast. Hitler was confident that any invasion in the heavily fortified and well-defended area could be easily repulsed. Which is why, when German sentries looked out over the grey waters of the English Channel two days later, they could hardly believe their eyes. The first of 1,200 warships were slowly coming towards them, but they were not heading to the Pas de Calais. They were on their way to Normandy.

Hitler, as was his custom, had taken a cocktail of sleeping pills the previous night, and did not wake up until midday. 'The Führer always gets the latest news after he has had his breakfast,' the duty adjutant snapped at an impatient Albert Speer. When he finally emerged, Hitler, still in his dressing gown, listened calmly as Rear Admiral Karl-Jesco von Puttkamer told him that a number of major landings had taken place between Cherbourg and Le Havre; more were expected. Hitler sent for the head of the armed forces, Field Marshal Wilhelm Keitel, and his deputy Colonel General Alfred Jodl, but all three agreed that this was a diversion, and nothing more than an Allied trick. Hitler opted to do nothing.

Colonel Hans von Luck, head of Kampfgruppe von Luck, was in the thick of the fighting on the coast, and desperately trying to inform his superiors that he was witnessing an invasion on an unimaginable scale. 'We were dismayed and angry that we had not been believed by the highest authority. And even by evening the Panzer divisions and reserve units stationed in the Pas de Calais were not to be withdrawn, on express orders from Hitler.' At 4.55 p.m. Hitler revealed his complete lack of understanding of the situation by giving the extraordinary order that the Allies' bridgehead was 'to be annihilated by the evening'. Perversely, he seemed almost relieved by the invasion: 'When they were in Britain we could not get at them. Now we have them where we can destroy them.' Later, Keitel admitted his mistake: 'If we had fully believed our radio intelligence interception we would not only have had the date of the invasion, we would even have had the exact time.' When Hitler and his generals finally realized their error it was, as von Luck put it, 'too late, much too late!'[2]

A furious Rommel met Hitler on 17 June in the gigantic concrete bunker near Soissons, in northern France, that had been designated the Führer's western HQ. By now over 600,000 Allied troops had landed in Normandy. Rommel was critical of Hitler's tactics, complaining, 'The battle is hopeless!' 'Just take care of your invasion front,' Hitler snarled in reply. 'I shall take care of the future of the war.' Thereafter, Rommel began to criticize Hitler openly, and lent his support to the 20 July plotters who were planning to assassinate the Führer. When Hitler discovered his treachery, Rommel, who was idolized by the German people, was given the opportunity to commit suicide rather than face a public show trial that would have resulted not only in his own death but also in the persecution of his family. Rommel chose suicide. Keitel revealed the truth about Rommel's supposed 'heart attack' only after the war.[3]

The Normandy landings shocked the Germans, but the news was received with jubilation in occupied Europe. Warsaw was abuzz with rumour and speculation. The success of the western attack meant, quite simply, that the war was coming to an end. The landings also came as a great relief to Stalin. Germany was now forced to fight on two fronts, and would have to divert resources away from the east. But, as ever, Stalin's reasons were not purely military. The pathologically suspicious dictator had feared that, despite Roosevelt and Churchill's assurances at the Tehran Conference in November 1943, they might actually invade Europe through the Balkans rather than France. Now he could remain true to the promise he had made to the British and American leaders: 'The summer offensive of the Soviet troops to be launched in keeping with the agreement reached at the Tehran Conference will begin in mid-June in one of the vital sectors of the Front,' he wrote. Stalin was careful not to mention exactly where the attack would take place, but he had already chosen his target. The Red Army was going to attack the German Army Group Centre, in Byelorussia.

Practising Murder

When Oskar Dirlewanger, the leader of one of the most notorious SS units in the war, was asked why he was behaving in such a brutal fashion in Warsaw in August 1944, he laughed. 'This is nothing,' he said proudly. 'You should have seen what we did in Byelorussia!'[4] He was right: the people of Byelorussia endured one of the most cruel and murderous occupations of the Second World War. The number of victims, particularly helpless civilians, is staggering. Nine million people lived in Soviet Byelorussia when the Germans invaded Russia in 1941, and two million of them, at the very least, were killed – by shooting, gassing, hanging, burning, drowning. A further two million were deported to the Reich as forced labour. Although there were exceptions, most were treated little better than livestock. On 21 August 1942 Hitler told the Nazi racial theorist Achim Gercke: '[Fritz] Sauckel [head of the deployment of forced and slave labour] told me a very curious fact. All the girls whom we bring back from the eastern territories are medically examined, and 25 per cent of them are found to be virgins.'[5]

The Germans killed civilians in 5,295 different locations in Soviet Byelorussia, with many villages being burned to the ground. The victims included around 700,000 prisoners of war, 500,000 Jews and 320,000 'partisans' or 'bandits', the vast majority of whom were unarmed civilians. The Germans deliberately mixed these groups together, killing Jews under the guise of the 'anti-bandit' war, or murdering peasants accused of 'helping Jews and partisans'. One German commander admitted that 'the bandits and Jews burned in houses and bunkers were not counted'. The victims were slaughtered with pitiless cruelty, and those not murdered outright often died as the result of cold, disease or starvation brought about by the German scorched-earth policy and the creation of 'dead zones', in which all living things, including people, were to be destroyed on sight.

The men who directed and oversaw the mass murder in Byelorussia included Erich von dem Bach-Zelewski, Oskar Dirlewanger and Bronisław Kaminski. Although they subsequently became best-known for their roles in the Warsaw Uprising, they learned their skills long before the summer of 1944. Indeed, in order to understand what happened in Warsaw one has first to look at the history of the killing fields of Byelorussia. It was precisely because Operation 'Bagration', the Soviet invasion of Byelorussia, was so rapid and successful in the summer of 1944 that so many of these hardened murderers were uprooted and suddenly available when Hitler and Himmler decided to put down the 'Schweinerei' in the Polish capital. In that sense the Warsaw Uprising became an extension of the policies that had been carried out in Byelorussia between 1941 and the summer of 1944. The personnel and the methods were the same; only the location had changed.

The sheer idiocy of German racial policy from a purely strategic point of view was never more clear than in Byelorussia and Ukraine. When they first arrived in the summer of 1941, the Germans were seen as liberators. Local people lined the dusty village tracks offering them bread and salt and boiled eggs, and winding flowers around the barrels of the advancing tanks. 'Women often came out of their houses with an icon held before their breast, crying, "We are still Christians. Free us from Stalin who has destroyed our churches." ' The inhabitants were relieved to be rid of Stalin, of the NKVD, of engineered famine and forced collectivization. Life under the Germans simply had to be better. Hans Fritzsche, who worked in Goebbels' Propaganda Ministry, was able to drive through villages near Kiev and Kharkov in German military uniform, 'alone, unguarded . . . I slept peacefully in farmhouses and was fed by the population . . . Yet three-fourths of a year later, that whole country through which I had travelled was full of partisans – villages were burned, people shot, hostages taken, and general terror ensued.'[6] Ukrainian Archbishop Count Andrij Scheptycky wrote to Pope Pius XII on 29 August 1942: 'When the German army first appeared to liberate us from the Bolshevik yoke, we experienced at first a feeling of some relief. But that lasted no more than one or two months. Step by step, the Germans introduced their regime of terrible cruelty and corruption . . . It simply appears that a band of madmen, or of rabid dogs, have descended upon the poor population.'[7] It is a testament to the brutality and barbarity of the Nazis' policy that they were able to turn entire populations against them in such a short time. But this racial element could not be tempered; it was the very basis of the Nazi ideology.

Hitler was obsessed by the idea of 'Lebensraum', and the need to conquer huge territories in the east for the resettlement of the German people. In 'Generalplan Ost' Himmler described how the conquered lands were to be 'Germanized'. The local inhabitants were to be either killed, transported to western Siberia, or kept as slaves. The Jewish population was to be completely annihilated – or, in Nazi terminology, given 'special treatment' – and the Slavic population was, according to von dem Bach at the Nuremberg Trials, to be reduced by around thirty million human beings. The conquered land was to be settled by Germans in new, romantic, medieval-style villages and towns, with officials set up in local palaces and ex-soldiers and deserving families given their own farmsteads in which to live out the pastoral idyll of Nazi mythology. There was no room for human empathy or compassion towards the victims of this massive undertaking.

Both Hitler and Himmler believed that cruelty and domination was a better way to control the east than any kind of benign rule:

collective punishment and mass murder would intimidate the local populations, and the instilling of terror would make the conquered people malleable and submissive.

In a secret speech of 30 March 1941, recorded in his diary by Army Chief of the General Staff Franz Halder, Hitler told his officers to forget old notions of honour and decency in the east. 'The war against Russia will be such that it cannot be conducted in a knightly fashion,' he said. 'This struggle is one of ideologies and racial differences and will have to be conducted with unprecedented, unmerciful, and unrelenting harshness.' In the terrible 'Commissar Order' of 6 June 1941, Hitler stated that Jews, Soviet officials and Red Army political commissars were to be executed on sight. Enemy civilians would not be protected by law, guerrillas were to be 'relentlessly liquidated', and all attacks by 'enemy civilians' were to be suppressed at once by the military 'using the most extreme methods'. The Barbarossa Decree outlined by Hitler during a meeting with military officials on 30 March 1941, and officially issued by Field Marshal Keitel, had called for a war of extermination of the political and intellectual elites of Russia. All normal codes of war were to be forgotten when it came to the conquered peoples of Eastern Europe. German officers were entitled to order the execution without trial or any formalities of any person suspected of 'having a hostile attitude' towards the Germans, 'collective responsibility' could be applied to the residents of an area where an attack had occurred, and German soldiers were to be 'exempted from criminal responsibility' even if their acts contravened German law. It was, in effect, a licence to commit murder. A Wehrmacht officer wrote: 'Today we had to take all of [the males] from the village that were left behind last time . . . You can imagine the wailing of the women as even the children were taken from them . . . Three houses in a village were set on fire by us, and a woman burned to death as a result. So it will be uniformly along the front in all the villages . . . It was a fantastic sight for the eye to behold, as far as you could see, only burning villages.'[8] Of all those involved in creating the terrible 'landscape of horror and death', one of Hitler's most willing and enthusiastic disciples was Erich von dem Bach-Zelewski.

'Skunk!' Hermann Göring would scream from the dock, to the surprise of all in the courtroom at Nuremberg. 'Swine!' Göring would erupt in a fury after listening to the testimony of his erstwhile colleague von dem Bach, who had turned witness for the prosecution. 'He is the bloodiest murderer in the whole damn setup!' Göring screamed again, waving his fist. Von dem Bach said nothing. 'He is selling his soul to save his stinking neck,' Göring went on, getting louder and louder. Jodl, equally angry, chimed in: 'Ask the witness if he knows that Hitler held him up to us as a model partisan-fighter. Ask the dirty pig that!' As von dem Bach stepped down, it seemed as if Göring was about to have a heart attack. His face was red and he could barely breathe. '*Schweinhund!*' he screamed. '*Verräter.*'[9]

Göring, though not one to talk, had a point. Erich von dem Bach-Zelewski became a master at rounding up civilians and killing them, and later, when labour was needed back at home, at sending selected people off as forced labour in the Reich. Byelorussia taught him how to control large civilian populations, a lesson he would put to devastating use in Warsaw. It is testimony to his ability to lie, to deceive and to appear respectable that he managed to convince the Allies to allow him to act as a witness at Nuremberg. This saved his life, although he had earned a place in the dock alongside Göring, Frank, Kaltenbrunner and the rest.

The chubby, jovial, bespectacled Erich von Zelewski, with his impish smile and dimpled chin, was born in Lauenburg in Pomerania in 1899. His mother was of Polish descent, a fact von dem Bach tried to hide in the Nazi years, and his father, Otto von Zelewski, was from a poor Junker family. His father died young, and the uncle who was meant to bring the boy up was in turn killed in the First World War; the young man himself joined up in 1915, becoming one of the youngest recruits in the German army. When the war ended he spent some years fighting against Polish nationalists in Silesia, and distanced himself from his Polish roots by changing his name in 1925 to the more Germanic-sounding 'von dem Bach-Zelewski'. He would, tellingly, change his name twice more: in 1940, when as one of Himmler's favourites he rid himself of the hated 'Zelewski' altogether; and again in 1946 in Nuremberg, when in his attempts to paint himself as a pro-Polish activist and the 'saviour' of Warsaw, his name returned to von dem Bach-Zelewski.

Changing his name to suit the circumstances was typical of von dem Bach. He was a pathological liar, adept at ingratiating himself with those in power, whether Himmler or the prosecutors after the war. Walter Schellenberg, head of SS military intelligence, said of him, 'He has the kind of personality that can't differentiate between the truth and lies. He gets himself so much into the whole thing he can't differentiate . . . Originally it was not the truth, but he so convinces himself – he's ready to die for it.'[10]

Bach joined the SS in 1930, and quickly became friendly with powerful colleagues including Kurt Daluege, Adolf Eichmann and Reinhard Heydrich. On 7 November 1939 Himmler made him Commissioner for the Strengthening of Germandom in Silesia, where his duties included mass deportations of Poles to make room for ethnic Germans being resettled in the east. In order to deal with the large number of now homeless ethnic Poles in his area, he proposed to Himmler that a concentration camp be built for the non-German inhabitants of the region. Obergruppenführer Arpad Wigand proposed a place called Auschwitz, and the camp was duly created in May 1940, initially for Polish Catholic prisoners. Von dem Bach visited the camp's commandant Rudolf Höss there shortly afterwards, dispensing advice on how many prisoners should be shot in reprisal for attempted escapes. After the war von dem Bach claimed that Auschwitz had been nothing more than a 'troop training centre' at the time; in reality he had been one of its creators, and was fully aware of what was done there.

After the invasion of the Soviet Union, Himmler made von dem Bach HSSPF – 'Higher SS and Police Leader' – in the region of Army Group Centre, which was pushing east through Byelorussia. It was an amazing elevation. Had the Germans conquered Moscow, as von dem Bach fully expected them to do, he would have reached the lofty heights of being HSSPF in the Russian capital itself. Vain, ambitious and anxious to keep in with Himmler, he embarked on an exhaustive series of journeys to execution sites throughout Central Europe in order to prove his worth. By August 1941 he had travelled from Minsk to Mogilev to Starobin – a total of nine sites at which mass killings took place.[11] He travelled even more the following year, doggedly going to the ravines and pits and trenches in which the innocent were shot in cold blood; men, women and children. He competed with his fellow HSSPFs to 'win' the 'killing score' in his region: in 1941 he proudly wrote to Berlin that he had 'passed the figure of 30,000 in my area'. On 28 July that year, after a meeting with Himmler, von dem Bach mounted an operation to comb the Pripyat marshes for 'partisans'. Himmler's oral instructions had left no doubt: 'All Jews must be shot. Drive the females into the swamps.' This *Aktion* lasted from 2 to 12 August, with 15,878 people killed and 830 prisoners captured. One of the most vicious and efficient officers in the *Aktion* was Himmler's protégé and Bach's friend Hermann Fegelein, who worked closely with von dem Bach throughout.

33

His cavalry brigade were ruthless when it came to rounding up and shooting civilians: they reported killing 699 Red Army soldiers, 1,100 partisans and 14,178 Jews in one sweep alone. The women and children who did not drown in the shallow waters of the marshes were shot. At Nuremberg Bach claimed that he had 'personally saved . . . 10,000 Jewish lives by telling them to hide in the Pripyat marshes'. The reality had been quite different.

Von dem Bach saw Himmler in Byelorussia on 15 August 1941. Film footage of this visit gives a hint of the power that Himmler must have felt in those heady, victorious days. He and von dem Bach were joined by Karl Wolff, chief of his personal staff, Otto Bradfisch, leader of Einsatzkommando 8 of Einsatzgruppe B, and Hermann Fegelein. Himmler, tanned and relaxed, processed through the streets of Minsk in an open Mercedes like a famous film star, every inch the conquering hero. On his arrival at the tall, white, modernist SS headquarters, with its enormous flag curling over the roof, he waved to the adoring employees who had lined up, cheering and smiling, on the balconies to greet their boss.

Von dem Bach took Himmler to a Soviet PoW camp on the outskirts of Minsk. Some of the emaciated prisoners tried to catch a glimpse of Himmler, while others lay on the ground, unable or unwilling to move. The Reichsführer SS started a conversation through the wire with a tall, handsome young man, but then, as if suddenly realizing that he was talking to a 'sub-human', turned quickly away, rubbing his nose with the back of his gloved hand.

The brutal treatment of Soviet PoWs is one of the least-known, and most terrible, crimes of the Second World War. Once captured, the prisoners were marched or forced to run to gathering points, or were transported in open freight wagons, 150 at a time; the wounded who could not keep up were shot immediately. 'What do you do with 90,000 prisoners?' asked one Wehrmacht soldier who filmed such a group. 'The majority were badly wounded, in a bad state, half-dead with thirst, resigned to their fate. Worst was the lack of water . . . Many many soldiers, what became of them? I don't know and it is better not to know.'[12] His amateur footage shows column after column of men, most of whom were destined to die of starvation or disease, trudging in columns stretching for kilometres in the hot, dusty landscape. 'Many of those without caps wore wisps of straw or rags tied to their close-cropped heads as protection against the burning sun, and some were barefooted and half-dressed . . . a long column of misery,' remembered one Wehrmacht soldier.[13]

Upon arrival the prisoners were herded into barbed-wire enclosures like the one Himmler visited with von dem Bach, perhaps with a few wooden huts or old barns as shelter from the extreme heat and cold. Sometimes, as in Stalag 352 near Minsk, they were crushed together so tightly that they simply could not move. There were no latrines, so they had to scoop up their own excrement and put it into barrels. Over 100,000 died there, their bodies dumped into pits. The Dulags, Stalags and Oflags of Byelorussia were centres of slow, agonizing death for hundreds of thousands of human beings who were essentially left in the open with no medical care, no protection and hardly any food. At Dulag 131 at Bobruisk, thousands of prisoners burned to death when one of the outbuildings caught fire; those who tried to escape were mown down. The guards tortured and humiliated the men, sometimes beating and shooting them for fun. At times they would throw a dead dog into the compound: 'Yelling like mad the Russians would fall on the animal and tear it to pieces with their bare hands. The intestines they'd stuff in their pockets – a sort of iron ration.'[14] Often fed only the entrails of horses, the starving men ate grass down to the earth, and chewed on wood. Some were reduced to 'lyudoedstvo' – cannibalism. One German soldier wrote that the Russians 'whined and grovelled before us. They were human beings in whom there was no longer a trace of anything human.' But dehumanizing the victims was, of course, the point.

After the PoW camp Himmler was taken to see an *Aktion* for himself. Einsatzgruppe B commander Artur Nebe had organized a small execution of ninety-eight men and two women for Himmler's personal viewing. An open grave had been prepared, and the victims were forced to lie in it in rows. When one group had been shot, the next had to climb down on top of those already killed. Von dem Bach recalled Himmler asking to talk to one of the prisoners, 'a young Jewish boy of twenty who had a Nordic appearance, with blue eyes and blond hair. Himmler called that boy aside from the pit where he was to be shot and asked him if he were Jewish.' When it became clear that the boy's entire family was Jewish, Himmler said, 'In that case I cannot help you.' The boy was executed along with the others. 'You could see,' von dem Bach added, 'how Himmler tried to save the boy's life . . . he was undoubtedly soft and cowardly.'[15]

Karl Wolff would claim that Himmler had been spattered by the brains of one of the victims of this *Aktion*, and had nearly fainted, but von dem Bach later denied this story. Even so, Himmler, having spent so much time in the distant luxury of Berlin, was clearly shaken by this encounter with actual killing. Von dem Bach pointed out to him that he had witnessed a 'mere hundred people' die, and that he had to try to imagine the pressures on those who had to kill thousands. When Himmler had collected himself he gave a speech to the executioners, praising their courage and appealing to their sense of patriotism in carrying out the hard tasks required of them. Although he had been touched by what he had seen, the action had been 'necessary' for Germany's future. The men should turn to the natural world for their model. Bedbugs and rats were living creatures, after all, but human beings had the right to defend themselves against such 'vermin'. The metaphor was obvious.

Von dem Bach was right to fear for the mental health of his murderers: he himself would have to undergo treatment for the psychological trauma he suffered after witnessing so much killing. In Byelorussia the extermination of the Jews was done in broad daylight, and often in sight of the local population. In one of many reports, a District Commissar in Slutsk described how a police battalion had 'fetched and carted off all the Jews . . . With indescribable brutality on the part of the German policemen as well as Lithuanian partisans (under the SS) the Jewish people, including Byelorussians, too, were brought together from their apartments. There was shooting all over town, and corpses of dead Jews piled up in several streets.' People had been 'buried alive', and the police had looted the town. 'The Byelorussian people, who had gained confidence in us, have been stupefied.' The SD complained that the Byelorussians were 'passive and stupid', so that it was 'virtually impossible' to persuade them 'to stage pogroms against the Jews'. In Minsk in 1942, Einsatzgruppe B decided to give Hitler a present by killing all the Jews in the city by his birthday, 20 April. The plan was stymied by the civilian occupation authorities under Wilhelm Kube, who wanted to save some Jews to be used as forced labour. On 1 March the Germans ordered the *Judenrat* – one of the councils which Jews were forced to set up in the occupied territories – to provide a quota of 5,000 Jews by the following day; when they did not, the Germans stabbed the children in the Jewish orphanage to death.[16]

Gerhard Bast, a member of Sonderkommando B, took part in the murder of Jews in and around Minsk. One eyewitness testified after the war how Bast's group had brought a group of Jews and gypsies in lorries and unloaded them near a freshly dug trench. 'It was mainly women and children who were shot, some of them with babies.' He could still picture the women 'nursing their children on the way to the pit to calm them down. At the pit the children were torn from their mothers and were generally shot first, in front of their mothers. Very small children were held up by one arm by the SD men, shot in the head, and then carelessly tossed into the pit like a log.'[17] Bast was one of the many from Sonderkommando B who under Artur Nebe had worked closely with von dem Bach, and who would flee Byelorussia in the face of the advancing Red Army in 1944. He ended up in Warsaw in August, just in time for the uprising.

It is almost beyond belief that von dem Bach would declare at Nuremberg: 'The whole crowd – Hitler, Himmler, Göring, Frank, Rosenberg, just to mention those who were responsible in the east alone – have blood on their hands. But I have none.' Bach saw himself as a humanitarian family man who called his wife 'Mutti' and was close to his six children, to one of whom Himmler was godfather. And yet to mark his first Christmas in Minsk in 1941, this proud father sent 10,000 pairs of babies' and children's socks, and 2,000 pairs of shoes, as a gift to children of the SS in Germany, items which had been stolen from the condemned children of the Minsk ghetto.[18] Some measure of his personal 'hands-on' participation is revealed in his own medical record. In early March 1942 he suffered a nervous breakdown, and had to be taken to the SS hospital in the erstwhile tuberculosis clinic at Hohenlychen, where he was treated by Ernst-Robert Grawitz, the SS chief medical officer and head of the German Red Cross. In his report to Himmler, Grawitz stated that Bach was 'suffering particularly from hallucinations connected with the shootings of Jews which he himself carried out and with other grievous experiences in the east'. When Grawitz asked him why he was under such strain, Bach replied, 'Don't you know what's happening in Russia? The entire Jewish people is being exterminated there.' By the end of 1942, the Germans had killed at least 208,089 Jews in Byelorussia, and Bach had participated fully.

The 'successful' treatment of Russian prisoners of war, and the mass murder of the Jews in Byelorussia, led to von dem Bach's next major promotion. As German brutality increased, so did resistance. The Germans had lost their chance to be treated as liberators, and had quickly turned themselves into loathed conquerors. As such, they were increasingly under attack by partisans. Something had to be done.

Von dem Bach and the Partisan War

The first partisans in Byelorussia were Red Army soldiers who had become trapped behind enemy lines in the first months of Barbarossa. While some of these joined the German side to avoid the atrocious conditions of the PoW camps, or out of conviction that Germany offered a better future, others remained loyal to the Soviet Union, and regrouped in secret to continue the fight. On 3 August 1941 Stalin recognized this phenomenon by declaring an official 'partisan war'. 'It is necessary,' he said in a radio broadcast, 'to create unbearable conditions for the enemy in the occupied areas.' By the spring of 1942 the central headquarters of the partisan movement had been created at Stavka, the headquarters of the Soviet armed forces, headed by Panteleimon Ponomarenko. Groups of partisans were trained by the NKVD, SMERSH (the acronym for the Soviet counter-intelligence agency, 'Death to the Spies') and GRU, the Main Intelligence Directorate, and dropped behind enemy lines, and as German oppression worsened their ranks swelled. Many joined to avoid being press-ganged by the Germans as *Hilfswillige* – literally 'those willing to help' – and there were increasing desertions from the ranks of German-controlled military and police formations: the entire 1,000-strong Volga Tatar Battalion came over to the Russian side in February 1943. Around 10,000 Jews from Minsk also tried to join: men with weapons were taken, but most women and children who were hoping for protection were turned away, and had to eke out an existence in the forests and marshes nearby; many were later caught in German 'combing' operations and killed.

The huge area of uncharted forests and swamps of Byelorussia was ideally suited to partisan warfare. Small mobile units could race through the marshes and outmanoeuvre the Germans, who would get lost on unmarked trails and whose vehicles would get stuck in the mud. The partisans had special swamp clothing and boots which helped them walk in the sodden landscape. Using methods more reminiscent of Vietnam than the Eastern Front, they fashioned reeds into breathing tubes so that they could submerge themselves underwater until danger had passed. By the end of 1943 the partisans controlled vast areas behind the German lines, with sophisticated facilities and airstrips where the Soviets could land with supplies and men; by 1942 they already numbered around 100,000. Having learned that the Western Allies would not be opening the second front within the year, Stalin held a party for the partisans at the Kremlin in September 1942. They were, he said, to become a serious element of Soviet strategy – 'a second front in the enemy's rear'.[19]

It soon became clear to the Germans that the partisans were more than a mere nuisance. As early as February 1942 Field Marshal Günther von Kluge, commander of Army Group Centre, complained to General Halder that far from limiting themselves to disrupting communications, the growing partisan bands were now attempting to bring 'entire districts under their control'. For Hitler this was intolerable, and his answer was to order even more brutality. In August 1942 he placed anti-partisan warfare under the jurisdiction of the Army Operations Sections from the High Command down. In Directive no. 46, 'Instructions for Intensified Action Against Banditry in the East', released that month, he vested responsibility for the operational areas in the General Staff, while the SS was given overall command and responsibility for the extermination of the partisans. There would be no attempt to win them over. Being 'weak' had only led to failure in the past. In a top-secret supplementary order to the 18 October 1942 'Commando Order', Hitler stated that 'Only where the fight against this partisan disgrace was begun and executed with ruthless brutality were results achieved which relieved the positions of the fighting front. In all eastern territories the war against the partisans is therefore a struggle of absolute annihilation of one or the other party.' As for enemy sabotage troops, they were to be exterminated, without exception, to the last man. 'This means that their chance of escaping with their lives is nil.' Hitler recalled watching as the 'red bastards' had placed children at the head of their march through Chemnitz in the interwar period in order to dissuade their opponents from attacking them. Faced with similar circumstances an officer must, he explained to Generals Keitel and Jodl in December 1942, be prepared to kill women and children in order to overcome a greater evil. Burning down houses with people inside was now a military necessity. On 16 December Keitel issued the last security order of the year. Partisans were to be eradicated like 'pests', and troops were granted the right to use all measures, even against women and children, if it led to success. They would not be punished, nor would they ever face trial. The level of brutality was set to escalate to astronomical levels.

When in the first days of August 1944 the beleaguered civilians of Warsaw were hauled from their homes and taken to their deaths

– men, women, children, the infirm, babies, the sick – they were executed to the cry of one word: 'Banditen'. Every single citizen of Warsaw, regardless of background, age or gender, was considered to be guilty by association – guilty because they were inhabitants of a city that had condoned the uprising. As they were all collaborators, they could be killed outright without question and without pity. This murderous treatment of so-called 'Banditen' was not invented in Warsaw, but had been pioneered in the east, and perfected under the watchful eye of von dem Bach himself.

It was Himmler who had dreamed up the use of the term 'Banditen'. Ever conscious of symbolism, he felt that the word 'partisan' conjured up far too positive an image, suggesting a noble freedom fighter romantically standing up to an evil invader. This would not do. In a pamphlet entitled 'Thoughts on the Word "Partisan" ' he decided to officially replace it with 'bandit'. This had suitable connotations of the underhanded opportunist, the lawless thug, indeed the very opposite of the brave rebel fighting for a great cause. The 'Jewish-Bolshevik evil of terrorists, bandits and outlaws' was to be completely eliminated. And if 'partisans' were now 'bandits', the war to annihilate them would also have a new name: the 'Bandenbekämpfung', or Bandit War. In September 1942 Himmler wrote a pamphlet outlining how the Waffen SS, the regular police force and the Wehrmacht would work alongside the SD and the SiPo (the security police) to rid the Germans of the menace. Their goal was to be the 'extermination', and 'not the expulsion', of bandits.[20]

Himmler needed someone to lead this fight. Von dem Bach, still disappointed that German reversals had meant that he had not become SS Police Leader in Moscow, brazenly put himself forward for the job. As long ago as September 1941 he had presented two papers at the first of a number of conferences dedicated to the theme of 'combating partisans', and he described himself as 'the most experienced Higher SS and Police Leader in the business'.[21] Himmler agreed. On 23 October 1942 he made Erich von dem Bach-Zelewski SS Plenipotentiary for the Bandit War, with the approval of the OKW, the Supreme Command of the Armed Forces; on 21 June 1943 he was promoted to Chief of the Bandit War (*Chef der Bandenkampfverbände*).[22] His deputy was to be the drunkard Curt von Gottberg.

Von dem Bach's star was rising, and it was clear to all in the inner circle that Himmler was grooming him for high office. He was given all the perks of enormous power – meetings with high officials on visits to Berlin, palatial headquarters in Mogilev and a palace in Minsk, chauffeur-driven limousines and even a Junkers 52 passenger transport plane directly from Göring – a huge status symbol in Nazi Germany, which implied that he had reached the realm of strategic command.[23] He was even given a new, grand-sounding code-name – 'Arminus'. 'I was very well known, respected, and beloved,' he said at Nuremberg, and his diary records a social life befitting his new status. As the brutal war raged around him he described evenings of cocktail parties and cultural events. He arranged for the latest films to be screened for his secretaries, and when after heavy fighting officers of the 14th Police Regiment needed a rest he gave them a free night at the Minsk theatre, with the whole building set aside for their use. Ballet, chamber music, opera and cabaret all played a part in his life, with many local artists given rations to keep them alive. He and Artur Nebe conducted 'actual exercises': the first was a search-and-destroy operation in a village near Mogilev; the second took place in a forest where they 'dug out' partisans who were later shot.

Von dem Bach was now in charge of a large organization dedicated to the fight against the 'bandits'. After the war he claimed that at its height his gleaming offices received 15,000 pieces of information every day, much of it intelligence from local villages and towns, on suspicious characters and possible collaborators.

This information allowed the Germans to create enormous 'bandit maps' of 'infested areas'. When an area seemed beyond control and resources allowed, it would be subject to an '*Aktion*', in effect a killing spree. Von dem Bach could draw upon army personnel – security divisions, units composed of indigenous collaborators, SS units, police regiments and Einsatzgruppen for as long as he needed them for any particular operation. In the military areas the same responsibility was exercised by the chief of the army's General Staff; in practice the two often overlapped.[24]

Killing so-called partisans became a part of everyday life: 'A partisan group blew up our vehicles,' wrote Private H.M., a member of an intelligence unit. 'Early yesterday morning forty men were shot on the edge of the city . . . Naturally there were a number of innocent people who had to give up their lives . . . One didn't waste a lot of time on this and just shot the ones who happened to be around.'[25] The Wehrmacht, too, participated in these killings. Wehrmacht soldier Claus Hansmann recalled an execution of partisans in Kharkov: 'The first human package, tied up, is carried outside . . . The hemp neckband is placed around his neck, hands are tied tight, he is put on the balustrade and the blindfold is removed from his eyes. For an instant you see glaring eyeballs, like those of an escaped horse, then wearily he closes his eyelids . . . one after the other is brought out, put on the railing . . . Each one bears a placard on his chest proclaiming his crime . . . Partisans and just punishment.'[26] Field Marshal Walter Model, soon to become the head of Army Group Centre, requested that partisans be executed out of sight of his office, as the sight of men hanging nearby was so unpleasant.[27] Murder of partisans and civilians was carried out on a grand scale in Byelorussia, to be sure, but one person who stood out even in that terrible time was Oskar Dirlewanger.

The Very Face of Evil

Like that of Erich von dem Bach, Oskar Dirlewanger's name will always be linked first and foremost with the Warsaw Uprising. He too did the majority of his 'practical training' in Byelorussia. Unlike the affable von dem Bach, Dirlewanger actually looked and acted like the murderer he was. His face resembled that of a vulture, with thin lips and deep circles under his cruel, almost mocking eyes, while his dark hair was cropped close to his bony, angular head. His violent tendencies got him noticed at an early age. After serving in World War I he joined the Freikorps, a volunteer paramilitary organization and temporary home to many future Nazis, where he made a name for himself beating up Communists in the regular street fights of the period. He attended Frankfurt University, earning a PhD in economics, and then joined the Nazi Party, becoming deputy director of the Labour Office in Heilbronn.

Dirlewanger seemed to enjoy stirring up trouble, and his position was in question almost immediately. The Führer of his SA-Group Southwest reported that for a full five months since joining the Labour Office Dirlewanger had been acting in an 'undisciplined way'. He had 'repeatedly had sex in the official car of the Labour Office with girls who were less than fourteen years old'.[28] Then on 15 April 1934 he 'drove the official car of the Labour Office into a ditch while completely drunk; on this occasion, a female passenger was severely hurt and he fled the scene of the accident'.[29] Dirlewanger was sentenced by the State Court of Heilbronn on 20 September 1934. At his trial it was noted that he had had sexual relations with 'several other women among them the twenty-year-old leader of the BDM [League of German Girls] group of Heilbronn'; also, he had 'used' the fourteen-year-old Anneliese 'four or five times in the period of February to mid-July 1934 in order to satisfy his sexual appetite'; during one of these meetings the girl had actually been wearing her BDM uniform.[30] Dirlewanger was kicked out of the SA and sentenced to two years in prison. But he had friends in high places.

Dirlewanger's old comrade, SS Brigadeführer Gottlob Berger, was outraged. 'The condemnation was absolutely unjust,' he said at Nuremberg. 'I turned to Himmler in a teletype, to the higher SS and Police Leader, and they had enough sense of justice to intervene and fetch him out again the next day. Then I sent him to Spain.'[31] Berger had salvaged what would turn out to be a most notorious career. Dirlewanger served in the Condor Legion, a unit of German volunteers who fought alongside the Nationalists in the Spanish Civil War, and in 1938, while he was away, he was investigated by the SD. Its report concluded that 'Dirlewanger must be called absolutely reliable as far as politics are concerned.' He returned from Spain in June 1939, and wrote to Himmler asking to join the SS. He was soon to get the promotion that would make his career.

When Adolf Hitler had lunch with his Minister Dr Hans Lammers in 1942 he introduced an unexpected topic to the conversation. 'It is ridiculous,' he said, 'for a poacher to be sent to prison for three months for killing a hare when there are so many real criminals who serve no time. I myself should have taken the fellow and put him into one of the guerrilla companies of the SS!'[32]

Despite his vegetarianism, Hitler had long had a strange admiration for poachers, and decided that with their particular skills of tracking and killing they might be useful in the fight against the partisans. On 23 March 1940 SS Gruppenführer Karl Wolff had informed Himmler that Hitler had decided to grant an amnesty for convicted poachers, and that they were to be organized into a special sharpshooter company. Eighty poachers were located and transferred to Sachsenhausen concentration camp. Someone had to head this unit, and Gottlob Berger thought of his old friend who now needed a job, and wrote to Himmler recommending Dirlewanger. Himmler agreed, and on 1 September 1940 the band of poachers was given the official name 'Sonderkommando Dr. Dirlewanger' (SS Special Battalion Dr* Dirlewanger), and was immediately sent to Poland to work with the SS. Amongst other things they excelled at carrying out the *Sonderbehandlung* ('special treatment') of victims – the Nazi euphemism used to cover crimes including mass murder – in Lublin. On 9 November 1941 Dirlewanger was promoted to SS Sturmbannführer.

Despite his good fortune, Dirlewanger could not stay out of trouble, and in January 1942 he was again under investigation, this time for corruption, rape and looting. SS Brigadeführer Odilo Globocnik criticized Dirlewanger not because he disagreed with what he had done, but rather because he could not control him, and wanted to retain power in the Lublin area for himself. In one incident Globocnik accused Dirlewanger of 'race defilement' for taking an attractive young Jewish assistant as his lover; the situation was made 'worse' because Dirlewanger repeatedly kept her from being sent away for 'special treatment'. At the same time, Dirlewanger was under investigation for crimes against Jews. Dr Konrad Morgen, the SS lawyer investigating the case, testified at Nuremberg: 'Dirlewanger had arrested people illegally and arbitrarily, and as for his female prisoners – young Jewesses – he did the following against them: he called together a small circle of friends consisting of members of a Wehrmacht supply unit. Then he made so-called scientific experiments, which involved stripping the victims of their clothes. Then they were given an

---

* Given that so many Nazis were uneducated thugs, they were always keen to advertise the fact if one of their own had had a higher education.

injection of strychnine. Dirlewanger looked on, smoked a cigarette, as did his friends, and watched as they died.'[33]

'This is a joke,' Dirlewanger claimed in his defence. 'It looks as if Brigadeführer Globocnik has made a question out of poisoning Jews in Lublin a subject of investigation. He is besmirching my name. He has tried to do this before. But he is not so lucky this time. It is true that I told a doctor from Lublin to poison these Jews instead of shooting them, but I did it to save the clothes, like coats, for example, which I sent later to Hauptsturmführer Streibel. These were clothes for work. The gold teeth were taken by the Director of the SSPF Infirmary from Lublin so that there would be material for teeth for members of the SS. All of these things were settled with Brigadeführer Globocnik, who then denied all the facts when the SD got involved. It is really a comedy in Lublin. In one trial I am said to have had intercourse with a Jewish woman. In another case I am not showing the correct attitude towards the nation, and I throw out my unbreakable ideology with a Jewess, and when it turns out not to be true I am accused of the complete opposite.'

Himmler decided that the solution was to quietly send Dirlewanger somewhere else, where his skills could be put to greater use. On 29 January 1942 the Chief of Staff of the headquarters of the Waffen SS placed Sonderkommando Dirlewanger under the direct control of the command staff of the SS Reichsführer himself. The Sonderkommando was refitted and sent to Byelorussia in February 1942. (While Himmler saw great potential in Dirlewanger, and wanted to use him, a problem was that he was being investigated by Dr Konrad Morgen – backed by Globocnik, who wanted to get him out of 'his' territory. Himmler spirited Dirlewanger off to Byelorussia as quickly as he could, although Morgen's dogged investigation into his activities continued throughout the war.)

The SS Sonderkommando Dirlewanger that arrived in Byelorussia consisted of around ninety former poachers, but it would grow rapidly. Within six months it would receive a few hundred political prisoners, criminals and psychopaths recruited from psychiatric hospitals and concentration camps, and would gain the reputation of 'exceeding all others', even amongst the SS, in 'brutality and depravity'.

Between February 1942 and June 1944 Sonderkommando Dirlewanger participated in over fifty of von dem Bach's anti-partisan raids. Some of these were small, with just a few dozen men attacking a single target area. After eighteen German soldiers had been killed in a partisan attack a young soldier, Matthias Jung, witnessed the reprisal: 'The whole place, everything [was destroyed]. Everything. Totally! The civilians who had done it, all the civilians who were in the place. In each corner stood a machine gun, and then all the houses were set on fire and whoever came out – in my opinion with justice!'[34]

The large 'actions' were giant sweeps into 'bandit' territory involving hundreds of men. There were various approved methods of attacking 'bandit-infested areas'. The main aim was to encircle an area and to capture or kill anyone within it. Von dem Bach referred to this as 'extermination by encirclement'.[35] The first and preferred form of the extermination of those caught was through combat. This was called '*Kesseltreiben*', or 'crushing the encirclement', and involved units proceeding through the area and slaughtering everyone they could find. The Nazis employed hunting terms to describe various methods of clearing a designated area; human beings were treated like animals.

This was by no means random or hurried killing. Areas with 'proven' bandit connections were targeted for destruction weeks, or even months, in advance. Agents were placed in villages and towns, with collaborators, *Hilfswillige* and others recruited as spies.

Signs of suspicious activity – the delivery of too much food, or strange movements at night – were noted. Before the *Aktion* began, the SS or police would arrive and check papers. Houses and barns were meticulously searched. A hidden weapon meant certain death; if there was an extra coat in the kitchen or too much food on the table the householders were shot.

On the fateful day the SS and police would surround the area and herd the inhabitants into the largest building in town – usually a church or hall. When everyone was inside it would be set on fire; anyone who tried to escape was shot. At Nuremberg, von dem Bach described the standard procedure: 'The village was suddenly surrounded and without warning the police gathered the inhabitants into the village square. In front of the mayor, people not essential to the local farms and industry were immediately taken off to collection points for transfer to Germany.'[36] Von dem Bach was careful not to mention that those who were not designated as useful slave labour were burned alive or shot.

The partisans, if indeed there were any in the area, often escaped to the woods in advance, leaving only innocent civilians behind. They were killed anyway, the logic being that if you couldn't kill the actual partisans, you could at least destroy the people who might be aiding them. From six to ten people were killed for each weapon that was found. It became mass murder on a grand scale: it is estimated that 345,000 civilians, many of them Jews, and only 15 per cent of them actual partisans, were killed in these operations, but there were probably many more who died without a trace. The reports speak for themselves. Von dem Bach's deputy von Gottberg wrote to Berlin after the relatively small Operation 'Nürnberg' on 5 December 1942, boasting that 799 bandits, over three hundred suspected gangsters and over 1,800 Jews had been killed. In all this only two German soldiers had been killed and ten wounded. 'One must have luck,' he quipped. One had only to recall Himmler's words of July 1942 'All women and girls have the potential to be bandits and assassins.'

Dirlewanger's first large-sweep operation was Operation '*Bamberg*', near Bobruisk, in March–April 1942. It was reported that he had proved himself with 'flying colours'. He met von dem Bach on 17 June, and was praised again for his work. Soon the brigade was involved in some of the biggest 'anti-bandit' operations in Byelorussia, which were given romantic-sounding code-names like '*Adler*', '*Erntefest*', '*Zauberflöte*' and '*Cottbus*'. Most lasted three to four weeks, and involved attacks against not only the Byelorussian peasant communities but also the remaining ghettos – '*Hornung*' ended with the liquidation of the Slutsk ghetto, and 'Swamp Fever' with that of the Baranovitsche ghetto.[37] The commander of the 286th Protective Division of the Wehrmacht, General-Leutnant Johann Georg Richert, congratulated Dirlewanger in front of von dem Bach after Operation '*Adler*'. The enemy had 'tried to escape capture by going up to their necks in the bog or by climbing thin branches of trees and viciously tried to break through. In many cases officers and commissars committed suicide to avoid capture.' Dirlewanger had ruthlessly hunted them down.

Operation '*Hornung*', in February 1943, was staged ostensibly to prevent the spread of 'bandits' in the Slutsk region. After careful reconnaissance, von dem Bach arrived at Combat Group Staff von Gottberg on 15 February to give the order to begin. Dirlewanger had just been put at von Gottberg's disposal – other units taking part were Einsatzgruppe B and the Rodianov Battalion, which came from the rear area of Army Group Centre and was also known for its ruthlessness. Five combat groups including the Dirlewanger Brigade were sent into the area with orders to kill everyone they could find, and to take all useful property. Dirlewanger primed his men not to shirk from killing civilians, who, he said, were guilty by association: 'Given the current weather it must be expected that in all villages of the mentioned area the bandits have found shelter.' All the houses in Dirlewanger's area were burned down, and cattle and food taken. Villages were utterly destroyed, along with their inhabitants – the official lists included dozens of place names, all carefully tallied up: 'Lenin 1,046 people, Adamovo 787, in Pusiczi 780 . . .' and so it went on. In all 12,718 people were reported killed, including 3,300 Jews murdered in the Słuck ghetto. Only sixty-five prisoners were taken in the entire operation. Later, when the Soviets exhumed the bodies they found no bullets or spent cartridges lying around. The victims had been burned alive in the barns.

In this terrible phase of the 'Bandit War' few prisoners were taken; indeed, only 3,589 people were taken for slave labour by the Sauckel Commission (in charge of processing forced and slave labourers) in the course of eleven major operations, in which at least 33,378 people were murdered.[38] It was straightforward slaughter. Gana Michalowna Gricewicz, who survived the destruction of her village, remembered feeling as if 'there was no one left in the world, that all had been killed'. The country around Slutsk was turned into a 'dead zone': all the people, animals and supplies were removed, and the area torched. Any person found there was to be treated like 'game', and shot on sight.

One of the most deadly 'actions' in which Dirlewanger participated was Operation '*Cottbus*', which started on the morning of 30 May 1943. The attack at Lake Palik saw 16,662 soldiers sent in to push a terrified civilian population in front of them, forcing them to fight with their backs to the water; the death toll was at least 15,000 people.[39] Bach's deputy von Gottberg praised Dirlewanger's innovation of forcing civilians to walk over minefields: 'The mine detector developed by the Dirlewanger Battalion has successfully passed the test,' he crowed.[40] Von dem Bach was delighted by this new technique, which had 'sent two to three thousand villagers flying', he said.[41] It soon became standard practice. Dirlewanger also continued in his sexual abuse of, and by now profitable trade in, women, noting that one group had 'enjoyed' catching many girls who had been trapped on the edge of Lake Palik. The victims were gang raped, and then sold to Dirlewanger's friends. Some were kept in makeshift prisons, to be abused later.[42]

Despite his successes in Byelorussia, Dirlewanger's brutality brought him negative attention once again. Wilhelm Kube reported a massacre in the village of Vitonitsch, complaining that bullet-wounded escapees were climbing out of their pits and seeking help in hospitals and clinics. Kube wrote in a report to Alfred Rosenberg, the Reich Minister for Occupied Territories, that in terms of turning the local population against the Germans, 'the name Dirlewanger plays a particularly significant role, for this man, in the war of annihilation he wages pitilessly against an unarmed population, deliberately refuses to consider political necessities. His methods, worthy of the Thirty Years War, make a lie of the civil administration's assurances of their wish to work together with the Byelorussian people. When women and children are shot *en masse* or burned alive, there is no longer a semblance of humane conduct of war. The number of villages burned during sweep operations exceeds that of those burned by the Bolsheviks.'[43] Kube's report was ignored. Dirlewanger was given even more men, this time hardened criminals from Dachau, Buchenwald, Mauthausen and Sachsenhausen. In order to impose discipline he had three of them shot in the back of the head in front of their new comrades upon their arrival. All the men knew that they would quickly share the same fate if they did not fall into line; at best they could expect to be sent back to the camps at the first sign of weakness.

Far from attempting to rein him in, von dem Bach and Himmler rewarded Dirlewanger. His grand residence in the ancient town of Lagoisk was perfect for entertaining. Unlike von dem Bach he was not one for ballet or theatre, preferring a '*Kameradenschaftliche Abend*' (comradeship evening), for which colleagues would be invited from the area, or flown in on his own Fieseler Storch aircraft. After drinks, the guests would be seated at the large table, the lights glinting off stolen glass and silver. The best pieces were sent to his storage facility near his home at Esslingen, in Württemberg, but there was enough left over to make life at headquarters bearable. To the sound of a gramophone playing songs like Dirlewanger's favourite '*Alle Tage ist kein Sonntag*', particularly pretty young women prisoners, specially chosen during round-ups, would be forced to serve the food and wine, and to endure the lurid attentions of the host and his guests. Dirlewanger would invariably get very drunk, and invite his guests to join in the rape, and often the murder, of these women. His officers were permitted to capture women during the partisan sweeps: a unit veteran, Waldemar B, certified that in one case 'the officers shut up eight women, confiscated their clothing, and in the evening took them to the castle, where they whipped them'.[44] A company of policemen operating with the unit was in the habit of taking women prisoners and selling them. A radio message sent by Dirlewanger on 11 March 1944 confirmed this trade: 'The Russian [women] requested by Stubaf. Otto will be captured on Monday and delivered with the next men to go on leave. The price is the same as that fixed by Ostuf. Ingruber in the Lake Palik woods. Price per Russian woman: two bottles of schnaps.'[45]

Dirlewanger's last 'sweep' in Byelorussia, Operation '*Kormoran*', took place in May and June 1944. It was never completed. On the night of 19 June the partisans who for so long had been hunted by the Germans set off a massive series of bombs and explosions, which heralded the beginning of the great Soviet summer offensive into Byelorussia. Hundreds of thousands of Germans, Dirlewanger included, would soon be scrambling to get out as fast as they could, as the house of cards collapsed around them. Dirlewanger had spent twenty-eight months in Byelorussia. His next stop was to be Warsaw.

2

TO THE VERY GATES OF WARSAW

———◦◦◦———

Those on the walls joined in the lamentations, knowing nothing, but sensing unmistakably the feeling of a great calamity. (Chapter XIII)

Bagration

As von dem Bach and Dirlewanger were slaughtering their way through villages on what would prove to be the final day of Operation '*Kormoran*', the regular soldiers of Army Group Centre were waiting nervously at the front. It was common knowledge that the Soviets were about to attack, but the troops were convinced that the main thrust would be directed to the south, against Army Group North Ukraine, and that they would be spared. When the young German infantryman Armin Scheiderbauer arrived in Vitebsk on 11 June 1944 he found the Byelorussian front surprisingly quiet. He was sent off to dig trenches, but felt an ominous and overwhelming 'sense of discomfort' out amongst the isolated platoons.

For others the waiting was torture. Willy Peter Reese, a twenty-three-year-old Wehrmacht soldier who would die in the fighting around Vitebsk, described the reality of filling these endless hours: 'Things and values changed. Money had become meaningless. We used paper money for rolling cigarettes or gambled it away indifferently. There was a feeling of impending gloom. 'Only a few sought intimacy, most drugged themselves with superficialities, with gambling, with cruelty, hatred, or they masturbated . . . Our comradeship was made from mutual dependence, from living together in next to no space. Our humour was born out of sadism, gallows humour, satire, obscenity, spite, rage, and pranks with corpses, squirted brains, lice, pus and shit, the spiritual zero.'[1]

At times Red Army reconnaissance soldiers dressed in German uniform would penetrate the line. When one soldier shot at and killed some members of such a party he found 'still clenched in their cold fists the opened razors with which they had planned to silently cut the throats of our sentries'.[2] At other times loud-speakers would blare at the German ranks from across no man's land: 'You are spilling your blood for Hitler. Nothing can save you from the carnage. Break from this army of Hitlerite oppressors, otherwise you will face destruction.'[3] These messages were met by bursts of machine-gun fire. In truth, although many Germans feared that the war was lost, 'it was widely accepted within the ranks of those fighting in the east that death on the battlefield was preferable to an unknown destiny in a Soviet prisoner of war camp'.[4] Morale was low; sometimes new recruits would be caught 'surreptitiously creeping along the earthworks, their hands held high in the air above the protection of the berm in hopes of receiving a *Heimatschuss*' – a wound that would get them home.[5]

The Russians were now equipped with new automatic weapons, including a short-barrelled submachine gun fitted with a high-capacity drum magazine.[6] The ordinary 'Ivan' was both feared and, in a strange way, admired. The image of the Russian soldier in his loose-fitting brown tunic, with his greatcoat carried even in the hottest weather to be used as a blanket or uniform, and his boots stuffed with straw, had an almost iconic status. The Soviets were admired for other things, too. They could forage and survive on what seemed like almost nothing. General Guderian's adjutant, Lieutenant Horbach, wrote a letter which was found by the Soviets on his corpse: 'You ask my opinion of the Russians. I can only say that their behaviour in action is incomprehensible. The most remarkable thing about them, to say nothing of their persistence and cunning, is their incredible stubbornness . . . The life of the individual means nothing to them.' Gottlob Biderman, a young Wehrmacht soldier, remembered coming across some Russians while he was searching for fuel: 'Inside the tanks we discovered three shivering Russian soldiers who had been standing up to their shoulders in oil for several days. Having been convinced that they would be shot immediately upon capture, they had chosen to die in the freezing temperatures or face the prospect of drowning in horrible conditions rather than surrender.'[7] Another, Harry Mielert, found two Russians hiding in a cellar in a burned-out village: '[They] had fed themselves on potatoes . . . they held out for four weeks, together with two dead bodies, their own excretions, their feet . . . frozen, and yet they still wouldn't venture out.' Erich Dwinger was amazed at the stoicism of the wounded Russians: 'Several of them burnt by flamethrowers had no longer the semblance of a human face . . . Not a cry, not a moan escaped the lips of the wounded . . . The shapeless burnt bundles advanced as quickly as possible [for supplies]. Some half a dozen of them who were lying down also rose, holding their entrails in one hand and stretching out the other with a gesture of supplication.'[8] But years of anti-Soviet propaganda had done their work, and not all

German soldiers felt respect for their adversaries. One, Wilhelm Prüller, wrote that 'It's not people we're fighting against here, but simply animals.'[9] Another spat that the Russians 'are no longer people, but wild hordes and beasts who have been bred by Bolshevism in the last twenty years'.[10] Erich Stahl felt that the Soviets' 'utter disregard for their own lives, that ruthlessness towards their enemy and themselves alike, was a riddle we had never answered'.[11]

The soldiers were frightened of the Russians for other reasons, too. The infantry commanders may not have reached the depths of depravity of a Nebe or a Dirlewanger, but their men were part of the same army, and had participated both directly and indirectly in the murderous policies in the east. 'On the way we torched all the villages we passed through and blew up the stoves,' wrote one retreating soldier. 'We had been ordered to spread devastation, so that our pursuers could find no shelter ... When we were issued a supply of cigarettes we lit them on burning houses.'[12] The Wehrmacht soldiers knew they could expect no quarter from the Red Army. Reese, who had left Germany two years before as a perfectly ordinary young man, saw how Russia 'was turning into a depopulated, smoking, burning, wreckage-strewn desert, and the war behind the front bothered me still more, because those it affected were non-combatants'. Yet he and his colleagues made 'a Russian woman prisoner dance naked for us, greased her tits with boot polish, got her as drunk as we were'.[13] In Russia the normal rules of warfare no longer applied: everything was permissible, as long as any criminal behaviour was directed against the racial enemies of Germany. White flags were used to draw Soviet soldiers to their deaths; red crosses on field hospitals were used for target practice. Soviet soldiers retaliated in kind, so that the brutality and depravity spiralled out of control. Atrocities were committed by both sides in a struggle that had sunk into a moral abyss so deep that little came close to it on any other front in the Second World War.

Despite von dem Bach's best efforts, partisans were harassing the Germans at every turn. The '*Banditen*' were hated and feared in equal measure, and the savagery meted out to and by them was terrible. This 'was not fighting any more, it was butchery. In the course of brief counterthrusts, we found our missing in little pieces. And we didn't take any prisoners either,' remembered one soldier. Men found their comrades stripped naked, having been beaten to death or dismembered. One came across a group of dead soldiers whose tongues had been nailed to a table. Generaloberst Georg-Hans Reinhardt, who would replace Model as commander of Army Group Centre on 16 August, in the midst of the Warsaw Uprising, fought the 'bandits' ruthlessly in the forests of Byelorussia, killing anyone he caught. 'There had been no time to bury the bodies. That was why long stretches were overwhelmed by a ghastly stench. It was said that hundreds of dead were lying in the woods. The July heat strengthened the smell of putrefaction. You had to pinch your nose and breathe through your mouth. Some men even put on their gas masks.' At crossroads it was common to find bodies hanging from posts or branches, their faces swollen and blue, their hands tied behind their backs. Reese remembered coming across such a scene: 'One soldier took their picture; another gave them a swing with his stick. Partisans. We laughed and moved off.' But later that night, two scouts disappeared into the woods and never came back, probably killed by 'bandits'.[14]

'Bagration', the great Soviet summer offensive, has not received the attention given to other battles on the Eastern Front, which is all the more strange as it was without a doubt the single most successful Soviet military operation of the entire Second World War. It also came as a complete surprise to the Germans. Stalin had decided that his attack should not be against Romania, northern Ukraine or the Baltic, but rather should go straight into Byelorussia. His aim was nothing less than the complete encirclement and destruction of Army Group Centre, which was situated in a bulge of occupied territory that jutted into the Soviet Union like an enormous balcony. This was, apart from anything else, the shortest route to Warsaw, and to Berlin.

On 14 May 1944, Stalin summoned his commanders to formulate a plan of attack. It was the most ambitious task he had yet set for the Red Army, and he assembled an extraordinary team with which to achieve it. One of his greatest strategists was the complex and controversial General Konstantin Rokossovsky, who had recently proven himself both at Stalingrad and at Kursk. In his surprisingly high voice for such a bearlike figure, he told Stalin that his 1st Byelorussian Front should attack Bobruisk along both sides of the Berezina River, creating a giant pincer to hit the flanks of 3rd Panzer Army and the 9th Army, and then encircle the 4th Army and destroy it. Stalin, who believed that there should be a single thrust against the German lines, disagreed, and twice sent Rokossovsky out of the room to 'think it over'. Foreign Minister Vyacheslav Molotov and Georgy Malenkov tried to convince him to toe the line, but Rokossovsky stood firm, declaring that he would rather be relieved of his command than attack as Stalin wanted him to. After the third discussion Stalin walked over to him and put his hand on his shoulder. The room froze, with those present convinced that Stalin was about to tear the epaulettes from his shoulders. Instead he smiled. Rokossovsky's confidence, he said, 'reflected his sound judgement', and he was to attack as he wished.[15] Stalin also made it very clear, however, that Rokossovsky would be blamed for any failure.

Rokossovsky's defiance revealed great personal courage. This was, after all, a man who had experienced the Terror first hand. The fact that he had been born in Warsaw, to a Polish father and a Russian mother, had made it easy for Lavrentii Beria, the notorious head of the NKVD, to accuse him of being a Polish spy, although in reality Rokossovsky had been targeted because he had openly favoured the innovative military methods of Marshal Tukhachevsky over traditionalists like Semyon Budenny. Arrested in 1937 for allegedly having conspired with another officer to betray the Soviet Union, he was dragged through a ridiculous show trial, during which it emerged that his alleged co-conspirator had been killed in the Civil War twenty years before. 'Can dead men testify?' Rokossovsky had asked incredulously. Imprisoned until March 1940, he was repeatedly tortured: his teeth were knocked out, leaving him with a steel denture, and his toes were beaten to a pulp with a hammer; he also had his ribs broken and endured a number of mock executions.[16] Despite all this, Rokossovsky never signed a confession; nor did he denounce any of his erstwhile colleagues. Unlike so many of his compatriots who perished in Beria's indefatigable 'meat grinder', Rokossovsky escaped with his life. He would soon be a pivotal figure in the fate of his home town of Warsaw, for it was he who would lead the Soviets to the gates of the city, and who would watch from across the Vistula River as the Germans crushed the desperate uprising in the summer of 1944.

Rokossovsky's argument with Stalin proved that the Red Army of 1944 was a completely different entity from that of 1941. Officers with talent were finally being promoted rather than being sent to the gulag, the ideology of an officer corps was brought back, and officers were given a certain amount of freedom from the NKVD. Propaganda abandoned dull, Communist rhetoric in favour of rousing talk of the Great Patriotic War and the fight for Mother Russia. Three years earlier Rokossovsky would have been shot for standing up to Stalin; now he was allowed to argue with the dictator face to face – and win.

Other things had changed too. The Soviets were producing more, and better, weapons than the Germans. By the time of the summer offensive they had introduced a new model of the T-34 tank, now with an 85mm gun; the SU-100, an update of the SU-85 anti-aircraft gun with lethal long-range 100mm barrel; and the Josef Stalin II tank, armed with a heavy 122mm artillery gun, that could wreak havoc on its German equivalents. Huge stockpiles of food, supplies and ammunition, and fleets of trucks, were brought to the front.[17] Massive quantities of Lend-Lease matériel from the United States were of enormous importance: American Jeeps whizzed around Byelorussia, and Studebaker US6 trucks were used to launch Katyusha rockets: at the same time Russian soldiers feasted on Hershey's chocolate and wieners stamped 'Oscar Meyer – Chicago'.

Stalin approved the final plan of attack against Army Group Centre in Byelorussia on 31 May 1944. The operation, he declared, was to be called 'Bagration', after the Georgian general whose heroic resistance at the Battle of Borodino was instrumental in reducing Napoleon's Grande Armée to such a crippled force that it could never mount an offensive against Russia again. General Pyotr Bagration himself had been killed at Borodino, but the name was a prescient choice. Operation 'Bagration' of 1944 would also change history, and when it was over the Germans in turn would be so weakened that they could not mount another significant offensive in the rest of the Second World War. It was the single greatest defeat ever suffered by the Wehrmacht, and in losses of men and matériel far exceeded those at Stalingrad. The Soviets would achieve blistering success, and would race westward at such speed that it surprised even Stavka and Stalin himself. At the same time, Stalin would launch the Lwów–Sandomierz offensive, drawing German reserves to the south to fight phantom armies. The summer of 1944 saw the loss of a million German soldiers on the Eastern Front. It was the success of Bagration and the Lwów–Stanisławów–Sandomierz operations that would lead to the Polish Home Army's ill-fated decision to begin the Warsaw Uprising on 1 August.

One of the reasons Stalin favoured a full-scale attack on Byelorussia was the element of surprise. His commander Marshal Georgy Zhukov, who had long enjoyed duck-shooting in the swamps near Parichi, understood that the Germans had dismissed the possibility of a Russian attack in the area, believing that the marshes were impassable. For Zhukov the landscape was 'crucial in shaping the course of the attack'. The front held by Army Group Centre was 1,000 kilometres long, with the ancient and beautiful cities of Mogilew, Orsha and Vitebsk strung along it like pearls on a necklace. The southern sector ran through the Pripyat marshes, an enormous 100,000-square-kilometre wetland, a maze of 'swamps and bogs, mud and mosquitoes, impassable for armoured vehicles without special knowledge and equipment'. The rivers Dnieper, Prut, Berezina, Svisloch and Ptich were also natural obstacles. The Germans, Zhukov said, believed that 'the wooded and boggy terrain would not allow us to move to Byelorussia'. He added wryly, 'the enemy miscalculated'.[18]

The next phase of the plan suited Stalin's devious nature perfectly. Having chosen his target, he set about deceiving the Germans with 'maskirovka' – a particularly clever and all-encompassing form of camouflage, misinformation and deception. All troops and equipment were to be moved up to the Byelorussian front in utter secrecy, while at the same time an entire mock front was to be created in Ukraine to fool the Germans into believing that Stalin intended to attack to the south. The plan succeeded brilliantly.

It is difficult to imagine the scale of the subterfuge. The movement of a staggering 1.7 million men in and around Byelorussia had to be done in utter secrecy. This monumental task was undertaken with deadly seriousness. No information was to be permitted to leak to the Germans. Correspondence, telephone conversations and telegraph messages were strictly forbidden. Front-line soldiers were not to know that they were going on the attack, but were told that they were holding 'defensive positions'; General Sergei Shtemenko ordered that 'front, army, and divisional newspapers published material only on defence matters. All talks to the troops were about maintaining a firm hold on present positions.'[19] The troops were carried in by train, but were often dropped a hundred kilometres to the east of their assembly points; in many places the move to the front line was ordered only two days before the attack began. There were to be no unauthorized people in the area, and the transport of troops and equipment was kept from the sight of the general public as much as possible: 50,000 supply vehicles moved at night in strict blackout conditions, and the construction of roads and pontoon bridges was done only after dark and under cover. Vehicles could not use headlights, but instead followed daubs of fluorescent paint on the tailgates of those in front; white posts were put by the sides of roads as night markers. No artillery fire was permitted. Tank crews being moved to the front were forbidden to wear their black uniforms lest they be spotted by German spies; officers had to dress as private soldiers, and even bathing in the open was forbidden. The enemy, as Rokossovsky put it, was permitted to see 'only what we wanted him to see.'[20]

All the while, the fronts were being secretly supplied under the noses of the Germans with immense quantities of matériel and equipment: nearly 400,000 tonnes of ammunition, 300,000 tonnes of fuel and lubricants, and 500,000 tonnes of foodstuffs and fodder were moved in. Five combined armies, two armoured armies, one air army and the 1st Polish Army were brought, up as were five independent armour, two mechanized and four cavalry corps out of the Supreme Command reserve, as well as dozens of independent regiments and brigades of all fighting arms. Eleven air corps were moved to new bases, and tanks equipped with heavy rollers were brought in to break through the minefields. As Zhukov put it, 'All these movements had to be done with great caution to prevent the enemy's detection of the preparations for the offensive. This was especially important since our intelligence reports showed that the German High Command expected us to make the first blow of the summer campaign in the Ukraine, not Byelorussia.'[21]

While the real offensive was being prepared in top-secret conditions, the Soviets worked equally hard to convince Hitler that the main summer offensive would be staged against Model's Army Group North Ukraine. As Byelorussia went 'quiet', the Ukrainian theatre was abuzz with manufactured noise and movement. Soviet air activity increased dramatically. German reconnaissance flights were allowed to pass over the lines and photograph the 'armies' that were gathering – armies which actually consisted of rubber tanks and mock gun emplacements. In a strange take on the Potemkin Village, only 10 per cent of the arms in the entire region were genuine. Heavy radio traffic was faked, and increased rail usage simulated. Small teams of men were sent out into the forests at night; when German planes flew over they shone torches into the sky, before moving forward ten kilometres and repeating the performance, to convince the Germans that the forests were crawling with troops. Major V. Vilensky was not the only one ordered to move his division back and forth to make it look as if ten divisions had been brought up. 'We'd move out at night, come back in the morning, sleep the whole day, and then repeat it all over again.'[22]

Hitler was completely taken in by the deception, but so too were General Kurt Zeitzler, chief of staff at OKH (the German Supreme Command), and Generaloberst Jodl, chief of staff of OKW. General Reinhard Gehlen, chief of the intelligence branch of OKH dealing with the Eastern Front – *Fremde Heere Ost* (FHO) – was so convinced by the troop movements in the south that he told Hitler the area north of the Pripyat marshes would be left out of any Soviet offensive altogether. Hitler mused that the Soviets might even 'refuse to fight' once they reached their own pre-war border. 'Soviet enthusiasm for a military advance is still out of the question,' claimed a German report. It was wishful thinking, but the Führer was insistent: Stalin would attack in the south, and he would hear no arguments to the contrary. Hitler believed he had the chance to achieve a major victory in Ukraine, and save the situation on the *Ostfront*.

Utterly convinced he was right, Hitler set about weakening Army Group Centre still further. Twenty-four of its thirty Panzer and mechanized divisions – 88 per cent of its tanks in all – were ordered to move south of the Pripyat marshes, along with half its tank destroyers. This left a mere 118 battle tanks and 377 assault guns against the cunningly hidden 2,715 Soviet tanks and 1,355 assault guns. There were, in fact, no actual tanks remaining in the so-called 3rd Panzer Army. German artillery was just as depleted, with 2,589 barrels against a staggering 24,383. The discrepancy in the air was also profound – the Luftwaffe had only 602 operational aircraft to the Soviets' 4,000, and the lack of high-octane fuel meant that many could not even take off. Hitler also slashed Army Group Centre to a mere 400,000 men, from its peak of one million. The Red Army had 1.25 million soldiers for the first phase alone – already a three to one ratio – but 2.5 million more were waiting just behind the front line. The Germans didn't stand a chance.[23]

Field Marshal Ernst Busch, commander of Army Group Centre, was one of Hitler's most sycophantic and obsequious generals. After meetings with the Führer, who by now was issuing ever more incoherent and impossible orders, the compliant Busch would tell his senior general staff officer Colonel Peter von der Groeben: 'I am a soldier. I have learnt to obey.' This blind obedience did Busch's career a lot of good, but it was a disaster for the men about to face the full might of the Red Army.

Despite Stalin's best efforts, information was starting to leak that the Soviets were up to something in Byelorussia. There had been slip-ups, as when General P.A. Rotmistrov, commander of the 5th Guards Tank Army, was reported by a Russian prisoner of war to have been spotted in the Smolensk area.[24] The Germans began to detect Soviet tanks and troops. General Jordan, commander of 9th Army, tried to convince Field Marshal Busch to persuade Hitler that something terrible was about to happen. The 9th Army Intelligence Summary of 19 June stated categorically that 'the enemy attacks to be expected on Army Group Centre's sector – on Bobruisk, Mogilev, Orsha and possibly southwest of Vitebsk – will be of more than local character. All in all the scale of ground and air forces suggests that the aim is to bring about the collapse of Army Group Centre's salient by penetrations of several sectors.' The report was ignored.

The staff of 9th Army were furious, but Busch remained steadfastly loyal to Hitler, flying to Führer headquarters only on 22 June, when the Soviet operation was just hours away. When Busch finally told Hitler that an attack of some kind was expected the Führer flew into an uncontrollable rage. The Soviets could not have deceived them; the Red Army was too weak to attack in both places; how dare he introduce such nonsense to a serious discussion? Busch was shocked by the dressing down, and scuttled back to Minsk, calling a hasty conference and telling his horrified generals that the Führer had ordered them to hold their positions at any cost. Worse still, they were to halt all construction on rear lines of defence. The German troops would have nowhere to go when the tidal wave came.

In a strange twist of fate, Hitler seemed bent on repeating Stalin's grave mistakes of 1941, refusing to listen either to those generals who were now trying to warn him of an imminent attack, or to the latest intelligence reports. As a result, Bagration was to become almost a mirror image of Barbarossa, with hundreds of thousands of German troops waiting like sitting ducks to be encircled, killed or imprisoned. One of Hitler's most ludicrous inventions, announced in Führer Order no. 11 of 8 March 1944, was the creation of 'Feste Plätze', or fortress cities. The idea stemmed from Hitler's First World War experience, and his determination that not a single piece of ground was to be given over to the enemy. It ran contrary to his earlier strategy – he had never wanted his troops to become bogged down in street fighting in Leningrad or Moscow, for example. Now, however, cities were to be designated as 'fortresses', and to hold out like medieval castles even when completely surrounded. Those trapped within them were to fight on until help came; if it did not, they were to die in a heroic orgy of blood, defending every last inch of ground in the name of the Fatherland. The latter scenario was the most probable, as by now there was little hope of holding any of these 'fortresses', or of saving the men and matériel trapped inside them. It was sheer madness, but as Albert Speer put it, 'by this time Hitler had started to issue orders which were clearly insane'; they were 'pathologically self-destructive', and their only result could be 'glorious' death.[25]

On 19 June, the complete failure of von dem Bach's anti-partisan warfare in Byelorussia was made abundantly clear. Despite being hunted down for thirty months, and despite at that very moment enduring the brutality of his Operation '*Kormoran*' anti-bandit sweep, the partisans detonated over 10,000 explosives in a massive coordinated action which paralyzed communication routes at the rear of Army Group Centre. Von dem Bach was shaken, and suspected that a Russian invasion was imminent. He was right. On 22 June the Soviets launched probing attacks to determine German strength along the front line, while engineering teams worked through the night clearing paths across the massive minefields in front of the German positions.

Many of the Germans did not know it, but that night was to be their last moment of calm. Some suspected that the Soviets might attack the next day – the third anniversary of Barbarossa. The atmosphere was tense. They sat in their grass-lined foxholes or prefabricated steel pillboxes, or in their bunkers furnished with stoves and beds and samovars, and lit fires to try to keep the infernal mosquitoes and midges at bay. Hot food, tinned liver and blood sausage with *Schmalzbrot* was washed down with tea, *ersatz* coffee or schnapps. Some read letters from home by the light of their Hindenburg candles; officers sat in more luxurious bunkers and stonewall shelters insulated with navy-blue overcoats stripped from the enemy dead.[26] Some sang songs to the accompaniment of harmonicas, smoked and drank whatever alcohol they could get. The smell of unwashed woollen uniforms, heavy leather equipment, grease and oil filled the air. Many of the infantrymen thought 'of wives and children, of mothers and fathers', and of the bodies of their fallen comrades 'lying still and cold' beneath their birch crosses. Some read the Bible. Many still hoped that the real offensive would break out further south, and that they would somehow be spared. But even those who feared the worst had absolutely no idea of the massive scale of the attack they were about to face. Very few of the Germans on the front line in Byelorussia that night ever made it home.

Just across from them, a staggering 2.4 million Soviet soldiers were preparing for battle. The front-line troops were told about the attack at the last possible moment during the obligatory evening Party and Komsomol meetings. So careful had the deception been that most were surprised to learn that they were going on the offensive in the morning, but morale was extremely high, and when they heard they cheered and sang and shouted slogans against the Germans. This was the anniversary of the Nazi invasion of the Soviet Union, and it was time for revenge. Whatever happened from now on, they were told, it was an honour to die in battle. The crimes of the German invaders had been seen by all of them – the burned villages, the dead women and children – now it was time to seize the moment and fight. Many sensed that they were to be part of a decisive moment in history. As one soldier put it 'It was better to fight than to sit around in the trenches – the mood was electrified.'[27]

The Great Offensive

At exactly 0500 hours on the foggy morning of 23 June 1944 General Ivan Bagramyan gave the order to begin. Suddenly the mist was ripped by the sound of fire. The Germans, having just washed and shaved in the early-morning light, didn't know what hit them. The concentration and magnitude of the opening barrage were overwhelming, as thousands of shells exploded and pounded and shook the earth around them. The noise was deafening, the vibrations of the ground like a series of earthquakes, an attack of 'unprecedented ferocity' in which 'the air was thick and the light was blocked out by smoke and debris', and a 'whirlwind of iron and lead' howled, 'slicing through anything it hit'. The first round penetrated six kilometres into the German lines, crushing the forward trenches; then came rolling or double rolling

71

barrages by hundreds of multiple-rocket launchers. Aircraft blackened the sky, pounding the German lines with rockets and bombs. Veniamin Fyodorov, a twenty-year-old soldier with the Soviet 77th Guards infantry regiment, watched the immense show of strength in awe: 'When you look ahead, you see bits of earth flying up into the air and you see explosions. As if you light a match. Flashes, flashes.' For the German soldiers it was hell: 'We threw ourselves into the deepest trenches. Earth and shrapnel struck our steel helmets.' German artillerymen mounted a feeble counter-attack, but the Russians targeted them with long-range artillery and blasted them to a pulp. A Russian signalman reported that 'the whole line was burning from the shell bursts, almost all positions were seen to be blazing'.

With the 'monstrous hurrah!' characteristic of the Soviet infantry, the Russian soldiers swarmed forward in their thousands, fourteen armies in all, with over a thousand infantrymen per kilometre of front. 'It was a sea of brown uniforms, our machine guns and explosive shells did no good, the Russians pressed forward, apparently oblivious to their losses.' The 'crazy attacks' and wild choir of Russian 'hurrahs' struck terror in the Germans. Gone were the massed Soviet charges of Barbarossa days: a German 9th Army report described these new waves as intelligent, with 'concentrated groups of infantry supported by highly concentrated and well-controlled fire from heavy weapons'. 1,700,000 combat and support troops were ready to push into the breach. After them came the T-34s and other tanks – along the four Soviet fronts an astounding 5,200 tanks and self-propelled guns had been prepared. There were 5,300 Soviet aircraft ready to pound the German lines. Then came 'the cries of the wounded, of the agonized dying, shrieking as they stare at a part of their body reduced to pulp, the cries of men touched by the shock of battle'.[28] Army Group Centre's War Diary reported in panic that 'the major attack by the enemy north-west of Vitebsk has taken the German command completely by surprise'.

The Germans in and around Vitebsk were in shock, and the 53rd Corps was barely able to hang on. After only one day of fighting Colonel General Georg-Hans Reinhardt, leader of the 3rd Panzer Army, proposed withdrawing, but Busch retorted that Hitler had ordered the city to be held at all costs. By the third day the Soviets had encircled the beleaguered men.

Reinhardt, who was soon to fight at Warsaw, was utterly shocked when he saw the Soviets bearing down on Vitebsk. The sheer number of men, tanks and planes was simply overwhelming. Reinhardt realized that the situation was hopeless, and begged Busch to ask Hitler for permission to fall back to the 'Tiger Line' east of Minsk. Hitler angrily refused. Within hours entire formations, including the 6th Corps' 299th and 197th Infantry Divisions, had simply ceased to exist. By evening two more German divisions were encircled, and another two were about to be. Major General Gollwitzer was trapped in the pocket, and pleaded down the phone for Busch to give the order to retreat. Busch told him he had to fight to the last man, snapping: 'The Führer has ordered it.' Generals Reinhardt and Zeitzler shouted at one another for over an hour before finally agreeing that all but one division could be allowed to make a run for it. In the meantime Gollwitzer disobeyed orders and tried to break out. He failed. He tried again in the evening, amidst the chaos of shelling and strafing from the air, but failed again, and was forced to watch as the ancient city went up in flames, 'the old Tsar's palace blazing and the ruined towers of the cathedrals and churches surrounded by brightly burning ruins of houses surmounted by thick black smoke'. The German 53rd Corps was wiped out; 17,000 survivors were taken into captivity, including Gollwitzer. The 4th Luftwaffe Field Division, which had managed to get out of Vitebsk, was mown down in the forests on the outskirts of the town.

A few months before Bagration, the great painter Marc Chagall had published an address to his beloved Vitebsk from his exile in New York. The 'saddened wanderer' could 'only paint your breath on my pictures', he said of his beautiful home town. Before the fires of 1941 and 1944 the ancient city that Chagall had known had been one of the gems of Byelorussia. Lying on the hills above the Vitba River, its spires and domes and ornate wooden houses had spilled down towards the bridges and out to the harbour. Few German soldiers would have known that this was the great artist's birthplace, but those few who had seen the pre-war exhibitions at the Sturm Gallery in Berlin would have remembered the swirling images of the city, with Chagall and his adored wife Bella floating in the sky above its chimneys and spires and rooftops. Chagall had wept when he heard of the destruction of the Jewish quarter in 1942. When he heard that the Soviets had surrounded the German occupiers he started work on a picture of his father's old house. But that, too, had already disappeared in the flames.

For the next three days 28,000 German soldiers were systematically wiped out in the area around Vitebsk. After his return from a Russian prisoner of war camp in the 1950s, General Gollwitzer wrote a bitter account of the terrible – and unnecessary – destruction of his men thanks to Hitler's insane 'fortress' policy and Busch's unwillingness to stand up to his master. 'Under Busch,' General Ziemke would later say, 'Headquarters, Army Group Centre had become a mindless instrument for transmuting the Führer's will.'[29]

And Vitebsk was just the beginning. Over the next few days four of Hitler's 'fortresses' would tumble like bowling pins. Orsha was next. Lying on the main Moscow–Minsk road, it held the

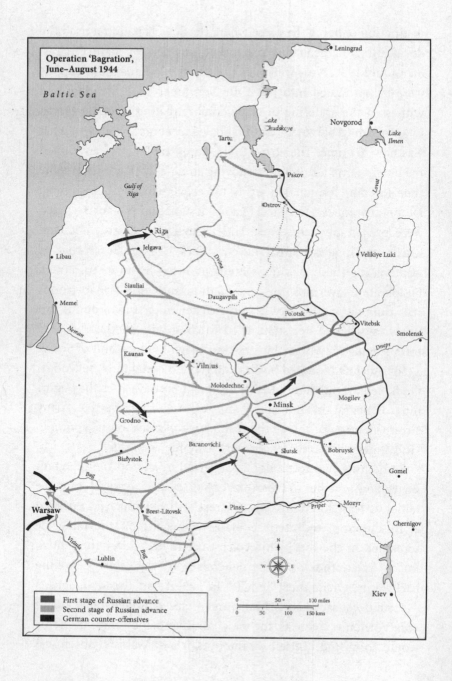

Operation 'Bagration',
June–August 1944

Baltic Sea

Leningrad

Lake Chudskoye

Novgorod

Lake Ilmen

Tartu

Pskov

Gulf of Riga

Ostrov

Riga

Jelgava

Libau

Dvina

Velikiye Luki

Siauliai

Daugavpils

Polotsk

Meme

Vitebsk

Smolensk

Nieman

Dnepr

Kaunas

Vilnius

Molodechno

Minsk

Mogilev

Grodno

Baranovichi

Slutsk

Bobruysk

Gomel

Białystok

Bug

Brest-Litovsk

Pinsk

Pripet

Mozyr

Warsaw

Chernigov

Vistula

Bug

Lublin

N
W   E
S

Kiev

First stage of Russian advance
Second stage of Russian advance
German counter-offensives

0   50   130 miles
0   50   100   150 kms

distinction of being the place where the Soviets had first used the devastating Katyusha multiple-rocket launchers, or 'Stalin Organs', on 14 July 1941. Now well over 2,000 of these punishing weapons were being hauled into place. In November 1812 Stendhal had witnessed the suffering of Napoleon's retreating forces at Orsha in an 'ocean of barbarity', but that paled by comparison with what was now to come. The Soviet 2nd Guards Tank Corps enveloped the city in a matter of hours, moving so quickly that it took some time for the German 4th Army to realize what was happening. Desperate requests to cancel Orsha's designation as a 'fortress city' were predictably refused by Hitler; finally, in despair, General Kurt von Tippelskirch disobeyed orders, lying to Busch that he was holding the line while secretly allowing his units to retreat. Desperation overtook the tens of thousands of German troops still trapped in the city. Panic-stricken men ran around, not knowing what to do; some tried to cling onto the last hospital train leaving for Minsk, but this was blown up by a unit of Soviet T-34s, hurling bloodied bodies and twisted metal into the woods. Orsha fell on the night of 26 June, only four days after the beginning of Bagration. But Hitler still refused to believe that Army Group Centre was facing the real Soviet offensive of the summer. 'The attack will come in northern Ukraine', he ranted.

Something had to be done. General Jordan and the reluctant Busch flew together to Obersalzberg on 26 June to try to convince Hitler at least to change his 'fortress' order. Hitler was enraged at this attempt to interfere. Banging his fist on the table, he screamed at the top of his voice that he had never thought of Busch as another of those generals who was 'always looking backwards'. Orsha must be held! In fact, it had already fallen.

Jordan was sacked on 27 June, and replaced by General Nikolaus von Vormann, who as the new commander of the 9th Army would soon find himself on the outskirts of Warsaw. Busch was removed the next day, and replaced by the foul-mouthed and abusive Field Marshal Walter Model, who would also play a pivotal role in the fight for the Polish capital. Those in FHQ called Model 'Hitler's fireman'; his staffers, who hated him, called him '*Frontschwein*', but as an excellent tactician and innovator he was the best choice for the moment. Later, Hitler would call him 'my best field marshal' and 'the saviour of the Eastern Front'. Rokossovsky, however, was not impressed. 'Model? We can take on Model too,' he said.

Hitler's decision to appoint Model would prove crucial for the fate of the Warsaw Uprising. By now, the constellation of generals that would soon meet on the Vistula was in place. Above all, it was Model's creation of a defensive line at the Vistula that would present the greatest challenge to Rokossovsky in August 1944, and that would have disastrous implications for the people of Warsaw.

The Soviets did not let up. The unfortunate men of Lieutenant General Rudolf Bamler's 12th Infantry Division and Major General Gottfried von Erdmannsdorff's city garrison had been chosen to be the human sacrifices in the next Soviet target – Mogilev. Von dem Bach, hearing of the Soviet onslaught, hastily abandoned his luxurious palace in the city, where Tsar Nicholas II had spent much of the First World War, and fled first to Minsk and then to Poznań. His staff worked at breakneck speed to move or burn the hundreds of thousands of documents outlining the deadly '*Banditenkrieg*' that had raged in Byelorussia on his watch. Most of the evidence of the mass murder of Jews, gypsies, 'partisans' and ordinary civilians was lost in the flames, or was captured by the Soviets.

Mogilev was completely surrounded on 28 June. General Tippelskirch ordered a reserve Panzer grenadier division to plug the hole east of the city, but the situation there was desperate:

'We've got nothing but holes here!' General Martinek yelled back down the phone. The trapped Germans were helpless. One Red Army soldier watched in awe as Soviet planes dived over the city, blasting away at the men trapped in it: the planes were so close that he could see the stars painted on their sides. 'The Red Army, defeated and shamed at Barbarossa, has been transformed into a technological marvel,' he said. 'And now we are in the Soviet rear! The Red Army passed by like a typhoon. The enemy has scuttled off in disarray. Even the Germans did not manage this in 1941!!' Bamler and Erdmannsdorff capitulated on 30 June; Stalin had the latter hanged.

In the great staggered offensive in Byelorussia it was General Rokossovsky and the 1st Byelorussian Front that were the last to go forward, in what proved to be one of the most dramatic attacks of the war. Rokossovsky had spent weeks constructing wooden causeways and corduroy roads through the 'impassable' swamps; his men had swum across lakes and rivers, using four-man LMN rubber rafts and MPK rubber 'swimming suits' which, with their built-in inner tubes, made the wearer look like some strange floating beast. They had made their way through the dense, tangled forests using special shoes to get them across the bogs, and had built a veritable flotilla of rafts and boats, as well as platforms for trundling machine guns, light artillery and mortars into position. The massive build-up of men and matériel had been so ingeniously hidden from the Germans that when the Soviets burst upon them on 23 June the 9th Army was taken completely by surprise.

Rokossovsky pushed forward in a perfect two-pronged pincer movement around the city of Bobruisk, and on 27 June he snapped the pincers shut. A hundred thousand soldiers of the German 9th Army were trapped. On 29 June 30,000 of them slipped out of the trap, but the Soviets quickly hunted them down; only 10,000 escaped back to the German lines. There was little that could be done to save those who remained. The 20th Panzer Division had only forty tanks left against Rokossovsky's nine hundred. 'Bombers of S.I. Rudenko's 16th Air Army cooperating with the 48th Army struck blow after blow at the enemy group,' Zhukov recalled. 'Scores of lorries, cars and tanks, fuel and oil was burning all over the battlefield . . . The terror-stricken German soldiers ran in every direction,' and the cries of the dying 'shook the strongest man'. The city, with its great fortress that had repelled even Napoleon, descended into chaos. 'Everywhere dead bodies are lying. Dead bodies, wounded people, people screaming, medical orderlies, and then there were those who were completely covered, who were not taken out at all, who were buried there straight away.' At 9 a.m. on 29 June permission was wrenched from Hitler to allow the 35th Army Corps and the 41st Panzer Corps to break out, but fifteen minutes later he changed his mind. Seventy thousand leaderless and confused soldiers awaited orders; some obeyed Hitler and fought, others tried to flee. The 134th Infantry Division reported that 'no trace of order remained. Vehicles and heavy armour were simply blown up and troops escaped *en masse* over the remaining bridges.' The division commander, Ernst Philipp, committed suicide in despair. At the very end, when the situation was completely hopeless, Hitler again gave them permission to break out. And then the last command arrived: 'Destroy vehicles, shoot horses, take as much ammunition and rations with you as you can carry. Every man for himself.' But by then they could no longer move. General Vincenz Müller ordered the men of 12th Corps to lay down their arms. He then walked over to his Soviet counterpart, General Boldin, and asked him how to surrender. 'It is very simple,' Boldin replied. 'Your soldiers lay down their arms and become prisoners of war.'

The Russians swarmed through the city, killing any Germans

they found hiding in the ruins. There were many atrocities and acts of revenge. A member of the 58th Regiment of the 6th Infantry Division who was hiding in a hospital reported: 'On 29 June the Russians occupied the infirmary . . . They went from bed to bed systematically, pointed their machine pistols at the wounded and emptied their magazines. A great clamour arose. Today I can still hear the screams for help of the wounded in their hopeless situation against the firing Russians. It was a bloodbath.'[30]

At the Berezina

The scenes of slaughter of the 4th Army along the Berezina River rivalled the fate of the Grande Armée in 1812. One German soldier recalled how, in 1941, an entrenchment party had found a Napoleonic eagle in the earth by the river, dropped no doubt as the Grande Armée had fled. 'The parallels with the Napoleonic retreat were now borne in upon us in a shattering way,' he said of the crumbling front. The Soviets squeezed the Germans up against the river and mowed them down. The living did anything they could to try to get across: some floated on pieces of wood, some who couldn't swim clutched onto those who could, until it looked as if 'bunches of grapes were sinking in the water'. At one section the Germans tried to force their way out to get to the river no fewer than fifteen times. General P.A. Tieremov, commander of the Russian 108th Infantry Division, recalled an attempted German breakout past the 444 and 407 Regiments. 'Despite the concentration of artillery no fewer than 2,000 enemy soldiers and officers walked into our positions. Artillery opened fire at seven hundred metres, machine guns at four hundred metres. The Nazis kept walking. Artillery shells were exploding in the middle of their formations. Machine guns felled entire rows of people. The Nazis walked on, stepping over the bodies of their soldiers. They walked to break through, and did not take anything else into account. It was a crazy attack. We saw a horrific picture from our observation posts.' General Gorbatov decided to use the events at Bobruisk to educate his troops. 'I crossed the railway bridge on the Berezina River adopted by the enemy for vehicle movement and I was shocked at what I saw. The entire field next to the bridge was covered with the bodies of the Nazis. There were no less than 3,000 . . . I changed the route of two divisions of the second line of attack so that they would walk past that railway bridge and see the work done by the comrades of the first line of attack. It gave them an extra six kilometres but they would be rewarded in the future because they had seen what could be done.'

The Germans held only one crossing on the Mogilev–Minsk highway, and utter pandemonium reigned as every kind of vehicle tried to crowd onto the bridge. 'There were fights and swearing; the military police were powerless,' recalled one soldier. Sturmovik ground-attack aircraft strafed the fleeing troops, killing them in droves. For those fortunate enough to get across alive, the other side of the river was equally chaotic. Infantrymen and officers of all ranks headed towards Minsk as fast as they could; many wore only their underwear, having stripped down for their swim across the river, and most were without boots, weapons or equipment. These so-called *Rückkämpfer*, alone or in small groups, were harassed by the hated partisans. One remembered finding a field station in which there were around three hundred untransportable men. Nobody, not even the doctors, knew where the front was any more. 'Partisans fell on the first-aid station. My courier and I ran several metres to the side and hid in the forest . . . later we moved back to the aid station. It was a horrible sight. As far as we could establish, everyone was shot or slain . . . we established that 400–500 lay dead strewn in the forest that day. Some of the wounded had been hit from behind with a shovel as they fled. This dreadful sight gave me the courage, in spite of my wounds, not to give up. I swore never to fall into the hands of "Ivan".[31] Others were harassed from the air. The Russians strafed them and dropped phosphorus, giving the evening sky an eerie glow. The morale of the Germans was at rock bottom as they struggled across the boggy Byelorussian terrain. 'We got to a bridge. Ready to blow. With savage shouts, we succeeded in driving the horses across the river . . . a mine laid by our sappers blew up drovers, horses, and the first of the guns. We didn't care. We understood that no one was expecting us to get through.'[32] By now, thirteen German divisions had been destroyed. That day, Rokossovsky was promoted to Marshal.

The escaping Germans found no comfort in 'Fortress Minsk'. The city, where von dem Bach and Himmler had met so confidently in 1941, and which had been slated by Hitler for destruction and replacement by a new metropolis to be named 'Asgard', was now in utter confusion. The streets leading west were clogged with soldiers and equipment, and ragged columns of evacuating civilians: 'Old and young women, children, pregnant women, single men, barefoot in ripped shoes with sacking wrapped around their feet. An endless column stretched backward and forwards, making all the time for the west. In some places the forest was already burning, a last barrier against the advancing Russians.'[33] Von dem Bach had made sure to invent some ailment or other so that he could fly out of Minsk to the safety of Poznań in good time. Oskar Dirlewanger and his men were almost annihilated, but managed to fight their way out of Minsk, and raced down the Lida and Grodno road towards Poland, their two-year murder streak finally at an end. Bronisław Kaminski and his 6,000-strong brigade, fresh from recent massacres at Borisov, fought their way out too, and also made a dash for the Polish border. All of them would soon surface in Warsaw.

Two days before the start of Bagration, Albert Speer had ordered that 40–50,000 boys aged between ten and fourteen who had been caught in von dem Bach's 'Kormoran' sweep be transported to the Reich. 'This action is aimed not only at preventing a direct reinforcement of the enemy's military strength,' he wrote, 'but also at a reduction of his biological potentialities as viewed from the perspective of the future. These ideas have been voiced not only by the Reichsführer SS but also by the Führer.'[34] The Red Army had advanced so quickly that the Germans had not had time to carry out Speer's order. Later, when the Soviets reached Minsk, they found several trainloads of these starving children crammed into railway carriages, still awaiting deportation to the Reich.

When Model arrived in Minsk to take command of Army Group Centre he found the city in an uproar. The Soviets were less than twenty kilometres from his headquarters, and there were no reserves to attack their bridgeheads. The Russians were racing to close the pincers around Minsk, just as the Germans had done, in reverse, in 1941. It finally began to dawn on Hitler that Stalin intended nothing less than the complete encirclement and anni-hilation of Army Group Centre. He still ranted that his generals had to hold out at any cost, but after a week of massive losses, he at last allowed German Panzer divisions to be diverted from Ukraine. The 5th Panzer Division, reinforced with a battalion of Tiger tanks, now went up against General Pawel Rotmistrov's 5th Guards Tank Army, hindering the Soviet advance. The tank battles raged for two days outside Minsk, and the Red Army suffered enormous losses, leading to Rotmistrov's dismissal; but the German losses – their forces were reduced from 159 to just eighteen tanks – were more serious, as they had nothing to replace them with. The Tigers and Panzers had bought Army Group Centre some time, but they could not stem the Soviet tide, and the fate of Minsk was sealed.

On 1 July the Nazis hurriedly blew up important buildings and key installations in the city. Fifteen thousand unarmed *Rückkämpfer*, 8,000 wounded and 12,000 rear-echelon staff from Army Group Centre headquarters were still trying to get out, and the 5th Panzer Army did all it could to hold the Soviets off a little longer. The gleaming white SS headquarters that Himmler had so proudly visited in 1941 were now empty – nobody bothered to burn papers any more, and files were tossed off the backs of trucks to allow room for a few more people. Only on the evening of 2 July did Hitler give permission for Minsk to be evacuated, but it was far too late. There were scenes of panic at stations as senior officers exploited their rank to get on the trains, 'claiming precedence for themselves'.[35] At dawn on 3 July, the 1st and 3rd Byelorussian Fronts encircled the remnants of two German armies, while the 2nd Byelorussian Front attacked retreating Germans from the east. Model had inherited a desperate situation, and even he could not save the troops of the 4th Army and the remnants of the 9th Army. 'Hitler and Stalin were very alike in some dreadful respects, but there is one fundamental point on which they differed absolutely,' Albert Speer would later say. 'Stalin had faith in his generals and, although meticulously informed of all major plans and moves, left them comparative freedom. Our generals, on the contrary, were robbed of all independence, all elasticity of action, even before Stalingrad. All decisions were taken by Hitler and once made were as if poured in cement, whatever changing circumstances demanded. This, more than anything else, lost Germany the war.'

Hitler insisted that Model force a reversal with a series of 'rapid hard counter-strikes'. But with what? The 9th Army was smashed to bits, the 4th Army had been surrounded, and the 3rd Panzer Army only had one corps left of its original three. The Soviets began to bombard the city: 'At 1600 hundreds of weapons opened fire with hurricane force. Thousands of tonnes of murderous metal flew over the German positions.' The city was clouded in a haze of smoke and dust.

The liquidation of the three huge groups of men trapped in the Minsk encirclement took eight days. Knowing that they must be either killed or captured, the Germans fought fanatically. In the next few days the losses on both sides were extremely high: only nine hundred of the 15,000 4th Army troops survived; only a fraction of the 100,000 trapped Germans ever made it back to their own lines. One Red Army soldier described tanks rolling over the bodies of the dead and wounded, making a 'bloody paste'. A German infantryman remembered the suffering of the horses, how they were 'ripped apart by shells, their eyes bulging out from empty red sockets . . . That is just almost worse than the torn-away faces of the men.' On 3 July the 2nd Guards Tank Corps broke into the city. Zhukov, who knew Minsk well, wrote: 'The capital of Byelorussia could hardly be recognized . . . Now everything was in ruins, with heaps of rubble in place of whole blocks of flats. The people of Minsk presented a pitiful sight, worn out and haggard, many of them crying.' Special composite detachments were formed to comb the woods and hunt down the thousands of Germans who had wriggled free; by 11 July the rest were killed or captured. To Hitler's fury, 57,000 German prisoners were taken, including twelve generals – three corps commanders and nine division commanders.[36] Finally, he seemed to sense what was happening. On 4 July he gave a speech in the Platterhof which sounded almost defeatist: 'If we lose the war, gentlemen, no re-adjustment will be necessary. It will only be necessary that every-body thinks about his own readjustment from this life into the next, whether he wants to do it himself, whether he wants to let himself be hanged, whether he wants to get a bullet through the base of the skull, whether he wants to starve or go to work in Siberia. Those are the only choices which the individual will then have to make.'[37]

The Germans' panicked retreat did not stop their ruthless scorched-earth policy. Himmler ordered that everything left behind was to be razed: 'Not a house is to remain standing, not a mine is to be available which is not destroyed and not a well which is not poisoned.' Villages were hastily torched and animals slaughtered; nothing was to be left for the Red Army. German soldier Harry Mielert watched as 'buildings and facilities were blown up by Pioneers. Everything roared, flamed, shook, cattle bellowed, soldiers searched through all the buildings.'[38] Once again the civilians paid the heaviest price, either being killed outright or left with nothing. 'Ruined villages, debris, and ashes marked our way. Behind us the last houses went up in flames, woods burned on the horizon, munitions dumps were blown up, and flares, shells and bombs went up like fireworks into the night sky.'[39] The policy sometimes backfired: the stragglers needed water, but the wells had been damaged or poisoned; at one well a retreating soldier saw 'a scummy mass with rotten wood and thorn-apple bushes afloat on it. Other wells had been blown up, and the last blocked off by mines. Tears of rage filled my eyes.' But 'we had been ordered to spread devastation so that our pursuers could find no shelter'.[40] The Soviet condemnation of Model as a war criminal, which led directly to his suicide in 1945, included the ruthless scorched-earth policies he sanctioned during this retreat.

The Soviet offensive had been so successful that some in the West doubted the reports of Stalin's triumph. Could it possibly be true that the Germans had suffered nearly half a million casualties, that 150,000 men, including twelve generals, had been captured, and that an astounding seventeen divisions of Army Group Centre had been wiped out in a mere two weeks? Stalin decided to prove to the world what he had done. In Operation 'The Great Waltz', named after a 1938 American film based on the life of Johann Strauss, he marched over 50,000 of the Germans captured at Minsk through Moscow. The vanquished had been loaded onto cattle trucks, and many had died from thirst or exhaustion on the way to the massive PoW camps that had been set up outside Moscow. Those who collapsed due to illness or wounds were shot. On 17 July the surviving prisoners were collected in the Central Moscow Hippodrome and the Dynamo Stadium. From there they were marched, led by their generals, through the streets of the city and into Red Square itself. It was a sobering sight. Muscovites watched quietly as the haggard men filed past, their fearful, downcast faces revealing the scale of their defeat. When a handful of young people jeered and threw stones at the prisoners, the Russian-born British war correspondent Alexander Werth noted that they were quickly restrained by their elders. The scene was too grave for that.

The Germans had been provided with a ration of greasy soup to give them energy, but their now starved digestive systems could not handle the fat, and many were stricken with acute diarrhoea. 'Thousands of the "*Vohna-Plennys*"* were unable to control their tortured bowels,' and soiled themselves as they trudged through the streets. In an act heavy with symbolism, Stalin had street cleaners follow the columns to sweep up the 'Nazi filth'.

As the German prisoners were being marched through Moscow, the Red Army was racing westward at a remarkable twenty-five kilometres a day. Stavka now realized that nothing stood between them and Poland and Lithuania. Despite technical problems,

---

* The Germanized version of the Russian for 'prisoner of war'.

stretched supply lines and exhausted troops, Stalin decided to exploit this momentum, and ordered on 28 June that Kaunas, Grodno, Białystok and Brest-Litovsk be included in Bagration.

Stavka now issued order no. 220126, directing the 3rd Byelorussian Front to take Wilno, a move which would bring the Soviets deep into Polish Home Army (AK) territory. This presented particular problems for both forces. General Bór-Komorowski, Commander-in-Chief of the Home Army, had long planned for uprisings to break out all over Poland in order to aid the Red Army to rid the country of the Nazis. The Poles hoped that by aiding the liberation of their country they would boost their claims to create an independent state after the war, and prove to the world that they were a force to be reckoned with. On 26 June the commander of the Home Army District in Wilno, General Aleksander Krzyżanowski, code-named 'Wilk', set out the plans for an uprising for that city. Called Operation 'Ostra Brama' – 'Gate of Dawn' – it involved the Poles of the AK attacking the German forces just as they were evacuating their last positions.

Like the Western Allies, the Poles had been amazed at the speed and success of the Red Army's advance, but they were well-organized and eager to fight to help liberate their country. The area around Wilno was ideal partisan territory. Vast forests and few roads had meant that they had been able to operate there even in the worst years of the occupation, with relatively little interference from the Germans; indeed, their main problems had come from rival Soviet-backed partisans, with whom they competed for matériel and influence. Over 12,000 Home Army men now gathered from Wilno and the surrounding area, but the roads were in chaos, as the city was being evacuated. The AK troops ran into retreating Germans and panicked civilians, or got caught up in local skirmishes; in the end, only about 5,000 of them actually made it to Wilno.

The German city commander, Luftwaffe Major-General Rainer Stahel, formerly city commander of Rome and a man Hitler trusted, had been ordered to hold Wilno with his 17,000 men. Stahel was not surprised when the Poles attacked on 7 July, just as the first Soviet tanks of the 3rd Byelorussian Front rolled into view. The AK were able to take part of the city centre, but were too weak to dislodge the Germans. As the Red Army began to close in, Model tried to persuade Hitler to change the designation of Wilno as a 'fortress city', but even after a series of long and violent arguments Hitler would not back down. Finally Model tricked him into thinking that the besieged troops had run out of drinking water – something Hitler himself had encountered in the First World War. He resentfully allowed a breakout, and Colonel General Reinhardt personally led the 3rd Panzer Army to create a passage through to the trapped garrison. But Stahel got only 3,000 of the 17,000 troops out; the rest were captured or killed, often in bitter hand-to-hand combat that lasted five days. The Germans surrendered on 13 July; the next day a jubilant Krzyżanowski reported to the government-in-exile in London: 'Wilno captured with great participation of the AK, which is in the city. Great losses and destruction. Relations with the Soviet Army correct at the moment.'[41] The Soviets flooded into Wilno on 15 July; Red Army and AK soldiers linked arms, sang and drank and celebrated in high spirits. The mood did not last. Within hours the NKVD had moved in. Stalin had no intention of allowing the Polish Home Army either political or military power, and had decided that it should be eliminated immediately.

On 14 July Stalin had issued Directive No. 220145, stating that all members of the Polish underground in Lithuania, western Byelorussia and western Ukraine were to be detained and disarmed. Ivan Serov, Lavrentii Beria's deputy, who was responsible for the massacre of thousands of Polish army officers at

Katyń in 1940, and who would later crush the 1956 Hungarian Revolution, was sent to Wilno to 'guarantee' that this was done. 'Wilk' and his officers were invited to discuss future 'terms of cooperation with the Red Army', but were taken prisoner instead; those who resisted were shot. Beria reported to Stalin that 15,000 AK soldiers had been disarmed, and requested his permission to hand those officers who had 'operative value' over to the NKVD, the NKGB and SMERSH; the rest were to go to NKVD camps 'lest they undertake the organization of numerous Polish underground formations'.[42] News of this treachery reached General Bór-Komorowski, who was now in the final stages of planning the uprising in the Polish capital. A few days later Beria moved Serov to Lublin to repeat the process there. Serov would then be sent to Warsaw, where he would have most of the AK soldiers or 'hostile elements' who fell into his hands either forced to join the Soviet-led Polish 1st Army, or sent to prison camps.[43] After the arrests in Wilno, Bór knew that Soviet treachery in Warsaw was a foregone conclusion. It was not a good omen.

General Stahel, on the other hand, was lionized by Hitler for his defence of Wilno against the advancing Red Army. That most of his troops had been killed was irrelevant: Stahel had held on, and that was enough. Hitler awarded him Oak Leaves to his Knight's Cross, and appointed him city commander of Warsaw.[44] But this was to prove irrelevant. Stahel would spend the beginning of the uprising under siege in the Brühl Palace, and Himmler would wrest control from him soon enough.

To Kill Hitler

The second extraordinary event to rock Germany in the summer of 1944, after the shock of Bagration, was the attempted assassination of Hitler on 20 July. The day after the collapse of Wilno,

Hitler had moved back to the stifling atmosphere of Rastenburg in order to be close to the front, swapping the homely Berghof for the miserable Wolf's Lair, which was situated in what even he called 'the swampiest, most climatically unfavourable and midge-infested region possible'.[45] During the flight he had kept the blinds of the aircraft drawn to spare himself views of destroyed German towns. But he made the move believing that 'As long as the soldiers know I am holding out here, they will be all the more determined in their struggle to stabilize the front'.[46]

Rastenburg was stifling. It was high summer, and the air was hot and sticky. The air-conditioning whined all day; even the guards wore mosquito-netting over their helmets. Hitler's secretary Christa Schroeder recalled the horrible boredom and isolation there: 'We sleep, eat, drink, and let people talk to us, if we are too lazy to talk ourselves.' Hitler seemed to turn in upon himself, sitting in his rooms isolated from the rest of the world. According to his doctor, Morell, who by now had him hooked on various drugs, Hitler had developed a kind of 'bunker mentality'. 'It was the only place he felt at home . . . the only place he could work and think.'[47]

Claus von Stauffenberg's failed attempt on Hitler's life at the Wolf's Lair on 20 July was to have dire consequences for the fate of the Warsaw Uprising. First, Hitler came out of the destroyed conference room believing that he had been saved by divine providence, and was destined to snatch Germany from the jaws of defeat. According to Christa Schroeder, he had had a premonition about the attack the night before. 'Nothing must happen to me,' he had told her. 'There is nobody who can carry on the business.' Just after the blast, Morell heard him shout, 'I'm invulnerable! I'm immortal!' Albert Speer found Hitler 'triumphant' in the days after the attack, believing that he had discovered the true reason for his failure to win the war: the treachery of his own generals. 'Now at last the great positive turning point in the war had come. The days of treason were over, new and better generals would assume the command.' Hitler, who had previously referred to the barbarity of the Soviet dictator, now praised Stalin for the Terror, claiming that by eliminating the former commander-in-chief of the Red Army, Tukhachevsky, and liquidating his General Staff he had 'made room for fresh, vigorous men', free of the tainted ideas of Tsarist times. Hitler even toyed with the preposterous notion that there had been 'treasonous collaboration' between the Russian and German general staffs. 'Now I know why all my great plans in Russia had to fail in recent years. It was all treason! But for those traitors we would have won long ago!'[48]

He continued to rant against the generals and the officer corps, becoming ever more paranoid until his death in the Berlin bunker in April 1945. As the US Strategic Bombing Survey later put it, the attempt on his life 'set in motion in the mind of that evil and uncertain man a chain of psychological reactions that separated the Führer from his advisers and friends and gradually undermined his psyche. In the end, these reactions trapped Hitler in the maze of his own obsessions and left him with self-destruction as the only escape.'[49]

The German commanders scrambled to outdo one another in the proof of their loyalty. Model was the first to write a note of condolence to the 'great man': '*Mein Führer*,' he said, 'we soldiers of Army Group Centre and Army Group Nordukraine have just heard with outrage and hatred of the criminal attempt against your life. We thank the Almighty that He kept you, and all of Germany through you, from unimaginable disaster.'[50] All the other generals followed suit, probably more to divert suspicion than out of genuine feelings of relief. They tried to ingratiate themselves in other ways, too. General Walter Warlimont, deputy chief of operations for the OKW, remembered how Keitel and Göring had announced that 'as an indication of the unshakeable loyalty to the Führer and of the close bonds of comradeship between Wehrmacht and Party, the Party salute is to be made obligatory for all members of the Services.'[51] The order was duly given. 'The traditional salute of touching the cap with the right hand was now forbidden, and the Nazi Party salute, thrusting an outstretched right arm forward, was made mandatory. This was observed with contempt and resentment by soldiers who honoured military tradition,' recalled Warlimont, 'and the order was taken as an insult . . . it was not uncommon to observe entire companies carrying their mess tins in their right hands to avoid being compelled to demonstrate their "loyalty to the party". Later, many soldiers would claim that the assassination attempt had 'not caused a tear to be shed' among their colleagues. They had fought on not out of loyalty to Hitler, but because they felt 'bound to our duty by the oath we had sworn as soldiers of Germany; to swear, with weapons in hand, to defend our country even to the sacrifice of our lives. Not even a change in command or policy could free us from this oath.'[52]

The failed assassination attempt would have a profound effect on the course of the Warsaw Uprising precisely because the German generals had been so deeply disgraced in Hitler's eyes. Top Nazis now vied and plotted for influence. Kurt Zeitzler, who had told Hitler to his face that his 'fortress city' policy was madness, had a nervous breakdown. Heinz Guderian replaced him as Army Chief of Staff on 21 July; his promotion even earned him a cover picture on *Time* magazine. Goebbels used the attempt as an opportunity to push harder for 'total war': 'It takes a bomb under his arse to make Hitler see reason,' he wrote.[53] This would affect both the use of slave labour from Warsaw during the uprising and the creation of the *Volkssturm*, or 'people's army', which was inspired in part by the Polish resistance.

The most chilling outcome of the failed plot to kill Hitler, and the one which would have the most significant influence on the future of Warsaw, was the meteoric rise of Heinrich Himmler and the SS. Himmler was now presumptive commander-in-chief of the army, commander of the Reserve Army (a group of units of trainees and older soldiers not yet released from service) and chief of army armament, as well as commander-in-chief of the Volksgrenadier Divisions. His new position at the head of the Reserve Army, in particular, gave him great power. Himmler saw 20 July as a chance to imbue the military with the Nazi Party spirit, and to kindle the 'fire of the people's holy war'. At last the Waffen SS was to be accepted as an equal partner with the army, navy and air force. National Socialist political officers were appointed to all military headquarters – a direct copy of Soviet practice perfected by the NKVD. Thus, when the uprising broke out only eleven days after the attempt on his life, Hitler would not turn to the army for help, but to his trusted and 'Treuer Heinrich', Himmler.

For his part, Stalin was elated when he heard about the attempt on Hitler's life, and summoned Zhukov to share the good news. 'If the mad dog isn't dead already he soon will be,' he said, tipping back a glass of champagne. For Stalin, Hitler's death would have meant chaos in the Third Reich, a collapse of German morale and a much easier and quicker road to Warsaw and Berlin. When Zhukov returned to his headquarters after the meeting, he issued two orders to his senior staff: first, he was to be informed when Hitler's death was confirmed; and second, the Red Army was to push even harder than before to defeat the Germans as quickly as possible.

Speed was important. If the Third Reich was going to implode, Stalin knew that he would have to act quickly to position himself politically in Eastern and Central Europe. The Soviet dictator was now waging an all-out political, as well as military, war. As the last of the German stragglers were being hunted down in the forests around Minsk, Stalin summoned Zhukov and General A.I. Antonov to his summer house outside Moscow. 'We are strong enough to finish off Nazi Germany single-handed,' he declared triumphantly. Zhukov said that 'no one had any doubt that Germany had definitely lost the war. This was settled on the Soviet–German front in 1943 and the beginning of 1944. The question now was how soon and with what political and military results the war would end.'[54] Later that afternoon they were joined by Foreign Minister Molotov and other members of the State Committee for Defence. Stalin asked Zhukov: 'Can our troops reach the Vistula without a stop, and in what sector can we commit the 1st Polish Army, which has acquired combat efficiency?' 'Not only can our troops reach the Vistula,' Zhukov replied, 'but they must secure good bridgeheads which are essential for further offensive operations in the strategic direction of Berlin. As for the 1st Polish Army, it should be directed towards Warsaw.' At this point, Warsaw was less than two hundred kilometres from the front.

News of the assassination attempt only fuelled Stalin's determination to set up the political structure he desperately needed before Germany collapsed completely or arranged a separate peace with the West. Always wary of his allies, he told the chief of the NKGB, Boris Merkulov, that 'as long as Hitler is alive the Allies will not sign a separate peace with Germany. But they will sign a peace at once with a new government.'[55] It was a time of frenetic activity. The day after the attempt on Hitler's life the 47th Guards Army reached the western Bug River. On the same day the Red Army formed the Polski Komitet Wyzwolenia Narodowego (Polish Committee of National Liberation, PKWN) in Chełm. Stalin announced that this was now the 'only legitimate Polish government' in place on Polish soil, essentially ending any chance of reconciliation between the Polish government-in-exile in London and the Soviets. The link between Soviet military conquest and political domination was becoming abundantly clear.

Zhukov was intrinsically involved in this political element of the war. On 9 July he had met Stalin and Bolesław Bierut, Edward Osóbka-Morawski and Michał Rola-Żymierski, Stalin's Polish puppets in the PKWN. 'The Polish comrades spoke of the plight of their people who had been suffering German occupation for over four years,' Zhukov recalled. He conveniently forgot the fact that the war had started in 1939 with the mutual Soviet–German dismemberment of Poland, and the mass deportation and murder of tens of thousands of Poles. 'The members of the Polish National Liberation Committee . . . burned to see their homeland free as soon as possible.' Stalin decided that the new government was to be based in Lublin.

This political decision to set up a puppet government in Lublin, the largest city in the area, explains why on 21 July Stavka ordered General Bogdanovitj to move away from his original target of taking Siedlce and turn instead towards Lublin. Stavka issued an order to Rokossovsky to capture Lublin no later than 27 July. This ran counter to military logic, but Rokossovsky was told to put aside his doubts, as 'the political situation and the democratic independent interests of Poland acutely required this'.[56]

On 22 July Rokossovsky's 1st Byelorussian Front broke through against 4th Panzer Army's weak defence. Hitler had designated Lublin another 'fortress city', but the term was virtually meaningless, as it was being held by a mere nine hundred men. Lublin fell on 23 July. On the same day the Soviets liberated the concentration camp at Majdanek. This horrifying place, with its huts and brick crematoria and barbed-wire enclosures, was now virtually empty. The ever-efficient SS, under the direction of camp commander SS Obersturmbannführer Arthur Liebehenschel, had evacuated 15,000 prisoners in the previous weeks, the last thousand sent on a pitiless 'death march' just one day before the Soviets arrived. The Soviets found only a few hundred survivors trapped behind the barbed wire; most of them were severely crippled prisoners of war. They also found gas chambers, stained blue by Zyklon B, which the Germans had not had time to destroy completely. Eight hundred thousand shoes that had been earmarked for shipment to German civilians lay abandoned in a dusty pile.

Also on 23 July, the Polish underground AK started another uprising, this time in Lwów. This most elegant of cities, with its splendid pastel-coloured neoclassical buildings, once stood at the very furthest reaches of the Austro-Hungarian Empire. It had always been a tolerant and welcoming place, with myriad religions and languages. Poles and Ukrainians, Jews and Germans, Russians and Armenians had all lived and traded and argued together there. Before the war its great university had contained one of Europe's most celebrated faculties of mathematics, including world-renowned figures such as Stefan Banach and Stanisław Ulam.

On 18 July the German civilian authorities and pro-Nazi Ukrainian troops fled, but Hitler ordered that the Wehrmacht troops hold the city. The Polish Home Army under Władysław Filipkowski was poised to rise up, but waited until the Soviet 29th Tank Brigade of the 4th Tank Army had actually reached the city limits. The Soviet attack on Lwów was part of the hugely successful Lwów–Sandomierz offensive, which in concert with Bagration forced the Germans from Ukraine and eastern Poland. That evening the AK began the uprising, capturing the main railway station and taking the large nineteenth-century fortress, which was still filled with German supplies. The Soviet approach to Lwów had been slowed by the weather and by fanatical German resistance around Brody, but unlike so many units trapped in

Hitler's 'fortress cities', the Lwów garrison decided not to stand and fight, and managed to escape on 26 July. The Soviet 10th Tank Corps entered the outskirts of Lwów on 23 July, and were joined by the 4th Guards Tank Army. The city fell to General Konev on 27 July, and the Soviet and AK troops cooperated in mopping up any Germans still left there. The Soviets congratulated their Polish comrades on their mutual victory. But the euphoria was not to last.

Vyacheslav Yablonsky was a member of an NKVD squad sent into towns and cities to raid Gestapo and SS headquarters before the Germans could destroy evidence of their crimes. Tearing into Lwów in his American Studebaker truck, he and his team of twenty men dodged the retreating Germans and broke into the Gestapo building, where they found documents containing the names of Nazi collaborators and other 'enemies of the Soviet Union', as well as all the information the Nazis had gathered on the Polish Home Army. Interrogations began immediately. 'Informers told us if somebody hated the Soviets and was a threat to us, and we would arrest him . . . they could be saying bad things about us or just thinking we were bad. Once arrested the normal sentence was about fifteen years of forced labour . . . we thought it was normal at the time.'[57] The Soviets arrested over 5,000 Home Army soldiers who had fought with them as brothers in arms only days before. Most were sent to the Miedniki gulag; those who remained were forcibly conscripted into the Red Army, usually into Stalin's Polish 1st Army. This was treachery on a grand scale, and served as another grave warning to General Bór-Komorowski. The Warsaw Uprising was only days away. But after the arrest of so many Home Army soldiers in Lwów, Wilno and elsewhere, Bór had absolutely no reason to put his trust in Stalin.

After the fall of Lwów the Germans tried desperately to stop the Soviet advance towards the capital. General von Vormann was told to defend the Vistula's central portion and the city of Warsaw with the reorganized 9th Army, but this was impossible. There simply were not enough troops. Von Vormann reported to Army Group Centre on 25 July that 'there is not a single German division between Puławy and Siedlce' – the area just east of Warsaw – while the road to Warsaw was not manned 'by a single German soldier'.

On the same day the 8th Guards Army reached the eastern bank of the Vistula and easily established a bridgehead across the river at Magnuszew, fifty-four kilometres south of Warsaw. The 2nd Tank Army was ordered to turn north towards Brest and Warsaw, so as to cut off the retreating forces from Army Group Centre. Generaloberst Walter-Otto Weiss, leader of the 2nd Army, realized that Brest was lost, and gave the order to try to free the Germans trapped there; the plan worked, but the men, including General-Leutnant Scheller, commander of the 337th Infantry Division, were captured in a second encirclement east of Janów Podlaski. Brest fell on 28 July.

With the Polish capital within its grasp, Stavka issued new orders to Rokossovsky. These prove without a doubt that despite all later denials, Stalin did originally intend to take Warsaw in August 1944: 'After the seizure of Brest and Siedlce the attacks on the front's right flank are to be expanded in the direction of Warsaw and the mission is to, no later than 5–8 August, seize Praga and occupy the bridge emplacement on the Narew's western bank in the area around Pułtusk and Serock. On the front's left flank, the bridge emplacement on the Vistula's western bank is to be seized in the area around Dęblin–Zwoleń–Solec. The seized bridge emplacement shall be used for attacking in a north-westerly direction and thereby neutralize the enemy's resistance along the Narew and Vistula and thus guarantee the successful crossing of the Narew by the 2nd Byelorussian Front's left flank and likewise over the Vistula by those armies which are concentrated at the front's central section. Thereafter, attacks shall be planned in the direction of Toruń and Łódź.[58]

It is thus clear that, as of 28 July, the Soviets fully intended to seize the two operational bridges to the north and south of Warsaw, and to encircle the city. Like Buda and Pest, Warsaw is divided in two main parts, with the poorer eastern suburb of Praga separated by the Vistula from the main part of the city on the western side. The Stavka plan never saw the western city as a high-priority military target; rather it was intended to encircle it from the north and south, and to crush the trapped Germans as had been done at so many 'fortresses' in the previous weeks. Storming the city centre by pushing front-line troops across the bridges and into the Old Town, which was what the Polish Home Army believed the Soviets would do, was dismissed for tactical reasons from the very beginning. It would have been costly and senseless, not least because the Germans had already mined the bridges over the Vistula. The plan was always to encircle Warsaw in a giant pincer movement; indeed, that is precisely how the city was eventually taken in January 1945.

By 27 July the Soviets were moving ever closer to Warsaw's eastern suburb, and the plan to take Praga was on course. The 2nd Tank Army overwhelmed the pathetically depleted 73rd Infantry Division, easily capturing Garwolin and taking General Frank prisoner. Further south, General Radziewsky approached Warsaw on 28 July with two tank corps, leaving a third to snake its way along the riverbank. The 69th Army began to cross the Vistula at Kazimierz Dolny. Stalin had also made sure to send the 1st Polish Army to the Warsaw area, above all for propaganda reasons; it was now outside Dęblin, waiting to help 'liberate' the capital.

By 29 July the Germans' situation appeared hopeless. The 3rd

Tank Corps was outrunning the panicked men of the 73rd Infantry Division scrambling to get back across the bridges and into Warsaw; that night the Soviets severed the railway line between Warsaw and Białystok. The noose tightened further. The next place to fall was the southern suburb of Otwock – a villa colony in the pine forests originally built in the 1920s by wealthy Warsawians keen on the pleasant summer climate there. The 16th Tank Corps moved in, and despite heavy fighting destroyed the German armoured train No. 74 and began to clear the area. On the morning of 30 July the 3rd Tank Corps moved towards Zielonka, with its main force taking the city of Wołomin. The Russians now set their sights on Radzymin, a pretty neoclassical town a mere thirty-five kilometres from Warsaw.

The bustling, leafy town of Radzymin, while most famous as the childhood home of the Nobel Prize-winning writer Isaac Bashevis Singer, has been at the centre of some of the most important battles in history. Napoleon's army was there, as were Lenin's and Stalin's and Hitler's. The 1809 Battle of Radzymin saw the Poles defeat the Austrians in a battle that set the Imperial forces reeling. In 1920 it was the location of 'the Miracle on the Vistula', still considered one of the most decisive battles of the twentieth century. Now the Red Army had returned. Stalin must have been wary of this approach to Warsaw, no doubt remembering the humiliation he had suffered there twenty-four years earlier. He had never quite got over the sting of Lenin's disapproval.

But he had no reason to worry this time. The Red Army seemed invincible. The 2nd Tank Army stood on the outskirts of Warsaw with over five hundred tanks and assault guns, and Rokossovsky's troops were already moving into the right-bank suburb of Praga, with its red-brick factories and working-class tenements that stretched the whole length of the city. The excited Warsawians believed that they were about to be rid of the Germans once and for all, and although many were mistrustful of the Soviets, there was a tremendous sense of anticipation. Stalin, Zhukov and Rokossovsky expected Warsaw to fall as quickly as the other cities had in the race through Byelorussia. But this time they were wrong.

Up until now the Soviet summer offensive had been a stunning success, vastly exceeding Stavka's original expectations. In a matter of five weeks Stalin had pushed the Germans out of both Byelorussia and much of pre-war Poland, destroying an unbelievable seventeen and damaging fifty Army Group Centre divisions in the process. Bagration was the single greatest Soviet victory in numerical terms of the entire war: final estimates would put overall German losses at over a million men. Hitler had never suffered a defeat like this before, and because of it he would not be able to mount another major offensive on the Eastern Front. Now the Soviets stood a mere five hundred kilometres from Berlin. But their luck had temporarily run out. The Germans were not yet entirely beaten, and thanks to Field Marshal Model, Operation 'Bagration' was about to come to an abrupt end at the very gates of Warsaw.

When Model took command of Army Group Centre on 28 June, the situation was dire. With the Soviets ripping an ever greater hole in the German front, he knew that something had to be done, and quickly. Rather than try to argue with Hitler about withdrawing and regrouping the disorganized mass fleeing Byelorussia, Model had issued orders to bring troops to the Eastern Front from wherever possible in Europe. The Russians were moving so quickly that by the time these troops began to arrive the Red Army had already crossed the pre-war Polish border. The German reinforcements could no longer be used in Byelorussia; but they could be sent to Warsaw.

Model was in the process of amassing a considerable force, meant to include eleven tank divisions and twenty-five others, including the Grossdeutschland Division, the 3rd SS Division Totenkopf, three infantry divisions from 'Heeresgruppe Nord', and the 12th Panzer Division from Ukraine. Ten new grenadier divisions were promised by the command leadership of the Reserve Army, along with the 6th Panzer Division, the 19th Panzer Division and the 25th Panzer Division with the 6th Infanterie-Division. The 'Hermann Göring' Fallschirm-Panzer-Division was called in from Italy. Two infantry divisions, the 17th and the 73rd, were set to arrive from the Balkans and Norway, along with the new 174th Ersatz Division.[59] Many of these men took a long time to reach the front, arriving only in late July or early August, but enough had been gathered near Warsaw by 28 July to enable the first German counter-attack of the entire summer to begin. Model's gambit would lead to the biggest tank battle on Polish soil during the entire war. It would take the Soviets by surprise, and stop them in their tracks.

This could not have come at a worse time for the people of Warsaw. The great Bagration offensive was to be forced to an abrupt halt at the very moment the Poles began their ill-fated uprising. Model, with his successful counter-attack, would hammer the first nail into the coffin of the doomed Polish bid for freedom.

3

OSTPOLITIK

———≫⊂≪———

Scipio, beholding this city, which had flourished seven hundred years from its foundation . . . now came to its end in total destruction.
(Chapter XIX)

The City on the Vistula

Warsaw has the fortune – or misfortune – to be situated at the very centre of the immense flat, sandy plains of Mazowia, along the Berlin–Minsk–Moscow road. Although this vast unimpeded landscape gave the fledgling settlement great advantages in trade, the lack of natural barriers meant that it was at the mercy of any army that marched through. And march they did. Austria, Prussia, Sweden and Russia invaded and occupied the city numerous times, and its destiny has been written as much by foreign armies as by Warsawians themselves.

Today, evidence of this often violent past is visible everywhere. It is there in the huge swathes of overgrown fields in Wola, where pavements and houses once stood. It is there on the ancient steps where Napoleon stood before leaving on his march on Moscow. It is there in the Tartar and Protestant and Jewish cemeteries, which stand as a testament to a history of openness, and in the beautiful Gothic and Renaissance buildings so carefully rebuilt after the war. It is also there in the hill of rubble – 121 metres high – which was created from the ruins of the city after 1945. Ghosts are everywhere, too. They meet in the Art Deco bar of the Bristol Hotel, or in the white halls of the Wolski hospital, or hover in the spaces between the 1950s housing blocks that criss-cross the former ghetto, once home to the second-largest Jewish community in the world. There, the silence is palpable.

Ancient Warsaw started as a trading centre. Everything, from amber and fur to timber and salt, was carried by barges on the Vistula or hauled by road to Germany, Holland, Ukraine and Russia. The settlement prospered. It had become rich enough by the thirteenth century to be named a seat by the Dukes of Masovia, and before long the skyline was punctuated by the pretty rooftops of the cathedral and the red-brick church of St Mary's, and by the merchants' houses, churches and high walls of the Old and New Towns. In 1596 Warsaw's star rose again when it was named capital of the now powerful Polish-Lithuanian Commonwealth, and the Polish court moved from gracious Kraków to the 'upstart' city in the north.

It was a time of great prosperity for the new capital. Aristocrats, merchants, traders and soldiers moved to the city, and with them architects from all over Europe who built glorious churches, administrative buildings and palaces along the Royal Way, each one more beautiful than the last. This time of peace ended with the coming in 1654 of the Northern Wars, in which Swedish and Russian armies burned and pillaged their way across Polish territory in a seemingly endless orgy of violence. The wars lasted for decades, the worst being the invasion by the Swedes, which came to be known as the 'Deluge' and which saw much of Warsaw destroyed. Half a century later, Poland began to rebuild. The new king, Stanisław August Poniatowski, began to renew Warsaw's battered cultural life. Dozens of institutions were founded in the eighteenth century, not least the Załuski Library – the first Polish public library – and the Collegium Nobilium, the predecessor of the University of Warsaw. But the peace would be short-lived. Poland's avaricious neighbours Austria, Prussia and Russia carved up the country between them in three separate partitions; by 1795 Poland had ceased to exist.

Warsaw's unlikely saviour came in the form of Napoleon Bonaparte, who marched through Poland in 1812 on his way to Russia. In 1807 he had created the 'Duchy of Warsaw', giving the Poles some autonomy at last, but his demise spelled another period of stagnation for Warsaw, this time under Russian rule. Tsar Alexander I was not particularly hostile to the city and allowed some development – the railways brought wealth, and new streets like Jerusalem Avenue were laid out. The Jewish population, which had numbered only 15,600 in 1816, was bolstered by mass migration of victims fleeing the pogroms in Russia, and had reached 337,000 by the end of the century.

In 1863, following the reign of the reactionary Tsar Nicholas I, an uprising against Russia ended in another humiliating defeat for the Poles. An oppressive military rule was imposed on the country, epitomized by the gigantic red-brick Citadel in Warsaw's Żoliborz, built after the first uprising in 1830, which was both an administrative centre and a vast prison. Thousands of Poles were sent to Siberia from its cells. Some growth was permitted under the Russian-born mayor Sokrates Starynkiewicz, who under Tsar Alexander III built the city's sewer system, introduced trams and street lights, and saw the creation of the Warsaw University Library, the Philharmonic Hall and the Polytechnic. Even so, when compared to the explosive growth of similar cities like Berlin and Vienna, Warsaw seemed stunted. By the end of the nineteenth century it had the reputation of being little more than a provincial city in the Russian Empire.

In most Western European countries 11 November, which marks the end of the First World War, is a day of mourning. But not in Poland. The 'war to end all wars' might have been a horrific conflict, but it freed Poland from despised Russian rule, and marked the beginning of a period of such energy and creativity and optimism that it remains unique in Warsaw's history. The era was not without complications. In 1920 Lenin invaded the new country in an attempt to bring Bolshevism to Germany by force: 'The road to worldwide conflagration will run over the corpse of Poland,' he said. To his surprise the Poles defeated the Soviet forces in the 'Miracle on the Vistula', the last time Russia would lose a war until its foray into Afghanistan in the 1980s, persuading Lenin to rein in his global ambitions and to pursue Communism in Russia alone for the time being. Poland also endured hyperinflation and other economic problems, political strife and ethnic conflicts, but none of this could dampen the sheer optimism felt by its young people, the so-called 'Columbus Generation', who were growing up in freedom at last.

Warsaw had now become an important capital city. It was a major centre of political, diplomatic and military life, and its two main airports and roads and rail lines and five bridges across the Vistula to Praga brought diplomats, dignitaries and people from all over the world to trade, work and live. The city had always been a melting pot, and it continued to welcome foreigners, whether refugees from Bolshevik Russia or, later, those fleeing Hitler's Germany. With its museums and concert halls, publishing houses and newspapers, museums and galleries, cabarets and film companies, it was a magnet for anyone who wanted to make a mark in the country. Its population increased from 700,000 at the turn of the century to 1.3 million by 1939.

✳   ✳   ✳

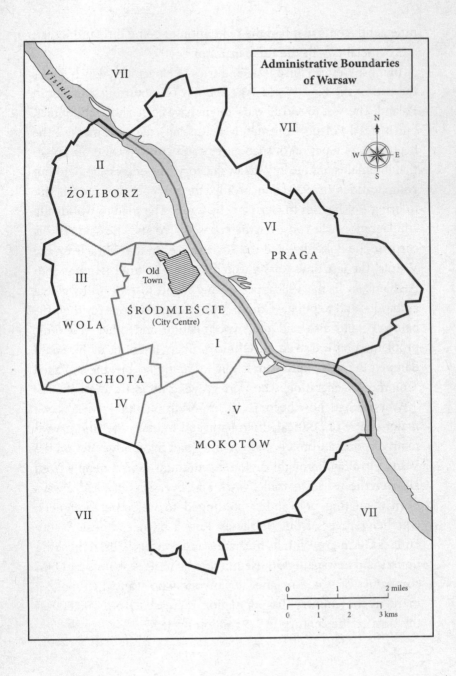

Administrative Boundaries
of Warsaw

Vistula

VII

VII

N
W E
S

II

ŻOLIBORZ

VI

PRAGA

III

Old
Town

ŚRÓDMIEŚCIE
(City Centre)

WOLA

I

OCHOTA

IV

V

MOKOTÓW

VII

VII

0   1   2 miles

0   1   2   3 kms

The massive influx of people created a need for housing, and Warsaw exploded outwards, with entirely new districts created beyond the boundaries once imposed by the tsars. The Warsaw Housing Cooperative constructed huge modernist complexes with all the latest conveniences, and gleaming hospitals and innovative schools were built. Public landmarks like the Sejm (Parliament), the ZUS insurance building and the grand new National Museum were built in the new modernist style, but the past was cherished too. The formerly drab façades of the Old Town were restored to their exuberant original Renaissance colours, and many other revered buildings such as the Warsaw Castle were given much-needed facelifts after decades of neglect by the Russian occupiers.

Science, culture, history and the arts were celebrated, and dozens of new institutions – including the Geological Institute and the Higher School of Commerce – opened their doors in the 1920s and 30s. When Madame Marie Curie, who had been born in Warsaw, opened her new Radium Institute in 1932 the whole city turned out to cheer her. It was a time of great innovation and excitement in science and the arts. Kazimierz Funk, then at Warsaw University, discovered B vitamins there, while Józef Kosacki, who invented the mine detector, worked with Rudolf Gundlach, who in turn had created an ingenious periscope which was later used in virtually every tank in the Second World War. Kazimierz Prószyński, who developed the film camera, listened to the first broadcast from Europe's most powerful radio station, opened near Warsaw in 1931. All scientific fields – biology, chemistry, anthropology – flourished. Jerzy Nomarski developed a way to look at live specimens under a microscope without damaging them, while mathematicians flocked to work with Stefan Mazurkiewicz, the genius who had broken the Russian ciphers during the 1920 war. Stanisław Mazur, Stanisław Ulam (who went on to co-design the hydrogen bomb with Edward Teller) and

Stefan Banach worked in Lwów, but greatly influenced mathematics in Warsaw. When the Nazis invaded they fired them all from their academic positions; Banach, one of the greatest mathematicians of the twentieth century, was forced to make his living during the war feeding lice in a laboratory.

Artists, actors, set designers and playwrights were drawn to Warsaw in the 1920s, and all the great stars performed there on their European tours. The city had the largest opera house on the continent, and everyone from Enrico Caruso to the Ballets Russes appeared on its stage. Warsaw also housed the National Theatre, the Mały and Nowy Theatres and the Wojciech Bogusławski Theatre, which produced all the classics – Shakespeare was a particular favourite. Newer venues like Momus, the city's first literary cabaret, and Leon Schiller's Melodram, a highly successful musical theatre, experimented with entirely new forms of entertainment. By 1939 there were literally thousands of cabarets and revues in Warsaw, their actors, directors and set designers fuelling a burgeoning film industry. After appearing in films like *The Polish Dancer* and *The Wife*, Pola Negri became the first European film star to be invited to Hollywood, where she became as famous for her fashion (turbans, red-painted toenails) as for her love affairs with the likes of Rudolph Valentino and Charlie Chaplin.

At the same time Warsaw grew into one of the world's leading musical cities, and was home to some of the twentieth century's most famous composers, not least Karol Szymanowski. The Fryderyk Chopin Piano Competition, still one of the most important in the world, was first held in Warsaw in 1927. Witold Lutosławski attended the first ever performance of Szymanowski's Third Symphony in Warsaw, the event that made him want to be a composer. But the road was not easy for many of the artists of that generation, a large number of whom would either lose their lives in or have to flee the conflagration to come. During the war

Lutosławski was forced to make a living playing the piano in the Café Adria alongside his friend and fellow composer Andrzej Panufnik – who later settled in Britain, where he would be knighted – and the original scores of most of his pre-war compositions were lost in the flames of the Warsaw Uprising. The composer Mieczysław Wainberg made his debut as a pianist in Warsaw in 1929, at the age of ten; a decade later his entire family was murdered in the ghetto, and he fled to Moscow. Moshe Wilensky was educated and worked in the city before emigrating to Palestine in 1932, and would become one of Israel's most important composers. But at the time, few realized that such grave danger was looming.

There was a sense of excitement, experimentation and daring in all the arts. Painting flourished, with artists, spurred on by the breathtaking movements sweeping Europe and helped by the Institute for the Promotion of Art and the Polish Artists' Club, being exhibited at the dozens of salons and galleries in Warsaw. Rytm ('Rhythm'), the Warsaw Association for Polish Artists, was rivalled by Blok, which attracted the avant garde. Józef Pankiewicz pioneered the colourist movement in Polish painting, while graphic art took on an entirely new direction through the eerie woodcuts of Władysław Skoczylas and the dark, swirling figures in Edmund Bartłomiejczyk's work. Jewish painters like Moshe Rynecki documented daily life in Warsaw; Jakub Adler first exhibited at the Polish Artistic Club in 1919, and returned to the city in 1935, having come under the influence of the 'Neue Sachlichkeit' movement in Germany. Roman Kramsztyk and Eugeniusz Żak found a public eager and hungry for new ideas.

Literature, too, enjoyed a renaissance. Dozens of clubs and salons sprang up in the interwar years, including the famous Pikador, where writers would meet to discuss the latest works by the likes of Stefan Żeromski, author of *The Coming Spring*, or Zofia Nałkowska, who dared to write about women, eroticism and sexuality. Skamander, a group of experimental poets, included the brilliant Julian Tuwim, Antoni Słonimski and Jan Lechoń in its ranks; their witty and perceptive analysis of the period remains extremely funny nearly a century later.

Tuwim's satire poked fun at a society which was changing beyond recognition. The glamorous women painted by Tamara de Lempicka, also born in Warsaw, epitomized the new look as girls threw out their corsets in favour of the unstructured clothes pioneered in Paris by Coco Chanel. To the horror of the older generation they began to wear make-up and have 'cigarette parties' and to dance the Charleston and the Shimmy in public. Dozens of new nightclubs catering to men in dinner jackets and women with stylish bobs, red lipstick and bias-cut dresses opened up in the city centre. Warsaw had its risqué side too, complete with drugs, drink and erotic dancing. Jan Kiepura sang 'I Love All Women' (in German) to adoring crowds, Zula Pogorzelska had a hit with 'She's Tipsy, That Girl', while night owls danced to dubious tunes with titles like 'Opium' and 'Sex Appeal'. Warsaw's cultural life may have been outshone by Weimar Berlin, but it was a daring centre in its own right, and embraced the new avant-garde ideas from Paris, Vienna and beyond. It also took on the exciting new mediums of radio and film, and an experimental television studio made its first broadcast in 1938.

Above all, Warsaw revelled in all things from across the Atlantic. The Poles have long had a love affair with the optimism and energy epitomized by the United States, and in the 1920s America was all the rage. Duke Ellington and Louis Armstrong were popular, and other black stars were invited to play in the new clubs. August Agbala, a Nigerian-born jazz musician, even stayed on in the city and ended up fighting in the Warsaw Uprising.

George Gershwin, Irving Berlin and Cole Porter were idolized, and their music was everywhere.

The first Polish jazz band, the Karasiński and Kataszek Jazz-Tango Orchestra, was founded in 1923. It became a sensation, playing in clubs like Morskie Oko and Wesoły Wieczór, and later touring Europe and the Middle East. Another famous band, the Petersburski and Gold Orchestra, regularly appeared in glamorous hotspots like the Adria, with its unique revolving dance floor. All of them recorded for the new Syrena record company, and provided the soundtracks for the hundreds of films being produced in the capital. Even the venerable Polish National Opera embraced the change, premiering the opera *Jazz Band, Negro and Woman* to great acclaim in 1934. Ironically, Warsaw's cultural life benefited when Hitler took power, as thousands of artists fled Berlin for the Polish capital; musicians like Ady Rosner, whom the British magazine *Melody Maker* called 'the Polish Armstrong', found safe haven there for a time.

Many of the most famous artists, writers, film-makers and musicians of the interwar period were of Jewish origin. The Jewish community had been an integral part of Warsaw society for centuries. Their lives revolved around the Great Synagogue in Tlomackie Square, designed by Leandro Marconi in the nineteenth century to hold 2,400 people, and later the vast Judaic Library, which opened in 1936. There were hundreds of smaller synagogues and 433 Jewish schools catering for a population which had reached 393,950 by 1939. Life was often hard, particularly for the refugees who had been forced to leave Russian-held lands, but there was also great wealth and a dynamic cultural life, from theatres and music to galleries and cabarets. The list of artists is vast. Władysław Szlengel, the popular songwriter of interwar hits and later the most popular poet of the ghetto, rubbed shoulders with the great Yiddish writer Yisroel Shtern, who was in turn a friend of Isaac Bashevis Singer. Gerszon Sirota, 'the

Jewish Caruso', sang in Warsaw before giving his sell-out concerts at Carnegie Hall. Groups like the Kultur Lige promoted Yiddish culture in a whole new way; set designer Boris Aronson, who eventually made his name on Broadway, the artist El Lissitzky and the sculptor Joseph Chaikov developed a new kind of Jewish modernism using abstract art and innovative techniques; the movement they founded would later be based in Warsaw.

Memoirs, photographs and films hint at the dynamism of the Jewish quarter before the Germans came. Nazi propaganda was keen to show Warsaw's Jews as poverty-stricken and the ghetto as filthy and disease-ridden, but history tells a different story. There was poverty, of course, but films show clean, elegant streets lined with beautiful apartments, and prosperous men and women wearing the latest fashions and heading out to go shopping or to the cafés, restaurants, thriving theatres and revues. The traditional Jewish world was changing, as many young people were choosing to study at Warsaw University, to join the army or engage in politics, often to the ire of their parents, who cherished tradition.

For the most part Warsawians loved their city, 'the Paris of the east', and many would remember this brief era as a joyous and optimistic time. For the vast majority life was better than it had been before the First World War, and people revelled in the new prosperity. A typical weekend in the capital would see couples strolling in Łazienki Park, going on a river cruise or swimming in the Vistula. Families took their beautifully dressed children to the zoo or to the fun park, stopping on the way home for an ice cream. In the evenings Warsawians and visitors flocked to the grand hotels – the Europejski or the Bristol – for cocktails and dancing before moving on to the opera or to one of the dozens of cinemas or theatres, while others headed to the neon-lit night-clubs to dance the night away.

The last pre-war President of Warsaw, Stefan Starzyński, had set out to make his capital a world-class city, and he succeeded. After many years of occupation the reborn capital city blossomed as the centre of Polish life. Warsaw had new roads, trains, housing, factories and institutions; its museums and archives, libraries and laboratories were rebuilt or improved, and science, the arts and culture flourished. It was the centre of Polish and Jewish writing, publishing, painting, film-making and photography, and new ideas were quickly embraced. The changes brought not only cultural renewal but also investment, with companies like Opel, Philips and Prudential moving into landmark headquarters which were often the envy of their counterparts in other European cities. Warsaw was a 'city of the future', and its trajectory was 'always up'. A 1938 exhibition at the National Museum, 'Warsaw – Yesterday, Today and Tomorrow', which celebrated this new identity attracted half a million visitors.[1] The generation that grew up in this climate could not imagine that it would end so suddenly. When it did, they were indignant. They knew that something wonderful had been cut short, and their anger prompted many who had come of age in the 1920s and 1930s to fight against impossible odds to regain their freedom. That generation was unique. It was also doomed.

On the morning of 1 September 1939 confused Warsawians awoke to the sound of aeroplanes flying overhead, followed by the crashing of bombs. Hitler had started his Blitzkrieg.

The German surprise attack on Warsaw was as quick and merciless as it was unexpected, and from the very beginning of the war the city was subjected to a campaign of terror bombing of a kind that had never previously been experienced anywhere in the world. It had been personally ordered by Hitler, who detested the Polish capital and all it stood for; indeed, his hatred was so great that when Generaloberst Franz Halder suggested to the Führer that Warsaw could easily be bypassed on military grounds he was shouted down. 'No!' Hitler yelled. 'Warsaw must be attacked!' The war against Poland 'will only be over when Warsaw has fallen'. Hitler set out his vision: 'how the skies would be darkened, how millions of tons of shells would rain down on Warsaw, how people would drown in blood. Then his eyes nearly popped out of his head and he became a different person. He was suddenly seized by a lust for blood.'[2]

The city was pounded for twenty-five terrible days. Then, on 26 September, nine German divisions attacked simultaneously, blasting their way into the city centre. The Warsawians had no choice but to surrender the next day. When he toured the fallen city in October, General Erwin Rommel was shocked by the devastation, and wrote to his wife that there was no water, no power, no gas and no food; 25,000 people lay dead in the rubble. But for Warsaw this was only the beginning.

The Terror

What followed was to become one of the most brutal occupations in all of Europe. In the next five years the Germans systematically rounded up and murdered millions of Poles, and Warsaw suffered terrible losses. The litany of crimes against the people of the city is overwhelming. By far the single greatest atrocity was the extermination of almost all of the capital's Jews, a crime so complete that by the time of the Warsaw Uprising there were only 28,000 left alive in the city, all of them, with the ghetto an utter ruin, in hiding on the 'Aryan' side.[3] Over 11,000 were able to leave Warsaw with the Gentile population after the uprising, most of them using false papers. Of the five hundred who remained behind, only two hundred would survive until January 1945, when Russians liberated the frightened and starving people struggling in the embers and rubble of the once great city.

The Jews of Warsaw had made the city their home for five hundred years, creating a rich cultural heritage which had become part of the very fabric of urban life. The old tombstones of the Jewish cemetery, which as in Berlin Hitler decided to spare, bear the names of thousands of people who, through literature or science or music, contributed in some way to the richness of one of the great European capitals. This old and dynamic community was targeted by the Nazis for complete annihilation.

The process began gradually. In October 1939 spiteful and humiliating attacks began against the Jews of Warsaw. The Germans themselves documented these attacks, which at first took place primarily against Orthodox Jewish men – thousands of 'tourist' photographs show innocent people being forced to dance by Nazi soldiers, or having their beards roughly cut off. The oppression increased. Jews were forced to move the rubble from bomb sites. There followed widespread organized theft of Jewish property, often by the Wehrmacht. By the end of November 1939 Jews were being forced to wear Star of David armbands, which in Warsaw were blue and white. In April 1940 a high red-brick wall began to rise around the newly created ghetto, and between mid-October and mid-November of that year the city was turned on its head as 113,000 Catholic Poles and 130,000 Jewish Poles were forced to leave their homes and move to either the new 'Aryan' or 'Jewish' districts of Warsaw. None of them had a choice, although many thousands of Jews chose to hide on the 'Aryan' side. On 16 November the Germans closed all the gates in the ten-foot-high brick wall and topped it with barbed wire, penning Warsaw's Jews in a thousand-acre prison in the centre of their own city. The Nazis had effectively created the largest ghetto in Europe. For the Jewish prisoners, communication with the outside world virtually ceased. As weeks turned to months, most of those trapped inside were reduced from the prosperity of their former lives as doctors and actors, tradesmen and journalists, to a basic struggle for survival, selling whatever they could to make a little money to get through another few hours. By 1942 the majority of Jews in the ghetto were existing on less than two hundred calories a day. Eighty thousand people – 10,000 of them children – died of starvation, disease or brutal treatment on the streets. Films and photographs, some taken by German 'tourist' soldiers, show the lonely deaths of emaciated children too weak even to move from the middle of the street. Their bodies were collected daily by handcart and thrown into mass graves along with the rest of the victims. It was pitiless cruelty.

For those strong enough to carry on, life was a ritual of humiliation, degradation and fear; people were pushed off high balconies, or beaten with rifle butts, or herded and whipped like animals for no reason. The Nazis and their henchmen, the *Jüdischer Ordnungsdienst* ghetto police, had absolute power over life and death, and a person could be stopped, interrogated, beaten or killed on a whim. Piotr Dembowski, who grew up in the ghetto, remembered guards forcing Jewish workers to 'fight each other or to sing (in Polish) the song praising the "golden Hitler, who taught us how to work". I remember the German Polish-language propaganda posters: "Jew=Louse=Typhus".[4]

In 'Grossaktion Warschau', which lasted only from 22 July until 21 September 1942 – a period of less than two months – a staggering 310,322 men, women and children were gathered at the Umschlagplatz and herded onto trains destined for Treblinka. This terrifying place was perhaps the most chilling and efficient of all the extermination camps.

In order to encourage people to go to the trains, the Germans cynically promised loaves of bread and free marmalade to the starving, and spread rumours of 'resettlement' to allay their fears.

Many desperately hoped that their lives would be spared; others suspected the truth. Władysław Szpilman remembered the terrible conditions at the Umschlagplatz, where those awaiting transportation were forced to wait sometimes for days for space on a train. It was hot, and there was no shade, food or water: 'People got lost in the crush and called to one another in vain. We heard the shots and shouting which meant raids were going on in the nearby streets. Agitation grew as the hour approached at which the train was supposed to come.'[5] Szpilman was pulled out of the crowd at the last possible moment and his life was spared, but he watched as his mother, father and siblings were crammed into the wagon that would take them to their deaths. As it rolled away he heard a Jewish policeman say to an SS man, 'Well, off they go for melt-down!' Szpilman remembered, 'I looked the way he was pointing. The doors of the trucks had been closed, and the train was starting off, slowly and laboriously. I turned away and staggered down the empty street, weeping out loud, pursued by the fading cries of the people shut up in those trucks.'[6]

Stanisław Aronson, the scion of a sophisticated and wealthy Jewish industrial family, managed to escape from the train taking him and the rest of his family to Treblinka. 'When the train stopped in the field I approached a small window in the top of our wagon. I was very thin and managed to squeeze through.' He made his way back to Warsaw, where he joined the elite AK unit 'Kedyw', and eventually fought in the 1944 uprising. As it happened, the first place he was ordered to attack was the school in Stawki Street, the very place from which he had been sent to Treblinka.

For those who did not escape from the trains, their fate was almost certain death. The horror of Treblinka is simply impossible to imagine. A glimpse of its depravity can be gleaned in a book, published by the Polish Underground Press in 1944, by Yankel

Wiernik, who managed to escape after working in the camp as a carpenter. Wiernik witnessed the sufferings of the Warsaw Jews who were not, as was the custom, sent directly to the gas chambers, but were treated with particular cruelty. Many were burned alive on the huge pyres lit to destroy the tens of thousands of bodies: 'Women with children were separated from the others, led up to the fires and, after the murderers had had their fill of watching the terror-stricken women and children, they killed them right by the pyre and threw them into the flames. This happened quite frequently. The women fainted from fear and the brutes dragged them to the fire half dead. Panic-stricken, the children clung to their mothers. The women begged for mercy, with eyes closed so as to shut out the grisly scene, but their tormentors only leered at them and kept their victims in agonizing suspense for minutes on end. While one batch of women and children were being killed, others were left standing around, waiting their turn. Time and time again children were snatched from their mothers' arms and tossed into the flames alive, while their tormentors laughed, urging the mothers to be brave and jump into the fire after their children and mocking the women for being cowards.'[7] The Nazis' desire to keep the horror of Treblinka secret meant that anyone who went inside as a prisoner had to die. Wiernik saw a German woman and her two sons, who had been put on the transport by mistake, sent to the gas chambers despite having identity papers proving that they were 'Aryan'. Of the 850,000 people sent to this terrible place, only forty to seventy Jews survived the war.

News of the fate of those who boarded the trains was, however, beginning to leak out. The Polish-Jewish politician and historian Emanuel Ringelblum and others had collected evidence of life in the doomed ghetto, and also of the mass murders in Treblinka and Chełmno. The Catholic Pole Jan Karski was smuggled into the ghetto, and later managed, dressed as a Ukrainian guard, to witness conditions in one of the transit camps. He and others in the AK tried to alert the world about what was happening. Their warnings were ignored. Nevertheless, as evidence mounted of the true destination of the Jews taken for 'resettlement', a resistance movement grew. It was to lead to the most tragic of all the uprisings in Warsaw's long history.

Comparisons between the Warsaw Ghetto Uprising of 1943 and the Warsaw Uprising of 1944 are inevitable, but it is virtually impossible to equate the two. Both were enormous and terrible tragedies, but in terms of motivation, hopelessness and desperation there is absolutely no equivalence between the tragic fighters of 1943 and those who decided to take up arms in 1944. The latter uprising was started largely for political reasons, to demonstrate to the world that the Poles had helped liberate their capital from the Germans and to prove that they deserved an independent state, free from German or Soviet control. The participants in the 1943 Ghetto Uprising had no such grandiose aims. Their choice had been made for them. They had been condemned to death because they were Jewish, and their struggle was not even one for survival. They were not interested in the kind of political or military objectives that preoccupied so many in the AK, nor did they entertain thoughts of any kind of victory. They had only two choices: to be murdered in Treblinka or to be killed, fighting with weapon in hand, in the tiny area remaining to them. Rarely in history has such a desperately tragic choice been forced on any group of human beings.

Mordechaj Anielewicz, organizer of the Ghetto Uprising, did not believe any of the German promises of 'resettlement'. By September 1942 all but 60,000 of Warsaw's Jews had been murdered in Treblinka, and despite the measures taken by the Germans to hide the truth, some now knew for certain what awaited them if they boarded the trains. The Jewish Combat Organization under Anielewicz began to gather weapons as best it could, and to organize to fight.

On 19 April 1943 the Germans descended on the ghetto with a force of 2,000 men. They had expected simply to terrorize their victims into getting on the trains, as they had in the past, but this time they were taken by surprise. The Jewish fighters, vastly outnumbered and with far fewer weapons than the thugs sent in to eject or kill them, had an intimate knowledge of the geography of the ghetto, including the sewer system, on their side. The battle raged for three weeks, with the desperate resisters first being hounded by German troops, and then forced from place to place as the ghetto was systematically burned. On 8 May Mordechaj Anielewicz and his girlfriend Mira Fuchrer, along with his staff, were surrounded at the ŻOB command bunker at 18 Miła Street. A monument now marks the site where they committed mass suicide in front of the SS troops who had been sent to kill them. As the Germans took over the ghetto a handful of fighters escaped through the sewers and were hidden on the 'Aryan' side of the city; a number went on to fight in the 1944 Warsaw Uprising as the 'ŻOB Group'.

Having defeated the resisters, the Nazis began to clear the ghetto. Anyone left alive was either killed on the spot or taken to Treblinka. On 16 May SS Brigadeführer Jürgen Stroop announced that the fighting was over. 'The Jewish quarter of Warsaw is no more,' he crowed. Himmler had the Great Synagogue on Tlomackie Street, a beautiful and imposing Leandro Marconi landmark, blown up to celebrate this great success. 'What a wonderful sight!' Stroop wrote. 'I called out "*Heil Hitler*" and pressed the button. A terrific explosion brought flames right up to the clouds. The colours were unbelievable. An unforgettable allegory of the triumph over Jewry.'[8] The rest of the ghetto was systematically destroyed. Photographs show a sea of rubble where homes and synagogues and shops had once stood. An entire history had been wiped from the map.

The destruction of the Warsaw ghetto was of importance to the genesis of the Warsaw Uprising of August 1944, not least because it was a grave warning of the depths to which the Nazis could sink. The AK had not contributed a great deal to the heroic fight at the beginning of the Ghetto Uprising, but in reality there was little it could have done. At that point the AK had few weapons to spare; some of its members also subscribed to the stereotype that the Jews were unable or unwilling to fight. By the end, however, the sheer heroism of the combatants had greatly impressed many in the AK, who were amazed that a small group of poorly armed Jews had managed to hold off the Germans for weeks under near-impossible conditions, with almost no help. Thirteen thousand Jews had died in the fighting, around half of them burned to death. The Germans had lost seventeen men killed and around two hundred wounded. ŻOB had been so effective in part because they had abandoned street fighting, with its high casualty rate, in favour of partisan-style warfare, with each burned-out building and the sewer network being used to the utmost advantage. At the same time, Warsaw's citizens had watched in horror from Świętojerska Street and Krasiński Square as Jews trapped by flames had jumped from the upper storeys of burning buildings. All Warsaw could hear the explosions and the sound of gunfire inside the ghetto, and stories of acts of bravery and self-sacrifice spread throughout the city. The uprising won the respect of the non-Jewish Warsawians, many of whom were deeply disturbed by what was being done to the Jewish population just beyond their reach.

The chilling fact was that in the space of a few months the Germans had succeeded in murdering a huge number of

Warsawians in the centre of their city, or deporting them to be murdered elsewhere. Despite the efforts of some individuals in organizations like Żegota, a code-name for the secret Council to Aid Jews set up by Władysław Bartoszewski, Zofia Kossak-Szczucka and others, few outside Warsaw believed the reports of what was happening, and precious little was done to help. In a moving speech at Warsaw's Jewish cemetery on the fortieth anniversary of the Ghetto Uprising, Józef Rybicki, commander of 'Kedyw', who later recruited Stanisław Aronson, described his feelings of helplessness at the time. 'There behind a wall, burning ghetto houses, detonations, shots, executions, murders. And from our side the pain and despair of powerlessness. It is like a mother who knows her child is dying and she can only suffer and despair that she can't help him. This feeling of despair and powerlessness stays with us forever as remorse.'[9] The Ghetto Uprising taught Rybicki just how badly armed the AK was. 'We couldn't give proper help, necessary help. In places that needed divisions we could only send groups or give some weapons. The Warsaw Uprising showed us later how weakly equipped we were.'

The treatment of the Jews and Roma in Nazi-occupied Europe was unique. No other peoples suffered the systematic hunting down, the remorseless quest for every last individual, the utterly pitiless extermination of each human being, and the knowledge that once they had been identified and caught there would be no mercy and no escape. Non-Jewish Poles did not suffer the extreme, unrelenting terror that led to the murder of so many Polish Jews. Piotr Dembowski, who was arrested in Warsaw on 7 April 1944 in a round-up in the district of Żoliborz, witnessed the different treatment meted out to Jews and Catholics at such a moment. Around sixty people were arrested, among whom were eight Jewish men and women who had been in hiding and who did not have the correct papers. 'We stayed together for a few hours in a transit cell in the Pawiak prison,' he recalled. 'We whispered. Later, "we" [the Poles] were turned into the Registrar's office and entered the regular prison, while "they" [the Jews] were led outside to the already destroyed ghetto. They knew and we knew that they would be shot that very day. That particular memory, the memory of my "automatic" reaction – "Thank God that I am not . . ." – has prevented me from ever forgetting the absolute distinction that existed in those terrible days between Jews and non-Jews.'[10]

Ethnic Poles also endured great discrimination and violence at the hands of the Nazis, albeit on a vastly different scale from the Jews and Roma. From the moment the Germans invaded the country, ethnic Poles were treated as *Untermenschen* – sub-humans – who were to be killed, deported or turned into slaves of the German master race. Hitler had made it very clear from the beginning that his troops were to send to death 'mercilessly and without compassion, men, women, and children of Polish race and language'. The Poles, and Warsawians in particular, were despised by both Hitler and Himmler, and from 1939 SS and police Einsatzgruppen arrested and killed anyone who stood in the way of *Generalplan Ost* – the Nazi plan to Germanize the east.

In June 1939 Hitler was invited to visit an architectural office in the Bavarian city of Würzburg. By chance his attention was caught by the designs for a new town planned to replace the current city of Warsaw. He gave his permission for the project to be pursued. The design, which became known as the Pabst Plan after one of its authors, envisaged the callous reduction of the city from 1.5 million inhabitants to a small German population of 130,000 people, with room for 80,000 Poles to be kept as slave labour on the left bank of the river. The Jews were to disappear altogether. Warsaw, with the exception of a few areas such as the Old Town, was to be flattened and replaced by a 'New German

City' which had been designed to resemble a medieval German settlement, complete with picturesque narrow streets and pretty timber-framed houses. The population was dispensable. The city was to become a symbol of the new Germany of the east.

Generalplan Ost was not reserved for Warsaw alone; indeed, the entire pre-war Polish population of thirty-five million was to be reduced to a mere three to four million uneducated 'peasants' who would be put to work in industry or agriculture. To this end the Germans swept through Poland in 1939, arresting the country's elite – tens of thousands of doctors and teachers, bureaucrats and landowners, clergymen and professors, journalists and businessmen, actors and priests. Many were murdered at killing grounds such as the Palmiry forest near Warsaw, or in the Pawiak prison in the city itself. The earliest such massacres were small – the first in Warsaw was in the suburb of Zielonka in September 1939, when nine people were executed because someone had put up a poster quoting an anti-Prussian song, but the numbers increased rapidly. In Wawer, another suburb of Warsaw, 107 civilians were shot in reprisal for the killing of two German NCOs. As it happened, Zielonka and Wawer would be the first two suburbs of Warsaw to be taken by the Red Army in July 1944. The sounds of battle from those districts would prompt the AK to start the uprising.

One of the Germans to take to the killing of the Poles with gusto was none other than Hermann Fegelein, whose 1st SS Cavalry Division carried out a number of mass shootings in the autumn of 1944. Fegelein had shown his disdain for the Poles early on, personally taking part in the execution of nearly 2,000 people in the Kampinos forest near Palmiry. The first of these, on 7 and 8 December 1939, saw eighty people killed. Later victims included the speaker of the Polish Parliament, the Olympic gold medal-winning athlete Janusz Kusociński, and the Vice-President of Warsaw Jan Pohoski. Pictures taken on the first day show the victims being led to their deaths in dressing gowns and pyjamas, as they had not been given time to get dressed.[11] Fegelein also shot a number of eminent Poles in the gardens of the Parliament Buildings in Warsaw.

This brutality only increased with time, and by the end of the war ethnic Poles were to be found in nearly every camp in the Reich. Erich von dem Bach-Zelewski called for the creation of Auschwitz in order to hold ethnic Polish prisoners; only later would it evolve into the factory of death for Jewish victims. The numbers of ethnic Poles killed are dwarfed by the sheer scale of the murder of Jews in the camps; even so, of the estimated 140,000 non-Jewish Poles imprisoned at Auschwitz, around 70,000 died, some as the result of barbaric medical experiments but most through disease, starvation and ill-treatment. Around 20,000 Poles were killed in Sachsenhausen and 20,000 in Gross-Rosen, 17,000 in both Ravensbrück and Neuengamme, and 10,000 in Dachau. Tens of thousands of the 100,000 Poles sent to Majdanek were killed there, and 30,000 died at Mauthausen. Few people today have heard of the sub-camp at Gusen, a place designed specifically to erase the intelligentsia of Poland through hard labour in the granite mines. Many died after being thrown into the Mauthausen quarry, the SS and kapos laughing as the 'parachutists without parachutes' writhed and twisted before hitting the ground.

As with any list of numbers, it is sometimes easy to forget that each figure represents an individual, a single person who was wrongfully imprisoned, brutally abused, and killed. Stanisław Nogaj, Gusen prisoner no. 43322, wrote that there were about eighty kinds of violent death in the sub-camp, where the guards were particularly cruel and sadistic, as if to heap humiliation on the 'effete' intellectuals and professionals who ended up as prisoners there. They included 'bullets, clubs, ropes, gas, poison, electrical current, hunger, being buried alive, burned alive, stoned to death, falling under trains, thrown from cliffs . . .' Sketches that survive from the camp show prisoners being crushed by stones, hung up by their hands and whipped, or chained by the neck like animals. Ludwik Bielerzewski, Gusen prisoner no. 48705, recalled the death of Father Laskowski, Director of Economy at the Seminary in Poznań. When the hated *Oberkapo Kastenhofen* Gustav Krutzky, known as 'Tygrys' by the inmates, asked Father Laskowski who he was, he answered that he was a priest. 'This answer was sufficient. They ordered him to lift a huge, hundred-kilo stone. When he was not able to lift it, "Tygrys" – one of the *kapos* who should be avoided at all costs, since a mere encounter with him heralded an inevitable death – together with his colleague, placed this stone on the back of the unfortunate prisoner. The stone fell, Father Laskowski was knocked down. The torturers beat and kicked the prostrated victim. When he got up with difficulty they weighed him down again. Another fall.' The *kapos* eventually killed him.[12] In another form of murder people were forced to strip naked and, in freezing winter weather, stand in the 'baths', where they were doused with cold water. Zbigniew Wlazłowski, Gusen prisoner no. 49943, risked his life to witness such an execution from Block 29: 'Unterscharführer Jentsch ran around with a riding crop in his hand, urged on the block leaders and encouraged the *kapos* to beat the resisters. Even he cut the naked bodies with a whip or shoved the prisoners with his leg under the ice-cold showers. The people froze, and the water unable to drain to the blocked sewers kept on rising . . . Most of them became weak, fell down, and drowned in the water then above their knees.'[13]

The Germans had other punishments for the Poles. Between 1939 and 1945 over 1.5 million were sent as forced labourers to the Reich. In another agonizing chapter, children deemed 'racially acceptable' were taken from their parents and given to childless couples in Germany. As Himmler wrote in his official report on the subject, 'racially valuable children [are to be raised] in the old Reich in proper educational facilities or in German family care. The children must not be older than eight or ten years, because only till this age can we truly change their national identification, that is "final Germanization". A condition for this is complete separation from any Polish relatives. Children will be given German names, their ancestry will be created by a special office.'[14] Twenty thousand children were taken in this way; one witness remembered 'the agony of the mothers and fathers, the beating by the Germans, and the crying of the children' as they were taken from their homes.[15]

Nowhere in all Nazi-occupied Europe was the 'extensive machinery of repression' as great as it was in Poland.[16] There were always at least 50,000 SS and police on hand to control the despised inhabitants, and as a result nowhere was safe. Local officials in tiny villages and towns could be targeted, or held hostage to be killed later, if a German was attacked. Life in Warsaw became particularly dangerous after September 1943, when Governor Hans Frank decided to hold random round-ups and public executions on the streets. His sole aim was to increase the terror in the hope of intimidating the 'bandits' of the Home Army.

When one walks the streets of Warsaw today, particularly the lovely area around Nowy Świat, with its charming buildings and luxury shops, one comes across grey concrete plaques every few hundred metres or so. Each commemorates thirty or forty people killed by the Germans. In photographs of these random round-ups one can see groups of well-dressed men and women, on their way home from work or off to see friends, cordoned off from the rest of the crowd. They would be put up against a nearby wall, and shot. At first the victims were simply executed, but as the Poles had the annoying habit of yelling patriotic phrases as they died, the Germans took to sealing their mouths with plaster of Paris, or pushing narcotic-soaked rags down their throats to keep them quiet.[17] As the war dragged on and clothing became more scarce, the condemned were forced to strip before they were killed; their bodies were then burned in the ghetto ruins. After evening curfew the names of those who had died were read out over the tinny loudspeakers that hung from posts throughout the city; people listened from their homes, dreading to hear the name of a friend or a loved one.

The Italian journalist Alceo Valcini, who lived in Warsaw for most of the war, remembered round-ups as late as July 1944. 'I met an old lady on a street who said, "Go away quickly! Round-ups!" With a beating heart and with my Polish friends I found shelter in the nearest gate. We walked upstairs and strangers opened doors, offering us hospitality for a few hours. Another time after one hour of waiting the concierge came and said that the Germans had gone. I was very touched by the solidarity.'[18] In total the Germans rounded up and killed 40,000 ethnic Poles in Warsaw in this way between June 1941 and September 1944. Erich von dem Bach admitted at Nuremberg that any officer with the rank of captain or higher had the authority to kill fifty to a hundred Poles for every German killed without referring the matter to a higher authority.[19]

The ethnic Poles and the Jews of Warsaw were targeted by the Germans in different ways and at different times, but it gives the Nazis a kind of victory to describe the deaths of the two groups as if they were entirely removed from one another. The murder of the Jews was unique in its extent and barbarism, but the whole of Warsaw was terrorized and destroyed, and its people murdered, throughout the war, albeit to different degrees. Five hundred years of Jewish culture were simply erased from the city centre in an enormous 'Grossaktion' that is hard to fathom in its sheer scale.

The total death toll in Warsaw, including Jews and non-Jewish Poles, amounted to 685,000 human beings. In 1939 Warsaw had had the second-largest Jewish population in the world after New York. Only 11,500 of them survived the war. What was done in the Polish capital was, as the historian Gunnar Paulsson has put it, 'the greatest slaughter of a single city in history'. For Warsaw, the deaths of so many of its citizens was a tragedy from which it will never truly recover; the end of so much life and the elimination of an entire culture completely and forever changed the character of the metropolis on the Vistula.[20]

It was precisely this rule of terror that instilled such deep longing for freedom in Warsaw, which is why, in the summer of 1944, the atmosphere in the city changed so radically. The citizens could hear the echo of Soviet guns in the distant suburbs of Wawer, Otwock and Zielonka. They knew that a German officer had very nearly succeeded in killing Hitler on 20 July; they knew about the Normandy landings, and were excitedly following the progress of the Allied troops in France via illegal radio broadcasts and underground newspapers. And above all, everywhere they could see the physical evidence of a defeated German army for themselves.

The German Retreat

The amazing success of Bagration had an enormous impact on Warsaw, not least because it turned the city into a mêlée of retreating German soldiers racing westward in their attempt to escape the hammer blows of the Red Army. Alceo Valcini watched from his tiny room in the Venice Hotel as groups of fleeing Germans made their way across Poniatowski Bridge and Jerusalem Avenue, and down Senatorska and Chłodna Streets. 'They weren't soldiers any more. They were remains of human beings, tired, frightened, passive, in a state of visible physical and moral depression. They were sweating, starving, covered in mud from head to foot, sitting on equipment pulled by horses or battered cars or peasant wagons with cows and dogs alongside. They had long beards and gazed with dimmed eyes . . . a shapeless mass of beaten soldiers.'

These were the stragglers who had escaped the encirclements and massacres in Byelorussia, and were desperately trying to get across the Vistula before the Soviets attacked again. These *Rückkämpfer*, the survivors of Minsk and Grodno and Vitebsk, limped through Warsaw in their ragged grey-green uniforms and cracked boots, their faces unshaven and their steps faltering. Gas masks and mess tins swung from leather belts, dented camouflage helmets shielded gaunt faces. A lucky few still had grenades in their belts, or submachine guns or anti-tank rockets over their shoulders, but some were barefoot, with no equipment at all, and a great many were covered in bloody bandages. It was like a medieval horde.

Confusion and collapse of discipline and order became the rule. 'We didn't attend to our dead. We didn't bury them either,' one soldier recalled of the flight. Sometimes the soldiers encountered officers fresh from Germany who clearly had no idea of the magnitude of the defeat. One infantryman who had walked for three days without rest was hauled up at a crossroads by a prim Oberst who yelled at him for his 'disgraceful' appearance. When the soldier tried to explain what had happened to his regiment, the officer made him use a piece of grass to point at the map so he did not touch it with his filthy hands. 'I found myself resisting the urge to toss the table and the map at him.' Gallows humour abounded among the completely demoralized soldiers: 'We are, with every step, capturing ground to the west,' they joked. They made fun of Hitler, too, referring to him as '*Grofaz*', an abbreviation of the title *'Grösster Feldherr Aller Zeiten'* – the greatest commander in history – that Keitel had invented for the Führer in all seriousness after the collapse of France.[21] Even those at the top began to doubt whether the Führer really could win the war – Rochus Misch, Hitler's bodyguard, said that he 'no longer believed in a final victory'.[22]

Misch did not, of course, voice his doubts, but by now the men of Army Group Centre were daring to say the unthinkable out loud. Drunken German soldiers could be seen staggering arm in arm down Marszałkowska Street in the heart of Warsaw: 'They paid no attention to discipline and were shouting at the tops of their voices: "I am sick of this war!" Officers who saw them turned pale, but looked away.'[23]

For their part, Warsawians were both shocked and elated by the sight of the bedraggled army. Could this really be the mighty Wehrmacht that had defeated them so easily in 1939? Poles quietly lined up along Jerusalem Avenue and Wolska Street to watch them file past. A few girls waved handkerchiefs and called out in mock sadness, 'Goodbye, goodbye, we will never see you again!' The gesture would have been unthinkable a month before. Given the sheer numbers plodding through the city, the retreat of the German soldiers was quite calm. The exodus of German civilians, however, was another matter.

There is little that compares with the corruption and the utterly venal attitude of the German colonizers in the east, and Warsaw was no exception. These men and women, often of low standing at home, took postings to far-off capitals where suddenly they found they could 'be somebody'. They were detested by those forced into subservience; this was particularly true of Warsaw, which before the war had a very large Jewish and non-Jewish professional class, a thriving university, a sophisticated cultural life and tens of thousands of highly educated men and women who looked on their new German 'superiors' with nothing but contempt.

Having murdered most of Warsaw's Jewish population the Germans had, by default, become the second-largest ethnic group in the city, with more than 16,000 *Reichsdeutsche* ('pure' Germans) and around 14,700 *Volksdeutsche* and *Stammdeutsche* (ethnic Germans). This did not include the hated SS and police units stationed there.[24] These German civilians were part of the advance party of *Generalplan Ost*, the new elite that was to create the foundation for the thoroughly Germanized city that was to rise from the ashes of the old Warsaw. Far from the prying eyes of Berlin and away from their own upright Nazi peers they quickly became drunk on privilege and absolute power, lording it over the citizens of Warsaw at every opportunity. Apartments and houses were seized at will, and entire German quarters created of this stolen property. Furniture, paintings, jewellery and other belongings were taken; unlike for the infantry, this was not considered looting. Trams, restaurants and parks were given signs reading '*Nur für Deutsche*' (Germans only), '*Kein Zutritt für Polen*' (No entry for Poles) or '*Spielplatz nur für Deutsche Kinder*' (Playground for German children only). The Germans ran everything that mattered, from government organizations to cultural institutions, from banks to businesses requisitioned from Poles, which were used for the German war effort – Warsaw was an important centre of manufacturing, from armaments and heavy industry to chemicals and electrical technology to foodstuffs. The Germans had enjoyed their status enormously. But suddenly, thanks to Bagration, it was all in imminent danger of collapse.

The German civilian authority managed to maintain order until early July, in part by restricting information about the actual situation at the front, but when news came that army support units on the eastern side of the Vistula were starting to withdraw, the cry of 'full retreat' went up. The sound of Soviet artillery was drawing closer, and the Germans in Warsaw, knowing full well what had happened to their counterparts trapped in Minsk and Vitebsk, simply panicked. Everybody wanted to get out.

The streets were soon impassable. Cars and wagons, filled to bursting with all manner of goods, clogged the German district. Factories were hurriedly dismantled to be sent to the Reich, and institutions were prepared for evacuation. Heavy transport cars were loaded with the archives of the German Red Cross, the Police Presidium and the SS.[25] Relocation companies were overwhelmed by the number of German apartments they were expected to empty. Trunks, packing cases and other huge boxes of loot were loaded onto wagons and sent to Poznań, Łódź, Vienna and Dresden, where it was thought the risk of bombardment was less. German officers appealed for calm, but civil servants acted as if 'they were all about to have heart attacks'.[26] Stanisław Aronson, by now working for the AK, noted that these Germans 'bore little resemblance to the master race'. Furthermore, the inhabitants of Warsaw 'were convinced that the German occupation was over'.[27] 'No one would have been surprised if the next day he heard that Hitler had committed suicide and Russia, England and America had accepted German capitulation.'[28]

The panic reached fever pitch when the Nazi-appointed Governor Ludwig Fischer and Mayor Ludwig Leist abandoned Warsaw on 23 July.[29] Stanisław Ruskowski, a Polish engineer who worked at the water board, was amazed when his boss, Director Elhart Ellenbach, and his colleague Engineer Jung announced that they were going to try to escape through their own lines to get home to Germany; they even ordered that he kill and prepare three pigs for the journey. Larysa Zajączkowska, an AK operative who worked undercover at a German office, noted: 'Documents had been taken out, destroyed or burned so there literally was nothing to work on. I was running from one office to another with mail as there were no Germans left to move it.' In one embarrassing incident, Goebbels' entire propaganda department secretly abandoned Warsaw, with the result that when the uprising broke out, the minister had no informers, and was forced to rely on short army reports until he could locate his errant employees and order them back to the city. One Gestapo chief who had delayed his departure to make sure his stolen goods were safely on their way to Germany was killed by the AK just as he was about to leave.[30] There were small acts of mercy, too, as when the German President of the Warsaw court ordered the release from Mokotów prison of more than one hundred German and four hundred Polish short-term prisoners before packing up to leave.[31]

Cars waited with engines running as the remaining Germans said goodbye, giving huge tips to their concierges as they left for the last time. 'I met some at Piusa Street,' remembered Stefan Chaskielewicz, 'going down the stairs with suitcases, fur coats, anything they could carry, telling me, "We have no time to lose, tomorrow in the morning the Bolsheviks will be in Warsaw." They left their apartments filled with furniture, pictures, carpets – sometimes they even left the doors open.' Dr Jerzy Dreyza, who worked at the Maltese hospital, watched as SS guards forced thirty Jews in striped camp uniforms to empty the basement of the house next door, which had been used as a store room. 'Lorry after lorry was filled with food and vodka and wine' for the journey west.[32] Eugeniusz Szermentowski remembered 'lorries and carriages with heavy horses loaded up to the sky with cases, suitcases and furniture all going down Jerusalem Avenue and Wolska Street. The Germans are quiet, and not dragging Jews out of apartments any more.'[33] That evening the roads leading west were completely blocked by German cars. An evacuation train was supposed to be leaving for Łódź, but then information arrived that the Russians were already in Radzymin. New columns of lorries appeared at the railway stations and in front of the big institutions as Germans looked for other ways out.

The evacuation affected non-German foreigners, too. They were told that they would be allowed to evacuate only on Tuesday, 25 July. 'The tiny corridor of the police office in Aleja Ujazdowskie was filled with people from all over Europe – Greeks, Bulgarians, Armenians, French workers, Belgians and especially White Russian émigrés trying to get papers before the Soviets arrived and arrested them. The German functionaries giving out passes were so tired they could hardly stand up.'[34] The railway stations were no better. Sister Tosia Hoffman saw 'piles of luggage left at the mail stations by German *Volksdeutsche*, but the trains to Łódź and Kielce have already been cancelled'. Poles were now forbidden to board any train leaving Warsaw. 'In some places Poles broke into now abandoned German warehouses, as on Długa Street where they stole clothes, or in Miodowa Street, where they took salt and flour. White powder lay all over the road.' Sister Hoffman was given bolts of stolen red and white cloth from which to sew armbands for the AK for the coming uprising.[35] Soviet reconnaissance planes and bombers began to appear over the city, lighting up the evening sky with rockets. Warsawians watched these so-called 'chandeliers', and broke into song.

The sudden, chaotic departure of the Germans was a boon for the AK, as it allowed them to prepare for the uprising with little fear of harassment. Stanisław Jankowski, one of the SOE-trained '*Cichociemni*' ('silent and dark') agents parachuted into Poland from England, was amazed at the sudden change in atmosphere in those hot July days. 'The city was full of "*Kałmucy*" or "*Hilfswillige*" – Russians who had worked for the Germans. For them the war was over. They sat with open uniforms drinking beer, their shirts undone, their belts and guns sitting in the corner.

They spoke a language we didn't understand, but they knew enough to negotiate. We got their guns with five clips for 2,000 zloty.' Jankowski even managed to buy weapons from the departing German police at Dworkowa Street, including machine guns with eight full magazines. 'With the right password and some money you could get anything.'[36]

An AK soldier who had been working for a company based in the Prudential building, Warsaw's only 'skyscraper', managed to steal a car from the fleet, as there were no Germans left to stop him. Teams of boy scouts moved around Warsaw distributing leaflets and carrying out reconnaissance, making detailed notes about German patrols and the fortifications around important buildings. At Okopowa Street they hung a string of white eagles from the tram cables as a defiant symbol of Polish national identity. To their surprise, the German police did nothing.

By 26 July the atmosphere in Warsaw was one of intense anticipation and excitement. Dr Zbigniew Woźniewski put benches in the lower corridors of the Wolski hospital so that patients could sit in comfort during the anticipated Soviet attack. Warsawians watched as German Pioneers prepared the Vistula River bridges for demolition. People laughed openly at posters announcing registration for the German school year 1944–45, or advertising a concert to be given by the SS Orchestra on 1 August. By 29 July Soviet radio had begun to call on the Poles to rise up against the Germans, and Warsawians joked nervously: 'Tomorrow we will have Russian guests here.' Many bars and shops with fruit and cool drinks remained closed, despite the sweltering heat. Blinds were drawn. People waited.

The obvious German panic and the sound of the approaching Red Army had convinced most in the AK that the Third Reich was in imminent danger of collapse, and that it was just a matter of days before Warsaw would be taken by the Soviets. They were wrong. In the final week of July, just days it seemed before the Red Army would be in their midst, something suddenly changed.

It was, at first, barely perceptible. But for those willing to look it became clear that the Germans had stopped running away. The loot-filled cars and lorries returned, along with their German occupants. The Nazis started to resume their jobs as if they had never been away.

The army, too, ceased to panic. The bedraggled soldiers were replaced by well-fed men in new uniforms. These fresh troops were not running from the east; on the contrary, they came from the west, and were marching towards Russia. An order was issued to 9th Army that 'All units which detrain in Warsaw will march eastwards in perfect military order through the city, and should preferably use the main streets. Their bearing should destroy all rumours among the local populace that we do not intend to defend the city.'[37] The Hermann Göring Division, likewise, arriving from Italy, was told to march smartly through the streets in an 'impressive' way before heading to the other side of the Vistula. Most Warsawians ignored these signs, although some were angry that the Germans seemed to be coming back. Eugeniusz Szermentowski complained that 'Every day we expect a call for the uprising and nothing happens . . . a week ago the Germans were running away and now they come back full of superiority and arrogance.'

There was another discovery too. The AK operative Larysa Zajączkowska had deliberately befriended the German director of the transport company where she was working undercover. Her boss knew a great deal about all goods and troops being moved in and around Warsaw, and when the Germans were fleeing *en masse* he had told her how many lorries and trains were leaving every day. Now, he said, all that had changed: 'They are planning to stop the Soviets to the north of the city. They have just concentrated two divisions there . . . One of these,' he added in an excited tone, 'is the Hermann Göring Division, which is secretly detraining in the forests on the outskirts of town.' Larysa passed this information on to her AK contact as quickly as she could. It was imperative that the AK understand, she said. The Germans were no longer retreating. They were going to turn and fight the Russians at the gates of Warsaw.

Her information reached the AK leadership, but it was not taken seriously. The die had been cast, and the AK was about to call for an uprising at the worst possible moment. Most tragically of all, they had been warned.

4

RESISTANCE

—◦◦◦—

One of the senators asked the ambassadors why they did not condemn their officers at the beginning of the war instead of waiting till they were beaten. (Chapter XI)

The Creation of the Home Army

That there would be an uprising against the Germans was a foregone conclusion in wartime Poland. Resistance against the Nazi tyranny was visceral. The country, painstakingly re-created after the First World War, had been invaded in 1939 and unceremoniously carved up between the Soviet Union and Nazi Germany. Warsaw had been mercilessly bombed, with 20 per cent of its buildings destroyed or badly damaged and over 25,000 people killed. After the city's surrender the Soviets and the Nazis had rounded up thousands of innocent people and imprisoned or killed them, making the Poles simultaneously victims of two of the most vile dictatorships in history. There was no alternative but to fight back. The need, the desire, for action was to exact a heavy price, but it would have been unthinkable for most young Warsawians to have turned their back on the fight. The patriotism

141

and the fervour to act led, rightly or wrongly, to the terrible events of August 1944.

The Armia Krajowa, or AK, was officially formed in February 1942, born of the shock of the German invasion and Blitzkrieg victory over Poland in 1939, and reinforced by the Soviet invasion that followed. Warsaw capitulated to Hitler on 27 September. On that tragic day seven Polish army officers gathered secretly in an apartment in the city and started the group (then called the SZP, or Polish Victory Service) that would become the AK. It was headed by General Michał Tokarzewski, with General Stefan Rowecki as second in command. The group contacted General Władysław Sikorski, commander-in-chief of the Polish armed forces and Prime Minister of the Polish government-in-exile, who was already in Paris, and were quickly established as the government-in-exile's Polish-based military wing.[1]

General Bór-Komorowski was preparing to escape to France too. 'Looking over Kraków, I saw the swastika flying from the Wawel, for centuries the residence of Polish kings. The walls of the houses were covered with German notices and orders. A couple of phrases seemed to recur in all of them insistently; one was "strictly forbidden" and the other "penalty of death". Just before he left, Bór met Tadeusz Surzycki, a respected member of the National Party (Stronnictwo Narodowe), one of Poland's dozen pre-war political parties, who convinced him to stay in Poland. 'One can hardly envisage the possibility of everyone going to France . . . We must fight in this country,' he said. He asked Bór to help set up a military wing of the National Party, but Bór refused. 'As a regular army officer, I recognised only one authority – my commander-in-chief General Sikorski, in Paris. I maintained that there should be only one military organization, common to all and independent of political opinion.' Equipped with false papers that listed him as a dealer in wood for making coffins,

Bór set about creating an underground army in south-west Poland. Even in those early, desperate days he felt that the entire nation stood behind him: 'A country, completely overrun by two invaders and torn in half, had decided to fight. No dictator, no leader, no party and no class had inspired this decision. The nation had made it spontaneously and unanimously.'[2]

General Tokarzewski went to the Soviet zone of occupation to determine whether or not resistance could be organized there, but he was arrested by the NKVD, and Rowecki (known as 'Grot') was placed in charge of the fledgling AK. Recruitment began immediately. The idea behind the underground army was that it should be all-inclusive. Every Pole who wanted to contribute would be included in the fight. The AK was to represent the entire nation.

The first members were largely army officers, but before long the net was cast far wider: doctors, workmen, engineers, teachers, farmers – in short, people from all walks of life joined the fight against the common enemy. Rowecki and Bór also recruited through pre-war political parties, so that, with the exception of fanatical right-wing nationalists and Communists, virtually all political points of view were represented, 'every class and profession'.[3] The AK was unique in its broad appeal to virtually every Pole, irrespective of background. The entire country was to join the fight.

Because of the need for absolute secrecy in the face of the Gestapo, people were recruited into small groups by friends or colleagues, and were not told about the work of other underground members. Stefan Korboński, who was soon to become the AK's Chief of Civil Resistance in Warsaw, had escaped from a Russian PoW convoy, and returned to Warsaw unsure what to do with himself. 'The idea of waiting passively until the end of the war did not appeal to me,' he said. 'I was, of course, like thousands of others at that time, thinking about some kind of underground activity against the Germans.' A friend, the former Speaker of the Polish Parliament Maciej Rataj, told him that a resistance organization was being set up. Within days Rataj had been arrested by the Gestapo, and Korboński was asked to stand in as his representative until he returned. A meeting was organized so that he could meet Rowecki: 'I entered a dimly-lit room, to be welcomed by a thick-set man in his forties . . . Our talk lasted for several hours, during which I was mostly a listener,' he recalled. 'At that time I was not aware that I was sitting in front of a man who was to be one of the most heroic figures of the coming struggle.'[4] Rowecki would play the decisive role in the creation of the AK; 'Bór' Komorowski replaced him after he was arrested by the Gestapo on 30 June 1943.

Jan Karski was recruited in a similar way. He too had escaped from a PoW convoy, and went to see an old friend in Warsaw, Dziepatowski, in the hope that he would help him find a place to live. Karski did not know that Dziepatowski was already working for the resistance. 'Conditions here are very bad,' he said. 'A man like yourself – young, healthy – is in constant danger. You can be picked up at any moment and sent to a forced-labour camp. You must be very careful. Avoid visiting your family. If the Gestapo learned about your escape it would mean the concentration camp. They may be searching for you already.' Dziepatowski handed him false identity papers. 'You are going to have a new name,' he said. 'Call yourself "Kucharski". The apartment I am sending you to is owned by the wife of a former bank employee.' Karski was still reeling from this information when he left to embark on his new life. 'Although I did not know it at the time, this was my initiation into the Polish underground organization. There was nothing extraordinary about it; nothing at all romantic. It required no decision on my part; no spurt of courage or adventure. It came about as the result of a simple visit to a good friend, dictated largely by my despair, gloom, and the feeling of being utterly at a loose end.'[5]

Thousands of young people were recruited like this. Stanisław Likiernik joined after attending secret university courses. 'I am not sure exactly how and when it happened, but eventually I became a full-time member of the underground. I received a small amount of money, enough to live on . . . I spent a lot of time cycling around Warsaw, meeting people, passing on and receiving intelligence in friendly shops, secret haunts and safe houses.'[6] Stanisław Aronson, having escaped from the train that was taking him to Treblinka, was recruited into the 'Kedyw' unit by its head Józef Rybicki after an interview in a friend's apartment; he became one of approximately a thousand Jews who fought in the AK during the uprising.[7]

The AK also had a large number of women in its ranks, many of whom had participated in the First World War and the 1920 war against the Bolsheviks as couriers, runners, nurses or drivers. When these conflicts were over they had refused just to 'return to the kitchen', and threw themselves into various paramilitary organizations like the Ochotniczy Legion Kobiet (Voluntary Legion of Women).

The most important source of female AK recruits was the Przysposobienie Wojskowe Kobiet (Female Military Training), or PWK, a paramilitary organization set up between the wars. By 1939 it had 40,000 active members and 1,500 instructors. An estimated million women had been through its rigorous courses, learning everything from first aid to how to shoot. Antonina Mijal was typical of its leaders. A crack shot, she had spent years directing training camps for the PWK. She was approached by Major Zofia Franio, and joined her new female sappers' unit in October 1940; in February that year she had become the liaison officer for Jan Kiwerski, the deputy commander of the sabotage unit of the AK, who had overseen the abortive attempt to assassinate Hitler during his visit to Warsaw in October 1939.

By the outbreak of the uprising the AK had over 300,000 volunteers, the vast majority of whom were young men and women who had for years dodged German round-ups and restrictions, waiting for the day they could fight back. They were from every imaginable background – politicians and peasants, professionals and students, workers and writers, musicians and army officers – all joining together in an outpouring of patriotism and indignation that the nation which had been re-created after the First World War had been taken from them. Twenty thousand Polish nurses, runners and snipers, sappers and soldiers would lay down their lives in the summer of 1944 in the fight for their capital city.

The Troublesome Poles

Partly because of the overwhelming brutality of the invading forces, there was no serious Polish political collaboration with Nazi Germany – no quislings or Polish SS divisions – during the Second World War. There were, of course, individual collaborators and 'Volksdeutsche' who worked for the Germans; there were also the despised 'Schmalcowniks',* who specialized in blackmailing and betraying Jews and their protectors. On the whole, however, the Poles supported the Western Allies, and unwaveringly shared their vision of freedom, democracy and self-determination. When Jan Karski joined the underground in 1939 he was told by his mentor 'Mr Borecki', a well-known lawyer in the interwar years, that the organization was nothing less than 'the official continuation of the Polish state'.[8] General Władysław Sikorski, the leader

---

* From *szmalcownik*, a Polish pejorative term derived from the word for 'lard'.

of the wartime Polish government-in-exile in London, said that 'we are fighting not only for an independent Poland but for a new democratic state assuring to all her citizens political and social freedom and progress'.[9] The Poles resisted German rule from the beginning of the war, and plans for an uprising evolved early. The most critical question was not if they should act, but how and when.

The Germans were well aware of the Polish history of rebellion, and dealt with all threats by increasing the terror. In February 1940 SS General Petri sent a study of the 1863 Polish Uprising against the Russians to Himmler, who found it so instructive that he ordered copies to be distributed to the Gestapo and to all SS and police battalion commanders at once. 'The only means of dealing with a Polish Uprising,' the report stated, 'is unmerciful severity applied at the first show of resistance. Any indecisive behaviour of the authorities [must] end in disaster.'[10]

Despite this, the Germans completely misunderstood the mentality of a people well acquainted with persecution and oppression, and did not realize that the more they pushed, the more the Poles would resist. Every Pole understood the wartime rules of behaviour which were formalized by the Directorate of Civil Resistance in 1942. Citizens were to hinder the Germans wherever and whenever possible. Quotas were to be fudged, armaments were to be sabotaged, equipment was to be improperly repaired. People learned not to pry into the affairs of those who might be working for the underground. Small acts of resistance, like daubing graffiti on prominent walls or placing flowers on the sites of destroyed memorials, did little more than raise morale, but they were important in maintaining the spirit of solidarity in the grim war years. After the defeat in 1939 a mass grave for unknown soldiers was dug on the corner of Marszałkowska and Jerusalem Avenue in the very centre of Warsaw, and hundreds of people lit candles for the fallen every day. SS Gruppenführer and Commander of the SS and Warsaw District Police Paul Moder realized the potential danger of such gatherings, and had the bodies moved and access to the site restricted. Warsawians nevertheless managed to surreptitiously light candles there every day until the uprising made it impossible. The 1942 Directorate even included the creation of underground courts of justice which heard cases against collaborators. They imposed – and carried out – the death penalty on a regular basis.

The Nazis tried and utterly failed to crush Polish culture. Many Germans held the strange notion that the further east one went, the less sophisticated people became; propaganda bore this out with carefully chosen photographs of filthy villages and houses in 'the east', with no electricity or running water, and with outhouses dotted around muddy back fields. In reality, Warsaw, with its embassies and theatres and museums, was a highly sophisticated and elegant city, and its inhabitants were often far more worldly than the young German soldiers sent there who had been brought up on a provincial diet of narrow-minded Nazi propaganda. Warsaw inhabitants lived in close-knit working-class communities, handsome villas or suburban flats; they loved their families and their neighbourhoods and their churches, and they followed the latest fashions, theatre and films as keenly as their counterparts in any other European capital. The young German soldiers sent to arrest eighteen-year-old Władysław Bartoszewski in April 1940, and send him on the second ever transport bound for Auschwitz, were astounded to find complete German editions of Goethe and Heinrich Heine on his bookshelves; it had not occurred to them that knowledge of German or French literature was commonplace among educated Poles. Despite the mass arrest of university professors in 1939 and the official ban on university education, hundreds of students clandestinely obtained degrees during the war, the courses being overseen by the underground Department of Education and Culture. Professors deported from the University of Poznań established a secret University of Western Lands in Warsaw, with 250 teachers and 2,000 students. Other scholars risked their lives to hold lectures in their flats: one student was sitting her final exams when the Gestapo burst in and arrested her teacher in front of her.[11] The Poles even created a successful underground medical school. Parents and teachers organized instruction throughout the country: over 5,200 teachers illegally taught 86,000 elementary school pupils and over 5,600 teachers taught 48,000 secondary school students in the 'General Government' (Nazi-occupied Poland). The work was dangerous, as the Germans arrested and executed a large number of Polish teachers: in late 1942 alone 367 were rounded up, most of whom perished in Auschwitz.[12]

When the Germans banned newspapers the Poles simply printed more; indeed, the underground press became one of the secret triumphs of occupied Poland, churning out everything from the latest speeches by Churchill and Roosevelt and interviews with key figures in the government-in-exile to warnings about local Gestapo and SS activity. It is estimated that around 690 titles were published in Warsaw alone; the AK publication *Biuletyn Informacyjny* reached its peak at 50,000 copies per edition.[13] Printing presses were carefully hidden, with secret spaces made by painstakingly removing earth from under buildings by basket. General Bór-Komorowski, the commander of the AK after 1943, visited one of Warsaw's seven large printing shops, buried underneath a perfectly ordinary-looking house. The printing press was in a stuffy room deep underground, its entrance concealed by a dusty slab of concrete, but as the workers had to arrive and leave at prearranged times, there was no way for them to step out for a breath of air. An elaborate signal system had been hidden in the walls. The presses worked away in the glow of a green light, a sign that everything upstairs was in order. If something did go wrong the old lady who acted as the guard would press a rusty nail in the wall, and a red light would turn on below. The machines would be stopped, and the workers would wait in silence for as many hours or days as it took for the danger to pass. The publications of presses like this one were distributed around town from empty beer barrels or factory cases loaded on the pushcarts used to transport everything in Warsaw in those days. An armed escort would always be nearby. 'If anyone insisted on seeing the contents,' Bór said, 'a shot was the only way of finishing the argument.'[14]

Poles were not officially allowed to listen to foreign radio, but illegal stations sprang up throughout the city like mushrooms; no sooner would the Germans close one down than another would appear. Some broadcast throughout the war. Władysław Rodowicz had a radio station hidden under the basement of his house on Forteczna Street in the pretty suburb of Żoliborz; it was never found, despite repeated raids. At the same time Stefan Korboński fed information from Poland to ŚWIT, a station actually located near London but masquerading as being in Poland. As a result of such stations, Warsawians were well informed about unfolding events, hearing about Stalingrad, Kursk and Normandy as the news broke; when a German defeat was announced, the people of the city quietly celebrated.

There was entertainment too. Theatres were created in cellars and factories and churches, and Warsawians put on clandestine performances of Adam Mickiewicz, Alexander Fredro, Molière and Shaw; these were augmented by poetry readings, recitations, political discussions and literary evenings. Puppet shows satirized Hans Frank and Ludwig Fischer; one group even re-enacted the death of SS and Police Leader Franz Kutschera on the streets of Warsaw, while others parodied Adolf Hitler in skits reminiscent of Charlie Chaplin's *The Great Dictator*. The Germans had expected the Polish people simply to forget their cultural heritage, and to go and dig potatoes or slave away in the mines, but this was impossible. One of the tragedies of the Warsaw Uprising was that so many talented men and women whom the Germans had singularly failed to silence between 1939 and July 1944 were killed in the inferno that followed.

By 1944 some Germans, particularly Hans Frank, Governor of the General Government, realized that the policy of increased brutality was not working. The war was coming to a close, and he, like many top Nazis, assumed that he would be able to play a role in the post-war world as an elder statesman and representative of Germany. Frank hoped that the Poles could be recruited to fight on the German side in what he believed would be a new conflict between the Soviets and the Western Allies, and tried to win them over by opening a few schools and allowing the return of elements of Polish culture; he even had Frédéric Chopin Germanically renamed 'Frederick Schopping', thereby allowing the composer's works to be played in public.[15] Frank's overtures came to nothing, as in reality he remained the insensitive overlord he always had been. He referred to his wife as 'the Queen of Poland', and had a swimming pool built for her in the beautiful Wawel Castle. He kept Leonardo da Vinci's *Lady with an Ermine*, one of Poland's greatest treasures, in his private rooms, and tried to take it with him when he packed up and left for Germany in 1945. He paid Poles, including Roman Polanski's mother, to work at the castle, but never deigned to speak to them as fellow human beings – they were slaves, there to serve his mighty court until they were disposed of. On any given morning he might sign a hundred death warrants or put his signature on the order for another transport bound for Auschwitz, then go in the evening to a concert by the orchestra in which a handful of

Polish musicians were allowed to perform for him. Himmler thought of Frank as 'too soft', and neither Hitler nor Himmler would sanction any cooperation with the hated Slavs. The Poles poked fun at him constantly. When he published his 'Days in Poland' pamphlet for the German Kultur organization, the underground printed a parallel brochure with a new ironic text. Frank's glowing section on *Kraft durch Freude* (Strength through joy) became an 'exhibit of manhunts and arrests at home combined with an excursion to view Polish intelligentsia in camps in Oświęcim, Dachau, and Oranienburg'.[16] His true colours shone through when the uprising broke out. He felt betrayed by 'his' Poles, and agreed that Warsaw was 'the point from which all unrest in this land is brought'. Like his masters, he approved of the complete destruction of the city.[17]

As the Allied advance on Nazi Germany continued, the military fight in Poland was spearheaded by the AK, under the auspices of the government-in-exile in London. Under Stefan Rowecki's leadership from 1940, the Home Army was soon operating throughout occupied Poland. Its structure mirrored the pre-war Polish army's order of battle, with units formed into divisions, brigades and regiments.

In order to avoid German reprisal killings, which sometimes amounted to a hundred or more innocent people for the death of one German, the AK focused primarily on intelligence and sabotage. General Kazimierz Sosnkowski, commander in chief of the Polish armed forces in London, held that intelligence-gathering was the most important task of the military underground. It was the Poles who first broke the high-security German Enigma codes, and who provided British and French intelligence with reconstructed Enigma machines on 25 July 1939, just before the outbreak of the war – Winston Churchill later told King George VI that breaking the Enigma code had been the main reason for the Allied victory. Later, the Poles sent detailed reports of the German concentration and extermination camps to the West; they even delivered parts of a captured V-2 rocket. The AK worked closely with the British centre for the coordination of resistance against the Germans in occupied Europe, the Special Operations Executive, or SOE, which in turn dropped weapons, ammunition and *Cichociemni* agents into Poland. Unlike the British Foreign Office, which became progressively more pro-Soviet and anti-Polish as the war went on, the SOE, whose operatives often worked in highly dangerous situations alongside Poles, had great respect for these unflinchingly pro-British resistance fighters. The Minister for Economic Warfare, Hugh Dalton, openly declared that 'I like the Poles,' while the Director of Operations for Western and Central Europe, Brigadier Colin Gubbins, was a close personal friend of General Sikorski, and got along well with his successor as the head of the government-in-exile, Stanisław Mikołajczyk.[18] Thomas Snowden, a British-Canadian operative who worked with his Polish counterparts in Sweden and elsewhere, was not unusual when he said that, aside from his navy colleagues, he would 'most trust the Poles with his life'.[19] Even the Germans acknowledged their effectiveness: in December 1942 Himmler complained that the Polish resistance was strong, well organized, and had become 'very dangerous' for Germany.

For the AK operatives, Warsaw was extremely dangerous. They had to be highly secretive, as any mistake would quickly lead to a knock on the door by the Gestapo. When Jan Karski was recruited by Dziepatowski, the mood turned very serious. 'You are now a member of the underground . . . should you turn informer or make any attempt to betray us you will be shot. Have I made myself clear?'[20] Everyone had a *nom de guerre*, and the organization was cellular rather than strictly hierarchical.

Operatives knew only their superior officer and a handful of colleagues, which meant that they could give away only a limited amount of information even if they were tortured. Some of the most vulnerable were the 'liaison women' who were used to maintain contact between underground workers; the nature of their work meant they could not remain in hiding like other operatives, but always had to be reachable. As Karski put it, 'of all the workers in the underground their lot was the most severe, their sacrifices the greatest, and their contribution the least rewarded. They were overworked and doomed. They neither held high rank nor received any great honours for their heroism. Most of the liaison women with whom I had the honour to work endured the common fate of their sisters. One of them was a young girl of about twenty-two or -three . . . A message smuggled out of the jail after her first and only interrogation described her condition . . . "when they carried her away, the lower half of her body was in shreds".[21] Despite all the precautions taken, many hundreds of AK operatives were captured, tortured and shot during the war.

After the betrayal and arrest of Rowecki in 1943, the AK was commanded by the short, slim and unassuming General Tadeusz Bór-Komorowski, who would soon be forced to make the agonizing decision about when to start the Warsaw Uprising. Born in 1895, he served as an officer in the Austro-Hungarian army before joining the new Polish army after the First World War. He became a career cavalry officer and commanded the Cavalry School at Grudziądz; a superb horseman, he led the Polish equestrian team at the 1936 Berlin Olympics. It was at the Games that he came to the attention of both Himmler's protégé Hermann Fegelein and General-Leutnant Hans Källner of 19th Panzer Division, both of whom would fight against him in the uprising. Bór was very effective in the conspiracy, but he was not a tactical commander.[22] Andrzej Pomian, one of the post-war founders of the Polish Independence Movement, first met him in London after the war: 'In my imagination he was a great symbol of heroism and so the first meeting with him was very disappointing.' Bór, he thought, had 'nothing of the heroic about him'. He was 'modest and simple', and carried the 'terrifying stigma of having made the decision to start the uprising'. Stanisław Jankowski, code-named 'Agaton', spent time in a prisoner of war camp with this 'tired, shy, polite and friendly man'. Colonel Józef Szostak, Chief of the Operational Bureau of the AK, who had been present on numerous occasions when the fateful decision was being discussed, said of him that he was 'honest, honourable and brave, but he had absolutely no qualifications to occupy the position that fate allocated to him. He was a pleasant, well-mannered and elegant cavalry officer . . . but no outstanding individual, and he did not tower over his subordinates in terms of character and valour.'[23]

The AK had been preparing for an uprising against the Germans from the beginning of the war, but that was not their only role: the organization was divided between those who were actively engaged against the enemy throughout and those who were dormant, waiting for the moment they would be called to fight. Most men and women in the AK had ordinary jobs and lived normal lives. Józef Garliński, who was a counter-intelligence officer, traded in old clothes as a cover. The handsome, tennis-playing operative was married to an Irishwoman who stayed in Poland throughout the war: 'We never spoke about my underground work,' he said, 'but she knew that I was deeply engaged in it and the old-clothes trade was only a front to hide my activities. She herself, in spite of my opposition, was involved in similar activities, although to a lesser extent.'[24] Włodzimierz Rosłoniec, who was in charge of guarding an arsenal of weapons at Krolewska Street, hinted about his work to his mother shortly before the uprising. She cut him short, saying, 'I am very happy for you, but don't tell me anything more, and I won't tell you anything about my activity – it will be better for both of us.' They agreed to name an emergency meeting point in case of trouble, but only admitted the extent of their involvement to each other after the war.

The AK contained a number of elite units, of which the most famous was 'Kedyw', a reprisal unit which consisted of men and women trained in sabotage, communications and even chemical warfare. Kedyw and other groups carried out hundreds of operations of sabotage throughout the war, and were so effective that General Siegfried Hänicke complained: 'My troops do not understand that when they are in the General Government they are not in the Fatherland, but in a region where the majority of the population is hostile to us and opposes us with violence.'[25]

Kedyw operatives came from many walks of life, although most were well-educated and from professional backgrounds. One of the most exceptional was Stanisław Aronson. Having escaped from the train taking him to Treblinka, he found refuge at the home of a friend of his mother's on the 'Aryan' side of Warsaw. It was there that he was introduced to a softly-spoken philosophy professor, Józef Rybicki, who turned out to be the head of Kedyw Warsaw. Rybicki realized that this sophisticated and worldly young man might be a good fit in Kedyw, and after a long 'interview' he asked if he would join. Aronson agreed, and was given a new 'Aryan' identity, a complete set of papers and the pseudonym 'Rysiek'. He was quickly accepted by the eight-member team of 'Kedyw Kollegium A'; the fact that he was Jewish was discussed only once, when a colleague asked him if he was from Kresy, 'or are you Jewish as we can't place you exactly'. When Aronson admitted his background she promised that they would all protect his identity, and the subject was never mentioned again. All of them understood the particularly grave danger Aronson was in, as the discovery of his true identity could result in betrayal, arrest and death.

Unlike most AK members, Aronson and his Kedyw colleagues underwent military training throughout the war. They were taught how to operate all types of weapons, from American Thompson submachine guns to German Schmeissers; they attended workshops analysing past operations; and they were trained by the dashing *Cichociemni* parachuted in from England. One of the more grim 'ruthless and dark' tasks undertaken by Aronson's unit was the execution of traitors sentenced to death by the underground courts, including Poles who collaborated with the Gestapo. 'Sometimes these actions took a few weeks to prepare. We hung around near the victim's house and observed his habits. We drew a map of the surrounding streets and alleys, and the layout of the building. When everything was prepared, we went to the victim's apartment . . . We then read the sentence and one of my friends carried out the execution.'[26]

The most famous Kedyw assassination in Warsaw was of Erich von dem Bach-Zelewski's friend and colleague Franz Kutschera (whose wife was the sister of Hermann Fegelein), who after a short time working with Bach in Byelorussia had been sent to Poland, where he became known as 'the executioner of Warsaw'. Kutschera, a tall man with a toothy grin and a neat Hitler moustache, was a fanatical enemy of all real or imagined 'partisans', and seemed to take great pleasure in identifying and exterminating centres of 'banditry', whether as SS and police leader in Mogilev or, from September 1943, in Warsaw. For him all Poles were expendable, and he energetically carried out the policy of mass round-ups and random executions on the streets of the city. It was for this crime in particular that he was found guilty by the Special Court of the Polish Underground State, a verdict approved by the Polish government-in-exile in London. The execution order was given by General Emil August Fieldorf ('Nil'), the commander of Kedyw for all of Poland. In a brilliantly coordinated attack in front of his residence next to the SS headquarters on 1 February 1944, Kustchera's car was blocked by another vehicle carrying four Kedyw operatives. Bronisław Pietraszkiewicz ('Lot'), whom Bór called one of his 'ablest soldiers', shot him in the head; one of his colleagues did the same to the SS driver. Within seconds the area came under heavy German fire, but the four men managed to drive off.[27] They raced across the bridge to the Hospital of the Transfiguration in Praga, where 'Lot' and 'Cichy' died of their wounds. The other two men, 'Sokół' and 'Juno', were later stopped by the Germans, and jumped into the Vistula to try to swim away. They were shot in the water.

Von dem Bach made a special point of having dinner with Kutschera's widow, and praising her late husband's glorious career, but the bold assassination in broad daylight had unsettled the Germans. Kutschera's replacement, Paul Otto Geibel, stopped the massive random street round-ups, although many Poles were still shot in the ruins of the ghetto and elsewhere. Wehrmacht soldiers were ordered not to walk on the streets alone, and the Germans became obsessed with secrecy around their top officials. Geibel's identity and movements were kept hidden from the Poles, and other top Nazis stationed in Warsaw stayed in the heavily guarded German areas as much as possible. Franz Grassler, a young attorney and deputy to Dr Heinz Auerswald, Commissioner for the Warsaw ghetto, complained that it was difficult even for Germans to contact their superiors, so conscious were they of rank and security: 'Auerswald was in his apartment and we were . . . housed in barracks . . . in the German House,*' he said. When important matters had to be discussed it sometimes took days

* Now Poland's presidential palace.

for a meeting to be arranged. It is not surprising that few Poles had ever seen the faces or knew the names of the high-ranking SS officials in their midst.[28]

Even so, the AK was effective at gleaning information about the top officials governing their lives. As part of her duties working undercover in a German-run office, Larysa Zajączkowska sometimes delivered mail to the glorious rococo Brühl Palace, now the headquarters of the police, the SS and the Governor of Warsaw Ludwig Fischer. It was one of the most closely guarded buildings in the city, but 'with the help of a few bars of chocolate, a few bottles of slivovitz and a packet of coffee I befriended Governor Fischer's secretary', Zajączkowska recalled. 'She had very simple tastes, and the greedy *Fräulein* could not imagine where I sent all the information she let slip out. For example, nobody knew who had replaced Kutschera after his death . . . It was a strict secret and the name was not even known to the Germans. Then one day a slim, balding officer was in the room and I whispered to Freda, "Who is he?" adding that I liked the look of him very much. She whispered, "That is General Geibel, Kutschera's successor." I reported this immediately.'

The AK asked Larysa to find out which cars Geibel used, with a view to another assassination, but this was extremely difficult, as after Kutschera's death the top Nazis changed their cars several times a day. When she finally obtained the information she was told that Geibel would not, after all, be assassinated, as 'the war is ending and the guilty will be judged by international tribunals'. Sadly, this was not to be. Although Geibel himself would die in a Polish prison, many of the worst criminals active in Warsaw – from Bach to Reinefarth, from Ludwig Hahn to Wilhelm Koppe and Heinz Auerswald, escaped punishment for the crimes they committed there.

.   AK attacks against Germans in Warsaw became more frequent as the Soviets drew ever closer to the city. In the fifteen months before the uprising, Aronson's Kedyw unit carried out more than sixty operations, many of them executions of Germans or collaborators; nearly half of his unit was lost in the process. Between November 1943 and May 1944 the AK killed 704 Germans; by the time of the uprising they were assassinating around ten people every day.

The Germans continued to fight the AK as best they could. One of their most successful operations was the betrayal of Stefan Rowecki to the Gestapo. He was taken to Germany on Himmler's orders, but despite being tortured, never disclosed any information about the AK. Himmler had him executed in Sachsenhausen when he heard about the outbreak of the uprising on 1 August 1944.

Rowecki's female colleagues routinely displayed similar courage. One of the most extraordinary groups, also part of 'Kedyw', was the all-female sapper unit under Major Zofia Franio. In 1940 Franio was given permission to recruit five instructors from the PWK. All the women, who included Antonina Mijal, had 'military knowledge, the psychological disposition and physical prowess to carry out the tasks'. Franio organized officers from the sapper corps to teach her recruits about explosives and incendiary devices, and in the autumn of 1940 three of the five instructors started their own sub-units, all of which became part of 'Kedyw'.[29]

One of these recruits was Antonina Mijal ('Tosia'), who soon became Franio's second in command. A beautiful young woman with jet-black hair and dark eyes – her great-grandfather's family had come to Poland from Spain with Napoleon's Grande Armée – she was recruited by Franio in October 1940. Mijal took part in numerous sabotage operations, particularly blowing up rail lines. She would leave town on the last tram, carrying the concealed bombs; on one occasion she transported them in stuffed toy monkeys. Her friend Irena Hahn remembered blowing up a train with her one evening and having to 'sneak back to Warsaw, which was very dangerous as the roads were already swarming with Germans lighting up the area'. On another evening they were walking home after training at Franio's apartment when they were stopped by a police patrol: 'The men searched Tosia's sack but didn't pay attention to the box under her arm. They let us walk away with Tosia still carrying the sample explosives. A few minutes later we had to stop; we couldn't speak.' Had the box been opened, both women would have been shot. Another time they were caught in a street round-up, and although Tosia managed to walk through the cordon Irena was stopped. 'Tosia came back for me, took my hand and snatched it from the policeman as if she was offended that he had grabbed me. He stood there rather confused but his colleague started to laugh at him and so we managed to slip away.'

Franio and Mijal ran twenty storage facilities and arms factories in and around Warsaw, not only overseeing production, but also moving arms to where they were needed, constantly risking arrest and imprisonment. According to Rybicki, 'there were no men involved, and there were never any complaints about technical standards or delivery'.[30]

Unfortunately, 'Kedyw' operatives were not representative of the entire AK. Stanisław Aronson, who served in the Israeli army after the war, said: 'People today think that the Home Army was a kind of military power, but it was not at all like that. It was an organization with a few hundred thousand members, however there were actually only small operational fighting units. In the Warsaw area there were probably around 1,000 soldiers who participated in diversionary actions.' At the beginning of the uprising the Warsaw AK counted 40,000 members, but only a few thousand were properly armed and trained.[31] Most of the others were young people frustrated by almost five years of

German occupation, but with scant practical knowledge or experience. They were desperate to 'do something', but they had had little or no training, and very few had weapons. This would prove to be a serious problem during the Warsaw Uprising.

Operation 'Tempest'

The first concrete plan for an uprising was released in September 1942, and was to be ordered by the Commander-in-Chief in London when German defeat was imminent. At first the Poles had hoped that victory would come from the west, and that British and American troops would overrun Germany and push into Poland, but as Soviet victories mounted after Stalingrad and the Western Allies delayed the invasion of France, it became clear that they would in fact be 'liberated' by Soviet troops from the east. The Poles were rightly wary of Soviet intentions, and much time was put into discussing the potential threat of the Red Army. In February 1943 Stefan Rowecki, whose mantra was that the Soviets 'will always be our enemy', drafted a new plan called 'Burza', or Tempest, which would unfold in three stages: an armed rising in the eastern cities of Lwów and Wilno, an armed attack in the area east of the Vistula, and finally a national uprising throughout the country. The idea was to harass the German retreat, to prevent reprisals against civilians, and to secure important cities for the émigré government before the Russians could take over. Rowecki's fears about the Soviets increased when Stalin broke off diplomatic relations with the Polish government-in-exile over the murder of 4,410 Polish officers at Katyń – and more than 17,000 elsewhere – by far the largest massacre of PoWs during the war. The graves had been discovered by the Germans in April 1943, and when the Soviets denied that they had committed the murders the Poles, knowing the truth, demanded a Red Cross inquiry. On 26 April Stalin used this 'insult' to break off relations with Sikorski's government, in mock fury at the Polish accusations. Rowecki decided that the Soviet threat to the AK was too great for an open uprising, and that Polish forces should conduct sabotage operations against retreating Germans, but remain under cover.

When General Bór took over command of the AK after Rowecki's arrest by the Germans in 1943 he reversed this order, deciding that the Poles should reveal themselves, in order to prove that it was they who had legal authority in Poland. General Sosnkowski in London reluctantly agreed, although he had no illusions about Russia's intentions. 'In my view,' he wrote to Bór on 11 January 1944, 'the final aim of the Soviet Union is to transform Poland into a vassal Communist republic or simply into the 17th Soviet republic.' He was right. Stalin had already mentally claimed Eastern Europe for himself. Furthermore, the Poles could not count on any real help from the Western Allies. At the Tehran Conference in November 1943 Stalin, Churchill and Roosevelt had determined the future eastern border of Poland at the so-called Curzon Line, which gave large chunks of Polish territory to the Soviet Union. Churchill suggested that Poland be given swathes of Germany as compensation. It was an ominous precedent. Not only had the Western Allies left the Poles out of the decision-making process, they had made it clear that however just their cause, they cared more about maintaining friendly relations with Stalin than they did about Polish concerns for the future of their country. Roosevelt in particular saw Poland as part of Stalin's sphere of influence, and his only real concern was to keep the issue of the future border secret from the millions of Polish-American voters until after the November 1944 presidential election. Documents released by the National Archives in September 2012 show that Roosevelt knew that the Soviets had in fact committed the massacre at Katyń, but was so determined to remain on good terms with Stalin that he lied to his own people, and in particular to the Poles. It was harsh treatment of a nation in such peril.

Churchill was sympathetic to Poland, but he was in a difficult situation. British power was waning in the shadow of the two emerging superpowers, and he was desperate to preserve what he could of his nation's influence. He understood that the West could not defeat Nazi Germany alone, and that one price for Soviet cooperation would be a change to Poland's eastern border. The sheer scale of the Soviets' military success led to irritation with the Poles amongst the Western Allies for not accepting the new international reality. The prevailing view was that the Soviets were paying for victory with the blood of millions of men, and that the 'Polish question', however embarrassing, could not be allowed to threaten Stalin's decision to carry on the fight. As Field Marshal Jan Smuts, Prime Minister of South Africa, put it to Churchill in March 1944, 'It would be calamitous if the Polish question were to sour Russian relations with Britain.'[32] Most senior officials in the Foreign Office agreed. Sir William Strang, Assistant Under-Secretary of State for Europe until 1943, felt that it would be in Britain's interest to accept Soviet supremacy in Eastern Europe: 'It is better that Russia should dominate Eastern Europe,' he wrote, 'than that Germany should dominate Western Europe.'[33] Stalin was in effect given *carte blanche* to do as he wished.

Despite their fears of Soviet intentions, the Poles did their best to help the Red Army in its sweep towards Warsaw. The AK attacked the Germans in Wilno, Lwów and Lublin as part of Operation 'Tempest', and assisted the Russians where they could. Stalin did not care, as he was determined not to allow the AK any kind of military or political victory. Early contacts between Red Army soldiers and the AK were usually friendly, but once the NKVD arrived – usually within a few hours – AK soldiers who revealed themselves were arrested, murdered, sent to the gulag or press-ganged into the Soviet-run army commanded by General Zygmunt Berling.* The Soviets used the recently liberated camp at Majdanek to intern 'dangerous' Polish nationalists. When the 'Committee for National Liberation' was set up in Lublin as the 'legitimate government' of Poland on 22 July, the announcement had been followed by a half-hour broadcast of the Polish national anthem. Stalin had laid his cards on the table. The Polish government-in-exile in London was to be undermined in every way possible, and its representatives in Poland eliminated.

As the Soviets' true intentions became clear, the pressure on the AK in Warsaw grew ever more intense. With the Red Army advancing rapidly towards the city, the fear was that if the AK did nothing the Soviets would liberate Warsaw, and Stalin would broadcast to the world that the Polish Home Army had been ineffectual – or worse, had even collaborated with the Germans. General Bór and a handful of colleagues began to convince themselves that the very proximity of the Red Army might give them the chance to include Warsaw in Operation 'Tempest'. With the Germans apparently falling to pieces and the Red Army approaching the eastern bank of the Vistula, the calls to 'do something' increased. That 'something' was to be an uprising in the capital.

---

* Born in Limanowa in 1895, Berling had been in Józef Piłsudski's Polish Legions in the First World War, after which he had joined the now reborn Polish army, advancing to the rank of major. He was in the Soviet zone when Poland was invaded in 1939, and like thousands of other officers had been arrested and was meant to die at Katyń; but he offered to help the Soviets, and his life was spared. After the Sikorski–Maisky Pact of 1941 he joined General Anders' army, but on his way out of the Soviet Union he deserted for the Red Army. The Poles court-martialled him and sentenced him to death *in absentia*, but Stalin liked him, and his Soviet star began to rise.

There was one big problem. In March 1944 Warsaw had been deliberately excluded from the plans of Operation 'Tempest' because, as Bór had put it, 'we wanted to avoid destruction and suffering of the civilian population and safeguard historical buildings'.[34] Some AK units remained in the city, but most of the arsenal had been moved to the main forces waiting in the forests. General Tadeusz Pełczyński, the AK Chief of Staff, said that 'we wanted not to fight in the towns to save them. A fight in Warsaw was not planned. But the nature of the war changed all that . . . the decision to fight in Warsaw was taken in mid-July when the front was approaching the capital very quickly. The authorities decided it was essential for Polish soldiers to free Warsaw from the Germans.'[35]

Pełczyński and his friend General Leopold Okulicki were the main architects of the revised plan. Born in 1892, the son of a sugar-mill technician, Pełczyński had been deeply involved in the AK from the beginning: it was he who handed over the Enigma machines to the British in 1939, and he had commanded numerous 'Kedyw' sabotage operations throughout the war. For him the choice was simple: either the AK could depart from Warsaw, leaving a no man's land in which the Germans and Soviets would fight one another, or it could help free the city and, as its rightful proprietors, extend a formal welcome to the Soviets.

For his part, Okulicki had few doubts about Soviet intentions. Arrested and sent to the gulag while serving in the Polish resistance, he had only managed to escape thanks to General Władysław Anders, who was released by the Russians to form an army made up of Poles captured by the Soviets in 1939 and 1940. Okulicki was parachuted back into occupied Poland in May 1944, and the fact that he had been sent on a special mission from General Sosnkowski in London lent his voice great weight in AK headquarters. But his view bordered on the messianic. Even if the

Russians did not come to help liberate Warsaw, he argued, the price of defeat would be worth it, as it would 'show the world' that the Soviets were the bearers of an 'inhuman policy which condemns half of Europe to future slavery'.[36] Both Pełczyński and Okulicki believed that waiting for the Germans to retreat would make the AK appear too weak and passive. The Poles had to show the world that they could fight in open combat, and that they had the right to a free and independent country after the war. All they had to do was to storm the German garrison and hang onto the city until the Red Army arrived. It seemed so simple.

On 21 July, General Bór bowed to pressure from Pełczyński and Okulicki and asked Jan Jankowski, the Government Delegate for the Polish government-in-exile, who was based in Poland but was in constant contact with London, to approve the decision to include the capital in the fight. The timing seemed perfect. That very night the German commander of Warsaw had announced that all German women, including those working for auxiliary organizations, should leave the city. The German community was in chaos as panicked civilians tried desperately to get out before the Russians arrived. Even SD units were leaving.

That same day, Bór sent what turned out to be a wildly optimistic telegram to London describing the situation on the front: 'The Soviet advance on this sector will be rapid and will reach and cross the Vistula in a further advance to the west without any effective or serious German counter-offensive . . . It appears certain that on the Eastern Front the Germans are incapable of taking the initiative from Soviet hands or of successful opposition. Recently we have observed more frequent signs of the disintegration of the German forces who are tired and show no will to fight. The recent attempt on Hitler's life, together with the military position of Germany, may lead at any moment to their collapse.'[37]

The AK High Command were by this time meeting daily at

their central headquarters on Pańska Street. Colonel Rzepecki, the head of the Information and Propaganda Bureau, was in favour of an early start to the uprising, not least because he felt it would help Stanisław Mikołajczyk's negotiating position with Stalin in Moscow. But he also believed that the Nazis were finished. During the meeting on 21 July he gestured to the window and asked his colleagues to look at the empty streets. The Nazis had gone; there were no armed patrols. 'The German army has ceased to exist,' he declared.[38]

A kind of fantasy seemed to grip many in AK headquarters. It was as if they could picture themselves standing in a Warsaw emptied of Germans, waiting on the proverbial red carpet to welcome the Soviets with a gentlemanly salute as a mark of mutual respect, power and goodwill. They had spent the war creating an underground army with the intention of rising up against the Germans, but now the chance had come to win a great political victory over Stalin as well. They did not stop to think that with only a few thousand poorly armed men they had nothing remotely like the military strength to defeat one, let alone two, of the greatest armies ever created should something go wrong; but there was no 'Plan B'. In those heady July days the AK leaders allowed themselves to believe that the Germans were now all but irrelevant, and that their primary task was to deal with the Soviets, as well as international opinion and the post-war world. The under-estimation of German strength would prove to be a terrible and costly error. Worse still, none of the AK High Command could later claim that they had not been told the truth.

There was, in fact, one important dissenting voice at the AK meeting of 21 July. Colonel Kazimierz Iranek-Osmecki, the Chief of Intelligence, was one of the most thoughtful and well-informed of the group that gathered daily to discuss and decide on Warsaw's fate. He was appalled to hear Rzepecki say that the German army was finished, and quickly gave a summary of the military situation gleaned from intelligence personnel around Warsaw. He said that the German units which had crossed the Bug River in the past few days were remnants of four divisions; two others had been surrounded at Brest, which meant that the German 2nd Army had been destroyed, and that the Germans could not defend Warsaw from an attack from the east. Furthermore, in the south the 4th Panzer Army seemed to have been demolished: 'The command headquarters of the army has sent unciphered dispatches to all units which means that they have either lost touch with them or the divisions have ceased to exist.' But then Osmecki made one of the most important revelations of the days leading up to the uprising. 'There is new unverified information that fresh Panzer units, as yet unidentified, have appeared on the right side of the Vistula in the forests between Wyszków and Jabłonna. Also, parts of the Hermann Göring Division, one of the best units of the German army, have arrived in Żyrardów. According to our intelligence the Hermann Göring Division was withdrawn from the Italian Front and moved by train to Warsaw. The first units have been moved in secret into the forests by Wyszków and Jabłonna.'[39]

Osmecki was asked about the significance of the troop movements, but replied that it was too early to tell. Then General Okulicki, who had no way of knowing any more than Osmecki about the German plans, confidently declared that the new forces were of no importance, because the tanks 'are simply there to protect the retreat of the 2nd Army'. Osmecki countered with a new piece of information. Intelligence had informed him that the 'German headquarters in Warsaw had demanded from the railway office the immediate dispatch of 2,000 empty wagons to remove factories from the city'. However, rather than simply send the empty trains from Berlin to Warsaw, as might have been expected, the headquarters announced that 'a few thousand wagons of ammunition and equipment will be sent in the nearest future to Warsaw' in those same trains. The wagons were to be unloaded, and only then sent back to Germany with the dismantled factories. 'A few thousand wagons of supplies and ammunition,' Osmecki said, 'suggests that the Germans are going to defend themselves.'[40] Again Rzepecki and Okulicki downplayed the idea, and referred to the attempt on Hitler's life the previous day, concluding: 'The German army could fall apart at any time.'

What they could not yet know was that far from removing Hitler, the attempt on his life had only fuelled his fanaticism and his desire to fight on. In his mind he had been spared for Germany by 'divine providence', and in the Wolfsschanze he railed against his generals and wrested even greater control for himself. But General Bór was swayed by Rzepecki and Okulicki, and called a state of alert for Tuesday, 25 July at the very moment Hitler's luck on the Eastern Front was turning in his favour. Warsaw's day of reckoning was drawing near.

During the next meeting, on Sunday, 23 July, Osmecki again tried to warn the AK leadership of the threat posed by the Nazis. He now had more information: 'There is a concentration of German forces to the north and east of Warsaw which is increasing all the time,' he said. 'Now we know that the elite Viking SS and Totenkopf Divisions have come.' Although the Soviets 'will ultimately defeat the Germans', he said, decisions about the uprising 'should be postponed' until the Germans had launched their counter-attack in the north.

This time, Osmecki's view was supported by the AK's brilliant Deputy Chief of Staff Colonel Janusz Bokszczanin, who was in Warsaw for a few days. But Okulicki and Rzepecki again declared that the Germans were in 'disarray' and were 'about to leave Warsaw'. Rzepecki even said that although it would be very bad to start the uprising too early, it would be 'considerably worse' to start it too late. 'In the first case we could hope to improve the situation, but in the second we would be condemned for good, and so would Poland.'

25 July brought a full meeting between Bór and his staff, Jan Jankowski, and General Antoni Chruściel, known as 'Monter', Commander of the Home Army units in Warsaw. Born in 1895 of peasant stock, Monter had served in the Austro-Hungarian army and then, after the First World War, in the newly formed Polish army. Józef Rybicki, head of 'Kedyw' in Warsaw, found him unsuited to the secret world of the AK. 'Meetings with Monter were particularly unpleasant,' he said. 'He was a typical *Zupak* – a boorish old soldier – with no understanding of conspiracy and its style of operations.'[41] Monter was 'always suspicious in an unpleasant way, distrustful and crude . . . We often exchanged strong words, which I could get away with as a civilian but which would not have been tolerated in the army officers.' Monter was overly concerned with superficial matters. He cared too much about military protocol and about his personal appearance, having new uniforms made and striking poses in front of onlookers. He was also obsessed by his place in history, and had a highly exaggerated view of his own importance. After the war he wrote to Stanisław Jankowski, who had by then become an architect in Warsaw, to try to get a memorial that he had designed built on one of the most important squares in Warsaw. In the crucial days leading up to 1 August Monter continued to underestimate German strength. His main concern was the weakness of the AK in Warsaw and the location of the Soviets, and he was against starting the uprising until the Red Army was in Praga.

Osmecki tried to emphasize the importance of German strength and the growing evidence that they intended to counter-attack against the Russians from Wyszków, to the north-west of Warsaw.

'This would have a huge effect on the capital,' he said, and again urged that the timing of the uprising be made dependent on the outcome of the Russo–German battle. He left the meeting quite dejected, with the feeling that he had not been heard. It was true. Far from heeding his warnings, Jankowski sent a message to London that the uprising was now imminent: 'We are ready at any time to launch the battle for Warsaw,' it said. He even requested that the Polish Parachute Brigade stationed in the UK be sent to Warsaw, and that the airfields near the city be bombed by the RAF. 'I will report the commencement of the battle,' he wrote. And that was all. There was no real discussion between Warsaw and London about what was about to happen; Bór and Jan Jankowski were effectively dictating policy to their superiors in the UK.

As he walked home after the meeting, Osmecki had a vision of the fate that he was sure awaited Warsaw. 'The sun was going down over Wola and lighting up the windows of the city. I stood on Sienna Street blinded by the reflection. Suddenly I remembered Bokszczanin's warning: "Believe me, the Russians will not come, they will leave us alone to the Germans." I was sure he was right, and that the city would once again be destroyed. As I looked at the sun reflected in the windows I saw a vision of fire consuming the city and heard the crackling of flames. This was very brief, but the feeling stayed with me and I had nightmares that night. I woke up in the morning feeling as if I was in a Greek tragedy. We were watching a horrifying drama unfold around us, but we could not avoid it; it was our tragic fate against which we could do nothing.'[42]

The point is that the AK could have done something, but they chose not to. Osmecki, Bokszczanin and Colonel Pluta-Czachowski, the AK's Chief Signals Officer, had warned Bór and the others about the German threat, but they were ignored. 'Destiny' had spoken.

Bokszczanin remains one of the unsung heroes of the AK at this pivotal moment in history. More than any other, he consistently spelled out the dangers of underestimating the Germans and above all of pinning their hopes on salvation by the Russians.[43] Bokszczanin's view was very clear and consistent: 'The first condition to start the uprising is to see the destruction of the Germans in Praga, on the left bank of the river. But that is not enough. You have to wait for the Russians to get the pontoons necessary to cross the river and start artillery attacks on the western side of the Vistula. You have to be very careful and double-check all the information especially to do with the 8th Army. The Russians can send patrols out so we think that they are attacking. We have to make sure that these are main forces and not bait.' Even Osmecki initially thought Bokszczanin was 'overdoing it', only later admitting that his fears about Soviet intentions had been well-founded. 'Bokszczanin understood everything, but he told us things we did not want to hear because to accept them meant that we would have to resign and not begin the uprising.'[44]

Osmecki wanted to delay the start of the uprising until the situation at the front was more clear, but he was not against it *per se*. 'As a man and a Pole I shared their passion and certainty that Warsaw could not be allowed to move from German hands to Soviet hands without us expressing our will to maintain independence, even if it meant we gave a great cry of rebellion and sorrow. Bokszczanin was right, but his arguments were unacceptable as they destroyed our whole *raison d'être*.' Jan Nowak-Jeziorański, the Home Army courier who heard Bokszczanin speak in those final days before the uprising, said that he was 'greatly impressed by this officer's coolness and assurance'.[45] But his attempts to warn the others came to nothing in the end, and his role has virtually disappeared from history.

The Decision is Taken

The arguments about what to do continued over the next two days, as tension mounted in the city. On 26 July Osmecki again stressed that three SS divisions had been sent into the Warsaw area, but Monter retorted that the German troops were of 'poor quality'. Given that he was referring to the Waffen SS Viking and Totenkopf Divisions, and Hermann Göring's own elite Luftwaffe division, he was either incredibly badly informed, or did not understand their significance: these elite units may have been under strength, but to refer to them as of 'poor quality' was ludicrous. Monter admitted that his own armoury was in a dire state, and was worried about the strength of the AK.

The mood among the Germans seemed to be changing too. On 27 July Governor Fischer, who had fled the city, suddenly returned, had the street megaphones switched on at 5 p.m. and announced that the next day, 28 July, at 8 a.m., all men between the ages of seventeen and sixty-five were to appear at gathering points to dig anti-tank ditches. The AK banned compliance, so only a few hundred people showed up. Even so, Monter was worried that the Nazis would start to round up men by force, thereby destroying the very fabric of the AK in Warsaw. To counter this he took the extraordinary decision to mobilize the armed forces and call the alert for the uprising without consulting the other members of the AK leadership. Orders were sent out, and the young men and women of the AK hurried to their designated areas, convinced that the fight was about to begin.

In reality, the Germans had neither the manpower nor the authority to enforce the order to dig trenches; both Frank and Fischer agreed to ignore the snub to their authority so as not to provoke the very uprising that they wished to avoid. With the Germans not reacting after all, Monter was forced to recall his order. But the false alarm sowed confusion and discontent among those who had struggled to get to their positions on time, and it was also to have a great influence on Bór two days later. To cancel the mobilization order a second time, he felt, would have a disastrous impact on morale. Monter's rash decision to act alone would therefore have fateful consequences on 31 July.

As for the call to Warsaw's male inhabitants to dig ditches, the AK High Command failed to ask themselves an important question: why, if the Germans were set to abandon the city, had they called for men to dig anti-tank ditches? This too hinted at a dramatic shift in German policy.

On 26 July the German panic in Warsaw had ceased. The columns of bedraggled soldiers had vanished, and the cars which had left in such haste, packed with belongings, began to return. Bureaucrats and policemen quietly reoccupied their apartments, and German functionaries reported for work as if they had never been away. The SS and police presence on the streets doubled and then tripled, and the pillboxes and bunkers next to important buildings and institutions suddenly bristled with troops. Many Germans who had fled illegally were arrested; Himmler even ordered that the President of the Warsaw court, who had released the prisoners from Mokotów prison without permission, be tracked down and shot. On 31 July all releases were stopped; two days later the thousand remaining prisoners were murdered by the SS.

The real reason for the change on the streets of Warsaw was down to Hitler. The Führer had been appalled by news of the exodus from Warsaw, and on 27 July he had ordered an end to the shameful retreat and declared it a 'fortress city'. The Germans were going to stay put. On the same day, he summoned Luftwaffe General Reiner Stahel to the Wolfsschanze. Stahel, the ex-Commandant of Rome and 'Defender of Wilno', was one of

Hitler's favourites, not least because of his vigorous defence of earlier 'fortresses'. Hitler 'gave me the Swords of the Knight's Cross with Oak Leaves and nominated me to the position of Warsaw Kommandant. My tasks were a) to maintain order and calm in the city and b) to support building of fortifications.'[46]

The AK leadership were unaware of Hitler's decision, and pressed ahead with their plans for the uprising. On 29 July the government-in-exile in London informed the Home Army that Prime Minister Mikołajczyk was on his way to Moscow for talks with Stalin, and that the AK were free to do what they thought best. The Government Delegate, Jankowski, received a message empowering Bór to start the rising at a moment selected by him, without having to consult the Cabinet in London. Mikołajczyk asked Jankowski to inform the government beforehand 'if possible', but in effect gave Bór the authority to do as he wished.

On the same day, the Polish Deputy Chief of Staff, General Stanisław Tatar, sent a dispatch to Warsaw informing Bór that his request of 25 July for assistance from Britain had been submitted to the 'highest authorities' in London. The response had been discouraging, to say the least. There was only a 'slight possibility' that the British would bomb sites in Warsaw, and 'little chance' that a squadron of Mustangs would be handed over. The next day Jan Nowak-Jeziorański, the extraordinary courier who had travelled between London and Warsaw throughout the war, reported to AK headquarters with more news from London. Nowak-Jeziorański clearly stated that the AK could not count on large-scale British help or the arrival of the Polish Parachute Brigade. He also said that the effect of an uprising on Allied governments and on Western public opinion would be 'negligible'.

During the meeting, Nowak-Jeziorański realized that nobody was paying any attention to him. He was constantly interrupted by the arrival of other couriers and messengers, and felt as if his warning about the lack of help from the West had been completely ignored.[47] He had told the AK leadership in Warsaw point blank that they would not receive any outside assistance should they begin the fight. Later, when the uprising began to go badly, this warning was conveniently forgotten, and the AK would bitterly accuse the West of not having done enough to help those suffering and dying in Warsaw.

A number of factors have been cited to justify the call for an uprising in Warsaw on 1 August 1944. One of the most commonly mentioned is the Soviet radio broadcasts at the end of July, encouraging the people of Warsaw to take up the fight. On the night of 29 July, for example, Radio Moscow announced that 'the waiting' was over. 'Those who have never bowed their heads to the Hitlerite power will again, as in 1939, join battle with the Germans, this time for decisive action . . . the hour of action has arrived.' However, such propaganda was commonplace, and there were never any direct instructions to the Home Army to rise up. Furthermore, why should the AK take Soviet propaganda broadcasts seriously when they had decided long before not to make contact with the Soviets themselves? On 26 July Colonel Pluta-Czachowski, the AK's Chief Signals Officer, had worried that the lack of operational liaison with the Red Army would cause grave complications, but Rzepecki had told him that the establishment of direct contact between the Home Army and the Soviet High Command was 'impossible'. In fact the AK had decided not even to try to make contact, pinning all hope for Soviet–Polish cooperation on Mikołajczyk's ill-fated visit to Moscow, and ultimately on Stalin's good will. To rely on a dictator who had repeatedly proved his animosity towards the AK was illogical, and a measure of the desperate situation the Home Army found itself in at the end of July 1944.

At 9 o'clock on the morning of 31 August the regular AK

meeting took place at Pańska Street, and Osmecki was called on to give a detailed account of the situation on the German–Soviet front. His conclusion was simple: 'The [Soviet] attack on Warsaw will not start for four or five days, and therefore to begin the uprising now would be wrong.' Osmecki left the meeting with the impression that everyone had been convinced by his report. Bór had clearly said: 'Under these conditions the fight will not start on 1 or 2 August.' The next meeting was scheduled for 5 o'clock the same afternoon, but Osmecki genuinely believed that Bór had decided to postpone the uprising until the situation was more clear.

Later that day Osmecki left his flat on Napoleon Square, bound for the 5 o'clock meeting. The Germans had staged a round-up near Marszałkowska Street, and it took him half an hour to cover the few hundred metres to Pańska Street. 'I had just received information that the German counter-attack would start shortly, but I was calm as I didn't think any decision would be taken.' He made his way into the building, fully expecting to report to the AK about developments along the front.

To his surprise, Bór was in the hallway getting ready to leave. There was nobody else there, and Osmecki asked if anyone else had even come.

'The meeting has ended,' Bór said. And then, as if as an after-thought: 'I gave the order to start the uprising.'

Osmecki was shocked. When he asked why, Bór said simply: 'Monter brought information that Soviet tanks made the break-through in the German bridgehead in Praga. He said if we don't start immediately we will be late. Therefore I gave the order.'

Osmecki later found out what had happened. The meeting had started earlier than planned, with only Bór, Pełczyński, Okulicki and Major Karasiówna in attendance. The atmosphere was relaxed, and they discussed Mikołajczyk's visit to Moscow. Then

Monter appeared. He had 'information that Soviet Panzer units had entered the German bridgehead and that Radość, Miłosna, Okuniew, Wołomin and Radzymin are in Russian hands'. Monter insisted on the immediate launch of the uprising, otherwise 'it might be too late'. Bór, who had rejected the idea only hours before, suddenly changed his mind. 'After a short discussion I came to the conclusion that it was the right moment to begin the fight. The Russian attack could be expected from one hour to the next,' he said. Jankowski was summoned, and Bór demanded that the operations begin in Warsaw immediately. This would 'transform the German defeat in Praga into a complete rout, make reinforcement of the German troops fighting on the eastern bank of the Vistula impossible, and in this way would speed up Soviet encircling movements which had started to the east, north-east and north of Warsaw'. Jankowski asked a few questions, and then said, 'Very well, begin.' Bór turned to Monter. 'Tomorrow at 1700 hours precisely you will start Operation "Burza" in Warsaw.'

The problem was that Monter's information had been wrong. The Soviets were not in Warsaw at all.

Osmecki approached Bór in the hallway. 'General, you have made a mistake,' he said. 'Monter's information is imprecise. I have the latest dispatches from my people on the ground. There is no doubt that the Praga bridgehead has not been broken. Conversely, they confirm everything I said in the morning. The Germans are preparing a counter-attack.'

In reality, the Germans had started the first counter-offensive of the summer, which stopped Bagration in its tracks. The Soviet offensive had finally been halted, at the very edge of Warsaw.

Bór collapsed on a chair, wiping his forehead. 'Are you absolutely sure that Monter's information is incorrect?' he asked.

Osmecki told him that a few Russian tanks may have moved

into Praga, but that the German bridgehead had not been broken.

Bór asked what he should do. Osmecki suggested he send a courier to Monter immediately to revoke the order.

'Do we have to revoke it again? Revoke the order?' Bór asked.

'Yes. You have chosen the exact wrong moment. You have to revoke the order.' Bór looked at his watch.

'At that moment Szostak came in. He looked at both of us, Bór in his hat and coat and me standing. When he heard what had happened he was furious that neither he nor Osmecki had been consulted. "This is madness," he said. "We will let ourselves all be massacred. You have to immediately revoke that order." '

Bór said only, 'Too late. We cannot do anything.' He sat helplessly, exhausted, with a pitiful look on his bloodless face. 'We cannot do anything more,' he said for the third time, with what appeared a combination of relief and tiredness. Then he stood up and left.

A few moments later Pluta-Czachowski arrived, and ran into Bór on the stairs. 'He knew immediately, and looked at us with silent questions and fears. I said: "It's done, we cannot do anything. Let's do all we can to reduce the losses. From this moment on every moment counts." I went to the door and Pluta said in a matter-of-fact voice: "Apropos – the German counter-attack has just begun." '

Most Poles who had been listening to the sounds of artillery approaching Warsaw believed that they meant certain and imminent Soviet victory over the Germans. But, for the first time since the launch of Bagration, the opposite was true. The Germans were fighting back. General Walter Model had just begun Army Group Centre's only major counter-offensive of the summer of 1944. The Battle of Wołomin is virtually unknown in World War II history, but it was hugely significant, as it halted Bagration and ended the rout of the Germans in Byelorussia and Poland. It was the largest tank battle on Polish soil in the entire war, with 450 German Panther and Tiger tanks wading into over seven hundred Soviet T-34s. The Germans had air superiority, but still the region between Wołomin and Radzymin was caught in a seesaw of attacks and counter-thrusts; the villages in the area were reduced to rubble, and the Soviets lost over two hundred tanks. The battle also helped determine the fate of the Warsaw Uprising. The German counter-attack made it impossible for the Red Army to take Warsaw in the first days of August; later it would provide Stalin with an excuse not to help the beleaguered city when he could easily have done so. The battle was therefore a pivotal moment in the history of the Second World War.

It is often said the AK leadership's lack of understanding of Stalin was their biggest mistake, but equally important was their ignorance of the German position at this crucial moment. Bór could not conceive that the Nazis would be able to turn around and fight back. He did not understand that the Germans on the Eastern Front were not going to lay down their arms with the Soviets rolling towards Berlin. In fact surrender was not an option for the average German soldier, and even those who now doubted Hitler fervently believed that the Red Army had to be stopped at any cost. Many German soldiers secretly believed that they would soon be joining forces with the Western Allies to wage war against the Russians.[48] But for now the feverish desire to protect Germany from the ravages of the Red Army would see the prolongation of the war in Europe for another nine bloody months.

The decision to start the uprising under such circumstances has long been a source of controversy, not least because of post-war politics. Even before the end of the war the Soviets began arresting, imprisoning and murdering thousands of members of the AK, and anyone else who might hinder Stalin's plan to rule

Poland. After the war, mention of the Warsaw Uprising and the AK was forbidden. Former AK members and combatants were arrested and killed, and the official line was that a group of irresponsible bandits had started an 'adventure' in Warsaw which had been brutally suppressed by the Nazis. Decades later, after the collapse of Communism, the pendulum would swing the other way, and the AK would be bathed in a heroic light in which these valiant fighters for freedom could do no wrong. The truth, as ever, lies somewhere in between.

The Poles were in an impossible situation in August 1944, caught between two of the most brutal and murderous regimes in history. Despite having been stalwart supporters of the Western Allies since the beginning of the war, they were marginalized and treated as a nuisance for standing up for the very freedoms that the West claimed had inspired the fight against Hitler. They were excluded from the Tehran Conference, and had not been told that their country would become the *de facto* property of the Soviet Union after the war. Roosevelt would do nothing to endanger his 'special relationship' with Stalin, while Churchill was too weak to influence the outcome, despite his pangs of conscience about Britain's loyal ally. And so this freedom-loving and independent nation was condemned by geography, by power and by politics to the mercy of Hitler and Stalin. The novelist Maria Dąbrowska watched, torn, as the Germans attacked the Red Army in August 1944: 'It is like 1941 all over again – all are going eastward. The Germans have apparently moved ten divisions to the Warsaw front. It is tragic to have to say that we hear of this with some relief, as the thought of a Bolshevik invasion is our utter nightmare.' It is precisely the hopelessness of the situation that makes the uprising so controversial. The heroism of the fighters and the civilians is not in doubt. But it is clear that many grave mistakes were made.

The greatest problem was that it was first and foremost a political and not a military operation. General Bór's claim that he had to call for an uprising because Warsaw was in danger of becoming 'a battlefield between Germans and Russians, and the city would be turned into rubble' is not borne out by the evidence. Ever since Stalingrad, and indeed in all the battles for cities during the Bagration offensive, including Vitebsk, Orsha, Minsk, Kiev and Lwów, the Soviets did not attack the cities head on, but encircled them, trapping the Germans in giant 'pockets' and finishing them off later. There may have been heavy street fighting, as in Vitebsk, but for the most part the civilians and the infrastructure were spared. There is no reason to think that 'Fortress Warsaw' would have been any different, particularly as it was so weakly defended.

The AK also misunderstood the Soviet plan of attack, believing that the Russians would take the east-bank suburb of Praga and then launch a frontal assault across the bridges into Warsaw proper, but this had never been Stavka's intention. Rather than worrying about when the Soviets would enter Praga and begin crossing the Vistula, the AK should have waited for the moment when the northern and southern Soviet pincers to the west of the city snapped shut, cutting off the Germans trapped within.

The AK, however, could not verify Stavka's plans, because they had no contact with the Soviets. 'We had to run the great risk of undertaking open action without any coordination with the Red Army command,' Bór said.[49] Any links between the AK and the Soviets had ended in the murder or imprisonment of the Poles. It had become clear after Soviet treachery at Wilno, Lwów and Lublin that Stalin wanted nothing less than to annihilate the AK and to put his own puppet government in place. He would destroy anyone who stood in his way. It was a measure of the AK's desperate plight that in July 1944 General Okulicki argued that if they did take over Warsaw before the Soviets entered the city,

Stalin would have no choice but either to recognize AK authority in liberated Warsaw, or to liquidate the AK using military force. Okulicki's view was that the Soviets might indeed murder the AK fighters, but that it would be impossible for Stalin to hide this crime from the international community. Such an act, he said, would shake the moral conscience of the world. What none of them seemed to realize was that, at the time, the world was just not interested. The Soviets had committed mass murder at Katyń, yet the Western Allies had deliberately perpetrated the lie that it had been a Nazi crime. The Nazis had murdered millions of Jews and others in the occupied territories, but despite the best efforts of Jan Karski, Szmul Zygelbojm and others to expose these crimes, and at the very least to bomb the rail tracks leading to Auschwitz, little was done. The response was always the same: the war must be won, and only then would Nazi crimes be stopped.

Bór was left with very few cards. If he chose to go ahead with the uprising, his only hope was that the Poles could prove their bravery and demonstrate national support for the AK and the legitimate Polish government-in-exile in London. 'By our own actions on the field of battle and the aid which we were thus able to afford the advancing Russians, a suitable foundation for reaching agreement could have been created had the Russians shown any good will.' But the Russians had not shown any good will, and they were not going to. Bór also hoped that the very fact of the uprising would cause Roosevelt and Churchill to change their minds and come to the Poles' aid: 'We believed that the Western powers would acknowledge our good will and our share in the battle and victory and that they would exert the necessary influence on the Soviets in bringing to bear at least part of the principles of the Atlantic Charter.'[50] But the Western Allies had already given in to Stalin, and would do very little to help.

Another argument used to justify the uprising is the mood of the people of Warsaw, who 'would never have understood an order to stop the fight; it would have been taken as tantamount to capitulation and quite unacceptable to the soul of the Polish community'. One has to ask whether offending 'the soul of the community' can ever be seen as justification for starting an action that leads to the destruction of a city and the loss of tens of thousands of civilian lives. The community was in favour of the uprising because they trusted their leaders and believed that the fighting would last only a few days. They believed that the Germans were 'finished', that the Soviets would soon move in, and that the Western Allies would send aid. They were wrong on all three counts. Bór, Monter and the rest had been told outright that the West would not offer any help, but they did not inform the population. They knew the treachery of the Soviets; again they were silent. And they had been told that far from being 'finished', the Germans were massing troops near Warsaw to mount a counter-attack against the Red Army which actually began before the uprising was launched. The general public were misinformed from the beginning. In the end, it was they who paid the price.

Many of those who made the fateful choice to begin the uprising were less than honest after the war. General Pełczyński said that Bór's choice was simple – he 'could have called off the fight and left the capital like a no man's land to be a victim of the German–Soviet battle, or he could decide to fight with the enemy and try to free Warsaw with the help of Polish soldiers. General Bór decided that the second option was the right one . . . Sixty-three days of heroic fighting confirm how this decision was understood by the inhabitants of the capital.' But that was not Bór's only choice. He could have waited until the situation at the front had become clear; indeed, he should have waited to strike until the Germans in Praga had been defeated by the Soviets. Instead he called for the uprising to begin at the very moment of Model's effective counter-attack against the Soviets, thereby leaving the population of the city to Hitler and Himmler, and providing Stalin with the perfect excuse to do nothing.

The idea of the Warsaw Uprising as a great, symbolic Polish gesture underlay the lack of military thinking. Okulicki displayed what Osmecki called this 'Polish madness' when he said that if the Russians did not come to help it would actually assist the Polish cause, as it would 'give the world proof of their perfidy. It will expose them to the world as what they are, as red fascists. Wilno, Lwów and the rest of the cities in which we were murdered did not open the eyes of the West, but our sacrifice this time will be so great that they will not be able to cover their ears and will not be able to not see and not understand, and will be forced to change this inhuman policy which condemns half of Europe to future slavery.'[51] A Polish tragedy was set to unfold before a largely indifferent world.

There were powerful voices against the uprising, including that of the remarkable General Władysław Anders. Born in 1892, he had been wounded and captured by the Russians in 1939, and incarcerated in the Lubyanka prison in Moscow. After the Germans invaded the Soviet Union in 1941 Anders was released under the Sikorski–Maisky Pact, and was allowed to form a Polish army in Russia. When he found out about the atrocities committed against Poles by the Russians at Katyń he was determined to get out of the Soviet Union, and in an extraordinary, epic journey he marched this army, largely made up of ex-gulag prisoners, through Central Asia, Iran and Palestine to Egypt, where they were incorporated into the British 8th Army. Anders knew the Soviets from bitter experience, and his view of the uprising was simple: 'You can never trust the Soviets – they are our sworn enemies. To hold an uprising whose only success depends on either the collapse of your enemy or help from another enemy is wishful thinking beyond reason.'

After the war Anders said: 'I kneel before the heroes who fought in Warsaw, however I think that the uprising was the biggest and most reckless catastrophe of Poland. It served the interests of the Germans and the Bolsheviks. It was not well prepared and there was not the slightest chance of success. It caused many thousands of victims and terrible suffering to millions of civilians, the destruction of the capital and its cultural heritage. It destroyed the institutions, the intelligentsia, it destroyed the fight for independence in the country, making Sovietization easier. The estimation of the situation was wrong . . . the uprising was not agreed upon with the Allies and there was no confirmation that the Allies could offer help.'[52]

Despite being a member of 'Kedyw', Stanisław Aronson was also critical of the uprising. 'We knew from the beginning that it was senseless. My division leader, "Stasinek" Sosabowski, the son of General Stanisław Sosabowski of Arnhem fame, had said that the uprising was evidently nonsense. We knew from the beginning that in the territory newly occupied by the Soviets, they arrested and executed soldiers from the Home Army participating in the "Burza" action. We concluded that even if the uprising was a success, they would arrest us and ship us off to Soviet concentration camps. Józef Rybicki believed that the AK should have gone down even deeper into the underground and waited for the Soviet occupation. The disaster caused by the uprising surpassed our worst predictions: sixty-three days of fighting instead of five or six as planned, the complete destruction of Warsaw and 200,000 civilians killed – a horrific mistake.'[53]

In a sense Bór was a tragic figure, pressured by his advisers into making a terrible decision at an impossible time. This decent and honourable man was trying to do the right thing, hoping to send a message to the world that Poland deserved its independence, but in reality he was in a lose–lose situation. If he had done nothing and the Red Army had liberated Warsaw, the Soviets would have claimed, as they had in the past, that the AK were proto-fascists and that only Stalin's puppet government, the Lublin Committee, represented the Polish people. And if, as indeed happened, the Poles rose up before the Red Army arrived, they faced utter destruction by the Germans. As Jan Nowak-Jeziorański put it, even if the greatest genius had been at the head of the AK, 'he would not have been able to find a solution to the tragic situation in which Poland found herself at the time. Once again we were crushed in a mortal embrace of two deadly enemies. No matter which decision the General would have taken – to fight or not – each enemy would turn against the nation, against the Home Army, or against the Home Army leader.'

What Bór did not know was that because of Model's success the Germans had bought themselves a little time. He could not have known that Hitler and Himmler were about to turn Warsaw into a terrible and deadly example. The city was to be destroyed forever, so that even if Germany lost the war it would never again stand as a hindrance to future German ambitions in the east. This was sheer madness on every level. Quite apart from the barbarism involved in liquidating a European capital city and its inhabitants, its culture and its history, the Germans could ill afford to waste precious resources on an 'Aktion' which was completely devoid of any military advantage or sense. It was the same kind of twisted logic that governed the SS camps and the murder of European Jewry, and the pointless and cruel death marches which took place only days before the end of the war in Europe. In his spiteful fury Hitler decided to wreak a kind of Biblical havoc on the unfortunate city, and its doomed inhabitants had no idea of what was coming. On the contrary, they prepared for the uprising in a spirit of optimism and hope.

5

THE UPRISING BEGINS

The time to strike is immediately after this meeting ends . . . when the blow will be the more terrifying and the enemy will be unprepared. (Chapter X)

Godzina W

The order to mobilize on 1 August came as a great relief to the members of the AK. After years of waiting, the young fighters were finally going to force the hated Nazis from their own cherished streets; they would be the heroes who would liberate the city and welcome in the Red Army as equals. Fifteen-year-old Julian Kulski, the son of the Mayor of Warsaw, who was in the group that fired the first shots of the uprising, recalled feeling that at last he was going to be allowed to do what he had dreamed of for so long.[1] The young fighters were fired up, and ready to lose their lives if necessary. They believed in their cause and they believed in their leaders, and they went to their positions eagerly. It was all a great adventure. Even in their old age some of these AK fighters would remember those early days as the best time of their lives.

The uprising was to begin at 5 p.m., or 'Godzina W' – 'Hour

W' – and when Bór issued his fateful order it was as if a switch had been turned on in Warsaw. Hurried telephone calls were made to the headquarters of each district, messages were sent by courier, runners criss-crossed the city, and AK soldiers and nurses rushed to their meeting points as quickly as possible. Józef Rybicki sent his runner to inform Stanisław Aronson that the uprising was about to begin. 'May God be with you,' he wrote at the bottom of the small piece of paper.

Suddenly the streets filled with young people, many in winter coats and bulky sweaters concealing weapons and ammunition. Some wore pre-war officers' boots and trenchcoats, but most could only find civilian clothes, as Polish uniforms had been banned by the Germans. They carried rucksacks filled with useful items – underwear, torches, food. Jadwiga Stasiakowa left her Praga apartment on 1 August and crossed the bridge by tram. 'People were saying that the Russians were very close and that they could hear cannons. The unbelievable tension and the hatred of the German occupiers was visible, and people on the street could not wait to take revenge.' The civilian population had not been told about the uprising for security reasons, but the atmosphere in the city was so electrified that many guessed that something important was about to happen.

Władysław Szpilman, author of the devastating memoir *The Pianist*, was hiding in an apartment in Niepodległości Avenue, in a German area, when his protector, Helena Lewicka, came to see him. She could barely contain her excitement. 'It is about to break out,' she said. Like many others, she believed that the fighting would last only a few days. So confident was she that Szpilman's ordeal would soon be over that she offered to take him to the cellar to protect him from bombing raids. Szpilman, still terrified of being exposed to the Germans as a Jew, which would mean certain death, declined. The decision would save his life.

Across town, a thirteen-year-old girl was playing in the family apartment when her brother's best friend burst in. 'Uprising,' was all he said. Her brother took his coat silently and left with his friend. He never returned.[2] One young man remembered hauling marmalade tins full of grenades onto a tram that day, and meeting a girl doing the same. They both knew what was in the containers, but joked loudly about 'buying provisions for the family'. Some young AK recruits flirted with nurses and messengers, while others strode to their posts in deadly seriousness. It had something of the air of the first days of the Great War, with girls pinning flowers on the jackets of their young men who were setting off to war. Like the First World War, everybody believed it would be over very soon. The tram drivers, the eyes and ears of Warsaw, roared out, 'The firm is going bankrupt today! We'll soon be getting visitors from across the river!'

The young AK soldiers gathering at their meeting posts were excited too. One of the most successful leaders of the Warsaw Uprising, Lieutenant Colonel Jan Mazurkiewicz, known in the AK as 'Radosław', felt 'feverish expectation' among his troops. Stanisław Aronson remembered the sense of freedom when he reached his post at the Customs Office in Wola. For the first time since joining the AK he could talk to soldiers from other platoons, and learn about their past missions and successes and failures. The room fell silent as they were given their orders. Aronson's 'Kedyw Kollegium A' was to take over a school at 5 o'clock, then move down Stawki Street to the Umschlagplatz and take the huge German warehouses at Stawki 4. 'It did not seem very difficult,' he said.

Nothing was too much to ask of the young fighters that day. These were, after all, members of the generation that had helped to revive the phoenix Poland after the First World War. The sense of national pride and patriotism was intense, but it was justified.

In a mere twenty years the Poles had re-created everything, from a freely elected government to a well-organized military apparatus and all the legal, political and cultural institutions that defined an independent democratic state. Poland was dotted with new libraries, housing associations, banks and railroads; there were now forty-one hospitals in Warsaw, with 10,682 beds. The country still had many political and social problems to contend with, but its capital had been transformed from something of a backward Russian-occupied outpost to a national treasure. Entire neighbourhoods, like Żoliborz, had been built from scratch to house the new professionals; journalists, military personnel and civil servants occupied elegant houses, and modern apartment blocks had been put up in poorer districts like Wola. Marcin Weinfeld's 1934 sixteen-storey Prudential building was Europe's second-tallest skyscraper, and quickly became a symbol of the modern city. It is no wonder that the insurgents made it a priority to fly the Polish flag from its lofty heights in the first days of the uprising.

Known as the '*Kolumbowie*', or 'Columbuses', for their pioneering spirit,[3] the young generation would do anything for their country, including laying down their lives for it. It was precisely this passion that made the uprising difficult for Bór and others to control. No logical argument or rational thinking could curb the pressure Poles felt to 'do something' to free their country, even if the timing was wrong or the conditions unfavourable. The Germans had invaded their beloved land, and murdered and enslaved the population, and now the Russians were threatening to force their way in and take control once more. The young longed to act, because they wanted to show the world that they deserved a free and democratic country; it did not occur to them that such a gesture might simply be ignored. It was this willingness to sacrifice themselves come what may that led them to the barricades in August 1944. And when the uprising failed, it was this sense of patriotism that caused many of them to defend the tragedy long after it was over.

Although the uprising was set to start at 5 o'clock, it was inevitable that with so many people moving to so many different meeting points, some things would go wrong. The first skirmish started three hours ahead of schedule, in the journalist quarter of Żoliborz, when a car loaded with illegal weapons was noticed by Germans on patrol near Krasiński Street. The music critic and AK soldier Zdzisław Sierpiński was in the car: 'We could see one another very clearly and they were looking at us as if calculating whether to attack or to pretend that they hadn't seen us.' The Poles were wearing suspiciously heavy winter coats, and when the Germans came for another look the AK fighters had no choice but to act. Julian Kulski was in a group helping to move weapons in Suzina Street. 'The Germans brought their vehicle to a screeching halt and opened fire on the men in the middle of the boulevard . . . the Germans, surprised by the fire on their flank from the other side of Krasiński Street, turned around . . . The firing was still fierce and bullets whined over our heads as we lay flat in the green centre strip dividing the boulevard. I kept firing back. "Wilk" wounded a couple more of them with his Sten gun, and the Germans withdrew quickly towards Powazki.' The Germans soon returned in trucks loaded with SS anti-insurgency commandos and began to fortify Żoliborz. It is ironic that the first tanks to appear on the streets that day crossed Plac Wilsona, a busy square in Żoliborz named after the US President who had been lionized in Poland for his role in re-creating the country after the First World War, but was despised by Hitler for his part in writing the Treaty of Versailles.

Despite the fact that heavy fighting soon spread throughout Żoliborz, the Germans did not yet realize that this heralded a general uprising in the city. Kulski, who was by then hiding in an apartment building near Plac Wilsona, remembered: 'machine-gun volleys exploded constantly. Every five minutes or so a bullet or fragment of a mortar shell would enter the room and strike the furniture or the walls.'[4] The Germans quickly secured the most vital transport links, including the Gdańsk railway viaduct, effectively cutting the district off from the rest of the city. Żoliborz would become the first of many isolated, reluctant 'islands' in a sea of German-held territory, lonely pockets in which the hapless civilians trapped inside would be forced to face the enemy virtually alone.

Skirmishes soon broke out in other districts. Some were avoidable, as when an over-excited boy from the 'Parasol' Battalion in Ochota threw Molotov cocktails at an SS pillbox.[5] Just after 4 o'clock, fighting started at Napoleon Square, and raged around the main post office and the Prudential building; the Germans fought back, but without conviction. Lieutenant 'Kosa', of Aronson's sister unit 'Kedyw Kollegium B', attacked and took the Victoria Hotel with ease. It was to become Monter's headquarters until capitulation.

The uprising proper broke out at 5 p.m. as planned. The entire city, from Wola to Praga, from Mokotów to the Old Town, erupted in waves of explosions, gunfire and movement. Civilians, many of whom had no idea what was happening, ran for cover as AK soldiers attacked their designated targets. 'Within fifteen minutes our city, one million strong, had joined the fight,' Bór recalled proudly.

In some places events had an almost theatrical quality, with young men stopping on the streets and simply beginning to fire at enemy targets as if this sort of thing happened every day. A kind of exhilarating chaos reigned amongst the AK in those first moments. The decision to give a mere twelve hours' notice had caused enormous confusion, as many only received their orders just before 5 o'clock. One high-ranking officer, a friend of General

Bór's, learned that the uprising had started when a barrage of gunfire interrupted his evening meal.[6] Many soldiers failed to reach their meeting points: only nine hundred of the elite 'Kedyw' soldiers came on time, and only half of the 40,000 AK troops managed to get to their posts at all. The nurse Anna Szatkowska and her group were trapped in their Old Town apartment because German tanks and armoured cars were blocking their front door. 'We could hear machine guns and grenades and single shots. It started to pour with rain. The evening came and in the twilight we could see the glow of fires.' They were forced to wait for three frustrating days until the Germans moved away.

Many AK soldiers found themselves cut off from their own platoons, and begged to join other units; only a fraction were accepted, because of the severe shortage of weapons. Jan Magdziak remembered carefully-drawn-up plans being tossed 'out the window'. It seemed that 'everyone was mixed up and misplaced. We were divided into numbered platoons which were supposed to act as independent units. As the situation became more difficult we fought without connection to other units, so we really had no idea of what was going on elsewhere.'[7] Włodzimierz Rosłoniec could not reach his platoon despite five days of trying, and joined another group on Marszałkowska Street. By then the fighting there was essentially over: the Poles had run out of ammunition, and the Germans had holed themselves up in the nearby Polonia Hotel. 'It was calm. The streets were covered in rubble, glass, broken tram cables and destroyed and overturned rickshaws and wagons. You could see traces of bullets on the walls of the houses.'[8] Hastily-drawn front lines marked by home-made barricades soon criss-crossed the city. Like the First World War trenches on the Western Front thirty years earlier, these accidental borders would in many cases remain in place until the bitter end.

Before the uprising, General Monter had divided Warsaw into

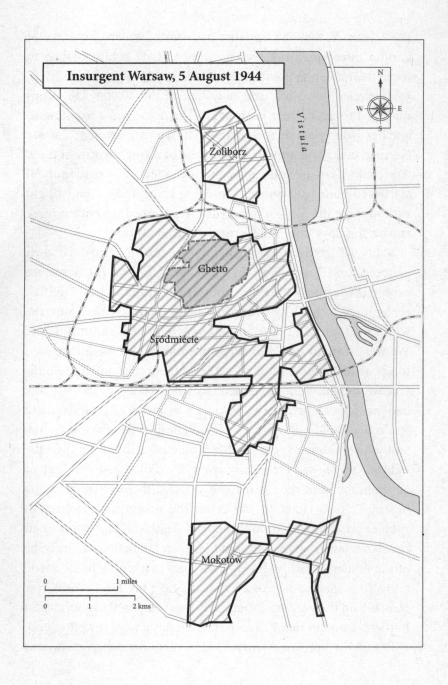

Insurgent Warsaw, 5 August 1944

seven districts, each with its own command structure and military objectives (see map, p. 108). Area I comprised the Old Town and the city centre; Area II the northern districts, including Żoliborz and Bielany; Area III was made up of the western working-class district of Wola; Area IV was Ochota, a villa colony to the south; Area V, Mokotów, was the largest, a well-to-do southern residential district which included the strongly fortified German police district; Area VI, Praga, on the east bank of the river, was heavily guarded by Germans awaiting the Soviet onslaught; and Area VII included outlying areas which did not play a decisive role in the first days.

AK formations in each area were divided into over forty battalions, subdivided into companies and platoons; some, like Battalions 'Parasol', 'Miotła' and 'Zośka', remain household names in Warsaw because of the heroic fight put up by their soldiers. Added to the AK soldiers were around 1,700 members of other resistance units, including the Communist AL (Armia Ludowa – the 'People's Army'); there was also a motley collection of foreign nationals, including Hungarian and Italian deserters who chose to fight on the Polish side. The British RAF Sergeant John Ward, an ex-German prisoner of war, also joined the Poles, and sent numerous eye-witness radio dispatches to the British government during the uprising. One hundred and fifteen Jews, of whom sixty-six were members of the AK, were to die in the uprising. Twenty of them had fought in the Warsaw Ghetto Uprising crushed so brutally by Jürgen Stroop and the Warsaw SS in the spring of the previous year.[9]

Monter's List

General Monter had drawn up an ambitious list of the most important targets to be achieved in the first hours, and had ordered the commanders of each district to send squads, often numbering as few as fifteen men, to take them one by one. Monter's plans were ambitious, to say the least. He fervently believed, despite contrary evidence, that the Germans were so demoralized and weakened after the 20 July plot that they were 'on the run', and would leave the city at the first sign of trouble. He also believed that the Soviets would move into Warsaw within a few days. These assumptions informed his entire strategy for the uprising. They led to disaster.

It is often said that the uprising 'failed' in its first days, because Monter was unable to take key installations from the Nazis such as bridges, airports, railway stations and police and military outposts, although in reality the AK never had the remotest chance of taking most of these positions. On 1 August Monter himself admitted that he had a mere 1,000 rifles, 1,700 pistols, three hundred machine pistols, sixty submachine guns, seven machine guns, thirty-five anti-tank guns and 25,000 hand grenades, and that he was 'worried' about his strength. After the first days of fighting the AK had captured six howitzers, seven mortars, thirteen heavy and fifty-seven light machine guns, 373 rifles, 103 pistols and twenty-seven Panzerfaust anti-tank weapons, but these were not nearly enough to take on heavily defended German areas. As General Anders put it, around half of the weapons the AK had on 1 August were 'pistols, short weapons, personal weapons which did not have any serious impact on the fight in the city against buildings, fortresses, barricades and the like. It was crazy to think that they could be successful when the Uprisers were equipped only with grenades.'[10] Monter's plans were reminiscent of that lack of military analysis that had led many Poles to believe that they were going to win the war against Nazi Germany in September 1939. He handed out his orders with gusto, but in reality most were little more than suicide missions.

Those European capitals which lie on great rivers, whether

London or Paris or Budapest, are divided by the waterways that flow through them, and dependent on the bridges that link their two sides. Warsaw is no exception. The earliest bridges in the city were simple wooden structures which came and went over the centuries, but by the time of the Industrial Revolution Warsaw had been transformed. The first railway bridge was built in 1875, the second in 1908. The city, which had been isolated on the flatlands of Central Europe, was now connected to the great cities of Vienna and St Petersburg, and from them to the rest of Europe. It began to grow, and new structures mirrored its new wealth. The 1864 Kierbedź Bridge, the first iron bridge on stone supports built over the Vistula, and one of the most modern in all Europe, had a dramatic five-hundred-metre latticework mesh which cast eye-catching shadows on the cobblestone road below. The Poniatowski Bridge was opened in 1914, and its eight soaring steel spans and pretty white neo-Renaissance towers became a landmark of the city; it was so expensive that even the writer Bolesław Prus, author of Stalin's favourite book, *The Pharaoh*, protested against it.[11] Sadly, however, these magnificent structures were not to last. Warsaw's bridges have been destroyed on numerous occasions, either to prevent the Russians from coming west, as happened during the Kościuszko Uprising in 1794, or to keep the Germans from going east, as happened in 1915 when the Russians demolished them all.[12] They were all hastily rebuilt, only to be destroyed again in the summer of 1944. This time they would disappear into the muddy waters of the Vistula because of bombs detonated by the Germans.

The Poles believed that when the Russians came to take Warsaw in the summer of 1944 they would cross the Vistula bridges and head directly into the city. They seemed not to have learned the lesson from Bagration. Zhukov and Rokossovsky intended to follow the highly successful pattern perfected during the summer offensive, namely to encircle the city, trap the Germans in the vast pocket, and finish them off later. Stavka called for the Red Army to take only the eastern suburb of Praga, and to leave the rest of Warsaw in German hands while developing the pincers to the north and south. This, in effect, made the bridges irrelevant to Soviet strategy.

The Warsaw bridges may have been of little tactical value to the Russians, but they were crucial to the Germans. They provided essential communications links to troops fighting on the eastern side of the river, and without them entire divisions would be cut off with little chance of escape. Furthermore, the counter-offensive then taking place at Radzymin depended on them for supplies and ammunition. As a result of their strategic importance the Germans had ensured that they were virtually unassailable. Poorly equipped AK troops were sent in anyway.

At 5 p.m. on 1 August the AK mounted an attack on the great Kierbedź Bridge. It was a disaster from the beginning. The 103rd Company from Praga attacked from the east bank, and AK Battalion 'Bończa', under the 'Róg' Group, based in the Old Town, rushed in from the Royal Castle to the west. Both were mown down in minutes.

A large fortified building stood squarely at the western end of the bridge. The Germans called it the *Schichthaus* – the layered house. It may have served as a German hospital, but it was also an important command post. A large bunker squatted on the riverbank nearby, its hundred soldiers covering the bridge. In order for the AK troops even to get near their target they would have to run out in the open for some hundred metres, overpower the bunker garrison and get past the *Schichthaus*. It was an impossible task. Most of the AK soldiers who tried that day were mown down before they even got close to the bunker.

The attack from the Praga side fared little better, as the AK soldiers ran into the Hermann Göring Division's 2nd Panzer Battalion and other units which were detraining at Praga's Eastern station. The Poles were no match for these elite troops, and were quickly defeated.

Battalion 'Konrad's' attack on the Poniatowski Bridge was equally disastrous. The huge structure could only be reached by advancing along a wide and clearly visible viaduct, making a surprise attack impossible. To make matters worse, the sappers from Oberleutnant Karl Eymer's 2nd Company of Pioneer Battalion 654 were putting down demolition charges on both bridges precisely when the attacks began. The twenty-nine-man platoon on the Poniatowski Bridge and the twenty-seven-man platoon on the Kierbedź Bridge made short work of the few AK soldiers who survived the initial onslaught.

Attacks on Warsaw's two airports were no more successful. The attempt to take Okęcie, which still serves as the city's main airport today, proved even more costly than the attacks on the bridges. Okęcie was defended by no fewer than eight hundred well-trained and well-armed Luftwaffe airport security men, and over half the AK's 'Garłuch-Gromada' unit – 120 men – died in the attack.* On 2 August the AK stormed Bielany airport in the north, this time going up against the Luftwaffe's Flak Regiment 80/Flak-Brigade X, as well as the airport security which had a total of 3,500 men. After five hours of fighting, seventy-seven AK soldiers lay dead; the survivors ran for their lives.

The list of failures mounted. Company 'Granat' attacked the strongly defended Luftwaffe bunker and anti-aircraft artillery positions known as the 'Flak Kaserne' with the loss of a hundred of its 120 men. Part of the 'Krybar' Group went up against the

---

* So strongly defended was Okęcie that in September 1939 a full Polish army battalion, supported by tanks, had failed to take the airport from its German occupiers.

German garrison stationed in the fortified grounds of Warsaw University. Two hundred and seventy soldiers of Hauptmann Uhlig's 7th Genesungs Kompanie and one company of the Sicherungs-Battalion 944, armed with tanks and heavy weapons, mowed the AK unit down; the German victory at the university meant that the Powiśle district was now, like Żoliborz, cut off from the city centre for the rest of the uprising.

Perhaps the most pointless losses occurred in attacks on the police and SS barracks. These were some of the most heavily defended areas in the General Government, and home to hundreds of SS, SD and Gestapo men who had no intention of dying at the hands of Polish insurgents. Monter had planned to take the entire police district in a single day, but this was utterly delusional, as to overcome such positions by force would have required heavy artillery and thousands of men, neither of which he had at his disposal. Once again small units of a few dozen men were mown down as they ran up to barricades, pillboxes and bunkers bristling with weapons. The 'Jeleń' Unit was sent to take the massive Gestapo headquarters on Rakowiecka Street, a huge complex defended by over 1,450 SS men, five Tiger tanks, four PzKpfeIVs and one Panzer from the Viking and Totenkopf Divisions. The AK men began by firing off some home-made mortars, but most of them were killed as soon as they moved into the open. The AK attack forced Geibel to hide in the Stauferkaserne bunker for an hour, but he was never in any real danger. Heavy fighting continued for hours around the Gestapo headquarters on Aleja Szucha, until German tanks were sent in to mow down the remaining AK fighters. The Poles fought with the utmost bravery, but it was clear that they never had a chance. It was a massacre.

The same was true of the attempt on the heavily guarded SS police barracks on Narbutta Street, where the well-trained soldiers of AK Regiment 'Baszta' were sent to their deaths. A third of 'Bałtyk' Battalion, commanded by Major Eugeniusz Landberger ('Burza'), lay dead on the street. Many had been killed by German tanks that had arrived only half an hour before.

The SS police barracks on Narutowicz Square in Ochota were attacked in the evening, but the eight hundred AK troops were forced to retreat against massive odds, leaving this as the third district to be cut off from the rest of the city. The AK district commander Mieczysław Sokołowski ('Grzymała') decided to retreat to the forests, leaving only three hundred troops under Lieutenant Gustaw on the barricades of Aleja Grójecka and Kaliska and Wawelska Streets. In Ochota too, the civilians would be left to face the Germans largely on their own.

General Bór himself nearly fell victim to this early chaos. The Commander-in-Chief had decided to set up his headquarters in a famous furniture factory at Dzielna 72, in the western suburb of Wola. The Kammler factory was housed in a large complex of buildings, and was well-known for supplying bespoke furniture to wealthy clients throughout Europe – in 1939 it had made a cradle for the then Princess Beatrix of the Netherlands. The building itself was strong and easy to defend, but unfortunately for Bór it was adjacent to a tobacco factory occupied by the SS. The Germans quickly became suspicious of the activity next door, and went on the attack. The 'Kedyw' unit under Lieutenant Colonel Radosław, which had been meant to protect Bór, had been unable to get to the factory on time, and when the fighting broke out they were forced to crawl through the attics of nearby buildings, reaching Bór and his staff just in time. Radosław repulsed the SS attack, but Bór had very nearly been killed. Furthermore, the AK's crucial radio transmitter had been damaged, which meant that Bór was not able to send news of the uprising to London until early in the morning of 2 August. The choice of the Kammler factory had other consequences, too, as by basing himself in this far-flung corner of Warsaw Bór had removed himself from the centre of power. General Monter was now in *de facto* control.

Monter's quixotic plans did not end in the city centre. In Żoliborz, too, his ambition far exceeded the means of his men. In one example, he ordered the ill-equipped 'Żaglowiec' Battalion to take the gigantic ex-Russian fortress known as the Citadel, the crucial Gdańsk railway station, the Traugutta Fort and the heavily guarded Chemical Institute, all in one day. In reality an attack on any of these heavily fortified German-held targets would have required thousands of well-armed troops to have even a chance of success. As AK soldier Andrzej Borowiec put it, 'ordering poorly armed and mostly inexperienced fighters against heavily fortified German positions in broad daylight smacked of criminal irresponsibility'.[13]

The huge brick Russian-built Citadel straddles the riverbank in Żoliborz like a gigantic red starburst. Even today this grim fortress's massive walls and ramparts still radiate a sheer brute power which betrays its original function. Built on the order of Tsar Nicholas I after the Polish Uprising of 1830, at the cost of a colossal eleven million roubles – paid for by the Poles as punishment for their defiance – it was always meant to be a symbol of control, of intimidation and punishment, and over the years its dank prison complex held thousands of political victims, from Joseph Conrad's father to the defiant Rosa Luxemburg. Perhaps the most notorious inmate was Feliks Dzierżyński, who after his release returned to revolutionary Russia to create the brutal Cheka. Dzierżyński always remembered his time there with hatred, and kept a picture of his beloved Rosa Luxemburg on the wall of his office in the Lubyanka in Moscow.

By the summer of 1944 the Citadel had become a powerful German military base, and with its heavily guarded walls and ramparts resembled nothing less than a red-brick Monte Cassino. At 5 p.m. on 1 August 218 poorly equipped AK soldiers gathered to attack this monster. The operation got off to a slow start. The head of one platoon had a heart attack and died; the head of the other did not show up. The brave soldiers rushed in anyway. At first they tried to make a hole in the main gate, but came under machine-gun fire from the towers. They tried again, this time attempting to blow the gate with an old Panzerfaust, their only heavy weapon. It did not work, and they were forced to retreat with the loss of many men.

The courage of the AK soldiers is not in doubt, but the scale of Monter's suicidal order to take the Citadel becomes clear when the AK attack is compared to that undertaken by the Red Army on 17 January 1945. By this time the Germans were manning the fortress with a skeletal staff of 250 men, but even so, Soviet reconnaissance deemed the Citadel so strong that it ordered heavy artillery to be brought in for the attack. Fortunately for the Russians, a local Pole informed them of a secret escape tunnel which the Germans had dug from the fortress to a bunker on the bank of the Vistula. Over a thousand well-armed Soviet troops supported by 76mm guns attacked and took the bunker, then crawled through the tunnel to the Citadel. They took the Germans by surprise from the inside, and flung open the main gates, allowing 2,000 more troops to storm in. Despite the overwhelming odds the Germans fought on for a further four hours, resorting in the end to vicious hand-to-hand combat.[14]

The AK troops lacked both the weapons and the experience to fight effectively against such an enemy. Janusz Brochwicz-Lewiński, who had earlier captured the palace by the steam mills on Żytnia Street, watched from its windows as the Germans began their counter-attack; when they brought a Panzer 88 into position, he knew the AK assault was doomed: 'My soldiers were between sixteen and twenty-four years old, more or less well trained, but it is difficult to compare them to soldiers who had three years of experience at the front . . . they were mostly students, teenagers from the Lyceum and Gymnasium. They were very patriotic and great fighters, but they didn't have experience.'[15] On the other hand, 'the Germans stayed calm. Most of them were from formations from the Eastern Front and very good shots.' Only a handful of the twenty-three young Poles in his charge survived.

Success and Liberation

There was one notable exception to Monter's list of failures, but it was unique, because the 'Krybar' Battalion had been able to work at taking its target from the inside for some time. The massive power station in Powiśle was the main source of electricity for the entire city, and had always been seen as an important target. The groundwork for taking the plant preceded the uprising, as AK members posing as ordinary workers were smuggled in. In a strange twist of fate they were helped in this by a German Lutheran pastor who happened to be in charge of personnel. The pastor had lived in the Polish town of Żyrardów before the war, and had become close to the Poles. He was so horrified by Nazi crimes there that he agreed to help the AK, giving dozens of insurgents false papers which allowed them to work 'legally'.

The complex was heavily fortified, and guarded by Wehrmacht, SD, Ukrainians, *Volksdeutsche* and police units. One hundred and sixty Germans slept on site; an additional twenty-five police and SD men were added in the summer of 1944 because of the fear of unrest. Undaunted, the Poles devised a detailed plan. Because of the heavy security, nothing could be brought into the plant before the actual attack. They began their work on 1 August.

At 3 o'clock that afternoon Krybar's men smuggled in ten kilograms of explosives, followed by grenades hidden in the wicker baskets ostensibly holding the monthly meat ration. Pistols were hidden amongst a batch of electricity meters, and machine guns were carried in under raincoats. At 4.55 p.m. the phone wires were cut and the special Gestapo line was redirected to an 'industrial guard' – an AK operative who spoke perfect German.

At 5 p.m. the sound of pistols, machine guns and bombs ripped through the massive concrete halls. The Germans were confused by the noise, and the AK quickly overran the SD quarters, turning on the steam valves so that the Germans could not see. Two Wehrmacht soldiers chose to drown in the basement rather than surrender. The Gestapo, now facing a general uprising in the city, telephoned from headquarters asking if everything was under control; the 'industrial guard' informed them in flawless German that 'All is in order.' The insurgents were then left alone.

The bitter fighting lasted for nineteen hours; in the end fourteen Germans were killed, thirty-five wounded and ninety taken prisoner, the rest having escaped by jumping out of the windows. As a result of this notable success the AK was able to keep the plant running until September, providing electricity for the entire city during the uprising.[16]

There were other successes in those first three days. The 1,600 well-equipped soldiers of five elite 'Kedyw' battalions – 'Czata', 'Miotła', 'Parasol', 'Pięść', 'Zośka' – 'Kollegium A' and the women's unit 'Dysk', led by Jan Mazurkiewicz ('Radosław'), who would distinguish himself as one of the most effective commanders of the AK, had taken a huge chunk of northern Wola. On the morning of 2 August a small German unit tried to advance on Radosław's 'Zośka' Battalion. The Poles had a PIAT (an English Panzerfaust) and anti-tank grenades, which so surprised the German tank crews that they abandoned their Panzers and were captured. These two highly prized vehicles formed the basis of the new 'Wacek Panzer Platoon'. Flushed with enthusiasm, Bór came out in person to see the trophies, and radioed London in buoyant mood reporting that the AK were 'successfully capturing tanks'. There would be very few more.

The first two tanks proved extremely useful, however, and were employed to great effect in Wola. The first target to be destroyed was the tower of the St Augustin church, one of the few structures left in the ghetto, which had provided the Germans with an ideal machine-gun position. Two shots from one of the tanks knocked it out.

Later that day 'Kedyw' attacked the vast Waffen SS supply depots at Stawki, killing the German guards and freeing a number of Jewish labourers. One of them, a doctor, joined 'Kedyw' despite the fact that he could only communicate with the Polish soldiers in Latin. For Stanisław Aronson the buildings brought back terrible memories: a year and a half earlier the Jews of the ghetto had been kept there before being loaded onto the trains for Treblinka, and it was the last place he had seen his parents alive. Aronson was struck by these thoughts for a fleeting moment as he fought to take the warehouses, but he consciously pushed the memories aside. 'There was no time for that kind of reflection now,' he said.[17]

Although tactically unimportant, the warehouses contained enormous quantities of food, which would help keep the beleaguered people of the Old Town alive in the weeks to come. Anna Szatkowska was one of many sent to get supplies for her temporary clinic: 'We took out as much as we could carry, rucksacks and sacks of rye, sugar, flour and tinned meat.' There was also a cache of SS uniforms, including the so-called 'Panterki', or camouflage smocks, along with trousers, hats, belts and rucksacks. Most AK soldiers had arrived in civilian gear, so the uniforms were useful, although not all of them wanted to don the clothes of the detested SS.

Szatkowska protested, but conceded tha: 'an order is an order. We grabbed what we could, I got trousers and a padded jacket in a huge size. We put our red-and-white armbands on over the top.'[18] Janusz Brochwicz-Lewiński of Battalior. 'Gryf' said: 'We all had German helmets and German *Panterki,* a belt, and suspenders and German boots.' The helmet saved his life when a bullet hit him on the chin a few days later in the fierce fighting in the Evangelical cemetery. Others, like Włodzimierz Rosłcniec, felt that the uniforms and the red-and-white armbands made his unit more like a real fighting force, and helped to 'give us mcre self-confidence'.

The Poles wore red-and-white armbands to distinguish themselves from the enemy, but the fact tha: the opposing sides had the same uniform caused confusion: sometimes truckloads of Germans would drive by and not fire or Poles, thinking that they were German, while at other times Poles or Germans fired at their own side. 'The Poles had started the uprising on 1 August,' German staff officer Hans Thieme complained. 'They killed single soldiers in the city and took over or surrounded our posts and institutions, they took over warehouses and armed themselves and took food and took uniforms so we didn't know which man was one of ours or which was the enemy – many Poles were wearing SS camouflage jackets.'[19] Walter Schroeder, a German anti-aircraft artillery surgeon, was captured by the Poles on 3 August as he was transporting a wounded colleague in a motor-cycle with a sidecar. 'I was stopped by four soldiers in German uniform. I asked the way to the hospital and got an answer in perfect German.'[20] It took some time for him to understand that he had been arrested by the Poles and was now a prisoner of war.

One of the most poignant successes in Wola was the liberation of Gęsiówka prison. This sinister place had been created on the bones of the Warsaw ghetto by SS Brigadeführer Jürgen Stroop, who had convinced Himmler that the wasteland could be harvested for building material and the old prison used as a concentration camp. Many of the Jews imprisoned there were not from the Warsaw ghetto, but were specialist craftsmen who had been brought in from all over Europe: as a result the signs in the prison were written in German, Polish, Hungarian and French. One of the prisoners' tasks had been to demolish what was left of the ghetto: one group had recovered thirty-four million bricks, while another was forced to carry the corpses of many thousands who had perished in the Ghetto Uprising to 45 Gęsia Street, and to burn them in the courtyard there. When the Germans had started to evacuate Warsaw in mid-July they had sent most of the prisoners – at least 4,000 – to Dachau, where the majority of them died. Those remaining in Warsaw knew that they would soon be killed. When the SS guards heard that the uprising had broken out they pushed them into one barrack and barked at them to lie face-down on the floor. 'If the "*Banditen*" come,' they were told, 'you will be shot.'

But the SS were too slow. On 5 August, using one of the captured tanks, the 'Zośka' Battalion launched a daring raid to free the prisoners. The AK men got inside the heavily fortified complex, knocked out the guard towers and blasted away at anything that moved. 'The Germans had either to surrender or perish.' In the so-called 'White House', a building in the central courtyard, the Poles came across a bizarre domestic scene – a long table covered in an elegant white cloth with a tureen of steaming soup on it, surrounded by open bottles of wine and vodka. The chairs were overturned, suggesting that the black-uniformed SS guards had only just managed to flee.

The Jewish prisoners were terrified to see men in German uniform coming towards them, but when they realized that these were Polish soldiers the prison erupted, with the inmates embracing their liberators, some with tears streaming down their cheeks. Lieutenant Wacek of the 'Zośka' Battalion remembered: 'At least a hundred prisoners had been drawn up military style in two long rows. As I approached a voice called out, "Attention! Eyes left!" One of them came to me and saluted; "Sergeant Sub-Officer Henryk Lederman, sir, reporting that the Jewish battalion is ready for action." ' The touched and astonished Wacek informed Radosław what had happened, and a number of the ex-prisoners joined Wacek's platoon. They included Corporal Filar, an electrician, and Rysiek and Ledermann, both mechanics. Many of the Jews joined the ranks of the AK. One, a Frenchman named Dawid Edelman, fell in battle on 5 August.[21] One of the Greeks became a tank gunner, while others worked producing armaments. Later, in the Old Town, another of the Greek Jews, who had been an opera singer in his past life, entertained the shattered civilians with his songs. But he like most of the others freed that day, was to die tragically in the weeks to come.[22]

The Old Town, Area I, also saw some successes in the first days. An ancient and beautiful place and one of the gems of Warsaw, the old part of the city sits high on an embankment which sweeps down to the river. The quarter had long dazzled visitors with its medieval square, its myriad churches and its tall merchant houses painted in cheerful pastel colours. The little cobbled streets, small workshops and modest apartments had never been of interest to the Germans, so the area was not particularly well guarded, and the AK were able to capture much of its central district quickly, with very little loss of life.

Its edges, however, were much more contentious. The Old Town was encircled by a belt of grand columned palaces, Warsaw's internationally renowned Opera House, the City Hall, and a plethora of imposing institutional buildings, from the Archbishop's Palace to the vast National Archives. The Germans used most of these buildings as offices, and they were determined to keep them.

By 2 August, heavy fighting raged in and around a number of key German installations, including the hospital-school on Barokowa Street, the ruins of the Warsaw Castle and the National Archives on Długa Street. The colourful AK figure Major Barry directed fierce battles at the Blank Palace, Theatre Square, the Polish National Bank and the Mostowski Palace. Willy Perner, a member of the Technische Nothilfe, a German organization for the protection of strategic facilities and infrastructure, had been sent to Warsaw from Berlin at the end of July, and was quartered in the Strasse der Polizei, in Aleja Szucha 23, when he was ordered on 2 August to go to the State Securities building. Bloody fighting broke out in the vast concrete structure, with Germans holding one floor and Poles another, as if in a giant layer cake. 'There were at least two hundred partisans against us,' Perner said of the vicious battle that day. He was wounded in the chest, and dragged himself to the attic, where he hid alone for twenty-five days, as he, like many of his colleagues, mistakenly believed that he would be killed if he were taken prisoner. The same was true of Hermann Fribolin, the Deputy Oberburgermeister of Warsaw and Brigadeführer Leist's deputy. Fribolin was captured at the Blank Palace; he had been so terrified of being executed as one of the hated German administrators that he had disguised himself as a Wehrmacht officer.

When the Poles could not take a building outright they laid siege to it, as happened at the venerable National Bank on the edge of the Old Town, which was defended by about forty well-armed German troops. To the annoyance of the German defenders, a client rang the bank from Kraków in the midst of the fighting, thinking it was business as usual, and asked for a sum of money to be sent immediately. 'Don't you know that we are under siege here?' the hapless guard yelled down the line. The trapped Germans realized that their situation was hopeless, and Stahel ordered them to withdraw. On the night of 4 August a lorry and three tanks pulled up, and were loaded with money, munitions and fifty-six German soldiers and civilian personnel, including three wounded. They buried the one soldier who had died in the bank and then left. The Poles stationed 180 troops in the building; the Luftwaffe would target it mercilessly until the collapse of resistance in the Old Town.

The regular bombing raids which became such a deadly feature of that summer in Warsaw began in earnest on 4 August. The Germans had complete air superiority over the city, and as the Poles had no anti-aircraft weapons, the Luftwaffe could do as they wished. For the Germans trapped and under siege the bombs were cause for celebration. Dr Krug, who was with Governor Fischer in the Brühl Palace, was 'relieved when they hit places where we knew there were nests of Polish defence'.[23] While the bombs were a sign to the Germans that they might soon be rescued, for the Poles they were to become a terrifying daily ordeal which killed and maimed thousands of innocent civilians in the coming months.

By 4 August, most of the Old Town was in Polish hands. From time to time the Germans tried to counter-attack, as when a column of tanks advanced along Krakowskie Przedmieście towards the Old Town. The Poles hit them with a barrage of 150 Molotov cocktails. Three of the tanks were disabled, and the remainder hurried back to the safety of the garrison, then holed up in the fortified university complex, where they were supplied by the Luftwaffe.

There were many other Polish successes, although mainly against non-military targets. 'Baszta' Regiment managed to take the Królikarnia Palace on 1 August; 'Kiliński' Battalion captured the Prudential building on the first day, to an outpouring of emotion, and on the second captured the employment office in Małachowski Square, as well as the main post office. In the Old

Town the AK captured the State Security building, the Blank Palace, the Arsenal and the Mostowski Palace, thereby turning the great Theatre Square into the new front line at the southern end of the Old Town. The Social Security building was captured in Czerniaków, while in Śródmieście, 'Chrobry I' took the Nordwache police station at the crucial junction of Żelazna and Chłodna, and after heavy fighting captured the Postal railway station and part of Jerusalem Avenue. The Court of Appeal building was captured after heavy fighting, and forty Germans were taken prisoner; the 'Dzik' Battalion took the City Hall and the prison in Daniłowiczowska Street. By the end of the third day the AK had captured over fifty square kilometres of territory, including a large chunk of Żoliborz, much of the Old Town, the southern part of Śródmieście and a huge sector of Wola. They had lost over 2,000 fighters, around 10 per cent of the force committed, compared to just five hundred German casualties. Warsaw now looked like a jigsaw puzzle, with much of its area controlled by the AK, but most vital communication hubs and other key positions still held by the Germans (see map, p. 196). Bór, realizing that his troops lacked the strength to continue the attack, ordered them to move onto the defensive while they waited for 'help from outside'.

Monter was quick to blame the AK for their failure to capture everything on his list, but in the end it hardly mattered. The real key to success, and the very thing which enabled the Poles to hold out against the Nazis for sixty-three days, had nothing to do with taking Monter's unreachable targets; on the contrary, it was the physical occupation of huge swathes of Warsaw, largely by the civilian population bolstered by small groups of insurgents, which caused problems for the Germans. The Nazis would have been able to recapture bridges and airports with ease, but the prospect of having to fight an underground army, hidden amongst tens of thousands of civilians in endless apartment blocks and office buildings which quickly came to resemble fortresses, was a true nightmare. It was the civilians who streamed out of their homes and began to build barricades on every street corner on the very first evening, and it was in this sense that the Warsaw Uprising became a mass phenomenon. The positive aspect of Monter's attacks was that they frightened many of the Germans into remaining on the defensive, giving the Poles a window during which to fortify streets and key buildings. The extraordinary combination of AK initiative, civilian participation and the German failure to act quickly and decisively in the first hours led to the prolongation of the uprising.

For the Germans this turn of events could not have been less welcome. Suddenly every street, every building, every room was a potential fortress. For many it conjured up memories of Stalingrad's bitter, hand-to-hand fighting for each basement and street. Worse still, this time the battle would not be against the Red Army, but an entire population of 'Banditen'. The Poles had taken over large areas of their capital. Now the Germans had to figure out a way of getting it back. Their solution would be diabolical.

The Taste of Freedom

Most Warsawians were oblivious to this looming danger, and felt that a great victory had been won. Maps were drawn and pinned up showing the 'free' parts of Warsaw – Żoliborz to the north, Wola to the west, the Old Town and the city centre at its heart, and Ochota, Czerniaków and Mokotów in the south. But a closer look revealed a more sobering view. Praga, on the east bank of the Vistula, had already been taken back by the Germans. Airports, bridges, main roads, railway stations, the SS and police headquarters, military installations – indeed virtually all the places that the Germans had fortified before the uprising – were still in Nazi hands, even if some, like the Brühl Palace, were isolated within Polish-held areas. 'It is not important that we didn't achieve our aims in the first days of fighting,' Włodzimierz Rosłoniec wrote on 5 August. 'Our faith in victory is still strong.'

The proud people of Warsaw revelled in their new-found freedom. Suddenly, after five years of brutal occupation they could leave their homes after curfew, talk out loud, read a Polish newspaper or wave a Polish flag without fear of arrest. On 2 August the AK managed to get the city's loudspeaker system working, and the population heard the rousing and beautiful Polish national anthem for the first time since 1939. People wept openly on the streets. General Bór spoke to his soldiers, calling on them to 'restore freedom in our county and to punish the German criminals for the terror and atrocities committed on Polish soil'.[24] 'It is difficult to recognize the city,' wrote forty-six-year-old lawyer Stefan Talikowski. 'People are crazy with joy, they hug one another with tears of excitement and are very emotional. You can see red-and-white flags, big and small, taken from the secret hiding places where they had waited for the days of freedom.'[25] One of the girls in his building took out 'two beautifully ironed national flags ten metres long' and put them up for all to see.[26] AK situation reports of 3 August praised the spontaneous cooperation between civilians, who 'are hanging out Polish flags', and volunteers, 'who are helping the AK in every way'. People sang patriotic songs like '*Rota*', written in protest against Prussian oppression a century before. 'The Germans will not spit in our face,' one line goes. German signs and swastikas were unceremoniously ripped from buildings, and pictures of Hitler, obligatory in every German office, were put on the barricades so that the troops would have to shoot at their Führer.

When the Prudential building was taken and the Polish flag

hoisted from it, people left their homes just to look at it, 'crying and laughing and spontaneously singing the national anthem'. A postal system was set up, complete with AK stamps and postboxes, which lasted in one form or another until the end of the uprising. Old divisions between people were eroded; everyone wanted to help. When Jan Rossman of the 'Broda' Battalion was ordered to capture the school buildings at Okopowa 5 he was amazed at the warmth shown by the civilians in the district: 'People from local houses welcomed us enthusiastically. They found ladders and rams to help get into the school and it was taken very quickly.'[27] Eulalia Matusiak, who would later be deported to Auschwitz, remembered having 'total freedom in our block' on the second day. 'Even in the basement it was a free Poland.' Her brother, who had disappeared some days before, came back 'in a helmet, with a white-and-red band on his arm, he had a gun, he brought some newspapers . . . there was joy.'[28]

From the first moment Warsawians pitched in to build anti-tank barricades throughout the city. 'Children, adults, old people all want to help. They carry what they have, paving stones, bricks, tiles, wood, heavy furniture, a child's pram, stone and sandbags.'[29] In scenes reminiscent of the Blitz in London, people who had lived as neighbours for years and had never talked to one another suddenly became friendly as they worked together to heap up the barricades. Tadeusz Szczęsny, a boy scout, spent hours building one on the corner of Karolkowa and Dworska, made of everything that could be collected from the surrounding streets: 'furniture, prams, wagons, carriages from the Hrubieszcowska Street carriage depot. It was as high as the small buildings in the neighbourhood. We were proud of it.'[30] The Government Delegation* had to issue an order

---

* The Goverment Delegatation for Poland, based in Warsaw, acted as the official representative of the Polish government-in-exile in London.

for people not to use valuable things like 'antiques, pictures and typewriters'. These amateur 'light barricades' were small, and could easily be crushed under the tracks of a Panzer, but army engineers were brought in to fortify important intersections like that of Młynarska, Wolska and Górczewska Streets. These became serious obstacles for the Germans.

The AK soldiers could do no wrong in those first days of freedom. They were the heroes of the moment, and they basked in the glory afforded to those who sported the 'Panterki' uniforms, armbands and helmets. Older men not involved in the Home Army asked if they too could have a weapon and join in the fight, but the answer was usually negative, as there were no guns to spare. The young fighters were given food, clothing, shelter and anything else they needed. 'As we were marching from the Umschlagplatz to Wola – one kilometre that was now free of Germans – thousands of people stood on the street throwing flowers and crying.'[31] The basement at Jadwiga Gronostalska's house had been used as a store room for AK provisions before the uprising; now packages were arriving by the dozen. A local village woman who had come to Warsaw on 1 August to sell her produce found herself trapped in the city. She took her chicken to the Maltański hospital and left it 'for the soldiers'.[32]

The desire to support the uprising was heartfelt and widespread. Temporary clinics were set up in people's houses; children were put to work ripping up sheets for bandages. Civilians learned to make 'filipinki' grenades – 'You just hammer an old meat tin, push in tiny pieces of iron mixed with explosives, and an expert puts the detonator on it.'[33] Stefan Talikowski made Molotov cocktails and hid them in the courtyard of his family's building: 'We made sixty in one day alone.'[34] Antonina Mijal's group and other teams stepped up weapons production from the increasing supply of unexploded bombs. The need was acute. When an AK unit met up at Jadwiga Stasiakowa's house, she noted that the young soldiers carried no explosives, and 'only four had guns'.[35] Scouts and other volunteers cheerfully organized canteens, gathered clothing from abandoned flats, dug toilets for refugees, gathered bowls, towels, soap and blankets, and organized accommodation in basements. Residents appointed special delegates for their blocks, and when bombing started on 4 August fire watches were created. Bunkers were prepared in basements all over town; water was stored and food distributed. Some buildings introduced strict sets of rules. One such, known as the '*Pensionat*', was almost like a strange subterranean hotel: 'Everyone had a place and could not change it. They had the right to have essential things with them during bombardments but they could not bring other possessions. There were small porches and ventilation holes where they were allowed to smoke cigarettes. There were a few dozen pickaxes and torches every few metres in case of danger. At night silence was enforced between 11 p.m. and 5 a.m. The highlight of the day was the communal reading of the Home Army newspaper; people came from different parts of the basement to hear the latest news'.[36]

Around six hundred people were living in the basement of Jadwiga Stasiakowa's building. 'We all worked to provide water and provisions wherever possible; we created places to cook.' One day she decided to break the rules and take a bath upstairs. She had just let herself into her ghostly apartment when suddenly a bullet came through the window, hitting the mantelpiece and knocking ash on her only blouse. She gratefully returned to the safety of the basement. 'We had enough food and water, and hoped that we would make it through for a few more days.'[37]

Tunnels were dug to other buildings so that there was no need to go outside, and entire neighbourhoods organized themselves into groups. 'I was given anti-aircraft defence,' remembered Stefan Talikowski. 'I went downstairs and upstairs checking posts in attics and approving fire equipment. We looked for snipers hidden on the roofs or in attics.' His building was used as the headquarters of 'Chrobry I' Battalion, led by Captain Gustaw Billewicz ('Sosna'). Like many civilians, Talikowski cooperated in every way possible with the AK members.

Not everyone was so fortunate, and even early on there were hints of the crisis to come. The decision not to tell the population about the start of the uprising had been necessary, but ordinary people had paid the price. Untold numbers were caught away from home when the battle lines were drawn. People returning from work or from visiting friends found themselves cut off from loved ones, often with no way of finding out what was happening to their families. The practice of leaving messages on a scrap of paper or scrawled in chalk across the door began in those first days. Many found themselves homeless in a wartorn city, often with no money, no food and no help. Even General Bór had chosen not to tell his pregnant wife that she should leave town – she was later caught up in the massacres in the Opera House and in Wola, although she miraculously survived. Thousands of children were left on their own when their parents were unable to reach them or were killed. Tadeusz Rybowski, a twelve-year-old who lived with his mother and his paralyzed grandmother, was lucky that his mother returned home before her usual time on the evening of 1 August: 'I really don't know what would have happened to us if my mother had not come back early that day.'[38] Halina Wiśniewska gave birth to a son at 1 p.m. on 1 August. She had no food; the child survived by sucking on sugar tied into old rags. 'From the outset, from the first day, the situation was terrible . . . Getting milk was completely out of the question . . . No one imagined the situation that later turned out. Everyone expected it to end shortly. The Germans were already fleeing and that would be the end.'[39]

Life at the new front lines was extremely dangerous. Stefania Chmielewska, who owned a sewing shop on the grand Krakowskie Przedmieście, was unable to get to her home on Kozia Street, even though it was only metres away. German tanks controlled the entire area, and a machine gunner on the roof of the Prime Minister's office shot at anything that moved.[40] Bodies littered the street by her shop, but nobody could reach them.

For many, the first days brought a glimpse of the tragedy that was to come. Some young AK soldiers found it all too much: the group gathered in Sabina Sebyłowa's building 'have dramatically few weapons. They don't have bullets as they have used them already. So they have revolvers without bullets and bullets which don't fit the revolvers. In the morning many of the boys just took off their red-and-white armbands and walked away. They left empty bottles beside the body of a colleague who had died of wounds in the night and was lying at the gate. It was pouring with rain and he lay in a puddle of water covered with a piece of cloth.'[41]

Many were horrified to see the first corpses lying in streets, gardens and courtyards. 'I saw them, the dead bodies of men, women, old and children, some dressed, some nearly naked and covered only with newspapers. After the euphoria and enthusiasm it is a shock and makes us quite depressed.'[42] Young women who had volunteered as nurses began to realize that their work was serious; suddenly these untrained girls were being called on to bandage maimed children or to try to ease the pain of terrible burns, a very common injury in the uprising. Halina Zbierska, a twenty-year-old nursing student at the Maltański hospital, started work on 1 August, when heavy fighting was just beginning around Theatre Square. 'During my first operation I was asked to hold the leg of an eighteen-year-old soldier as it was being amputated. I was fine until they started to saw through the bone. Then the leg came away in my hands. I fainted.'

There were many other victims. Jadwiga Stasiakowa's building was in the direct line of German fire, and nobody dared to go out onto the street. But the AK soldiers needed to make contact with headquarters, and as the phones did not work, they asked for somebody to act as a runner. A young girl called Wanda volunteered, but she was shot in the stomach as soon as she left the building, and lay in the street bleeding. Finally a boy who could stand it no longer ran from the cellar and pulled her to a temporary clinic, where she soon died. 'There were six hundred of us in that basement, and we all felt very depressed after that . . . it was a feeling of terrible isolation.'[43]

But for most the mood remained buoyant. 'The news is good,' Anna Szatkowska wrote confidently on 2 August. 'The Warsaw centre is in our hands except the main arteries, there is fighting in the peripheral districts, the Soviet army is already close and will soon enter Praga, and the Allies will support us.'[44] Larysa Zajączkowska remembered hearing rumours that the Germans were going to blow up the bridges. 'There was the constant muffled sound of artillery so everyone thought that the Russians were going to come.'[45] The radio station 'Anna' reported that the Soviets were practically in the city. An internal AK report noted sternly that people were ignoring the dangers and were getting drunk and celebrating: 'It may be necessary to write propaganda to dampen the enthusiasm and remind people that the Germans are still in the city.'

As for General Bór, despite niggling worries about not having achieved all his aims, he reported to London on 3 August that 'the mood and morale of leaders and soldiers is fantastic. Civilians cooperate with the fight with enthusiasm. Many barricades have been built on the streets. National flags fly over the places taken over. We fight effectively against heavy tanks, we have destroyed or disarmed a number of them.'[46] The next day he reported to

London that although the Germans had started to burn houses along the main artery, Jerusalem Avenue, 'the civilians cooperate in the fight and even unarmed young people build barricades with enthusiasm. Women serve and fight with the men, everybody is very obedient and dedicated.'

On 5 August, British Halifax bombers that had flown from Brindisi dropped twelve loads in the cemeteries held by the AK. The packages contained much-needed machine pistols, Sten guns, ammunition, grenades and an anti-tank PIAT. Here was further proof that help was on its way. The population celebrated, and waited for more.

But 5 August was to be the high point for the AK. It had 16,000 people under its command, outnumbered the German garrison three to one, and controlled over 125 square kilometres of territory. The euphoria was not to last. The Germans, who had been surprised by the scale of the Polish attacks, had been slow to respond, but they were beginning to get organized. Warsaw was going to be made to pay for its insolence.

6

'HIMMLER HAS WON'

In war, gentlemen, that which is expedient is alone advantageous.
We are told that this city is still powerful. So much the more ought
we to be on our guard against treachery joined to power, and to
crush the power in time since we cannot extinguish the treachery.
(Chapter IX)

The German Response

When the first shots of the uprising rang out in Żoliborz, SS and
Police Leader Brigadeführer Paul Otto Geibel dismissed them as
a 'local skirmish', but when fighting started to spread into
Śródmieście, Mokotów and Czerniaków he knew something was
wrong. At 4 o'clock he put the 5,000 SS police and SD personnel
on full alert. The Germans had dozens of heavily fortified headquarters and barracks located throughout the city, many protected
by bunkers and guard posts. The SS and police were told to secure
these areas, including the SS and Gestapo headquarters, the
Governor's Palace and the German quarter. But they did little
else. The German garrison was severely understaffed, morale was
at rock bottom after the exodus at the end of July, and none of

the Germans was keen to lose his life to a sniper's bullet just before the Soviets came. The journalist Stefan Kisielewski was at Piłsudski Square, then called Adolf Hitler Platz, when he heard gunfire. 'I took out my white handkerchief and moved past the armed Germans. Of course I was afraid but they didn't even pay attention to me, instead they looked up at the sky or over the rooftops with unseeing eyes.' The unwillingness and inability of the Germans to act quickly and forcefully allowed the AK and the civilians to take control of huge areas of Warsaw in those first days, and by the time help came it was too late for a quick German victory. The scene was set for a long and agonizing fight.

The Germans' passivity is surprising, given that they had long suspected that the Poles were planning an uprising of some kind. By 1942 the so-called 'Officers' File' of Polish underground activists contained the names of 30,000 suspects, while the 'Uprising File' started in February 1944 had 40,000 for the Radom area alone. SS Obergruppenführer Wilhelm Koppe, who had recently outdone himself by murdering 30,000 tuberculosis patients because they posed a health hazard to the General Government, had suggested that the German forces exert greater control over the roads, as the Poles were likely to use bicycles during a revolt. SS Brigadeführer Walter Bierkamp of Einsatzgruppe B told Hans Frank in February 1944 that the Polish underground was very well prepared, and that the 'enemy apparatus' functioned in a 'well-organized and military way'.[1] Koppe informed Himmler on 25 July that the government-in-exile in London had called for an uprising, and that, contrary to earlier information, it would start not in Kraków but in Warsaw. Reinhard Gehlen's German intelligence service had warned on 1 July that 'In our judgement the plans for revolt, given the Polish character, incline towards a strong but not overestimated possibility.'[2] The OKH, too, was concerned. By the summer of 1944 Warsaw was the last major city between the Russian front and Berlin, as well as an important transportation hub to the troops on the other side of the Vistula. On the evening of 25 July the 9th Army Diary stated nervously that 'it is known there are preparations for an uprising but there is no information about the date of the breakout and there is no information about how advanced those preparations are'. Dr Ludwig Hahn, the Chief of the Security Police, said later of the uprising: 'We in the HQ of the Security Police were not at all surprised by it.'

The Germans were also slow to react because they underestimated the numbers and the organization of the insurgents, and believed that any unrest would be easily contained. The staff of Army Group Centre thought that the insurgents would wait until relations with the Soviet-backed PKWN government had become clear: 'We do not expect the uprising to be a significant event.'[3] The Governor of the Warsaw District, Dr Ludwig Fischer, completely misreading the Poles as usual, requested that General von Vormann give Warsaw 'a show' to demonstrate the 'resolute plan to keep the city'. In an order released on 26 July, all units which were regrouping at Warsaw, above all the Hermann Göring Division, which was on the move from Italy, got the order to 'march ostentatiously' through the main streets of Warsaw. The Poles had been 'impressed', Fischer concluded: 'the situation in the city is much calmer'.[4] In reality, Warsawians paid little attention to this gesture, as they were much more interested in the approach of the Red Army and their plans for the uprising. Still, Fischer insisted that 'his Poles' would not revolt.

The Germans had prepared the city in case of attack, but this was standard procedure throughout the occupied territories. Warsaw had been divided into five districts, A to D on the west bank and E – Praga – to the east. Each region had its own barracks, leadership, equipment, provisions and an arsenal. This was an advantage in that the Germans were safe from a concentrated attack on a single area, but it was a disadvantage in that the districts could easily be cut off from one another. There was one place, however, that was virtually unassailable: namely the police district, bordered by Aleja Ujazdowskie, Klonowa and Flory Streets. The sinister Aleja Szucha lay at its heart. It was one of the most loathed places in the city.

It is difficult now to understand the sheer size of the Nazi apparatus of terror based in Warsaw's police district at the time of the uprising. The commander of the Security Police oversaw dozens of departments, from administration under SS Hauptsturmführer Arthur Füssel and the Security Service under SS Sturmbannführer Dr Ernst Kah, to the Gestapo under Walter Stamm and the Criminal Police under Harry Geisler. Each of these was in turn broken down into smaller administrative units – the Gestapo, for example, had its 'Hostile Activities and Sabotage', 'Religious Bodies, Masons and Jews', 'Émigrés, Hostages, Foreign Labour' and other sections, each headed by its own SS Hauptsturmführer or Obersturmführer. There were over 150 SS officers, each of whom oversaw dozens of subordinates. The officers lived luxurious, quite unreal lives in flats and houses furnished with paintings and goods stolen from the Poles. They had their own shops, and ample supplies of food and drink, including regular shipments of wine and spirits from France; the women met friends for coffee, and in the evening watched the latest films from Germany or spent time in the clubs and restaurants that were designated 'Nur für Deutsche'.

The list of residents at the time of the uprising reads like a ghastly Who's Who of SS criminals. Standartenführer SS Dr Ludwig Hahn, with his chubby face and large blue eyes, looked the very picture of innocence, but he was quite the opposite. After the war he boasted: 'I could do ten, twenty, thirty, forty death sentences in an hour, maybe even more.'[5] From his office in Strasse der Polizei 25 he ran the Gestapo, the SD and the Criminal Police from 1941 until the end of the uprising, reporting not to the SS and Police Leader of Warsaw, but directly to Ernst Kaltenbrunner, Reinhard Heydrich's successor as head of the RSHA, the Reich's Security Office, in Berlin.[6] And yet he was elegant and sophisticated; he and his charming wife Charlotte, known as 'the *Kommandeuse*' by the German staff, tried their best to lead a cheerful social life, organizing drinks and dancing parties for their friends. Charlotte found this something of a challenge, as her husband was so busy organizing deportations of Jews to Treblinka and executing the inmates of Pawiak prison, but theirs was a good marriage; she would conceal her husband's identity in West Germany after 1945, allowing him to build a quite different career as the vice president of an insurance company. This was not unusual: after the war Wilhelm Koppe took his wife's name – Lohmann – and became the director of a chocolate factory in Bonn.

SS Sturmbannführer Thomas Wippenbeck was another resident of the police district. Jokingly referred to as 'the hangman' by his colleagues, his favourite pastime was to go into the cells and murder the prisoners, sometimes calling on his friends SS Oberscharführers Franz Bürkl and August Albers to join in. Together they hanged around 150 people, and then claimed that the victims had committed suicide. A British prisoner of war, Sergeant Hickman, was murdered in this way, as was Henryk Pogoriely, winner of the silver medal at the 1936 Munich Chess Olympics. Pogoriely's wife and small son were also killed.

Others in the police district included SS Untersturmführer Karl Brandt, a notorious sadist, and Obersturmführer Norbert Tripps, who was responsible for implementing Kutschera's infamous public executions in Warsaw. It was Tripps who killed the sick women and children in Pawiak prison in July 1944; he disappeared after the war, and was never brought to justice.[7] SS Unterscharführer Engelbert Frühwirth also killed civilians, including forty-two 'redundant' Jewish workshop employees whom he gunned down in cold blood as the Germans were fleeing Warsaw in July 1944. He died in Vienna in 1964, having also evaded justice. Frühwirth and his men seemed to enjoy their work: after murdering 223 people near Warsaw one evening they returned home in the empty lorries singing loudly and congratulating themselves on a job well done.[8] Brigadeführer Paul Otto Geibel, one of the very few who would later be sentenced to life imprisonment for crimes committed against the civilians of Warsaw, and Wilhelm Rodewald, the last commander of the Schutzpolizei in the city, were also important residents. The men of the SS and SD in the police district had unlimited power over the citizens of Warsaw, and they had felt all but invincible. As a result they were enraged by the attacks that broke over the city on 1 August 1944. But they quickly learned that it was one thing to round up unarmed civilians and murder them in cellars and prisons; it was quite another to face an enemy that was actually fighting back.

Banditen in Warsaw

News that something untoward was happening in Warsaw came in over the radio just after 5 o'clock in the afternoon of 1 August. General Stahel found himself in the embarrassing position of being locked in the Brühl Palace, surrounded by attacking '*Banditen*', with no way out. He announced a state of siege and commandeered all military, SS, police and other German offices to do 'whatever necessary' to keep order. Ludwig Hahn recalled: 'We immediately began to arrange our defence. Everybody, leaders and men alike, seized their weapons. We set up a heavy machine

gun in the doorway.'[9] Oberdienstleiter Tiessler sent a telegram to
Martin Bormann saying there had been some 'incidents' in
Warsaw and that a few police posts had been attacked, as had the
post office. 'So far it appears we are dealing with Communist
rebels as they have red armbands,' it read.

Himmler was informed at 5.30, but the facts were sketchy; half
an hour later Koppe called Geibel from Kraków complaining that
Himmler was irritated and 'wants answers'. The police unit
commanders met at the headquarters of the Ordnungspolizei and
waited for information. While Stahel paced angrily in the Brühl
Palace, Geibel cowered in the basement of Aleja Szucha 53,
listening to the battle raging outside. Neither really knew what
was happening. Geibel was particularly frightened when he
learned that the Poles had taken the SS casino next door. He
demanded – and got – the immediate back-up of a Wehrmacht
company as well as four Tiger and one Panther tank from the
Waffen SS Viking Division. He also managed to get the megaphones working, and called on the citizens of Warsaw to turn
their backs on the 'criminal and mad' people who were leading
the revolt. He added that if shots were fired from a building 'it
will be demolished'. The Poles ignored him. Stahel ordered Geibel
to stage a counter-attack from the police district to free him from
the Brühl Palace. The Germans tried to get to him via Nowy
Świat, but Polish platoons threw grenades at the columns, setting
the tanks on fire; their crews managed to retreat, but they were
badly burned, and most died. The remaining Germans abandoned
their vehicles and ran for their lives; some hid in Marszałkowska
118–129 and were later captured. Geibel and Stahel agreed that
it was too dangerous for troops to move through the city without
reinforcements. Stahel reported this to the 9th Army, and
requested a rescue as soon as possible.

General von Vormann, who had only recently been made

commander of the 9th Army, responsible for the Warsaw district, was stationed in the nearby little town of Skierniewice when a telegram arrived from Stahel at 6 p.m. informing him that 'organized disturbances' had broken out in the capital. After a series of reports, one reaching him by motorcycle courier from Wola, he called an all-night staff meeting which concluded that 'the revolt of the Polish bands should be put down by the police because the army is in such a difficult position'. General Helmuth Staedke, Chief of Staff of the 9th Army, disagreed. 'The position of the army will be compromised if the uprising is not put down [by us], especially as there are front-line units still in Warsaw – parts of Panzer Division Hermann Göring which is moving to the front, and the 19th Lower Saxon Division whose units fought in Radzymin . . . and the SS Viking Division which is moving to the front.'

Hans Frank argued that the army should have acted right away, as it had in the Praga district, where the uprising was quelled immediately. Instead of relying on the police and the SS, they should have sent the Panzers of the 2nd Battalion of the Hermann Göring Division or the 4th East Prussian 1st Regiment to the Brühl Palace; but they 'did nothing', and missed the 'Kampfsekunde' – the 'combat second' – which might have allowed them to stop the uprising in its tracks. 'The delay gave the Poles time to get organized,' and the Warsawians used it to build barricades throughout the city, making it extremely difficult for the Germans to move. It was this delay that led to the pointless lengthening of the uprising,' Frank concluded. He was correct in theory, but the reality was that no troops could be spared for Warsaw. At that very moment Walter Model was attacking the Red Army, using every available force, including the Totenkopf and Viking Waffen SS Divisions, and the Hermann Göring Division. It was this severe shortage of highly trained troops that led to the tragic use of special SS forces under Himmler's command to crush the Warsaw Uprising. In that sense, the timing could not have been worse for the people of the city.

The troops who had been caught by the uprising while detraining in Warsaw were desperate to get out as quickly as they could. These soldiers had no desire to get involved in Stalingrad-style street fighting, which the German infantrymen loathed. Model was scathing about the 'Bonzen' (bigshots) who had provoked the uprising in the first place: 'All these people who have led to this, through their corruption and their shameless treatment of the Polish people, should now clean up the mess. This is not a job for my troops.'[10] He was determined to get all his men out of the city as quickly as possible. On 3 August he told Heinz Reinefarth: 'Simply burn down the city 1,000 metres on both sides of the road. Show no consideration. Otherwise we will be unable to fight our way through.'

The situation was very dangerous for these troops. On 1 August a column of SS Totenkopf Tiger tanks had been attacked, and several were lost. The rest managed to get out across the Poniatowski Bridge and make their way to Radzymin, where they joined von dem Bach's old rival Herbert Gille of the Viking SS, who was headquartered in the little palace of Jaktory near Radzymin, now in the thick of some of the fiercest battles seen on Polish territory during the war.

The situation for the 2nd Battalion of the 1st Regiment of the Hermann Göring Division was more complicated, as they were trapped with twenty T-IV Panzers in the western district of Wola. One of the only AK successes in the district of Ochota was the capture at Barska Street of the Hermann Göring supply head-quarters, which had arrived on 31 July. The Hermann Göring men had no interest in talking to local Nazi officials, whom they considered to be corrupt shirkers who avoided facing the enemy at the front. They had no idea of the trouble that was brewing; indeed, most went out sightseeing on 1 August, and so were away from the barracks when the uprising broke out. When the AK stormed the building; the commanding officer was killed in the fighting.

The rest of the 2nd Battalion, under Generalmajor Wilhelm Schmalz, tried to break through to the Poniatowski Bridge on 2 August. The attack near Górczewska by the 3rd Battalion of the 2nd Parachute Panzer Grenadier Regiment, the 2nd Battalion Panzer Regiment of the Hermann Göring Division and the 4th Division of the Panzer Artillery Regiment reached a point only two hundred metres from the main defence position of the AK 'Parasol' Battalion, but the Poles pelted the heavy tanks' steel hulks with Molotov cocktails, and the Germans were forced to retreat. The next day they tried again, threading their way through residential streets which were blocked by barricades made of overturned trams, paving stones, iron gates and piles of earth. The Poles bombarded the tanks once again, and after numerous vain attempts to crush the barricades the Germans forced three hundred civilians to march next to the column of tanks, and to dismantle the barricades along the way. The Poles, afraid of hitting the innocent civilians, stopped throwing bombs and watched as the tanks crashed their way over the barricades in Chłodna and Barokowa Streets. The column turned into Towarowa Street and onto Jerusalem Avenue, where the tanks shelled the Train post office before heading towards the Poniatowski Bridge. When the Hermann Göring Division tanks finally reached it they released the civilians and headed to the eastern bank of the Vistula as fast as they could go. They rejoined the rest of the 1st and 2nd Regiments of the Hermann Göring Division under Oberst Kluge and Oberst von Necker at Radzymin, where they would help to defeat the Soviets.

Model Strikes Back

That battle saw ferocious fighting around Radzymin and Wołomin. Model's desire to get his troops out of Warsaw had been based on genuine need. The strength of the Germans' resistance surprised the Russians, who until then had been cutting through Army Group Centre like a hot knife through butter. On the night of 28–29 July the 29th Panzer Corps clashed with the Soviet 2nd Tank Army at Wołomin, the fighting so fierce that the noise could be heard in Warsaw. The Hermann Göring and 19th Panzer Divisions slammed into the 8th Guards Tank Corps and 3rd Tank Corps – among the German dead was Heinz Göring, the Reichsmarschall's nephew, who was killed in action on 29 July in the village of Pogorzel, east of Warsaw. The 3rd Tank Corps, already weakened by Model's earlier attacks, could not withstand the hammer blows meted out on 2 and 3 August – one anti-tank company alone reported destroying thirty-four tanks, a feat recorded in the 9th Army Daily Order. The 4th Panzer Division and SS Viking Panzer Division joined the battle, annihilating the 3rd Tank Corps and severely damaging the 8th Guards Tank Corps.

Model had achieved the near impossible by halting the Soviet advance into the Warsaw area. Two hundred and forty-three Soviet tanks had been completely destroyed, and over two hundred put out of action. Guderian realized the importance of the victory: 'During the period from 26 July to 8 August 1944 9th Army reported the capture of 603 prisoners and forty-one deserters, the destruction of 337 tanks and the capture of seventy guns, eighty anti-tank guns, twenty-seven mortars and 116 machine guns. Such figures are considerable, particularly when it is remembered that during the period in question 9th Army had been constantly withdrawing.'[11] More important, however, was that the counter-attack stopped the Soviets in their tracks:

'the Russians did not advance beyond the Vistula and we were consequently granted a short breathing spell'.

Model's gain was Warsaw's loss. The attack effectively foiled any plans the Soviets may have had for taking the city in early August; it would have been physically impossible for the Red Army to have reached it in the first days of the uprising. As Guderian put it, 'We Germans had the impression that it was our defence which halted the enemy rather than a Russian desire to sabotage the Warsaw Uprising.' Stalin quickly used this temporary setback on the front as an excuse to deny aid to the AK and the people of Warsaw. This effectively gave the Germans free rein to finish off the city as they wished.

As the Hermann Göring troops left Warsaw to get to the front, two battalions of the 4th Regiment of the East Prussian Grenadier Regiment and roughly a thousand troops with a Panzer unit brought in from Zegrze were ordered to try to restore order in Warsaw. These troops crossed the Poniatowski Bridge, entering the city on 3 August. The AK were not equipped for anti-tank warfare, and the Germans quickly captured Platoon 1139, which had tried to stop their crossing: all of the men were gathered together and executed. The tanks rolled forward into Jerusalem Avenue, firing at anything that moved. They took over the Bank BGK on what is now Rondo de Gaulle, and by evening had occupied Jerusalem Avenue from Nowy Świat to Marszałkowska, setting the buildings on either side of the street on fire. Despite their apparent success the Germans suffered heavy losses, and refused to stay in their positions at night. The regimental commander turned the National Museum into his headquarters. Four thousand innocent civilians were brought in as hostages; many would later be killed.

In those early days of the uprising the fate of those captured depended very much on chance. Civilians rounded up at Jerusalem

Avenue 19 were used as human shields, and forty men and two women were shot by the East Prussian Grenadiers. At Bracka 17, eleven men were taken out and shot. At the same time a group of men who had been rounded up at the corner of Marszałkowska Street were allowed to escape, thanks to a sympathetic Silesian soldier. There were other incidents of kindness. Maria Adamska remembered the Germans occupying her street on 3 August: 'A group of Polish men with raised hands stopped at our house. The Germans allowed us to give them food and shaving gear before they moved on.' When German troops appeared at Sabina Sebyłowa's building, a young girl came forward with her hands behind her neck as a sign of surrender. 'The German shouted at her to put her hands down as she might fall and hurt herself.'[12]

That evening the Poles captured the pastor of the 400th Battalion of the East Prussian Grenadiers, Walter Brunon Dolingkeit, who told his AK interrogators that the Germans had been ordered to kill all men, whether in or out of uniform, to remove women and children to safety, and to burn down the buildings on either side of Jerusalem Avenue. On 1 August Wehrmacht officer Hasso Krappe was with the Lower Saxon 19th Panzer Division at the Gdańsk railway station when they were shot at from nearby buildings. They arrested nine people, some of whom were wearing red-and-white armbands, but released them 'because we didn't know what to do with them'. They then got out of Warsaw as quickly as they could, 'happy not to have lost anyone'.[13] Wacław Nowowiejski of 'Żmija' Platoon remembered a strange quiet after the first attacks: 'The Germans did nothing. We were lazy. We went to the gardens in the neighbourhood to pick vegetables.'[14]

The Warsaw-based SS units, on the other hand, reacted more violently, committing mass murder from the first day. They were furious that the Poles had dared to challenge their authority, and lashed out in a bitter, furious rage. On 2 August twenty men from the fortified Stauferkaserne on Rakowiecka stormed the Jesuit monastery across the road, claiming to have heard shots coming from within. They herded the Father Superior and the priests into the boiler room, threw in grenades and shut the door. Father Alexander Kisiel had managed to hide: 'Terrible explosions followed. Bricks, plaster, wood and glass fly, and terrible cries ring out. As if in response the SS men stand in the doorway and spray bullets into the whirl of bodies which slowly becomes silent. After some time two German-speaking people came in looking for watches. I could hear pistol shots again. When silence fell the survivors fled. Thirty-five people died, including eight women and one little boy. The Germans poured petrol on the bodies and burned them.'[15]

On 1 August part of the 'Granat' Battalion attacked Mokotów prison and liberated around three hundred of the inmates, but the SS retook it the following day. Obersturmbannführer Martin Patz, notorious during the uprising for torturing and murdering civilians, gave the order to kill the remaining prisoners; after the war he was tried along with Karl Misling for the deaths of 794 prisoners, for which he was given a four-and-a-half-year gaol sentence. At the same time the SS murdered around five hundred civilians in Fort Mokotów. Geibel ordered the SS to comb through houses looking for AK suspects, and groups of SS fanned out from Rakowiecka Street and into the neighbourhood beyond. On 2 August they took 18–25 Madaliński Street, and began to shoot men in the streets and courtyards in plain view of the terrified residents. On 3 August the net was thrown wider still, and apartment buildings in a dozen streets in the area were stormed. Hundreds of men were hauled from the buildings and shot; a number of women and children unlucky enough to get caught up in the fray were also killed. Obersturmbannführer Dr Ludwig Hahn took command of a battalion of seven hundred SS men who murdered civilians on Aleja Szucha. This group would kill 2,000 people on that street alone during the uprising; Hahn shot many of them himself.

The AK fought back, and the German casualty rate began to climb, reaching over six hundred in the first two days. A number of SS officers were killed in the fighting, including members of the Criminal Police. It was a kind of justice: each one of them had actively participated in the crushing of the Ghetto Uprising sixteenth months before.[16]

The Germans had been aware of the planned uprising, yet their reaction in the first days of August was chaotic at best. The blame lay with Hitler. When he designated Warsaw a 'fortress city' on 27 July, he had meant it. There were to be no more rumblings about retreat, no more treasonous releases of prisoners, no more talk of giving ground to the Soviets, and certainly no tolerance of any 'Banditen' activity. Hitler had chosen Reiner Stahel to control Warsaw because, according to legend, he could cope with anything. In the Wolfsschanze, Guderian witnessed Hitler's absolute faith in this ascetic Austrian when Stahel was appointed to his new position: 'This general had become famous defending other fortresses and was perceived as a very strict and dynamic man who was able to liquidate such an uprising very quickly. I was present when Stahel got the order to suppress Warsaw. This was just before he departed for the city. Many formations which were already in Warsaw were put at his disposal.'[17]

Stahel had made his name as the Commandant of Rome and the 'Defender of Wilno', and had held ten of Hitler's 'fortress cities'.[18] He arrived in Warsaw only a short time before the uprising began, and had little chance to get to know the city. On 1 August his garrison numbered only 13,000 soldiers, rather than the 36,000 promised to him; as Hans Frank put it, 'the garrison existed only on paper'. Even Goebbels realized the danger, writing in his diary on 28 July: 'General Stahel has been given the task of holding Warsaw. But if he has no troops he can't do anything on his own any more than he could in Wilno.'[19]

Hitler's Rage

Hitler was informed that there might be trouble in the Polish capital, but he dismissed the threat. On the night before the uprising began he met General Walter Warlimont at the Wolfsschanze; the only thing he was interested in was Model's counter-attack against the Red Army east of Warsaw. He wanted to prove to the Turks and the Hungarians, the Romanians and the Bulgarians, that he was still in control. 'If they can be convinced that we can stick it out, they will not lift a finger.'[20] He did not mention Warsaw. When he was told the next day that the Poles had started an uprising he was furious, and determined that they would pay for their insolence. Hans Frank wrote in his diary that Secretary of State Dr Josef Bühler had passed on a message from Hitler. The Führer was 'very determined to suppress the uprising by all possible means', he said.[21]

Hitler was, by now, quite deranged. The Führer had been much more affected by the 20 July attempt on his life, both physically and mentally, than Goebbels' propaganda allowed, and was bent on revenge against all of his enemies, real or imagined. On the day the uprising broke out Hitler's doctor wrote of 'Patient A' that his condition was 'still dominated by injuries suffered on 20 July', and that blood was seeping through the skin on his arms and buttocks.[22] Stuck in the unhealthy gloom of Rastenburg, the damp rooms filled with the drone of the air-conditioning, the windows closed because of the plagues of mosquitoes and midges, he was going ever more mad.

The 20 July plot had other consequences too. Along with his customary porridge and two thick slices of bread, Hitler's breakfast now consisted of an ever increasing number of pills taken with a glass of orange juice – his 'anti-gas' tablets alone contained half a gram of strychnine, half a gram of deadly nightshade, and one gram of gentian. As a response to the pain caused by his injuries, he was now being administered cocaine by Dr Giesing under Dr Morell's watchful eye. 'It's as if I am not ill at all,' Hitler said after his treatment, later joking that he hoped he was not turning into a drug addict.

Everyone who visited Hitler in those early days of August commented on his decline. Warlimont said that 'it seemed as if the shock had brought into the open all the evil of his nature, both physical and psychological. He came into the map room bent and shuffling. His glassy eyes gave a sign of recognition only to those who stood closest to him . . . On the slightest occasion he would demand shrilly that "the guilty" be hunted down.'[23] Erich Hartmann, who was to end the war as the highest-scoring fighting ace in history, saw the Führer on 3 August. 'Hitler was not the same man. This was just after the bomb plot to kill him, and his right arm was shaking, and he looked exhausted. He had to turn his left ear to hear anyone speak because he was deaf in the other one from the blast.' During the conversation Hitler attacked the quality of his generals, saying again that they were the reason for failure on the front and adding that 'God had spared his life so that he could deliver Germany from destruction.'[24] Guderian complained that 'the deep distrust he already felt for mankind in general, and for General Staff Corps officers and generals in particular, now became profound hatred'.[25]

It was this angry, suspicious man who was given the news of

the uprising on that muggy summer evening of 1 August. At times like this, Guderian recalled. Hitler seemed to lose all self-control: 'His fists raised, his cheeks flushed with rage, his whole body trembling . . . He was almost screaming, his eyes seemed about to pop out of his head and the veins stood out on his temples.'[26] Guderian would watch Hitler lose his temper over Warsaw a number of times, particularly after being briefed by Himmler and Fegelein.[27]

Germans were being attacked all over the Polish capital by well-organized and armed 'Banditen'; worse still, this was happening just as Model was attacking the Soviets, at a time when Hitler wanted to appear strong and in control. The events unfolding in Warsaw might threaten supply lines to the front; they might also lead to an uprising throughout Poland and inspire 'Banditen' elsewhere. Furthermore, they were a painful, urgent reminder that Hitler was losing his grip over his 'Lebensraum'. It was one thing to be forced to abandon some far-off Russian village, but it was quite another to have to relinquish the territory over which he had gone to war. There was no doubt that 'Fortress Warsaw' must be held against the Soviets 'at any cost', but in order to do this Hitler had to crush the uprising. And for this he turned not to Guderian and his generals, but to Heinrich Himmler.

For Himmler, the July plot and its bloody aftermath had been a blessing in disguise. The Reichsführer SS had been trying for years to increase his power over his rivals in the Wehrmacht, and at last he had a chance. On 3 August he wrote in his diary that Hitler believed that the generals were to blame for all the failures on the Eastern Front: 'The generals are not opposed to the Führer because we are experiencing crises at the front. Rather, we are experiencing crises at the front because the generals are opposed to the Führer.'[28] As a reward for his loyalty, Hitler gave Himmler the military promotion he had longed for, in the form of command of the Reserve Army. He was also given control of the Abwehr and of the V-weapons installations, most notably that at Peenemünde. Himmler wanted more, however, and the Warsaw Uprising gave him the opportunity he needed to prove his military credentials.

Himmler had also misjudged the AK in Warsaw; indeed, he had been so confident that it would do nothing that on 17 July he had sent the 22nd Police and SS units based in the city to the Eastern Front, and had even ordered Colonel Haring's experienced street-fighting police unit to Grodno.[29] Ernst Rode, the chief of Hitler's personal staff, testified at Nuremberg that SS Gruppenführer Koppe had shown him, Himmler and Guderian the so-called IC secret report which included counter-intelligence information about potential unrest in Warsaw. 'They did not try to stop the uprising,' Rode claimed, 'because Himmler was deeply convinced that given the situation it would not break out.'[30] According to Rode, on hearing of the uprising Himmler 'immediately sent a telegram to the commander of KL Sachsenhausen' with the order to kill General Stefan Rowecki. He then rushed to see Hitler.

Hitler was still raging in the Wolfsschanze, in a state of delirium. Himmler tried to calm him down. 'My Führer,' he said, 'the timing is unfortunate, but from a historical perspective what the Poles are doing is a blessing. After five, six weeks we shall leave. But by then Warsaw, the capital, the head, the intelligence of this former 16–17 million Polish people will be extinguished, this *Volk* that has blocked our way to the east for seven hundred years and has stood in our way ever since the First Battle of Tannenberg [in 1410]. After this the Polish problem will no longer be a great historical problem for the children who come after us, nor indeed will it be for us.'

Himmler's words clearly made an impression on Hitler, who

used very similar phrases in the following weeks. In a talk with General-Leutnants Westphal and Krebs on 31 August he would argue that he had to carry on the fight until there was 'a peace tolerable for Germany which will safeguard the existence of this and future generations'. And later that same day he stated that he was trying to 'secure the life of the German nation for the next fifty or one hundred years'. But the earlier exchange made it quite clear that both Hitler and Himmler now believed that the war was lost. The crushing of the Warsaw Uprising had nothing to do with military victory; it had to do with the racial future of Germany. One thing was clear: the new Europe would not contain a city called Warsaw. The Polish capital was to be totally destroyed.

Hitler and Himmler discussed how to accomplish this task as if it were a normal military operation. Hitler's first idea was to 'remove all German forces from Warsaw to the outlying areas', and then 'with mass use of all aircraft of Army Group Centre including communications aircraft' to 'raze Warsaw to the ground and crush the centre of the uprising'. He demanded an audience with General-Leutnant Robert Ritter von Greim, the First World War flying ace and last commander of the Luftwaffe. Von Greim told Hitler that the plan was unworkable, as there were too many Germans trapped in the city who would also be killed; furthermore, he lacked the resources for such an operation. Hitler would have to find another way.

Guderian claimed that he had put himself forward for the task of retaking the city. Warsaw, after all, was firmly in the Defence Zone of the 9th Army, and according to the internal order of General von Vormann, General Major Gunter Rohr had already been nominated to the position of Army Kommandant and been given a fine set of rooms in the Saski Palace as his headquarters. However, Guderian reported that Hitler was in no mood to listen to him, not least because his troops were fighting in Model's counter-offensive. Guderian claimed that he 'requested that Warsaw be included in the military zone of operation; but the ambitions of Governor-General Frank and the Reichsführer SS Himmler prevailed with Hitler'. As a result of this in-fighting, 'the Reichsführer SS was made responsible for crushing the uprising'.[31] Himmler had won.

The Order for Warsaw

On 1 August 1944 Hitler and Himmler released their now infamous Order for Warsaw, which stands as one of the most barbaric documents of the war. Ernst Rode testified at Nuremberg on 28 January 1946 that he had seen a pencil-written copy of this terrible order. 'Every citizen of Warsaw is to be killed including men, women and children,' it read. 'Warsaw has to be levelled to the ground in order to set a terrifying example to the rest of Europe.'[32] The order clearly stated that 'no matter how the Poles will behave, even if they behave according to international law', the judgement was 'final'. In short, Hitler and Himmler had decided to slaughter the inhabitants of an entire European city, and then to remove all traces of its existence. Quite apart from its vindictiveness, the idea was sheer madness. For one thing, it was unlikely that such a crime could remain hidden from the eyes of the world. The Nazis had murdered hundreds of thousands of innocent Jews in or near cities and towns earlier in the war, but they had been in complete control of those territories at the time, and had favoured extermination camps for killing on such a scale so close to home – even when liquidating the Warsaw ghetto they had murdered their victims in the top-secret confines of Treblinka rather than in the less deniable pits and shallow graves favoured in far-off Byelorussia.

To order the annihilation of the population of an entire city in broad daylight so close to the front and so late in the war was insane. But as Guderian said, Hitler had by now completely lost his sense of proportion. It was his madness that accounted for the 'very harsh orders for the prosecution of the fighting and for the treatment of Warsaw'.[33]

It was Himmler, however, who added that all the inhabitants of the city should be killed. In his conversation with Stahel on 27 July, Hitler had said that in the event of an uprising the city should be crushed using great force, and that men who sympathized with the uprisers were to be killed. Women, however, were to be sent to work, and children were to be spared.[34] On 1 August Hitler told Himmler that the city was to be completely destroyed.[35] Von dem Bach testified at Nuremberg to Himmler's contribution: 'The order to level Warsaw to the ground was the Führer Order, while the order referring to the civilians and participants of the uprising came from Himmler.'[36] Bach claimed that on 5 August he met Reinefarth, who told him that he had been given 'a clear order that he is not allowed to take PoWs and that every inhabitant of Warsaw must be killed . . . women and children also'.[37] This order had come from Himmler. This helps to explain why, in the first days of the uprising, before the order was known, so many civilians were spared. The mass murder started in earnest only after Himmler's order had reached Reinefarth and others.

This was not the first time that Hitler had threatened the destruction of a metropolis. Paris was spared in 1940 because he decided that his new Berlin – 'Germania' – would be even more imposing than its French counterpart. Hitler revisited the idea of flattening Paris in August 1944, telling Model that 'in all history the loss of Paris has meant the loss of France'. As a result, 'the first signs of revolt are to be harshly put down, by blowing up entire street blocks, by public execution of the ringleaders, or by evacuation of any districts involved, as only this will stop things getting out of hand. The Seine bridges are to be prepared for demolition. Paris must not fall into enemy hands – or if it does, then only as a field of ruins.'[38]

Leningrad and Moscow, too, were to have been levelled and their populations starved to death. Rudolf-Christoph Freiherr von Gersdorff, a counter-espionage officer for Army Group Centre, recorded a visit by Professor Franz Six of Einsatzgruppe B to Borissow in July 1941: 'He reported that Hitler meant to create the eastern border of the Reich at the Baku–Stalingrad–Moscow line. To the east a fire-strip would be created in which all life was to be wiped out. Around thirty million Russians were to die by hunger through the removal of all food from this huge area. Anyone taking part in this action would be forbidden under the punishment of death to give even a piece of bread to a Russian. The big cities from Leningrad to Moscow were to be levelled to the ground; head of SS von dem Bach-Zelewski would be responsible for the execution of these measures.'[39] Many of the ancient and beautiful settlements in Ukraine and Byelorussia were likewise to be destroyed; Minsk was to be rebuilt as a mock German village. On 5 October 1941 Alfred Rosenberg's adjutant Werner Koeppen was invited to dine with Hitler. Himmler, who had just returned from a tour of the east, told the gathering that in Kiev the people looked poor and proletarian, and that 'we could easily dispense with 80 or 90 per cent of them'. It was only the defeat in the east that prevented Hitler from carrying out these terrible plans.

Warsaw was different. Now, finally, the Führer had the chance to fulfil his dream, and it clearly excited him. Himmler boasted that after his conversation with Hitler on 1 August, 'I . . . gave orders for Warsaw to be totally destroyed. You may think of me as a terrible barbarian. I am, if you like, but only if I have to be. My orders were that we were to burn down and blow up every block of houses.'[40] Hitler had some idea what this would entail: when looking at aerial photographs of Warsaw with Guderian and Fegelein during a military conference a month later, he pointed to the ruins of the ghetto, which Jewish slave labourers had been forced to clear since May 1943. This area was to become a large park, which the Reichsführer SS had modestly decided to call 'Himmler Park'.[41] 'For the ghetto, my Führer, it took us I believe a half a year,' Fegelein said, grossly underestimating the time it had taken to clear the shattered streets.[42]

The generals did not object to the Order for Warsaw. But after the war a wave of collective amnesia swept over them; indeed, if one were to rely on the self-serving memoirs and autobiographies that appeared in the 1950s and '60s in both Germany and the Soviet Union, one would be forgiven for thinking that the Warsaw Uprising had not happened at all. One of the most creative in this respect was Guderian. When reminded at Nuremberg of the order to destroy Warsaw, he answered that at times it was 'very difficult to recognize if an order which we got was against international law . . . it is also difficult for generals because they didn't study international law'. Asked what made an order requiring his troops to shoot women and children difficult to understand with regard to international law, he replied that, indeed, according to the Codex Paragraph 47, the order 'should not have been obeyed'. Later in the trial, Guderian claimed that he had not heard about the order until after the war. This was a lie. The prosecutor read him Hans Frank's diary entry stating: 'Guderian said to the General Governor that he gave his assurance that everything will be done to come with help for Warsaw [i.e. to free the trapped German troops] – and then the verdict [Hitler's order] will be passed ruthlessly.' Guderian retorted that he had 'never used the word "verdict" '. Later he changed his story again, admitting that he had indeed heard Hitler say that Warsaw was to be destroyed, but adding, 'I thought it was only a metaphor.' This too was untrue. At the military conference in the Wolfsschanze on 1 September 1944, Guderian complained to Hitler about the problems his troops were encountering while fighting in Warsaw; Hitler suggested that the Luftwaffe drop mines on the buildings to destroy AK hiding places and help the men on the ground. Guderian knew perfectly well that Hitler's order was not a metaphor.[43]

The reality was that by issuing this fateful order, Hitler and Himmler had turned the Warsaw Uprising into an integral part of the racial war which was being carried out with utter ruthless-ness throughout occupied Europe. Despite the shrinking of the Reich and the approach of the Red Army, at this point in the war Himmler was still working around the clock to eliminate his racial enemies while he still had time, and in particular to exterminate the remaining European Jews. Anne Frank was arrested on 4 August 1944, the Łódź ghetto was liquidated on the same day, and Hungarian Jews were still being transported to Auschwitz during the conflict. Any sane commander would have put all his resources into the decisive battles at the front, but both Hitler and Himmler continued to expend time and energy on their murderous racial policy, attempting to 'cleanse' Europe before the Soviets and the Western Allies took over. The destruction of Warsaw became part of this SS war, and an extension of the 'Banditenkrieg' which it had so recently been forced to abandon in Byelorussia. Himmler mounted a massive 'Sonderaktion' in what was to become the only major German ground combat operation run almost completely by the SS in the whole of the Second World War.[44] And he had just the men for the job.

The Appointments

In an isolated patch of forest sixty-five kilometres north of Rastenburg lies a strange set of ruins, with massive, moss-covered hunks of concrete jutting out of the ground like the vertebrae of some prehistoric monster. This complex of bunkers and huts may have been smaller than the Wolfsschanze, but it was of vital importance. It was known as Hochwald, and was Himmler's headquarters in East Prussia and the nerve centre of the racial war in the east. On the night before the uprising Himmler held a special meeting in his dank concrete quarters. He invited Colonel General Heinz Guderian and Erich von dem Bach, who later claimed that this was his first ever meeting with the great commander. Himmler's colleagues from Byelorussia were together again, too. Curt von Gottberg came with his underlings Bronisław Kaminski and Oskar Dirlewanger, and there were toasts all around when Kaminski was promoted to the ranks of Brigadeführer SS and General Major.[45] After the war, Guderian denied that he had been there that night.

The real purpose of the meeting was to find von dem Bach and his henchmen something to do. The portly hypochondriac was becoming desperate; on 15 July he had written a melancholy letter to his wife complaining that he was 'still sitting in Gansenstein' like a 'pensioner without a job', reduced to swimming and going for long walks through the summer fields, and musing that it was 'unbelievable that the Bolsheviks will soon be speeding through here'.[46] Von dem Bach's greatest fear was that he would end the war in semi-retirement, and would therefore be denied a position of importance in the post-war administration which he, like many top Nazis, desperately wanted to be part of. He had been pushing Himmler to create a *Kampfgruppe* so that he could take up the fight in Poland, but to his annoyance the decision was delayed until the situation at the front became clear.[47] For weeks he had been pressing Himmler for an appointment. The Warsaw Uprising solved his problem.

Von dem Bach was lounging in a deckchair in the pretty seaside resort of Sopot on 2 August, watching the waves wash over the shore, when he was called to the telephone. He would later tell his wife that he had been in exactly the same place, doing exactly the same thing, in 1914 when he had been called to go immediately to Berlin at the start of the First World War. This time he was told that there was a great 'Schweinerei in the GG' – a great mess in the General Government. He was to return from his vacation at once. Bach left Sopot immediately, and met Himmler on 4 August in Kraków, where he was put in charge of the suppression of the uprising. His career was looking up.

At the Nuremberg trials von dem Bach lied about the timing of his appointment in order to distance himself from the crimes committed in the early days of the uprising. 'I think if I can well remember that it was around mid-August' that he was asked to 'take over the leadership in the fight against the uprising', he said. He put the responsibility for the first two weeks of fighting squarely on General Stahel's shoulders. The truth is rather different. Bach recorded in his diary, which was not available at Nuremberg, that he was appointed on 4 August 1944, and that he arrived in Warsaw not in the middle of the month, but the very next day.

He did admit at Nuremberg to knowing the contents of Hitler's order to destroy the city. On 26 January 1946 he was asked, 'Did Hitler and Himmler gave you an order to suppress the uprising at any cost?' 'Yes, sir,' he replied. 'Did you get this order orally or by telegraph?' 'Verbally, on the telephone.'[48]

Himmler and Hitler both considered von dem Bach an obvious

choice for this unpleasant and difficult task. He had proven himself the consummate 'bandit hunter' in Byelorussia, and they wanted a tough and experienced killer. Ernst Rode said at Nuremberg: 'I think that Hitler and also Guderian wanted von dem Bach to conduct a Warsawian massacre . . . Bach was perceived as a very strict officer, and they counted that he would ruthlessly suppress the uprising. They thought that only the nearness of the [German] army might be an obstacle – which was in fact a reason that Bach didn't report to the Wehrmacht.'[49] In his diary von dem Bach griped that the Warsaw posting was probably another '*Himmelfahrtskommando*' – suicide mission – like his stint in Kowel some months before. He had managed to get out of that tricky situation by claiming that he had to have a haemorrhoid operation, and had left Herbert Gille and the Viking SS to defend the Kowel pocket alone. Hitler had been so angry that he had only allowed Himmler to give Bach the lowly Bandenkampfabzeichen in bronze on 3 July 1944, for having served twenty-eight days in combat. It had been a demeaning put-down.[50] Gille, on the other hand, received his Knight's Cross in April 1944, and would soon become the most highly decorated Waffen SS officer in the war.[51]

Von dem Bach pretended that Hitler's snub had meant little, but this vain, self-pitying man makes it clear in his diary that he thought his treatment had been unfair. He hoped that the uprising would give him the chance to redeem himself. Any sign of praise from the Führer was eagerly lapped up; he was delighted when Fegelein came to see him on 13 August and told him that Hitler had 'sent his personal greetings and recognition to me'. Two days later, after talking to Himmler, he boasted: 'I am now Commander General of the Warsaw Area [*Kommandierender General im Raum Warschau*], everything is under me, Wehrmacht, SS, police and civilian administration.' Furthermore, he said proudly that

'Himmler has again promised me the Knight's Cross when Warsaw is conquered.'[52]

The forces under von dem Bach's command were already considerable when he took over on 4 August. Himmler had ordered a number of units be transferred to Warsaw, including some of von dem Bach's most brutal and experienced anti-partisan fighters from Byelorussia, under the command of the cruel SS Gruppenführer Heinz Reinefarth. On 2 August Himmler had flown to Poznań to talk to the Gauleiter of the Wartheland (the western zone of Nazi-occupied Poland) Artur Greiser and the Commandant of 21 Military District General Walter Petzel. He ordered that a police group be sent to Warsaw, consisting of two and a half companies of motorized police, a company of motorized gendarmerie and a company of SS soldiers. A battalion of cadets from the 5th Officer Infantry School under the command of Major Reck was also sent, along with the 608th Army Security Regiment. The 3rd Regiment of Cossacks and 572 Battalion of Cossacks were ordered to follow, although there were very few cossacks amongst them; many were simply Russians who had deserted to the German side – the title 'cossacks' was an attempt to romanticize their origins and make them racially acceptable in the German army. Von dem Bach remembered, 'the commander of the Cossacks of 9th Army 3rd Regiment was an ex-White Russian officer, a complete alcoholic'. Their battle value was 'low', and they had a tendency to drink to excess and 'little understanding of military discipline'. This was true, too, of the Kaminski Brigade – also known as SS Sturm Brigade RONA – which was made up of Russian defectors. Indeed, around half of the Nazi forces sent to fight in Warsaw were not ethnic Germans, but Azeris, Russians and some Ukrainians (the Poles mistakenly blamed the latter almost entirely). Many were deeply hostile to the Poles, and treated them accordingly.

Himmler had managed to gather this motley collection of SS and police units, criminals and foreign nationals from all over the Reich at the last minute, and the vindictive nature of their task was apparent from the beginning. A German fireman from Köpenick testified after the war that Himmler had personally ordered his unit to go to Warsaw on 2 August not to put out fires, but to light them.[53] The real purpose of the mission was made abundantly clear by the inclusion of the most ominous name on the list, that of Oskar Dirlewanger. He and his men had been recovering in the town of Łyck, near Rastenburg in East Prussia, after their unseemly rout from Byelorussia. Himmler personally ordered Dirlewanger to go to the Polish capital, adding two units of Azeri collaborators to his brigade.

Dirlewanger's forces started to arrive in Warsaw on 4 August, an advance guard of one battalion with 365 men. Two more battalions, a submachine-gun company, a mortar company and an anti-tank company followed. In all the regiment had sixteen officers, 865 men and a detachment of 677 Azerbaijani troops by the time it was ready to move on Warsaw.

On the same day an officer from the Hermann Göring Division, which had been 'on loan' to General Reinefarth for one day, approached Dr Leon Manteuffel and the director of the Wolski hospital Professor Zeyland, a world-renowned specialist in the treatment of tuberculosis. 'We are about to leave and are not going to do anything to you,' the officer said, 'but the SS groups are coming, and the situation will be terrible.' He urged the doctors and anyone who could walk to get away as quickly as possible, and to hide. But where could they go? Hitler had thrown a ring of steel around Warsaw, and nobody, not even women or children, was allowed to leave; those who tried were shot.

The officer had been telling the truth. Within hours, Professor

Zeyland was lying dead on the floor of his office, having been killed by one of Dirlewanger's men. Unlike so many doctors, patients and staff in his hospital, Dr Manteuffel would narrowly escape execution. He would live to write one of the most moving testimonies of the uprising. The terror had begun.

7

THE MASSACRE IN WOLA

Do not defile your reputation by an act so horrible to do and to hear, and which you will be the first in all history to perform.
(Chapter XII)

Reinefarth Begins

The murders in the Wola district of Warsaw on 5 August 1944 constitute the largest single battlefield massacre of the Second World War. The death toll was so catastrophically high because the Germans who attacked the innocent people of the city wanted it that way. This was not, as Heinz Reinefarth would later claim, a simple military operation designed to clear a transportation route through a large city. On the contrary, it was an SS-led 'Aktion' meant to punish, to terrorize and to kill the population of a district of Warsaw as a deterrent to the rest of the city. The brutal destruction of life and property was also meant to send a clear message to any other would-be rebels in occupied Europe not even to contemplate attacking their German masters.

The self-important Hans Frank was in his office in the Wawel Castle bright and early on the morning of 5 August. He was in a cheerful mood. The attack on the '*Banditen*' of Warsaw was set to begin at last – five days too late, in his view, but still better than nothing. At 8.05 he sent a telegram to Reich Minister Lammers predicting imminent victory: 'The German special groups will begin their operation today at 10 a.m. in three places,' he said, getting the time hopelessly wrong. 'We can be sure that the uprising will be suppressed in the next few days.'[1]

Himmler, too, was happy. The trusted 'anti-bandit fighter' Erich von dem Bach-Zelewski was on his way to the city; in the meantime, thousands of troops were massing on the western edge of Wola under SS General Heinz Reinefarth.

Reinefarth seemed every bit the quintessential SS officer, with piercing blue eyes, a prominent duelling scar and an emotionless although rather high-pitched voice. He had started army service in the 1920s in the Freikorps, before joining the Nazi Party in 1932. He had fought in Poland and France, and in 1942 he joined Himmler's staff. Following the 20 July plot, after demonstrating his unstinting loyalty to Hitler, he was made Higher Police and SS Leader for the Wartheland. On 1 August Himmler promoted him again, to coincide with his new assignment in Warsaw. He was now Gruppenhführer SS and General Police Lieutenant. Von dem Bach was jealous of Reinefarth's rank, and of his very close personal relationship with Himmler. 'He was overpromoted,' he griped after the war.

Reinefarth was less confident than his masters about the timing of the attack on Warsaw. Not all the troops had arrived by 5 August, and the city was in turmoil; he proposed to wait another day. But General von Vormann of the 9th Army insisted that the attack start immediately, as he had just learned that the Soviets were bypassing Praga and heading south, threatening the worsening situation at the Magnuszew bridgehead. He desperately needed to keep the west–east connection open through Warsaw.

It was von Vormann who gave the order to attack Warsaw on 5 August.[2]

A two-pronged attack was developed from the west, with the intention to push through the Warsaw suburbs and reach the Vistula in two days. The Kaminski Brigade was to be sent in from the Ochota district via Jerusalem Avenue to the Poniatowski Bridge, while Reinefarth's Kampfgruppe of 4,000 men was to attack Wola and drive through Plac Piłsudski to the Kierbedź Bridge. Reinefarth divided his force into three groups – the first under Schmidt in the north, the second under Reck in the centre, and the third under Dirlewanger in the south. Kampfgruppe Reinefarth spent the early hours of that Saturday assembling on the western edge of town. Most Warsawians woke up on the sunny morning still hopeful that the Soviets were coming, and that their ordeal would soon be over. Their hopes would quickly be shattered in what turned out to be one of the most terrible days of World War II.

Reinefarth's orders were clear. According to von dem Bach, the General was given instructions by Himmler personally. They read: '1. Captured insurgents ought to be killed regardless of whether they are fighting in accordance with the Hague Convention or not. 2. The part of the population not fighting, women and children, should likewise be killed. 3. The whole town must be levelled to the ground, i.e. houses, streets, offices – everything that is in the town.'[3]

Reinefarth had made sure his troops were psychologically primed for the task. As they arrived in Warsaw they were told about innocent Germans who had been attacked and killed by the 'Banditen'. The people of Warsaw had started this fight, he said, and had brought retribution on themselves. A rabid hatred was whipped up, so that even children were seen as 'guilty'; soldiers were told that they were expected to fight against the entire population, because all were to blame. The message was everywhere: the Nazi newspaper the *Volkische Beobachter* claimed that Warsawians had developed an 'underhanded' way of fighting, as they were dressed 'partly in German uniforms to confuse the soldiers and to sow chaos'. There was no mention of the fact that the Poles were only wearing German uniforms because they were not allowed to have their own. 'Because they behave in ways which do not respect international law they are outlaws.'[4] This theory of collective guilt took deep hold, and many Warsawians went to their deaths being told that they deserved their punishment.

Even so, there was great confusion even amongst the Germans who were trying to justify what they were doing. A Viennese doctor told Dr Kubica at the Karol and Maria hospital: 'You are angry because of what we are doing, but you are wrong. We were cruel in Russia. We are not being cruel here.'[5] On the other hand, a German soldier yelled to a young girl just before she was killed: 'German women and children are dying because of you, so you must also die!'[6] A group of civilians forced to wait in a warehouse prior to their execution were silenced by an SS soldier who fired his pistol into the air. This time the Soviets were invoked: 'You are all *Banditen!*' he yelled in Polish. 'You have attacked the Reich even though Hitler was trying to protect you from Bolshevism!' Some had a more simple message. When Dr Joanna Kryńska was being marched, as she thought, to her death, Reinefarth's staff doctor Major Hartlieb told her, 'There is a Himmler Order to execute all Poles in Warsaw no matter of age or sex, and Warsaw is to be erased to show the rest of Europe what it means to rise against the Germans.'[7] None of the Germans in command appear to have asked themselves why, when the war was nearly over, they returned to the Polish capital not merely to clear the important transportation routes to the east for their troops, but to annihilate the population and to erase the city from the map.

On the contrary, there was an element of self-pity in the German attitude, with soldiers angry that the Poles had 'forced' them to act in this way. When Dr Manteuffel was sent to a makeshift hospital in Wola on 5 August, 'a tall middle-aged army doctor from the Wehrmacht, with light blond hair and a handsome, serious face, said: "Dear colleagues, why are you doing all of this when the war is almost over?" ' Reiner Stahel, however, had no illusions. Whilst in captivity in Moscow in 1945 he wrote: 'I want to state that the responsibility for the suffering which was inflicted upon Warsaw civilians rests not only with Germans but also with the Home Army leaders who triggered civilians into a fight which was destined to fail. They did it to achieve their selfish aims.' He added as an afterthought: 'I couldn't stop the repression of German soldiers against Polish civilians. The problem was, he did not want to stop the repression. It was part of the overall plan.

The Germans had chosen non-German troops who were likely to be particularly hostile to the Poles. At Nuremberg Ernst Rode admitted that SS and police units had deliberately been used to crush the uprising and to do 'the dirty work' so as to spare the Wehrmacht. 'Dirlewanger and the eastern volunteers' were used on purpose 'to save valuable German blood'. This, he said, was confirmed in an order sent to H. Gepp at Army Group Centre.[8]

For his part, Reinefarth approached the problem with the cold-ness of a logician. 'It was clear when I arrived in Warsaw that orders to crush the uprising in forty-eight hours were impossible to fulfil because the entire population had been "zum Kampf gerustet" ' – armed for battle. He later claimed that his only action had been to 'fight to free up one or two streets through to the Vistula', the transportation artery that ran from west to east, part of a nearly 2,000-kilometre line from Berlin to Moscow. He failed to mention the special orders he had received from Himmler in the first days of August.

German staff officer Hans Thieme, a law professor and a captain in the 203rd Division in charge of intelligence, was assigned to Oberst Schmidt's Sicherheitsregiment 608 under Reinefarth on 2 August, and saw Reinefarth in action during the uprising.[9] Thieme thought Reinefarth a truly evil man. He was first and foremost a technocrat, he said, elegant, refined and handsome, but with no iota of remorse for the lives he was taking. When faced with hundreds of Warsawians being led to their deaths, Reinefarth was annoyed because they were getting in his way; but it did not occur to him to stop the killing. 'There was Reinefarth, this elegant officer with the Knight's Cross and wonderful manners who said: "Look at this, gentlemen, these refugees are our biggest problem. We don't have enough ammunition to kill all of them." He was completely calm, and just shrugged his shoulders.'[10]

The *Aktion* began at 7 a.m., in an orgy of violence. Artillery fire and explosions ripped through the air as the Germans unleashed the attack on Wolska Street, or Litzmannstadtstrasse, as the Germans then called it. 'Finally we moved to the unhappy capital city,' Thieme remembered. 'The police blocked all the roads and only the army were allowed to enter. We had already heard that terrible things were going on, and all the detonations and fires were a hint.'[11] Schmidt's Sicherheitsregiment moved towards the northern cemeteries. A group of three motorized police companies entered the city to the south of them, while two Dirlewanger battalions and an Azerbaijani battalion moved up Wolska Street. The Germans pushed into the four square kilometres of Wola, with its apartment buildings, factories, workshops, tram depot, dozens of stables, and large Catholic, Jewish, Evangelical and Calvinist cemeteries. They were urged on by their commanders: '*Schneller! Los!*'

A young Wehrmacht soldier, Matthias Schenk, remembered

the first moments of battle: 'When we entered Warsaw the Poles were shooting but not visible' Despite the danger, he was ordered to move forward. 'We jumped through the broken window of a house and noticed a woman and a man lying dead. They had been shot in the forehead.' When they stormed the first houses they saw 'civilians lying everywhere, women and children all shot in the head'. Part of Schenk's battalion ran into Polish positions; some lorries were burned and a number of his colleagues were killed. 'Few of us believed in victory by now. There were some fanatics – young Hitler Youth guys – but they were shot like field hares.' But men like Schenk had no choice other than to fight: 'I had to kill otherwise I would have been killed. But I can never forget,' he said. 'It is not easy to shoot a person or to kill someone at close quarters. In Warsaw we fought one-on-one in houses and cellars and sewers. It was hell.'

The attack came as a shock to the civilians of Wola; indeed, when the firing started some thought it heralded the beginning of a Soviet breakthrough. The reality quickly set in, as the horrified residents watched as building after building was surrounded and destroyed. Twelve-year-old Jerzy Jankowski was in his home with his mother and two siblings when the Germans arrived at the building next door. 'The sight was terrifying. The fear paralyzed us and took our breath away. Over a dozen soldiers ran into the building and began looting. Then shots were fired and there was shouting: "*Raus! Wychodzitie skorej!* ['Get out!' in Russian] *Schnell!*" All the people in the house ran to the exit, where they were again given orders: "*Hände hoch! Ruki wierch! Pod stienku!* ['Hands up! Against the wall!' in Russian]" A line was formed by the wall of the building facing the street; the people faced the wall and held their hands in the air. A Storm Unit stood a few metres away with submachine guns in their hands. People started to cry out "Mercy!" The horror intensified. For a moment there was silence, with only the sound of ammunition being reloaded. Then they were shot.'[12] The few AK soldiers tried to defend the area as best they could with sniper fire and Molotov cocktails, but the strongest forces had been positioned near the cemeteries in the north, leaving little firepower at the point of the German attack. The SS troops were able to move over 2,000 metres into Wola before they faced the first small barricade manned by the Polish Socialist Party. This was quickly wiped out by tanks.

It was terribly hot. 'Not one drop of rain fell during my time in Warsaw,' one German remembered.[13] But by now it was impossible to see the sun. Flames, smoke and dust blocked the sky, 'heat from the burning houses made our progress quite impossible, the wind blew up clouds of biting smoke which hid everything'. The sound of explosions and screams filled the air. At the same time von Vormann, cooperating with the Luftwaffe's General von Greim, ordered the 1st Aircraft Division to start dropping incendiary bombs on the district. Flames licked through windows and over the houses; entire streets were soon on fire.[14]

For the terrified civilians there was no escape. Many hid in cellars or tried to find hiding places in courtyards and garages, but once the Germans surrounded them they were doomed. Guns were pointed at the gates, doors and windows to the call of 'Raus! Raus!' The inhabitants were gathered in the courtyards and told to line up against a convenient wall; then they were executed. The Germans threw hand grenades into the basements, killing those who had not come out, and the buildings would then be set on fire. If anyone tried to escape they were shot. The fear, the agony and the human suffering endured in house after house was appalling. Children saw their parents die in front of them before they themselves perished in the flames; people were taunted and beaten before being killed, as if they were to blame for the destruction being meted out to them. Dozens of buildings were destroyed, and hundreds of civilians burned to death or gunned down.[15] 'Warsaw is burning all over,' Governor Fischer said proudly on 5 August. 'Burning the houses is the best way to liquidate the insurgents.'[16]

There is a tendency to look at historical events such as this with a cynical eye. The memory of propaganda about supposed German First World War atrocities in Belgium still lingers, as does the suspicion that eyewitnesses exaggerate or remember incorrectly. In this case, however, the evidence is overwhelming. The inhabitants of Wola were systematically killed along Wolska Street, Górczewska, Płocka and others, leaving a blood-drenched red line through the district. Enough eyewitnesses survived the hurried mass killings to testify before the war crimes tribunal in Warsaw after the war. But the most terrible proof lies in the mausoleum in Sowiński Park in Wola, where 1,120 kilograms of human ash are buried – all that remains of more than 40,000 people killed in that tiny area in the first week of August 1944.

It is not just the fact that people were murdered in their thousands that distinguishes the Warsaw Uprising from other conflicts; it is the bestiality that accompanied these murders that makes it so terrible to recall. Morality was turned on its head. Sadists were free to do whatever they wanted, and the more brutally they behaved the more Himmler praised them. Human life became utterly meaningless. The victims were violated and murdered in ways meant to degrade and belittle them. On 5 August the Germans attacked everything and everyone in their path. No human being was spared.

The AK tried to resist. 'Agaton' (Stanisław Jankowski) was on Górczewska Street during the first wave of attacks, and went to an upstairs room to relieve one of the soldiers. The man could no longer hear, because he had been deafened by the gunfire.

Agaton prodded his shoulder and he turned around, his face white with dust and his eyes red. 'He pointed at the building opposite and said: "*Niemcy*" ' – Germans. Agaton was handed the gun, and fired his first shots of the uprising. 'I could see Germans trying to run along a small fence through a garden . . . I didn't expect them to be so close and so I shot very calmly.' He was very aware of the shortage of ammunition: 'I repeated to myself I can only shoot at targets that are visible and that I can hit.'[17] Stefan Talikowski remembered trying to mount a defence in his apartment block: 'We pulled out a piece of asphalt from the middle of our courtyard and dug a tank trap; we prepared sixty petrol bombs in one day. The leader of Battalion "Chrobry" led by Captain Sosna was quartered in our house.'[18] The AK mounted counter-attacks at Plac Opolski, and at Górczewska and Chłodna Streets. 'Czata', 'Hal' and 'Miotła' Battalions fought back, but they were soon forced to retreat.

The Germans began to move into Wola proper, to areas of dense working-class housing and small to medium-sized factories. The massive red-brick Wawelberg blocks at Górczewska 15 were built at the turn of the century by the philanthropic businessman Hipolit Wawelberg as one of the first cooperative settlements in the city. Wawelberg's aim had been to create a true, tightly-knit, community, complete with a school and public baths, and he had succeeded. German troops surrounded the buildings and sealed the gates within minutes of their arrival. Hand grenades were lobbed into the large basements, and the huge complex was set on fire. There was barely time for the residents inside to think. Those trapped upstairs tried to jump to safety: 'People were burning alive and engulfed in flames and ran to the windows. Nobody upstairs could escape from the fire; they were all burned alive.' Those on the ground floor tried to get out the doors, but were shot as they emerged: 'The main entrance was full of the bodies of those who had tried to get away from the flames,' one eyewitness recalled. 'I saw among them women with babies at their breast.'[19] People next door could hear the cries for help and the screams of the dying, but could do nothing to help them.

Sheer terror spread throughout Wola as people tried desperately to escape to other districts. The next buildings to fall were the Hankiewicz Houses at Wolska 105–109. After surrounding them the SS lobbed in hand grenades and threw in a 'white incendiary powder which they carried with them in large bags. Everyone was burned alive or killed by hand grenades. No one could escape.'[20] The injuries caused by fire were particularly grim. One group of around thirty men and women who had been coated with the inflammatory substance struggled down the street. 'Their clothes had caught fire at once, especially the women's light dresses, and several of them could not go on. Their suffering was terrible, some of their eyes had been burned out, others were little more than an open wound on the whole body.'[21]

Building after building, cellar after cellar was forced open in this way, and all the people – mothers with children, old women, toddlers, teenagers – were pushed outside to the waiting troops. 'I was living at Wolska 132 when a group of Germans entered the house,' one young mother remembered. 'We were taken to Wolska Street and immediately saw piles of dead men, women and children, the inhabitants of the buildings at Wolska 128–129 who had been executed there. When our group got to the pile of dead bodies the Germans on Wolska Street by the railway tracks shot at us . . . When the police shot my son I could feel his blood dripping on me, and that is probably why they thought I was also dead.'[22]

One man watched from a window as the Germans gathered the civilians from the cellars at Płocka 28 and executed them in the courtyard with a machine gun. 'Next door I saw the hands of a few dozen people just above the wall. After a series of shots the hands disappeared.'[23] At the same time Stefan Talikowski watched as the troops rampaged through the houses. 'The Germans were plundering our flats, some were drunk and these guys with wild faces and machine pistols in their fists were very crude . . . some were carrying plates of eggs under one arm, sausages and wine . . . one broke the neck of a bottle and drank it with his companions.'

Fifteen-year-old Ryszard Piekarek was among a group hiding in the basement of a building in Wawelberga Street when he heard German voices shouting from ground level. Everyone froze. The glass of the basement windows was broken, and hand grenades fell into the crowd. They exploded, and fragments cut into people's bodies and ricocheted off the brick walls. The wounded cried out for help as the crowd started to push towards the exit, stepping on the fallen bodies of friends, neighbours and family. Once they reached the outside they were herded to the property's gate. 'Drunk "Ukrainians" in uniforms of German police stood beside every staircase and in the courtyards – they had their sleeves rolled up . . . each had grenades and automatic weapons and they swore and hit and shot people. They put us into two rows and we were forced into the second courtyard. We saw fifty or sixty dead people lying in puddles of fresh blood, men, women and children, and beside them some suitcases. I recognized the highly respected porter of our building.' A woman with a baby bent down to try to pick up one of the suitcases, in which she had put her savings. 'A Ukrainian with Mongolian cheekbones in an SS uniform shot her and the child. As she was dying in agony the SS man pulled her away by the hair, she was still holding her child. He opened the suitcase with the money in it and made a gesture inviting the other troops to help themselves. They were all laughing.'[24]

Piotr Dolny remembered being in a kind of trance when the SS arrived at his home in Młynarska Street. 'They told us to stand with our hands above our heads and then one of the SS men aged around thirty went down the line shooting into the back of the men's heads. I was at the end and I fell down and lost consciousness for around six hours.'[25] The bullet went through his jaw. He was the only one in the line to survive.

The killing continued throughout the morning. A Catholic priest watched from a window just before midday as the Germans took the building across the road. 'They executed all the inhabitants on the pavement in front of it, I suppose about sixty to a hundred people.'[26] Bogdan Duda, who worked as a porter at Wolski hospital, was arrested at his apartment in Wolska 11. 'They stole watches, money and jewellery at the gate. One Ukrainian asked for my watch, and when I said I didn't have one he hit me so hard in the face that I fell down.' Bogdan was taken to the courtyard at Krochmalna Street 90, where twenty freshly killed corpses lay in a row. 'I was in a group of fourteen people from my building. They ordered us to stand close to a pile of dead by the fence and to face the gate. There were four soldiers in front of us . . . When they opened fire I fell down even though no bullet had touched me. I lay on my side, leaning on two dead bodies with the blood and brains of one of them on my clothes. After the salvo the sub-officer approached each person and I heard him shoot each of them. He spoke Ukrainian and also German. He stood by my legs and shot my neighbour. I was lying just beside him and he probably thought the bullet got me as well.'[27] Dr Joanna Kryńska remembered 'drunk Germans in front of every house and streets covered in dead bodies. I didn't enter Bema Street but could see a group of 150 people, mostly women and children, against a wall. After I passed I heard salvos. After a few hours I saw the dead bodies in the same place.'

The violence was relentless. Jan Grabowski remembered the execution by German military police of all the blacksmiths who lived at Wolska 124. His building was the next to be emptied. 'The group from our house numbered about five hundred people. When I got there with my family people were already lying down . . . The Germans started to shoot with a machine gun and rifles and also to throw grenades into the crowd of people lying there.' Every half-hour another group was brought in, in a process that lasted six hours. 'A military policeman walked over my body three times. I was not injured but my wife and children were murdered. I heard a military policeman give the order to kill my five-year-old son, who was crying; I heard a shot and the child was silent.'[28]

Killing on this scale takes a great deal of time and energy, and by midday Reinefarth realized that the task of murdering civilians in their homes and basements was slowing him down. He decided that it would be more efficient to herd them away from the front line in large groups, and to kill them in a more organized fashion.[29]

By 1 o'clock in the afternoon a number of execution sites had been chosen. In normal times they were simply parts of the industrial landscape of Wola: the tram depot on Młynarska Street, the macaroni factory at Wolska 60, the railway viaduct at Górczewska 15, Sowiński Park, the Franaszek and Ursus factories and the foundries at Wolska 122–124. Now their names would be forever linked to the massacre of innocent civilians.

The method was remarkably simple. Shocked and terrified civilians were rounded up outside their homes and led at gunpoint to a factory hall or courtyard, where they were penned like animals, with no chance of escape. When the Germans were ready the civilians would be divided into groups of about fifty and brought to the execution site. Then they would be shot. Hans Thieme remembered some soldiers being excited by these killings, seeking out the execution sites and joining in the shooting.[30] Some took photographs for their scrapbooks back home.

The viaduct at Górczewska 15 was one of the first sites to be used. The victims were shoved into the hall of a nearby factory, and after being robbed of jewellery and other valuables, were gathered into groups that were led to the viaduct every half-hour. Górczewska is a wide street with tram tracks running down its middle, and that was where the machine guns were set up. The victims were pushed to the north side, up against a steep embankment, and then shot. Aleksandra Kreczkiewicz remembered: 'We were herded together. I stood on the outskirts of the group while at a distance of about five metres away our tormenters quietly made ready to fire a machine gun while another took photographs . . . A volley of shots rang out, followed by cries and groans. I fell wounded and lost consciousness. After a time I recovered my senses. I heard them finishing off the wounded; I did not move, pretending to be dead. They left one German to keep watch. The murderers set the neighbouring houses, large and small, on fire. The heat scorched me, the smoke choked me and my dress began to burn. I tried cautiously to put out the flames.' She managed to slip away and hide; most in her group perished.[31]

One of the worst aspects of these executions was that the victims were forced to stand next to, and sometimes even to climb onto, the corpses of those who had already been murdered. As they approached the piles of bodies they realized what was going to happen to them, and would panic. Parents pleaded with the SS to let their children go, others tried to hug one another and say goodbye, but all too often the barrel of a gun would be shoved between them. Those who broke away and tried to run for it were gunned down. When Ryszard Piekarek approached the viaduct he felt sick at the sight; at the same time he realized that there was nothing he could do. 'I could see around three or four hundred murdered civilians lying in a pile more than one metre high, with a thick layer of congealed blood beside them.' He was the only survivor in his group of fifty victims.

In Sowiński Park today stand 177 massive concrete headstones inscribed with the names of some of the victims of Wola. Three children are listed on one of them: Wiesław, Ludmiła and Lech Lurie. They were aged eleven, six and three. In 1957 a middle-aged woman in a headscarf and sunglasses was interviewed for a programme made for Polish television. One could see, despite the black-and-white footage, that her face had prematurely aged. Her voice, taut with emotion, was unnaturally hoarse. Wanda Lurie spoke briskly, almost as if she did not want to hear what she herself was saying, but the few words she spoke were devastating: 'I was taken to the Ursus factory with my three children,' she began. 'They shot each child in the head with a revolver. I was heavily pregnant. I lay amongst the bodies for three days in a pool of blood.' And then she broke down. 'I cannot talk . . .'

Eleven years previously, Wanda Lurie had testified to the Central Commission for the Investigation of German War Crimes in Poland about the massacre in the factory, of which she was one of the few survivors. Her testimony bears witness to the fate of more than 5,000 people who were killed in that bleak factory yard.

Wanda's husband was away, and she was alone with her three small children when the Germans came to Wawelberga Street on 5 August. Her apartment block was emptied, and the inhabitants were herded towards the Ursus factory, where they were kept standing in front of the entrance surrounded by armed guards. Groups were separated from the crowd and taken in, and Wanda could hear the sound of crying and begging from inside. She hung back, hoping that they would not kill a heavily pregnant woman, but as she approached the gate in her turn she realized that the situation was hopeless. 'There was no chance of being saved,' she said. 'In our group there were about twenty people, mainly children between ten and twelve years old; children without their parents.' They were forced into groups of four and were pushed towards the heaps of bodies. She recognized friends and neighbours already lying dead.

Wanda had some gold with her, and tried to buy her way out, but although the Ukrainian guard seemed willing to consider letting her go, the German supervising the executions would not hear of it. 'When I begged him to let me go he pushed me off, shouting "*Schneller!*" I fell when he pushed me. He hit and pushed my elder boy, shouting "*Schneller*, Polish bandit." This is how I came to the place of execution, in the last group of four, with my three children. I held my two younger children by one hand and my elder boy by the other. The children were crying and praying. The elder boy, seeing the mass of bodies, yelled "They are going to kill us!" and called out for his father The first shot hit him, the second me; the next two killed the two younger children. I fell on my right side. The shot was not fatal. The bullet went into the back of my head from the right side and went out through my cheek. I spat out several teeth. I felt the left side of my body growing numb, but I was still conscious and saw everything that was going on around me. I witnessed other executions lying there among the dead . . . it went on with group after group until late in the evening.'

Wanda Lurie lay there as the Germans walked on the corpses, kicked them, turning them over, finishing off those who still gave any sign of life and stealing valuables'. They took her watch. She noticed that they did not touch the bodies with their bare hands, but wrapped rags around them. They were drinking vodka the whole time, and singing.

The executions stopped the next day, but the Germans came back with dogs. 'They walked and jumped on the corpses to see if any of the supposed dead were still alive. On the third day I felt the child move in my womb. I was determined that this child not die, and I looked around to find a way to escape.' She managed to crawl out from under the blood and the bodies once the Germans had left, and hid in a cellar; she eventually ended up in the Pruszków transit camp. Her son Mścisław was born on 20 August 1944, and is now an active campaigner to honour the memory of those who died like his siblings in Wola. When it was over 'the whole courtyard, about fifty metres square, was so thickly strewn with dead bodies that it was impossible to walk without stepping on them. Half of them were women with children, often with infants. All the bodies bore traces of robbery.'[32] The horror of dealing with so many dead was terrible. Matthias Schenk remembered that 'when you burn the bodies, you can hear noises, like groaning, and at the time I thought the people were still alive. It was all the flies and insects.'[33]

Many other mass executions took place in Wola that day. A machine gun was set up in the courtyard of the macaroni factory at Wolska 60, and hundreds of civilians were herded there and shot. Over a thousand civilians were murdered in Sowiński Park. Wacława Szlacheta was taken there, and put near the fence by the gate. The Germans had set up three machine guns. 'They fired into us. I fell to the ground. I was not wounded. Corpses were falling on my legs. My youngest daughter, Alina, who was lying next to me, was still alive. As I lay there I saw and heard German soldiers walking between the bodies, kicking them to see if anyone was still alive. Anyone breathing was killed with a single shot of a revolver . . . A soldier went to the baby carriage in which my neighbour Jakubczyk's twin babies were lying and shot them.'[34] A witness described the scene afterwards: 'Those executed were mostly women and children, including pregnant women. The position of these bodies, lying in a row, showed it was part of a mass execution.'[35]

One hundred people were gunned down in the courtyard of the Michler works, another hundred on Ptasia Street. Over a thousand people were herded together at the tram depot at Młynarska. Janina Rogazińska watched as the SS 'opened fire on the crowd. After the first salvo some people who had been only wounded began to get up. Then they threw the grenades.' Dr Manteuffel saw the aftermath on 7 August: 'Close to the tram depot we saw another place of execution. About fifty bodies lay there, one beside the other, men over fifty, women and children up to the age of fourteen.'

The Franaszek factory at Wolska 41–45, which produced specialized photographic equipment, was important enough to be mentioned at the Nuremberg Trials in connection with German expropriation of Polish industry: 'We took samples of the manufacture of film paper and films to be examined in Germany,' a Berlin official reported in 1939, 'and to decide if production should continue in order to augment German capacity.'[36] The factory had been kept running, and its owner, Kazimierz Franaszek, had even been permitted to work there. He would witness the mass execution on his grounds. 'We must remember,' he said, breaking down during the war crimes trial in Warsaw in 1946.

Włodzimierz Starosolski, a chemist and technical manager, remembered the streams of refugees coming to the factory for shelter at the beginning of August, drawn by the bunker and the first-aid post on its grounds. By 3 August the SS had already rounded up around two hundred of these people and taken them away for execution, and on 5 August they returned and set fire to all the buildings, with the exception of the photography department. 'Those trying to escape the flames were shot. I knew a number of the people killed in front of my eyes, including a porter and a wounded woman who were burned alive.' The SS ordered the factory area cleared, and around five hundred people were

The Wola Massacre: The German Attacks, 5–6 August 1944

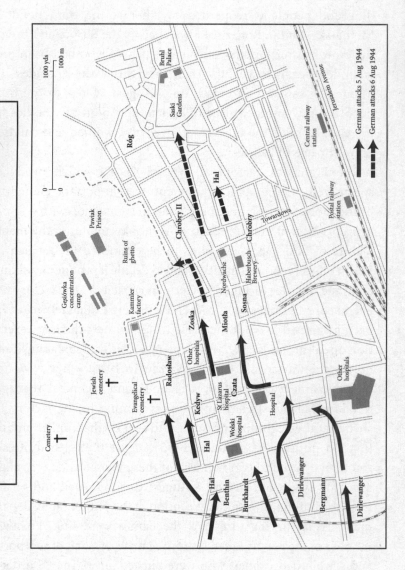

German attacks 5 Aug 1944
German attacks 6 Aug 1944

1000 yds
1000 m

Cemetery

Jewish cemetery

Evangelical cemetery

Gęsiówka concentration camp

Pawiak Prison

Ruins of ghetto

Kammler factory

Róg

Saski Gardens

Bruhl Palace

Chrobry II

Hal

Radosław

Other hospitals

Zoska

Kedyw

St Lazarus hospital

Czata

Miotla

Sosna

Nordwache

Haberbusch Brewery

Chrobry

Towardowa

Central railway station

Postal railway station

Jerusalem Avenue

Hal

Wolski hospital

Hospital

Other hospitals

Hal

Benthin

Burkhardt

Dirlewanger

Bergmann

Dirlewanger

taken to the tram depot at Młynarska 2, where they were executed.[37]

Włodzimierz hid under the water station in the basement, and survived. On 6 August he crept upstairs in Building M, from which he could see the whole factory. 'Around 11 a.m. two SS military trucks appeared on the main courtyard, each with about thirty people inside. They were executed. The people in the bunkers were then hauled out and executed along with people brought in from Wola.' More and more people were brought in. Afterwards, bodies lay everywhere. They were 'all twisted together, some of them one beside the other, others lying separately on their own at the edge of the courtyard spreadeagled with their hands reaching towards the wall as if in a last attempt to survive. They must have been driven into the courtyard and then hand grenades thrown in, as the bodies were mangled in a terrible way. The others who had not been killed instantly were lying in disarray, cringing in fear or pain . . . Thousands of fat blue flies were on the dark drops of blood and the holes left by the shooting.'[38]

A plaque now commemorates the victims. 'From 4 August until 4 October the Germans shot and burned around 6,000 inhabitants of Wola including the female volunteer fire brigade of the factory,' it reads. Over half of the victims were women and children who had come to find shelter. There were almost no survivors.

The SS were proud of the death rate. One SS man from Holland, a patient in the Wolski hospital, boasted on 5 August: 'We have already killed around 7,000 people.' The suffering was terrible. 'Evidence of German bestiality to Warsawians was everywhere . . . there were dead bodies lying in piles, and some had been mashed by cars and were pushed aside like rubbish. A woman lay half naked on the street, her body already stiff. Piles of banknotes flew in the air. There was screaming and the sound of gunfire as the Dirlewanger men shot into the people next to our column.

We walked through puddles of fresh blood . . .'[39] There were heartbreaking scenes of children lying dead still hugging their favourite toys; family pets were tortured in front of their owners before they too were killed; horses neighed in terror as the flames engulfed them alive. After a round-up, personal possessions lay strewn on the ground; suitcases and bags and pieces of clothing lay in heaps dotted with the smaller, more personal items testifying to a life – photographs, hair ribbons, books, letters. As Hans Thieme put it, these were not poor peasants, but well-dressed, well-educated people who, only days before, had been living relatively normal lives.

The Dirlewanger Brigade

As the troops moved forward, Reinefarth complained once more about the numbers of civilians he had to kill. In a recorded phone conversation with von Vormann, he said, 'What are we to do with those who are arrested – we have more arrested than ammunition.' Von Vormann asked about losses. 'Our losses are six killed, twenty-four badly wounded, twelve slightly wounded; losses of the enemy including those shot are more than 10,000.'[40]

News of the mass executions spread rapidly; before long the streets of Wola and beyond were filled with piles of bodies, and surging with throngs of panicked residents who knew that if they stayed where they were they faced certain death. This slowed the Germans down.

It became clear in the first day or so that many of the troops brought into Warsaw were not really suited for this kind of fighting. Von dem Bach would later describe Schmidt as 'towering' above all other commanders in the Warsaw battle, and his troops as 'capable front-line soldiers with years of experience'; even so, they proved to be of little worth in Warsaw, as they had no knowledge of street fighting.[41] But Hans Thieme visited Schmidt in his quarters in a disused petrol depot, and thought him 'not a very good officer'. He was clearly enjoying his promotion, and 'savouring the feeling of importance. His new role boosted his ego. Many units had to report to him now, and the police treated him with sophisticated politeness.'[42] He may have enjoyed the attention, but he and his men accomplished little.

Worse still were the police units sent from Poznań, who were more used to arresting unarmed people in the middle of the night than fighting a real enemy. 'The battle-readiness of the police companies was low,' von dem Bach said. 'They were of little help and had no enthusiasm for the fight. If they were used in the attack they needed heavy weapons to clear their way. If a block of flats occupied by the enemy was not completely destroyed by artillery or by flamethrowers, the police would not dare go near it.'[43] Even the Schmidt troops, von dem Bach noted sadly, lacked enthusiasm for the fight – the 'Freude am Handwerk', or 'delight in their trade' of the Dirlewanger men.[44] In his old comrade in arms from Byelorussia, here at last was a man he could trust.

Oscar Dirlewanger had been relaxing in the little East Prussian town of Łyck after his narrow and hasty escape from Byelorussia. These quarters were conveniently close to both the Wolfsschanze and Himmler's headquarters, and while he and his men had been enjoying themselves carousing until the early hours every night, he had also met up with his old friends von dem Bach, Himmler and Kaminski.[45]

Himmler ordered Dirlewanger to Warsaw immediately after hearing about the uprising. It is a measure of Dirlewanger's self-confidence that he blatantly disobeyed, going instead to a party in Berlin; it is a measure of his importance to the Reichsführer SS that Himmler did nothing more than send him a terse note: 'As much as I am satisfied with your endeavours, as I recently told you personally,' Himmler wrote on 4 August, 'I must express my displeasure that, despite having been warned to proceed immediately to your regiment on the aeroplane which was reserved for you, you spent several more hours in Berlin. I am used to prompt and immediate obedience. H. Himmler.'[46]

Dirlewanger's troops were more compliant. The first battalion arrived via Modlin on 3 August, and the rest were there by the evening of the 4th. The Sonderkommando had grown considerably while it was in Byelorussia. As well as his own troops, Dirlewanger had an SD commando led by SS Untersturmführer Heinrich Amann, and on 8 May nearly 3,000 eastern Muslims from the North Caucasus were assigned to the unit.[47] Russian soldiers, former members of the Red Army – either deserters or ex-prisoners – from the rank of private to lieutenant, and from both the army and the air force, also joined them, as did two Azerbaijani units which were added in East Prussia.[48] Dirlewanger also had the Battalion Bergman and the 1st Battalion of the 111th Unit, the 1st and 2nd Battalion Heavy Machine Gun Company, a company of mine-throwers and an anti-Panzer company. Others included German criminal prisoners hauled out of the camps, some of the most brutal men in the brigade. On 27 May, 182 came in from Auschwitz; on 5 June, 293 were sent from Oranienburg. The Sonderkommando was also used as a punishment battalion, and 1,900 new recruits were sent from the SS Straflage in Matzlau. Georg-Wilhelm Eggers was one of these, a former SS Hauptsturmführer from Hildesheim who, in a drunken stupor, had fired off his service pistol on 22 February 1944 in the pretty university town of Göttingen. He had been demoted to the rank of private and sent to prison for three months. On 2 August he was forced to report to the Sonderkommando, just in time to fight in Warsaw.[49] It was an assignment from hell itself.

Dirlewanger knew precisely what he was expected to do in the doomed city. According to Ernst Rode, Himmler gave Dirlewanger 'all authority and power to kill whoever he wanted to according to his wishes'.[50] This hardened criminal, fresh from the 'Bandit War' in Byelorussia, was given *carte blanche* in Warsaw.

Dirlewanger's cruelty was legendary even before he got to the Polish capital, and he and his men were disliked by most of the other troops. Reinefarth detested Dirlewanger so much that the two had once almost had a duel, and they avoided meeting one another in Warsaw. A Waffen SS soldier, tank commander and winner of the Knight's Cross wrote after the war: 'All soldiers, even those in the Waffen SS, distanced themselves even during the war from the Dirlewanger Brigade. This brigade consisted only of sentenced members of the Wehrmacht and the Waffen SS and they were used in fighting against partisans . . . which was especially cruel and hard. As far as I know no soldier wanted to end up on those missions'. He concluded that it would be difficult to find any information about the brigade after the war, as 'when the subject is mentioned there is a reluctance even to talk about it'.[51]

At the same time, the Dirlewanger gang was grudgingly admired for its suicidal bravery. It was eminently useful. One SS soldier recalled that whenever the situation in Warsaw became critical, 'sooner or later the unit "Dirlewanger" surfaced. In a normal time any loyal citizen, whether a private person or in the police, would have taken this monster into custody away from the streets and would have locked him up . . . This man dealt with incredible harshness and granted no pardon'.[52] The soldier described an attack on a building held by Polish sharpshooters in which half the SS men taking part had been lost. 'That's when the Dirlewanger crowd was brought in. The horde arrived, took one look and stormed in. About fifty men rushed across the street. Around thirty remained lying there, no longer moving. The remainder disappeared into the building, and over the next ten minutes both corpses and the living flew out of the windows of the fourth and fifth floors. The Dirlewanger guys did not bother to give speeches. This is how the houses of Warsaw were cleaned up.'

One of the most extraordinary eyewitness accounts of Dirlewanger and his methods comes from Matthias Schenk, a young German-speaker from the part of Belgium that Hitler had integrated into the Reich. Schenk was recruited into the Wehrmacht in 1944, at the age of eighteen, hoping to become a lorry driver. Instead he was assigned to the 46th Assault Brigade, becoming the youngest in his unit.

After short basic training, Schenk and his brigade were loaded onto trains at the end of July 1944. Rather than being sent to France, as they had hoped, they found themselves heading east, through a land of 'small villages, flat fields, houses with straw roofs'. They were on their way to the Eastern Front. It was very hot, and the soldiers in the train were drunk. They were just coming into Warsaw when they heard shooting. Schenk's wagon was hit, and a few of his colleagues were killed. A German covered in blood ran towards them, yelling that an uprising had broken out in Warsaw and that they had to proceed on foot.

The fight in Warsaw was to be Schenk's first experience of combat. It was a horrifying trial by fire.[53] He was sent into the fray immediately. As a sapper, his job was to blow up doors, gates or any other obstacles in the way of the soldiers. 'Lieutenant Fels ordered us to explode the doors of the houses from which the most shooting came, but we were caught by gunfire on two sides and had to hide in a courtyard garden overnight waiting for help. The next evening the infantry came to the rescue but we made no progress. Then an SS unit arrived.'

These SS men were unusual. 'They looked very strange. They had no markings of rank on their uniforms and they smelled of vodka. They attacked right away with a loud "hurrah" and they died by the dozen. Their commander, dressed in a black leather coat, was at the back of the unit yelling at his people to attack.' A tank appeared, but it was hit. A second tank arrived, but its crew hesitated to move forward. 'We were covering the front as the SS expelled people from their homes and placed them around the tank, forcing some to sit on the top. It was the first time in my life that I had seen such a thing. They were shoving a Polish woman in a long coat. She was cuddling a little girl in her arms. The people crowded on the tank tried to help her to get up. Someone took hold of the girl. As he handed her back to the mother the tank jerked forward, the girl fell and was crushed under the tracks. The woman began to scream in terror. One of the SS guys sneered at her and shot her in the head. The tank moved on. People who tried to escape were killed by the SS.' The attack was successful, and the Poles were forced from their shelters. 'They came with their hands raised and calling out "Niz partisan!" I heard the SS commander in the black leather coat yell to his men to kill everyone, including women and children.'

Schenk was sent off to attack a building; when he returned he was disgusted by what he saw: 'The bodies of the Poles were lying on the street. There was no place to move, and we had to step on them to pass. The corpses began to decompose very quickly in the heat. The sun was covered by smoke and dust and there were flies and insects everywhere. We were sweating and covered in blood and Lieutenant Fels the stupid fanatic yelled, "Where have you been, cheeky swine?" while praising the SS for having done such a good job. I could not eat anything. We were vomiting.'

In the barracks, Schenk was told that the SS man in the black coat was Oskar Dirlewanger, and that his men were criminals. 'At the time we called him a butcher, but very quietly, because it was very easy to be hanged in the Dirlewanger Brigade.

Dirlewanger had this habit of hanging people every Thursday, Poles or his own people, it didn't matter. He often kicked the stool away himself.'

After only a few days in combat, Schenk found himself assigned to one of the worst roles he could possibly have had – as an assault sapper in an SS platoon of the Dirlewanger Brigade. He had no choice but to fight, or to be shot himself. Even so he managed to retain his humanity, expelling people from buildings rather than killing them outright, and then lying to Fels about it. For him there was a marked distinction between the Wehrmacht and the SS. He recalled a moment when a girl came out of a building and said, 'I am not a partisan.' 'We Wehrmacht guys lowered our guns. Then Dirlewanger came. His men fired the first volley but he stopped them. "Not bullet but butts," he said. The child was beaten to death.'[54] All the German troops knew that they had to carry out Dirlewanger's orders, but Schenk detested the Dirlewanger crowd: 'They looked like low-lifes, scruffy with torn uniforms, some without weapons which they then took from the dead. In the morning they got vodka, we sappers as well, and we drank it on an empty stomach as before an attack you do not eat. If they shoot an empty stomach you have a chance to survive, but if it is full you die in agony.'[55]

Everything was upside-down in Dirlewanger's world. Common humanity meant nothing to him, and the very symbols of a civilized society seemed to provoke the most violent reaction in him and his men. He had had a great deal of practice at killing civilians in Byelorussia, so by the time he got to Warsaw burning people alive or torturing them or hanging them for sport was almost second nature. Dr Joanna Kryńska, who was spared in the massacres at Wolski, became his translator. 'All that is going on in Warsaw with the civilians is nothing compared to what happened in Russia,' he told her in early August. 'There the soldiers didn't leave anyone alive and murdered and raped women.' He said that 'this had been necessary for German victory. We are talking about nations which are less important than Germans. Slavic people are *Untermenschen*.' He also explained to her that his units had been specially trained to crush partisan activity.[56] When the highly respected Dr Manteuffel from the Wolski hospital first encountered Dirlewanger's men, one of the sub-officers greeted him with the words 'Our Führer's orders are to send you straight to hell.'

Unlike the Red Army, the Wehrmacht was not particularly known for rape, because of the 'racial' implications. In most units this was true even during the uprising. On one occasion three young girls were singled out by members of the SiPo and SD, forced to drink alcohol and then raped. After raping one of the girls Ludwig Hahn ordered that she be executed; when no one volunteered, Hahn shot her himself. SS Obersturmführer Ulrich Stern, who witnessed the crime, was disgusted and upset not because his superior had murdered an innocent girl, but because he had committed a '*Rassenschande*' – the crime of racial defilement – by raping the Polish girl.[57]

In the Dirlewanger Brigade, however, rape was the norm. 'When we forced ourselves into basements,' Schenk recalled, 'the Dirlewanger men followed and the women were always raped. Sometimes a few of the men raped the same woman one after the other without putting down their weapons. In one basement Dirlewanger's men burst in. One took a woman. She was pretty and did not scream. He raped her, pressing her head down into the table with one hand and holding a bayonet in the other. Afterwards he cut her blouse open. Then he cut her from her stomach to her throat.'[58] After raping his victims, Hauptsturmführer 'B' was known for putting hand grenades in the vaginas of Warsaw women and detonating them.[59]

'Tradecraft'

One of the most terrible features of the Dirlewanger Brigade was the wilful murder of children. Schenk witnessed a number of such killings, including a massacre at the Orthodox Children's Home at Wolska 149 on 5 August. 'A lot of children were standing on the stairs with raised hands. Lots of children. All with their little hands in the air. We looked at them for a while until Dirlewanger appeared. He ordered that they all be killed. They killed them and then stepped on the children's bodies, smashing their little heads with the butts of their guns. The stairs were covered in blood.' A plaque now commemorates the 350 children who died there.[60] Similar scenes took place during the destruction of the hospital for female orphans run by the nuns of St Vincent de Paul, which was burned to the ground. Schenk witnessed Dirlewanger take a small child from a woman who was standing in a crowd on the street. 'He lifted the child high and put it into the fire. Then he shot the mother.' A Catholic priest watching from a window on Wolska saw how Dirlewanger's soldiers 'grabbed hold of one woman with a small child who in fear was visibly running away from the burning house, and threw them both back through the window into the flames'.[61]

Dirlewanger's men took pride in their 'tradecraft', as von dem Bach called it. A small girl of around twelve, with torn clothes and dishevelled hair, appeared from a basement long after the other inhabitants had been assembled in the courtyard. Schenk motioned to her not to be afraid as she stood by the wall, unsure of where to go. 'She raised her hands and said, "*Nicht Partisan.*" She walked with raised hands. She was squeezing something in one of them. She was very close when I heard a shot. Her head bounced. A piece of bread fell from her hand. In the evening the platoon leader, who was from Berlin, came up to me and said proudly, "It was a master shot, wasn't it?" He smiled, very full of himself.'[62]

Stanisław Kicman was a small boy in short trousers and summer sandals when he and his mother were forced out of their apartment and taken to St Wojchiech church. He recalled: 'There were already lines of dead bodies. People were crying, calling out. I was not sure what to do and asked my mother what was happening. "Don't worry my little child," she said. "It won't take long." She took me in her arms and cuddled me close to her. "Close your eyes," she said. "It will not hurt." '[63] Another witness, from Elekcyjna 8 in Wola, remembered the death of his wife and son: 'They ordered us to leave the cellars and to march through Sowiński Park at Ulrychów. Then they started to shoot us as we passed. My wife was killed instantly; our child was wounded and cried out for his mother. Soon a Ukrainian came and killed my two-year-old child as if he were a dog.'[64]

Wiesław Kępiński was hiding in the basement of the Orthodox church with his family and a group of ninety other people. On the afternoon of 5 August the Germans came. With cries of 'Raus' they forced the civilians to walk to the road. 'My father was at the front of the line, my mother, my siblings and I at the end. We all knew that we were going to die. We had no time to say goodbye, no time to say anything.' They were made to stand in front of the embankment and watch as a machine gun was set up on the tram tracks in the middle of the road. All the people, fathers, mothers and children, were shot. 'I was hit but not killed, and by chance was able to flip over the little wall behind the execution site.' Wesław always wondered if his mother had seen him escape just before she died. Like so many other children, he found himself on his own in the wartorn city.[65]

A young girl also survived this massacre. Maria Cyrańska remembered hiding with her parents when 'around 5 p.m. the German soldiers entered the church. They ordered us to leave. We were brought to Wolska Street and then I saw on the tram tracks machine guns prepared for execution . . . A few minutes later a car full of Germans came, then another, and they all had weapons and all of them shot at us. I was wounded in the left arm, the chin and the temple. The person beside me moved a little and the German soldiers went down to see if he was alive and when they saw he was they shot him. A German soldier stood on my back. I could feel the tread of his boot.'[66] Hans Thieme saw the debris, suitcases, clothes and beds in the church some days later. 'Where were the people? I left the basement and walked around the church and got to one of the gravestones. The people were here. These innocent refugees who had dared to find shelter in a house of God had been gathered in the cemetery and shot. Men, women, old people and children, all of them.'

'Very often children came to us,' Matthias Schenk recalled. 'They couldn't find their parents, and wanted bread. A Polish boy brought us food when we were on guard duty . . . If I had cigarettes I gave them to him. One time an SS guy was passing. He called to the boy to follow him. After a while I heard a shot. I ran. The dead boy was lying on the stairs. The SS guy pointed his pistol at me. He looked at me very long and hard before walking away.'[67]

There was an element of pure sadism in the Dirlewanger Brigade. At one point they designated a crippled twelve-year-old boy their 'mascot' in Wola. 'He had lost one leg but could jump very fast on the other one,' Schenk recalled. 'He was very proud of this. He always jumped around the soldiers, one way then another. We said it was for luck. He helped us out a little. One day the SS men called out to him. He jumped over eagerly. They were laughing, and told him to jump towards the trees. From far away I saw that they had put two grenades into his bag, but he didn't notice. He was jumping away and they laughed at him, shouting, "*Schneller! Schneller!*" Then the boy blew up.'[68] The Dirlewanger men laughed at the sport.

Schenk was not alone in being disgusted by all of this. German Lieutenant Peter Stolten, a teacher's son, had been moved from the relative civility of the Western Front in France in August 1944 to the fight in Warsaw; he was to die on 24 January 1945 near Allenstein in northern Poland. He wrote to his parents from the Polish capital: 'Warsaw shows the true face of war. I am used to male bodies, but when I see torn female bodies and see how lovely they were once, when I see children whose innocence is there no matter which language they speak . . . (You will say for certain that I should not and am not allowed to write like this.)'[69]

Churches and religious buildings seemed particularly to goad Dirlewanger's men. The nuns' house at Górczewska 9 was attacked on 5 August: 'The courtyard was a dreadful sight. It was a place of execution. Heaps of corpses lay there. I think they must have been collecting there for some days as some were swollen and others killed recently. There were bodies of men, women and children, all shot through the back of the head.'[70] Three thousand two hundred people were murdered in the nuns' garden at Wolska 27–29. Tadeusz Klimaszewski saw that the well was filled 'not with water but contorted dead bodies. The number of dead was so high that we knew there were not bodies of just the people who lived here . . . most were male, and we started to think that women and children had survived this mass execution, but after clearing the area around the well and courtyard we went to another part of the garden to a wall covered in bullet holes, and there was another pile of dead bodies. Very small children and toddlers were lying there in the tight embrace of their mothers, the older ones were lying close holding the sleeves and parts of their mothers' coats. In the middle of this group lay an old man with a stick, on which was a white flag.'[71]

The SS treated all symbols of Polish culture with complete contempt. In the Karol Boromeusz church on Chłodna Street,

Stefan Talikowski saw them relaxing and joking after a murderous day. 'German officers were sitting outside, they were sitting on the church pews. They were laughing and observing the street and on the square in front of the church were collecting valuables, jewellery, watches and rings which were dropped into special trunks.' One man resisted. 'A German soldier pushed him to the nearest gate and shot him there.'[72] Władysław Stępień remembered women being raped in St Wojciech church on Wolska Street.[73]

Schenk, too, remembered Dirlewanger's particular scorn for religion. 'We blew up the back door to a monastery – very heavy – that led to a cellar,' he recalled. 'A priest was standing in front of us. He had a communion wafer and a chalice in his hands. Acting on impulse – I don't know –.we genuflected and took the communion. A third from our group ran in and did the same. Then the SS men stormed in and there were the usual shots, screams and groans. The nuns were in habits. A few hours later I saw that priest in Dirlewanger's hands. They drank wine from the chalice, the wafers were scattered and broken. They were urinating on a cross leaning against the wall. They were torturing the priest: he had a bloody face, torn cassock. We took that priest from them, it was an impulse. They were surprised, but so drunk that they didn't know what was happening. The next day they didn't remember at all.'[74]

'The Hospitals are Burning'

The killing spree in Wola extended to the hospitals. Their destruction had been sanctioned by the SS and the Wehrmacht. Generals von Vormann and Reinefarth both knew about and condoned the attacks; on 3 August Major Reck, under Reinefarth's command, gave an acquaintance a special pass so he could get his wife out of one of the hospitals as soon as possible. 'You should evacuate your wife as the hospital is to be burned and blown up,' Reck told him.[75] Dirlewanger may have carried out these vicious attacks, but as with everything else that took place in Wola, the crimes were sanctioned from above.

The hospitals of Wola were well known before the war, not only throughout Poland but also in the rest of Europe. The Wolski hospital, housed in an imposing brick building, was headed by the great Professor Janusz Zeyland, who had worked in Paris for many years and was a world expert on pulmonary tuberculosis in children; his publications are still in use today.

Dirlewanger's men arrived at the hospital at 2.30 on the afternoon of Saturday, 5 August. Dr Zeyland, who spoke perfect German, was ordered to go into his small office to the left of the entrance along with the hospital's director, Dr Józef Piasecki, and its chaplain, Kazimierz Ciecierski. They were put behind the desk and shot. The Dirlewanger men then raged through the hospital, rounding up doctors, nurses and the sick. The hospital quickly became a killing ground as drunken troops rampaged from floor to floor. Before long bodies were everywhere, on the floors, on the beds and in the corners, bodies lying or half sitting, leaning on the wall, hanging from the metal railings of the beds half naked, in hospital gowns torn to shreds. The bed linen, pillows and comforters were spread on the floor, sticky from blood which turned into black puddles on the floor.'[75]

They did not kill everyone *in situ*. Four hundred people, many of them in a pitiful state because of their wounds or illness, were forced to walk to various places of execution. One woman later testified that, after being rounded up in the cellars with a group of patients, doctors and nurses, they were marched to the tunnel in Górczewska Street. 'We were ordered to form rows of twelve people, and were then driven into the yard of the building by the viaduct. At the entrance Ukrainians (six in number) shot from close range at every person who entered, and thus the dead fell into the flames of the burning buildings. I saw clearly, when waiting my turn in the first group of twelve people, doctors, assistants in white aprons and also (if I am not mistaken) priests being shot. Amongst the doctors was Professor Grzybowski. Then the wounded and sick in the other rows were driven to their death, and when people were brought on stretchers first that person was shot and then the stretcher bearers. It was only by a miracle that I escaped death. When I was pushed to the entrance in the group of twelve I lied to one of the officers that I and my two companions were *Volksdeutsche*, as I speak German well. So the German ordered us to fall back and follow him. He led us to a German first-aid station there. About five hundred people were shot in my presence, many from the Wolski hospital.'[77]

Father Jerzy Zuchoń, a missionary from Kraków and a patient at the time, watched in horror as the Dirlewanger men broke in and pulled the sick out of the basement where they had sought shelter. 'The procession was dreadful; the doctors leading, then the assistants, then the patients staggering along, supported by those who were stronger.' They were led to a factory hall by the viaduct at Moczydlo where, group by group, they were forced to go in after having given up their watches. 'After a moment we heard shots. As there was no fighting nearby we knew that an execution was taking place near us. The well-known sound of machine-gun fire was heard, and later single shots. There was no doubt that those who had been led out had been shot. Being a priest I told those present the fate that probably awaited us, and gave them absolution.' Zuchoń managed to hide, but 'the party of doctors was led to death before my eyes. I was told later that the executions took place inside and in the courtyards of burning houses at several places in Górczewska Street. In the last group I saw Professor Grzybowski, Dr Drozdowski, Dr Sokołowski and Dr Lempicki led out for execution.'[78]

Dr Bernard Filipiuk also survived the killings on Górczewska Street. 'The place of execution was a large yard. I was standing there for about fifteen to twenty minutes. I saw how every group of twelve men was executed by shooting in the back of the neck . . . I have to underline that not only men were executed in Górczewska Street . . . In my twelve was a woman. She was holding a baby in her arms which must have been around one year old. She asked the Gestapo soldier to kill her baby first and then her. He smiled, but said nothing. The child was whimpering and crying long after its mother was executed.'[79]

All patients were to be killed. One young man had been wounded in both legs and could not walk, so two other patients were made to carry him on a chair. The German guard became irritated by the fact that this was slowing down the column, and the carriers were ordered to leave him on the corner of Górczewska and Płocka. Suddenly the patient heard a shot. The chair on which he was sitting fell apart, and he landed between the bodies of others who had been killed earlier. He survived by playing dead.[80]

Another group of young men were marched to Górczewska Street, where they were ordered to dig a pit. 'They were brought in groups of twenty-five; they had no shirts and held their hands in the air.' The young men were lined up facing the pit, and were shot in the back of the head. 'The bodies would fall into the pit and the next would be brought in. No one screamed, begged or resisted. Several hundred men were killed that way.'[81]

After the Germans had massacred the Polish patients and most of the staff of the Wolski hospital, it was decided to spare the building and use it to treat German wounded. Dr Woźniewski was put in charge. In the afternoon of 5 August a German arrived at his office, guaranteed his safety and asked quietly, 'Which of the bodies is the professor?' Woźniewski, who had not been told that Professor Zeyland had been murdered, did not understand the question. The German led him into the professor's office, and Woźniewski saw the bodies of his friends for the first time. He was overcome: 'You could see traces of bullets . . . Zeyland was lying in a puddle of blood.' He could not calm down, and the German gave him a cigarette, motioning towards the Dirlewanger troops still roaming the halls. 'Don't show how upset you are to the primitive horde,' he said. 'It is a war, and you Poles started this uprising; you must be the victims of this war. I can only assure you that this was a mistake, as the professor was not supposed to be killed.'[82]

Dr Woźniewski decided to bury Professor Zeyland in the hospital garden. A young German doctor named Pucher arrived, and, after acknowledging Professor Zeyland's illustrious career, said sadly, 'This is terrible, this is really terrible.' Pucher insisted on staying while the professor was buried, but halfway through Woźniewski noticed a wounded man trying to get into the court-yard. His lower lip was torn, his mouth was filled with blood and tissue, and he could not speak. After Pucher had gone, Woźniewski helped the man to the building. The patient wrote three words on a piece of paper: 'Execution at Młynarska'. His name was Jan Napiórkówski, an employee of the hospital who had been rounded up for execution. He had been shot in the back of the neck, but the bullet had gone through his mouth, destroying his palate. After the uprising he returned to the Wolski hospital to thank Dr Woźniewski for saving his life.

Another of Dirlewanger's targets on that day was the St Lazarus hospital, two blocks away. This modern four-storey building had been a proud symbol of the Wola neighbourhood in happier times, but from 1 August it had become a haven for refugees; by 5 August the hospital contained around three hundred patients and over a thousand refugees.

Dirlewanger's 111th Regiment's 1st Battalion 'Azerbaijan' and

2nd Battalion 'Bergmann' attacked at 10 o'clock that night. The occupants heard voices and then yelling outside. They had no idea what was happening. Suddenly the SS troops forced their way into the grounds from Wolska Street, blocking the exits and ordering everyone to give up their weapons, watches and jewellery. Then the killing began.

Maria Wanda Suryn watched in terror as the SS started the slaughter in the basement: 'I saw grenades thrown in by three soldiers . . . there was no way to escape. The civilians were pushed into Room 2 and the boiler room, and the soldiers built a barricade of benches between Rooms 1 and 2. Mothers with very small children and an ill nun were in Room 2. They started to throw grenades there first.' The doctors and nurses stayed with the patients. The doctors were the first to be taken outside and executed – all of them were shot in the back of the head.[83] 'The Germans threw grenades and mines and poured petrol and set it on fire. Around six hundred people were burned. The whole hospital building was burned down after they had removed all the Germans who had been cared for by the Poles.'[84]

Those in the hospital who could not walk were murdered in their beds; many were killed in the cellars, and around 335 people were shot in the courtyard. Wanda Łokieček was in a group of girl scouts, all between the ages of fifteen and eighteen. 'There were fifteen of us in all . . . They ordered us to move a few steps forward as they executed us in groups . . . I heard shots and fell down, so did the girls round me with their heads smashed.'[85]

Sixteen-year-old Wiesława Chełmińska and her mother had gone to visit her sister, a patient in the hospital's wing on Leszno Street, close to the front line. By then those who could be moved had been put in the basement; her sister was in the hospital kitchen. When the SS soldiers entered the basement they ordered all those who could move to leave. 'We obeyed; only the badly

wounded, including my sister, remained. We were sent to the courtyard and ordered to stand close to the wall . . . I heard shots from
the basement area and saw the SS shooting wounded patients . . .
after a while the SS started to call people from our group. We were
told to go back into the basement, and after a while we could
hear shots. When there were about thirty people left in the group
my mother and I were taken to the basement . . . we could see
blood on the floor and in one of the areas by the entrance lay a
pile of bodies around a metre high . . . They ordered us to climb
on one pile of bodies. My mother climbed up first and I saw the
SS man shoot her in the back of the head and watched as she
fell. Then I climbed and fell down without waiting for the shot.
He shot anyway and I was wounded in the right arm. In the end
there were about twenty layers of bodies . . . I knew by the clock
on the wall that it was 1 a.m. when the SS men left. I don't know
when the Germans started the fire, but at 2 a.m. I felt the rubber
soles on my shoes starting to burn, so I left the pile of dead
bodies.'[86] Later witnesses 'found the bodies of the murdered
patients and of the staff in the hospital wards in beds, on the
staircases, in the passages and in the cellars . . . Most of the bodies
were in the cellars where people had been burned.'[87]

One of Poland's leading paediatric hospitals, the Karol and
Maria, was located at Leszno 36. Many wounded AK troops,
particularly from the 'Parasol' Battalion, had found shelter there,
and this made it a particular target for the Dirlewanger Brigade.
It was encircled on 6 August, and Władysław Barcikowski
watched terrified as the SS men pushed their way into the quiet
rooms at 4 o'clock that afternoon. 'Most were in German uniform,'
he said. 'They had belts of ammunition and had the blank expres-
sions of real killers. They murdered in cold blood. The Germans
amongst them told us to leave the pavilion. We wanted to take
a small child lying in his bed in traction. The Germans shouted

at us that we could not take him. To this day I hear the terrified and horrible despairing cry of this helpless two-year-old boy. The wounded were left by themselves. They were later shot in their beds.'[88]

The Dirlewanger troops gathered up personnel and patients and pushed them outside. All were convinced that they were going to be executed. A group of around a hundred people were being pushed down Młynarska Street when the column was suddenly stopped. 'A German runner with some new order came. They put a machine gun in front of us, we thought this was the end . . . After a while a soldier picked up the machine gun and a German sub-officer asked, "Where is the director of the hospital?" I was close enough to hear, and knew a bit of German. One doctor replied: "The director of the hospital is not present." The German said, "I give you one minute to think about it. If the commandant won't appear all doctors will be shot." It was a dramatic moment. We stood, petrified, in this group of doctors. Suddenly one man came forward. I don't know if he said anything, but for the German it was not necessary. The German took him by the elbow and walked him a few steps away. At a sign from the German a "*Własowiec*"* picked up the machine gun and within seconds the doctor had fallen, his head smashed.'[89] Dr Włodzimierz Kmicikiewicz had chosen to sacrifice himself to save the others. Sixty children were ordered to move out, and were meant to be taken to the Wolski hospital; all but one ran away in terror; their fate is unknown. The hospital was burned.

It was clear even on 5 August that the fight for Warsaw was going to take longer than Himmler and von Vormann had expected, and that the Germans would need hospitals for their sick and wounded. It was this consideration that saved the Wolski hospital

---

* A Russian- or Ukrainian-speaking soldier in German uniform. The Poles, mistakenly thinking that men from General Vlasov's army had been brought to Warsaw, called them '*Własowcy*'.

from being burned down after the massacres on 5 August. It also saved the St Stanisław hospital at Wolska 37 from destruction.

The St Stanisław hospital was run by a quick-thinking director, Dr Kubica, who from 1 August had ordered all Polish insurgents to leave their weapons at the door. When the Dirlewanger troops came at 3 p.m. on 5 August he was able to claim that there were no insurgents in the beds, and that as a centre for infectious diseases, his hospital had no operating facilities, and therefore could not aid the AK. 'It is neutral,' he said.

One witness remembered the moment. 'We all thought we were going to be murdered. The Germans expelled a few people to the street and shot them, including a doctor (Dr Jan Barch), but at this moment Dr Kubica came. He was from Silesia and spoke German. He was a dynamic and well-built man, and he was clever. He started to shout and behave like a corporal. He made such an impression that they stopped the murders.' Reinefarth spared the hospital, and it would later have the dubious distinction of serving as both Reinefarth's field hospital and Dirlewanger's headquarters.

The young Viennese doctor Major Hartlieb, from Kampfgruppe Reinefarth, ran the hospital for the Germans. He was soft-spoken and handsome, but he was also cruel. 'Why did you bring them?' he yelled at the soldier escorting Dr Kryńska and a small group of medical personnel towards him on 5 August. 'We don't need any Poles, and now we have to execute them!' However, when Dr Manteuffel appeared that same afternoon, having narrowly escaped death by firing squad, Hartlieb was delighted. '*Ihr name ist Manteuffel!*' he exclaimed. '*Sie sind also Deutsch!*'[90]

Oskar Dirlewanger set up his headquarters in the hospital on 9 August. He chose the best rooms for himself, and ordered them to be furnished to the highest standard, using looted goods from nearby houses. Dr Manteuffel remembered Dirlewanger as tall, strong and well-built, with an olive complexion and a cold, piercing gaze. Given Dirlewanger's usual cruelty, Manteuffel was very surprised on one occasion when he pointed to a wounded Polish civilian and, rather than ordering his execution, said, 'Get this man some help – a compress or bandages. He helped to get a German soldier out of the fire.'

Dr Kryńska, who became Dirlewanger's interpreter, gained an insight into this most brutal of men. Dirlewanger was arrogant, opinionated, and extremely powerful. He believed completely in the German racial mission to 'cleanse' the east, and was very proud of his friendship with the Reichsführer SS. 'Dirlewanger told me that he was a friend of Himmler's,' Kryńska recalled, 'and all the officers used to say that he was a very important person'. He was also extremely greedy, and looted incessantly: 'During his stay until the end of September beautiful carpets and silver were brought in from houses in Warsaw.'[91] Many of these things were sent to his warehouse in Germany, to join the objects already stolen from Byelorussia; Dirlewanger's looting was sanctioned by Himmler himself. Dr Wesołowski remembered being pushed by 'a man carrying a huge suitcase filled with silver cutlery down the corridor'. Dirlewanger 'ordered the man to sort through the goods for him'; it was a daily occurrence.

This officially permitted looting reached every level of the German occupiers. The city was slated for destruction, the argument went, so the troops might as well take whatever they could carry. In the Protocol of Interrogation of General Reiner Stahel in Moscow in 1945, Stahel admitted: 'When it became clear that German soldiers were robbing the houses of the inhabitants I released an order according to which soldiers could take all they wanted from houses which were already on fire . . . I must admit I let them rob . . . as I knew that we could not stop the German soldier from doing that.' Poles were routinely robbed before they were sent to their deaths or to detention. Watches were a particular favourite, and it was common to see broken fingers and twisted arms after rings and bracelets had been ripped off. 'At Wolska 60 the Dirlewanger troops stole everything – watches, rings, earrings, suitcases, parcels, autumn and winter coats ... very often earrings were pulled off flesh, and when they took rings they broke the women's fingers.' Dr Kryńska protested when a 'Commission of Telephones' walked into the hospital and started taking all the phones; on another day a group came in demanding the typewriters. The doctors took to hiding equipment in small shelters in the sewers in the hospital basement, but that did not stop the looting. 'One day an Oberartzt from a German field hospital came to our operating room, and to our distress took our most beautiful kits of instruments with sterilization canisters.'[92] The doctors could do nothing to protest. In early August Dr Hartlieb issued the order that 'All hospital equipment including telephones, medical equipment, microscopes and all other technical material from all the hospitals in Warsaw is to be seized, packed and sent to Germany.'[93]

Although it had not been the scene of a massacre, killing continued at the St Stanisław hospital. Dr Manteuffel recalled: 'In the first week the Gestapo came and ordered the evacuation of a large group of men from the hospital; Dr Kubica risked his life pulling people out – they were mostly doctors, including me.'[94] The hospital was reserved primarily for German patients, and any Poles hidden there were in grave danger. On one occasion 'the SS took two young AK prisoners of war and hanged them on a tree in the hospital courtyard. They decorated their dead bodies with red-and-white flags.'[95]

Dirlewanger worked closely with the Gestapo, whose headquarters were located in a house in Sokołowski Street, near the St Wojciech church. He often asked Alfred Spilker, the head of the Warsaw Gestapo, for help in 'cleaning up' the hospital. German doctors would be forced to go from bed to bed choosing patients to fill the quota, usually taking those suffering from tuberculosis and young Polish men hidden by the hospital personnel. The victims were taken to the Gestapo or to St Wojciech's.[96] Spilker ran an extermination facility at the Pfeiffer tannery at Okopowa 58–72, today the site of an upmarket shopping mall. Five thousand people, including victims from the hospital, were killed there throughout the uprising by Spilker's Sonderkommando and Reinefarth's Kampfgruppe.* News of the destruction of the Polish hospitals reached the West. On 11 August John Ward radioed to London: 'The German forces have brutally murdered wounded and sick people both men and women who were lying in St Lazarus hospital in Wolska Street, Nr. 18, and Karol and Maria hospital in Przejazd Street, Nr. 5.'

A New Approach

For all their brutality, or perhaps because of it, the Dirlewanger Brigade only managed to advance four hundred metres on 5 August. Even Dirlewanger's official reports acknowledge the difficulties. SS Sturmbannführer Weisse of the Dirlewanger Brigade was recommended for a decoration for his work that day: 'On 5 August the SS Regiment Dirlewanger under SS Sturmbannführer Weisse fought along Litzmannstadtstrasse [Wolska Street] towards Warsaw. Most severe street fighting developed, and there were heavy losses . . . Towards the evening of the first day of battle enemy resistance increased. SS Sturmbannführer Weisse made the decision to attack and destroy the enemy barricades and minefields during the night. By the

---

* On the first day of the uprising Reinefarth organized a battle group in Poznań consisting of SiPo and SD security units, which he brought directly to Wola; he was responsible for the largest massacres of civilians in the first week.

morning of 6 August some hundred metres of ground had been regained.'[97] The fighting was fierce as the Germans moved closer to more heavily fortified AK strongholds. 'Most severe street fighting with heavy losses developed. After only a few hundred metres, the attack threatened to come to a standstill. Heavy barricades and bunker-like fortified buildings forced our men to fight for every foot-length of space.'[98]

Reinefarth's decision to gather prisoners in large groups and shoot them away from the fighting had freed the Dirlewanger men from having to murder them themselves, but things were still moving too slowly. Dirlewanger wrote: 'The attack in the afternoon of 7 August threatened to come to a standstill in the ruins of the burning houses. Collapsing buildings and debris were an obstacle for all the men fighting under SS Sturmbannführer Weisse. In the evening of 7 August he decided to advance more quickly by setting all the buildings in the area on fire and then advancing behind the flames. We hope that by 8 August 1944, he will be able to fulfil his orders and reach his destination, the Markthallengelände.' Dirlewanger was referring to the Hala Mirowska market stalls. They did indeed reach their destination at noon on 8 August.[99] Over two hundred people were burned alive in the process.

The long, red-brick, neo-Gothic market stalls still stand in Wola, resembling two small nineteenth-century railway stations. For over a century they have housed little shops selling everything from meat and cheese to flowers, toys and pet supplies. They were still operating in the summer of 1944. When the Dirlewanger men broke in on 8 August, they killed everyone: 'SS Untersturmführer Schreiner led a group on the right side of the market hall which allowed us to block the enemy retreat, resulting in their complete annihilation,' Dirlewanger reported proudly.[100] The Hala Mirowska witnessed an orgy of violence. Zenon Piasecki was one of a group of civilians who were led there just after the massacre had taken place. 'I noticed close to the wall of the cool room piles of dead bodies.'[101] Men, women and children had been murdered there. Their suitcases and bags were neatly piled up to one side of the entrance.

Dirlewanger's men did not linger, but tried immediately to push through to the Brühl Palace to free General Stahel and Governor Fischer. They fought on from the Hala Mirowska through the Saski Gardens, killing everyone in their path. They reached the palace on 9 August: 'The German war flag of the Army City Commander was waving several hundred metres east of the Markthallengelände,' Dirlewanger wrote. 'Weisse made the decision to push through the heavily occupied area in a last attempt so that a connection to the army units could be established.' They made it through, and triumphantly entered the palace grounds. Dirlewanger described the 'joyous scene' as Sturmbannführer Weisse 'rolled into the courtyard standing on the tank of the Army Commander. He was greeted rapturously.' The dozens of Germans pinned down under constant fire in the palace had been running out of food and water, and had been convinced that they were going to die. Governor Fischer, General Stahel and the trapped civil servants were evacuated in a column of cars protected by tanks. The AK put them under heavy fire; Fischer was slightly wounded, and Vice-Governor Dr Herbert Hummel and another aide were killed, but most escaped unscathed, grateful that their ordeal was over.[102] Dirlewanger was praised by Himmler for this great victory; his soldiers got completely drunk.

In the next days Dirlewanger's troops began to secure the surrounding area. Matthias Schenk was sent in to set explosives at a building near the Brühl Palace when he heard a voice shouting 'Don't shoot!' in German. The doors opened, and a nurse appeared holding a tiny white flag. The building was being used as a temporary clinic. 'We entered with fixed bayonets. It was a huge room with beds and mattresses on the floor. Wounded people were everywhere, including Germans. The latter begged us not to kill the Poles. A Polish officer and a doctor and fifteen nurses from the Red Cross surrendered the military hospital to us. The Dirlewanger people were coming in behind. I managed to push one of the sisters behind the door and lock her in. I heard after the war that she survived. The SS men killed all the Polish wounded, smashing their heads with their rifle butts. The German patients were crying and shouting in despair not to shoot the Poles who had cared for them. The Dirlewanger guys began to molest the nurses, ripping their clothes off. We were driven out to go on guard duty. We heard women screaming.'

Schenk was still on duty when he heard the roar of a crowd from Piłsudski Square, then known as Adolf Hitler Platz. 'It was the sort of noise you would hear at a boxing match,' he said. 'My friend and I climbed the wall to see what was going on. There were soldiers from different units – Wehrmacht, SS, Cossacks from the Kaminski units, Hitler Youth boys – whistling and yelling. Dirlewanger was standing there with his people and laughing. Then the nurses from the hospital were pushed through onto the square. They were naked and had their hands on their heads. Blood was running down their legs. The doctor was dragged along behind them with a noose around his neck. He wore a rag, red probably from his own blood, and a crown of thorns on his head. They were all brought to the gallows; a few bodies were already hanging there. They put a noose around the neck of one of the nurses; Dirlewanger himself kicked over the pile of bricks on which she was standing.'[103] The worst was yet to come. 'The others were hanged by their feet and then shot in the stomach.' They were not dead; a Wehrmacht soldier shot them in the head to end their suffering.[104]

Schenk was disgusted by Dirlewanger's behaviour, but Himmler was amused by him. 'Dirlewanger is unique,' he said in Poznań on 3 August. 'When he began to run out of men I said to him, "Listen, try to find people amongst the hooligans in concentration camps and amongst professional criminals." The discipline in the unit is in many cases like the Middle Ages, with beatings and such things, and if someone has doubts that we will win the war he is killed immediately at the table. You can't manage such people behaving any differently.'[105] Himmler knew and approved of Dirlewanger's 'medieval' disciplinary practices because he got results.

As Himmler pointed out, Dirlewanger's success was due in part to his brutality towards his own men. When a quota of fresh German prisoners from the camps were brought in to replenish troops lost in Warsaw, Dirlewanger took the opportunity to teach them a lesson. Franz Hobelsberger, a former Sachsenhausen inmate who had recently deserted and been recaptured, was hanged from the gallows in the centre of the roll-call square, with all the new recruits in attendance. The significance of the gesture was not lost on them.[106] On another occasion Dirlewanger executed a group of men for leaving the unit without permission. 'For the execution the whole battalion had to stand there, forming an open square. The approximately twenty men were kneeling in the middle, stripped down to a shirt, and were shot in the neck by the chauffeur of the battalion commander. Light was provided by car headlights.'[107]

Some men were so desperate to get out of the Dirlewanger Brigade that they wrote to Himmler begging for help. One junior non-commissioned officer who had been taken prisoner by the Poles in Warsaw but had managed to escape and rejoin the brigade wrote: 'I have now one wish. I want to be transferred out of the unit Dirlewanger. What have I done that is so wrong that I must serve under such people who loot and get drunk, and if one doesn't participate in it, they shun you? I don't have any enemies in the unit, no, but please do not misunderstand me, dear Reichsführer, ten years have passed since I made a mistake and in the ensuing ten years, in private life as well as in the military, I have demonstrated that I have faithfully done my duty according to my oath, and I will continue to do so . . . However it is a strange feeling when you have to be with comrades from the concentration camps who have spent six to eight years behind prison walls. Dear Reichsführer, I truly believe that I have suffered enough because of a mistake which I unfortunately made.' It was signed 'My Honour is Loyalty. Heil Hitler. Andreas Schillinger.'[108]

A political prisoner recruited from a concentration camp recalled hurrying a horse-drawn ammunition cart through a barrage. 'Dirlewanger was watching through binoculars. He stopped me and accused me of being a coward because I did not shoot back. When I replied that nothing had prompted me to do so he beat me so that I fell to the ground covered in blood. Three days later I was given an additional thirty lashings due to cowardice in front of the enemy and by order of Dirlewanger.'

That the Dirlewanger Brigade was used as a punishment battalion was admitted by Gottlob Berger at Nuremberg. When asked if men in the unit had the chance 'after proving themselves to have their status and the right to bear arms restored to them', he answered, 'Yes,' adding that any sentence against the man in question would be quashed.

'In June of 1942 I was transferred to administration in the concentration camp of Majdanek,' one soldier wrote. 'I expressed the desire to leave and was transferred to the Buchenwald concentration camps as company leader because as a soldier and officer I did not want to be a murderer of innocent women and children. I then gave cigarettes to prisoners working there amongst other things and this was reported to the commander. After a heated argument I got drunk and did not report for duty the next day.' As a punishment the soldier was taken into custody and sent to the Dirlewanger Brigade, with a chance to redeem himself.[109]

Dr Bruno Wille, who was also transferred to Dirlewanger as a punishment prisoner, detested the unit: 'SS Oberführer Dirlewanger had unlimited control . . . Dirlewanger dealt directly with Himmler, with whom he enjoyed an especially preferred position . . . Dirlewanger took care of everything himself, greatly misusing his authority over life and death no matter if it concerned somebody who had a prior record or not, whether it concerned a member of the concentration camp, army or former SS. Punishment consisted only of thrashing or death, while the leadership of the whole battalion was based on corporal punishment.'[110] Ernst Rode testified to Polish prosecutors after the war that the Dirlewanger men were 'rather more a bunch of swine than soldiers'. Von dem Bach, too, tried to distance himself from Dirlewanger after the war, accusing him of hiding his crimes so that one could 'never prove anything' against him. 'His reports were full of lies,' he said. In reality von dem Bach was close to Dirlewanger throughout. He used him, relied on him, and nominated him for numerous high decorations and honours.

Hitler, who was given detailed reports about the uprising and the excesses committed in Warsaw, continued to heap praise on the Sonderkommando and on Dirlewanger throughout. Guderian, on the other hand, was disturbed by reports of his excesses, and even SS General Hermann Fegelein, not known for his squeamishness, corroborated reports that Dirlewanger was using unacceptable methods to control the city. Hitler refused to act; indeed, the Führer himself awarded Dirlewanger the Knight's Cross, Germany's highest award for bravery and military achievement, for his performance in Warsaw. For Hitler the crimes committed against civilians were irrelevant; on the contrary, he was impressed by the toughness of the fighters. The death toll in the brigade was enormously high. Dirlewanger lost 2,712 men in Warsaw; only 648 survived. His unit had the highest military effectiveness of any group in the city, and did most of the attacking; it also had by far the highest death rate. This was important to Hitler.

As in Byelorussia, however, Dirlewanger's casualty list was dwarfed by the numbers of his victims. Between 5 and 6 August the Dirlewanger Brigade and the rest of Kampfgruppe Reinefarth murdered between 30,000 and 40,000 civilians in Wola; most were killed in cold blood. There was little remorse among the German generals: Stahel wrote a report whilst a prisoner of war in Russia entitled 'Uprising in Warsaw: A Personal Testimony of General Reiner Stahel'. In it he estimated that 8,000 to 10,000 people had been killed on 5 August, but casually admitted that the number could be 'much higher, even double'.[111] During his interrogation in Moscow he claimed that the death of so many civilians 'is a natural result of street fighting. That is why I see nothing particularly significant in the fact that civilians suffered in so many cases . . . I admit that German attack groups led by SS Brigadeführer Kaminski and Dirlewanger Police Unit raped women, shot civilians and robbed houses . . . I couldn't stop German soldiers from repressions against Polish civilians'.[112] His testimony is the definition of understatement.

The sheer brutality with which the uprising was put down in the first days of August had broader repercussions. The Nazi puppet Romanian Prime Minister Ion Antonescu saw Hitler at Rastenburg for the last time on 5–6 August. It was not a pleasant meeting. The Führer was in one of his fits, and raved about Warsaw incessantly; he described the mass killings in detail, including the murder of civilians, the burning of buildings and the destruction of entire blocks – he even showed Antonescu photographs of the carnage.[113] Antonescu was clearly shaken. After his return from

Rastenburg he declared to Turkey's chargé d'affaires that it was neither possible nor in Romania's interest to try to detach itself from Germany. He was convinced above all by the 'intensity and the violence of the German reaction against the Warsaw Uprising he had seen'. Antonescu saw the horror in the face of the Turkish representative as he described the images Hitler had shown him. The Romanian leader did not believe that his country could decouple itself from Germany 'without suffering consequences as terrible as those that were developing in Warsaw, where the German action was still going on'.[114] The Warsaw Uprising had already played a role in international affairs. It would do so again.

8

THE FATE OF OCHOTA

Spare the city which has done you no harm, but, if you please, kill us, whom you have ordered to move away. (Chapter XII)

The Kaminski Brigade

As Dirlewanger was cutting his violent swathe across Wola, another SS group was using its own brand of terror to clear the Ochota district to the south. The Kaminski Brigade had also honed its skills in Byelorussia under Erich von dem Bach-Zelewski, yet they were quite different from the Dirlewanger men. These were not Germans but Russians, and their story reflects the tragic dilemmas thrown up by their country's history. The First World War, the cruel Revolution and the triumph of Lenin and Stalin had ripped the old Russia to shreds. Many millions, including Kaminski and his followers, had fallen into the Bolshevik 'meat grinder', languishing for years in the prison system, usually on trumped-up charges. Many of those who survived were motivated by the desire to rid Russia of Communism, even if it meant collaboration with the Nazis. Kaminski's dream ended not with the end of Stalinism, but in a terrible descent to utter barbarism in Warsaw in the summer of 1944.

Had the Germans entered the Soviet Union in 1941 promising to destroy the Soviet regime rather than vowing to kill thirty million Slavic '*Untermenschen*', hundreds of thousands of Russians and other nationals would have joined them. But Hitler and Himmler could not envisage such cooperation in the heady early days of victory. Local populations which might have been conciliatory were ravaged, dispossessed and murdered instead, and came to detest the Germans whom they had initially seen as liberators. Even so, there were some who detested Bolshevism so much that they saw the Nazis as a lesser evil. Bronisław Kaminski was one.

Kaminski had good reason to hate Stalin. Although he claimed to have been born in Poznań to a German mother, he had faked this biography in order to ingratiate himself with the Nazis. In reality Kaminski was born in 1899 in Vitebsk to mixed Polish-Russian parentage. Having a Polish mother made him a 'foreigner' and thus a secret-police target; the fact that he had been educated in St Petersburg and was a 'bourgeois' chemical engineer made him doubly suspect. He was arrested as a foreign agent in 1935, and sent to the gulag for five years. Kaminski was lucky in that he ended up not in one of the Taiga hard-labour camps, but in a Sharaska laboratory, where his mind was put to use; in this he shared the fate of thousands of other Soviet scientists, from Andrei Tupolev, the great aircraft designer, to Sergey Korolyov, who would later direct the Soviet space programme. Kaminski ended his sentence in Lokot, near Bryansk, south-west of Moscow, and had made his home there by the time the Germans marched in.

Nazi brutality had quickly pushed many Russians in the area into the fast-growing partisan movement. The Germans severely underestimated the '*Banditen*' problem, and they had also failed to understand the importance of Bryansk, which lay close to Moscow and was crossed by three railway lines. By September 1942 the partisans were causing serious disruption in the area: the Germans counted two hundred demolition attacks in one month alone. Something had to be done.

On 16 July 1941, shortly after the beginning of Barbarossa, Hitler had declared: 'We must never let anyone but Germans carry arms . . . not the Slav, not the Czech.' But it soon became clear that the shortage of manpower in the east would make this dream of racial purity impossible to realize. On 1 March 1942 General Max von Schenkendorff complained that he did not have the resources to fight the Soviet partisans. Standards were quietly relaxed, and by the end of the year the ranks of the SS were filled with foreign nationals. There were many in the SS who despaired at this 'muddying' of the pure Nordic race: Zvonimir Bernwald of the SS Handschar Division remembered: 'A number of the older SS men turned up their noses at these newcomers,' while Carlheinz Behnke complained that their 'fighting morale was not like ours'.[1] But the SS had no choice as the war took its toll. As Kurt Sametreiter of the SS Leibstandarte Adolf Hitler recalled, 'Ninety per cent of my regiment had been wiped out.' Replacements had to come from somewhere. Erich von dem Bach was an early advocate of such recruitment: on 3 July 1944 he would even have a meeting with the Grand Mufti of Jerusalem to try to raise a formation of Muslim recruits from the Balkans; some of these later fought in Warsaw.[2]

Kaminski offered his services to the Germans in their battle against the Bolsheviks. At first he made a name for himself by protecting the grateful men of Organization Todt, who were sent out in hostile territory to keep the rail lines operational. In return for keeping them safe from surprise attacks, they gave Kaminski all the spare equipment they could muster, turning a blind eye to these semi-legal transfers. By 1942 Kaminski had enough men and matériel for nine infantry battalions, split into three regiments totalling some 9,500 men.[3] The Germans began to use his forces for ever more important 'anti-partisan operations'. By 1943 he controlled five infantry regiments, an artillery battalion and two tank companies of twenty-four tanks; most of the men were Russian deserters and escaped PoWs, along with some Ukrainians. Kaminski's unit began to wreak havoc amongst the partisans of Bryansk, as the Germans used it in the large sweeps meant to clear the area in preparation for the intended 1943 summer offensive.[4] These operations were given romantic-sounding names like 'Zigeunerbaron' (Gypsy Baron), 'Freischütz' (Fire at Will) and 'Tannenhäuser' (Fir House), but that hid the brutal truth of the destruction of entire villages, and the deaths of thousands of innocent civilians who got in the way.

Army Group Centre rewarded Kaminski for his increasing success, and set him up as the new 'Bezirksverwaltung', or Native Administrator, of the Lokot region. It was the first time that the Germans had allowed a Slav such autonomous local power, and from their perspective it was a successful bargain – Kaminski got the chance to run a local self-government, and they were offered protection from the partisans. Kaminski tried to please his German masters, talking up the idea of creating a 'National Socialist Russia', but in reality he and his followers cared little for Nazi ideology, and wanted nothing more than to get rid of Stalin and restore basic freedoms, above all the rights to own property and to freedom of religion. He named his militia RONA – the 'Russian People's Liberation Army' – the military wing of his 'Russian National Socialist Party'. He even tried to create a kind of Utopia in his small patch of territory, setting up schools, hospitals and civic centres under watchful German eyes. But the dream was not to last. The tide was turning inexorably against the

Germans, and the Eastern Front was disintegrating fast. Far from winning a great victory in the summer of 1943, the Germans lost the Battle of Kursk, the greatest tank battle in history. This, even more than the defeat at Stalingrad, marked the military turning point of the war.

In July 1943 the Red Army was approaching Lokot at breakneck speed, and Army Group Centre advised Kaminski that he should move his group westward as quickly as possible. Everyone connected with Kaminski's unit knew that by siding against Stalin they had written their own death sentences, and that they would never be forgiven for having collaborated with the Germans. The villagers demanded to be taken with them, and Kaminski was forced to move not only his 20,000 soldiers, but also 25,000 civilians. Tearfully they piled their belongings on wagons and began to wind down the dusty summer roads, taking their cows, sheep and chickens with them. The Germans had promised that Lokot would be theirs forever, but now they were homeless. Morale plummeted, and many deserted to the partisan side.

When Erich von dem Bach returned to Byelorussia in May 1942 after a bowel operation, he had flown over burning partisan villages near Mogilev; the very sight gave him 'an itchy finger' for action.[5] A year later, however, the partisans were stronger than ever, and he needed help. In September 1943 Kaminski was ordered to go to Lepel in Byelorussia, which had the heaviest concentration of partisans in all of von dem Bach's territory. The unit, along with thousands of villagers on their carts and horses, arrived in due course, and moved into empty 'ex-partisan' buildings. It was not to be the paradise they had longed for. Kaminski's people were treated with disdain both by the locals and by the Germans: 'Along the whole route we had very serious problems with provisions . . . the Germans treated us very badly. This was caused by the fact that soldiers and their families who got almost no food began to dig potatoes on the march and sometimes took other goods. Wagons often broke down so soldiers simply took new ones from inhabitants.[6] Morale was so low that a group of Kaminski's own men tried to kill him and join the partisans. When he learned who was responsible he flew his Fieseler Storch, supplied by Army Group Centre, to the headquarters of his 2nd Regiment, grabbed the mutinous commander by the throat and strangled him in front of his men. He then had several other plotters hanged in the yard.[7]

After Kaminski's retreat from Lokot the RONA group was promoted to the rank of brigade, and became part of the 2nd Panzer Army under General Rudolph Schmidt. It was officially part of Army Group Centre, but in reality von dem Bach put Kaminski under SS Brigadeführer Curt von Gottberg, head of the SS and police for Byelorussia. Gottberg was close to Dirlewanger, and was protected not only by von dem Bach but also by Himmler, who championed him despite serious indiscretions in his past. He assimilated Kaminski's entire brigade into the Waffen SS, and gave Kaminski the uniform and rank of an SS brigade leader. Kaminski agreed to this on condition that if his men had to move again he would be permitted to take the Lokot civilians with him. Gottberg agreed.

When Stalin had called for a general guerrilla uprising against the Germans in August 1941, Hitler retorted: 'This partisan war has some advantages for us. It enables us to eradicate anyone who is against us.' Himmler believed that the army had been too soft on the '*Banditen*', and that the only way to deal with them was by extermination. Gottberg took Hitler and Himmler at their word, and initiated a new strategy, turning Byelorussian partisan round-ups into little more than full-scale attacks against the civilian population. 'In the evacuated areas all people are in future fair game,' he said. After his first operation, '*Nürnberg*', he proudly reported on 5 December 1942: 'Enemy dead 799 bandits three hundred suspected gangsters over 1,800 Jews. Our losses two dead and ten wounded.' One German soldier had been killed for every 1,450 'bandits'. One can only imagine the slaughter.

As such brutality increased, so too did anti-German resistance amongst the local population. Major General Haseloff, chief of staff of the General Government's military district, reported an increase in 'banditry' from December 1943 to July 1944. Railway lines were being attacked, particularly those between Warsaw and Minsk; over 6,000 'bandit' actions had been recorded during that time, and maps of rail lines were covered in 'x's, each denoting an incident.[8] Von dem Bach's response was to step up the terror still further, and Kaminski was expected to perform. One of Kaminski's largest 'anti-bandit' operations in Byelorussia was 'Regenschauer' (Rain Shower), launched in the Ushachi region on 11 April 1944 under the broader Operation 'Frühlingsfest' (Spring Festival). By now Kampfgruppe von Gottberg consisted of around 4,000 Germans and 20,000 'native' militiamen, including 6,000 Cossacks and Kaminski's men, who were sent against over 10,000 partisans. 'Despite determined resistance the operations succeeded in dispersing and largely annihilating the partisan brigades which had controlled the region since 1942,' the report gloated. Kaminski's men were praised; over 7,000 'partisans' had been killed, which in practice meant that once again thousands of innocent people had been slaughtered. The erstwhile Russian freedom fighters were learning to become little more than cold-blooded murderers.

Kaminski participated in the final anti-partisan drive in Byelorussia, Operation 'Kormoran' ('Cormorant'), launched on 22 May 1944. This was meant to clear the area north of Minsk, and it too became a slaughter of the innocent. 'While the partisans fought stubbornly at times their resistance lacked cohesion and they were slowly pressed into a small swampy area and cut to pieces,' the official report read.[9] By now Kaminski's RONA soldiers were beyond caring. As SS veteran Gerhard Stiller put it, they were 'after several years so deadened that they did not even notice it any more, they'd bump someone off just like that'.[10]

Operation 'Kormoran' was cut short by the arrival of the Red Army in the summer of 1944. Suddenly von dem Bach's 'anti-bandit' fighters, so used to meting out violence behind the front lines, were themselves in real danger. Von Gottberg was ordered to stand and defend Minsk, but he ran away when the scale of the Soviet attack became clear; many German officers were executed for less, but again Gottberg was protected by Himmler; he would eventually commit suicide in Allied captivity on 31 May 1945. For Kaminski the situation was increasingly dire. His brigade lost over two hundred soldiers in the fighting in the Polotsk lowlands, and many more deserted. When Minsk collapsed in a panic, the RONA Brigade and its accompanying columns of miserable civilians were forced westwards once again. The Kaminski Brigade was now officially turned over to Himmler, as it had proved of no use in front-line fighting. It was moved to Częstochowa in occupied Poland, and told to wait. All hope of returning home was now gone, but Himmler tried to keep up Kaminski's spirits. On the day before the Warsaw Uprising began he made him SS Brigadeführer and General Major. Kaminski spent the evening drinking with Himmler, Dirlewanger and von dem Bach at the Hochwald, celebrating his new role as head of the 29th Waffen-Grenadier-Division der SS (Russische Nr. 1).

News of the uprising changed Himmler's plans, and on 3 August Kaminski received the order to go to Warsaw. He was sent first to the village of Raków with 1,700 combat-ready troops, while the Russian civilians, many of whom were members of the men's families, were left behind in Racibórz. When asked by some

German officers why they had come, they answered, 'We were brought here to die.' The men were not keen to go to Warsaw. 'We pretended that we had no equipment to fight – you could see the obvious unwillingness to fight. All of us were thinking about the families which had been left just like that.'[11] A regiment was created of only unmarried men under the command of Major Ivan Frolow.

Frolow was a complicated character, tough, ambitious and vain. On 4 August the regrouped units started to move to the Warsaw area, and after 4 p.m. Kaminski's communications officer appeared in the headquarters of the 9th Army with the announcement that 2,000 of Kaminski's soldiers were ready to move into the city. Their orders were to go into the Ochota district from the southeast, and to fight through to the Poniatowski Bridge. But they did no such thing.

The RONA 'Clowns'

As for so many civilians in Warsaw, most of those in the wealthy and elegant district of Ochota had no idea that an uprising was about to begin. Melania Bischof, who worked in Wola, was abruptly sent home from work with no explanation. She picked up her two-year-old son at the Górczewska Street crèche, and got home just before 5 o'clock. She was shocked to hear the sound of gunfire. The residents of Cecelia Orlikowska's building were 'surprised by the breakout of the uprising but with more astonishment than enthusiasm', while Franciszka Pilewicz, a hairdresser, left her salon on Barska Street when she heard shooting, and managed to get to her apartment at Grójecka 48, where her children were playing in the courtyard. She took them down to the basement. 'I got the feeling that most of the inhabitants, myself included, were surprised by the uprising,' she said. Zofia Piotrowska had decided to go shopping in town, but when she went onto the street a young man told her to go home immediately. 'I wanted to know what was going on, but he just repeated that I was to go home. I returned to my staircase as fighting started'. Maria Antoniewicz was also stopped by a young man walking past the church of St Jakob: 'Be home by 4 o'clock and do not leave,' he said.[12] Her husband was just walking in the door at 5 o'clock when they too heard guns. 'Young people with red-and-white armbands were running towards SS police headquarters at the Dom Akademicki and bumping into people coming home from work. Shots rang out. Civilians tried to hide, but a number died on the streets. A woman from Barska Street was killed while on her way home, but she covered her baby with her own body and saved its life. A horse, terribly badly injured, went careering through the streets.'

But for many the uprising was welcomed with enthusiasm. In Barbara Śliwińska's home in Częstochowska Street, people cele-brated because 'we thought it was the end of the occupation'. But with only four hundred troops in the Ochota district the AK was very weak, and there was little they could do to fight back. Within hours the AK had lost its connection with Śródmieście, and Sub-Colonel Grzymała decided to leave Ochota and regroup rather than be slaughtered. The majority of soldiers left on the first night; those who remained in position in the two 'redoubts' at Wawelska and Kaliska Streets did not realize that their colleagues had retreated and that they were now trapped, a vulnerable mix of civilians and combatants. They fought fiercely, holding these two positions for some days, but the Germans had control over the rest of the area, with heavily armed troops stationed in the Higher Army School and the Sappers' School, an SD battalion at Koszykowa Street, two companies of security police in the Dom Akademicki – a huge complex of dormitories belonging to the

University of Technology – and Plac Narutowicza, and SS units in former school buildings at Wawelska, at Tarczyńska, and on the corner of Raczyńska and Niemcewicza.

Despite the overwhelming German presence, the first days in Ochota were relatively calm compared with what was to follow, and the civilians were lulled into a false sense of security. The SS did round up some people on 2 August, but these attacks were concentrated primarily on buildings in which suspected 'Banditen' were hiding. Ryszard Sitarek remembered the SS executing seventeen men at Tarczyńska Street 19, and then setting it on fire 'as punishment for the fact that someone was apparently shooting from the building'. The survivors set up an improvised camp in the garden, and waited in the stifling summer heat for something to happen. There was, as yet, no real sense of panic. Outside Janina Idaszek's home on Siewierska Street the Germans built a barricade and 'shot everyone who appeared', but people simply avoided the area. Jadwiga Freistadt's husband was one of a few dozen men from Ochota used a 'human shield' on a tank covering a transport of German wounded heading for the airport. Sixteen-year-old Maria Wodzińska was with a group in the cellar of her home at Grójecka 48 on 3 August when they heard cries of 'Raus! Raus!' They were lined up by the SS: 'We all thought it was the end. One man could not take it, and fell to his knees begging for his life.' But they were not executed; instead they were taken to the Security Police headquarters at the Dom Akademicki on Plac Narutowicza. By 4 August over five hundred civilians had been herded there, including young children and two women who had just given birth. The German police and SS had been stationed in Warsaw for some time, and were fairly lenient towards the population. 'Conditions were tolerable. The Germans who were guarding us were not brutal,' Maria Antoniewicz recalled. 'Some of them even gave portions of food to the children.' At one point

German tank drivers appeared with watches and jewellery and called out, "Trophies from Warsaw!" They actually offered these things to the crowd, but nobody wanted them.'

Maria Wodzińska was befriended by a Silesian soldier who spoke Polish very well. 'You remind me of my sister,' he told her, and brought her dry bread in his helmet which he discreetly left in the corner. Franciszka Pilewicz was brought to the Dom Akademicki from Barska Street, but by the time she arrived it was so crowded that the only place she could find room to lie down was in the orchestra pit. 'It was surreal. We were allowed to walk around, but could not leave. A barrel hidden from sight was the only toilet.' They were given black coffee and watery soup, although the women could earn extra food by helping clean up; some people used the coffee to wash in. 'An Austrian soldier brought some sugar for my children,' Franciszka recalled. But this period of relative calm was not to last. The RONA Brigade was moving towards Ochota. They, along with Dirlewanger's men, would commit some of the most terrible crimes of any of the units sent to quell the Warsaw Uprising.

Heinz Reinefarth launched his attack on Warsaw at 8 o'clock on the morning of 5 August. Seventeen hundred RONA troops, all young unmarried men, and a four-hundred-man police battalion were set against the four hundred poorly-armed AK troops in Ochota. At first the RONA men did not show up at all; they had found two partly burned-out buildings on the edge of the district, and had started looting and drinking from the first moment they were in action. The Germans were astounded by the motley group that did finally turn up. They did not have proper uniforms, but were dressed in a ragtag mixture of outfits. Many only had a clearly hand-sewn white band with the cross of St George or 'RONA' written on it; a large number of them had no ammunition, so were incapable of fighting. Von Vormann insisted they proceed, but added the 743rd Unit of Hetzer Panzerkannonen as back-up. German reports were scathing about their lack of progress: 'Kaminski's unit, which began its assault at a more leisurely 9.30 a.m. on 5 August only advanced 300 metres,' the first one read.

Kaminski's men were by now demoralized, dispossessed and homeless. As far as they were concerned, they were being sent into Warsaw not to fight, but to take some kind of reward for the years they had fought for Germany in the east. It was the first time most of them had ever seen a major city, certainly a large Western capital, and they were amazed by what was for them extraordinary wealth. The district they were ordered to take was prosperous and filled with attractive, well-appointed flats and villas on pretty tree-lined avenues with cast-iron lamp posts, ornate postboxes and cobblestone pavements which would not have been out of place in Paris or Berlin. Most residents had comfortable homes complete with running hot and cold water, bathrooms and the elegant furnishings, paintings and other amenities typical of a sophisticated European household of the day. The Russians had never seen anything like it. Nor had they ever encountered people like the inhabitants of Ochota, well-dressed men and women with beautifully cared-for children dressed in cool summer clothes.

It is no wonder that when the residents of Ochota first saw the RONA soldiers approaching, some found it hard to take them seriously. 'They did not look like an army,' Hanna Paradowska recalled, 'they looked like circus characters. They had uniforms in different colours and sizes, shirts in different colours as well. They often wore the hats of Warsaw postmen, probably because of the shiny pieces on the front. Their machine guns hung from pieces of string rather than leather. They all had lots of looted watches on their wrists . . . Despite the fact that our situation was tragic it was impossible not to laugh at them – they were grotesque.' Henryk Poborski remembered a group of Kaminski men coming towards his home: 'They were dirty, in shoes and uniforms torn into pieces and grenades strung around their necks and machine guns hanging on rope.' Some had steel helmets, some soft caps. They had ammunition belts slung around their shoulders, and their faces looked old before their time. Only the RONA patch, with its distinctive cross, sewn on their left shoulders gave away their identity.

The RONA Brigade descended first on the Staszic and Lubecki housing estates and the neighbouring streets, robbing, murdering and raping as they went. Maria Adamska was with her thirteen-year-old son in the basement of her building on Opaczewska Street when the RONA men first appeared on 5 August. 'They told us to leave the basement and took us to the building at Grójecka 104, where a huge crowd had been gathered. A young Polish man was standing just behind me. A RONA guy took him and shot him in the back of the neck with a revolver for no reason at all.'[13] The Grójecka buildings were targeted early, with dozens of RONA men swarming through the apartments looting and looking for alcohol. They took 160 boys and men, pushed them into the cellar, shot them in the back of the head and then threw in grenades. This was repeated in a number of buildings, which were then set on fire.[14] Genowefa Lange, then nineteen years old, was forced to march past her former home: 'It was already burning. The old ladies who had been left there were shot by the RONA men.' One ex-RONA soldier admitted after the war: 'I killed Polish citizens who tried to hide.'[15]

When the uprising broke out, eleven-year-old Alodia Prejzner's parents were trapped on the other side of the city, and their children faced the RONA onslaught alone. 'The Germans announced that we would be killed as someone was shooting from the roof of our home, Grójecka 20. One lady who had worked for the Germans in Poznań reacted hysterically, yelling she should not be killed, nor should the women and children. The officer ordered that we be moved to the other side of the street; we saw the men being taken to the entrance of the basement, and on the threshold they were shot in the back of the head; the bodies were later burned.' The residents were forced to pour petrol around the building and help set their own homes on fire.

In all the brutality there were, at times, glimmers of kindness. Janina Golecka was forced to gather at Grójecka 104 with dozens of other people. A young RONA soldier who 'could not have been more than twenty ran around the basement crying like a child and saying "Warsaw is burning. My God, what will become of all of you, you will be killed!"' When Lech Kilicki was expelled from his home his mother began to cry, and a RONA soldier gave her a package of smoked bacon. Fifteen-year-old Wojciech Kucharski was in a group of thirty men, all of whom were to be shot. His sister begged a German officer to spare her brother's life. 'How old are you?' the German asked him. 'Twelve,' he lied. The German slapped him twice on the face and kicked him, but then pulled him out of the group of the condemned.

In this first wave of attacks, almost all the young men were shot immediately. When Władysław Zgulczyński was being chased by some of Kaminski's men he survived by jumping from the highest floor of an unfinished building on the corner of Grójecka and Spiska. His fall was broken by a pile of dead bodies. Those who did not leave the buildings as ordered were burned alive, or shot as they tried to escape the flames. Ryszard Lemiszewski was expelled with 150 other people, and ordered to walk down the street with a white flag; thirty young men were chosen from the group and taken behind a fence. The others saw their hats flying in the air as they fell to the ground. The killing was often carried out in a particularly sadistic fashion: Jadwiga Freistadt was being marched down the street when she watched, horrified, as a RONA soldier took a young woman and her baby from the crowd. 'He held the baby's legs and smashed the body on the wall.' For a young girl who only days before had been living a fairly ordinary life it was a shocking sight.

Major Ivan Frolow, who oversaw these operations, admitted on 16 July 1946 that the uprising had indeed been crushed 'by very cruel methods. Many civilians died in the basements of buildings, also because of artillery and bombing by aircraft.'[16] But Frolow maintained that the Kaminski Brigade 'had not participated in executions. The fact that civilians were executed *en masse* was something I did not know.' This was an outright lie. It is true that mass murders of the sort taking place a little to the north under Reinefarth and Dirlewanger were less common in Ochota, but thousands of people were murdered there; the main difference between Dirlewanger's men and Kaminski's was that the RONA troops were too busy looting and raping to move the front line forward, or to gather tens of thousands of people and shoot them down. A more truthful picture was painted by Alexander Pierhurow, a Kaminski officer who testified in 1946 that 'Germans and the members of the special Kaminski Brigade unit entered buildings, they robbed and murdered many people and senselessly attacked women, children and old people. The wanton execution of Polish citizens which was never punished was very common.'[17]

The Radium Institute

In 1925 the great scientist Marie Curie visited her native Warsaw for a very special ceremony at Wawelska 15. She had decided to found a 'Radium Institute' in her home town, and had donated the substantial gift of a tenth of a gram of pure radium for medical use there – a prize which was carefully hidden from the Germans during the war. By now Curie was one of the most famous scientists in the world; a great chemist and physicist who invented the term 'radioactivity', the first woman to win a Nobel Prize, and the first person to win Nobels in two fields. The institute was opened to great fanfare on 29 May 1932, with a beaming Marie thanking everyone who had helped make her dream a reality.

This noble heritage was turned on its head when the Kaminski Brigade attacked the Radium Institute in an episode which has come to symbolize the very worst of the crimes committed during the Warsaw Uprising. Other hospitals were targeted by Reinefarth's troops to be sure, and many patients and staff were murdered, but what took place at this hospital was particularly vile, not least because some of the victims were made to suffer over a period of fourteen terrifying days before being murdered.

The first attack on the Radium Institute began at ten in the morning on 5 August, when around a hundred RONA soldiers approached from Wawelska Street. Jadwiga Bobińska was on Korzeniowski Street when she heard a roaring noise: 'A crowd of strange-looking soldiers were coming towards us in uniforms we did not recognize. After a while we heard the sound of Russian. They were Russians.' The men rushed into the hospital, yelling at the terrified patients and shooting at random. About ninety patients and eighty members of staff and their families were in the building. First the RONA men raided the pharmacy, and drank all the rubbing alcohol; when that ran out they got into the ether. By now raging drunk, they went from room to room, looting and stealing valuables from their terrified victims. Then they started raping staff and patients; many of the latter were bedridden women suffering from terminal cancer but that made no difference. Another group, mostly staff, were driven into the hospital garden and forced to march to the Zieleniak camp in Grójecka Street; many of the women were taken away at night and raped.

Ninety patients and staff were trapped in the hospital building. RONA soldiers guarded the complex, and shot at anyone trying to leave. They returned to rape all of the women patients on the ground floor; the victims were then shot and their mattresses covered with petrol and set alight. Three women – an X-ray assistant, a nurse and a patient – managed to slip out of the building; two of them were caught, taunted, repeatedly raped and then murdered. Their blood-soaked bodies were dumped in the garden.

The Kaminski men then set the hospital on fire, but it refused to burn outright, and the sixty or so surviving patients and staff tried to shield themselves from the smoke and heat. Over the following days the RONA men came and took the younger women away; again they would be raped and then killed in the garden. At other times they would try again to set the building on fire. They were always drunk.

Reinefarth issued an order that all hospitals were to be looted, and German soldiers were duly dispatched to collect all the equipment from every one in Warsaw, including the Radium Institute. When the looting party arrived they found the terrified women trapped in the building; they begged to be allowed to move to safety. The Germans looted the hospital of all its remaining equipment, then announced that they were unable to help the prisoners, as it was not in their power to do so. It was a death sentence. On 19 August the RONA soldiers returned and the remaining patients were shot. The seventy people, mostly doctors, nurses and other staff, who had been taken to the Zieleniak camp were brought back to the Institute, where an officer shot them in the back of the neck. Their bodies were heaped in a pile, covered with petrol and burned. Only one woman employee who had managed to hide in the building was able to testify to the Central Commission for the Investigation of German War Crimes in Poland in 1946 as to what had happened in the hospital. RONA Brigade officer Alexander Pierchurow said during his interrogation in 1946 that they had crushed the uprising in a 'bestial' way. 'The methods which were used shocked the world.'[18] The events at the Radium Institute bore that out; in all, around 170 patients and staff were murdered, the women often after having been raped, and the hospital was finally burned. Those who lived nearby could hear and sometimes see what was being done there. Rumours spread throughout Ochota. Nobody knew what was going on, but hopes of an early victory were fading fast. There was no news of imminent liberation by the Soviets. People began to fear the worst.

Zieleniak

Before the war the Zieleniak land at Grójecka 95 had been one of the biggest farmers' markets in Warsaw, with stalls spread over an area the size of a football pitch selling everything from meat, vegetables and fruit to furniture and fodder. In the uprising it was to become a makeshift concentration camp, and another place of terror.

As the Kaminski men cleared the houses and apartment blocks of Ochota, they found themselves burdened with thousands of people who had to be dealt with. Unlike Dirlewanger they were loath to shoot so many people, not for humanitarian reasons but because to do so would be a time-consuming and messy business that would take them away from more profitable activities. The people had to be taken somewhere. Zieleniak was the answer.

Eugenia Wilczyńska was one of the first inmates in the camp. On 5 August the inhabitants of her building were made to leave the coolness of their cellar and lined up against the wall, with a machine gun trained on them. 'There was no doubt that these were our last moments.' The tension grew as mothers and children began to scream. Suddenly one of the women with a child in her arms risked her life to break through the cordon and run off towards the road. At the time a group of old German officers was riding on horseback from Okęcie down Grójecka Street. The woman ran to them, kneeled and begged them in German not to kill them. The officer ordered the RONA men not to shoot, but they retorted that they had been told to evacuate all of the apartments, and as they had nowhere to put the people, they had to be executed. One of the old officers pointed at Zieleniak market, a large area completely enclosed by a high red-brick wall. The RONA men understood. Before long the hapless civilians were being pushed into the abandoned lot. The tall grass, already yellow in the blistering August sun, was soon trampled underfoot.

RONA Brigade headquarters had been set up in the Polish Free University on Opaczewska Street, but a group of the men moved into the Zieleniak administration building and put sentries in the old caretakers' huts. 'We saw lights there all the time and heard the music from gramophones and the yelling of drunken soldiers.'[19] Eleven-year-old Wiesława Chmielewska remembered that they 'drank vodka all the time. There was a huge amount of vodka.' They also took over the Hugo Kołłątaj secondary school building next door, from which they could control the entire area.

Everybody who encountered the RONA Brigade experienced one thing in common: robbery. One of the main reasons Kaminski's men were such exceptionally bad fighters was that their prime interest was looting. When a building was taken over they would evacuate the civilians and plunder the apartments. First they would drink all the alcohol they could find, then they would steal anything they could carry. Most had never seen dwellings like these before, and took everything, including door handles and kitchen taps. All the booty was loaded onto Kaminski's special transports, which he lied were to be used for his 'Free Russia Fund'; in reality the spoils were to be split between himself and his men. If the troops could not take something, they destroyed it: sixteen-year-old Kazimierz Tomaszewski was almost crushed on his way to Zieleniak when a grand piano came flying out of a window. By now the streets were littered with discarded clothes, toys and kitchen utensils abandoned by the soldiers in their quest for more valuable booty. Alexander Pierchurow testified on 8 July 1946 that 'the scale of robbery was immense – every soldier of the Kaminski Brigade had fifteen or twenty watches up his arm whenever he got back from a raid'. Later, the people of Ochota were repeatedly robbed of the few possessions that they had managed to grab before being forced from their homes. In the coming months of homelessness and poverty even a meagre piece of jewellery or a watch could mean the difference between getting food and going hungry. The plundering of these last possessions condemned many to a great deal of suffering.

Those who resisted having their possessions taken were killed. Genowefa Lange remembered being terrified 'as the Kaminski men wanted to cut my finger off to get a ring. A woman helped me by giving me a piece of soap.' When Count Czarnecki refused to be searched, a RONA soldier slapped him on the face. The Count slapped him back. Four RONA men held him down, and a fifth shot him in the back of the head.[20] Countess Niemojewska, aged seventy, had her fingers broken when the Kaminski men took her rings; she was taken away and did not return.[21] 'Everyone was robbed on the way to Zieleniak,' Alodia Prejzner remembered. 'A RONA soldier took my mother's gold watch and hit her and said, "I will kill you if I find something." He searched through her hair, but my mother saved her wedding ring by hiding it in the belt of her light black coat.' Others were equally ingenious: Anna Mizyk, who had been married only two months, saved her wedding ring by hiding it under a scarf; Irena Cherbichowa hid jewellery in her leg bandages. Lech Kulicki, who lived near Zieleniak, watched as 'women's earrings were simply ripped through their flesh'. Ryszard Lewandowski's father was killed when the RONA men found a torch in his pocket; Maria Antoniewicz watched a RONA soldier beat a man to death with a rifle butt because he refused to be searched.

Once at Zieleniak the horror increased. A few hours before, these people had lived in houses and apartments only minutes away, and Zieleniak had merely been the place to go for the weekly shop. Now they found themselves walled in on a barren field from which escape was impossible. By the end of 5 August over 8,000 people had been crammed in; the number would grow to 20,000 in the coming days. Honorata Wolska was taken to Zieleniak straight from her home on Opaczewska Street; her mother was so shocked by the sight that she started to laugh hysterically. Her father slapped her hard in the face to stop her so that they would not attract the attention of the RONA men.

Irena Obraniak said that even the Germans were wary of the RONA soldiers. 'They were always drunk, they were dirty and had watches from their wrists to their elbows.' Their quest for alcohol was ceaseless. Cecylia Orlikowska remembered some RONA men breaking into a store on Grojecka Street and starting to drink, but being furious to find that it was vinegar and not vodka; they murdered a group of civilians out of spite. Their thirst could sometimes be useful. Jadwiga Bobińska recalled one of her neighbours being so shocked at the appearance of the RONA soldiers that she forgot to take her child from her home; she promised a soldier vodka if he would let her go back for the baby, and he agreed.

Others survived out of luck. Lech Kulicki's father had been separated from the rest of his family when they were expelled from their building. When he saw them later he was so happy that he started to run towards them. A soldier in German uniform saw him and raised his gun: 'Son of a bitch, you are laughing,' he said, aiming at him. Lech's mother shouted at the soldier, distracting his attention long enough for her husband to slip back into the crowd. They ended up in Zieleniak together, and survived the war.

Even at this late date, Kaminski's men were still trying to enlist new recruits. As the couple were being moved to Zieleniak a RONA soldier spotted a Russian ring on Władysława Dziegała's husband's finger. 'They started to speak in Russian – my husband spoke it very well – and the man tried to convince him to join them, promising him that he would be nominated to become an officer. My husband rejected the offer.' The infuriated RONA soldier took his ring and threw away his house keys as well. 'You won't be going home again!' he shouted.

Zieleniak camp was a makeshift solution, with no provision for the number of people now being herded in; there was no shelter, no food and no electricity. In the daytime it was unbearably hot, but in the August nights the temperature dropped, and the people, most of whom were dressed in light summer clothes, shivered in the open air. The ill, the elderly and the very young suffered most: Czesława Kawałkowska was one of many who lost her newborn baby in Zieleniak.

There was no water whatsoever in the first days, and people risked their lives to get to an old paddling pool in the school next door, part of the 'Jordan Garden' playground. The water was filthy, as the RONA men used it to clean their dirty dishes. They also took potshots at the desperate people; many were injured or killed, their bodies left to rot in the sun. On 6 August some soldiers brought a barrel of water into the camp. People grabbed empty food cans from a ditch and stampeded to fill them: 'It was chaos, and the RONA guys started to shoot into the crowd so people had to queue; if someone stepped out of the line they were shot.'[22] After some days a tap was installed, but the prisoners were not allowed to use it; they had to scoop water from a trough below.

Very little food was provided, and it was dangerous to forage for anything beyond the camp, although courageous children went through holes in the wall at night and into the fields to dig up beetroots and potatoes.[23] The Kaminski men shot at them for sport. On 8 August the RONA men decided to 'feed' the camp by driving a herd of cows inside. 'The cows stampeded and started to trample us. Drunk RONA guys sat on the walls and began to shoot at the cows and into the crowd; they only stopped when the cows lay dead. The starving people tore into them for meat.' The RONA men shot if they saw flames, so many people ate the meat raw. Thirteen-year-old Halina Szczepanik was with her three siblings, one a six-month-old baby; the only food her parents managed to get during the week they were in Zieleniak was one piece of raw beef and some potatoes. 'I don't know how I managed to get a piece of meat without a knife,' Lech Kulicki recalled, having pulled a slab from one of the cows. 'We found two old marmalade tins and cooked the beef in those, with some vegetables and a few potatoes. Each person from our group got a mug of hot fatty soup.' Henryk Poborski managed to get a piece of raw meat, which his father warmed up in a tin. 'We bartered a second piece of meat for a bit of water.'

Most, however, had no food, no water, no provisions, and had been robbed of whatever belongings they had taken from their condemned homes. They suffered terribly. Women gave birth on the ground, with little medical care, and a number died.[24] Natalia Stawiarska remembered an insect-infested shed where the babies were born: 'a woman was giving birth to a baby with no water and a doctor crawled in to help her but did so in complete silence so as not to provoke the RONA soldiers.'[25] One of the doctors who helped deliver babies in Zieleniak was herself killed by a grenade. 'Her own baby was smashed against a fence.'[26] Genowefa Lange watched, helpless, as a RONA soldier stabbed a newborn baby with his bayonet.

Executions were common; from time to time RONA soldiers would gather a group together and pick out every tenth person to be shot for some real or imagined offence. An increasingly large mound of corpses littered the entrance to Zieleniak, and dozens of bodies lay along the nearby roads or by the walls. Halina Sosińska remembers that at the beginning they tried to bury bodies individually, but after a few days it was hopeless, as the bloating corpses covered with black flies became putrid in the sweltering summer heat. Over a thousand people died in the camp in the first two weeks.

One of the great tragedies of the Warsaw Uprising was the number of children who were separated from or lost their parents, and had to face the dangers of the city alone. Antoni Pacholski's father had decided to take his three boys to work on 1 August and had left them at the office to deliver one last load of bricks just before 5 p.m., but he did not come back. They would later learn that he had died in Dachau. Strangers took the boys to the church of St Jakob, where the priests from the orphanage took them in, and they ended up in Zieleniak. Eugenia Wilczyńska's mother was supposed to join her two daughters in their bunker when the bombing started. She never came back. Jadwiga Dąbkowska saw two daughters helping their ill father; 'one of the Germans noticed that he could not walk, so he was taken out of the group and shot; his body was thrown onto a potato field and the girls were left alone'. Sixteen-year-old Maria Wodzińska's father was also shot by Kaminski's men as they marched to Zieleniak; she was not allowed to say goodbye, but had to walk on as if nothing had happened.

Rape

Perhaps the worst aspect of Zieleniak was rape. Attacks against women and girls were frequent; indeed, the raping started even before the victims reached the camp. Ryszard Sitarek fought as Kaminski soldiers tried to take his twenty-three-year-old sister when they were expelled from their home at Tarczyńska 19. One Russian hit him hard in the stomach with a rifle butt, but he managed to gain the attention of an SS man standing nearby and, using the few German words he knew, persuaded him to save his sister. Few were so lucky.

Rape was simply a way of life for the RONA men, who saw the women of Warsaw as a prize they had earned for years of service to Germany. Zieleniak was the most convenient place to commit this crime, as thousands of women were trapped there for the choosing. From the first night soldiers walked around shining torches on people huddled on the ground. Eerie bright circles landed on terrified faces, and girls and women were simply hauled away.[27] They were often raped in the allotment area or behind the wall, but could be taken anywhere, including to the market toilets. Irena Obraniak's friend had two daughters, aged eight and eleven: 'A RONA man wanted to take one of them, but my friend offered herself instead. We could hear her screams and cries all night, and in the morning they shot her anyway. Her husband lost his mind.' There was terrible cruelty in all the RONA soldiers did. Honorata Wolska watched as one man took a twelve-year-old girl, killed the mother who had offered herself in the child's place, and raped the girl beside her dead mother's body.

Eugenia Wilczyńska hid on the second night as the Kaminski soldiers raced around the market in pairs picking out pretty young girls. 'The next day we could see the dead bodies of those same girls in the ditch. The parents were crying and shouting, and some were shot. Neighbours tried to calm them, putting their hands over their mouths so that they would not be murdered too.' Ryszard Lemiszewski recalled that some women were taken more than once; 'often those who came back were so traumatized that they were unable to speak'.

Jerzy Skwarek saw a seventeen-year-old girl killed because she did not want to leave her mother to go with one of the soldiers. 'The mother had pleaded with them: "What are you doing, she is only a child." The soldier killed the girl right there and then took the mother away. She never returned. Women were also raped in the square in front of everyone, and those who raped them were drunk. The form of the rape depended on how drunk they were.'

Wiesława Chmielewska saw a RONA soldier pull a woman from his group. 'She was begging for help from the people around her, but nobody dared do anything. Then she got up and stood there in front of the soldier and then slapped him very hard in the face. He took out his pistol and shot her.'

The Kaminski men showed a mocking cruelty towards their victims. On 7 August a group approached the parents of some pretty young women and 'requested' at gunpoint that they be allowed to take their daughters. 'We will bring them back,' they promised. The next morning they brought the devastated young women back along with 'gracious' gifts; one of the fathers was ceremoniously given a box of underwear as a present.[28]

Zofia Piotrowska remembered RONA soldiers dragging a young woman away from her husband and baby; the husband began to scream, and the soldiers told him they would kill him if he didn't stop. She came back after some time. 'She had been beaten, her clothes were torn to pieces and she was crying spasmodically, having been raped by nine RONA men.' Zofia also saw an eleven-year-old girl who had been raped and beaten by RONA soldiers lying beside the wall; her mother was kneeling and holding her in her arms. The girl died that night. When Kazimierz Tomaszewski went near the administration buildings he saw gruesome evidence of RONA bestiality. 'Six bodies of naked young girls with wounds on their necks just beside their ears and around their eyes, some had had their breasts cut off and others had bottles between their legs.' Lech Kulicki, twelve years old, went to the school to fetch water. 'Three or four RONA guys were sitting at a table just beside the wall. A woman was kneeling under a table beside them, holding her intestines in both her hands.' He heard just before he left Zieleniak that RONA men had burned the bodies of over eighty women in the gymnasium of the school.

The Kaminski men simply did not care who their victims were. The Germans found that they had raped 'Volksdeutsche' women who were supposed to have been protected; and Zofia Piotrowska remembered coming across a group of Czech women who had been raped in the school. Kazimierz Tomaszewski, then sixteen, recalled RONA men forcing boys to masturbate in front of them. Even women who had just given birth were taken away and raped, as were very young girls. Henryk Poborski remembered seeing the bodies of girls who had sometimes been raped by more than ten men lying against the wall. 'They were half naked, many had been shot in the stomach or the chest.'

Women learned to disguise themselves in order to survive this hellish prison. Thirty-year-old mother of two little girls Halina Jedyńska was told the minute she entered Zieleniak not to show herself, and quickly put a scarf over her head. Natalia Stawiarska changed into men's clothing; Maria Adamska 'put mud on my face and messed up my hair'. Seventeen-year-old Janina Idaszek's mother 'put scarves on our heads so we looked like old women', while Maria Piekarz plastered mud and dirt all over her face and put a pillow under her dress. One husband scratched his skin to make it bleed, and then smeared blood all over his wife's clothes and on fake bandages to make it look as if she had been wounded. Marta Czerniewiçz's mother cut her hair to make her look like a boy.

Families desperately tried to hide girls and women at night. Halina Szczepanik, who had seen many women and girls being pulled out of the crowd by soldiers on their way to Zieleniak, was covered by a dirty blanket and her four younger siblings lay on top of her. Maria Piekarz, who was incarcerated in Zieleniak for several weeks, avoided being raped by being covered in rags, with her sister's five children and other members of her family lying on top of her. Irena Obraniak also avoided being raped by her family sleeping on top of her; in the morning they had to massage her and slap her skin in order to get her circulation going again. Maria Adamska helped hide a pretty seventeen-year-old girl who was on her own; 'other girls who were spotted and refused to go with the RONA men were murdered in a bestial way'. Nineteen-year-old Genowefa Lange's father dug a hole in the ground in the middle of the market, and she lay in the dirt covered by pieces of wood with her father on top. Alodia Prejzner saw a woman roll up a number of young women in a huge living-room carpet that had somehow ended up in the camp; family and friends took turns lying over it to hide them. Some friends hid their child in a cushion and put fake humps on the wife's back and chest to make her look disfigured. Girls were hidden in wooden cupboards from the school.[29] Lech Kulicki remembered hiding his mother from the RONA soldiers: 'I only had a small jacket and shorts, as did my brother, my father was in a shirt with no jacket, and my mother had a summer dress and a coat which we used as a blanket. We slept on the ground with my mother in the middle, my brother and me on either side and my father on top to hide my mother.' These elaborate ruses saved many girls and women from being raped, but the soldiers still found plenty of victims. Henryk Poborski remembered RONA men spotting two girls hiding under layers of blankets. They were taken away.

Amidst all the horror there were moments of kindness. One RONA soldier told a young girl that he would not rape her as she reminded him of someone at home. Natalia Stawiarska was stopped when she went to the school to get water. 'A RONA soldier wanted to rape me, but I begged him, and for some reason he didn't do it but protected me as I carried the water back.' Maria Adamska remembered that on 6 August 'two RONA guys came to me and I had my hair down and was not yet dirty and looked quite all right. One paid me a rude "compliment" and took my hand and started to drag me away; my son started to shout very loudly and didn't want to let go of me and one of the RONA guys said, "Leave her, maybe we'll find a younger one," and I was saved.' When a Kaminski soldier started to drag Czesława Kawałkowska's daughter away she pretended to show him great respect, calling him 'Herr Offizier' and behaving with deference. The soldier kicked her hard a number of times, but then let her go.

The Wawelska Redoubt

Von dem Bach and von Vormann were becoming increasingly incensed by Kaminski's behaviour. They were informed daily about events in Zieleniak and elsewhere, and knew that his soldiers were drunk and disorderly most of the time. Kaminski had been in Ochota for eight days, but was nowhere near the Poniatowski Bridge; indeed, his troops had advanced by only a few city blocks, and seemed to have stopped fighting altogether in favour of raping, looting and getting drunk. They had not even managed to take the two 'redoubts' at Wawelska and Kaliska, despite the fact that these were held by only a few dozen poorly armed insurgents. As von dem Bach put it, 'The capture of a liquor supply was more important for the brigade than the seizure of a position commanding the same street.'

For the civilians trapped in the two redoubts the wait was agony, not least because they were being pounded from the air and by German artillery. Wanda Skrzeszewska had been hiding in the basement of her apartment building in the Wawelska redoubt since the beginning of the uprising. 'After five years of occupation the inhabitants of our block were very close, like a family. One man was completely terrified of the sound of the bombs, so we put an iron pot on his head as a joke to calm him down.' On 8 August her husband, who worked for Błyskawica radio station, managed to get through to her on the telephone in their building. She had hoped for a cheerful message, but instead he was in despair, and broke down on the phone. 'Everything is going wrong,' he said. 'We can't expect anything good to come of this now.' He had called to say goodbye, and to thank her for the love and happiness they had had together. She was heavily pregnant, and now understood that she and her daughter Basia would have to face whatever was coming alone. At this early stage of the uprising people still had candles, food and water, but the pounding of the bombs and the fear of what was going to happen next made life almost unbearable. Some people began to turn against the AK, and to blame them for having started the uprising.

The German attack to drive the AK from Wawelska began in earnest on 10 August, and although they fought bravely, the Polish troops under Jan Mazurkiewicz ('Radosław') did not have a chance. The Germans smashed the few city blocks with everything from mortars and anti-tank guns to concentrated clouds of machine-gun fire; then the tanks were brought in. The trapped civilians sat in terrified silence as explosions rocked the buildings to their foundations. 'The next day, 11 August, hell began,' remembered Wanda Skrzeszewska. 'We in the basement were terrified, and we panicked. The AK insurgents left the district via the sewers. Then the RONA Brigade came. They started by dropping grenades into the basements. We ran from one place to another like rats, with the feeling that nowhere was safe. Basia cuddled me, but I could not lift her because of the pregnancy. At around 7 p.m. it fell silent. We were ordered to leave the basement. I was in my worst dress, a summer coat, and had a tiny suitcase in which I had documents and clothes for the child which would be born at any time. I hid watches and gold inside a corset. I was robbed of the watches. Later I tried to bribe a RONA man with a cup and saucer, but he was not interested.' The inhabitants were rounded up and taken to Zieleniak.

The second redoubt, at Kaliska, was defended by Unit 'Gustaw' along with a group from the 'Parasol' Battalion. Andrzej Ulankiewicz was with the latter: 'All the windows at ground level had been barricaded with sandbags or barred to prevent access. Some drunken RONA men decided to get to us by climbing up the iron drainpipes. When they got to the second floor they were of course liquidated by our sentries. The enemy, true to form, never attacked at night. We only heard the sounds of their debauchery – screams of raped women and the crying of those being murdered. We saw people being doused with gasoline and burned alive in part of the Radium Institute at Wawelska Street. We realized that we had to fight to the very end, as we would all be killed without mercy by this vicious band of thugs.' At one point a Polish sergeant downed a telephone pole onto a tank at Barska Street, forcing the Germans to retreat for a time.

The Kaminski men proved to be so useless in the fight that a unit from the SS Galizien Division was sent in to finish the job. The AK soldiers continued to pelt German tanks and Goliaths with Molotov cocktails and *filipinki*, even knocking out a few of the latter, but the Germans were steadily gaining ground. Andrzej Ulankiewicz watched from a window as the Goliaths hit his building with their deadly payload of TNT: 'The vastness of destruction was unbelievable . . . this corner section of the solidly built edifice was reduced to little more than a one-storey heap of rubble . . . Outside the unrelenting and indescribably intense fusillade from all types of enemy weapons made it clear that our only possible salvation lay through getting to the storm-drainage system.'[30] The civilians had no such way out. 'I could hear women's cries and the desperate prayers for the dying. A large group of civilians were gathered there awaiting their tragic fate. In the light of burning candles I could see the faces of deathly scared people.'[31] An eighteen-year-old insurgent who had been shot in the stomach was brought to the basement at Barska Street. 'A doctor wanted to operate, but there were no conditions or tools to do so and the boy died, and his body was wrapped in a kelim rug.'[32] 'One woman whose child was killed went mad, and walked around and around calling out her name.'[33] Fourteen-year-old Bożena Grzybowska trembled in fear as her building was overrun: 'I lost my beloved grandmother, who was shot, and then my house was destroyed.' She was taken to Zieleniak. The AK defence in Ochota was finally broken on 11 August.

After the war, Major Frolow tried to restore the reputation of the Kaminski Brigade, claiming that it was he who had taken the area: 'The unit reported to me, and it was because of me and my troops that Ochota was cleansed of rebels. I cannot say how many insurgents were killed in the fights, as nobody bothered to count.'[34] Whatever the truth, Kaminski's men were now free to do as they pleased in Ochota, and they took the opportunity to drink, to loot, to rape and to burn.

Władysław Szpilman was hiding in Ochota as the RONA men rampaged through the district. As a Jew he was forced to conceal himself from everyone, including the Poles, for fear of discovery. When his building was set on fire he remained inside, choking on the smoke pouring into his attic hiding place. The next day he crept down the stairs: 'The floor below me was already burnt out, and the fire had died down there. The door frames were still burning and the air in the rooms beyond shimmered with heat. Remains of furniture and other possessions were still smouldering on the floors, leaving white heaps of ashes as the glow died out where they had stood. As I came down to the first floor I found the burnt corpse of a man lying on the stairs; its clothes had carbonized on it, and it was brown and horribly bloated.' Once outside, he dodged German patrols in his search for a new place to hide. 'The broad roadway was lit up by the red glow of the fires. It was covered with corpses, and the woman I had seen killed on the second day of the rebellion still lay among them . . . Germans were constantly passing by, alone or in groups, and when they did I stopped moving and pretended to be another corpse. The odour of decay rose from the dead bodies, mingling with the smell of the fires in the air.'[35] He found a new hiding place, but was constantly in danger from the parties of RONA men intent on looting buildings before they were burned out. On one day alone 'the Ukrainians entered the building three times to search for loot in the undamaged parts of the flats. When they had gone I went down to the flat where I had been hiding for the last week. The fire had spared nothing but its tiled stove, and the Ukrainians had smashed that stove tile by tile, probably in search of gold.'[36] Hours later he watched as the SS and Ukrainians rounded up people from another building. 'People carrying bundles on their backs, mothers with children clutching at them, were driven into this cordon. The SS and the Ukrainians brought many of the men out of the cordon and killed them in front of everyone for no reason at all, just as they did in the ghetto while it still stood.' Before long the area had been completely cleared of civilians, leaving him alone, starving and vulnerable in the ruins. 'I went down to the mezzanine floor and looked out of the window. Below me were hundreds of burnt-out villas, an entire part of the city now dead. The mounds of countless graves stood in the little gardens.'[37]

Von dem Bach

When Erich von dem Bach-Zelewski arrived in Warsaw on 5 August, the city was already a terrible sight. 'Houses burning all around and mountains of corpses in the streets,' he wrote. He went in search of his detested rival Reinefarth, and found him next to piles of bodies by one of the Wola cemeteries. 'Reinefarth leads a Kampfgruppe. Very orderly, and with better nerves than I,' Bach said, referring to the thousands of civilians lying dead in the streets. 'But then again,' he griped, 'he has been resting since 1940.'[38]

After the war von dem Bach would claim that he was so disturbed by the mass slaughter perpetrated by Reinefarth that he immediately gave the order to stop killing women and children. On 26 January 1946 he testified: 'When I got to Warsaw I saw a group of civilians taken to the cemetery and shot by members of Reinefarth's *Sturm* group . . . I intervened right away.' Q: ' . . . You forbade the execution of the civilians?' Bach: 'Yes, I forbade it and I stopped the executions. I personally went to Reinefarth and I informed him of the situation. Then I focused his attention on this mass of uncivilized people and the mess of what they are doing, and the fact that his units are executing innocent civilians. The first thing he said was that he had received a clear order that he is forbidden to take PoWs, and that every inhabitant of Warsaw must be killed, including women and children. Then I immediately cancelled Himmler's order.' Q: 'You cancelled the order of your superior? It was Himmler's order.' Bach: 'Yes, that was Himmler's order. Pure and clear order.'[59] In his diary he wrote: 'I have saved the lives of thousands of women and children even though they are Poles. The bloody and terrible fight goes on. We fight in danger and even so I will lead the fight in as humanitarian a way as possible.'

Von dem Bach's action had an immediate effect in Wola. Lines of people who were waiting in the stifling heat to be pushed in front of a machine gun watched incredulously as officers appeared on motorcycles and ordered the would-be executioners to let the prisoners go. Most of the men were still killed, but women and children were gathered up and sent 'to the rear' for deportation. In those grim and terrifying hours even this was something of a miracle. After his meeting with Reinefarth, von dem Bach went to his next stop: Ochota.

The thousands of prisoners crammed into the Zieleniak market were surprised when German officers suddenly appeared in the camp. The civilians were ordered to gather on the cobblestones in the centre of the area, kneel down in neat rows and raise their hands above their heads; the men were ordered to remove their hats. Many thought they were about to be executed. To their relief they learned that they were about to receive an important visitor instead.

Von dem Bach was, as ever, determined to make an entrance, and arrived in the camp with great fanfare. He got out of his car and stood in the middle of the kneeling crowd, tall, portly and elegantly dressed, with his round glasses glinting in the sunlight.

His speech did not last long. The Poles were to understand that they had started this violent uprising, and could not blame anyone but themselves for what was happening now. Furthermore, they were to remember that for any German killed in Warsaw, forty Poles would die. But he was a humanitarian man, and had stopped the mass executions. He would now see to it that everyone was 'relocated' from Warsaw as quickly as possible.

The speech did little to settle people's nerves; nobody knew if they could trust him. Afterwards, a Polish lawyer who spoke German was permitted to talk to von dem Bach privately, and told him about the looting and the rapes in Zieleniak. Von dem Bach half-heartedly agreed to send German soldiers to guard the camp, and conditions did improve for one day, but then things returned to normal. When Janina Idaszek complained in German to one of the soldiers about the barbaric treatment meted out by the RONA soldiers, he said, 'You wanted an uprising, and now you have one.' For all the filth, lack of food, water and shelter, and with the bodies of RONA victims already piling up by the gate, von dem Bach said of his visit to Zieleniak: 'I did not notice anything particularly wrong there. Everything was perfectly fine.'[40]

After the war, von dem Bach was keen to appear 'the saviour of Warsaw', and he repeatedly talked about his decision to stop the executions as having been motivated by his 'humanitarianism'. This is unlikely. Bach was the ultimate careerist, and thought above all in terms of his own power and position. By the summer of 1944 everything he did was done with an eye to what would happen after the war. He realized that the Soviets would soon be occupying all of Poland, and that the war was lost; indeed, he wrote to his wife musing on the imminent Russian onslaught, words that would have been seen as treasonous had they been discovered. Like many top Nazis, Bach believed that he would survive to play a leading role in the post-war world; he also hoped that the West would ally itself with Germany in a fight against Bolshevism which might open up a career path for such a distinguished veteran of the anti-Soviet war. He was determined to create a new image for himself, one that would make him acceptable to the Allies as a future German leader. He knew that it would not do him any good if film crews were to capture images of tens of thousands of babies and children and mothers rotting in the hot sun on the streets of Warsaw in the late summer of 1944. It was not that he was squeamish – he had sanctioned the deaths of tens of thousands of people in his day – but he knew that in this case it would be difficult to hide the truth.

At Nuremberg von dem Bach claimed that he had been moved by a sudden wave of compassion and humanity to defy Himmler's order and save the people of Warsaw. 'I intended to suppress the uprising using political means,' he said. 'That is why my first decision was to cancel Order No. 1 and not to fulfil it no matter what the consequences.' He was simply lying; indeed, there is good reason for Göring's obscene outburst of fury at von dem Bach's Nuremberg testimony.[41] There is absolutely no possibility that von dem Bach would have had the courage to revoke such an order on his own initiative; he must have secured Himmler's permission to revoke the order to kill all civilians before talking to Reinefarth on 5 August. The question, then, is not why von dem Bach revoked the order, but why Himmler allowed him to do so.

The period of the Warsaw Uprising seemed to mark a turning point in Himmler's life. In the early years of the war he had been utterly faithful to Hitler and to all that the SS stood for, but things had changed so much by the late summer of 1944 that even Hitler's 'Treuer Heinrich' was starting to have doubts. Himmler was now certain that the war was lost, and did not know what to do. He was a nervous wreck, and his behaviour became erratic, contradictory and unpredictable. One minute he would declare his absolute loyalty to Hitler, and the next he would speculate about his own place as Hitler's successor; one day he would pledge to fight with the Führer to the end, and the next he would be negotiating a secret peace deal with the West. When he was with Hitler and the likes of Kaltenbrunner, who were determined to kill all the Jews without mercy to the bitter end, he portrayed himself as the unflinching SS racial warrior; yet in early 1945 he would be sending out feelers to Count Bernadotte of Sweden to negotiate the release of some Jewish prisoners. Indeed, the Warsaw Uprising coincided with Himmler's secret initiative to stop the extermination of the Jews altogether. According to Rudolf Höss, the former Commandant of Auschwitz, Himmler decided to 'discontinue the Jew-extermination in the autumn of 1944'. SS Standartenführer Kurt Becher, chief negotiator in Himmler's bizarre attempt to barter a group of Jews for some trucks,* placed the start of Himmler's change of heart at mid-September 1944, precisely when the Warsaw Uprising was at its height.[42] At this point Himmler was vacillating wildly in his proclamations, bargaining with Bernadotte to free Jews, and then reversing his decision and yelling that the inmates of the camps would not be allowed to emerge as victors: 'They will go under with us! That is the clear and logical order of the Führer and I will see that it is carried out thoroughly and meticulously.'[43] A week later Himmler again changed his mind, agreeing not to pass on Hitler's order that all the camp inmates be killed. This increasingly erratic behaviour may account for von dem Bach's ability to convince Himmler to stop the slaughter of the women and children of Warsaw in early August 1944.

Bach had powerful arguments at his disposal. First of all, the SS did not have the manpower to finish such an 'Aktion' in such a short time. Von dem Bach had seen at first hand what 'processing'

---

* See page 546

victims on such a scale actually entailed, and had been one of the first to point out to Himmler the psychological damage it did to his men to have to kill so many civilians at one time, face to face and in cold blood. One of the founders of Auschwitz, he had from the beginning been a strong advocate of murder by gas so as to spare his men the dirty task of having to kill at close quarters. When Himmler gave a speech explaining why the Jews had to be killed in their entirety, he said: 'We were forced to come to the grim decision that this people must disappear from the face of the earth. To organize this assignment was our most difficult task yet. But we have tackled it and carried it through, without – I hope gentlemen, I may say this – without our leaders and their men suffering any damage in their minds and souls. That danger was considerable, for there was only a narrow path between the Scylla and Charybdis of their becoming either heartless ruffians unable any longer to treasure human life, or becoming soft and suffering nervous breakdowns.'[44] Von dem Bach had been instrumental in sparing the feelings of the executioners. He could not have put it better himself.

It was not just the killing. Bach also knew from experiences in Treblinka and elsewhere the enormous difficulty of disposing of several hundred thousand corpses at a time without the 'correct' facilities. Did he really want the Allies to march into Warsaw to find piles of half burned bodies because the SS had not been able to hide the evidence? Treblinka had posed enormous problems for the Germans, who had resorted to building gigantic pyres of the dead which often did not ignite; the SS had only just managed to eliminate the grim remains of the camp and plant saplings on the ash-covered ground before the Soviets came. But Warsaw was not Treblinka. The eyes of the world were upon the city, and the mass murder and disposal of such a large number of people in secret was unfeasible by August 1944.

Von dem Bach had another reason to preserve the civilians: their potential value as slave labour. With very few exceptions the people still living in Warsaw were not Jewish, and therefore did not automatically qualify for extermination. Bach had long been trading in human beings for labour, and had met Fritz Sauckel on a number of occasions, the last being in Mińsk just before the Soviets arrived, when they had discussed new quotas for forced labour for the Reich. Both Sauckel and Albert Speer had requested that Bach send ever more labourers to Germany; he had even set up a transit camp specifically for women and children in Byelorussia.[45] When Bach took over command in Warsaw, Sauckel and Speer asked him to provide workers from the civilian population, and again Bach agreed. As a result, the uprising brought about the biggest and the last major operation to move people from Poland to work in the Reich.[46] Had the population been Jewish, there is no question that they would have been murdered, or at least the attempt would have been made to kill them all, as was happening in Hungary at the time. But the SS had already exterminated nearly all the Jews of Warsaw, and the remaining Poles, slightly higher on the Nazi racial pecking order, could be sent to work instead. The decision to use so many women, including those with children, rather than able-bodied men was also significant. By this stage of the war there were murmurs about the danger of having so many young foreign men in Germany, who if fortunes changed might act as a fifth column for the Allies and help create another 'stab in the back' attack from within. This is part of the reason why so many men from Warsaw were either executed in the city or sent to camps, while a disproportionate number of women were sent to the Reich.

Whatever his reasons, von dem Bach did manage to convince Himmler to stop the slaughter in Warsaw. On 9 September Himmler sent Hans Frank new instructions for the treatment of 'insurgents and civilians' in the city: 'Men who participated in the uprising or who probably did are to be located in concentration camps . . . all those people who surrender together with women and children are to be sent to work camps in Germany.'[47] It was quite a *volte face*. A short time later, Himmler elaborated on his new vision for Warsaw. Suddenly the once vilified city was being called the 'capital of betrayed Poland . . . Resistance had burst out as the Poles believed that Germany had lost the strength to break the insubordination of this city of millions behind the German front.' But despite crushing the uprising, 'it was thanks to German humanity as well, to be sure, to the prudence of the Polish General Bór . . . that the last quarter of a million Polish men, women and children in the middle of the cauldron were allowed to escape certain death in the street fighting of this blazing hell'. Not only was Himmler denying any responsibility for creating this 'hell' in the first place, he had transformed himself from 'anti-bandit warrior' to a great 'humanitarian' who, like von dem Bach, had 'saved thousands' from certain death. Clearly he too had his eye on the future. Surely he would be rewarded for his humanity after the war.

Himmler had another reason to respect the Polish fighters; indeed, the declaration about Warsaw was part of his 18 October Leipzig speech during which he announced the creation of the *Volkssturm* to the German people. He had become obsessed with the idea of raising an auxiliary force for the defence of the *Vaterland*, and the valiant fight of the insurgents in Warsaw had clearly impressed him. The poorly equipped AK, with only meagre weapons and little battle experience, had defended the battered city with surprising success. If every German could fight as hard as the people of Warsaw, perhaps they too could stave off defeat and buy time for some last-minute miracle to end the war in Germany's favour? Himmler's belief that he would play a role in

349

the post-war world carried him through, although he continued to 'switch violently between fanatical loyalty to the person of the Führer . . . and a vision of himself as the Führer's successor nego- tiating an alliance with the West against the Russians. Even that idea was split between his hope of proving himself acceptable by releasing prisoners and, on the other hand, using his important group of prisoners as "hostages" to force a bargain.'[48] Himmler continued to waver until the end. On 21 April 1945, after trying to send peace feelers to General Eisenhower, he talked about his dream of founding a new National Unity Party without Hitler's by now cumbersome presence, completely unaware that the Allies would never dream of negotiating with one of the greatest criminals who had ever lived.[49] But at the very end Himmler's true colours came through. Minutes before he committed suicide in captivity on 23 May 1945 he was shown pictures of piled corpses and living skeletons found at Buchenwald. The British intelligence officer in charge asked for his comments. 'Am I responsible for the excesses of my subordinates?' he asked. Shortly afterwards he bit down on the cyanide capsule concealed in his mouth and died.[50]

Only Hitler remained true to his vision of what was to be done to Warsaw. He continued to insist that all men be executed and the city utterly destroyed, reissuing this order on 19 September 1944. The Polish capital was to be emptied of all inhabitants, and every building was to be blown up. For Hitler there was to be no reprieve for the hateful city. Interestingly, the writing was on the wall for RONA leader Bronisław Kaminski as well.

Kaminski's men had turned out to be utterly hopeless in Ochota, unable to fulfil any of their military objectives and constantly running into trouble with German troops on the ground. Any successes were due to the presence of a company of *Sturm* sappers who had been sent in to support them; it was these troops who managed to fight their way through to Jerusalem Avenue, to Sawicki Square, and on 12 August to Starynkiewicza Square. Kaminski's men followed them and immediately set about looting the gynaecological clinic and robbing, raping and murdering the staff and patients of the Hospital of Baby Jesus. On 13 August the group made it to Chalubiński Street, Nowogrodzka and Wspólna. Kaminski's men settled in and refused to go any further. The looting, raping and drinking continued unabated.

Tension between Kaminski's men and the Germans increased to the point of violence: Major Frolow testified after the war that his troops had shot German soldiers in Ochota for getting in their way. There were other problems too, as when it was discovered that the Kaminski men had raped two young *Kraft durch Freude* girls, who as Germans were supposed to have been protected.

A furious von dem Bach met Kaminski again on 9 August, and set up a German commission to look into the matter of his men's behaviour in Ochota. The meeting that followed in Zieleniak between the Germans and Kaminski became so loud that the people on the square could not help but overhear; indeed, the dispute was 'so violent that a drunken RONA soldier shot between one of the Germans' legs'.[51] On 11 August the Germans shot twelve RONA soldiers for insubordination.

Bach had had enough. Kaminski was called to German headquarters at Ożarów, outside Warsaw, to account for his behaviour. An officer who was present heard his defence: he and his men had fought for the Germans for years; they had been forced from their homes, and had nothing to show for their loss; they had been promised a free hand in Warsaw as compensation for their long years of service. 'There were fierce arguments, and Kaminski was put in his place,' he recalled. Kaminski returned to Warsaw but did not change; one soldier remembered seeing him on the balcony of his headquarters, a bottle of vodka in one hand and two women on his knees. His command was officially cancelled on 19 August, and Leutnant August Weller of the German 9th Army saw him leave Warsaw laden down with chests full of booty. His men stayed in Ochota under Major Frolow.

On 27 August von dem Bach talked to Fegelein, who also detested Kaminski and had regularly briefed Hitler on RONA's conduct. It is likely that Kaminski's fate was sealed during that call. The next day Bach travelled to Łódź to participate in a military tribunal investigating Kaminski. A death sentence was passed, and Kaminski was executed either immediately or the following day. When von Vormann talked to Colonel General Georg-Hans Reinhardt, the newly nominated leader of Army Group Centre, over the phone on the evening of 29 August, he said, 'The Kaminski question has been taken care of.'[52]

Frolow was perturbed by Kaminski's sudden disappearance. Kaminski had told him a few days before that he and his chief of staff Ilya Szavykim had been called to meet some German authorities at headquarters, and when Kaminski did not return Frolow demanded answers, and refused to obey orders. After the war he recalled: 'After two or three days a German general appeared and told us that Kaminski and Szavykim had been killed by partisans close to Kraków.' Frolow and his men were highly suspicious, and demanded to see the bodies. The Germans, caught out, quickly reconstructed the scene of a fake partisan attack. Kaminski's car was pushed to the side of a road near Kraków, riddled with bullets, and covered in goose blood.

The Germans now tried to buy Frolow off. All charges of insubordination against him were dropped, and he was officially made the leader of the RONA Brigade. He was even awarded an Iron Cross Second Class, ostensibly for his fight against the partisans near Vitebsk in June 1944. The Germans did not know that he had already helped himself to another honour.

During interrogation in 1946, Frolow admitted that when he heard that Szavykim and Kaminski had been killed he went to Szavykim's office and, while rummaging through his private papers, discovered that the dead man had been awarded the Iron Cross First Class. 'I erased the last name and Szavykim's patronymic, and using a typewriter with German letters typed in my own last name and patronymic. I already had an Iron Cross First Class medal in my possession, which I had stolen from a German officer who had been killed – he had been communication officer on my staff. I did all of this to wear the Iron Cross First Class so as to get the trust of the German leadership, as I was counting on the fact that after Kaminski's death I would be nominated to be the leader of the brigade.'[53] Frolow and the rest of the RONA Brigade had been moved out of Warsaw on 26 August, first to Fort Traugutta and then to Truskaw in the Kampinos Forest.

After the war von dem Bach again tried to portray himself as a humanitarian who had done the world a great service by ridding it of the hateful Kaminski. He was 'nothing more than a political hooligan', Bach said, an 'upstart' who had dreamt of a fascist Russia and who had even fantasized about becoming the Russian Führer. 'In reality Kaminski only really cared for alcohol and women. He hated no people more than the Poles.' Von dem Bach conveniently forgot to mention that he had happily used Kaminski's men in Byelorussia for years, and had recommended him for promotions and honours. All that was to be erased from history.

Von dem Bach was not the only one to suffer amnesia when it came to Kaminski and his men. Fegelein briefed Hitler almost daily on what was happening in Warsaw during the uprising, and even Guderian informed him of the excesses of Kaminski's men. Robbery, too, was officially sanctioned. 9th Army reports carefully totted up the spoils from the city: on 29 August one stated, 'In Warsaw currently every day between two and three hundred wagons are loaded with textiles, fat, equipment and engines.'[54] The goods were bound for the Reich. In his Nuremberg affidavit Wilhelm Scheidt, a retired German army captain who worked in the War History section of the OKW from 1941 to 1945, said: 'I remember that at the time of the Polish revolt in Warsaw SS Gruppenführer Fegelein reported to Colonel General Guderian and Jodl about the atrocities of the Russian SS Brigade Kaminski which fought on the German side.'

Heinz Guderian tried to exonerate himself after the war, claiming that he had tried to intervene; but much of this was sheer invention. 'Some of the SS units involved – which, incidentally, were not drawn from the Waffen SS – failed to preserve their discipline,' he wrote. 'As for the Kaminski Brigade, it was composed of former prisoners of war, mostly Russians, who were ill-disposed towards the Poles; the Dirlewanger Brigade was formed from German convicts on probation. These doubtful units were now committed to desperate street battles where each building had to be captured and where the defendants were fighting for their lives; as a result they abandoned all moral standards.'[55] While this might have been true in Wola, it certainly was not the case in Ochota, where Kaminski's men faced almost no resistance during their savage days of looting and raping.

Guderian claimed to have told Hitler to have the Dirlewanger and Kaminski units removed from the city. 'To begin with Hitler was not inclined to listen to this demand of mine. But Himmler's liaison officer, SS Brigadeführer Fegelein, was himself forced to admit: "It is true, my Führer. Those men are real scoundrels!" As a result he had no choice but to do as I wished.'

The idea that Hitler had to obey Guderian is utterly ludicrous; Hitler had no qualms about the violence meted out to the civilians of Warsaw, and Dirlewanger was not removed; on the contrary, he continued to murder, rape and pillage almost until the end, and was later highly decorated for his actions. Guderian attempted to cover his tracks further by claiming that it was von dem Bach who 'took the precaution of having Kaminski shot and thus disposed of a possibly dangerous witness'.[56]

It is possible that Kaminski was killed at the request of his most hated rival, General Andrey Vlasov, who also led an army of the anti-Stalinist 'Russian Liberation Army'. Berger, Schellenberg, von dem Bach and SS Gruppenführer Otto Ohlendorf had all recently had meetings with Vlasov, and it is possible that he agreed to hand his men over to Himmler if Kaminski was removed. Himmler had been scathing about Vlasov only a year before, but the situation on the front was now so dire that by the time he met him on 16 September in the Reichsführer's field headquarters in East Prussia, he was forced to back down, and secured Hitler's approval to incorporate Vlasov's anti-Soviet formations into the SS.[57] Vlasov, who had expected to meet 'a second Beria', was greatly taken by Himmler: 'Quiet modest, nothing of the gangster boss like Dr Ley . . . He more or less apologised for having so long been taken in by *Untermensch* theories.'

The Vlasov experiment did not work out, as there were too many in the SS and elsewhere who opposed Russians holding such high positions. Some of those around Hitler, including the trusted Bormann, were trying to sue for a separate peace with the Soviets. In his secret wartime diary, Guy Liddell, deputy head of Britain's MI5, wrote on 26 September 1944 that 'Werner Naumann Staatssekretär for Propaganda in German has had a conversation with the Japanese on the various problems with which Germany is now faced. It was made clear that while peace with England or America was out of the question Germany would not be averse to peace with Russia if a favourable opportunity had occurred. It was mentioned that Hitler had specially refrained from putting Vlasov's army into the field, as he felt that once he had done so he would be unable to get rid of these people if the situation suddenly underwent a change.'[58] This was untrue: Hitler could not stand Vlasov, nor would he have sued for peace with Russia; but some of his closest circle were trying to do just that, and they may have successfully blocked the integration of Vlasov's army into the SS.

Vlasov may have played an indirect role in the Kaminski saga, but in the end Kaminski's death was probably caused by simple insubordination. Hitler and Himmler did not object to his violent methods, but they expected obedience. Von dem Bach was more than happy to have him eliminated.

The RONA men did not fare well after their removal from Warsaw. The remnants of the brigade were sent to Truskaw, on the outskirts of town, and in one of the most successful AK attacks of the uprising were largely destroyed on the nights of 2 and 3 September by the 'Dolina' Unit. Those who escaped were transported to Błonie on 15 September, and rejoined the rest of Kaminski's men, who in turn were meant to be incorporated into the 29th SS Grenadiers Division. This transfer was never completed: many of the younger soldiers chose to join Vlasov's army instead, while the others stayed on to protect the beleaguered civilians of Lokot. After the capitulation of the Third Reich all the soldiers who had held Soviet citizenship before 1 September 1939 were handed back to the Russians. It is doubtful that many survived Stalin's wrath.

Pruszków

Having stopped the mass murder of women and children in Warsaw, Bach now had to find something to do with the home-less civilians. The option of letting them return to their homes apparently did not occur to him, and he never wavered from

Hitler's order that Warsaw was to be emptied of its population and razed to the ground – his humanitarian principles clearly reached their limit when it came to disobeying Hitler's direct orders. On 6 August von dem Bach opened the Pruszków transit camp, to the west of the city, which according to the Chronicle of the 9th Army was to be a 'camp for the refugees from Warsaw'. Wehrmacht officer Colonel Kurt Sieber was nominated as commandant, but it was SS Sturmbannführer Gustav Diehl, the SS camp commandant, who wielded real power from his office in the large green railway car in the centre of the camp. It was this brutal Gestapo thug who decided the fate of all the inmates. The '*Durchgangslager*', or Dulag 121, was to become another place of profound misery. Ninety per cent of the people forced to leave their homes in Warsaw were 'processed' there before being sent on either to concentration camps, to forced labour in the Reich or, for the lucky ones, to some village or town in the General Government. Von dem Bach had made it very clear that nobody was to be permitted to stay in Warsaw. And nobody would be allowed to return home.

The next stop for the traumatized survivors of Ochota was the transit camp at Pruszków. As the trains rolled out of Warsaw, the dark skies, thick with smoke and cinders from the burning city, gradually gave way to the sunny green of the countryside. It was a shock to discover that life was going on here as if nothing was happening in the capital. Marta Czerniewicz was amazed at the world she saw after the hell of Zieleniak: 'There were girls in summer dresses, people gathering tomatoes and fruit; I could not understand that such a normal world could exist so close to Warsaw, one where you could move freely and the wild world we had seen did not exist.'

Wanda Skrzeszewska, heavily pregnant, and her young daughter were also sent to Pruszków. 'I was so surprised being far from

Warsaw that people were living calmly and did not know about the terrible things that we were going through in the city. I had been convinced that all of Poland was fighting.' Twelve-year-old Lech Kulicki remembered the journey to Pruszków as a kind of dream: 'I noticed a man working in a field through the windows. The picture has stayed in my mind; I will never forget it until the end of my life. Everyone thought that all of Poland was undergoing the same kind of hell – that it was not only in Zieleniak or in Warsaw.'

For many Ochota residents the horrors did not end in Pruszków. A high percentage of the first trainloads of prisoners from Wola and Ochota were sent to the camps as a sop to Himmler and Hitler. After experiencing the horrors of Zieleniak, nineteen-year-old Honorata Wolska was taken to Buchenwald, where her father died; she and her mother were then moved to Bergen Belsen, and later to a linen factory in the Harz mountains. At the end of the war the Gestapo ordered that all prisoners be executed, but the director of the factory refused to kill his workers. He in turn was about to be executed by the Gestapo when the Americans arrived just in time, saving all of them.

Fifteen-year-old Wojciech Kucharski went from Pruszków to Netzweiler via Auschwitz; his mother, sister and aunt were also sent to Auschwitz. Ryszard Lemiszewski was sent from Pruszków to Oranienburg; Bożena Grzybowska's father died in Oranienburg, while she and her mother were sent to Ravensbrück. Most of the residents from Barska 5 were sent to Auschwitz: twelve-year-old Henryk Poborski was sent to Pruszków and then to Buchenwald; thirteen-year-old Bogdan Bartnikowski ended up in Sachsenhausen; thirty-year-old Ryszard Sitarek and his twenty-three-year-old sister were sent to Auschwitz; seventeen-year-old Janina Idaszek was sent to Buchenwald with her mother and three young siblings. Many of the residents of Ochota never returned.

To the end the Germans refused to take responsibility for what they were doing to these innocent civilians, turning the situation around to lay the blame at the feet of their victims themselves. Maria Piekarz was about to leave Zieleniak for Pruszków when a German officer turned to her and said in perfect Polish, 'You see? You got what you wanted.' Ten thousand people died in Ochota at the hands of the RONA Brigade. Many thousands more lost their lives in the camps and as forced labourers in the last months of the war.

9

'MOUNTAINS OF CORPSES'

———❦———

Hunger wasted Hasdrubal and the Carthaginians . . . first they ate their pack animals and after them their horses and boiled their leather straps for food . . . there arose a destructive and painful pestilence among them in consequence of living in the stench of putrefying corpses. (Chapter X)

The End of Wola

By 8 August Hitler was becoming impatient. The *'Banditen'* were still fighting in the north of Wola, and Guderian was worried that anti-German violence might break out over the entire country.[1] The unease was fuelled by inept German intelligence reports: 'Today about 16:30 one can expect the outbreak of an uprising in the General Government,' wrote the Alien Forces East Counter-Intelligence Unit, inaccurately, on 9 August.[2] More worrying was the pressure from the Eastern Front. The troops in Praga could no longer be supplied from Warsaw, and were forced to use the circuitous Modlin route; Guderian feared that even this might be cut off if the violence spread.[3] The fact that the German escape route over the Warsaw bridges had been inhibited affected the morale of the troops, who now feared that they would be 'trapped like rats' like their comrades on the Berezina river if the Soviets came.

Bach spent the night of 8 August conferring with von Vormann. They must have been trying to figure out how to procure more help for their fight in Warsaw, as the following day they unleashed a two-pronged attack. Bach told Himmler that unless they got more troops it would take weeks to clear Warsaw. Von Vormann sent a secret telex to Field Marshal Model at 6.20 in the afternoon, in which he attempted to make the military case for reinforcements. 'The danger is increasing,' he said. 'We are talking about having to fight from house to house. The street fights in the large city are leading to high losses. The current state of affairs is not acceptable to the troops in the east in the long run. Supplies which now have to go via Modlin could be cut off at any stage unless we find a way to secure the route.' It was obvious how dangerous the situation would be for the bridgeheads in Warsaw in the case of failure. 'We have only 3–4000 against 1.5 million,' von Vormann wrote. 'Von dem Bach has already reported the same thing to Himmler,' he added, as if to remind Model of the rivalry between him and the Reichsführer SS. They both wanted the forces in Warsaw to 'be supplemented by a full-value division with a lot of heavy weaponry'. Furthermore, 'dispatching further police forces is urgently needed as the Army Group can only have at its disposal a few gathered Cossack units'. But nothing happened. Guderian's troops were busy fighting the Soviets, and could not spare the men. Himmler managed to cobble together a force of 618 Wehrmacht soldiers, two Guards companies of 120 men each, the Benthin Battalion of Grenadiers, consisting of nine officers and 536 men, and a company of 142 men from the SS school in Braunschweig, but he was scraping the bottom of the barrel: one of the new units, supposedly a heavy-machine-gun platoon from

SS Röntgen Sturmbann Posen, was in fact made up of X-ray technicians and sanitary workers from an SS hospital. These untrained men joined the Schmidt group, and prepared for battle.

The moss-covered old cemeteries at the northern edge of Wola stand as silent witnesses to Warsaw's long and rich history at a crossroads of Europe. The Jewish cemetery, which stretches over thirty hectares and which Hitler decided not to destroy, is now woefully run-down, but its richly decorated tombs, headstones and mausoleums are still visible through the overgrown trees. To walk there is to get a glimpse of the sheer diversity of the Jewish community that existed in Warsaw before the Second World War. Thousands upon thousands of writers, journalists, doctors, soldiers, scholars and merchants rest in its quiet glades; Ludwik Zamenhof, who created Esperanto, lies near the humanitarian Hipolit Wawelberg, who built the apartments so brutally destroyed by Dirlewanger on 5 August 1944. Next to this is Powązki, the beautiful Catholic cemetery, which in turn lies alongside those for Protestants, Russian Orthodox and Muslims; the headstones in the 'Tartar cemetery' have inscriptions in Turkish and Arabic. The eighteenth-century Evangelical cemetery, with its Enlightenment tombs and chapels, contains the bodies of many non-Protestants who in the true spirit of tolerance were buried there regardless of their faith. These quiet and serene places were soon to become the incongruous locations of the final battles for Wola. Two days after Bach's talk with Himmler, German tanks were blasting away at the ornate monuments, obliterating many that had stood for hundreds of years.

Von dem Bach sent the Schmidt group to attack the last strongholds in Wola. Fierce battles raged around the Hala Mirowska market stalls and the Haberbusch brewery, with its crucial supplies of barley. Captain Wacław Stykowski ('Hal') and the soldiers of the AK's 'Chrobry' I and II fought for every building and street, counter-attacking and regaining lost positions in the middle of the night. Plac Żelazna Brama and Hala Mirowska changed hands several times, and there was bitter hand-to-hand fighting in Towarowa and Chmielna Streets. The lack of water meant that the raging fires spread quickly, and some AK soldiers were forced to retreat. Groups commanded by 'Hal' and Captain Gustaw Billewicz ('Sosna') retreated to the Old Town to regroup and continue the fight.

The civilians were terrified to see their protectors go. Stefan Talikowski, who had become friendly with Captain Sosna's men, watched as 'the AK retreated very quietly without saying anything to anyone. In the early morning of 7 August I asked the leader of the patrol what was going on; he said they were retreating to the Old Town and the Germans were coming.'[4]

Although many were forced to retreat one man, the professional Polish officer Jan Mazurkiewicz ('Radosław') was preparing for a fight.[5] His group, which included 'Kedyw', had started the uprising in Wola with around 1,600 trained and well-equipped soldiers in six battalions – 'Czata', 'Miotła', 'Parasol', 'Pięść', 'Zośka' and 'Kollegium A' – along with the women's unit 'Dysk'. The battalions were led by professional officers, including Captain Stanisław Jankowski ('Agaton') and Adam Borys ('Pług'), leader of 'Parasol', both of whom had been trained in Britain and dropped into Poland before the uprising. Pług and Agaton, who had last seen one another in Scotland, were delighted to meet up again, despite the difficult circumstances; Pług even managed to distribute a shipment of Wehrmacht-issue boots that he had found just before the fighting began.[6]

The last battles began in earnest on 10 August, when Colonel Schmidt consolidated his attack on the Lutheran and Calvinist cemeteries. The AK men were hiding amongst the headstones when they heard the tanks creaking into position. Agaton remembered hearing birds chirping in the trees just before a gaping hole was blasted in the cemetery wall. Janusz Brochwicz-Lewiński, who was in a group of twenty-three men from the 'Gryf' group, said: 'I had the feeling that I would not survive the cemeteries. The silence, the gravestones, the atmosphere.' But there was no time to think. Shells and bullets began to ricochet off the headstones, destroying the trees and sending branches down on the heads of the insurgents. Nurses tried to get the wounded out, but when the shelling became too much they used the small benches normally kept beside the graves to make steps down into the catacombs. Many of the coffins deep in the old tombs were made of metal, and these were now used as operating tables. When the Germans began to bomb the AK positions with Heinkel 111s, the nurses covered the patients with their stretchers.[7] Companies under 'Radosław', 'Rafael', 'Lot' and Wacek fought back, ducking bullets and moving from one gravestone to the next; pieces of masonry – the arms, wings and heads of angels – exploded onto the men.

The Germans pushed on into the Jewish and Catholic cemeteries on 10 August, with Schmidt, Reck and Dirlewanger urging their men forward. The 9th Army Daily Report revealed surprise at the scale of Polish resistance: 'They defend themselves everywhere and very fiercely,' it read. 'They use highly effective tactics of close fighting, so they allow the *Sturm* groups and support troops and even tanks to get to a certain place and then destroy them by accurate fire. Soldiers and wounded who escape the fighting report that the deaths are caused almost exclusively by head wounds.'[8] The Germans also used snipers. Lewiński found that 'the enemy was so well hidden that I almost could not see them. They were well experienced soldiers from the Eastern Front who knew how to camouflage themselves by attaching leaves to their uniforms . . . they were excellent shots and hid in the branches of the trees or in corners between the gravestones. These soldiers had very good sights attached to their guns, and they searched for their targets. I became the victim of an excellent shot who nearly killed me.' Lewiński had been hiding beside the Halpert chapel in the Evangelical cemetery, one of the most beautiful family crypts in Warsaw, when he was wounded in the chin; the brave AK nurses carried him to the Old Town under fire. His wound was so dreadful that he could only be fed through a tube; when a nurse first changed his bandage she fainted.[9]

The nurses are among the unsung heroes of the uprising. They were often very young and untrained women who risked their lives in perilous conditions to bring the AK wounded to safety, and they were treated with pitiless cruelty if captured by Dirlewanger's men. Anna Szatkowska left the safety of the Old Town and was guided to Wola by a 'Parasol' runner: 'The fires are so huge and bright that it is as light as it is in daytime. The moon shines and its cold silver light mingles with the hot flames of the fire creating a wall of strange sparkling blue dust in the sky.'[10] She worked in a team carrying the wounded back through the ruins of the ghetto to the safety of the Maltese hospital in the Old Town.

The 5 August Allied drop of supplies into the cemeteries was followed by a second drop of thirty-six parcels on the night of 8–9 August.[11] The British and Polish pilots had been forced to make a perilous non-stop 1,300-kilometre flight all the way from Brindisi, as Stalin had refused them permission to land on Russian-held territory. These drops, although infrequent, would become a feature of the uprising, and the brave pilots who risked their lives for the city were rightly hailed as heroes. The supplies were gratefully received, but were not sufficient to have any real effect on the outcome of the uprising. The drop on 5 August had included British-made PIAT anti-tank guns, but not enough ammunition; worse still, around 50 per cent of all matériel sent to the city during the uprising fell into German hands. Stahel was scathing about the drops after the war: 'Some contained civilian clothes, and cigarettes from Havana, Cuba,' he said. 'On one night alone we got around forty of them.'[12] Even so, this first overt show of Western support boosted morale in Warsaw, giving people hope that the Allies might, after all, take up the fight. The drops also had an unsettling effect on the Germans, particularly when the second was followed by an announcement from London warning them that 'all people both military and civilian who commit crimes against international law, against human beings and Home Army soldiers, will be found and punished after the war'.

For Radosław, however, the drops provided too little too late: 'The general mood in the units of my group is pessimistic and bitter because of the lack of weapons for the past eight days,' he wrote to Monter. 'We fight alone with no help from our quarter-master nor from the Allies. There is a problem as to what to do with soldiers who want to fight but for whom we have no ammunition. The second problem is connected with civilians, who despite terrible conditions here are still being protected only by the soldiers. I think it is a scandal that nobody from the Government Delegation has appeared in the area to care for the civilians. The soldiers see this and make comments about it.'[13]

The Germans were fighting with great brutality. Józef Czapski of 'Parasol' Battalion was captured and forced to become a human shield: 'They took my helmet and fire axe and I was made to walk with the others in front of the tanks. The Germans shot at our barricade, leaning their weapons on our shoulders as we walked.'[14] Stanisław Aronson, fighting in the 'Radosław' group, witnessed the last fights in Wola on 11 August. 'We faced very precise mortar and grenade fire,' he recalled. Aronson was operating a heavy machine gun with another soldier, and as the Germans increased their fire he yelled, 'OK, now we will be hit!' Seconds later he was wounded. He woke in a basement hospital in the Old Town, and miraculously survived the uprising.

The footsoldiers of Kampfgruppe Reinefarth pushed past the cemeteries as Colonel Schmidt moved to Gęsia Street. They attacked and won back the warehouses at Stawki, which Aronson and 'Kedyw Kollegium A' had won so easily on the first day. Radosław and 140 other AK soldiers were wounded; 115 were killed. The remaining tank in AK hands broke down, so they burned it to prevent it from falling into German hands.[15] They had to retreat through the ruined ghetto. Unlike in Ochota they could not use the sewers, as, to their horror, they had discovered that they were filled with the bodies of Jewish victims killed during the Ghetto Uprising. They escaped into the Old Town through the rubble and under heavy fire. It was the end for Wola.

The desperate fights for the cemeteries had not been in vain. By resisting so fiercely Radosław had delayed the German attack on the Old Town by a week, and had allowed Colonel Karol Ziemski ('Wachnowski'), the commander of 'Grupa Północ', the Northern Group, time to organize his defence. But for the people of Wola the news that Radosław had retreated led to feelings of utter despair. They were on their own.

The Flight from the West

The mass murders in Wola had backfired on von dem Bach and Himmler, as the terrified civilians of Warsaw were now prepared to do anything rather than fall into the hands of the Germans. Their instincts were correct. Von dem Bach might have halted the mass executions, but almost all Polish men were still shot on sight, and in reality it was impossible to rein in someone like Dirlewanger. Anna Szatkowska saw columns of people running north, trying to escape: 'They say that huge fires rage in Wola and that there are mass executions . . . they are killing without distinction between civilians and insurgents.'[16]

Von dem Bach and his friend Hauptsturmbannführer Alfred Spilker, head of the Warsaw Gestapo, knew that it was going to be difficult to get the people to trust them. Spilker had agents dressed like Poles circulating among the crowds. 'Some of the *Banditen* are afraid to give up as they fear they will be massacred by Tartars and Cossacks,' he reported back to the SS. And yet he casually concluded his report: 'eighty people to camps, 336 bodies burned'. Clearly the civilians still had good reason to be afraid.[17]

The refugees streaming from Wola did not get much help from the civil authorities. The AK deliberately withheld information, and forbade passage from one district to another without the correct papers, to prevent the spread of panic. Monter argued that civilians should be forced to stay in their districts, because without them AK morale would plummet, but he did little to help them once the AK soldiers had retreated.[18] The leader of a patrol of the Military Social Information Service met 2,000 refugees huddled in the church at Grzybowski Square, and 1,500 in the Palladium cinema at Złota, and his situation report was bleak: 'there is an atmosphere of apathy and depression; there is a lack of food and sanitation'. Wacław Zagórski wrote in his diary: 'Yesterday 7 August the main wave of refugees from Wola moves through Elektoralna and Leszno Streets. First single silhouettes in the early dawn light, half running and half walking in scruffy torn clothes, blindly going with ash on their faces, men and women who managed to get out from the hell . . . then come families with bundles and toddlers in their arms.'[19] The journalist Klaudiusz Hrabyk was angered by the treatment of the refugees:

'A huge column of people came down Ogrodowa Street. They were all very depressed and did not want to talk. We heard that the Germans and their Ukrainian colleagues were killing everyone. The AK staff refused to give any information about it and did not want to tell us what was really going on; in Wola they even refused me, although I am an accredited journalist. I asked officers from the staff just beside the court of law buildings at Ogrodowa, and they too refused to give me information.'[20] Jan Rossman watched as the crowds began to run: 'some talked of trying to slip out of Warsaw altogether.'[21] Hitler had forbidden anyone to leave his 'fortress city' without authorization and many would-be escapees were killed trying, but by the end of the uprising around 10,000 people had succeeded in passing through the German lines, some of them having been helped to safety by German soldiers willing to turn a blind eye to civilians, and in particular by the Hungarians, who although allied to the Germans were sympathetic to the Poles and refused to take part in crushing the uprising.[22]

The massacres in Wola, and the chaos that followed, sowed seeds of doubt amongst the civilian population. 'People are starting to say it was crazy to start the uprising,' noted an official AK report.[23] 'Lidzki' wrote in a report on 8 August that 'Civilians are in depression . . . the intelligentsia criticize the fact that the uprising was started so early. Teenage young people are still enthusiastic, but generally there is fear of the fate of the uprising and the fate of the city . . . They fear and hate the Germans, the women fear above all the German Gestapo and the Ukrainians.'[24] Monter seemed not to grasp what had happened in Wola. On 8 August he heaped praise on the good citizens of Powiśle, Żoliborz and other districts as yet untouched by the terror for their exemplary and patriotic behaviour. Of the people of Wola, who had just lived through one of the worst massacres of the Second World

War, however, he said: 'They have calmed down, but they brought chaos and psychological problems.'[25]

Those who could not get out of Wola hid for as long as they could, scuttling from one basement to another as the Germans moved through. Władysław Stępień and his group thought they had found a safe place, but soon learned that the Germans were getting closer. 'People came to us, including a Jew who had been hiding at Wronia 52, who said the bodies of the murdered were being burned. We decided to move to another basement. It had been burned out already, and a skeleton lay in the corner. It was difficult to get in, as the steps and hall had already been destroyed, but the basement was intact . . . We sat there knowing above all we had to be quiet so as not to attract attention. The area around us was almost empty, although we could sometimes hear Germans going down Ogrodowa Street.' When they were finally discovered they were herded to St Wojciech church in Wola, next to Spilker's Gestapo headquarters, which was being used as a temporary transit camp. 'The women in our group were taken away and raped.' The Germans joked: 'The Gestapo are doing some examinations today.' They were then all sent on to the camp at Pruszków.[26]

The Germans occupied all of Wola, rounding up anyone left behind. Men were routinely shot, leaving columns of mostly the elderly, women and children, who were sent via St Wojciech's to Pruszków, and an uncertain fate. The German officer Hans Thieme watched as they trudged by in their hundreds: 'There were people with deadly tired faces without a trace of hope, eyes swollen with smoke and tears, faces covered with soot, the picture of complete exhaustion, despair and fear. The police walked beside them with guns.' Buildings were burning like 'gigantic torches', singeing eyelashes and eyebrows. The smoke was stifling, and people tripped in the darkness.[27] Spilker organized a special group to

Hitler detested Warsaw, and had already agreed to the Pabst Plan, which called for its destruction and re-creation as a German city, in 1939. The Polish underground had plans to assassinate him during this victory parade on 5 October 1939, plans which were foiled when the SS had all houses along the Führer's route evacuated.

Three key events set the stage for the Warsaw Uprising: 1. The extraordinary success of
the Soviet summer offensive – 'Bagration' – which was Hitler's single greatest defeat and
brought the Soviets to the gates of Warsaw; 2. The 20 July plot to assassinate Hitler;
3. Walter Model's surprise counter-offensive against the Soviets only a few kilometres from
Warsaw, hours before the uprising began. Here, Soviet troops advance on Warsaw in the
summer of 1944.

Proud AK troops marching to battle on 1 August 1944. 'Agaton' leads his platoon.

First day of the uprising. When the uprising broke out most civilians were taken by surprise; many were caught in the crossfire whilst trying to get to safety. Here a man tries to make a run for it across the street despite the corpses nearby.

On the first day of the uprising the citizens of Warsaw built barricades on every major street. Here a person is running behind the barricade at Marszaticorska and Zlota streets.

German troops who entered the working-class district of Wola in early August under Heinz Reinefarth engaged in the indiscriminate killing of men, women and children.

Heinz Reinefarth (standing, center), who ordered the first wave of massacres in Wola. He later achieved high office in Germany and was never charged for his crimes.

An Azeri unit sharing sausages with their German colleagues – over 50 per cent of the troops brought in to crush the uprising were of non-German origin. Many were Russians and Azeris.

Men, women and children killed on 5 August 1944 in the largest battlefield massacre
of the Second World War. Note the papers – implying that the bodies had been searched
for valuables.

Wanda Lurie and her son Mścisław.
Wanda, then heavily pregnant, was shot
during the massacre at the Ursus factory
in Wola on 5 August 1944. Two of her
children were killed but she miraculously
survived; Mścisław was born during the
uprising.

Dirlewanger Brigade troops advancing. Perhaps the most brutal fighting unit in the German army was unleashed on Warsaw on 5 August.

Hala Mirowska – one of the sites of mass murder by the Dirlewanger Brigade which Tadeusz Klimaszewski was forced to clear of bodies with the 'Cremation Commando'.

Warsawians in the liberated parts of the city revelled in the first days of freedom, and Polish symbols were put up everywhere. Germans, enraged by the raising of the Polish flag at Starynkiewicza Square, shot at it in an attempt to destroy it, as they could not reach it on foot.

A Junkers landing at the main airfield at Okęcie – others are waiting for payloads of bombs to be loaded for another raid. These continued around the clock, causing terror and destruction among the civilian population.

Hitler personally oversaw the crushing of the Old Town, which had more in common with a medieval siege than modern warfare. The largest self-propelled siege gun ever built, the 'Karl' mortar, was positioned in Sowiński Park to fire on the Old Town. The aerial photograph overleaf shows the tracks needed to move the 'Karl' into position.

Warsawians were forced to leave their homes, often being given only a few minutes to gather any possessions. Most were robbed on their way to Pruszków transit camp.

Ochota – women being taken to Zieleniak camp. Hundreds were raped in the former farmers' market by the soldiers of the RONA Brigade.

By mid-August the Germans had stopped most (but not all) mass executions; young men suspected of being in the AK were still executed, as were all Jews; women and children were forced to Pruszków camp, from which many were sent to concentration camps, including Auschwitz and Ravensbrück, or as slave labour to the Reich. Below, a group of civilians cross Żelazna Brama Square as tanks move the other way towards Chłodna Street.

Among the most terrifying weapons were the mortars called *Krowas*, or 'bellowing cows' – the Allies nicknamed them 'Moaning Minnies' for their haunting sound. When filled with incendiary liquid they burned people alive. Note the number of used crates for shells.

The *Krowas* carried either high explosive or incendiary shells; the photograph shows a victim of an incendiary bomb.

A 'Goliath'. These miniature tanks, loaded with explosives and piloted by remote control, were very effective in destroying barricades.

The hulking Panzer train patrolled the border of the Old Town. It was virtually unassailable, and its constant bombardments caused enormous damage.

Clearing the Old Town. An attack on the Kamienne Schodki, the Stone Steps. First flamethrowers were used; then the infantry moved in.

The scale of destruction caused by Hitler's siege and the massive bombing raids made fighting in Warsaw all the more dangerous. Here two German soldiers clamber over the rubble in the Old Town.

At times a strange courtesy existed between combatants. Here Germans remove their dead during a short ceasefire using stretchers provided by the AK. The Poles were praised by Wehrmacht soldiers for caring for the German wounded.

The death toll in the city was so great that it became difficult to find space to bury the bodies; bombing raids often churned up those who had been laid to rest. Here a number of old gravestones and a birch cross mark a mass grave in Długa Street.

Previously unpublished photographs showing swastikas painted on the roofs of buildings in Ochota to prevent German planes from bombing their own positions. Red crosses mark German hospitals.

The Western Allies attempted to aid the Warsaw insurgents by dropping supplies by air; they were hindered by Stalin's decision not to allow Allied planes to land on Soviet airfields.

An AK soldier emerging from the sewers into German hands on Dworkowa Street. He and his 140 companions were shot by their captors.

From a plane, German soldiers prepare to drop leaflets informing Warsaw's citizens of the surrender and ceasefire.

A German soldier guards members of the Polish resistance after the end of the uprising. The terms of the capitulation agreement guaranteed prisoner of war status for the insurgents.

After capitulation the people of Warsaw emerged from their cellars and
bunkers filthy, exhausted and often starving. They had been shot at, bombed,
burned and buried under rubble; by the time they went to Pruszków many had
lost loved ones and all their possessions.

The AK in Warsaw was unusual in that it included a high number of women, working as
nurses, explosives experts and runners. Here two AK nurses leave the city as prisoners of
war in October 1944.

Over 30 per cent of the destruction of Warsaw took place after capitulation. Here, in a bizarre act of misplaced reconciliation, Erich von dem Bach-Zelewski presents a box containing Chopin's heart to the Archbishop of Warsaw.

On the day of capitulation, 3 October 1944, General Bór-Komorowski was taken to see Bach, who believed with Himmler that the Poles might be persuaded to join them in 'the coming fight against the Bolsheviks'. Bór rejected his proposals out of hand.

German troops with flamethrowers setting fire to buildings around Warsaw Castle. The castle was destroyed between 8 and 13 September, after the capitulation of the Old Town, as it was a symbol of Polish national identity.

watch the columns and pull out anyone who looked Jewish; Irena Janowska, a fourteen-year-old girl scout, saw Jewish victims being 'led to the side, and killed'.[28]

Those refugees who managed to reach the Old Town were astounded to find people living comfortably in their apartments and houses, as if nothing at all was happening in Wola. In a pattern that would be repeated again and again as each district of Warsaw fell, the people of the area that had been targeted by the Germans had to face the fact that the rest of the city had no idea what was going on just out of their sight. The refugees were amazed to see people enjoying their evening meals or chatting in cafés over *ersatz* coffee. Organizations were set up to help the refugees, and much work was done by the Red Cross, the churches and the scouts, but the traumatized victims of Wola were often disbelieved, and sometimes even treated as panic-mongers. The people of the Old Town did not yet realize that they would soon share their fate.

The Germans began the systematic looting and destruction of Wola. 'Agaton' remembered his last view of the district, with its bombed buildings cut open as if by some giant knife, their colourful insides hanging in the sky: 'On the fifth floor a bath is shining in the sun although the rest of the apartment is gone. When you look up you can see furniture, pieces of wood, bricks, metal beams, window frames. We walked very slowly and carefully, leaving the first traces in the dust.' He passed the body of a young AK soldier next to a barricade. 'Someone has put a broken picture over him to cover his face.'[29]

The SS and Gestapo stationed in Wola had a break from the fighting, and were determined to enjoy themselves. They raided the flats, hauling beds and chairs out to the cooler courtyards, from where they could oversee the evacuation and the looting. 'The SS took over buildings that were still standing . . . We saw filthy overgrown drunk soldiers from the RONA group in court-yards on piles of duvets and comforters. They made loud, noisy camps there with a lot of vodka and wine, and we could see them half-conscious, their eyes bloodshot from alcohol.'[30] But there was work to do too. Not a drop of rain would fall for a month, and the temperature in Warsaw was over thirty degrees. The dusty air shimmered in the heat of both the sun and the fires. Forty thousand corpses lay in this furnace, rotting and bloating. The stench was unbearable. Rats proliferated, and clouds of flies settled on the bodies. The Germans, always paranoid about the threat of epidemics, knew that the area had to be cleared. Above all, Himmler wanted to hide all evidence of the terrible crimes that had been committed against the civilians of Warsaw. It had to be done quickly, for as von dem Bach wrote in his diary on 9 August, the Russians might come at any minute.

The Funeral

Two years after the Wola massacre, in August 1946, Warsaw was only just beginning to awake from its terrible ordeal. Shards of shattered buildings pushed up through dusty mounds of rubble, once-wide boulevards were still little more than tracks zig-zagging through damaged brick and twisted steel. The people who had been so callously expelled from their city were coming back. Most had lost everything, and lived in whatever shelter they could find, but they wanted to return to their homes, and re-create what had been lost. Antonina Mijal, who had spent the uprising making AK explosives from unexploded German bombs, lived in a room with two walls open to the elements, and knitted sweaters which she bartered for food. But she was optimistic; within five years she would finish her degree, and would become a highly respected paediatrician.

The city was coming back to life in other ways, too. Signs urging inhabitants to 'Rebuild Warsaw' sprang up amongst the rubble, and the people, desperate to resurrect their city lest Stalin declare a new Polish capital in Łódź, threw themselves into one of the most remarkable civic regeneration projects in history. But as they cleared rubble and dug out ruined buildings, they made some terrible discoveries An enormous pile of ash, several metres thick, was found at the Wenecja Park in Wola, once a playground for children. More such piles were discovered throughout the district – at the Ursus factory, at Okopowa, at the Franaszek factory, along Wolska Street, at Aleja Szucha and the Marie Curie Radium Institute. Two tonnes of human ash were discovered in the military library in Aleja Ujazdowskie, where thousands of bodies had been heaped on pyres made from the beams of the destroyed building. In many cases the Germans had put earth on top of the ash in order to try to hide it.

The Red Cross was called in to sift through these grim piles, in the hope that at least some of the remains might be identified, but the task was hopeless. They found tiny things – wedding rings, chains, pen knives, medallions, clips for holding up stockings, even AK armbands that had not been completely destroyed by the fires – but it was impossible to identify individuals.[31]

6 August 1946 was a day of great sadness. The remains of the murdered victims were put into a hundred simple wooden coffins and carried by mourners into the church at Plac Zbawiciela. After Mass, tens of thousands of people spilled out of the church, grim-faced and crying. Warsawians lined the route bowing their heads as the ten army trucks carrying the coffins passed by, their canvas tops stripped back so people could see. The onlookers began spontaneously to throw their simple bouquets of daisies, corn-flowers and wild roses; there were so many flowers on the coffins by the time they reached the crypt that they were barely visible.

All of Warsaw had come out to mourn the dead. Normally restrained Warsawians sobbed convulsively or hugged perfect strangers for comfort; even men in the honour guard were crying. For all his effort, Himmler had not succeeded in hiding the Nazis' crimes.

When von dem Bach arrived in Warsaw on 5 August 1944 he was struck by the sheer number of dead lying in the streets: 'Bergen von Leichen', he wrote in his diary – 'mountains of corpses'. He must have talked to Himmler on or before his arrival about stopping the mass executions, and he must also have discussed the need to clean up the city. Von dem Bach had a problem. He knew from experience how difficult it was to deal with human remains; how were the SS supposed to dispose of 40,000 corpses in an urban setting? Himmler took control. The clean-up operation was to be done under his guidance, but he would rely on people who had first-hand knowledge of the problem.

Himmler had faced a situation like this before, on an even greater scale. In the spring of 1942 he had attempted to hide the evidence of the millions of Polish Jews who had been murdered during Operation 'Reinhard', using prisoners to exhume the mass graves and burn the bodies. These unfortunate men were given the official title 'Leichenkommandos', and were put under SS Standartenführer Paul Blobel.

The first experiments for 'Sonderaktion 1005' were carried out at Chełmno, where incendiary bombs were thrown onto the exhumed corpses. This proved ineffective. Eventually it was discovered that the most efficient way to destroy the bodies was to make huge pyres, using iron grilles. The 'Sonderaktion' officially began at Sobibór in May 1942, and when they had finished their grim work the prisoners who had carried it out were executed. The same grisly task was undertaken at Bełżec in December 1942.

Himmler then tried to destroy the evidence at Treblinka. Eight hundred thousand people, many of them Jews from the Warsaw region, had been murdered in that pitiless camp. At first the SS simply poured oil on the opened graves and tried to burn the by-now decomposing corpses, but only the top layer caught fire. Himmler called in Blobel's experts.

It was typical of the SS to use the knowledge gained in one camp to solve a problem faced in another and this was no exception. Heinrich Mathes, the commander of Camp III at Treblinka, recalled the arrival of SS Oberscharführer Herbert Floss to deal with disposing of the evidence of mass murder. Drawing on the knowledge gleaned by Blobel and the 'Leichenkommandos', Floss set up a new regime at Treblinka. 'He was in charge of the arrangements for cremating the corpses. The cremation took place in such a way that railway lines and concrete blocks were placed together. The corpses were piled on these rails. Brushwood was put under the rails. The wood was doused with petrol. In that way not only the newly accumulated corpses were cremated, but also those taken out from the graves.'[32] This help from the experts proved crucial. 'The burning of the corpses received the proper incentive only after an instructor had come down from Auschwitz. The specialists in this profession were businesslike, practical and conscientious.'[33]

Himmler now drew on experts who were in Warsaw to set up the crews that would carry out the grisly task in the Polish capital. The most obvious person was Ludwig Hahn, SiPo and SD commandant in the city, who would later receive the Iron Cross for his work during the uprising. He had participated in the destruction of the Warsaw ghetto, and had personally sent hundreds of thousands of Warsaw Jews to Treblinka. He was also very well informed about the problems the SS had encountered there. The second man was Alfred Spilker, head of the Gestapo in Warsaw. He too

375

would help to supervise the teams. On 10 August, after a conversation with Himmler, von dem Bach had a meeting with Police Commander Geibel, and contacted men of the so-called 'Ghetto Crew' who had taken part in the liquidation of Warsaw's Jewish quarter. On 13 August he flew to Lötzen and met Fegelein, who reported to the Führer directly after the meeting; von dem Bach then met Himmler. Everything was ready to go.

Himmler's SS 'experts' clearly decided to treat the district of Wola as a kind of sub-camp. It was well suited for this. It was a relatively small area, now completely cut off from all the other districts of the city and from the outside world, and it was swarming with SS and Gestapo men. Although it was modelled on the Leichenkommandos, the group operating in Wola also had a great deal in common with the Sonderkommandos.

The Sonderkommandos in the death camps (not to be confused with the SS Sonderkommando killing squads) were made up of Jewish prisoners who were selected to do the most filthy, degrading and disgusting tasks, including the disposal of murdered victims. The men of the Sonderkommando tended to be well fed, and to have access to extra supplies such as medicines, clothing and other 'luxuries' unthinkable for the other prisoners, and they were not subject to random execution, although they were slated for eventual extermination: Himmler designated them as 'Geheimnisträger' – those who bore secrets – and as such they all had to die. Their life expectancy was about four months. Of the hundreds of men forced to labour in the disgusting Sonderkommando units in all the Nazi death camps, fewer than thirty are known to have survived.

With Himmler's blessing, von dem Bach had ordered the creation of new units on 8 August 1944. They were to be called *Verbrennungskommando*, or 'Cremation Commandos', and were to be made up of groups of fifty Polish prisoners, healthy young men who were to be guarded at all times and put to work clearing up the streets. The Wola group was to be garrisoned at the old railway barracks in Sokołowska Street, next to Spilker's Gestapo headquarters; SS Obersturmführer Neumann was put in charge.

One of the prisoners, Tadeusz Klimaszewski, served in the Wola Verbrennungskommando for most of August, and miraculously escaped shortly before it was liquidated. After the war he wrote a memoir about his time there, in which he describes the ghastly work he had been forced to do. His record is unique, not only because he is able to document the sheer scale of the murders in Wola, but also because, unlike the Jewish prisoners in the Sonderkommando, he and his men lived and worked with the SS guards, and got to know them a little. Although they were aware that they would be killed in the end, a relationship developed between the prisoners and their guards. Klimaszewski was able to observe the Germans, record their conversations and gain insight into their views on everything from the promised Nazi 'Wunderwaffen' ('wonder weapons') to the Allied bombing of German cities. He has left a snapshot of a small group of SS men working in Warsaw in the last year of the war, at a time when German morale was crumbling, and even they were struggling to find any justification for what they were doing to the people of the city.

Verbrennungskommando

In the summer of 1957 Klimaszewski was shown a film shot on the North Frisian Islands, off the German coast. It was made by Annelie and Andrew Thorndike, and was called *Holiday on Sylt*. The film opened with predictable shots of people sunning themselves on the beaches and playing in the sparkling water. Later, pictures of Westerland, the main town on the island, flashed onto the screen. A distinguished-looking man, with close-cropped grey hair and dressed in a well-cut suit, was shown working at his desk. This was the town's proud *Bürgermeister*, who had been elected to office in 1951. He was destined for even higher things, and would soon be elected a member of the Landestag of Schleswig-Holstein. The man was none other than Heinz Reinefarth. Next, the film showed a large auditorium dominated by a gigantic iron cross hanging above the stage. This was an SS rally held near Würzburg in 1957. Eight thousand 'old combatants' chanted as the guest speaker, SS leader 'Panzer Meyer', spoke about the 'old times'. Klimaszewski watched as 'the same people who had been in Warsaw, in Aleja Szucha and Pawiak, and in Majdanek and Auschwitz', cheered and clapped their former comrade. It was the image of the SS men enjoying the wealth and freedom of post-war West Germany, and in particular of Reinefarth's new and untroubled life, that prompted Klimaszewski to write his book documenting what had happened in Wola. As he put it, he did not want the memories 'to be mine alone'.[34]

Klimaszewski had had an unusual career. After the First World War he had joined the French Foreign Legion, and fought in North Africa and Indo-China. Just before war broke out, he had returned to Poland to join the fight against the Germans. When the uprising began he was living in an apartment at Graniczna 14 in Wola, and had moved into the basement with the other residents, hoping somehow to survive. As it turned out, his building was one of the worst places to try to hide, as it lay precisely in Dirlewanger's path to the Brühl Palace. By 7 August all the buildings nearby were burning, and Dirlewanger was fighting for the adjacent Hala Mirowska market halls. 'Nobody bothered to close the gates to the block at night,' said Klimaszewski. 'Nobody could sleep anyway.' They listened in terror as the fight grew closer.

The Germans surrounded the building on 8 August, and forced the residents to leave the basement and line up against a wall. A tall, slim SS officer with a prominent duelling scar and cold, lifeless grey eyes stood in front of them. Klimaszewski would later learn that this was SS Leutnant Thieschke, the leader of the group, and that he wielded absolute power of life and death over his prisoners. He was accompanied by a short, fat, red-faced Feldwebel named Hans Bethke, who immediately began shouting at the civilians: '*Raus! Schneller! Gottverdammt!*' A man tripped in the confusion. Thieschke went up to him, took out his revolver and shot him in the head. The now terrified group was marched to the nearby Saski Gardens, one of the loveliest parks in Warsaw. 'Turn around!' Bethke shouted, 'On your knees!' They all believed that they were about to be executed.

But their lives were spared. Dirlewanger had decided that the people of Graniczna 14 were to become 'human shields' to guard his Tiger tanks during the attack against the barricade at Plac Bankowy. They were made to line up in eight rows in front of three tanks, and walk forward. The metal hulks bumped their backs, and they cringed in fear as the tanks began to fire shells at the Polish front line. Hot air pushed them forward, and they were deafened by the noise. The Poles at the barricade stopped shooting when they saw the civilians. Only one person was shot – a German soldier, whose helmet rolled around on the pavement like a cooking pot.

When the group returned from this ordeal, Leutnant Thieschke surveyed them with his cold eyes. 'He lit his cigarette very slowly and pointed at one, then another. "*Du, komm,*" he said. Our ears were so sensitive that we could hear the sound of his pistol moving against the leather holster.' After a time he looked directly at Klimaszewski. ' "*Komm,*" he said.' Klimaszewski moved out of the group, certain that he would now be shot. When fifty men had been called out, Thieschke gave an order. The rest of the group, including those from Klimaszewski's cellar, were shot. He watched, helpless, as their bodies 'buckled as they fell softly to the pavement'.

The group was forced to march. They moved 'like machines', with no idea where they were going or what was going to happen to them. Wola was burning, and clouds of smoke stung their eyes and seared their lungs. Shards of glass from breaking windows 'cut into our arms and hands'; roofs caved in and tiles fell into the flames as they passed. It was an inferno. Suddenly Thieschke ordered them to halt. They found themselves next to a huge crater in the road. A pile of bodies lay next to it. 'The officer showed us on his watch that we had twenty minutes to finish the job. He pointed to his pistol, and then to the ground.' They understood. Their job was to push the bodies into the crater, and cover them up.

The bodies were of civilians in ordinary summer clothes. They had been killed some days ago, and had already started to decompose. The men were disgusted and horrified. They did not want to touch the corpses, but they could see the officer standing by and looking at his watch. They knew that if they did not do something they would be shot. 'A few of us started to drag bodies to the hole and push them in. Stinking water splashed on the officer's boots. We took stones and rubble and bricks and twisted iron pipes and put them on the bodies.' Thieschke stood over them the whole time, checking his watch as they worked. After twenty minutes he looked up. 'Halt!' he yelled. Clearly, they had passed the 'test'. They were allowed to rest a while, although without food or water, before being moved up the street to the old red-brick market buildings, the Hala Mirowska.[35]

For Klimaszewski that first day passed in a haze. One minute he had been in a dark basement surrounded by people he knew, the next his friends had been murdered and he found himself in a cavernous brick hall surrounded by SS men barking orders. Despite all his experiences in the Foreign Legion he was unable to process what was happening.

A huge shell had gone through the roof of the market hall and blasted a hole in the floor, exposing the maze of rooms in the basement below. As Klimaszewski's eyes adjusted to the dim light, made yellow by the stained-glass windows, he could see piles of luggage and clothing placed neatly by the entrance. Then he saw the bodies. The halls were filled with the contorted forms of the dead, as far as the eye could see. Everything was coated in thick, sticky red blood, and the stench made Klimaszewski want to vomit. The eerie light from the windows threw terrifying colours onto the ashen faces of the dead.

One of the sub-officers approached the group. 'Who can speak German?' he asked. A young man stepped forward. '*Ja gut,*' the German said. 'Now you are *Kapo.*' He looked at the men. 'You are not going to be killed,' he said. 'No more "*pyk pyk*".' He pointed to his pistol. And then he told them what they were expected to do. '*Alle Leichen weg*' – all bodies to be cleared – he barked, pointing at the huge hole in the floor.

Klimaszewski was horrified by the inhuman things he and the crew were being forced to do. Apart from the nature of the work, these were fellow Warsawians, whose bodies should have been treated with respect. But he understood that he had to carry on if he was to have any hope of surviving even for another few days. The men started to move the bodies, but they were heavy and difficult to grasp. The blood had mixed with the dirt on the floor, making a slippery paste, and it was hard for the men to keep their balance. They tried tying rags around their hands to keep from touching the corpses, but the cloth was soon drenched with blood. The Germans made them take their shirts off. Someone found a cart, and they put the bodies in it two or three at a time and then dumped them in the hole. At every turn Klimaszewski saw evidence of the last seconds of life frozen before him – the grey-haired man trying to push himself to the back of the crowd; the face of the father saying goodbye to his child. At one point he broke down, thinking that the corpse he was turning over was that of his own father. The *kapo* told him quietly to pull himself together, 'or you will also be killed'.

As the men continued their grisly task the SS turned their attention to the piles of clothes and suitcases by the door. They were laughing all the time. Klimaszewski watched in disgust as 'One of them, short with a bald head, took out women's clothes and put on a tight summer dress and pushed cloth in the front to create breasts. He performed a cabaret, pretending to be a showgirl, and all the SS guys laughed. After a while he pirouetted, stepped on a dead body, lost his balance and fell. He got up, still sticking his hip out like a woman. We could see blood on the dress.' At one point Klimaszewski noticed a man hiding between some barrels, a mining engineer with whom he had built barricades in the first days of the uprising. The engineer was afraid of being captured by the Germans and begged to be allowed to join the commando. Klimaszewski told him to take off his shirt like the others, and start to work; Feldwebel Bethke would notice that evening that the group had grown by one, but he did nothing. The men were given six canisters of petrol and forced to burn the bodies, something which for Catholics was abhorrent.

When the job was finished the men, still in shock, were taken to their temporary quarters in the railwaymen's house in Sokołowski Street. They exchanged names and personal details – not out of politeness, but because they knew they could be killed at any time, and that a survivor might be able to pass information on to their families. This marked the end of Klimaszewski's first day in the Cremation Commando.

The next morning, after they had been given food and water, Thieschke came to talk to them. 'I have saved your lives, and you should be grateful to me,' he said. 'You will show your gratitude through good, honest, decent work. This borough is full of the bodies of people and animals, and they breed disease and infection for Germans and Poles. It is in our common interest to remove this cause of epidemics as soon as possible.'

With that, they were taken to the Franaszek factory. It was a shocking sight. Over a thousand civilians had been killed there on 5 August, and the men were overcome with fear and horror.

'We entered the space, and were at first blinded by the sun. We were suddenly hit by an unbearable stench. Then I realized that as far as I could see there were just bodies. They must have squeezed them in, as many as possible, and then thrown grenades, as it was a horrible massacre, the ground was full of holes and explosions, the walls of the courtyard were covered in bullet marks, there were small personal items like briefcases and bread and hats lying there. The mass murder had to have been committed some days ago, as the August sun had made the bodies bloat up. There were thousands of fat flies everywhere, everything was coated in a kind of stinking jelly with the noise of thousands of flies. We were completely terrified . . . We were horrified, disgusted, nauseous.' The Germans left them alone to get to work, but made sure to lock them in so there was no chance of escape. The tall, dark-haired mining engineer who had joined the group at the Hala Mirowska broke down in tears. 'Don't clean it up, don't do it,' he said. 'The war is nearly over, we need to leave them here and let people see it, they must lie here, we will bring people from the whole world and let them see it.'[36] Klimaszewski understood what he meant. The horror of having to put these bodies in massive pyres and destroy the evidence of their lives was terrible. But it had to be done.

It soon became clear that 'their' Germans had experience of such tasks. They explained to the Poles how to stack the corpses in neat piles, placing pieces of wood between the layers so they would burn. The technique was remarkably similar to that perfected at Treblinka. After some hours the pile in the courtyard was several metres high; one group handed bodies up to a second, positioned on top of the pile. The engineer leaned against the wall in despair as the bodies went up to a third layer, a fourth layer. Tears ran down his cheeks, tracing lines in the grey dust on his face.

When Leutnant Thieschke saw the engineer he asked the *kapo* why the man was not working. The young Pole tried to save the engineer's life by claiming that he had become nauseous because of the air. '*Na ja*, if he is sick he must go to hospital,' Thieschke answered cynically. He took the engineer away through the gate.

When Thieschke came back a short time later, the pyre was almost finished. The Poles were ordered to put earth on the ground to cover up the blood, then to pour petrol over the gigantic pyre. At the last minute the *kapo* and two others were ordered to fetch another corpse. 'It was the engineer. His body was limp. There was blood dripping from his mouth.'

In the coming days the Cremation Commando was forced to gather and burn the corpses of thousands of men, women and children who had been massacred in Wola. They built a pyre in the garden of the Russian Orthodox church, and burned corpses all along Wolska Street. 'Everywhere we went there were bodies,' Klimaszewski recalled – in courtyards and buildings, in gardens and on side streets. The worst thing was finding the bodies of women and children, such as a group of refugees in the garden of the Wolski hospital. A white flag still fluttered in their midst. All the bodies had been robbed, irrespective of age or sex; their clothes were torn, the pockets pulled out, their suitcases and bundles plundered and the unwanted things left to blow around in the wind. As the group burned the bodies in the garden they heard the SS men laughing in the distance. They were playing cards.

There were ever more bodies, and 'pyres, pyres, pyres'. At some sites they had to walk on corpses three layers thick; at others the blood had mixed with the earth, creating a thick purple muck that sucked at their shoes. One day they found a large cart with rubber wheels, and two horses. The Germans put armchairs on the back, and the Poles drove them 'to work'; the cart was then used to move bodies to the pyres until evening, when they all returned to Sokołowski Street. The Germans told the Poles to look for sites where there was already lots of wood; they also knew exactly how much petrol to pour over the bodies to get them to burn, and how long the process would take. Once again, it was clear that they knew what they were doing.

The prisoners had been frightened to talk at first, but soon began to feel more confident. They would whisper to one another at night, and got to know each other a little. 'Despite the situation all we could think about was food and sleep, and yet we talked and joked; if we had not we would have gone mad. This simple secret of survival explains how people can cope with the hell of the camps or long-term imprisonment, of bombing and of war.'[37] The group was a cross-section of ages and professions: there was Franek, nicknamed 'Dziobaty', with a pockmarked face, whose job was to spray-paint cars, and who had been in one of the camps. There was a delicate man who was a teacher, a tram driver, a barrister named Mańko, and tall, blond Edek, who was a coachman. The most knowledgeable of them all was a Jewish man who had escaped from the ghetto.

The Cremation Commando was based on the camp Leichenkommandos and Sonderkommandos, and as such the SS men were always careful to give them hope that they would live. Klimaszewski and his crew were treated well and given good rations, water and even alcohol. 'The SS guys told us we were not in any danger. They assured us that when the work was done and the district cleared after the *Banditen* capitulated we would have the right to choose proper work for ourselves.' Leutnant Thieschke even offered them jobs on his German estate after the war.[38] Some of the men wanted to believe these lies, and were lulled into a false sense of security, arguing against escape attempts or anything else that might anger their minders. But others had more experience.

Edek had a clear understanding of how the Germans worked. 'They will shoot us anyway,' he said. 'We have to remember that. When we finish our job they won't need us.' The former camp prisoner Dziobaty agreed: 'It was the same in the KZ with the Himmelkommando,' he said. 'It is their system. We won't even know where or when. Maybe tomorrow or the day after or in a few days they will tell us to march, we will take our equipment, nobody will suspect anything, only they will know. Maybe they will tell us to prepare a pile and prepare everything to set a fire, and when it is all ready they will gather us just like that and then they will shoot us.'[39]

In the beginning the Jewish man, clearly terrified lest his secret be discovered, had hardly ever spoken: Klimaszewski only realized he was Jewish when the Germans allowed the blood-soaked men to bathe in an ornamental pond one day. The man had refused to take off his clothes, and Klimaszewski had naïvely asked if he was afraid of getting sick. 'He turned to me, his eyes silently begging.' Klimaszewski finally understood, and quickly started a conversation with some others to divert attention away from him.

The rest of the men soon learned the truth, but nobody informed on him – a constant danger for any Jew discovered in Warsaw even at that late date. 'We are all in this together,' they said. The Jewish man admitted that he had managed to escape from the ghetto, and had seen what the Germans were capable of. 'I know what they were doing in the ghetto,' he whispered one night. 'Just before they started to kill people they would spread information about work and about the need for more workers. They created new groups. And then . . .' The men believed him. 'If he was in the ghetto he knows the Germans much better than we do,' they agreed.[40]

This particular conversation had been provoked by the fact that the Germans had rounded up fifty new prisoners in order to create another Verbrennungskommando. The Jewish man was worried: if they were creating a new group, perhaps they had decided to liquidate the old one. As Zenon Piasecki, another Cremation Commando survivor, put it after the war, 'We were told that the Germans killed the workers after a while and a new group was put together. They did it to hide the crime. They did not want witnesses.'[41]

The next day the Jewish man's suspicions were confirmed, albeit not in the way they had feared. Leutnant Thieschke had been asked to recruit a new group of men for Reinefarth, but was then told that they were not needed after all. Edek, who took care of the horses, had watched secretly as Thieschke argued with two other officers near the stables. '*Ich brauche keine Leute mehr* – I don't need any more people' – one officer had snapped at Thieschke. 'We don't either,' the second said. 'You can do what you like, *mein Lieber.*' After the officers had left, Edek watched as the fifty men were led away. 'They all died,' he said. 'Even the three guys who were sent for water.'[42] Klimaszewski felt a sense of foreboding. The men began to look for opportunities to escape, but it was virtually impossible. They were trapped in Wola, and were always guarded. They were forced to work without shirts, and as they were often covered in blood they would have stood out on the German-held streets. They also knew that if just one of them escaped, the rest would be killed.

The SS Men

Most Sonderkommando prisoners in the death camps slept and worked some distance from their German minders. The Verbrennungskommando was different. Klimaszewski and his team lived together with the same group of SS men day in and day out, and sometimes even ate the same food. Although the 'master–slave' relationship never changed, they began to get to know one another. 'I often observed the Germans who guarded us,' he wrote. It is this insight into the workings of the SS at close quarters that makes his testimony so valuable.

'With the exception of the fat Bethke and Feldwebel Hans the majority of the SS were quite intelligent,' Klimaszewski noted.[43] The rest had 'at least an average education and some more than that'. The most important man in the group was the tall, slim commanding officer, Leutnant Thieschke, a lawyer in civilian life who owned a huge estate in Germany.[44] His face had an expression of cold indifference, his sharp cheekbones and the long duelling scar on his chin giving it a horrifying grimness. Corporal Hans Bethke was short and chubby; whenever he spoke his voice would rise, he would turn red and a string of swear words would follow: '*Donnerwetter! Gottverdammt!*' The NCO, with his slim, pale face, was a musician, while Erik, with dark hair and gold-rimmed glasses, had been a teacher. There was a young botany student called Konrad; a sportsman, the massively built Kurt; and Feldwebel Franz, who had a sadistic streak. The old Feldwebel

Hans was a veteran of the First World War. Between them they represented all layers of German society. They worked closely together, and always came back to the group if they had a break, and to eat or sleep.

Von dem Bach had chosen men who had experience both of the camps and of the ghetto. 'Thieschke and Bethke and tall Kurt were very disciplined, and their eyes were everywhere – often when we were somewhere in an abandoned courtyard or street we suddenly met them allegedly by accident, or they appeared unexpectedly in the rubble or in the windows of burned houses. We knew that we were being guarded by the best SS guys, who must have had lots of practice in the ghetto or in the concentration camps observing people who were frightened and exhausted but always ready to grasp at even the slightest chance of salvation.'[45]

In the beginning the Polish 'Banditen' meant nothing to the group of Germans. On one occasion the men were forced to climb a barricade under Polish fire and clear it away.[46] Feldwebel Franz tried to make a young boy lie in front of his machine gun, but the boy refused. 'Komm!' Franz said, hitting him on the neck with a piece of iron. The boy, now injured, could barely move. 'Du frecher Kerl,' Franz snarled. The boy was made to lie down, and Franz placed the legs of the machine gun on his body. The SS men cheered. 'Richtig, Franz! Gute Arbeit! – Well done, Franz! Good work!' 'Was glaubst du? – What do you think?' he called back. 'Besser als Sandsack! – Better than a sandbag!' The boy was later wounded in the stomach, and was left behind at the barricade. Klimaszewski and the others assumed that the Germans had shot him, but a few days afterwards the men of the Cremation Commando found his body, and realized that his fate had been much worse. The corpse lay on the ground in the centre of a large black stain. His hands were raised to his face, which was still intact, but his body was nothing but a runny mass. The Germans had literally melted him, using some hydrochloric acid that they had found on the barricade that day.

By now Wola had been cleared of combatants and civilians, and the SS men could relax. From time to time long lines of refugees would march past under guard; Thieschke enjoyed picking young men out of the groups and shooting them for sport. The SS men lounged around in comfortable chairs, smoking and drinking and playing cards. They looted incessantly. Feldwebel Hans was from Silesia, and could speak a Polish-German dialect. On one occasion he ordered a Pole to remove the ring from a dead woman, but her finger was bent back and it could not be done. Hans took his pistol, shot the finger away and took the ring. '*Echt Gold,*' he said. '*Russisches.*' He undid his uniform and took out a leather bag already heavy with loot. '*Na ja, stimmt.*' Then he looked up. 'Why are you looking at me like that? This is war, and who survives and lives gets everything, and he who has a cold arse doesn't need gold anyway.'

One day when the men had finished work, Hans made the whole group sit around him in a circle. Nobody wanted to do it, but he insisted. 'It is my forty-eighth birthday,' he said, 'and there are forty-eight of you. I was supposed to have forty-eight candles on my cake, so you can drink to my health and then I can blow out each one of you.' He was laughing. Holding a bottle in one hand, he took out his pistol with the other. He must have seen the fear in the men's faces. 'No, don't worry,' he laughed. 'Just a joke.' He got increasingly drunk, and began to talk quite openly, telling the men that they should loot just like he did. People are predictable, he said, and always take their most valuable possessions with them when they are forced to leave their homes – jewellery, gold, money. 'Don't show it, hide it,' he said. 'In the meantime you can give me something as well, a ring or a signet – I will go on holiday to Frankfurt very soon, and I will have fun there. When there's war you need to live quickly, there is no time. Everything is expensive, schnapps, hotel girls.'[47]

More worrying for the men was his warning not to work so fast. '*Langsam*,' he said – 'Slowly.' 'I am an old front-line fox. I am in my second war. Do not rush. You have good food, drink – a lot – that is important. Work *schluss* – finished – then you . . .' His voice tailed off, but they knew what he had meant. When the bodies ran out, they would be killed.[48]

Clearing away dead bodies and hauling them up onto the pyres was exhausting and emotionally draining wherever they worked, but clearing the Wolski hospital had been particularly harrowing. Dirlewanger's men had been violent in the extreme, and the wards, operating theatres and offices were filled with the contorted bodies of dead patients, doctors, nurses and staff. The staircase had been destroyed, and the Commando was forced to throw the corpses out of the first-floor window. At first they had refused to desecrate the dead in this way, but the *kapo* had insisted, suggesting that they collect all the mattresses and blankets they could find so as to make a soft area on which the bodies could land.[49] It had been horrible work, and when it was finished the men were deeply shaken, and drenched in blood. The Germans, in a rare show of sympathy, gave them a scrubbing brush so they could get clean.

The sight of the murdered patients and doctors in the hospital had clearly affected the SS soldier Erik, the dark-haired teacher. He was from the Saarland, which had recently been heavily bombed, and Klimaszewski knew that he had lost a close member of his family in a raid. That evening the Germans let the Poles sit near them in the courtyard as they ate their cutlets and downed their schnaps and wine. Bethke started to talk about the Allied bombing raids, and argued that although civilians might die, the raids did not affect military production, 'which is the most important thing in the war'.

Erik took his glasses off and listened with an ironic smile as he cleaned the lenses. Finally he could contain himself no longer, and turned on Bethke. '*Armee Armee Armee!*' he yelled. '*Mensch!* This is stupid. What does an army mean without a society behind it? So what if we stand on the Vistula or the Danube or wherever else if there are only ruins and cemeteries waiting for us? I wonder what your reaction will be, Hans Bethke, when you win the war with a chest full of medals and you return to a city which no longer exists? Did you ever think about that?'

Bethke tried to answer, but Erik started in again. 'This is all just shit, man!' he yelled, gesturing around. 'War is war, but we should leave civilians in peace!'

They could all see the hatred in Bethke's round eyes. 'It is not good when an SS soldier gets tired of war,' he snapped. Erik bent towards him, his face pale then pink with anger: 'You, Hans, are a specialist in war with Jews and civilians, and you got decorated for that,' he spat. 'You also got loot in your pocket. But yours is safe war, Bethke.'

Thieschke had been listening in silence, but now he turned on the teacher in a fury. 'I order you to stay calm. You are talking to your superior. And I want to focus your attention on the fact that in the army we do not need philosophers. It is dangerous.' Thieschke took out a cigarette. He was trying to appear calm, but Klimaszewski could see that his hands were shaking in anger.[50]

The next confrontation between Erik and Bethke was over the fate of a young girl. The SS men were directing a group of civilians when Bethke pulled the girl aside, telling her to wait for him. As Bethke addressed the crowd, Erik helped her escape. When the Feldwebel noticed that she had disappeared he flew into a rage: 'Wo ist das Mädchen?' he screamed, grabbing Erik by his uniform. 'Erik slapped his hand away. Bethke put his hand on his pistol. Erik did the same, and they stood there looking at one another with boundless hatred.'[51]

Despite this in-fighting, Klimaszewski was amazed by how ordinary these men could be when they were not working. 'They had discussions about life, their families, art, paintings, literature and music. They seemed to be different people at that moment, their faces softened, the grim tension disappeared and their eyes got some human warmth. If they had taken off their uniforms and hats with shiny metal skulls and put on some civilian clothes they would have been just a group of nice, well-behaved people with whom you could talk and take real pleasure in their company. How easy it was to imagine them as respected trustworthy people from their neighbourhoods as good fathers, sons and husbands. They were perfectly suited to wholesome German households with beautifully maintained gardens, morning slippers and pipes and glasses of beer and the elegant clean streets of their towns.'

But this peaceful image was constantly shattered by the reality of life in Wola that August. 'How many times did they shoot frightened pigeons and cats and dogs and horses just for sport, or shoot into windows just to hear the sound of broken glass? They dropped grenades into abandoned flats just to hear the explosion, and set fire to houses for fun and used portraits and paintings as target practice.'

They were callous even to their own. 'Very often when we were clearing up we came across the bodies of dead German soldiers and officers. If our SS guys realized that there were no other Germans around, they told us to burn those bodies as well. They didn't take off their metal number tags and they didn't take their documents. They wanted everything completely burned in a meticulous way.'[52] At the same time, Thieschke would go from one execution site to the next, taking photographs of the piles of bodies lying on the ground. Hans told them, 'The propaganda office will pay well for those pictures, especially now that the Eastern Front is coming. It is the best proof of Bolshevik cruelty towards civilians in the occupied country.'[53]

Worst of all was the sheer inhumanity of these normal-looking men. They had no regard for human life, and a complete lack of empathy for those who suffered and died at their hands. Reinefarth epitomized this when he complained to von Vormann that he was frustrated, as he had 'more civilians than ammunition': for him the victims were not human beings, but simply a technical problem that had to be dealt with.

By the third week of August the Commando had burned all the bodies around Wolska and Chłodna, and had just about cleared Elektoralna. As they moved east they drew ever closer to the front line. Their work was almost done, and the SS men were becoming increasingly nervous. For them August had been something of a holiday, with two weeks of drinking and looting while the men of the Verbrennungskommando built the funeral pyres. They knew that they would not be allowed to stay in Wola much longer, and that with such a shortage of men at the front they might actually be called on to fight. 'Our SS men,' Klimaszewski said, 'realized that this was the end of the happy days.' He was right. The Commando reached the front line on 23 August.

Klimaszewski had no time to think about his fate or that of the others. That afternoon Thieschke pulled him and two other men, Mańko the barrister and the tram driver, out of the group. They were told that they were to walk to the City Hall, which was in Polish hands, check what was behind the sandbags in the courtyard, and then return to the group. The Germans controlled the Opera House on the other side of the street. The three Poles were being ordered to walk straight onto the front line.

'*Also, alles ist klar?*' Thieschke asked. 'I will wait here for twenty minutes. If you don't come back . . .' His lips twisted in an evil grimace.

The three men had no choice but to go, but Thieschke ordered that a red flare be sent up, and the German cannon at the Opera House stopped firing. Klimaszewski reached the sandbags surrounding the City Hall with the others, and looked over. A single soldier was lying there with his gun, a boy with a thin face covered in dust and with a bloodstained bandage on his head. Mańko said, 'Don't shoot.' The boy was taken aback to hear Polish, but immediately told them to lie down and not to move. When Mańko tried to tell him that they had to get back or else the other members of their group would be killed, he hissed, 'Be quiet or I will shoot you.' The look on his face told them that he meant what he said. Mańko tried again: 'Listen, you young shit soldier or whatever you are, don't you understand that if we don't go right away our people will be killed?' But the boy insisted that they stay there until his commanding officer came back. After an interminable wait they heard the German cannon start firing. 'It is already too late,' Mańko said.

Klimaszewski and his companions were now on the Polish side of the front line. What he had seen over the past two weeks had made him more determined than ever to fight against the Germans, and when Radosław learned about his experience both in the Foreign Legion and in the Commando he allowed him to join 'Czata 49' under his command. Klimaszewski had crossed the lines just in time to take part in one of the most vicious fights of the uprising: the battle for the Old Town.

The remaining men of the Verbrennungskommando were shot. By destroying the evidence of the bodies in Wola, Himmler believed that he had covered up the crimes committed there. Klimaszewski's invaluable testimony of life in Wola during August 1944 would prove him wrong.

10

HITLER'S WAR AGAINST THE OLD TOWN

———◦◦◦◦◦———

They had neither allies, nor mercenaries, nor supplies for enduring a siege, nor anything else in readiness for this sudden and unheralded war, while by themselves they could not prevail against the Romans and Masinnissa combined. (Chapter X)

The Fortress

When Bernardo Bellotto first arrived in Warsaw in 1764 as King Stanisław August Poniatowski's new Court Painter, he was deeply moved by the beauty of the Old Town. This jewel in the crown of Warsaw, one of the gems of Europe, stood high above the Vistula, its dramatic skyline of towers, spires and domes spilling down towards the river below. Bellotto set about documenting the city as his uncle Canaletto had Venice, creating an extraordinary series of paintings which now hang, as was intended, in the Warsaw Castle. In these masterpieces the city is rendered in soft greens and golds and pinks, preserving in great detail the beauty of its graceful churches and tall, colourful houses and exquisite palaces nestled together in the busy and bustling capital. The paintings would prove invaluable in the reconstruction of

Warsaw's Old Town after 1945, because by then everything that Bellotto had known had been destroyed.

With Wola now taken, the Germans turned towards the river, and focused on the Old Town. This area was important because of its proximity to the Vistula, and above all because of the Kierbedź Bridge, which was vital for the supply of the troops in Praga and beyond. The Old Town had to be defeated, and fast.[1] Reinefarth was not daunted. Wola had fallen relatively quickly, and he had no reason to think that the small district by the Vistula would be any different. But he was wrong.

The fiercest fighting around the Old Town in the first weeks of August 1944 took place in an area measuring ten square kilo-metres, and shaped rather like half an onion, with the Vistula at its base and concentric rings running around the tiny medieval core. The outermost layer consisted of the no man's land bordered by the Traugutta Fort and the Gdańsk railway station to the north, the former ghetto to the west, and Senatorska Street and the ruins of the Warsaw Castle to the south.

The next layers were made up of imposing swathes of grand eighteenth- and nineteenth-century buildings put up after the 'Swedish Deluge' had destroyed so much of the city in the 1650s. Famous architects had been called in from all over Europe, and the great white columns and grand façades were testimony to their skill. The pediment reliefs and statues on the glorious Krasiński Palace, one of the most beautiful Baroque buildings in the city, were carved by the great Prussian sculptor Andreas Schlüter, who created the famous Amber Room in Peter the Great's palace in St Petersburg, and whose works graced the most pres-tigious buildings in Berlin. The Nazis renamed Krasiński Square in his honour, although that did not stop them from pulverizing the palace in 1944. There were exquisite structures at every turn – the romantically named rococo Palace of the Four Winds at

Długa 40; the Blank Palace, hiding its pretty façade behind enormous wrought-iron gates; the great Mostowski Palace and the Bank Polski, both Corazzi masterpieces. With their thick walls, high gates and heavy doors they would all prove to be mighty fortresses; each would be the scene of desperate fighting in the coming weeks.

Further in still was the New Town, which was developed in the fourteenth century. Marie Curie was born in one of the handsome houses on Freta Street surrounded by the churches of St Jacek, St Francis, and the Holy Spirit. The most lovely of all was St Kazimierz's at the edge of the square, with its glistening white walls and glorious copper-domed roof, designed for the Sisters of the Sacrament by the Dutch-born Tylman of Gameren, architect of some of the most important Baroque buildings in all of Poland. Theirs was a silent order, but they would break the oath for the first time in three hundred years to run a hospital in the crypt during the uprising. On 31 August 1944, thirty-five nuns and over a thousand people would die there in a bombing raid.

At the very heart of the district lay the small, dense medieval city – the Old Town itself. It was a natural fortress. This was one of the few European cities to have retained its original walls, punctuated by massive gates including the sixteenth-century Barbikan built by the Venetian architect Jan Baptysta. Inside lay tiny, winding streets, lined by charming, narrow houses and shops, and the modest fourteenth-century Gothic St John's Cathedral, which rubbed shoulders with the soaring St Martin's church. Further down was Piekarska, or 'Little Hell', where witches were once burned, and Wąski Dunaj, a small street which was at the core of the original medieval Jewish quarter long before the artificial ghetto was set up by the Nazis. Then, suddenly, the little alleys opened up into the Old Town square, with its parade of shops and cafés and tall houses reminiscent of Amsterdam, but with exuberant painted façades. It was an atmospheric meeting place which had once housed fairs and markets and special feasts and celebrations of all kinds. Finally came the Kamienne Schodki, the long steps down to the river, from which Napoleon had stood staring pensively towards Moscow on the eve of his Russian campaign.

Reinefarth assumed that the fight for the Old Town would take little more than a week, but he had not counted on two important factors. For the first time the AK troops had had time to prepare fortifications, carefully designed barricades and well-hidden nests for snipers. Furthermore, the Poles were being led by two of the best commanders in the history of the AK – Jan Mazurkiewicz ('Radosław'), fresh from the fights in the cemeteries, and Colonel Karol Ziemski ('Wachnowski'), who was in charge of the Northern Group – 'Grupa Północ'.

'Radosław' was born in 1896 in Lwów. His idyllic childhood in that most picturesque of cities had been cut short at the age of nine when his father had been killed saving people from a fire. The young man had joined Piłsudski's renowned 1st Brigade of Legions, the Polish armed force created in 1914, and after a distinguished career he was made leader of the 'Kedyw' Group, one of the most prestigious postings in the AK. His friend 'Wachnowski' was educated in Lublin, and fought in the Russian army in 1915. Showing promise, he was sent to officer-training school in Kiev, then fought on the German–Russian Front in Romania and Byelorussia. In May 1918 he went to Warsaw to continue his studies at the University of Technology, and continued his military service. In 1920 he participated in the decisive Battle of Radzymin, which prevented Lenin from bringing Communism to Berlin. By 1942 he had been made Colonel Monter's second in command in Warsaw, and on 7 August 1944 Monter made him leader of 'Grupa Północ', in charge of the defence of the district in and around the Old Town. He had quickly reorganized its units to await the German onslaught.

These two talented leaders gave no quarter. From the beginning they fought bravely, earning the respect of their men and often serving with them on the front line. Wachnowski had three main groups spread through the quarter: Radosław's 'Kedyw' Group, which included the legendary battalions 'Czata 49', 'Miotła', 'Pięść', 'Leśnik' and 'Waligóra'; the 'Kuba' and 'Sosna' groups; and the 'Róg' Group. Altogether he had around 8,000 troops waiting behind well-constructed barricades and lodged deep in key buildings.

On 11 August the Germans began their attack, aiming for key points at the Krasiński Gardens, the Mostowski Palace and the barricades in Leszno Street. But to their surprise they ran into resistance at every turn. The Poles fought ferociously at the barricades in Podwale, Świętojańska, Piwna, Senatorska and Miodowa Streets, around the City Hall and in the Blank Palace. When the Germans retreated the Poles pursued them; there was bitter hand-to-hand combat in a number of buildings, and the warehouse on Stawki changed hands several times. German morale was low, and they made little progress.

One of the worst aspects for the Germans was the snipers, who caused physical and psychological damage in their endless game of cat and mouse. 'Agaton' was in position at the border of the ghetto ruins: 'The Germans had been so efficient destroying everything there was no shelter – it was a dead zone in the centre of burning Warsaw.' In the morning he noticed an enemy soldier 'so convinced that the area was in German hands he didn't even try to hide. He took off his uniform and started to shave. I could have shot him immediately. I had him in my sights and it would have been enough to pull the trigger.' Agaton did shoot eventually. 'To this day I don't know if I regret or am happy that I missed that shot.'[2]

Wacław Zagórski, also of 'Kedyw', showed a film crew from Biuletyn Informacji Publiczne (BIP), the Polish propaganda unit, around his sniper's nest.[3] It too was in a dead zone, 'full of burnt-out ruins with some lonely black chimneys and smoke above the rubble'. They could see a column of horse-drawn wagons, women walking in a line on either side of them, each one's hands on the shoulders of the woman in front. 'This is a human shield,' he explained. A group of Germans were sitting behind a high wall on the other side of the street. 'They have bare chests and are taking a bath with buckets of water; another group is drinking coffee from their canteen.' The cameraman asked why the Poles didn't shoot them straight away. 'We don't have ammunition . . . We have to keep these few dozen shells until the Schwabe attack.'[4] When the enemy finally made a move, the Poles fired at the last possible moment. The Germans retreated. Stanisław Likiernik remembered snipers firing from the church at Kościelna Street. 'Two German soldiers tried to hide by using the back of a sofa as a shield. Two almost simultaneous gunshots and both soldiers were flat on the ground with the settee as their ready-made coffin.'[5] For the moment the AK seemed to be keeping the Old Town safe.

The lack of German progress led to a false sense of security amongst the people living inside the 'fortress'. Agaton found the borough full of life, 'crowded with civilians reading newspapers and listening to music; the AK made announcements over the megaphone, civilian organizations were hard at work setting up food posts so people could get something to eat a few times a day'. There was enough water, the churches were full, and people made altars and prayed together in their courtyards. At one point eighteen newspapers were being published, albeit often on a single sheet. Agaton noted, too, that the AK was still highly regarded by the civilian population. 'Our scruffy uniforms evoked respect and interest. Soldiers were given the salute. Passwords were checked on the barricades. Refugees from Wola asked if we knew anything about the fate of their streets or houses.'[6] The AK were heroes, as one Warsawian remembered: 'We loved our army, the strange army of intelligentsia and workers and teenage boys with helmets covering their eyes and young girls serving Warsaw.'[7] There were ample supplies: 'A runner brings food and even chocolate. We have not had chocolate since the beginning of the war. The label says *"Nur für Wehrmacht"* – Only for the Wehrmacht. It made us laugh.'[8]

Refugees came in from Wola, convinced that they would now be safe. In his memoir of the uprising, Miron Białoszewski said of the Old Town: 'it was already a famous redoubt. Impregnable. Barricades. Serpentine streets. Not for tanks. Stare Miasto is strong. Its walls are solid. Thick.'[9] People felt secure; when they greeted one another they would say, 'Today is the twelfth day of the uprising,' as if it would soon be over. 'We were constantly listening for the Russians – was the ground trembling? Were they in the air . . . . where are they?'[10]

Old Town resident Aniela Pinon Gacka felt sorry for the refugees, who were 'so much worse off than we are. They came to us in the first days, through the ruins in the middle of the night. We helped by giving them food and putting mattresses in the basement.' The newcomers' stories of atrocities were not taken seriously. 'We really did not believe them and could not accept that in our century the German nation . . . could behave in such a bestial way.'[11] Grażyna Dąbrowska remembered that 'people were not particularly willing to accept them with children and luggage, not willing to look at these tired, frightened people.'[12] They did not realize that they would soon share their fate.

Janina Lasocka was one of hundreds from Wola grateful to have made it to the apparent safety of the Old Town, where she found shelter in the archives of the Courts of Law: 'Families used the shelves to create little spaces for themselves, and the documents were used as mattresses.'[13] After the chaos of Wola, life seemed almost normal. 'There was the clamour of children playing at the roundabout at Plac Krasiński – they could run away if they heard the sound of a plane.'

Jews also found refuge there. One of them recalled: 'At last I was only in danger in the same way as all the other inhabitants of Warsaw. Now even coming out in public didn't lead to certain death . . . For the people around me I was one of them and not someone especially marked out.'[14] Dr Jerzy Dreyza was looking for food when he found a group of mostly Greek and Hungarian Jews and two members of the hospital staff locked in a basement next to the Maltese hospital. The SS had forced them to clear out the warehouses during the panic at the end of July. They were to have been shot, but the soldier in charge had locked them in the basement instead. 'It saved their lives. We gave them civilian clothes and protected them in the hospital. They eventually left for Bielańska – we don't know what happened to them.'[15]

There were some anti-Semites amongst the members of the AK. Captain Wacław Stykowski ('Hal') used his position to become a kind of 'gangster warlord', and murdered at least twelve Jews near his quarters at the Haberbusch warehouse.[16] The Old Town units, on the other hand, seemed relatively free of this plague. The 348 Jews freed from Gęsiówka prison and a group of Hungarian Jews who had been kept in a school in Niska Street were 'unanimous in their desire to join the uprising and fight the Germans'. Eleven of the Hungarian Jews became sappers for the AK; most of them were to die in the fighting. Captain Miciuta praised the fifty Jews under him in the 'Zośka' Battalion as 'heroic', and would not forget their bravery in battle.[17] 'Antek' Zuckerman recalled that 'I didn't sense anti-Semitism even once, neither from the civilian population nor from the AK; the opposite was true.

The AL admired us and the AK showed us camaraderie. We were with them on the barricades.'[18] Marek Edelman and his group, who had fought in the Ghetto Uprising, also joined the Communist AL.[19] His 'ŻOB' Battalion manned its own barricade in Mostowa Street until the fall of the Old Town; many escaped at the last minute through the dangerous sewer to Żoliborz.[20]

The Jews from Gęsiówka made a lasting impression on many of the residents. Anna Szatkowska remembered: 'On 8 August I entered the gate and noticed a crowd of strange people with shaved heads dressed in striped uniforms . . . they were mostly from Hungary and seven from France and seven from Greece. One looked at me and said, "I am a lawyer from Budapest." He spoke in German. Another prisoner with a very intelligent face and grey hair whispered in German, "Please forgive me that I stopped you but my daughter looks like you and I just wanted to shake your hand." I spoke French with some who were happy to hear their language.' The neighbours rallied around and gave them soup and cigarettes. 'Amongst the young Greek Jews was a tenor from the opera in Saloniki who sang beautiful Greek and Italian opera songs for us.'[21] People gathered in the courtyard to hear his exquisite impromptu concerts.

In those early days there was still soup to give. Władysław Świdowski ('Wik Sławski') was in charge of organizing the civilian population, and departments were set up to provide food, collect clothing for the needy and take care of health matters and burials. The city authorities organized fire-fighting teams and groups to dig wells and latrines, and distribute powdered milk to infants. House committees were set up to look after food and supplies and to control looting and drunkenness. Wachnowski appointed Colonel Stefan Tarnawski to be medical chief of the Northern Group, in charge of hospitals. There was even a postal service.[22]

Brochures outlined how civilians should organize themselves

in their blocks: 'Everyone should keep basements and staircases clean,' one read. 'You must keep quiet hours between 8 p.m. and 8 a.m. Smoking is forbidden during these times. Sleeping areas should only be in basements and not in corridors. Oil lamps should be provided. Group prayer should take place before 8 p.m.'[23] These rules were obeyed in the early days; there was still a feeling of cooperation, and people still believed that they would be spared the worst, as the Soviets would surely come. Wacława Buzycka was working as a clerk in the City Hall, which was now on the front line. 'I typed notes for civilians as the engineers went out under fire to repair the sewer system.' In the first days they had treated one another with the usual formality, but they soon 'switched to the informal Stanisław or Józef . . . we were worried about food running out, although we still had supplies from Stawki'.[24] They could hear the sounds of fighting nearby, but there was no sense of panic.

People felt the urge to live life in the moment, and romance blossomed. Special arrangements were made so couples could marry without the usual paperwork. Piotr Osęka wrote of 'young boys with over-the-top pseudonyms, many of whom had nothing to do but walk around flirting with nurses . . . you knew when a young nurse was in love, because if the young man's unit was sent to fight she would go along'.[25] 'Under the pressure of the fighting the intensity of emotions broke through. I know an eighteen-year-old nurse who thought I was a hero. We didn't drink alcohol but if we found an empty flat we slept with one another, giving ourselves completely.'[26] This idyll was not to last.

On 12 August the Germans attacked again. Reinefarth sent his troops in from three directions, with a combined force of 3,000 men: Schmidt from the north, Reck from the west and Dirlewanger from the south. Vicious fighting broke out in various places, but the Poles continued to frustrate all German attempts to move forward. The AK would let them come close and then knock out their vehicles with PIATs, Molotov cocktails, home-made *filipinki* grenades and even fourteen-kilogram anti-tank guns that had been dropped into Warsaw by the British. When Dirlewanger attacked from the ruins of the Royal Castle his new Hetzer armoured vehicles were pelted with *filipinkis*; when they retreated the remaining troops were shot down by snipers. Whenever there was a lull in the fighting the Poles counter-attacked, often taking back barricades and posts that the Germans thought they had secured days or even weeks before. The Germans tried to attack Leszno towards Bielańska, but were repulsed; they attempted to get into the Old Town via the Krasiński Gardens, but 'Czata 49' defended it; rather than moving forward, Reck lost the Mostowski palace to 'Wigry' Battalion. Dirlewanger's men pushed into the Canonesses Convent at Plac Teatralny, but were held back when they tried to go towards the market. The AK refused to relinquish the barricades at the famous Old Town streets of Podwale, Piwna and Świetojańska.

The Germans tried again, this time using women as human shields against the barricade at Leszno, but again they failed. The AK barricades proved highly effective, especially in the cramped streets. The fighting was particularly brutal in the south, as Dirlewanger threw his men against the Polish lines time and time again; the barricade at Piwna Street blocked the way to the Old Town Square, and Dirlewanger was determined to take it, but the men of the 'Wigry' Battalion had constructed it in such a way that the attackers were forced into a funnel only a few metres wide, making it impossible for tanks to get through. Dirlewanger never succeeded in taking it, despite the huge loss of life there. On 12 August one of his men, SS Untersturmführer Schreiner, was praised for his bravery: 'He was at the front of his men when they stormed a building in the Dlugastrasse which was heavily occupied by bandits and barricaded. Despite a severe counter-attack, in which Schreiner was shot in the chin, he succeeded in setting the building on fire. The bandits inside, who were defending themselves desperately, were completely annihilated.'[27] Despite such successes, the narrow stone streets of the ancient fortress and the dogged determination of the Poles not to give an inch of ground proved too much even for the well-armed German troops.[28]

The German commanders in Warsaw subtly blamed Himmler for the military failure. On 13 August the 9th Army Diary complained that despite heavy fighting, safe passage to the Kierbedź Bridge had not yet been provided, and that 'the artery in the east is still unusable'. Von Vormann wrote to Army Group Centre that day that 'the 9th Army must learn to exploit the area gained if we are going to push through to the Vistula'.[29] Stahel was not sure they would succeed: 'this part of Warsaw is densely built up and extremely difficult for us. It is impossible to see even with aerial reconnaissance . . . It is impossible to see the Polish defensive positions or where enemy weapons are located.' This was a war 'in three dimensions with the soldiers having to move between streets and courtyards, always looking upwards to the roofs and downwards to the cellars'. When they attacked 'we moved forward blindly', and the attack and defensive positions were so close together that the fighting 'very quickly turned into hand-to-hand combat'. Polish morale was 'high', so that 'although we had superior weapons and more troops the AK had the will to fight. It was impossible to destroy them and the use of mortars was very difficult. Buildings create natural anti-Panzer defences and the narrow streets become even smaller the more you move into the city centre.'[30] Attempting to take Warsaw's Old Town was like fighting for a medieval fortress, with its tiny streets, houses with thick, heavy walls, deep cellars and catacombs, and an entire underground network of streets and passages connecting one end of it to the other. Even Himmler complained about the 'maze of passages and catacombs which we can hardly imagine.'[31]

The German death toll was surprisingly high: 9th Army Daily Reports listed 157 dead and 915 wounded on one day alone. Worse still, as Stahel had pointed out, the troops had no will to fight. Few wanted to be finished off by a sniper's bullet in Warsaw, and ordinary soldiers detested this kind of fighting in a city. They sometimes refused to attack at all. Jerzy Dreyza, a doctor at the Maltese hospital, was astounded when a German soldier walked into his room. 'He dropped his machine gun and ammunition belt and said, "I am sick of it," and asked me to take him as a PoW. I told him to work as a nurse for his German colleagues.'[32] A confidential Wehrmacht report admitted that progress was slow because of morale, and said that officers should see it as their top priority 'to encourage men to fight and to do everything to inspire the men to fight. The will to fight should be rewarded and particularly creativity such as finding shelters, secret passages and the like.'[33] The problem of morale was so serious that Guderian was impelled to bring it to Hitler's attention at the Wolfsschanze.

'There is a deficit of officers and NCOs,' Guderian said. 'The problem with NCOs is critical.' Fegelein agreed: 'We have men but no leaders, above all no NCOs. The ratio of casualties between men and NCOs is two to one. For every two men one NCO falls.' Guderian chimed in: 'The fight for houses costs an unusually high number of NCOs. When the officers and NCOs don't leap out the men refuse to move forward.'[34] In the official 9th Army Report of 13 August Leutnant August Weller complained: 'We do not note any major improvements in Warsaw.' It was becoming clear that the battle for the Old Town would be neither quick nor simple. But Hitler had a plan. If the fight for Wola had been fought using Himmler's methods, that for the Old Town would be masterminded by Hitler. It was to be an old-fashioned siege

– a Malta or a Saragossa. Above all it would demonstrate to the world the consequences of rising up against the Third Reich.

Hitler's Siege

In 1248 the English philosopher and scientist Roger Bacon wrote about an amazing new substance which was revolutionizing warfare the world over. It was called gunpowder. 'We can compose artificially a fire that can be launched over long distance,' he said. 'It is possible with it to destroy a town.'[35] This mixture of saltpetre, charcoal and sulphur had been discovered by the alchemists of China's Tang Dynasty, reaching Europe in the twelfth century via the Muslim armies of West Asia. By the fifteenth century extraordinary weapons were in use, including large siege guns which could hurl stones against once-impenetrable walls and gates. A renegade Hungarian Christian made the Ottoman Sultan Mehmed a bombard so enormous that it had to be hauled by fifty oxen for his siege of Constantinople in 1453. It could fire a ball weighing up to half a tonne. This was the kind of warfare Hitler instinctively understood.

Hitler had always liked the idea of destroying places he did not approve of. He said casually over lunch one day that 'St Petersburg must disappear utterly from the earth's surface. Moscow too.'[36] Shortly afterwards he noted that 'Switzerland is nothing but a pimple on the face of Europe and cannot be allowed to continue.' Methods of mining and bombing cities fascinated him; he told Grand Admiral Raeder on 26 August 1942 that 'multi-storeyed buildings are reasonably safe against a direct hit from a bomb, but not against the subsequent blast . . . An air raid such as those against London would have a devastating effect on New York. It would be physically impossible to clear the debris and it is not possible to build air-raid shelters.'[37]

Warsaw was the only major city in which Hitler actually got

to put these plans into action. The post-war notion that he was uninterested in the uprising was untrue; in fact he personally oversaw the war against the Old Town, and was regularly briefed on the situation there. When Fegelein complained that 'one has to turn entire blocks of houses inside out' lest the Poles retake the ruins, Hitler pointed at aerial photographs of the area: 'Here . . . when something is burned out,' he said, 'when the houses are burned out they are no longer useful for resistance. They are just walls, and if mines were dropped they would collapse straight away.' He thought for a moment. 'How many mines do we have?' he asked. 'Eight or ten thousand?' The bombs were, in his words, intended to *'schmeissen das Dann kaputt'*.[38]

He did not stop at mines. 'A mass of new technical weapons must be deployed' if the fortress was to be taken.[39] The array of technology, including many of Hitler's *'Wunderwaffen'*, employed to obliterate this tiny piece of ground was mind-boggling. It was as if the Führer wanted to showcase his power just as he had during the siege of Sevastopol in 1941–42, during which 750 pieces of siege artillery blasted away for an entire month: when the siege was over the city had looked like the moon. Now the Old Town was to share its fate. To bring in this kind of weaponry, at enormous expense and effort, so late in the war against such a relatively insignificant target – above all, one filled with 75,000 innocent civilians and only a few thousand troops – was absolute madness; but Hitler's attack on Warsaw had never been motivated solely by military necessity. In a phone conversation with Model on 14 August, Guderian said, 'Hitler attaches special importance to the use of this equipment in street fighting with the goal of destroying the city completely.'[40] Hitler wanted to prove that he was still strong, and he wanted to deter other would-be insurgents. But above all, he wanted to grind Warsaw into dust. The Old Town was the perfect place to start.

*   *   *

'Stawki has fallen!' The news spread like wildfire on that fateful 13 August, and everybody knew what it meant. The Old Town was now completely surrounded, and the people within it were trapped. Later that day a tragedy occurred which transformed the mood in the district for good. From now on the overwhelming emotion amongst the ordinary people would be fear.

There is a strange, incongruous, black metal strip attached to the outer wall of St John's Cathedral in the Old Town, a piece of tank track divided into segments like the shell of some ancient insect. It is a memorial to commemorate the tragedy of 13 August 1944, the day the Old Town received its own modern version of the Trojan Horse.

The Germans had spent the day attacking AK positions around the Old Town, and at 6 p.m. they turned their attention to the strong barricade that blocked Podwale Street. Three StuGIII assault guns rolled forward, fired straight into the AK position and then quickly moved away to make room for a strange, tank-like vehicle, the likes of which the Poles had never seen before. This was a Borgward BIV, one of Hitler's 'Wunderwaffen' and the largest of the Germans' remote-control demolition tanks.

The idea was simple. The driver brought the 'tank' close to its target, dismounted, and then sent it the final few metres by radio. It would drop a load of explosives held in a large metal box on its front, and then be piloted back to safety to be used again. But this time, something went wrong.

As the Borgward approached the barricade, AK soldiers from 'Gustaw' Battalion fired at its driver. The engine might have jammed, as the soldier abandoned the vehicle and ran away. The triumphant Poles made a passage through the barricade and drove the Borgward straight to Bór's headquarters at Kiliński Street. People flooded out of their homes cheering and shouting, not realizing that its explosives were still in place. One hour later the bomb exploded. It was deadly.

When Anna Szatkowska got to the site she found a 'huge mass of human remains, rubble, pieces of wood and iron'. There were 'terrifying screams of the victims calling for help – people in pain, burned black, blinded and impossible to recognize . . . Pieces of human bodies hang from broken eaves, there are pieces of bodies on the street, on roofs, everywhere . . . one of the tank tracks flew over the roof to Wąski Dunaj Street.'[41]

The buildings around were soon filled with wounded. Burned and blinded people 'lay in corridors, on the stairs, in the base-ment, on newspapers or sacks as there are no mattresses or blan-kets. Their faces are swollen, black from smoke and fire and yellow from disinfectant powder'. To her horror Anna found the 'delicate hand and long blonde hair' of her friend Antonina, a fellow nurse, who had died by their house. Another friend, 'Cień', looked terri-fying, his face burned and his hands so swollen he could not bear for his fingers to touch one another.

The Government Delegation requested that civilians help search the squares, courtyards, balconies and roofs for remains, stressing the threat of disease in the blazing August heat. Traumatized relatives searched in the rubble for their loved ones, 'but with only body parts they were impossible to identify . . . everything is covered in blood and sand and flies'. The dead were buried in two graves: one contained whole bodies wrapped in paper, the other unidentified arms, legs, torsos and heads. Three hundred people were killed as a result of this single 500kg explosion. The siege had begun in earnest.

Generalfeldmarschall Robert Ritter von Greim was the last commander of the Luftwaffe, appointed by Hitler on 26 April 1945, after Göring was dismissed for treason. His glory was short-lived. Greim was captured by the Americans whilst fulfilling Hitler's order to arrest Heinrich Himmler, also for treason, two days later. He committed suicide on 24 May. Greim's right-hand man in Warsaw, Oberleutnant Hans-Jürgen Klussman, had an altogether more peaceful end. After receiving the Knight's Cross on 9 November 1944 for doing such a stellar job in the Warsaw Uprising, he returned to Germany and died peacefully in Lower Saxony in 2009. Both of these men had inflicted tremendous damage on the people of the Old Town. It was they who controlled the planes.

Ritter von Greim had sent Messerschmitts and Junkers Ju-87Ds over Warsaw on 1 August. The Messerschmitts flew 204 sorties early that month, dropping 1,580 tonnes of bombs, but then Greim pulled them out. With complete aerial domination, they were no longer needed to protect the more vulnerable Stukas. The damage done by the Luftwaffe in Warsaw was made worse by the fact that it could so easily have been stopped. Stalin could have taken control of the skies over Warsaw in August 1944 with little effort. He could have bombed the airports, making it impossible for the Germans to take off; he could have shot down the Luftwaffe planes; and he could have destroyed the gigantic guns Hitler was even now moving into the city. Instead he chose to give the Nazis freedom of the skies. The last Soviet plane flew over Warsaw on 31 July; the next would not appear until well after the defeat of the Old Town. The German pilots could do whatever they wanted. They went hunting.

The Stukas which flew so relentlessly over Warsaw measured only eleven metres long, but they did an inordinate amount of damage through their incessant bombing and the deliberate strafing of civilians. They were based at Okęcie, from where Klussman personally ordered 711 Ju-87D sorties over the Old Town.[42] People were regularly shot at, as if in some cruel blood sport: 'The plane was flying very low . . . I even saw the blinking of fire from the machine gun . . . I could see the silhouette of the German pilot. I felt no fear as it was so sudden, although most people around me were wounded. A second plane appeared and this time I hid under an old train track. When it flew away I noticed a Jewish man in prison uniform, one of the Jews who had been released from Gęsiówka prison. He was groaning and spoke in an unknown language. The Germans were clearly using huge shells because he had a hole in his thigh and blood was spurting on the spilled sugar. Another old man was lying a few steps farther on, he was on his side trying to grab his intestines and push them back inside. They were mixed with sand.'[43] Janina Lasocka remembered a group of girl scouts from Mokotów who came to the Old Town to fight 'for Poland and Warsaw'. Their enthusiasm soon dimmed: 'We did not expect it to be so terrible,' they said. 'One day the Stukas came and targeted the left wing of our building. All of the girls were hit and died.'[44]

The planes took off without fail from 6 o'clock every morning, strafing civilians and dropping their bombs every half-hour. At midday the pilots took an hour off for lunch, and then they returned, dropping load after load until 7 p.m. They could fly very low, making their aim very accurate: Schmidt, Reck and Dirlewanger could request attacks on specific targets. 'German intelligence knew almost immediately that our headquarters had been moved,' Jan Rosner recalled. 'They started to bomb right away.' Nowhere was safe. Bombs dropped by the Stukas could make their way into the narrowest spaces, blowing up people who had felt secure in their courtyards or cellars. 'The whining of the bombs was distinguished immediately from the roaring dive of the planes; you waited a moment, just an instant. That moment was the actual hit. After it came a thud, or rather an explosion. And after that – a smashing, crashing, shattering of something.'[45]

Miron Białoszewski was offered a room in a ground-floor flat when he first arrived from Wola, and was just about to go to sleep when the planes came. 'Suddenly a shell hits the corner of the building. Then a second, a third, a fourth; nothing else, only shells. And flames. Everyone jumps up. Dashes into the courtyard . . . with suitcases, children, knapsacks . . .'[46] Sub-Officer Kurzyna of 'Czata 49' remembered two of his friends celebrating their marriage; only two days later they were buried alive in a Stuka attack at Mławska Street.[47] One young boy who acted as a runner for AK soldier Jacek was shot at and burned while carrying papers to the Central Historical Archives at Długa. When Jacek found him his skin was black and his eyes had been burned out. 'Don't tell my mother I lost my eyes,' he begged. 'First bury me and then tell her.' But when Jacek went to the boy's home there was nothing left but a pile of rubble.[48] Father Parysz remembered his sorrow after persuading Brother Dolorista, a very quiet twenty-year-old, to go out into the garden to get some air after spending weeks cowering underground. He was cut down by Stuka fire minutes after leaving the cellar; he died that afternoon.

Sometimes the bombs did not detonate: when a 250kg shell fell beside the Capuchin monastery it was carefully buried in the garden by Jews from Gęsiówka. Anna Szatkowska was cooking for her hospital when a Stuka dived over her building at Kilińskiego. A bomb went into the ruins just behind their wall, and they cowered in terror waiting for the explosion. 'Later we saw it, a 250kg bomb lying just behind our cooker.' They were told to keep it cool, but as there was no water 'we poured red wine on it instead'.[49]

These unexploded shells were a godsend to the AK weapons manufacturers. Over eight hundred grenades were produced from them between 10 and 18 August alone, but as the area held by the AK shrank, the weapons factories had to move or close down.

The best-known of them was run by Sylwester Łyszyński in the bowels of the Symons Passage; later it moved to the basement of the Krasiński Palace.[50]

The bombing exhausted everyone: 'Rescuing, digging out, extinguishing fires, helping – it was difficult, but people did it . . . it was made impossible by new bombs falling all the time, more fires being set. Or rather, it was hopeless. A vicious circle. At someone's cry "Planes!" we rush to a cellar, a shallow crawl space housing a workshop for glass cylinders and bombs. A crush. Panic. Prayer. Explosions. The rumbling, bursting of bombs. Groans and fear. Again they fly low. And explosions, they're probably bombing the front, we crouch down . . . And suddenly something rocks our house. Window frames, doors, glass panes are blown out. Explosions. The end? Still more crashes. Even more explosions.'[51] The planes made life extremely dangerous for the people, but they were not enough for Hitler. It was time to bring in the big guns.

It had become clear that Panzers were too cumbersome and too vulnerable to move through the narrow streets of Warsaw. The solution was to be found in the heavily armoured assault guns, the majority of which had been developed after the disaster at Stalingrad. These guns were behemoths. The SturmPanzer IV, or 'Grizzly Bear', was a huge, squat vehicle which had 100mm of armour on its front. It could move in very close to the enemy, smashing anything in range with its 150mm howitzer. Ten arrived in Warsaw on 13 August.[52] Another monster, used for the first time in Warsaw, was the gigantic sixty-five-tonne Sturmtiger, a heavily armed assault weapon whose 380mm rocket launcher belched gigantic shells from its ugly snub-nosed barrel. Two were sent to Warsaw. The only known film of the weapon in action was taken from the Kierbedź Bridge on 19 August, and it gives a sense of its awesome power. The camera follows the 345kg shells as they fly through the air; entire buildings crumble to dust. The German audience is delighted.[53] Other weapons were added. Over forty agile Hetzer JagdPanzer 38s arrived in August, anti-tank guns with high-velocity 75mm guns – one of the Führer's personal favourites.[54] The Goliath, another of the 'Wunderwaffen', was a miniature tank which zigzagged around on narrow tracks like a child's plaything. It might have looked amusing, but the little tank was deadly: it carried between sixty and a hundred kilograms of TNT, and could be driven by remote control straight up to enemy positions; a single Goliath could tear down the wall of a building, or blow a barricade into the sky. The AK learned how to disarm them by throwing grenades at their control wires. The young German officer Peter Stolten lost his crew twice this way: 'My own Goliath killed our soldiers for the second time,' he wrote to his father. 'The enemy shot at us detonating a thousand kilos of explosives just three metres from my vehicle . . . I lay for hours, blinded, amongst the groaning wounded.'[55] Ninety of these minia-ture tanks were sent to Warsaw in August alone.

But breaking down barricades was not enough for Hitler. His unadulterated hatred for Warsaw was reflected above all in the super-heavy siege artillery now brought in, some of which had originally been designed for use against the Maginot Line. The small, medieval Old Town was to be pounded into the ground by some of the largest weapons ever known. It really was like breaking a butterfly on a wheel.

The guns arrived thick and fast. On 1 August the Panzerzug 75 was rushed from production at nearby Rembertów to the edge of the Old Town. This huge machine looked more like a gigantic slug than a great train, with armour covering everything from its wheels to its 105mm howitzers. Captain Franz Eaon commanded this unassailable brute, sending it back and forth along the track by the Gdańsk station only metres from the Old Town as it fired relentlessly at buildings, streets and people. Klaudiusz Hrabyk was amazed by the size of one of its unexploded shells: 'it lay on the ground huge and shiny and so big you had to jump over it to get past'. Shortly afterwards, Major Reck put up a fixed rocket launcher in the Saski Gardens which could send off forty deadly 57kg incendiary bombs in as many seconds. On 18 August flame-throwers of the SS Jäger-Abteilung arrived, along with a 61cm howitzer; Krone Battalion was brought in with a further 150 flamethrowers. The SS also received batteries of 105 and 150mm howitzers, two 210mm mortars and two 280mm howitzers. They even set up a boat on the Vistula which pounded the city from the east. By mid-August the force concentrated on the Old Town was already astounding, but there was more to come.

On 28 August 2012 a gigantic shell was found at a construction site in central Warsaw. A large chunk of the city was evacuated as it was carefully made safe. It was the shell from a 'Karl Mörser Gerät' – a weapon which still has the power to terrorize nearly seventy years on. The 'Karl' mortars were enormous: they are still the largest self-propelled weapons in the history of warfare.

The Rheinmetall company produced only seven of these giant guns in the entire course of the war. Each was eleven metres long, weighed over 120,000 kilograms and required a crew of more than a hundred men just to move it. Air superiority was a pre-requisite for its use, so it could only be brought out when it was safe to do so – at Sevastopol, at Brest-Litovsk, and now in Warsaw. Even long-suffering Leningrad, which endured so much, was at least spared this particular torture.

The first to arrive was called 'Zui'. It came by train in three sections, and was mounted on a concrete pad which can still be seen in Sowiński Park today. Its shells, carefully packed in indi-vidual wooden crates, weighed an astounding 1,577 kilos each, and could blast through concrete bunkers several metres deep.

Fifty-six were fired from Sowiński Park alone; when the first one landed in the Krasiński Gardens the enormous explosion, which looked 'like a volcano', caused panic.

The effect on the civilians was devastating. A direct hit would bring down any nearby building. One shell exploded next to a crowded cellar, leaving a crater 'half the length of the street. It's bad. The crowds panic. With packages, bundles. They run about. Some towards the gate. Others, away from the gate.' People were buried when the massive shells fell on houses and apartment buildings, and nothing could be done to save them. 'We saw people digging out something white. We all knew that when instead of a cellar or houses there's a hole . . . many people have perished. So they'd bombed through to the cellars after all.'[56]

As Hitler's 'Wunderwaffen' began to pound the tiny district from morning to night, the atmosphere changed drastically. People became increasingly frightened and pessimistic. 'Thinking about what was going to happen accounted for at least half one's thoughts. The other half was taken with immediate needs – food, shelter, clothing.'[57] It was clear that the Germans meant to destroy the Old Town building by building, and its inhabitants along with them: 'The houses were already losing their normal contours, their height, the lines of their façades.'[58] Irena Orska wrote of her horror at the destruction: 'the beauty built up through centuries of Polish history was burning to ashes before our bloodshot eyes . . . the slenderness of the fourteenth-century Cathedral of St John, and Knight's Street, the narrowest in the Old Town, and the polychrome of the ancient Market Place . . . I cried in helpless rage.'[59] The sudden sound of masonry collapsing or a roof falling in was terrifying in itself. 'The whole area was filled with smoke and dust from falling houses, it was difficult to breathe because of the heat. We could not see the sky or the sun.'[60] After the bombing raids people held damp rags to their faces so they could breathe; one woman wrapped her one-year-old daughter's head in her blanket, as she was afraid she was going to choke.[61] Wacław Zagórski was at Wachnowski's 'Northern Group' headquarters in the Central Historical Archives on 20 August, when a mine exploded across the road. 'We were covered in dust, rubbish and glass, and for five minutes I didn't think we would get out of this tomb alive . . . Yesterday I was covered in rubble three more times, and this morning once.' Two days later, 'two hundred people are buried under Miodowa 7–9'.[62] It was dangerous to be out in the open even for a few seconds, but with the arrival of the immense guns even the subterranean world was unsafe. Everyone was afraid of being buried alive.

Daily survival became increasingly difficult. In the beginning the civilian authorities as well as religious orders had organized free soup kitchens. 'We would stand in line at the Dominican convent on Stara Street for soup . . . everyone knew everyone else. Friends. It was even pleasant . . . Only there were those aeroplanes. We would dive somewhere into the shadows. And then once more on those steps. Holding our mess-kits.' But the massive attacks ended all that. 'On 13 August it was all over with those thin soups . . . just being outdoors became impossible.' In a few days the Dominican convent and its soup kitchen were gone, 'nothing but a heap of red bricks, dust and the steps'.[63] The Capuchins had distributed the food which they had previously sent to their brothers in Dachau, but they too had been forced underground. Father Kwiatkowski was in charge of dividing their meagre supplies between the four hundred people sheltering there, but food was running low: 'We had only enough flour, grits and dry bread for a few more days.' A baker from Wola volunteered to work, but there were serious problems finding water: 'The nearby well was under constant German fire.'

Desperate people turned elsewhere for food. 'Whatever did not escape, fly away, burn up, cave in, die, was hunted down. Cats disappeared. Dogs disappeared.'[64] The price of horsemeat soared to 250 zloty per kilo; the sight of hooves piling up in buckets outside the communal kitchens became the norm. 'We found an utterly terrified horse in a small shed. Its body was covered in shrapnel and it was terribly thin although it refused to eat anything. It was killed for meat.'[65] Dog stew was also popular: Klaudiusz Hrabyk recalled that 'There were quite a few dogs wandering around, and when I brought a dog I asked one of my colleagues, a butcher called Doar from the Philips factory, to butcher it, but when he saw the dog he said he wouldn't do it. Finally he said he would if someone else killed the dog. The meat was delicious, although at the beginning nobody wanted to eat it . . . later we all did except for one runner.'[66]

Foraging for food was extremely dangerous. 'In the course of two or three days things had changed so drastically that dashing at full speed into the yard to pick two pumpkins and rushing back with them into the stairwell entrance had become terribly risky,' wrote Miron Białoszewski. He and a friend decided to risk running upstairs to get a bag of flour from one of the burned-out flats. 'We were terrified that there would be a shelling.'[57] Hunger began to take its toll. One man met a friend who had found a tin of meat. 'He asked me not to tell his hungry wife.'[68] At the same time there were extraordinary acts of generosity. When one of the directors of the Bank Polski fell ill with dysentery, Janina Lasocka, who had had a nervous breakdown, felt guilty that he was getting nothing to eat. 'I try to brace up and organize food. I go through the hole in the wall to the Capuchin monastery . . . In the bunker you could starve sitting on gold. I fight with myself and go to the first brother priest and tell him we have wounded. He smiled and took me to a chamber and gave me a piece of bread and a little sugar.' But her action was in vain. When she returned to her bunker 'it had been bombed and it was too dangerous to stay there any more. Men were on the roof trying to put out the fire with sand.'

The lack of water was catastrophic in the stifling summer heat. The Germans stopped the water supply in the first weeks of August, and not a drop of rain fell on that tinderbox during the entire siege. The civilian authorities oversaw the drilling of wells, but no sooner was one working than it would be buried under rubble; those that did function were put under constant German fire.[69] There was an attempt to impose order on the usable wells: 'Hospitals between 4–5 a.m. and 8.30–9 p.m., kitchens from 5–6 a.m. and 3–4 p.m.; military 6–7 a.m. and 10–11 p.m.; civilians 7–15 and 16–20'. A quartermaster was put in charge, but as the bombing increased the system descended into chaos. When an attack began people had to hide; when they moved back their slot was gone. Anna Szatkowska had no water for her hospital from 14 August: 'We will have to rely on wells, but they are all being buried under the rubble of bombed houses and only a few have been dug out and are usable.'[70] There was always a long queue for water at the Land Registry building. 'The well is constantly under siege, people wait with pots and buckets; snipers kill a few people every day. It is a challenge to get water but people have to do it.'[71] It seemed to the battered inhabitants that conditions could not get any worse. But then, on 15 August, another weapon was introduced into Warsaw. It was horrifying.

The Americans called them 'Moaning Minnies'; the British called a mortar barrage a 'stonk'. Seventy per cent of British and Canadian casualties in France in June 1944 were caused by the German 'Nebelwerfers', rocket launchers which could fire high-explosive rounds at amazing speed and to devastating effect. Almost their worst feature was the terrifying shriek their shells emitted as they hurtled through the sky; an eerie cry, repeated over and over, which could cause even battle-hardened troops to panic. A 1944 British report held that 'the morale effect of . . . the Nebelwerfer is so great that the introduction of a similar weapon might well be considered on this ground alone'.[72]

In Warsaw they were known as 'Krowas', or 'cows', as the noise sounded like dozens of beasts crying out in their death throes. Irena Orska called them 'the most terrifying of all the weapons the Germans used against the Home Army in Warsaw'.[73] One can only imagine the fear they caused amongst the trapped civilians of the Old Town.

The first of them to be used in Warsaw was a six-barrelled rocket launcher. Shells could be fired from specially tilted metal racks.[74] They came in their own packing crates, and when the Soviets arrived they found thousands of their discarded wooden cases lying in gigantic piles on the edge of the Old Town, a testament to the number of shells launched from there. They were sometimes equipped with delayed fuses, which allowed them to sink into a basement before exploding; others were filled with sticky jellied petroleum, which splattered on everything and caused atrocious burns. These bombs were designed to destroy life in the most ruthless way, and they succeeded. Untold thousands died in the Old Town, often in agony. 'Victims had their faces burned the colour of a mahogany wardrobe, covered with strips of gauze bandages . . . they were covered in bandages all over and walked stiffly like totem poles, constantly moving because they had been burned alive and could not keep still – they were still living and yet were not alive'.[75]

The mere sound of the Krowas caused immediate panic: 'You could hear the noise six times, then silence, before the series of six explosions hit,' Agaton recalled. 'The worst thing was the quiet just before . . . every time they fired I measured, following the silence in fear.' Then the impact. If the shells landed nearby you couldn't breathe. 'I could feel the thick brick dust in my mouth and ears and eyes. It actually glued your ears and mouth shut.'[76]

'The explosion sets fire in buildings and all around – people burn like torches or are badly burned if the liquid from the weapons explodes . . . Today it caused enormous damage and killed many people at Freta Street and the New Town Market Square. The church of the Sisters of the Sacrament is on fire along with the hospital.'[77] Zbigniew Stypułkowski was baffled by his first Nebelwerfer attack. 'I was lying in bed after a service and we heard this unknown sound . . . Then silence. Then the noise repeated very quickly six times again.' Suddenly he saw flames flying towards him, but just as they reached him they were sucked back. This was typical of *Krowa* attacks, which caused a rapid change in air pressure after the blast which actually imploded people's lungs. 'The windows and doors were burned to ashes and were covered with very thick oil.' A group of people from Wola had found shelter in the entryway of a building. 'An hour later I saw the cinders of the twisted burnt dead bodies on the pavement.' One of the AK runners had been sprayed by the oil. 'She managed to run to the first-aid post for help but died in agony a few hours later.'[78]

Adam Bień, a lawyer and First Deputy Chief in the Government Delegation, saw a group of people carrying an object on Jasna Street. 'As I got closer I saw something on a stretcher that had been a human being before. Now it was only a black charred corpse, with a charred head and face and shining eyes. It was a person who had been burned by a *Krowa*.' 'I have seen people with flat faces whose noses or ears had been melted away,' another Warsawian remembered. 'A piece of flesh would be burned away as if sliced off but without bleeding. These "melted" people suffered unspeakable tortures as they were burned alive. Few, with their bodies disfigured, their faces hideous to look at, escaped death.'[79]

The *Krowa* attacks continued into the night. Even sheltering underground was no guarantee of safety: 'Crash crash crash six times. God how those walls moved . . . fires, windblasts, flying walls, people with children in their arms hurling themselves *en masse* in the direction of the water barrel, to the narrow passageway leading to the far cellars, and people from the far cellars rushing into our shelter.' Then their building was hit. 'Something shuddered. Things began crashing down above us. The ceilings from the second floor broke through onto the first . . . Is this it already? Yes, it's hard, only will it strike from the head? To the feet? Will it knock you flat? If only it could be quick.'[80]

The *Krowas* and other incendiary bombs fuelled the fires that were already burning all around. A fire brigade had been organized at the Central Historical Archives, but as the Germans had destroyed the pumps, the men were forced to use sand. 'Fire is burning everywhere. It is so hot the asphalt is melting.' It was a constant struggle to control the flames: 'Now the planes come. They scatter bombs. And bomblets. Incendiary . . . There are about twenty of them . . . they are smouldering and hissing. And the wall is already on fire.' 'Another house is on fire, just one huge fire about three storeys high. Beams groan, collapse. Nothing can help this time.'[81] Warsawians mourned whenever a much-loved landmark disappeared: there was real sorrow when the front of St John's Cathedral collapsed, and when Zygmunt's Column, the symbolic twenty-two-metre-high monument to the Swedish King of Poland, was toppled. 'The Old Town is so pounded by artillery and mines that only ruins will be left . . . Yesterday the Krasiński Palace burned late into the night. That was horrible. The same with the Palace of the Four Winds and hundreds of others . . .'[82]

In the first week of August the sight of a dead body would have been shocking to the inhabitants of the Old Town, but by the third week it was the norm. Indeed, the death toll was so high that the Government Delegation had to publish rules as to how to bury the dead: 'identify the dead person, write down the name and leave the information on the body. A piece of paper should be attached to clothes with name, surname and address, and where the body was buried, the second copy to be passed to the Kommissariat as soon as possible along with valuables . . . bodies should be put in order lying in a natural position; people should put a sign where the head is using a cross or piece of wood with the surname, name and address of the person.'

These rules worked in the early days, but as the number of dead quickly rose into the hundreds, then into the thousands, nobody could cope. 'When the number of bodies is very high . . . a ditch should be dug one metre deep . . . the bodies should be put one on top of the other. Each body should then have its own piece of wood on which should be written information, and the number of dead.'[83] But the sheer numbers were so high that even this system broke down. Before long 'we were burying bodies all day', one woman remembered.[84] As the area available for burials shrank and the number of dead rose, it became impossible to find places for them. 'Kedyw' soldier Stanisław Likiernik recalled trying to bury a fallen comrade: 'I saw a hole and put the body there and then heard someone shouting, "Oh shit! They stole our grave!" '[85] Makeshift cemeteries competed with latrines and wells for empty pieces of ground.

Soon bodies lay everywhere. 'I will never forget the rows of people lying on the floor at the church of St Jacek, all of them wounded, many completely naked, others just had pieces of cloth on them. The church had been bombed and pieces of the walls had fallen on the floor, half-burying the patients.'[86] It was a similar scene after the bombing of the church of the Sisters of the Sacrament: 'Rubble is still smoking and between it lie dead bodies not yet collected. Some have been covered by a piece of material or paper, others are naked, deformed, terrifying.' Grażyna Dąbrowska remembered the dying and dead in the bunkers. 'The worst were the weak, alone and helpless, whom nobody cared about. They had nobody to tend their bodies when they died, so they were put close to the walls with paper or cloth over them, waiting for someone to bury them or to put some pieces of broken wall over their bodies.'[87] Worse still were the orphaned children, themselves often injured, who lay in the darkness, sometimes still clinging to the bodies of their dead mothers. Dąbrowska was convinced that she too would die, and made a cross for herself so that at least her grave would be marked.

Hundreds were buried in the rubble; sometimes the muffled cries of the injured could be heard from under the debris for hours after a raid. When Izolda Kowalska's house collapsed on top of her she was dug out after one day, but her husband died.[88] Heavy mortars caused entire buildings to collapse, as at Kiliński 3, where all the civilians sheltering in the cellars were crushed under their weight.[89] The human cost was high: children, parents, babies died – the bombs did not discriminate. When the Germans attacked an AK position in the apartment buildings on Bonifraterska with four Goliaths, five tanks and two Typhoons, only two officers survived. The best of Warsaw's poets were killed in the fighting. Cadet Zdzisław Leon Stroiński ('Chmura') and Tadeusz Gajcy ('Topór') died under the buildings at Przejazd Street. The most famous victim was Krzysztof Kamil Baczyński, the young bard of the 'Columbus Generation' who wrote so passionately against the horrors of war. On 4 August he was standing at a window of the Blank Palace when he was shot in the head by a sniper; his pregnant wife was killed on 1 September when a shard of glass pierced her brain. Baczyński believed that the only human force strong enough to defeat war was love; his

'Elegy for a Polish Boy' ended with the prophetic lines: 'Before you fell you hailed the earth with your hand, did it soften your fall, my sweet child?' When his friend Stanisław Pigoń heard the news of Baczyński's death, he said bitterly, 'We belong to a nation whose fate it is to use our diamonds as bullets.' Writers, musicians and artists were falling; one man was shot while reading his precious copy of a book by Aldous Huxley; a surgeon tried to operate on him, but the only equipment he had was a locksmith's drill. German PoWs dug his grave.[90] And yet somehow the human spirit endured. 'One night in the silence,' Klaudiusz Hrabyk recalled, 'I heard someone playing Chopin from the ruins of a destroyed tenement house.'[91]

Some tried to help. The brothers of the Capuchin monastery dug out dozens of people buried in the ruins; others went to the bunkers to hold Mass, listen to confessions and give communion. 'By the end of August it was unbearable,' remembered Father Kwiatkowski.[92] Father Parysz cared for the wounded in the Old Town. 'I went through the basements and through underground corridors from one building to another, and that way could go under the entire district . . . I heard a sixteen-year-old girl say to her father, "I have to die for my country, but I am so afraid." ' The danger was omnipresent. 'One day there was a huge explosion during Mass in the basement of the Garrison church. I heard a woman crying. Her husband had just taken communion and now lay dead in her arms.'[93]

The Underground City

By the third week of August everyone had moved into the basements. 'It was a kind of torture for people . . . We were based in Długa 23, but I tried to avoid the basement there as I was afraid of being buried alive.'[94] The civilians hiding in the basement of the Krasiński Palace organized a day of hair washing. To their horror they found that 'we girls with long hair had lice. There was not enough water to wash again so we hid our hair under our caps.'[95] People were 'crowded in corners of basements without water, little food and terrible hygienic conditions made worse because of fire and the exhaustingly high temperatures.'[96] 'We sat in darkness as the windows were covered to protect us from shrapnel,' Janina Lasocka wrote. 'A candle is lit only if someone is about to die or has died or when the Stukas are coming. One can say it doesn't matter if you die in darkness, but all feel that a candle must be lit anyway. When an attack begins it becomes so quiet you can hear your heart beating.' After her husband was injured by a piece of shrapnel, she tried to find a doctor. 'Someone said there is a pharmacy at Senatorska. I was stopped by soldiers at the barricade. "He is not the only one who is wounded, and you are not allowed to enter the area," they said.' She managed to talk her way through, but when she came back the barricade had been destroyed and the soldiers were gone.[97]

For Adam Bień the cellars were like something out of Dante. 'I saw crowds of people sitting in dark basements, praying aloud to a black cross hanging on the wall. I saw women in black, silent and resigned, kneeling next to the coffins at the gates of Warsaw apartment buildings. I saw how quickly and in what shallow graves coffins were buried.'[98] There was 'no food or water; we were in a crowd of old ladies, we couldn't wash. I went to sleep in my clothes and did not shave. We lived like animals.' When Klaudiusz Hrabyk visited his boss and his family, who were hiding in their basement in Kiliński Street, he was shocked: 'You had to lie on your hands and crawl just to get in. The man lived in this hole with his family of small children, and behind the basement wall lay the bodies of people who had been buried alive.'[99] 'There was no water, sewer, light, ventilation or food. The narrow, dirty corridors were crowded with possessions; sometimes in the candlelight we could see pale, thin faces. We could see the ill and wounded, children were crying.'[100]

Gone were the days when the refugees from Wola seemed like panic-mongers. Grażyna Dąbrowska, who had looked at the refugees with pity three weeks before, now understood. 'All of us sat in the basement with nothing but the things we had on our backs. We made friends and shared provisions, as we didn't know if we would make it through the next day. We kept an eye on children if someone needed to go and forage for food or try to get water.'[101] All notions of privacy broke down. Communal latrines were dug, and people used them in full view of others, chatting all the while: 'All the doors to the outhouse were gone. No one paid any attention to anyone else. Nor was anyone embarrassed.'[102]

The Old Town had become a vast underground city, with an 'endless number of corridors, cellar rooms with and without pillars, passageways, exits to the staircases, corners, separate vaults, store rooms, bins, sub-basements, passages leading to the boiler room with its many pipes and sewer mains, and a tunnel under the garden plots with pumpkins and tomatoes and potatoes'. The food was, by now, nearly impossible to reach. Miron Białoszewski walked through the underground passages talking to people he knew, like the young couple who had a cricket living in their wall – a small symbol of life. Another friend, Leonard, could no longer stand the bunker, and announced that he was going to the Sisters of the Sacrament, where he later died.[103] Others ended up in surreal hiding places: 'We found shelter in the Russian Orthodox church priest's quarter . . . in the destroyed apartment with its walls blown out and the floor covered with rubble we found a soft armchair from the destroyed library and a piano. And in the calm of the night a few boys played the Polonaises and the Nocturnes, the music flying out over this unreal world.'[104]

Others tried to organize a 'normal life' like the women in the basement of the Krasiński Palace. 'Mrs Borejsza invited some of the AK girls to visit her as if she lived in a normal home . . . She shared her jam and cooked food. She asked for only one thing in return. "Don't leave us here alone with the Germans," she begged. "Just let us know when you are going to retreat." Unfortunately, none of us honoured this dramatic request.'[105]

The bombing raids increased in ferocity, and ever more people were badly injured by the fires and the shrapnel. By the end of August doctors, nurses and volunteers were working heroically to try to save the lives of the many thousands of maimed, burned and injured. Dr Stefan Tarnawski, who had been the leader of 'Kedyw' in Kraków, had been called to Warsaw to lead the field hospital in 'Grupa Północ'. He faced an impossible task.

The Old Town had the Jan Boży and Maltański hospitals, as well as stations such as 'Długa 7', the surgical hospital in the former Ministry of Justice, with six hundred beds But as the bombing increased and the number of injured skyrocketed, the hospitals overflowed, and temporary wards were set up in cellars, basements and any available space; there was even one in the famous Fukier's restaurant in the Old Town Square, founded in the sixteenth century by the Fugger family from Augsburg. The 'hospital' at the corner of Rybaki and Boleść was typical: 'The cellars were dark, with narrow stalls and vaults for coal and potatoes. Signs were posted along the narrow corridors to the potato bins. "Ward 5; Ward 6". And in the corridor itself lay the wounded. That, too, was a ward. Some people were lying on the cellar floor.'[106] They lay on blankets and wrapping paper.

Nurses and other personnel were constantly being called upon to help move the wounded. When Anna Szatkowska was told to get some patients from Długa 5, she found that 'the stairs were destroyed and swinging back and forth. The roof and chimney were gone. There were just the remains of two dead soldiers and one wounded boy who whose body was burned all over and who had open fractures on both his legs.' They put the boy on a stretcher. 'A Stuka came over and shot directly at us. We took the patient down the broken stairs and got to the gate. At that moment the building collapsed around us.' They managed to get him to the hospital just as a *Krowa* attack began. 'Ewa is hit by a brick, I have shrapnel in my leg.' The boy died just before he was to be operated on, and Dr Morwa, the surgeon, asked, 'Why do you bring people to me who are going to die anyway? You can see I can't do anything here!'

By now doctors had stopped taking terminally wounded patients. When Anna Szatkowska collected another soldier from the barricade at Piwna who had a stomach wound she was turned away from four hospitals. 'Finally the Sisters of the Sacrament accept us. But by then our patient has died. They give us another patient, a civilian maybe twenty years old with wounds all over his body.' He too is dying, and they leave him with a priest and two women rather than take him directly to the morgue. The civilians promise to stay with him in the stifling heat until he dies.[107]

One nurse came across a wounded youth whom she had known before the uprising. 'He was hit in the lower stomach and thighs. I tried to put some bandages there, but this sixteen-year-old boy would not let me take off his pants. I explained that I was a nurse and wanted to help, but he pulled them up as I pulled them down. Finally he fainted and I put on the bandages and took him to the first-aid post.'[108] Later she had to carry a very tall wounded soldier on her own: 'I took him on my back, and his legs dragged on the ground, and I hung his pistol and book with maps around his neck, but it was so long it reached my knees . . . we were a perfect target for the Germans.'[109] A group of nurses found a

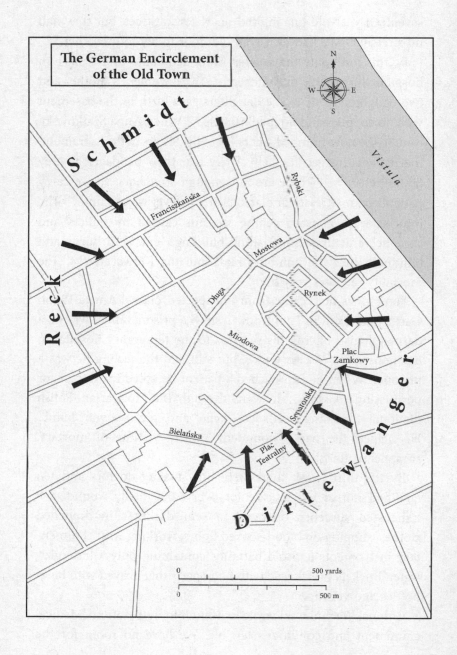

The German Encirclement of the Old Town

Schmidt

Reck

Dirlewanger

Vistula

Franciszkańska

Rybaki

Mostowa

Długa

Rynek

Miodowa

Plac Zamkowy

Senatorska

Bielańska

Plac Teatralny

N
W E
S

0 — 500 yards

0 — 500 m

seventeen-year-old girl injured on Nalewki Street, but they had no stretcher. 'We had to use an old door to try to move her.'[110]

By this time only the severely wounded could find a place in hospital. 'Just beside our kitchen are three women, a mother and two daughters. One of the daughters gave birth in the basement with no supplies and no medical help.'[111] When Anna Szatkowska went to the now-bombed-out crypt of the Sisters of the Sacrament, the patients begged for help: 'They tear their bandages as they try to get up . . . There are not enough stretchers, so we carry patients on mattresses or blankets or whatever we can find.'[112] The injuries were ghastly: gaping wounds caused by bullets and shrapnel, fractures from falling buildings, cuts and burns and blindness after the bombing raids and the *Krowa* attacks. The mortality rate was very high.

Sometimes help came from unexpected places. Aniela Pinon Gacka had taken in Jews from Gęsiówka prison, one of whom, a dermatologist, offered his services to the temporary hospital in her house. 'He was very nice, but still had the feeling he was a prisoner. When he approached a patient he asked the doctor for permission to work. He went through the Hungarian–Polish dictionary, learning words like "hello" and "give me your hand".' He helped the badly wounded, 'mostly victims of mortars, shrapnel wounds'.

By the third week there were only twenty doctors and ten qualified nurses left to care for over 6,000 badly wounded.[113] Exhausted surgeons operated in semi-darkness in drenched clothes, slipping on blood-soaked floors, working with rudimentary instruments and old bathtubs containing only a little grey water. Buckets overflowed with body parts that heaved with bluebottles and vermin.

Colonel Wachnowski wrote to Monter in desperation: 'Medical equipment and conditions terrible. We have no room for the growing number of wounded and not enough surgeons.'[114] Some supplies were sent into the Old Town via the sewers, but it was a drop in the ocean. When drinking water ran out at Długa 7 they used red wine instead. 'We got patients totally drunk and then amputated or took out a bullet.'[115] Bandages were now made out of paper. 'Patients die of everything now – infection, dysentery, operations without anaesthetic; there is not even basic hygiene as there is no water, electricity time or resources or personnel to clean and to wash. The incidence of tetanus is growing.'[116] Irena Orska saw the boy soldier who had been praised by Bór for destroying a tank lying near death in a hospital in the Old Town.[117] 'The patients' wounds are full of insects and they stink horribly. Sometimes we all feel helpless and ask ourselves why nobody wants to help us, why the Allies don't come.'[118]

When she first started nursing in the Old Town Anna Szatkowska had found the local people very helpful. 'It was populated by craftsmen, workers, some wealthier shop owners. They did a lot to assist the AK.'[119] Three weeks later, everything had changed. When she tried to find a place for wounded soldiers to sleep in a basement in Kiliński Street, people balked at taking them in. 'It was now full of people who had also lost their homes. When they saw the patients and realized it would be even more crowded they protested, and started to make critical comments about the AK fighters.'[120]

Stanisław Likiernik was hiding across the road from his unit when their building was blown up. 'Blasts . . . deafening noise . . . falling bricks . . . black dust.' His men were buried under the rubble. One of them, a seventeen-year-old volunteer, was buried up to his neck, and was crying out in pain. 'We started digging him out, but we couldn't manage on our own. I ran into the nearby Franciscan church. The crypt was crowded. "My boys are buried, I need help!" Nobody stirred, not a soul.'[121] An official government document reported that 'homeless civilians lie in bunkers, famine, terrible hygienic conditions, lack of organization, lack of help, growing possibility that there will be an epidemic, defeatism and even outright hostility to the AK. The civilians in bunkers are very passive, some don't eat for two or three days.'[122] It was extremely hot. 'In the evening, the heat inside must have exceeded forty degrees centigrade. The scarce water was reserved for the wounded.'[123] Despair was taking hold of everyone: 'The fact that we were so unsure of our lives, the lack of faith in a happy ending, the feeling of total helplessness. Famine, illnesses and the lack of the most basic things created an atmosphere of apathy and depression. Religion became hugely important, and people prayed in front of improvised altars in every basement. At the same time they were not always good to one another. There were robberies of food and other things.'[124]

The AK felt the change. A runner from 'Kedyw' said, 'I saw day by day the hatred towards soldiers grow amongst civilians. How much grief and bitterness was caused by the tragic conditions. In one of the courtyards mothers with children said to us, "You, bandits. Leave us alone." ' Gone were the days when people had joined in to build barricades in the streets, cheering them all the way. 'We could feel the enthusiasm waning and being replaced by dislike, even hatred.'[125] The AK were now seen to be privileged, with better food and more water than the civilians. Because they were actively involved in the struggle, they could feel that they were fulfilling some kind of mission, 'whereas ordinary civilians just felt useless'. People resented the lack of reliable information, and stopped reading official news-sheets. They looked in vain for signs of movement on the other side of the river. 'When no help came, people began to blame the AK for starting the uprising and causing this suffering and the deaths in their families. Some did not see that the people they were blaming were themselves just tired and exhausted boys.'[126] The AK press officer, Major Zagórski ('Gromski'), wrote in an official report: 'The Home Army is unable to win by itself, nor is it able to secure help from the outside in sufficient measure for the fighting to be brought to a close. In this condition the only solution is the help of the Bolsheviks, which is now anticipated with longing.'[127] But still the Russians did not come.

In August 1996 a new sculpture was unveiled in Warsaw. It was made of stone from a monument to Polish airmen which had been destroyed by the Germans in 1944. The new memorial was dedicated to the pilots, most of them volunteers, who died trying to bring aid to the beleaguered people of Warsaw in the summer of that year.

It was dangerous work. In all over 250 British, South African, American and Polish airmen died trying to get supplies to the city, and over half the drops fell behind German lines. Such losses were particularly painful in the besieged Old Town: at one point over ten packages landed in the former ghetto; the agony of seeing them 'so close but not being able to get them was awful'. Captain Roman Chmiel, who made drops over Plac Krasiński on 13 August, could see the Old Town from a great distance that night: 'It was burning all over. A terrible view, really terrible.'[128] Another pilot recalled that 'the navigator said we didn't need to give a course to the pilot as we could see Warsaw from so far away. We could see the burning city, the black places meant for us that those areas were still in German hands. The houses and streets were covered in smoke. I never thought a city could burn like that. It looked terrible, like a hell in which people were burning. I had never been under such strong artillery fire, you could hear bullets hit the plane as if the Devil was throwing beans at it.'[129]

On the night of 13 August one of the planes was shot down in Miodowa Street, in the heart of the Old Town. Father Parysz went to the scene: 'I gave absolution to the pilots, who were still alive at that moment,' he said. 'They were taken to the hospital at Długa 7, and died later.' It was a measure of the desperation felt by the population by then that night after night women would brave the fires and the *Krowas* to lie on the streets of the Old Town and point their torches into the air in the shapes of an arrow and a diamond, to guide the Allied planes to the drop zones. But there were only five drops in the whole of August.

Doubts were increasingly voiced about the uprising, and about the competence of the AK leadership. Bór had been in his head-quarters when the Borgward BIV blew up with such devastating effect at Kiliński Street. 'During the explosion Bór Komorowski was at the window watching the "tank",' recalled Major Zenon Tarasiewicz, an officer of the Second Department of Kommenda Główna AK (Information). 'The explosion threw him to the floor and he was injured.' A number of other people were also hurt, and there was panic in the room. 'For the first time since the beginning of the uprising he raised his voice and said, "Calm down, please!" Silence fell. Then there was a second voice, very quiet, but heard by all. "We have just been given the first smart order from our leader." Bór heard it too, but did nothing.'[130] Jokes began to circulate about him: '*Nie bedzie Warszawa, będzie Bór*,' which meant 'There will be no Warsaw, only Bór' – his pseudonym being a word for an ancient forest.

People now feared the worst. When Miron Białoszewski said goodbye to a friend, she replied, 'Don't cry, you won't live anyway.'[131] Father Rostowski, the Jesuit chaplain, stayed with the patients and soldiers, and gave communion on the barricades. 'He helps us, as every day we see more clearly that we will never leave the Old Town alive.'[132] The poet Jerzy Ficowski, author of *A Reading of Ashes*, which was later illustrated by Marc Chagall, refused to glorify his time in the Home Army: 'I went to the uprising out of a sense of duty and not because I had a passion or a mission,' he said. 'I thought that I had to participate, but I won't deny that it was one of the most tragic events in my life, and I don't think of it as a beautiful page in my biography or in the history of my city or my country, but rather as the biggest, bloodiest hecatomb which we have experienced. Nearly all of my friends died.'[133]

The Noose Tightens

Hitler's colossal weapons continued to pulverize the Old Town, but the progress of the German troops on the ground was still very slow. The Wehrmacht seemed almost to enjoy Himmler's embarrassment. General Krebs wrote to General Staedke on 21 August, sneering: 'Warsaw hobbles.' Staedke sent back a veiled critique of Himmler: 'The reasons lie in the command, which is below standard.' Von dem Bach and Rohr might be 'good enough', but Reinefarth and the lower ranks were 'brave but lack the necessary and precise knowledge of street fighting. SS and police units are insufficiently trained for these activities.' Himmler, who had never commanded even a platoon before, was now the head of the Reserve Army, and longed to prove his worth as a field commander. The criticism stung.

Von dem Bach, too, was getting edgy. Hitler had personally appointed him supreme commander in Warsaw on 14 August, in charge of every organization in the city. He could barely contain himself, lording it over his rivals at every turn. 'I rule over the military, the Wehrmacht including General Stahel, the police, the SS and the civilian administration,' he crowed in his diary. He even stopped a furious Reinefarth from sending reports directly to Himmler, insisting on seeing them first. Everything had to go through him now; the term 'von dem Bach Korpsgruppe' was used for the first time in the 9th Army Diary on 15 August – it would be a regular feature thereafter. Himmler again promised von dem Bach the Iron Cross once Warsaw was conquered.

On 18 August von dem Bach decided to try something new. He sent an SS representative, complete with white flag, to Królewska Street at the Saski Gardens, with a letter to be passed on to Bór urging him to 'stop the senseless and suicidal resistance'. If the offer was rejected, Bach added helpfully, the city would be destroyed. Bór did not take this proposal seriously. The German behaviour in Wola had erased any trust he might have had in them and in his view capitulation at this stage would have been the equivalent of sending civilians and soldiers to certain death. 'Above all,' Bór said, 'I hoped that the Russians would restart their attack and take over Warsaw. I decided to leave this letter unanswered.' General Georg-Hans Reinhardt, who had just replaced Walter Model as commander of Army Group Centre, also drafted a leaflet ordering Warsawians to 'surrender and give up your weapons'. These were dropped from the sky into the burning city, but again there was no response. The Poles were still waiting for a miracle.

At 5.30 on the afternoon of 18 August Reinefarth declared that as Bór had not responded, it was time to attack: 'The main aim now is the fast and complete destruction of the *Banditen* trapped by the Schmidt, Reck and Dirlewanger Brigades in the Old Town.' Himmler, desperate to save face, had been cobbling together as many men as possible to send into battle, but by now the once 'pure Aryan' representatives of the SS were more likely to be *Hiwis*, or press-ganged eastern prisoners. Dirlewanger's Kampfgruppe received two Azeri battalions with 1,300 men, as well as the 3rd Cossacks shock group of collaborating Asians, cossacks and criminals, with a total of fifty-five officers and 2,772 men; Himmler sent an additional 1,500 prisoners from concentration and punishment camps, many of whom had never been in combat. Dirlewanger was also sent the 579th Cossacks Unit and the 580th Russian Cavalry Unit. There were specialists, too, like the 608th Security Unit from the 203rd Security Division – a highly experienced and very brutal force used to protect the rear of the army, as well as the 500th Motorized Battalion of *Sturm* sappers, trained in city fighting. Between them Rohr, Dirlewanger, Reck and Stahel had a force of 13,400 men, and a powerful arsenal that included everything from Hetzer ('Baiter') tank destroyers to nearly a hundred Goliaths.

The general attack on the Old Town began in earnest on 19 August. 'First came the planes, then the artillery,' recalled Bór. 'The most dangerous was fire from the Panzer trains, and the greatest destruction was caused by fire from the *Krowas*. Artillery fire went on non-stop from morning until midday, and then the attack itself began. The first line was with Goliaths. Their task was to destroy barricades and the walls of buildings. Behind the Goliaths were Tiger tanks, which put our positions under direct fire. Only after this did foot soldiers move in.' Bitter hand-to-hand fighting broke out in a number of key buildings, including Bank Polski and the Mostowski Palace.

Civilians cowered in their shelters as explosion after explosion destroyed anything still standing. The AK fought ferociously for every centimetre of ground, but the battering was too great. Slowly the Germans began to push the Poles back, squeezing the troops and the trapped civilians into an ever smaller area. Even so, on 21 August German soldier August Weller wrote: 'Polish *Banditen* in Warsaw fight fanatically and fiercely. The results achieved by our units after three weeks of fighting are pathetic despite the support of numerous and most modern types of weapons.'

The situation for the AK and for the civilians was increasingly dire, as the city was literally smashed to pieces before their eyes.

AK press officer Major Zagórski's group had to 'change our headquarters as we were being shot at like ducks in a row. Linked to
the shrinking terrain the fire from the mine throwers and grenades
results in ever higher losses.'[134] Bombs pounded in day and night,
and people were dying in their thousands. Monter decided that
the only hope was to cut through the German lines and create a
passage to the north, so that the troops waiting in Żoliborz could
come to their aid.

On 13 August Agaton had miraculously survived the perilous
journey through the German lines and into Żoliborz. He was
shocked to find that life there was completely normal. 'It was only
eight hundred metres away, but it was like a different world . . .
there was even glass in the windows.' The locals were amazed that
he had made it – he was given dinner and a free shave, and treated
like a hero. The purpose of his mission was to meet Colonel
Mieczysław Niedzielski ('Żywiciel') and organize a simultaneous
attack on the Gdańsk railway station from Żoliborz and the Old
Town.

In reality, this operation was unwinnable. The station formed
part of the heavily guarded border between the Old Town and
Żoliborz, and was bristling with machine-gun nests and anti-tank
guns, barbed wire and bunkers. The great, hulking Panzer train
patrolled constantly. The first attack was attempted from the
Żoliborz side on the night of 19 August, but failed. Eighty per
cent of the men were lost. The second was led on 21 August by
Żywiciel from Żoliborz and Major Władysław Janaszek ('Bolek')
from the Old Town. It too was a disaster. Kampfgruppe Schmidt
had been forewarned, there was a full moon that night, and the
fires of the burning city made it easy for the Germans to see the
AK troops creeping towards the tracks. Rockets came at them
from all directions, and red flares were dropped to mark them
out for the German artillery. Only a handful of men from Żoliborz

reached the tracks, and they were then mown down. In the south the Germans trained five cannon and machine guns on the men from the 'Zośka' Battalion; five hundred men from the Old Town were lost. An Einsatzkommando report describes the treatment of the prisoners: '46th Sapper Battalion transferred eighteen *Banditen* who surrendered with arms in the air in a battle post between Żoliborz and the Old Town on the night of 21–22 August. In accordance with orders all eighteen prisoners were shot following interrogation.'[135]

The German onslaught on the Old Town was now relentless. The ground shook, fires burned everywhere, and the sky was black with dust and smoke. The gigantic Mint building, held by Group 'Leśnik' and Radosław, which was crucial to the defence of the northern sector of the Old Town, was bombarded constantly by the Panzer train. On 27 August Schmidt sent 1,600 troops supported by assault guns to attack it, and in scenes reminiscent of the grain elevator in Stalingrad, two hundred AK soldiers fought the Germans in bloody hand-to-hand combat for each floor. Schmidt's men finally took the building on 28 August. They immediately went to the cellar, and murdered all of the wounded Poles. It was a grim foretaste of what was to come.

Now there was nothing to stop the Germans from getting into the Old Town from the north. The situation was equally dire to the south-west. Simon's Passage – the shopping arcade which had belonged to Stanisław Aronson's family – was blown up, and two hundred soldiers from the 'Chrobry' Battalion were buried there.[136]

The Germans began to close in around Krasiński Square. The palace had been hit on 27 August, when its northern wing collapsed, covering a first-aid post filled with wounded soldiers. 'The dust was as thick as London fog. We found one body, then another, and worked fast to dig them out . . . After a few hours we decided to stop digging – it was too late to save these people.

Twenty-seven in the battalion died; they were exhumed after the war.[137] By 1 September the palace was 'burning so brightly it was like midday in the evening'. The Germans were using flame-throwers to torch anything in their path. Desperate attempts to save paintings, objects and books had long been abandoned; sculptures, statues and silver perished in the flames.[138]

As the noose tightened, ever more people were forced to move to avoid falling into German hands, but there were no new places in which to hide; even if they found a spot there was now no food or water, and temperatures were still around forty degrees. People fainted in the heat; children cried as they were pulled by desperate parents to yet another dark, crowded place. 'It was a herd instinct . . . the people from one cellar went to the one next door, and the people from next door went over to the first . . . Little by little, the territory of our Stare Miasto redoubt began to shrink; at times the barricades and trenches had to be moved back.'[139] Jan Rosner remembered that 'people were going crazy because of the bombing'. There was 'unbearable heat' in the cellars: 'the wife of the wounded man wore a slip. Who cared about a slip by then?'[140] As the intensity of the attacks increased, people were being killed by the blasts, by incineration and by suffocation. Captain Rozłubirski ('Gustaw') recalled: 'People lay on the streets killed by *Krowas*, very often torn into pieces and often without clothes, which had been blown off. Nobody took care of them. People were in shock, and the dead bodies did not matter. They passed the dead with indifference, moving from one part of Stare Miasto to another like mice in a cage. The units supposed to be defending Stare Miasto were thinking only about one thing: to get out of the district, to escape this hell.'[141]

By 25 August the Luftwaffe was constantly attacking an area by now no larger than three square kilometres. 'It was impossible to get used to the planes. Every fifteen to twenty minutes . . .

They didn't care what they hit as long as they destroyed everything. So the same ruins were hit for the third time, the fourth time. Even the ruins were disappearing.' The city was disintegrating; tall buildings were reduced to their foundations, with mere shards sticking out: 'gutters, brackets of sheet metal hung from holes in the balconies or from nothing at all'. Hundreds of dead bodies were rotting under the masonry, and the ground was thick with flies. 'The ruins stink.' Survival was a question of luck. One man went to look for a cup for water; when he came back, a burning hot piece of shrapnel was embedded in the spot he had been sitting on minutes before. People were buried alive with horrifying frequency, but nobody had the strength to dig them out any more. 'The condition of life for the population was worsened by the destruction of twenty further houses . . . the administration authorities cannot cope any more. Starosta, the head of the civilian authority in north Warsaw, is young and inexperienced. There is no water or gas, and the latrines are so stuffed that people have started relieving themselves everywhere. The stench is horrible, but you don't see any building of public latrines as there is nowhere to build, on every square there are tombs, and their number is mounting from hour to hour.'[142] People simply gave up. 'Where could we go? We were in the ruins . . . Either they'll hit us directly or they won't. If it's a direct hit they'll break through. There will be no miracles here.'[143] Even relatives stopped burying the bodies of their loved ones: 'A woman died in the cellar and her family carried her to the courtyard. They put her down outside and just left her there.'[144]

To the Sewers

By now Bór had virtually ceased to lead. Agaton visited him at the former Ministry of Justice in Długa 7, and was shocked by the state he was in: 'I entered the room, dark walls, shelves of books, their golden spines shining in the candlelight. Further in was a bed with a grey blanket. Bór was wounded and had a bandage on his head. He had problems speaking.'[145] On 25 August the leadership realized that the situation in the Old Town was hopeless. Bór and the rest of the government were to leave for the relative safety of the city centre; Bór was far too great a prize to be captured by the Germans. On that day Warsawians learned that Paris had been liberated. 'It filled me with unmitigated envy,' Stanisław Likiernik said. 'There they get rid of them in three days, while we will perish here before Warsaw is free.'[146] Meanwhile, the escape route that would become legendary in the history of the Warsaw Uprising was about to come into service. Bór would be in the first group to sneak out *under* the German lines, using the sewers.

Warsaw's nineteenth-century sewer system, designed by the British engineer William Lindley, had been much admired in its day. It was extremely well built, and in many places the red-and-mustard-coloured brick tunnels reached over a metre in diameter, large enough for the average person to get through; some were bigger still. As the uprising was only meant to have lasted a few days, the sewers had never featured in any AK plans, but when parts of the city were cut off in early August, this underground maze became their only possible link with other districts.[147] Municipal employees were called in to look at maps taken from the archives; Jewish fighters who had used the sewers during the Ghetto Uprising gave practical advice.[148]

In the first weeks most of the sewers were impassable, as the waste levels were too high; it was only when the Germans started clearing and destroying huge swathes of the city, and cutting off the water supply, that the level went down. When Monter sent the first runner from the city centre to the Old Town via the sewers, a distance of just over 1.5 kilometres, it had taken her eighteen hours to reach her destination. But before long the route from the Krasiński Palace to Warecka in the city centre had been improved, and equipped with ropes, signs and street names; Lieutenant Edward from the 'Kuba' Group even laid a telephone line which worked until 1 September. By the third week of August the AK were moving limited supplies to the Old Town, and some runners, often slim young girls and boys, became experts at getting back and forth in record time – 'Zyta', who made the journey every day in ninety minutes, was nicknamed 'the Queen of the Sewers'; it was not an insult.

On 25 August Bór took one last look at the ghastly ruins of the burning city from his office in the Raczyński Palace at Długa 7, staring for some time at the cathedral burning in the distance. Then he left. He was accompanied by a group of forty people, including the city's civilian administration, the Deputy Prime Minister, Jan Stanisław Jankowski ('Soból'), and the Chairman of the National Unity Council, Kazimierz Pużak ('Bazyli'). They carefully made their way to Krasiński Square, and the tunnel that they hoped would lead them to safety. 'The manhole leading to the sewer was only two hundred yards from the German lines, and under constant fire from their grenade launchers and heavy machine guns,' Bór recalled. 'Bent over, I crossed the fifteen yards or so at the double, and climbed down, slipping and stumbling, and found myself in complete darkness.'

With Bór gone and the area that had not yet been taken by the Germans shrinking by the day, on 30 August an increasingly desperate Wachnowski ordered a final attempt to break out above ground, this time to the south. One group was to create an artery to the city centre by attacking Plac Bankowy, another was to go through the sewers to attack the German lines from behind, and another was directed towards Krochmalna Street and Plac Mirowski. Again, it was hopeless. The AK ran into barricades, machine-gun fire and artillery barrages, and dozens of men were killed. Captain Andrzej Romocki ('Morro') and his unit from the 'Zośka' Battalion found themselves caught behind German lines, but in a now legendary display of bravado they removed their red-and-white armbands and marched straight past the Germans and back to their own lines. As they approached the Polish barricades they yelled, 'We're from Radosław! Don't shoot! We're Poles!'[149] They were greeted with hugs and tears of joy; in the evening they all sang hymns of thanksgiving. But the rest were not so lucky. The failure to break out meant that there were now only two options for the people trapped in the Old Town: evacuation through the sewers, or capture by the Germans.

Once Wachnowski decided to evacuate the AK through the sewers, he moved fast. Around 4,500 people, of whom 1,500 were armed soldiers, were given passes and a precise time at which they were to gather at the manhole on Krasiński Square. Every two hours the section leaders were to allow groups of fifty into the area, which by now was under guard and cordoned off with heavy concrete slabs to protect it from both German fire and desperate civilians. The Germans were only a few hundred metres away, and were pounding the area with everything they had. And when the civilians had found out about the evacuation, the entire Old Town had erupted in panic. Nobody wanted to be left behind.

The AK had deliberately not told the civilians about the escape route: 'I remember when Dr Bilewicz came in and said that they had found a way out through the sewers, but they were keeping it secret from the civilians for now.'[150] They wanted to be sure that the Germans did not discover and destroy this last lifeline, but they also wanted to keep the panicked crowds from trying to escape through it. The logic was simple. There were far too many civilians trapped in the Old Town to get them out through the sewers, and there was no room for them in the city centre, where there were already shortages of food, water and accommodation. The escape route was to be reserved for the AK and its affiliates only.[151]

Secrecy was of course important, but the way in which the evacuation was carried out caused bitterness, resentment and terror in those forced to remain behind. As Agaton put it, 'What happened in the streets of the Old Town on the night of 31 August was no longer part of an organized uprising, it was chaos.'[152]

There were problems from the beginning. A fierce disagreement broke out between Monter and Wachnowski about the movement of the wounded. Monter forbade their transportation through the sewers, for fear that they would block them, but Wachnowski disobeyed his orders, and ordered Dr Tarnawski to scour the AK hospitals for patients who could be taken out.

The soldiers who were too sick to move were to be disguised as civilians, in the hope that the Germans would leave them alone. Wachnowski remembered: 'I ordered a huge number of wounded soldiers to be dressed in civilian clothes with false documents and to be moved to different basements and bunkers. The rest of the badly wounded people, four hundred, were sent to small hospitals in Długa Street. Food and medicine was gathered for the patients.'[153] AK nurse Janina Kwiatkowska chose to stay in the Old Town to take care of her badly wounded sister. 'On 1 September I started to cover the traces that these were military casualties. I took away weapons and documents and changed uniforms for civilian clothes. We put a sign on the front that read "Hospital of Social Security" in German and Polish.'[154] A few civilian patients were brought in, including two women about to give birth.

Stanisław Aronson, who had been wounded in the lung and had a leg in plaster, recalled: 'I was very bitter and frustrated about the fact that I had to stay and wait for death. A few colleagues came to say goodbye to me. Then silence.'[155] Only a very few, including the chaplain at the hospital at Długa 7, Father Rostowski, and a handful of nurses, volunteered to remain; the rest were needed to carry the wounded out through the sewers.

The first official group arrived at Plac Krasiński on the night of 31 August. Only those with special passes could get anywhere near the area. All of Długa was blocked to civilians as 4,000 AK people crowded in. There were scenes of desperation as mothers with sick children, or young men fearful of execution, unsuccessfully begged Major Barry's military police to let them through the checkpoints. Jan Rosner remembered trying to get to the manhole at his allotted time: 'It was madness. We went to Plac Krasiński. Długa was filled with soldiers, the wounded . . . The chaos was unbelievable. We were led by one guy from the Socialist Party, but he was not dynamic enough to push his way through the crowd. Another guy from our group had dysentery . . . I recognized many more people trying to get in who were not on the list, the wives and friends of the bosses. The group was now much bigger than it was meant to be. I am fourth in line after the people leading us. There is heavy fire from the direction of Krakówskie Przedmieście. We are protected by a small barricade, so we have to crawl towards the drain. A Major Barry is there with a Sten gun. He orders me to step back because of the shelling, and says he will shoot me if I don't obey. I heard he is a brave officer, but his nerves are shot. Barry is paralyzing everything with his shouting, and shoots into the air with his Sten gun trying to defend the entrance to the drain. Then there is a bombing raid. We stand at a gate which gives no protection, and after a while Major Barry opens the sewers and lets us in, although the situation is in fact the same as it was before. We have just lost half an hour.'[156]

For Rosner, the descent into the sewer was preferable to the chaos on the streets. 'It is dark. We walk for ten metres and then enter the water to make space for the next group. More people. Cold, dirty waste water up to our knees, but after a while you forget you are in the sewer, and after what we had just experienced above ground we feel relieved. I feel as if I'm waiting in some station for the metro. I have just read *Les Misérables*, and remember Jean's walk through the Parisian sewer. I think also of the Jews who tried to leave the ghetto using the sewers.'[157]

As the drains narrowed, movement became more difficult. 'We go with candles . . . then to a very narrow sewer where we have to bend down. The walls are sticky . . . it is exhausting, especially for tall people. Then to an area where the water is very high. It is disgusting.' Some found it hard to carry on. The tunnels became ever lower, and the bricks scraped their backs. The smell was overwhelming. At times they stepped on dead bodies. 'The walls are covered in slime. We move on holding with one hand the back of the person in front of us, the second hand to feel the wall. Later we have to crouch to walk. It is tiring. One of the people in line loses consciousness, a two-metre-high lieutenant who was wounded in the face; the soldiers around help him move on.' It was worst for those trying to carry the wounded. 'It was ghastly – if someone lost their strength and fell the whole group stopped and were all trapped.'[158] They had to be extremely quiet as they passed under German positions; sometimes when they reached storm drains they could hear the Germans talking to one another.

Maria Stypułkowska, a runner for 'Parasol', remembered: 'We were not allowed to touch the walls. We had a rope, which helped, attached to one another's belts. The smell was so overwhelming that when I left the sewer at the city centre I lost consciousness.'

For those carrying stretchers, the journey took at least five hours. 'Wounded and exhausted men and women would fall and drown. In a few hopeless cases the medics spared their suffering with lethal injections of morphine. It was a nightmarish journey.'[159]

When they reached the manhole at Warecka, they had to be pulled out, grateful to have made it alive. 'We are helped out by people and lie on the pavement without moving. We are dizzy from the fresh air.'[160] Agaton had entered the sewer under German artillery fire with a group of wounded soldiers, most of whom were on stretchers. 'When we finally emerged the first thing I saw was a girl standing at the exit in shiny boots, navy trousers, a small pistol in a leather pouch and a clean white blouse and a red band on her arm and a navy hat on her head. I was so fascinated by her clean boots.'[161]

Jan Rosner remembered: 'I got out on Nowy Świat. It was paradise. Summery sky and sun, evening was coming and the world was smiling and sunny. People were nice to us, we got food. I found a knife and scraped the layer of smelly dried muck from my legs. People recognized us by our smell.'[162] For some, the sight of the city centre was shocking: 'There are normal real houses, a road, leaves. Trees! . . . You can hear explosions but it is as if they come from a different planet. We feel like strangers in this normal world and are convinced we cannot live in it . . . when we get up we leave stinking muddy puddles. We are given soup and clean socks, a bowl of water and soap and then a royal breakfast of bread, graham crackers and honey labelled "*Nur für Wehrmacht*".'[163] 'The houses are normal, normal walls, shop windows . . . people are clean, with combed hair. It doesn't look like war. They look at us with astonishment and respect.'[164] Those in the city centre heard the stories of the agony of the Old Town with the same interested detachment Old Town residents had earlier felt towards the refugees from Wola: 'We hear comments about the Old Town, about the suffering of the people there', but somehow it was not 'real'.[165] About 4,500 people made it to the city centre through the sewers between 31 August and 2 September; around eight hundred made the perilous journey through the sewer to Żoliborz. For those left behind in the Old Town, the agony was incalculable.

News of the evacuation spread rapidly and everyone tried to think of some contact in the AK they might use to gain a place in the escape groups. 'That was our dream. To get through to Śródmieście. The legend of the sewers, or entering with passes obtained through friendships and only in the highest circles . . .'[166] Zofia Zamsztejn-Kamieniecka was one of the Jews freed from Gęsiówka prison: 'The worst bombing was better than prison and camp. When I realized that the Old Town was soon going to fall my fear was boundless. After such a great moment of freedom I would again be in the hands of the criminals.'[167] She did not make it onto the list.

Stanisław Podlewski watched as the enormous, ghostlike crowd of those who feared they would be left behind emerged 'from basements, bunkers and all possible shelters, groups of people with their bundles started to leave these places. They walked along the streets which were now mountains of rubble with only the remains of foundations and black chimneys. The lights of rockets shone on these desperate people who were dirty and exhausted and run-down. Wounded patients are carried on chairs, stretchers, children's prams, in arms and on stools. The narrow Długa Street and the tight corridor by Kino Miejskie and Daniłowiczowska Street are overflowing with people . . . the sound of groaning, yelling, the cries of starving children, people calling for one another in the darkness, the fights of those who are drunk, people swearing, all create a picture of the apocalypse.'[168] In the end the crowd was packed so tightly that people simply couldn't move. 'We were amazed that so many people had managed to hide and survive the dreadful fires, bombs, lack of food and lack of water.' It was virtually impossible to reach the manhole cover. 'It was like rye in a field, blown by a summer storm. Those who were weak simply fell and hundreds stepped on them.'[169]

At 3 o'clock in the morning of 2 September Wachnowski finally left, along with all the soldiers and staff of Grupa Północ. Radosław left an hour later, and Barry followed. Lieutenant Colonel Tomków's 250 well-armed men had been keeping the Germans at a distance of at least 250 metres. They left at around 5 a.m.

With the military gone, the civilians stampeded in. Those AK who had not been able to get into position realized they would not make it; Halina Kidzińska-Zdanowicz of the 'Parasol' Battalion was forced to return to her shelter; others tried to get down into different sewers, and a number were lost.[170]

Around 7 a.m. an air attack covered the manhole with rubble. People clawed it away and started to go down again. Then disaster struck. At 9 a.m. the Court of Appeal building was bombed. The entire structure came down with a great crashing sound, covering the manhole and hundreds of people. Those nearby watched in horror as their loved ones were buried alive, and despaired as their last hope of escape disappeared under the ruins. They could hear the Germans coming. Within half an hour the Schmidt *Sturm* group was fighting its way into Krasiński Square. Confronted by the enormous crowd, they took 6,000 men, women and children prisoner. The Germans were amazed at their state: 'They are exhausted, emaciated from lack of water and food. They are near death.'[171]

Reinefarth's men fanned out, moving cautiously for fear of attack. They did not yet realize that most of the AK soldiers had left, and people could hear them asking, 'Where are the *Banditen*?'

For the Germans the Old Town was a sobering sight. In the

previous two weeks, besides the bombing raids from the planes, over 3,500 tonnes of shells had fallen in the artillery barrage of an area less than two square kilometres.[172] The entire district was burnt out, and hardly any buildings were left intact. Piles of smouldering rubble blocked streets and alleys, and the stifling air was thick with dust and the sickly-sweet stench of rotting corpses. Clouds of flies settled on pools of blood, and rats feasted on the remains of the thousands left unburied. Some 35,000 people, filthy and starving, cowered in cellars, basements and bunkers, fearing for their lives.

When von dem Bach heard that the Old Town had fallen he was ecstatic, and sent a triumphant telegram to Himmler: 'Reichsführer, I report to you that today before midday the northern *Kessel* [cauldron] of Warsaw was completely taken by us. Currently some civilians and prisoners of war are being taken out. One hundred and fifty German soldiers have been released and sincerely welcomed in Reinefarth's headquarters.' Further reports confirmed that 'the whole area north of Adolf Hitler Platz is now in our hands'.

Bach was annoyed that so many insurgents had escaped down the sewers, and ordered the Listening and Boring, and the Boring and Mining, companies to destroy the tunnels. He then went to see the battlefield for himself, driven in his grand car to Adolf Hitler Platz, his perfect uniform and polished boots in stark contrast to the filthy and exhausted civilians made to stand before him. He could not refrain from making one of his 'humanitarian' speeches, although it fell rather flat, given that thousands of people lay dead in the ruins behind him. 'You will be well treated,' he assured the crowd. As ever with von dem Bach, this was only partially true.

The 'cleansing' of the Old Town was to be different from the killing frenzy in Wola. German priorities had changed. The Reich was shrinking fast, and the supply of slave labour was drying up. Hitler decided that there was no point in killing any Warsawians who could be put to work; the people of Warsaw were to constitute the last substantial pool of slave labour captured by the Germans in the Second World War.

Von dem Bach supported this plan. When Geibel had criticized him on 18 August for trying to negotiate a peace with the 'Banditen', Bach had snapped back, 'Would you oppose a Führer Order? The Führer told me, "500,000 workers will move into Germany as soon as we have won this battle." '[173]

The civilians were now to be 'processed' to evaluate their suitability for labour. Those fit to work were to be sent to Pruszków, and on to camps or to the Reich. Those too ill or infirm, and those suspected of having fought in the AK, would be killed.

In the beginning there was hope that the Old Town would be spared mass executions, and in the early days the signs were positive. The Germans reached the Maltese hospital on that first afternoon. 'A tank appeared at 2 p.m. and started to shoot at the hospital. There was cannon fire, and machine-gun fire. When they stopped the barrage an SS Obersturmführer came in.' The officer asked if there were any German prisoners being held there. He was taken upstairs, where the PoWs were being tended by the hospital staff. 'The wounded Germans started shouting at the SS officer for firing at the hospital.' The treatment of the German wounded probably saved the Polish patients. Dr Jerzy Dreyza remembered: 'an SS guy prepared to shoot me. He loaded his gun but another said, "Leave him. He is a doctor here." '[174]

Then Dirlewanger's men arrived, 'swaggering around like great heroes. At midday Obersturmführer Lagna called me over. He looked at his watch and said, "You have two hours to clean out this dump." I objected, as I had badly wounded men and no stretchers. "I don't care. At 2 o'clock this hospital will be burned down." I could do nothing. The Germans were very aggressive. They took a wounded Polish officer outside and shot him in his bed in the garden. They hit our radiologist with their rifle butts.' Miraculously, the doctors were given permission to move the ill to other hospitals, and they moved fast before the Germans changed their minds.[175] Civilians came out to help as the hospital staff struggled to carry patients, still in their beds, through the streets.[176] At one point they were stopped by a group of cossacks from the Ostlegion. 'Two sub-officers approached me and pointed at the sick. "Rebels!" one of them said. "Rebels like you!" "If you were wounded I would carry you, too," I said. "You speak well," one said, and left us alone.' The Wehrmacht generally behaved reasonably well: 'A sub-officer approached one of our nurses, a young girl who was carrying one of the beds. He took her place and carried it for her. Another German sub-officer did the same. These soldiers also helped to protect us from the other units which were passing us all the time.'[177] But few of the patients were so lucky.

The Germans had started to murder 'undesirables' even before the capitulation of the Old Town: 350 people were executed in the Theatre Narodowy on 9 August, and after the war witnesses saw 'bones, hair, teeth, pieces of clothing, shoes, documents. I think there must have been women amongst the victims as there were pieces of dresses.'[178]

There were 5,000 civilians and 2,000 insurgents lying in cellars, bunkers, hospitals and makeshift clinics. AK officer Adam Borkiewicz wrote that as the Germans moved in on 2 September, 'The mass executions and rape began immediately . . . those wounded, incapacitated by their wounds or old . . . were executed.'[179] Matthias Schenk came across a wounded soldier lying on the ground: 'I gave him water from my bottle and ran to explode the door – the SS guys were behind me. When I came back Dirlewanger stopped me and said, pointing at the wounded man, "Did you give this swine something to drink?" I noticed only then that there was a red-and-white armband on the German uniform. "Shoot him!" Dirlewanger ordered. I stood motionless. I was sick of the whole mess, and Dirlewanger was so mad that I couldn't even understand what he was saying. The wounded man looked at me – I will never forget that look . . . One of Dirlewanger's people took my pistol and shot the man. Dirlewanger was shouting at me, saying he would execute me, but some Wehrmacht soldiers appeared and told him that he would be court-martialled if he didn't stop.' As Dirlewanger argued, Schenk took the chance to run away.

Zbigniew Galperyn ('Antek'), from 'Chrobry' Battalion, had felt utterly helpless when Barry's military police had come to St Jacek's church on 29 August and led anyone who could walk to the sewers. Two hundred badly wounded men had to stay behind in their beds, alone and defenceless. The Germans came on 2 September. The patients lay in complete silence, not daring to move as the SS walked around them. One of the Germans pointed at a young boy. 'I saw you shooting at us,' he said. The patients realized that they were doomed. The SS returned with petrol, splashed it everywhere, and set the building on fire. 'We were choking in thick smoke while lying in the sacristy.' A nurse managed to move twelve of the patients into the garden with the help of another man. 'The most severely wounded . . . could not be saved. Soon the vault collapsed, and those who remained were burned alive. In 1946 their skeletons were found still lying on their burned beds.'[180]

The largest AK hospital in the Old Town was located at Długa 7, in the massive Raczyński Palace. The imposing neo-classical building had served as the Ministry of Justice before the war, and had been headquarters for 'Wigry II' Battalion, and also for Bór between 13 and 20 August. The Cathedral surgical hospital on its lower floors housed over 450 badly wounded patients.[181] On 1 September Dr Kowalski ordered that all uniforms and weapons be taken away and the patients dressed in civilian clothes. Then they waited.[182]

Early on the morning of 2 September Barbara Blanka, a nurse, stepped outside to go and look for food. Suddenly she saw her first Germans. 'I froze. They are coming towards me from Kiliński Street.' She thought about running, but they were too close. 'Come here,' they say in Russian. 'I think quickly. I am in civilian clothes, wearing the red dress I started the uprising in and will now probably finish it in. I try to control my horrible fear. "*Banditen?*" they ask. "No *Banditen*," I say, explaining that I am merely going to the hospital to take my sick husband some tea. They search me skilfully, removing my watch and ring; they tear open my blouse and take my medallion.' After a short while a Wehrmacht officer joined them. The Germans were clearly baffled by the fact that there seemed to be no AK soldiers in the Old Town. ' "*Banditen, wo sind die Banditen?*" he asks. I answer in bad German that there are no *Banditen* here.' He seemed to believe her. 'Suddenly we hear planes circling overhead. "*Schnell! Schnell!*" he shouts. He shoots three flares into the air. The planes circle one more time around the hospital and then go away.'[183] Before long other Germans arrived with an enormous swastika flag which they stretched out over the courtyard to prevent further attacks.[184]

The nurses were given permission to go to look for food. 'We came across Wehrmacht soldiers, mostly from Silesia, who gave us sweets, dry biscuits, cigarettes and a bottle of wine on which was written "*Nur für Kranke*". They even took us to a demolished field hospital at Kiliński 5 which was full of supplies. "It will all be burned, so you had better take it," one said. He added, "I am Silesian. Don't worry, Poland will still exist after all this." '[185]

When the nurses returned to the hospital the staff were taken to the courtyard for interrogation. Dr Kowalski realized that it would be impossible to pretend that this had been a civilian hospital, and told the Germans: 'I felt obliged to treat everyone, including German prisoners of war.'[186] To their surprise they were told that any patients who could walk should leave immediately. Stanisław Aronson, who had been lying in the basement, managed to hobble out using two old brooms as crutches, thereby saving his life.

The Germans then ordered the nurses to scour the area and move all seriously wounded people to Długa 7. Father Rostowski, the chaplain, learned that there were a number of wounded lying unattended in the cellars at Kiliński 3, including scouts from the 'Gustaw' Battalion and the runner 'Kośka': 'her leg had been amputated and she was badly infected with tetanus'. One of the nurses, 'Ala', had trouble getting to her: 'Luckily a Wehrmacht soldier came and lent us his torch.'[187]

The nurses went to the cellars next door. 'The wounded lying down there in complete darkness are totally quiet until we yell out we are there to help. Then, slowly, they start answering. When they realize who we are they look upon us as saviours. All of them want to go to hospital. There are a dozen or so, all terribly wounded in the stomach or legs. We move them in darkness and put them on stretchers. We try to light matches, but there is no oxygen so the flames go out. Thankfully the Wehrmacht soldier comes back with the torch and helps us again.' The nurses returned for the patients upstairs. 'The first floor is on fire and a half-naked boy is crawling to get away from the heat. The Germans shake their pistols at him and yell, but they do not shoot him. We manage to move all of these patients to Długa 7 on blankets and stretchers.'[188] The seriously wounded were put on the first and second floors. Others were moved in from makeshift clinics and hospitals. But it was all in vain.

'At around 1 o'clock a furious SS officer comes racing over from Plac Krasiński. His name is Captain Kotschke and he has two Iron Crosses and two ribbons. He runs into the courtyard screaming to the SS men, "You have to clean out this building in ten minutes." ' The SS men didn't even stop to think, but started running. 'They go racing to all the floors, pushing the sanitary workers and nurses out of the way . . . We know that something horrible is about to happen.'[189]

The Germans quickly blocked the entrance to the hospital. Then the shooting started 'They used pistols and Schmeissers in a brutal way to threaten the patients,' one nurse recalled. Janina Kwiatkowska ran to a window and looked out: 'All of Kiliński Street to Miodowa was one big sea of flames. The house closest to us at Dluga 9 looked like a burning torch. I was afraid it would set us alight. The wounded woman lying next to the window started screaming in an inhuman voice. I looked down at the first floor and saw an SS officer with red hair under his cap. He looked at his watch and gave an order.'[190] The SS men started to throw grenades into the cellar. 'I put on my white coat and ran back to the first floor. I saw a soldier with a pistol in his hand finishing off the wounded. Our tiny "Ninka" grabbed the SS man's hand to stop him from shooting her husband; he shot him anyway and then shot her. The SS started to burn the staircase with rags soaked in petrol. I disobeyed the order to go downstairs, and went to the second floor. I heard shouts and the muffled sound of grenades which must have come from the cellars.'[191]

She waited on the second floor. 'We remained completely silent, and we could clearly hear the sound of the soldiers' hobnailed boots as they ran upstairs. Two SS men came in and shouted in Polish, "Wstać!" But nobody in the room could stand – the very best one of them could do was to lift his head. One of the SS men with a pistol in his hand started to walk past the wounded, checking everyone. One man was in agony because of severe loss of blood. The SS man kicked him and then bent down and shot him twice in his open mouth. He moved to the next man and kicked him. He moaned. The SS man shot him straight in the face. I shouted in German, "For God's sake, don't shoot!" He turned around and jumped towards me, I could see his bloodshot eyes. "Are you German?" "No, I am Polish." "Get out, you bandit!" He grabbed me by the neck and kicked me full force down the stairs."[192]

The SS killed all the patients on the first and second floors that day, over four hundred people. But the cellars were different. The Raczyński Palace was a huge building, with a vast underground maze of windowless storage rooms and vaults. The doctors had deliberately put the most severely wounded as far in as they could before they had left. Many lay silently in total darkness, waiting.

When the shooting started upstairs a few of them decided to try to escape, but the Germans caught them at the gate and pushed them back. An SS man lifted Jerzy Chybowski into the air and threw him back into the cellar so hard that he became wedged between the wall and an AK soldier lying there with both of his legs in plaster. After a while two SS men came to finish them off. One shone his torch around, and the other shot with his rifle. The first to be killed was the man with his legs in plaster. He was shot in the head, and his brains splattered all over Jerzy's face. The SS men came down the steps to take a closer look. Jerzy tried to play dead, but the Germans were too experienced to be deceived, and shot him three times. The bullets shattered his teeth, hit his arm and went into one of his lungs. When blood spurted out of his mouth the SS men thought he was finished. 'We need someone with a Schmeisser down here; we can't do it with a rifle,' one of them said. Then they left.

Jerzy crawled away in the dark, and was found by one of his friends, Henryk Kleniewski, known as 'Little Henry'. Despite their horrific injuries both men managed to rejoin the other wounded patients deep in the vaults. The Germans came down a few times looking for loot, but did not venture further in.

After some days the Germans began to light blankets covered in petrol and push them down the coal chutes. The cloth did not burn, but did remove the oxygen from the air. 'It was very hot, and the dead bodies started decomposing very quickly.' There was a terrible stench, and a complete lack of water. They feared discovery, but without help they knew they would die. Finally, in desperation, one of the women started shouting in German, '*Kamaraden, wir sind hier!*' The Germans found the emaciated woman and took her to a temporary hospital being run by Carmelite nuns, where she told the medical personnel that there were still survivors lying in the basement at Długa 7. They persuaded a German doctor to intervene with Colonel Schmidt, and the little group of wounded was pulled out of the basement, and saved.

Jerzy Chybowski still didn't trust the Germans, and remained hidden in the gloom after the others had left. An SS man came to the cellar. 'He shouted at the top of his voice, "Whoever is alive announce yourself, as we are leaving and that will be it." Then I said, "I am still alive." The Nazis did very many horrible things, but this German behaved not like an enemy but like my dearest friend. I looked disgusting. Not only did I have blood and dried brains all over my face, but I was completely covered in shit, as I had diarrhoea and was lying on the bed and had just had a bowel movement. I was too weak even to try to move. And this German came over and gave me a big hug, even though I was so revolting. Then he moved me to the window and pushed me out. I can only imagine what his uniform must have looked like and how much he must have stunk.'[193]

There were other strange incidents. Olgiert Cemerski ('Remec'), a patient at the Crooked Lantern hospital at Podwale 25, named after the restaurant there, was one of fifteen patients who were taken outside on their stretchers and laid on the street; those left behind in the basement were murdered. When the SS men came back, Remec stretched out his arm in the direction of their commanding officer and made the sign of the cross. 'What are you doing?' asked the German. 'I am a priest,' he lied. 'Just before you shoot us, I wish to forgive you and bless you while I can.' This quick thinking saved his life: the German was so surprised that he allowed the patients to be evacuated to the Wolski hospital.[194]

In general, however, Dirlewanger's men showed no mercy. The killing continued at the smaller hospitals at Podwale 23, 11 and 46 – the so-called Black Swan, where thirty people were killed. At the hospital at Freta 10 sixty people were gunned down, along with the staff.[195] The wounded were killed at Miodowa 23, and around a hundred people were shot at Wąski Dunaj: their burned ashes were found piled in a bathtub after the war. A group of Jews who had been released from Gęsiówka were shot at Plac Krasiński. The Einsatzkommando under Major Reck, supposedly the most humane of the German leaders in Warsaw, reported shooting fifty-four people and burning fifty-one bodies in one raid alone.[196]

After the war, people tried to find out what had happened to their loved ones, writing desperate messages in chalk on walls near where they had last been seen. 'Musza Majewska lay in this hospital with an amputated leg and Lala Sawacka ("Irma") also with amputated leg please send message to Milanówek address.' Below this, someone had written: 'They were shot and burned by the Germans.' Another message read: 'Henryk Walewski lay in this hospital – tall, blond, wounded in the collarbone – please send message to his family.' And below: 'I saw the patients being executed in this hospital.' Some of these tragic messages are preserved in the Warsaw Museum in the Old Town Square.

There is, at least, some kind of record of those murdered in the clinics and hospitals of the Old Town, but many of the thousands of wounded lying unable to move in the basements and cellars died forgotten and alone. The Germans went from building to building, ordering people at gunpoint to leave their hiding places. Those who were too afraid or too badly injured to come out were shot, burned, or killed by hand grenades dropped in through the grates. 'We could see their boots high up in the cellar windows . . . they dropped several grenades into the cellars . . . Explosions. Clouds of dust. Then silence. The dust and smoke were choking us . . . A short series of machine-gun fire hit the walls next to the windows.'[197] Hundreds died in this way.

The Germans wanted slave labourers; they did not want to have to care for burn victims, or people with broken backs, or blinded by the *Krowas*, or too old or ill or frail to work. One elderly invalid was lying on her bed when the SS entered her flat. They set her mattress on fire, but her frantic son grabbed her and carried her outside to the courtyard. The SS then burned the house down. The old woman could not walk, and was shot.[198]

She was not alone. Stefania Chmielewska was working at an institute for disabled women and girls run by nuns at Przyrynek 4. The Germans burst in on 29 August: 'They were very brutal and told us to leave. The ladies who could not be moved were murdered.' The SS killed them by throwing grenades through the windows. 'In March 1945 I returned to the house. It was burned out and I could see into the basement where the chapel was. The old ladies were lying there.'[199] A number of men who had been herded in with them were taken to the first floor, where the Germans took their identity cards and divided them into three groups. The first, which included those who had worked for German institutions, and the second, who were from other cities, were spared. The third group were taken into the next room, where they were shot in the back of the head. 'This is how my father and my husband were killed,' recalled Leokadia Chołodowska.[200]

For some, survival was a matter of luck. Wacława Makowska, then sixteen years old, remembered the Germans coming to her building. 'We were separated into men and women; I was with two other women from our group who were taken to the garden at Pokorna Street, where we had to move the bodies of dead German soldiers . . . The Germans discussed in front of us if they should shoot the whole group, or just the men. Suddenly one shouted to us girls in Polish, "Get out of my sight!" We turned and ran towards the train station as fast as we could. I could see the salvo from a machine gun as the others were shot.'[201]

The pattern was always the same: 'We heard "*Raus! Los! Schneller!*" We left the cellar. We all looked the same – dirty, skinny, unshaven, our clothing in rags. We were all surprised that here in the ruins we could see the sun. We had spent weeks with dirt, famine, fear and darkness . . . some people took luggage, trying to save valuables like furs and jewellery, silver and pictures, but they had to leave most of it; they simply did not have the strength to carry it.'[202] Everyone was filthy and starving: 'my husband is no longer my charming husband – his clothes in rags, his black hair sticky with blood, a dirty bandage and a long beard. The men are put into lorries and taken away.'[203] The rest were marched to St Wojciech church, which was now being used as a temporary transit camp.

Spilker's Work

The columns of refugees were watched by the Gestapo and the SS, and some people were plucked from the crowd: 'It was like Golgotha. Germans checked, and anyone who looked as if they had been wounded in the fighting was taken out and shot – they also shot those who were too badly wounded, or were of advanced age, or who were wearing any military dress.' A man called Milewski was killed because he was wearing riding boots; another because an SS man found some coffee beans in his pocket which might have come from a German food store. They were either killed in the street or taken behind a wall and shot there.

'We were guarded by SS men who spoke Russian,' Stefania Chmielewska recalled. 'We were robbed during the march. An officer pulled a fourteen-year-old girl from her mother and raped her. They were very brutal and rough with us.'[204] Another refugee remembered the 'murders and rapes' along the way. 'When the column stopped the Germans robbed us. Officers and soldiers chose people they didn't like the look of and did very brutal checks. In some sectors rows of soldiers yelled "*Banditen*" at us as we walked by.' Women had to carry belongings and babies in their arms under exhausting conditions. 'There were moments when the heat of the fires from the burning houses was so hot we couldn't get through, and the wind blew the smoke towards us and we could not see. At one point a bomber flew over; panic and chaos ensued, and we all fled, leaving the old people and the ill behind; nobody cared for them.'[205]

Father Parysz of the Capuchins had endured weeks 'in dust, no water, people running out of food, diarrhoea and people exhausted and nervous and frightened. Then the Germans came. They expelled everyone from the bunkers, ordering us to stand on the street. People were led by German soldiers with machine guns . . . one of them pulled me out of the column and took me to the ruins of a house. I was afraid and heard someone whisper, "He will kill him." ' Fortunately, the soldier just took his watch. '"*Væ victis* [Woe to the vanquished]," I thought as I walked through the ruined city.' At St Wojciech church they were told that anyone found with a weapon would be killed. A young German soldier took a pair of nail scissors out of his pocket. 'He pointed to me and to my beard. He probably wanted to cut it, but one of the Germans said "*Lassen sie*" – let him go.'[206]

Dr Edward Kowalski was marched from Długa 7 to St Wojciech's, and ordered to set up a clinic there. 'The Gestapo officer from Aleja Szucha and the Sicherheitsdienst der Kampfgruppe Reinefarth were in the vicarage house. This was Commandant Hauptsturmführer Spilker. Behind the vicarage was a prison overseen by SS Sub-Officer Müller, who had been in Lublin. He was tall, with brown hair and black eyes – he looked like a former policeman.' Dr Kowalski had a team of nine orderlies. The church was in an atrocious state: 'Everyone was gathered there, young, old, wounded . . . specialists like Müller were in the front choosing victims, especially young people who looked as if they might have participated in the uprising, as well as anyone suspected of being Jewish.'[207]

The Gestapo ran a prison behind St Wojciech's, next to the building where Klimaszewski and the Verbrennungskommando had been imprisoned. Stefania Chmielewska was pulled out of the crowd by the Gestapo along with five men and two other women. 'We were brought to the commandant, I don't know his name but he was about forty years old, well built, tall, with blue eyes and a cloudy gaze. He carried a riding crop. He asked where we were from and our opinion of the uprising. Another Gestapo man was in the room, as well as a man typing. The commandant left a few times, and then we could hear shouts and roaring from the rooms next to us.' After their interrogation they returned to the hall. 'A group of young men, stripped to the waist, were kneeling in the corridor, and also girls with their clothes torn to pieces. The men had their hands tied with barbed wire, and they were bruised and bloody and bore traces of torture . . . the commandant looked at our faces and then began to hit the men with his riding crop.' Stefania was lucky: her group was allowed to return to the church. It is most likely that the prisoners she had seen were executed.[208]

The church itself was 'filthy, overcrowded, it smelled terrible and was filled with wounded people, with children and old people who were physically and emotionally exhausted'. Most of the very badly injured had been murdered in the Old Town, but there were hundreds of serious cases left to treat, people with dysentery, severe burns, fractures and shrapnel wounds. When the bandages were finally cut on one soldier's leg pus gushed out, and he almost fainted, not from the pain but from the smell of his own putrefying flesh. Another man had tetanus, and screamed in agony for two days before he died. Dozens of children who had lost their parents cried in fear; they had no idea what to do or who would take care of them. Some were helped by people whose own children had died or disappeared. Mothers tried to comfort their children, but had nothing to give them; some held dead babies in their arms. The people who had emerged from their dark hiding places had endured weeks of terrifying bombs and fires, and many were completely exhausted. 'They were in dreadful fear of what would happen to them,' remembered Dr Kowalski. 'The SS walked around these poor helpless civilians shouting at the top of their voices and hitting them with their batons. We started work immediately. We cleared up around the main altar and made a work station. We found a blanket and duvets and told the wounded to lie around the altar. We gathered medication and bandages, and I did what I could. Day after day, night after night came new nightmares, the result of a big city being evacuated under such conditions. People were so tired after the fighting and bombing, and I saw a whole range of human tragedies before me. There were scenes as if from the Bible.'[209]

Some of the German soldiers – often young Silesians recruited into the Wehrmacht at the eleventh hour, who could speak Polish – tried quietly to help the Poles. 'The Germans brought a lorry to a column of refugees and offered to drive the wounded and the weak to the train station,' remembered Stefania Chmielewska. She wanted to help two nuns onto the truck, as one had a problem with her heart. 'As we approached the car one of the soldiers said to me in Polish, "Don't get in." Then I figured out they were to be executed.'[210]

The murders continued, with people randomly picked from the crowd and shot. 'In Żelazna I saw a group of murdered people who could not have been the victims of the bombing, as the bodies lay in piles.'[211] By far the worst ordeal faced by the people of the Old Town was the sub-camp set up by Spilker in the Pfeiffer tannery on Okopowa Street. Thousands of civilians – many of them unfit for work in the Reich, including the elderly, pregnant women, the frail and the sick – were taken there and murdered.

Stefania Chmielewska had also passed through the Pfeiffer factory on her way to St Wojciech church. She was lucky to survive. 'We were divided into two groups . . . the SS officer did the selection . . . I was in the group closer to Okopowa Street, and behind the net were old ladies, disabled, nuns, old people – around three hundred in all. I asked the officer not to separate me from the group of nuns and he asked, "Do you want to work?" and when I said yes he ordered me to join the group of younger people instead. We were kept in the garden until 5 o'clock without food or water. The children had found some pieces of carrots, but the SS men took them away. It was very hot, and children and women fainted, but the soldiers did not let anyone approach the pump in the garden. The commandant came and led the other group away.' Stefania's group was released and sent to St Wojciech's. 'As we left we could hear shots.' Not one of her friends in the first group was ever heard of again. They had been executed. Despite von dem Bach's claims that the murder of civilians had been stopped, Spilker continued to kill innocent civilians just as he had in the first days in Wola. His team of SS men were officially under Reinefarth. Their work was sanctioned by both von dem Bach and Himmler.

On 29 November 1945, German prisoner Willi Fiedler was interrogated at PoW camp no. 2228, near Brussels. His papers showed that he had served in the 5th Company of the 102nd Transport Battalion – Battalion-Nachschub-Turkiestan – from 1942 until October 1944. During the uprising he had been stationed at Modlin, near Warsaw, and had been driven into the city every day as part of a work detail. His group was made up of seventy men from Turkmenistan who were working at the Pfeiffer tannery. During his interrogation he gave a detailed description, complete with maps and accurate drawings of what happened there.

As the columns of refugees were marched out of the Old Town, Spilker and his underlings scoured the crowds looking for Jews, possible combatants and those who were unfit for work. Any they spotted were taken to 'Gate F' of the Pfeiffer factory. They never came back.

At first Fiedler knew nothing of the activities taking place only a few metres away, but one of his fellow workers was curious. 'A sub-officer from Turkmenistan, Mischa, followed them to see what was going on,' Fiedler recounted in his testimony. 'He managed to find a hole in the wall, and saw Polish civilians being forced to get onto piles where they were executed and burned.' Fiedler went to see for himself, but an SS man saw him and told him to leave immediately. 'The army has nothing to do here!' he barked. Fiedler persevered, and eventually managed to see an execution for himself through the hole in the wall. 'Civilians were herded into the yard. They sometimes followed orders and did what they were told; others had to be forced onto the piles. They were executed by SS men with machine guns.'

He returned a second time, and watched as groups of between a hundred and 150 people were brought into the yard. They were divided into smaller groups, which were then forced in turn to go into a second yard and lie on the bodies of those who were already dead, and shot. 'Some of them were pulled by the hair and then they were shot by SS men in the back of the neck. The next group was supposed to climb on the dead bodies, or they were pulled there and shot. And so on and so on until the whole pile was full and all the Poles had been executed. I saw nine or ten layers of dead in one pile, women with babies were executed together with them.' Once again Fiedler was caught. 'One of the guards saw me and said, "You shouldn't be seeing this or you could get into trouble." '

About thirty SS men lived in 'Building D' on the factory site, and took advantage of their position by trading in goods stolen from their victims. Fiedler got to know them a little. 'I asked one of the SS men if he didn't feel bad about shooting women and babies. The man was smoking a cigarette, and said, "The Polish nation must be exterminated. I don't care about them." '[212] Fiedler testified that around 5,000 Poles were killed during the time he worked at the tannery. He confirmed that 'the SS belonged to the Reinefarth *Sturm* group'.[213]

Spilker disappeared after the war; his wife claimed that he had been killed in a bombing raid in Krems, on the Danube, but his body was never found. The Pfeiffer tannery remained a ruin after 1945, and was only torn down in the 1990s to make way for the shiny new Klif shopping mall. The human remains found there were buried in the mass graves in Wola.

Reinefarth continued to murder civilians, albeit not on the scale of Wola. Oberleutnant Eberhard Schmalz was sent to Warsaw in August, and reported to Reinefarth at SS headquarters. 'The SS had lined up against a wall about forty or so Polish men, women, and children of all ages. I distinctly recall a young woman holding hands with two small children. It was clear to me what was about to happen. I confronted the SS commander as to why these people were about to be shot. He replied that they were being executed in reprisal for Germans who had been killed in the uprising. He also informed me that it was none of my concern. Shortly after, the hostages were shot before my eyes. I was disgusted.' When Schmalz later told his fellow officers what he had seen in Warsaw he was warned by a friend that 'I had better keep my stories to myself or I could find myself in an unpleasant situation'.[214]

The Old Town was slowly cleared of its remaining residents, many of them ill or wounded, and with their nerves shattered. After they had gone, there was nothing left but the outlines of what had once been buildings, surrounded by heaps of stinking rubble. The death toll had been high. Thirty thousand men, women and children lay buried in shallow graves or under the ruins. The Germans looted what they could, and then abandoned the wreckage. Hitler had prevailed in one of the most horrific sieges of the war, but in his victory he proved, as the great historian Hanns von Krannhals put it, that there is nothing worse in warfare than to fight in a besieged city populated by innocent civilians. The young German officer Peter Stolten was 'sick of it all'. He wrote to his father: 'Even if the spirit of the fight is brave and may achieve a great deal, weapons will always win . . . Is history fair?' he asked. 'Not here.'[215]

Hitler, Himmler and von dem Bach did not enjoy their victory for long. On 29 August news reached them that the Soviets had retaken the little town of Radzymin, and that Herbert Gille and his Viking SS Division had been forced to leave their headquarters at Jaktory and race towards the Vistula. The Red Army was on its way to Warsaw.

II

THE ALLIES, HITLER AND THE BATTLE FOR CZERNIAKÓW

We abandon all else and have recourse to prayers and tears, the last refuge of the unfortunate, for which there is ample occasion in the abundance of our calamity. (Chapter XII)

The First Battle of the Cold War

'The Warsaw Uprising,' wrote Colonel Teske, one of Model's staff officers, 'was the beginning of the Cold War between East and West.'[1] He was right. The terrible battle in the Polish capital was not just a fight for Polish freedom; it was also the first in a series of rifts between East and West which would come to shape the post-war world. The uprising laid bare the differences between Poland's desire for a Western-style democracy and freedom, and Stalin's brutal ambitions to Sovietize post-war Central and Eastern Europe. It was the first time that the two mutually exclusive world views came into open conflict; this ideological struggle would only end with the collapse of the Berlin Wall in 1989.

On a busy Warsaw street at the northern border of the Old

Town, sandwiched between a hotel and a 1950s housing block, is a dramatic monument. It is made of a long iron rail track which runs up a slope to an open railway car, filled with heavy iron crosses interspersed with Orthodox crosses and Stars of David. The names of little-known towns and villages are written on the railway ties. These are the places in the Soviet Union where hundreds of thousands of Poles perished between 1939 and 1941, during the Nazi–Soviet non-aggression pact.

The German invasion of Poland on 1 September 1939 was followed on 17 September by the Soviet invasion from the east. The armies of the two dictators descended on the hapless country like rapacious beasts. As the Nazis set out to Germanize 'their' territory, the Soviets, led by the NKVD head Colonel Ivan Serov, began to 'eliminate socially dangerous and anti-Soviet elements' in their own zone of conquest. Around 500,000 Polish citizens were taken from their homes and pushed onto trains in one of four mass deportations; 100,000 would die in captivity. All 'bourgeois' Poles were suspect, but army officers were considered to be particularly dangerous to future Soviet control. Beria himself called them uncompromising enemies of the Soviet Union for whom no rehabilitation was possible. 'They are anti-revolutionaries and should be sentenced to death,' he declared. In April 1940, at Stalin's behest, 22,000 captive Polish officers were taken to the Katyń forest, Mednoye and Kharkov, and shot one by one. It was the largest massacre of officers of a captured army in the history of warfare.

This horrific crime revealed the moral depths to which Stalin was capable of sinking when it came to Poland. To his annoyance, however, it did not remain hidden deep in those mass graves. In April 1943 the Germans began to dig in a clearing which, they noticed, had been carefully covered with newly planted saplings. After finding the remains of some of the officers who had so mysteriously vanished in 1940, they called in the Red Cross, who proved the identity of the men. Stalin had been caught red-handed.

Instead of admitting his guilt, however, he turned the tables on the Germans, claiming that the officers had been killed by Hitler. When the Polish government-in-exile asked for an investigation, Stalin blustered in feigned outrage, and used the affair as an excuse to break off relations with the 'London Poles' for good. In the following years he undermined the legitimate Polish government at every turn, while trying to cajole the Western Allies into recognizing his own Communist puppet PKWN instead.

'False face must hide what the false heart doth know,' Lady Macbeth famously said. Both Churchill and Roosevelt were informed of the fact that Stalin was responsible for the massacre, but they feared that if they confronted him with the truth he might abandon the war effort in the east, or make a separate peace with Germany. It was not a decision taken lightly. Churchill gave Roosevelt a document written by Owen O'Malley, the British Ambassador to the government-in-exile, in May 1943, in which he said: 'We have in fact perforce used the good name of England like the murderers used the little conifers to cover up a massacre.' Even so, he concluded that given the Soviet sacrifice in the war, 'few will think that any other course would have been wise or right'.[2]

The British Foreign Office was generally anti-Polish at the time, and with NKVD spies like Guy Burgess and Donald Maclean occupying influential positions there, the Poles had little chance of convincing the establishment that their cause was worth fighting for. Churchill and Roosevelt both felt that the need to keep Stalin in the war outweighed the injustice being done to the Poles. Not everyone agreed. Sir Alexander Cadogan, Permanent Under-Secretary at the Foreign Office, was critical of the moral dilemma that Britain had allowed itself to get into by not telling the truth about the murders immediately: 'How can the Poles be expected to live alongside the Soviets after Katyń?' he asked.[3] Churchill and Roosevelt knew that the 'London Poles' were supported by the vast majority of the Polish people, and were the legitimate representatives of their country, but they also felt that if they were to keep Stalin 'on side' they would have to be willing to sacrifice the Poles. As the American diplomat and historian George Kennan put it, the Allied victory in the war was 'mortgaged from the very beginning by the fact that the Allies were not strong enough to defeat Hitler alone and had to take advantage of the power of the Soviet Union . . . They had to compromise with the political aims of the Stalin regime. This placed them in a false and hypocritical position. And Poland was the place where this became most evident.'[4]

The sidelining of their loyal ally continued in Tehran in November 1943, when talks were held to determine the post-war boundaries of Europe. The Poles were not invited, and nobody told them it had been agreed that they would effectively lose half of their country to the Soviets. The head of the government-in-exile, Stanisław Mikołajczyk, suspected the worst, and announced that he would not accept territorial losses after the war. There was a twist, however. The Western Allies had decided that they would not recognize frontiers which had been established by force; as a result the government-in-exile was urged to accept the lie about Katyń and open up a dialogue with Stalin in order to come to a 'mutual agreement' about the frontiers. In effect, the Poles were under pressure to participate in, and give the seal of approval to, their own demise.

For the Poles the situation was dire. They had been staunch allies of the West from the first moment of the war, but were now being told they had to agree to terms which were simply unacceptable to them. Not only were they meant to approve the hated Curzon Line, and agree that the officers at Katyń had been murdered by the Germans; they were also being asked to abandon the legitimate London-based government in favour of Stalin's puppet PKWN, and even to renounce their pre-war constitution. They were being asked, in effect, to agree to the complete Soviet domination of their country and their people, and to do it willingly and without making a fuss. They simply could not do this. Churchill and Roosevelt mistakenly read this as Polish 'intransigence', and became increasingly irritated by their ally. As Kennan put it, the Western Allies were less sympathetic to the Poles 'precisely because they did work so hard to defend their independence, which was an embarrassment to them'.[5]

The problem was compounded by the fact that the British were now losing power not only to the Soviets, but also to the Americans. Churchill inherently distrusted Stalin, but Roosevelt believed that he had forged a special friendship with 'Uncle Joe', and this worked against the British Prime Minister. Roosevelt and Stalin held three private meetings at Tehran, in which the President granted Stalin all he wanted in Poland and the Baltic States, without asking for anything in return. By the time the 'Big Three' met, most important matters had already been decided, and their sessions became, according to Roosevelt's interpreter Charles Bohlen, 'little more than harangues between Stalin and Churchill, with Roosevelt sitting them out and seemingly enjoying them'. Bohlen was not impressed: 'Roosevelt should have come to the aid of a close friend and ally, who was really being put upon by Stalin.'[6] Roosevelt even made tasteless jokes at Churchill's expense: 'I began to tease Churchill over his Britishness . . . Winston got red and scowled and the more he did so, the more Stalin smiled. Finally Stalin broke into a deep guffaw, and for the first time in three days I saw the light. I kept it up until Stalin was laughing with me, and it was then I called him "Uncle Joe".'[7] As the historian Keith Eubank put it, 'Roosevelt had insulted Churchill who admired him, and demeaned himself before Stalin who trusted neither man. In his craving for Stalin's approval and friendship, Roosevelt imagined the joke had been on Churchill and that Stalin had laughed with him. More probably Stalin had laughed at the President of the United States belittling an ally to find favour with a tyrant.'[8]

Roosevelt's interest in the Poles did not extend much past the need to secure the Polish-American vote in the coming presidential election; indeed, he told Stalin that six or seven million Poles lived in the United States, and as a practical man he didn't want to lose their support. Shortly after, he told a visitor to his country residence at Hyde Park in New York State that he was 'sick and tired' of the Poles and other Eastern European peoples clamouring about their boundaries and sovereignties. 'I'm not sure that a fair plebiscite, if ever there was such a thing, wouldn't show that these eastern provinces would prefer to go back to Russia.'[9]

It is unlikely that either Churchill or Roosevelt could have done much to change the outcome of the war in the east, and certainly Roosevelt, unaware of the looming implications of the Cold War, did not see it as being in the American interest to do so. Unfortunately, however, they did not even try to gain small concessions for the people about to fall under Stalin's heavy yoke. Evidence shows that the Soviet dictator could be pressured up to a point, as Churchill proved during the uprising itself. Stalin had various contingency plans as to what to do with the conquered territories, depending on the success of the Red Army, the stance taken by the Allies and the situation on the ground. But as there was no pressure put on him by the West until Churchill's wrangling with him during the Warsaw Uprising, the Soviet dictator believed there had been a tacit agreement to allow him to do what he wanted in 'his' sphere of influence.[10]

The Polish situation became even worse after the Red Army crossed the pre-war Polish border on 6 January 1944. By now the

Americans and the British had essentially abandoned the country to the Soviets. The British government told the Polish government-in-exile that the logistical problems of intervening in Eastern Europe were enormous, while the Americans declared that the Eastern Front was a designated theatre of Soviet operations, and that Poland must somehow 'make a deal' with the Soviet command. Some in Britain even welcomed the Soviet presence. Foreign Secretary Anthony Eden thought that Stalin should be given something in return for the sheer scale of the Soviet sacrifice in the east, a view supported by senior officials like the diplomat Sir William Strang, who said it would be 'in Britain's interest' to accept Soviet domination of Eastern Europe. The problem was that it was not the British, but the Poles, who would pay the price.[11]

The half-truths and platitudes continued apace. When Churchill met General Anders in Polish military headquarters in northern Italy on 26 August, he said: 'We guaranteed and made a pledge to Poland as to its existence as a free, independent state, totally sovereign, strong, large, that the citizens living within it might live happily and with the possibility of free development without any foreign influences threatening it from the outside.'[12] Anders responded: 'We cannot trust Russia since we know it well, and we know that all of Stalin's declarations that he wants a free and strong Poland are lies . . . As they enter Poland . . . they disarm the soldiers of our Home Army, they shoot dead our officers and arrest our civil administration, destroying those who fought the Germans continuously since 1939 and fight them still.' Churchill answered: 'We will not abandon you and Poland will be happy.'[13] Roosevelt was also evasive. On 6 June 1944 Polish Premier Mikołajczyk landed in Washington to seek support from the President. Roosevelt chose not to tell him that he had already conceded Poland's eastern territories to Stalin at Tehran, promising instead that 'a strong and independent Poland will emerge'.

As the Western Allies concentrated their efforts elsewhere, Stalin continued to plan his takeover of Poland. On 21 July 1944 the Polish Committee of National Liberation (PKWN) had been set up under the chairmanship of Edward Osóbka-Morawski. The next day Radio Moscow announced its manifesto, in which the Polish government-in-exile in London was called 'illegal'; legal power was to be given to the Polish-Communist PKWN – the 'Lublin Poles' – instead.[14] At the beginning of August a State Committee of Defence meeting was held at which Stalin said: 'The Polish Committee of National Liberation was created and it will form its own administration. Keep in close touch with this Committee. Do not recognize any other political authority on Polish territory.'[15]

Stalin had created the foundation of a new government, but he still faced a serious obstacle in the AK. He had never come across anything as well-organized or powerful in his sweep through Eastern Europe, and in his eyes these people were bitter enemies who had to be controlled or destroyed. As a result, when the Red Army moved into Poland in the summer of 1944, AK soldiers who revealed themselves were arrested, imprisoned, killed, or press ganged into joining Stalin's own 'Polish Army', or 'Berling's Army'. On 2 August 1944, the day after the uprising started, the Soviet General Rokossovsky released a very detailed order to the units at the front about the disarming of the AK: 'The army units which are part of the Home Army or similar organizations certainly contain German agents and should be immediately disarmed. The officers of those units should be interned and the privates and sub-officers should be sent to a separate reserve battalion in the Polish Army of General Berling.'[16] It was quickly becoming clear that the Soviet sweep through Eastern Europe was bringing a new kind of oppression. At this point, few people in the West really cared.

Just hours before the uprising broke out, Prime Minister

Mikołajczyk travelled to Moscow at Churchill's behest to meet Stalin and to try to iron out an agreement on the post-war borders. The day before he landed, Churchill had made a speech in the House of Commons which he knew would be reported to Stalin, emphasizing that 'gallant Polish divisions are fighting the Germans in our armies'. But he also urged the Poles to be 'friendly to Russia'.

Churchill's words made little difference. Stalin was not particularly interested in meeting the representative of a government he despised; indeed, it was just before Mikołajczyk's arrival that the Soviets announced the agreement recognizing the PKWN. Stalin had told Oskar Lange, the Polish-born NKVD spy who had won Roosevelt's confidence, that Mikołajczyk was a 'man of weak will'. The hapless Prime Minister did not stand a chance.

When Mikołajczyk landed in Moscow on 31 July, things went badly from the start. He was snubbed at the airport, and told that Stalin was too busy to see him. The Soviet Foreign Minister Molotov looked at him and asked, 'Why did you come here?' When he asked if he could see Stalin, Molotov told him that he should talk to the Lublin Poles instead, adding that the London Poles had such a negative view of the Soviet Union that there could be 'no talk of cooperation'.[17]

The first meeting between Mikołajczyk and Stalin was a disaster. News of the uprising had just reached Moscow, but rather than broach the subject straight away, Mikołajczyk droned on about a 'four-point programme' of Polish–Soviet cooperation, only mentioning events in the Polish capital at the very end. When he did get around to it he said, 'I now have to ask you to order that help be given to our units fighting in Warsaw.' Stalin replied that he would give any 'necessary orders', which in fact meant nothing. He then asked Mikołajczyk why he had not mentioned the Lublin Poles in his speech, to which the Polish Premier answered that the London Poles were the true representatives of the Polish people, as it was they 'who for five years had carried on the struggle against Germany'. Stalin was not pleased. When Mikołajczyk finally stopped speaking, Stalin asked coldly, 'Have you finished?'[18]

The second meeting, on 9 August, was warmer, but according to the official translator Vladimir Pavlov, Mikołajczyk was clumsy in his dealings with Stalin. At one point he asserted that the Germans would soon be expelled from Warsaw, and that he would arrive in the capital as the legitimate Polish Prime Minister. The Soviet leader had heard it from the mouth of his enemy: the London Poles meant to return to Poland in triumph after defeating the Germans. Stalin made light of this, chiding Mikołajczyk that his army was too weak to liberate the city: 'What kind of army is that, without artillery, tanks or air force? It doesn't even have enough small arms. In modern warfare such an "army" has no meaning. These are small partisan units, not regular formations. I heard that the Polish government has ordered these units to expel the Germans from Warsaw. I cannot imagine how they are going to accomplish this – their forces are not up to it. As a matter of fact these people do not fight against the Germans but only hide in the woods, as they are incapable of doing anything else.'[19] Even so, Mikołajczyk's statement may have contributed to Stalin's decision not to come to Warsaw's aid. The last thing he wanted was a triumphant return of the London Poles to their capital city.

Mikołajczyk was clearly anxious about the situation in Warsaw, and asked why the 1st Byelorussian Front had halted in front of the city. Stalin had his answer ready. 'The German counter-attack has made further progress into Warsaw impossible,' he said. He gave a detailed description of the attempts to create the bridge-heads and the reasons for the setback. 'At the beginning everything was going well . . . but then the Germans attacked the bridgehead with two tank divisions.' He emphasized that the Germans in

Praga had 'three Panzer divisions plus footsoldiers', and concluded: 'The Red Army will without doubt win and will take over Warsaw, but it will take longer than expected.'[20]

Stalin was well aware of the crimes being committed in the city itself. 'The rising has no chance of success,' he declared. 'The insurgents have no weapons . . . The Germans will kill everybody.' Then he said, 'I am very sorry for those Poles.'[21] In this wistful moment he offered to help, and even undertook to drop a Soviet communications officer in Warsaw to make contact between the AK and Rokossovsky; on 16 August Stalin wrote to Churchill that he had sent the officer as promised. This was probably a lie, as there is no record in the Russian archives of any help being sent to the insurgents in Warsaw in August 1944.[22] Captain Kalugin, a Soviet officer who claimed to have been sent by Stalin to help the AK, and by extension the London Poles, turned out to have been working independently.[23] The Poles and the British sent Stalin precise details of where weapons and supplies could be dropped, but no Soviet planes appeared. Stalin had clearly decided not to help the AK or its leaders in London. 'Please note that the Soviet government does not accept the Polish government with which relations were broken some time ago,' he said. 'The Soviet government maintains relations with the Lublin government with whom we have signed an agreement and whom we help. You need to consider that.'[24]

Mikołajczyk had known before he left for Moscow that an uprising could not succeed without outside help, but he had hoped that the very fact it had broken out would prompt Stalin to send aid. On the contrary, Warsaw became a hostage to the Soviets, with terrible consequences. As Mikołajczyk was about to leave Russia, he had asked Stalin for some words of consolation for the fighting Poles. 'One should distrust words,' Stalin snapped back. 'Deeds are more important than words.'

Looking back at Mikołajczyk's trip to Moscow, it is unlikely that it would ever have taken place had Stalin been aware of the early success of the uprising. Like the Germans, he probably believed that it would last only a few days, and was surprised that the Poles managed to hold out for as long as they did. He had lied to Mikołajczyk on 9 August about sending help because it did not occur to him that the Poles would hang on long enough for the promise to have to be kept. But if Stalin's true aims were difficult to understand in Moscow, they certainly were not in Poland. His intentions became painfully clear on the battlefields outside the Polish capital, and in the brutal, dirty and deadly Battle for Warsaw.

The Battle for Warsaw

The Warsaw Uprising is usually portrayed as an isolated event, as if it were somehow unaffected by the battles which raged around the city in the summer of 1944. In reality, the fate of Warsaw was determined by what was done – and not done – by the armies nearby in what the Germans called 'the Battle for Warsaw'. The uprising was linked to outside events from the very beginning. It started because of the success of Bagration, it was prolonged because of Model's counter-attack, and it was doomed by Stalin's decision to abandon the insurgents and send the bulk of his forces to fight in the Balkans and East Prussia instead. But the starting point was Bagration.

When the Soviets planned their 'great summer offensive' in the early months of 1944 there was no mention of Warsaw – nor indeed of Poland – as it seemed simply too far away. It is clear from the 22 May 1944 plan that Stavka did not believe that the Red Army would get anywhere near the western Byelorussian border by the end of the summer; on the contrary, they thought they would be lucky if the front moved between seventy-five and 160 kilometres, with a possible maximum of two hundred kilometres. The Soviets covered that distance in just ten days. Nobody was more surprised than Stalin himself.

As the Red Army sliced its way through Army Group Centre, Stalin began to realize that he might get not only Vitebsk, Minsk and Lwów, but Warsaw too. The sheer success of Bagration changed the city's fortunes forever. The Vistula Line was mentioned for the first time at Stavka headquarters on 8 June 1944, and an excited Stalin was present at the meeting. The Normandy landings had just begun, which played a role in the direction of the following attacks. So too would the 20 July assassination attempt against Hitler.

The Soviet archives reveal that Stalin knew about the underground activities of the German officers, but his real concern was that they might actually succeed in killing Hitler. In a conversation with the chief of the NKGB Vsevolod Merkulov, Stalin said, 'As long as Hitler is alive the Allies will not sign a separate peace with Germany. But they will sign a peace with a new government.'[25]

On 21 July Stalin told Zhukov that his new task was to take eastern Poland and to incorporate Lwów into the Soviet sphere of influence. He then asked if he could get to the Vistula; Zhukov said yes. He was true to his word. By 23 July the Germans had been pushed out of Lwów, and the 2nd Guards Tank Army was only a hundred kilometres from Warsaw. On 27 July Rokossovsky received the order to attack towards Warsaw, the first time Stavka had actually mentioned the Polish capital by name.

The new plan envisaged taking Warsaw in a giant flanking manoeuvre, seizing bridgeheads to the north and south of the city and trapping the Germans inside the 'cauldron'.[26] Stalin's excitement was palpable. The Germans had not tried to stop the Red Army in any meaningful way that summer, and there was no reason to think they would start now. On 29 July Stalin promoted a beaming Rokossovsky to Marshal as a reward for Bagration, just in time for him to lead a procession into Warsaw as a victorious liberator. At the same time, Zhukov was made the strategic coordinator and leader of three fronts.[27]

It is important to note that with the exception of the eastern bank district of Praga, Warsaw itself was never seen to be of particular importance to Soviet strategic plans. This made it easy to abandon the idea of taking the city when things began to go wrong. Zhukov's aim was always to secure the bridges to the north and south of Warsaw, so that once the Red Army had taken the Balkans it could gather combat strength in central Poland and prepare for the offensive against Berlin. This plan was first drawn up in the summer of 1944, and was indeed put into practice in January 1945. It was also obvious that the chances of gaining the bridges in the city by storming them from the Praga side were virtually nil. The Germans had mined them, and the approach roads were covered by 88mm guns and bunkers; bizarrely, both the Germans and the Poles persisted in the belief that the Soviets would try to enter Warsaw this way, and many histories of the uprising still make the same error. The original plan was that Warsaw would be taken in a huge pincer operation involving six armies.[28] But then everything changed, and Stalin's miraculous summer came to a sudden end thanks to Walter Model.

The Soviets were shocked when the Germans suddenly started slamming into them at Radzymin and Wołomin. The 19th and 5th SS Panzer Divisions devastated the 3rd Tank Corps at Okuniev, marking the beginning of three months of relentless fighting in the 'Battle for Warsaw'; indeed, fighting continued in some pockets until November.

The Battle for Warsaw is now all but forgotten, as it has been overshadowed by the uprising, but in fact the two were interconnected from the beginning. Operationally, the Battle for Warsaw was one of the most complicated of the entire war, and losses in the swathe of territory ringing the Polish capital – not including the actual fight for Praga or the uprising – were staggering. Between 1 and 15 August the 1st Byelorussian Front lost 166,808 dead and wounded, and the 1st Polish Army 13,272. The German 2nd and 9th Armies lost 91,595 men.[29] Equipment losses, too, were high. Between 1 and 10 August the 2nd Tank Army lost 284 tanks, of which 133 could not be repaired; the 2nd Panzer Army Gruppe von Saucken alone destroyed over two hundred Soviet tanks in the first week of August, and nearly five hundred were destroyed in total, making it the third largest tank battle on the Eastern Front, and the largest ever fought on Polish soil. And the fights themselves were terrible.

In Warsaw today, one is often given the impression that the Soviets spent the month of August 1944 lounging on the other side of the Vistula, watching as the uprising was crushed by the Germans. This may have been true in September, but it certainly was not true at the beginning of the previous month. Model's counter-attack made it physically impossible for the Red Army to have been in Warsaw, or even in Praga, until at least the third week of August. Stalin would later use the battles as an excuse not to help Warsaw, but when he told Mikołajczyk that he had encountered problems getting to the city he was not lying. There is little that the Red Army ground troops could have done to help the insurgents when the uprising began.

Model's counter-attack may have come as a surprise, but Red Army superiority was so overwhelming that at first Stalin decided to fight on. Plans were duly drawn up to take Warsaw at a slightly later date.[30] A report written by Rokossovsky and Zhukov on 8 August contains a detailed four-point plan outlining the proposed

Warsaw operation, which proves that both Soviet generals assumed that they would continue the fight for the city once the bridgeheads had been established: 'The front could begin the operation to take Warsaw only after the creation of a bridgehead at the Narew, so only after 10 or even 20 August,' it read. 'The bridgehead in the south must be enlarged and strengthened by a Panzer army to be taken from Koniev, which would be incorporated into the 1st Byelorussian Front. After this is done there should be a break of five days to prepare, and the Warsaw operation should begin on 25 August to get to the line Ciechanów, Płońsk, Sochachew, Skierniewice, Tomaszów, and to finish by taking over Warsaw. Three armies would be needed in the northeast of the pincer together with one Panzer army and even a cavalry army, and in the southern part of the pincer Polish units should be used to march along the western riverbank towards Warsaw.'[31] At that point Stalin agreed. According to the plan of 8 August, Warsaw was to be liberated between 25 August and 1 September. But then he changed his mind.

By mid-August it had become clear that the attack on Warsaw had been abandoned, or at least postponed. Instead of moving forward, the Red Army troops poised to take Praga went onto the defensive. Rokossovsky did not move his right flank on 25 August as planned, and his left flank only took over Praga on 14 September. All discussion at Stavka headquarters about attacks on the German bridgehead to the north of Warsaw ceased until 4 October. There were other signs, too. In the second half of July a pontoon unit with the latest equipment from the American Lend-Lease programme had been incorporated into the 2nd Guards Tank Army, and was meant to move tanks across the Vistula at both the northern and southern bridgeheads. In the first two weeks of August, however, the bridges were removed and sent to the 8th Armia Gvardia at Magnuszew, further proof that Radzievsky's army was not going to cross the river at all.[32] Then, against all military logic, this force was suddenly removed from Warsaw.

There is no written order cancelling the Stavka plans of 8 August. This can only mean one thing: Stalin intervened personally. It is most likely that he abandoned the plans because of the Warsaw Uprising.

It is often said that the Red Army was too weak to carry on the fight into Warsaw, but the evidence does not add up. The fact that Stalin first approved the 8 August plan means that neither he nor his generals believed that the Russian troops were too exhausted to fight for Warsaw. There is no evidence in the Ministry of Defence Archives in Moscow that the offensive had to be stopped for military reasons; on the contrary, the generals assumed that they were going to carry on [33] Lieutenant General Chuikov of the 8th Guards Army told General Popov over the telephone: 'Despite the defence of the Germans my army is able to break through and execute the previously planned march on Warsaw.'[34] In the course of their conversation Chuikov repeatedly said, 'Please inform Rumiancev' – a secret code-name for Stalin. Chuikov wanted to send the message to Stalin that he was able and willing to get to the city.

The Soviets did indeed suffer a temporary setback thanks to Model, but the Germans were still vastly outnumbered, and a mere shadow of the swaggering army that had goose-stepped into Poland in 1939. True, Stalin had concentrated the bulk of his forces in the Balkans and East Prussia, but the remaining units were more than a match for the depleted 9th Army and Gille's SS forces. Von Vormann estimated that the Soviets outnumbered the 9th Army in the first week of August by seven to one foot soldiers, four to one artillery, and seven to one tanks.

Another argument often used to justify Stalin's decision to stop the offensive was that Soviet supply lines were too stretched, as the railways had not yet been repaired. In reality the Soviet railway units, many of them made up of crack NKVD troops, were extremely efficient: thirty-five independent railway brigades, comprising more than 270,000 soldiers, who worked day and night to repair the lines. By 28 July they had already fixed the section between Minsk and Brześć; by 7 August the railway between Lublin and Dęblin had been changed to Russian wide-gauge tracks, and the rail node in Lublin was almost intact. As the Red Army swept through it captured dozens of working locomotives and hundreds of wagons, some still packed with equipment, loot and slave labourers awaiting transport to the Reich. Even von Vormann grumbled that the Soviets were reconstructing the railway lines at such a pace that they had 'already rebuilt the connection between Siedlce and Lublin'.[35] Problems with provisions tended to be the result of the general chaos at the front and complications like looting; the latter problem was so bad that Zhukov was forced to release a special order on 19 July forbidding soldiers from dumping army equipment in favour of 'old cars that take a lot of fuel, furniture, chairs, carpets, beds', which were no use in the fight.[36] By 6 August the 1st Byelorussian Front was being sent 625 wagons of ammunition, 282 cisterns of petrol, a dozen wagons of food and thirteen wagons of vodka.[37]

One controversial point has to do with Soviet control of the air. It is true that the Soviets did not control Warsaw airspace at the beginning of August, but they were already moving field airports into central Poland, and the problem could have quickly been solved. Von Vormann wrote that the Russian planes were 'very close to the front and the 9th Army; there are sixty enemy airfields with 2,400 planes ready to be used . . . the Russians maintain such a strong presence with their fighters that it is impossible even to do reconnaissance'.[38] Again he was exaggerating, but by the end of August the Soviets had thirty-three field airfields no more than 150 kilometres from Warsaw, and good airports at Brześć, Międzyrzecz and Mińsk Mazowiecki. Over a thousand planes were relocated there from Byelorussia, planes which could easily have been used over Warsaw.[39] Stalin might not have wanted to take the city itself, but he certainly could have shot down the German Ju-87D bombers that caused such damage; he could also have knocked out the airports and railway stations, blasted at the Karl mortars, the Panzer trains, multiple-rocket launchers and tanks, and generally caused chaos for the Germans; he could also easily have created an air bridge of weapons and supplies in those early days when the Poles controlled so much of the city. Instead, from 1 August, Soviet aircraft were forbidden to fly over the Polish capital, with the exception of reconnaissance planes from the 16th Air Force; and even then, only the most politically trusted pilots were given permission to do so.[40] Stalin's hostility to the uprising was becoming increasingly clear.

Stalin and the Uprising

We know from his first conversation with Mikołajczyk that Stalin heard about the uprising no later than 2 August. The subject was clearly of great interest to him. Far from being some kind of sideshow, Stalin considered the uprising and its outcome to be of critical importance, so much so that he demanded information about it be put on his desk on a daily basis. Konstanty Tielegin, the NKVD general assigned to Rokossovsky, was ordered by the Secretary of the Political Bureau, General A.S. Stcherbakov, to telephone in reports about Warsaw and about Berling's Army every day. This was unusual, as the Political Commissar at the front usually released only weekly written reports. Stalin was personally managing almost every aspect of the political fight for

Poland, even signing seemingly trivial orders, such as a demand that Zhukov give the PKWN in Lublin a thousand tonnes of seeds, or that General Bulganin give the PKWN five hundred American Lend-Lease cars, 350 motorcycles and 430 trucks.[41] He knew that the uprising was crucial to the political future of Poland, and he intended to use it to his advantage.

Stalin went through a number of phases with regard to the uprising. In the first days, as we can see from his conversation with Mikołajczyk, he believed that the AK was too weak to sustain a fight, and would quickly collapse. When it became clear that the Poles were holding on, he became actively hostile. In this he was greatly influenced by General Tielegin, whose daily reports were unremittingly negative about the AK. Tielegin repeated time and again that the AK was deeply anti-Soviet, and even invented stories to bolster this view. On 20 September he sent Stalin a telegram stating that 'General Bór has released a secret order commanding the AK to take over all units which support the Lublin government,' a claim which was patently untrue. He also underestimated the number of AK fighters, saying at one point that there are 'no more than 1,000 armed AK men in Warsaw'.[42] Tielegin was simply telling his master what he wanted to hear, but it made Stalin even less inclined to try to help the insurgents who had started this '*Lekkomyslna awantura*' – reckless adventure.

The AK's unexpected success did create a problem for Stalin, however. If the Red Army carried on and took Praga immediately, he would be under enormous pressure to offer some assistance to the Poles. It was simpler to stop moving and claim that the very real German counter-offensive had been too strong, then wait and see what would happen. Stalin was now focused on the Balkans, where the 2nd and 3rd Ukrainian Fronts were poised to launch a new strategic offensive; the 4th Guards Cavalry Corps were withdrawn from Warsaw, leaving only the 47th Army at

Praga. Zhukov now argued that Stalin had so weakened the forces around Warsaw that they would no longer be able to break through the German front line at the Vistula; even the Germans noticed a brief respite at the front. John Stieber, a seventeen-year-old Irish-German in the Hermann Göring Division, was amazed when, having been pounded by the Red Army for days at Wołomin, he 'heard the explosions in the city behind me while all was quiet at the Russian lines in front of me'.[43]

The silence was not to last. The Red Army might have assiduously avoided the approaches to Praga itself, but Stalin was determined to clear out the east bank of the Vistula, and terrible fighting continued to rage on the outskirts of Warsaw throughout the uprising. Soviet progress was slow. This was due in part to the fact that Stalin had withdrawn so many troops, but it was also because the Soviets were up against highly mobile, motorized elite troops, including the Viking SS Division under Gille. They were determined not to let the Red Army reach the river. It took over a month for three Soviet infantry armies to advance the mere forty-five kilometres from Mińsk Mazowiecki to Serock, even with the support of a tank corps and an air fleet; progress was even slower as they neared the Vistula.

The battles for the towns and villages around Warsaw that August are little-known now, but they were some of the most ferocious of the war. Places like Ossów, Radzymin, Wołomin, Tłuszcz and Stanisławów were taken and retaken several times, often after brutal close-combat fighting. On 10 August Rokossovsky set about destroying the German 'balcony' that protruded from Stanisławów to the Bug River. General Popov attacked Stanisławów, but the Germans fought back, and the little village was pulverized as it changed hands fifteen times. By 12 August the Soviets were directing long-range artillery along the Wołomin–Tłuszcz line, pounding the area into a dusty hell: 'They lay siege to the terrain with heavy disruptive bombardment,' one German soldier recalled. 'On the road a car burns – black clumps, the stink of burning flesh, blood, rags, sun, dust – and even this soon flies. The first wounded: bloody bandages, open combat-jackets, day-old beard stubble, eyes strangely open, the lightly wounded on their way back. Camouflaged tanks stinking of earth, oil, gas – in front of us a drawn-out crash – the brutal impact of shells fired from enemy heavy artillery units.'[44]

Despite severe shortages of ammunition and fuel, the Germans launched counter-attacks on 15 August; Ossów changed hands six times, and again the soldiers were reduced to hand-to-hand fighting with bayonets and knives. Further north, Ewald Klaptor's Panzer crew had so little ammunition that they were forced to sit in their tank and watch as the Soviets took potshots at them: 'The Russians marched past us in a column on the railway embankment. Everyone up there took what he had – whether a hand grenade or submachine gun – and fired at us. Our crews had to sit by and clench their teeth as they were only allowed to fire in extreme necessity.'[45] SS Hauptsturmführer Flügel was forced to call off tank patrols altogether, as they were down to their last shells: 'Around 1400 we heard an explosion in the direction of my non-operational tank.' They rushed over, only to discover that 'after the crew had fired off the last of its ammunition, they had blown themselves up along with the tank.'[46]

The Germans attempted another counter-attack on 20 August at Radzymin, to hold the road to Białystok, but it was hopeless: 'In front of us a traffic jam . . . a shell howls in over us – Now in front of us, hands grab hold of tucked-in heads, the earth groans, trees are cut down, heat and dust, and then too soon another crash but this time in a cluster of houses out on the left.'[47] The Soviets were simply too strong. Herbert Gille looked out from the balcony of his headquarters in the little palace of Jaktory and saw fighting raging on three sides: 'I witness some of the most intense fighting I have seen in the war,' he said. The 9th Army Daily Reports between 18 and 22 August showed that Gille managed to destroy 249 Soviet tanks and tracked artillery, but this was a mere drop in the ocean: on 29 August he reported to army staff that he was under 'a massive infantry attack in numbers never before witnessed accompanied by waves of air attacks'. The next day the Soviets attacked Radzymin from the north and east. After more Soviet air attacks the Germans took up defensive positions in the now destroyed buildings of the once primarily Jewish town, its 2,500 Jewish inhabitants long since murdered at Treblinka. The pretty church founded by Eleonora Czartoryska was bombarded from all sides as the Germans cowered in the houses next door. A hole was blasted through a wall of the building where Isaac Bashevis Singer had lived, killing a handful of soldiers; the elegant childhood home of the linguist Jan Baudouin de Courtenay was utterly destroyed. After bitter street fighting the Soviets finally pushed the Germans out. Gille and the 4th SS Panzer Corps were slowly forced back to the so-called 'Wet Triangle', the small patch of ground on the east side of the Vistula bordered by the Bug and Narew Rivers. There they fought on fanatically with their backs to the river until 1 November. Over 40,000 Red Army soldiers died in the attack for that tiny area only thirty kilometres north of Warsaw.[48] But despite the heavy fighting all around, the road to Praga had remained uncontested.

On 29 August Stalin decided that the time had come to act, and consulted Stavka about operational plans in the Warsaw area. While still concentrating on the Romanian front, he agreed at last that it was time to take Praga, clear the eastern bank of the Vistula, and then shift onto the defensive at the riverbank. Help for the Warsaw insurgents was not even mentioned.

The suffering of the people of Warsaw was simply irrelevant to Stalin; indeed, he seemed to feel a kind of *Schadenfreude* in their destruction. On 6 August he had said to PKWN activists in Moscow: 'The losses amongst Warsaw are nothing unusual compared to the destruction in Soviet cities like Leningrad and Stalingrad.'[49] Poland's post-war Communist leader Władysław Gomułka recalled: 'Stalin was a ruthless politician, and he understood what a tragedy the destruction of Warsaw was for the Poles . . . but then he would recall how many cities like Warsaw were destroyed in the Soviet Union and how many millions of Soviets died and how many soldiers of the Red Army died.'[50] He was not touched in any way by the suffering of the Poles.

There is no doubt that if had Stalin had given the order, the Red Army could have liberated Praga much earlier – certainly between 10 and 14 August. Thanks to his 'wait and see' policy the attack did not take place until a month later, and even then it was meant only to tidy up the eastern bank of the Vistula, never as an offensive to take Warsaw itself.

The attack on Praga was scheduled to start on 10 September. It was to be carried out by the 70th and 47th Armies, the 8th Guards Tank Corps and the 1st Polish Footsoldiers Division of the Polish Army. The Soviets had 98,000 men in the 47th Army and 49,454 in the 70th Army alone, with a staggering thirty-five tanks per kilometre of the front where the main thrust was to take place. The Germans had about 60,000 men spread out between Serock and Międzylesie, and only one tank per six kilometres of front. The men of the 19th Panzer Division were exhausted and running out of equipment. Their only advantage was that the delayed Soviet attack had given them time to build a formidable defensive line. Praga measured around forty square kilometres, much of it surrounded by railway viaducts, factories and other obstacles. The Germans had used old World War I bunkers and added new anti-tank barriers and minefields. Soviet records of the interrogation of German PoWs state that 'the work to strengthen the fortifications had lasted for weeks with local people forced to labour on the trenches . . . They were connected with one another by ditches in front of which were barbed wire and minefields. Deeper in lay strong machine-gun nests and defence positions connected to one another by ditches and wooden and concrete bunkers. Praga was a fortress.'[51]

It had to be. Hitler had ordered that Warsaw's eastern suburb was to be held to the last man. But what the Führer did not know was that after the fall of Radzymin the morale of the Germans in Praga was crumbling. Panic akin to that last seen in June at the height of Bagration had taken hold. None of them wanted to be trapped in Praga when the Vistula bridges were blown; none of them wanted to fall into the hands of the Soviets.

The sense of panic was not restricted to the soldiers in Praga. The Germans on the western side of Warsaw also believed that the Russians were about to cross the river and attack the city itself. Looting increased enormously – the number of trains leaving Warsaw piled high with stolen Polish goods topped three hundred a day. Von Vormann said: 'We have to take over the west bank of the river as soon as possible to isolate the insurgents . . . It is the most important task for Bach.' He sent a warning to Bach and General Hans Schirmer, who had just replaced Stahel as German commander of the city, to hurry up and get Warsaw under control, so as to safeguard the bridges. 'Not a single Soviet tank shall be allowed to pass!' he yelled down the phone. On 10 September the 9th Army Report read: 'At 8.30 a.m. the enemy attacked the south-eastern part of the bridgehead . . . they may be trying to make a connection with the insurgents.'[52] That same day, the Soviets began to pound Praga itself. The fight for Warsaw's eastern suburb had begun.

The Battle for Praga

By now everything Stalin did in Warsaw had a political angle, even down to the choice of men used in the attack. He deliberately chose to use the 1st Polish Army, so that he could later claim that the Poles had freed themselves. The participation of Polish soldiers was one of the fundamental concepts in Stalin's strategy of Sovietization. It would also play well to the international community.

General Zygmunt Berling was an excellent choice as the leader of this army, precisely because he did not have a Communist background. Stalin watched him for some time before personally appointing him commander of the first unit of the Polish People's Army – the 1st Tadeusz Kościuszko Infantry Division. In March 1944 Stalin released Order No. 292277, incorporating Berling's poorly equipped and poorly trained army into the 1st Ukrainian Army, thereby excusing them from the fights in Byelorussia. Clearly they were more useful to Stalin alive.

Berling became an important political pawn. His background allowed Stalin to argue to doubters in the West that there really was an authentic Polish army in the Soviet Union. For his part, Berling believed that he could save Poland from becoming a Soviet republic if he served Stalin faithfully. He worked hard to stay in the dictator's favour. When Polish soldiers began to collect money for a statue to the victims of Katyń which pointed the finger of guilt at the Germans, Berling kept quiet, despite having nearly been murdered there himself.

Berling's 60,000-strong force, which included a number of women fighters, had been recruited largely from Polish areas that had been forcibly incorporated into the Soviet Union. They were by no means all Communist sympathizers: many had been press-ganged into service against their will.[53] Ludwik Skokuń was in Piława Dolna when the Soviets arrived on 1 May 1944. 'The 1st

Polish Army front was near Sobótka-Janowska and the Russians ordered that the Poles be press-ganged into the Berling Army, the Ukrainians to the Red Army. They took everyone without exception between eighteen and sixty years old. My father dropped me at the station and said, "Go, but come back." ' It took Ludwik ten days to get to the barracks at Sumy, in Ukraine. He had no training to speak of, and was made 'responsible for reconnaissance', which meant being placed 'seven kilometres ahead of the battery; before artillery began to fire we had to check terrain and point out enemy positions'.

They were indoctrinated from the start. 'The fact that the Polish soldier was so politically conscious was linked to the fact that political officers did a very good job from the moment the first division was formed. They organized meetings and published articles about the liberation of Warsaw and how much it would mean for the liberation of the country.[54] For all the Polish symbolism, Berling's Army was always a Soviet operation. Most of the officers were Russian, and a serious language barrier existed until the Political Department forced the Russians to learn some Polish and take lessons in Polish history and geography; it even organized traditional Polish Easter celebrations to integrate officers and men.[55] Relations between Rokossovsky and Berling were strained. Rokossovsky did not deign to mention Berling in the section of his memoirs that dealt with Warsaw; for his part, Berling described Rokossovsky as an alcoholic who deliberately hindered his attempts to liberate the city.[56]

Such differences were pushed aside on the eve of the Praga battle. Over the previous weeks groups of Soviet soldiers and officers who had been in 'the great battles of Moscow and Stalingrad' had come to speak to Berling's men about the coming victory: 'These speeches by the Soviets increased the fighting spirit of the Poles and imbued them with a sense of power. The soldiers were secure in the knowledge that they would win.' Posters and cards carried pictures of German helmets with bullet holes in them, or of cheering women and children waving flowers. 'Victory is ours!' they read. The talks were all about the inevitable triumph of the Red Army in the coming liberation of Poland: 'Corporal Siwicki told our group: "Poland will be a country of happy people because we are creating this country on our own." '[57] The greatest honour came when Marshal Rokossovsky visited the 1st and 3rd Footsoldiers Divisions and gave a morale-boosting speech. 'So, are we going to take Praga?' he yelled. 'Yes sir!' came the raucous reply.

The 1st Polish Army at Praga counted more than 6,000 soldiers, with 102 tanks and sixty-six fighter planes. One Polish soldier recalled: 'At a quarter past eleven all field radio stations and telephones released the order to prepare artillery fire. At the same time we heard both the Polish and the Soviet batteries: "*Za Warszawę! Ogon!*" – "For Warsaw! Fire!" – and hundreds of cannons blasted . . . One of the Polish leaders was mortally wounded. His last words were "Go for it!" '

An immense artillery barrage rained down on the German lines. Katyusha rockets began firing, the signal for the attack to begin. Sappers had cut paths through the barbed wire and destroyed minefields the night before; now the tanks began to roll forward along the marked trails, supported by cannon and footsoldiers. Morale was high, and the men of the 1st Footsoldiers Division chanted, 'We, the 1st, will enter Praga first!'

The people of Praga had heard the sound of the Soviet guns moving ever closer in the preceding weeks, and were prepared for an attack, but the sheer scale of the artillery barrage came as a surprise. Civilians ran to the cellars as the ground shuddered, entire buildings moved and glass broke in the windows. The German soldiers seemed equally frightened. Gustav Börg recalled:

'An unending thunder can already be heard – it increases with every kilometre, soon houses are shaking.' Then the guns. 'Gigantic flames appear over the eastern horizon, like a forest bending before a storm. A curtain of shells rush up towards the sky. It has begun.'[58]

The 47th Army, with the Polish 1st Infantry Division under General W. Bewziuk and the 70th Army, attacked the German 70th Grenadiers Regiment head on, and quickly broke the first line of defence. By 11 September the Poles had crossed the second line, and by the 12th they had severely mauled the 19th Armoured Division. The final assault, on 13 September, saw Polish units attack the central part of Praga, reaching Listopada 11 just before midnight.

The civilians trapped in Warsaw could not believe that the Germans were being pushed out so easily, and feared reprisals or worse. Bożena Grzybowska was in her house in the elegant district of Saska Kępa when the Germans set up their guns on the pavement outside on 10 September.[59] 'We sat in the basement listening to bullets and bombs, and suddenly heard an explosion; a cloud of dust came, and the house literally sank. The Germans had blown up the radio station at Grochowska Street.' The bombing continued until 13 September, when the Germans parked a Tiger tank by their house. 'Soviet artillery fired all night, and the Germans answered.' But by morning the German troops were panicking. 'We could see small groups of Germans running towards the river in helmets . . . they were fleeing. The artillery stopped at around 6 a.m. on 14 September. We went out in front of the house and could not see any Germans. I cannot say how touched we were when we realized that they had gone . . . the street was full of shrapnel, broken glass, unexploded bombs, and in the morning sun we could see a young Soviet soldier sitting on the pavement with his rucksack. Groups of excited people stood around him trying to give him food and cigarettes and wanted to talk, but he did not react – he fell asleep, he was so tired because of the fighting – he fell asleep as soon as he sat down.'[60]

The Germans had quickly realized that it would be impossible to defend the district with only one Panzer division. They were short of everything – ammunition, guns, and above all infantry to man positions against the massive combat forces storming Praga. Dozens of Germans were spotted scrambling to get to the river, where fierce fighting raged at the bridgeheads. Fighting broke out at the Zoological Gardens, where soldiers of both sides raced around the animal cages in bloody close-combat fighting. The many Jews who had been hidden there by the director of the zoo were terrified lest they be discovered at the last moment, but they were lucky. The Germans were intent on only one thing – getting across the bridges before they were blown up.

Von Vormann reported the desperate situation in Praga to Army Group Centre, and Reinhardt asked for permission to withdraw. Hitler refused. On 13 September Vormann was told to form a new defence line from Bródno to Marki with the 19th Panzer Division, the 73rd Infantry Division and the Hungarian 1st Cavalry Division, but the Germans knew that this order was ridiculous – by now even the Soviets were commenting on the number of enemy soldiers dropping their gear and running across the bridges.[61] Letters taken from PoWs captured in Praga mirrored this pessimism. One, sent to Obergefreiter Kuhlmann from his relatives in Bremen, read: 'The war will pass, the most important for you is to stay alive . . . just stay alive.' Grenadier Otto Kohlwegen wrote an ironical letter to his family: 'The victorious end is coming and very soon I will be at home.'[62] 9th Army headquarters sniped that the 73rd Infantry Division had not shown the correct 'Sturm spirit' during the fighting, but how could they? Gösta Borg remembered how in those last days 'the forces shrank together, equipment complements were worn down, divisions most often numbered a combat strength cf no more than a thousand men. The violent pressure left no time for a new tactic. Moreover, the high command was unwiLing to admit that the Soviet massive-assault tactical strategy caLed for a re-evaluation of the war's fundamental conditions.'[53] As they swarmed towards the bridges, many German troops realized that the Vistula was lost, and so too was the war.

The new leader of Army Group Centre, General Reinhardt, decided that the 4th SS Panzer Company, the 19th Panzer Division and the 1st Hungarian Cavalry Division could abandon Praga. Amidst scenes of utter chaos, those soldiers still in the area dumped everything and ran as fast as they could to get to the bridges. By 15 September all of Praga was in Soviet hands.

The units of the 1st Army were praised, and the Kościuszko Division was singled out for its bravery. General Lieutenant Czykin, Chief of the Political Department of the 1st Byelorussian Front, wrote on 15 September: 'In the fights for Praga the 1st Division of Berling's Army, led by Colonel Bewzyuk, fought from the first to the final moment of the attack . . . They all wanted to be the first to enter Praga . . . The soldiers' mood was very battle-hungry and optimistic. Officers and soldiers constantly repeat that no matter the cost they want to be the first to enter Warsaw. It was such a great unit that they were able to fight against Wehrmacht and SS units.'[64] Between 10 and 15 September alone the 47th and 70th Armies lost around 7,000 men; the Polish 1st Infantry Division lost 353 dead, 1,406 wounded and 109 missing. The Germans lost around 8,500 men and fifty-five tanks, many of which were simply abandoned in the rush to leave.

For the Germans there could be no more potent symbol of their humiliating defeat than the destruction cf the huge bridges on the Vistula on 13 September. The great Poniatowski Bridge was blown up at 4 p.m., after a first attempt had been foiled by damaged cables. The two railway bridges went up in the evening; the Kierbedź Bridge was blown up at midnight. Rokossovsky had tried to get his troops to the bridges, but he was too late. He, along with Berling's superior, the Polish army's chief commander General Michał Rola-Żymierski, and the Soviet representative of the PKWN General Bulganin, went to an observation point in Praga to see the historic sight for themselves. Afterwards he was prompted to write that 'the best moment to have started the uprising would have been during this moment of the Soviet offensive'.[65] Stalin was delighted that Praga had been liberated. In the Daily Report *Rozkazy Dzienny Stalina* (Stalin's Order), the units which had participated were given permission to call themselves '*Praskie*' – from 'Praga'. A 224-cannon salute was fired in Red Square to honour 'the heroic units of the 1st Byelorussian Front including those of the 1st Polish Army, led by General Lieutenant Berling'.[66] On 16 September an article in *Pravda* stated that 'the soldiers of Tadeusz Kościuszko's division fought arm in arm with soldiers from Riazan, Volgograd and Irkutsk!'[67] In his report given to members of PKWN on 15 September Rokossovsky repeated again that the 'enthusiasm of the soldiers was enormous'.

There was euphoria on the streets of Praga when the civilians realized that the Germans had gone. They raced out of their homes, laughing, crying and embracing one another. 'There was a joyful atmosphere, red-and-white, and also red flags appeared on the buildings.' On that first night the Soviet and Polish soldiers sang and danced together; bonfires were lit and copious amounts of vodka downed in celebration. But there were ominous signs, too. On 15 September Rola-Żymierski announced: 'Soldiers! The Tadeusz Kościuszko Division has, together with our brothers from the Red Army, in the early morning of 14 September, by means of storming, captured an entire suburb of our city – Praga! . . .

On the other side of the Vistula, in bloody flames of fire, there burn entire districts of our capital city. In Warsaw everyone struggles . . . They fight and curse the London-based government for this premature uprising.'[58]

It was soon clear that the Soviets had not brought liberation in any true sense of the word. The NKVD quickly took over the German barracks at Rembertów, turning the forbidding building into their headquarters and setting up Special Camp No. 10, for processing anyone suspected of being in the AK. They began to round up 'suspicious Poles' immediately.[69] One wounded AK soldier, Zbigniew Rylski, managed to swim across the Vistula on the night of 23–24 September despite his injuries, and was sent to the military hospital in Otwock. 'A few days there was enough to see that our [AK] boys were being transported away in an unknown direction. A doctor advised us to run away in the middle of the night.' When another AK soldier got to Praga he was struck by the calm, and by the 'green trees and late summer flowers in the gardens'. He was taken to a field station where he was forced to give up his gun. 'I was sent to the hospital of the Polish 1st Army in Anin which was set up in some villas and tents.' One of Berling's soldiers warned him: 'AK soldiers were arrested in Lwów, and it may happen in Warsaw.'[70] He eventually joined Berling's Army and fought on to Berlin.

The Fall of Czerniaków

'I think that it is pretty obvious,' Hitler complained on 31 August, 'that this war is no fun for me. I've been cut off from the world for five years. I've not been to a theatre, a concert or a film. I have only one job in life, to carry on this fight, because I know that if there's not an iron will behind it, the battle cannot be won.'[71] Two weeks later, with the fall of Praga, the 'iron will' had received another blow.

Hitler had dictated that Praga be held 'to the last man', and he was livid when it was taken. He found his scapegoat in von Vormann. 'Since 1 August we have lost 9,000 men,' Vormann had complained to Reinhardt the day before. 'How can the army possibly maintain Warsaw and face the battles to come?' This 'defeatist talk' was reported to Hitler, who ranted that Vormann was 'incompetent' and lack the necessary 'will' to fight. General Wilhelm Burgdorf listened to the anti-Vormann tirade in the Wolfsschanze before being sent off into the night to dismiss von Vormann personally on Hitler's behalf, effective immediately. On 20 September, General Smilo Freiherr von Lüttwitz took over as the new head of the 9th Army.

The Germans in Warsaw had watched with horror as the Soviets had moved into Praga. Von dem Bach was deeply depressed: 'I must get Warsaw before the Bolsheviks,' he scribbled in his diary. He worried for his future. Rumours reached him that he was being criticized at the highest level for not having taken Warsaw. 'Praga is lost,' he wrote, 'so we fight like in Kovel, in every direction. And Praga hangs like a millstone around our necks.' It was, he wrote, a '*Himmelfahrtskommando*'.[72]

The appointment of Lüttwitz did not bode well for von dem Bach. Lüttwitz hated Himmler and loathed von dem Bach, calling his Korpsgruppe a '*gefährlich schwachen Fremdkörper*' – a dangerous, weak foreign body – at the Vistula front. Reinhardt agreed. He slapped Bach on the wrist for not taking the riverbank, and implied that neither he nor Himmler was fit to lead soldiers in battle. Lüttwitz told Bach he would take over defence of the Vistula line himself; Bach was told to hurry up and clear the district of Czerniaków, which was crucial because it lay along the riverbank to the south of the Old Town. By controlling this area the Poles controlled the bridgehead where the Soviets would land. It had to be taken, and quickly.

In theory this should not have been too difficult. Czerniaków might have been an old district – Solec, or 'Salt', Street was named after the medieval salt warehouses that had once stood there – but it was not a natural fortress like the Old Town, laid out as it was with wide streets and avenues dotted with large apartment houses, factories, schools and hospitals. Little had happened in Czerniaków and the enclave of Powiśle in August, and the civilians there had been spared the worst of the bombing; most were still even able to use the upper storeys of their apartment buildings. But that was all about to change. Czerniaków was now the only territory standing between the Soviets and the rest of Warsaw. The Germans were determined to crush the insurgents there before the Soviets could cross the river, while the Poles were determined to hang on until their allies arrived. This dramatic double race against the clock would lead to some of the most fierce and vicious fighting of the entire uprising.

Czerniaków was well defended, although the AK suffered from a severe shortage of ammunition. The southern sector was held by the 'Kryński' Battalion, with its front line at Przemysłowa Street, while the north-central districts were held by the 'Broda' and 'Czata' Battalions. The six hundred well-trained and experienced troops were joined by five hundred of Radosław's men, including soldiers from 'Kedyw' and 'Parasol' straight from the battles in the Old Town, by now the most experienced street-fighters in Warsaw.

Piotr Stachiewicz, one of Radosław's men, had left the Old Town through the sewers and arrived in Czerniaków on 4 September. He and his colleagues from the 'Parasol' Battalion were amazed to find the district intact, with people living almost normal lives. He moved into quarters at Zagórna Street as part of a company that reported to Captain Ryszard Białous ('Jerzy'), commander of the 'Zośka' Battalion. After the deprivations of the

Old Town, Czerniaków seemed like the height of luxury: Stachiewicz was able to take a bath for the first time since leaving the sewers. Radosław set up his headquarters at Okrąg 2 as the men dug tunnels between buildings, set up barricades and even established a hospital in the massive PKO Savings Bank building. In those first days the atmosphere was relaxed, even jovial. Food of a kind was still available: Stachiewicz remembered that on his first night they enjoyed a feast of roasted horse. Zbigniew Rylski went to the basements where the civilians were preparing food: 'One old lady was looking for her cat. Finally everyone sat down to eat, and the food was fantastic – bouillon and pieces of meat out of a fairytale. She was still looking for her cat. We had eaten it.'[73] Stanisław Likiernik spent the first days in Czerniaków 'resting'.

But the calm did not last. After taking Powiśle the Germans started to move their firepower towards Czerniaków even before the fall of Praga. Mortars, rocket launchers, heavy machine guns, even the Karl mortar, were turned on the little patch of ground by the river. On 11 September a massive barrage rained down on the AK soldiers and the hapless civilians, crushing buildings and churning up gardens and the sand along the river. The German attack began in earnest the following day. Von dem Bach ordered Dirlewanger in from the north, with orders to seize as much territory as he could as quickly as possible. He reverted to his old methods. The Anglo-American announcement that the AK troops were to be treated as part of the regular Polish army and protected by the Geneva Convention was ignored; as Stanisław Likiernik put it, 'This new exalted status proved illusory, at least in Czerniaków.'[74] All young men and 'suspicious' women were shot, along with hundreds of civilians who got in the way; as in Wola and the Old Town, Dirlewanger's troops drank, looted, raped and murdered their way through the district.

The Germans vastly outnumbered the AK in Czerniaków. Dirlewanger alone had two battalions of his own men, plus two Azeri battalions of 507 men, a battalion of the Eastern Muslim Regiment of 575 men, the Walter Police Battalion with five 20mm anti-aircraft guns, and two tank companies – in all around 2,500 men. Kampfgruppe Rodewald, which was sent in from the west, and Kampfgruppe Schaper, which went in under General Rohr from the south, had a combined force of 2,000 men.

The Germans were determined to clear the area quickly. Dirlewanger pushed his men forward into the Czarniakowski port, the gasworks on Ludna Street and the St Lazarus hospital on Książęca Street. By the end of the day he had surrounded the district, cutting it off from the city centre and trapping those civilians who had not managed to flee. Another attack followed the next day, with the German infantry supported by two tanks and two armoured cars. The AK were forced back to the Social Insurance Office building, and pushed out of the post office. Dirlewanger took the burned-out St Lazarus hospital, massacring the patients he found there, and then attacked the gasworks. It was then that the Vistula bridges were blown. That could only mean one thing: the Soviets had taken Praga.

'Zojda called me over,' one AK soldier recalled. ' "Come and see! You won't see anything like this for the rest of your life!" The columns of the Poniatowski Bridge, around three hundred metres from our positions, are moving – suddenly they fall into the river with a loud crashing sound.'[75] An excited Włodzimierz Rosłoniec climbed up onto the roof of the 'Peking' building. 'People are standing around. And then a large explosion. A fountain of water shoots high up in the Vistula and then, suddenly, the central part of the Poniatowski Bridge crashes into the water.'[76] Jan Rosner also saw the bridges disappear. 'The Russians have broken through their front!' he wrote. The sight thrilled Bór, too, who had been contemplating surrender to the Germans, plans which were now put on hold. A surge of optimism and hope coursed through the AK. 9th Army counter-intelligence reported: 'The will to fight in the AK has found renewed strength because of the Red Army in Praga and they hope for help.'[77]

The news that Praga had fallen at last was greeted in Czerniaków with jubilation. The AK soldiers now began to fight with a dogged determination impressive even by the standards set in the Old Town. They improved their barricades, put snipers on the rooftops and attacked from the deep trenches hurriedly dug between crucial buildings. Despite their massive numerical superiority, the Germans' attack ground to a halt.

Lüttwitz had not expected this. On 14 September he telephoned General Rohr to reprimand him for the delay, and ordered an attack on the riverbank that night. Rohr told him it was impossible under the circumstances, and General Staedke asked for permission to wait until reinforcements arrived.[78] Lüttwitz reluctantly agreed. The 146th Panzer Grenadier Unit, which attacked on 15 September, proved no match for the AK, and at 9.35 that evening General Vokel was forced to report that 'despite heavy fighting the small buildings and factories are not yet in our hands'. Dirlewanger had suffered heavy losses, and had only managed to take over the small factory area next to Wilanowska Street.[79]

The fighting also took a heavy toll on the AK. One hundred and forty people were lost from 'Parasol' alone: 'Mirsky killed, Luty killed, Adjutant Lt. Kaktus killed.' A high number of casualties were women – nurses, runners and scouts: 'Runners Nina, Janina, Rena, Margoszata died 14 September,' one list read.[80] Despite the sheer tenacity of his troops, Radosław had no choice but to shorten his line and pull his forces back towards the river. The Poles gathered in Ludna Street, on the corner of Solec and at Wilanowska Street, which led to the riverbank. A network of deep tunnels was dug between key buildings, but the Germans bombed them mercilessly. Ludna 7 was hit, and the entire building caved in, burying over fifty people in the rubble; the Poles worked all night to put out the fires but there was no water and the victims perished. The Germans put the massive residential buildings at Solec 20, 20A and 22 under heavy fire, but as they moved in for the attack the Poles, who had not yet fired due to lack of ammunition, suddenly began to shoot out of the windows. The Germans retreated in a panic. Fighting carried on late into the night. The gardens at Szalkowa, near the viaduct of the Poniatowski Bridge, were filled with ripe fruit, tomatoes and vegetables, but lay in no man's land. At night Germans and Poles crept out to gather food, hoping not to bump into one another in the darkness; from time to time bullets ripped through the gardens.

By 14 September Radosław had moved most of his forces to the area by the river, while the defence of the riverbank itself fell to Jerzy's battalion. Captain 'Motyl's units were sent to control Okrąg and Ludna; the remains of the 'Kryński' Battalion were to be in charge of Zagórna and Czerniaków. The Poles took up positions in sturdy buildings, including the garages and the cork factory at the back of Ludna and Solec Streets; the Germans worked through the night, drilling into basements and roofs in preparation for the next attack. Radosław was under heavy fire: 'I lost all officers,' he wrote. 'After three days there are around one hundred dead, three hundred wounded, and I am able to maintain my position only because in the last three days we attacked at night – we have twenty PoWs* although this is not very helpful. We are exhausted, cut off and have no help. We have about ten bullets for each machine gun, twenty for p.m. [submachine guns] and 50–100 for LKM [light

---

* Members of a Wehrmacht battalion from Germany.

machine guns] so we can maintain our position until morning and then there will be a tragedy – or comedy?'

The next day was worse. 'The German attacks are stronger and stronger and the fact that we survived today I can only describe as a miracle. I have about 150 exhausted people . . . the fact that we are here without help, ammunition or connection with the outside world has a very bad effect on morale . . . The Germans are penetrating very deeply. They are trying to cut me off from the river. They are putting pressure from the western area. Today on one section I had eight attacks, each supported by four tanks and a hurricane fire of mortars and the Luftwaffe . . . I will wait for a miracle or the fact that tanks will kill the rest of my people.' Despite a few half-hearted attempts to reach them from the city centre, Radosław's group and the other units trapped in Czerniaków were essentially left to fend for themselves in what seemed a hopeless situation.

The German attacks became ever more ferocious. Heavy mortar shells landed on the strongholds at Solec, and the Germans attacked houses in Ludna. They brought three tanks and around 150 infantry up to the PKO building; the AK repelled a number of assaults. 'A tank opened fire and the Germans attacked under its cover . . . Kryst, posted on the first-floor balcony, greeted them with grenades. Several Germans fell and the rest retreated. A body remained lying in the middle of the street. At great risk and against my explicit orders, one of our girls, Irys, crawled out of the cellar window to get his rifle and ammunition. She was in luck.'[81] Despite such bravery, the Poles were too weak to fight back. Radosław knew that without help he and his men would be pushed into the Vistula. In desperation he sent a messenger across the river begging the 1st Polish Army to come to his aid. And then, everything seemed to change.

The first glimmer of hope had come on 14 September, when

Soviet planes had appeared in the sky above their heads. Dogfights broke out between Soviet and German fighters, the people of Warsaw unable to believe their eyes as the planes darted through the sky. Then Soviet aircraft began to fly low over the city, and container after container tumbled out of them. Fifty-kilo sacks were dropped from the Po-2 planes called 'terkotki' or 'Kukuruzniks', which sounded 'like motorcycles': between 14 and 28 September the Russians dropped fifty tonnes of supplies. The official report sent to Stalin by Rokossovsky on 2 October stated that the total number of flights was 2,435, and on paper the amount of supplies dropped to the Poles on the ground was impressive: 'One artillery piece, 1,378 machine pistols, 159 mortars, 505 anti-armour rifles, 170 carbines, 522 short carbines, 57,640 rounds of ammunition for anti-armour rifles, 1,312,600 pieces of ammunition for carbines, 1,360,984 rounds of ammunition, 75,000 rounds of ammunition (7.5 and 7.7mm), 260,600 rounds of ammunition for Mausers, 312,760 pieces of parabellum ammunition, 18,428 hand grenades, 18,270 German hand grenades, 515 kilos of medical supplies, ten field telephones, 9,600 metres of telephone cable, one field telephone station, ten batteries for field telephones, twenty-two batteries, 126,681 kilograms of foodstuffs.' They even dropped American tinned meat.[82]

But there was a problem. The Soviets did not use parachutes, claiming that they made the drops too inaccurate, and as a result most of the supplies were destroyed upon landing. One AK soldier made eye contact with the pilot who dropped a load next to him on the shore in Czerniaków. It was filled with 'kasza', or buckwheat, but the canister broke, and the food became mixed with sand. Janusz Zawondy watched as a 'beautiful new Soviet long-barrelled anti-tank rifle bent into a pretzel when it hit the ground'. Bór criticized the drops, but in reality the use of parachutes would have made little difference. Constant German anti-aircraft fire made it extremely difficult for the Soviet planes to fly low over Warsaw, and the area then held by the AK was so small that had parachutes been used much of the matériel would have drifted into German hands anyway. The drops did boost morale among both the AK and civilians, however, and rekindled hope that the Soviets were now intent on helping them.[83]

The next apparent miracle happened as a result of Radosław's desperate appeal for help on 14 September. The next day, to his surprise, an officer from the Polish 3rd Infantry Division crossed the river, turned up at his headquarters and informed him that troops from Berling's Army would begin to cross the Vistula that very night. A relieved Radosław ordered his men to redouble their efforts to protect the bridgehead so the soldiers could land unimpeded.

The soldiers of the 3rd Infantry Division – the least accomplished of the Berling units – had only just arrived in Praga when they received orders that they were to cross the river and fight for their countrymen on the west bank of the river. Morale was high; all were keen to help liberate their capital. Bożena Grzybowska remembered talking to the Berling troops who had been billeted in her family's house in Praga: 'People were friendly and said goodbye to them and even looked with pity on the boys who were going to die.'

At 4.30 a.m. on 16 September, three hundred soldiers of the 3rd Infantry Division began to cross the river in small NLP boats.[84] They brought much-needed equipment with them: fourteen machine guns, sixteen anti-tank rifles, five anti-tank guns and eight mortars. When they landed they met the delighted AK forces at Solec and Okrąg Streets. There was an 'instant feeling of brotherhood'; nobody seemed to care that one group was Soviet and the other from the AK; they were all in the fight together. Tadeusz Targoński crossed in the first landing party. 'When we got near the shore we jumped into the water up to our knees to find shelter. The lads from the uprising gave us a lot of help. They were much more poised than we were.' The AK were stunned to find women fighters in the group. 'I remember a beautiful, heroic woman of the Berling Army, Janina Błaszczak, who led soldiers into battle,' one recalled, referring to a Second Lieutenant Commander of 3rd Romuald Traugutt Mortar Company. Andrzej Wolski ('Jur') of 'Zośka' Battalion recalled the first contact with her: 'Soldiers, major officer, the captain of artillery reconnaissance, two radio stations, telephonists, lads with Russian automatic pistols. And loads of ammunition. And the girl – the officer.'[85] Radosław greeted the Berling troops, confident that they were the advance party of a major offensive into Warsaw. Włodzimierz Rosłoniec said that the arrival of the 'Soviet Poles' gave the AK men 'new hope'.

On 16 September another nine hundred troops crossed the river, followed the next night by 1,200 more. But things had already started to go wrong. The Germans had been waiting for a general offensive across the Vistula.[86] They failed to spot the first crossing at night, but by dawn they were on full alert. Artillery was quickly brought up, and soon the river bubbled and splashed with falling bullets and mortar shells. General Stanisław Komornicki watched as the Germans massacred the Berling men crossing on the second day: 'From the riverside escarpment you can see by the glow of the fire boats pushing off on the other side of the river. After a while the water is illuminated by the light of German missiles . . . German mortars burst and splash into the water sending fountains jetting high into the air. The glare of searchlights moves over the water showing soldiers desperately struggling to overcome the currents. Almost every boat is found by a searchlight. Heavy machine guns and cannon spray them with bullets. One hears the dreadful cries of injured men. Wrecked boats plunge into the depths. The heads of men swimming emerge here and there. Only one boat reaches the bank we are waiting on. It is bullet-ridden and starts sinking.'

By the morning of the 17th the Germans were in control. The 9th Army Daily Report read: 'From midnight we have an attempt at a Soviet landing to the centre of the *"Banditen"* defence . . . Thanks to the immediate use of strong fire from heavy weapons at the correct moment, which was already known, the enemy could not force the river.'[87]

The AK in Czerniaków were worried. The river crossing seemed amateurish. The Soviet artillery on the east side of river had for the most part remained silent; the Russians had not even attempted to attack the German Stukas bombing the riverbank where the Berling troops were trying to land. Something felt wrong. After the initial successful landing, the Germans killed or injured most of the Soviet troops who attempted to cross the river; the seriously wounded were taken to the hospital at Zagórna 9, where they were later murdered by the SS.

Those few who made it across the Vistula uninjured turned out to be totally unprepared for conditions in Czerniaków. On 17 September Włodzimierz Rosłoniec was ordered to conduct sixty of Berling's soldiers to his superior, Lieutenant 'Bicz' (Whip). They were 'well-meaning', he said, but it was clear that they were not going to be able to stop Dirlewanger and the German onslaught. Mieczysław Nitecki recalled meeting the Berling soldiers for the first time: 'The meeting was very heartfelt and they apologized many times for coming to our aid so late . . . Compared to us they were really well-armed – to the teeth . . . [but] they had no experience in street fighting. Very often, despite their heroism, they were wounded or killed.'[88] Tadeusz Targoński recalled that they were brave, but were not used to the conditions in the city. They were essentially boys from remote villages for

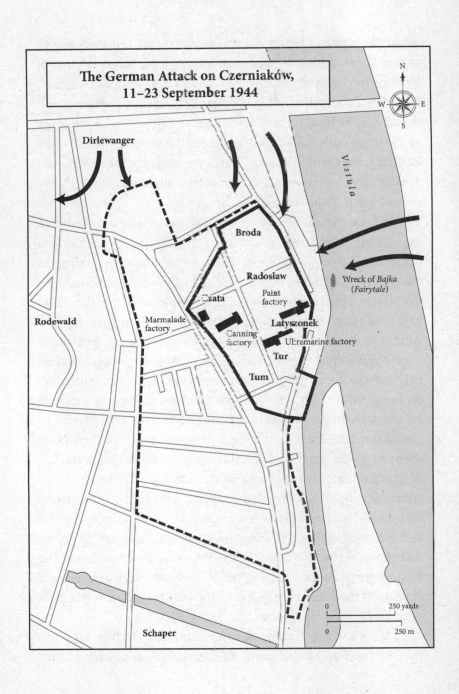

The German Attack on Czerniaków,
11–23 September 1944

Dirlewanger

Vistula

Broda

Radosław

Czata

Paint
factory

Marmalade
factory

Canning
factory

Latyszonek

Ultramarine factory

Wreck of *Bajka*
(*Fairytale*)

Rodewald

Tur

Tum

Schaper

0		250 yards
0		250 m

whom the 'maze of rooms, staircases, basements and attics as well as top-floor extensions was a novelty'. They had experience of fighting in the open, not in the *Rattenkrieg* of urban warfare. Stanisław Likiernik recalled meeting 'several men speaking with the characteristic accents of eastern Poland [who] had no training in close urban combat and sustained enormous losses.'[89] The Berling troops fought bravely, but it was clear that they were not going to make a difference to the overall situation.

Just when hope seemed to be fading once again, another 'miracle' happened. On 18 September Warsawians looked into the sky and could not believe their eyes. Dozens of American planes were flying high above them, silver fuselages glinting in the sun. As parachutes began to drift down people came out into the streets, shouting with joy in the belief that at last the Allies had sent Polish paratroopers to their rescue. On that day 117 American Boeing B-17 'Flying Fortresses' dropped 1,284 packages over Warsaw. But it was another false dawn. The Poles watched helplessly as the canisters drifted gently to the ground, more than 80 per cent of them out of reach. The Germans got a welcome boost of weapons, medical supplies and food – even Hershey's chocolate. Likiernik saw 'several containers which had been dropped several days back by Allied planes. There they were, full of ammunition, dressings and food rations, with parachutes still attached – our badly needed supplies, delivered to the wrong address.'[90] This latest disappointment led to even greater depression amongst the tired and battered people of Warsaw. The hope that more aid would come in the following days sustained the fighters for a short time, but before long lethargy and despair enveloped the bunkers once more. The false hope had, it was said, been worse than no hope at all.

The Soviet and American drops and the Berling landings spurred the Germans to finish off Czerniaków as quickly as they could. On 18 September they attacked Okrąg 2, a Goliath destroying the front of the building with an enormous crashing sound. Dozens of people were buried. The Germans pushed in from all directions, taking over the tinned-meat factory and the crane factory behind Wilanowska Street. When the dust had settled, people who had been hiding started to run away in panic, flattening themselves into ditches or crawling through basement tunnels and passages. The slightly wounded were moved to the ground floor at Wilanowska 12 as the AK fought for the building's stairs, hall and cellars. The basement was full of wounded soldiers and civilians. The Germans lobbed in grenades, then shot those who were still alive where they lay.[91]

That night the Germans attacked the cork factory, the ultra-marine factory and the Społem food warehouses next door. Sub-units of 'Czata 49' fought alongside Berling's men to defend the ultramarine factory; the Dirlewanger men set sulphur on fire and fanned the fumes towards the insurgents. 'The soldiers quickly dug a ditch so the burning sulphur flowed into the river . . . instead of forcing the Poles out the stench pushed the Germans from the factory instead.'[92]

By 19 September the Dirlewanger Brigade, bolstered by tanks and artillery, had started to make progress again. Mieczysław Nitecki remembered there were six Berling soldiers in his group. 'After the fights at Okrąg between 17 and 19 September only one officer and four soldiers from the AK and two soldiers from Berling's Army were left.'[93] Dirlewanger attacked the trenches and buildings held by the men of 'Czata 49' and 'Broda 53'; after vicious fighting he reached Wilanowska Street.

Trapped civilians sat petrified with terror in the cellars as the fighting raged around them. On 18–19 September the Germans closed in. Nurse Lidia Kowalczyk-Strzelecka ('Akne') was with her husband, who had been shot in the lung. They had been married in a romantic ceremony in the Old Town on 2 August, but it seemed a lifetime ago. They were on the third floor of a burning house: 'smoke already covered the floor and I feared he would choke. I knew there were civilians in the basement and went to the cellar to get four men to move him. Nobody helped. I didn't have a choice but to force them at gunpoint.'[94]

On 19 September Berling's Army began to retreat back across the river. Radosław, who had been wounded, realized that the situation was hopeless, and ordered those of his troops who were able to walk to join him in an escape through the sewers. He had the others moved to the riverbank, in the hope that the boats coming to collect Berling's men would take them too.

A nurse from 'Parasol' saw Radosław just before the retreat. 'He was lying in a huge room deep in one of the basements. We had managed to get a lot of bedding from the German district. Radosław ordered that because of the terrible conditions and the lack of ammunition all wounded patients who could not move themselves be taken by medical personnel to the riverbank so that they could try to get across to Saska Kępa, or go via the sewers to Mokotów.[95] He ordered the medical staff 'to carry the wounded to the river and load them onto the boats'. When Włodzimierz Rosłoniec heard that Radosław had decided to leave through the sewers, he was shocked: 'I did not want to believe it, as it meant that Czerniaków must soon fall.'

Radosław moved out quickly. Maria Stypułkowska was in the group of two hundred men and women who left Czerniaków that night. 'We went out onto the road. On one side they were raking the bridge from the Sejm Hill, and on the other side they were firing from Praga. Never in my life was I so scared. The explosions came every few minutes, after which the Vistula was all lit up by the rockets which dropped on us, and also by the flares.' She was grateful to get to the sewers, which would take her to safety: 'We entered the storm drain on the morning of 20 September. The journey lasted a few hours, starting at 12.30 a.m. on 20 September and ending at 6 p.m. that day.' For his part Mieczysław Nitecki found the sewers a terrible ordeal. The Germans had tried to disrupt the traffic underground: 'It was very difficult to pass through, as there were barriers of barbed wire; the Germans had mined the route and were firing into the passages.'

When they finally made it to Mokotów the Radosław soldiers were stunned to find the people there still living peacefully, and deluding themselves that they might somehow make it through the uprising without losing anything. Radosław's troops, who had now fought in Wola, the Old Town and Czerniaków, had no such illusions. Two days after their arrival, von dem Bach attacked Mokotów.

For those left in Czerniaków, the district became a living hell. The Germans continued to attack along Wilanowska and Zagórna Streets, while the Poles defended the area around the Syrena port and the houses on Wilanowska. Still hoping that the Soviets would launch a full-scale attack across the river, the defenders fought ferociously, and Dirlewanger managed to gain only a few metres between Okrąg and Wilanowska Streets. By 21 September the Polish rearguard under Captain Jerzy of 'Zośka' Battalion held only a few buildings along the river, but they repelled every attack, fighting viciously from house to house on Wilanowska, Idzikowski and Solec Streets. The German General Vokel reported that Wilanowska and Solec had houses with at least four hundred people in the basements; his men captured one of them, taking 130 AK soldiers alive.[96] The remaining insurgents under Jerzy fought alongside the soldiers of 1st Polish Army under Major Stanisław Łatyszonek, but only a patch of riverbank and two houses – Solec 53 and Wilanowska 1 – remained in Polish hands by the end of 21 September. The next day, with no ammunition left, Jerzy decided to attempt a breakout. A large group of wounded stumbled or were carried to the riverbank; Jerzy and four members of 'Zośka' Battalion wearing SS uniforms manage to pass themselves off as a German patrol, and walk though enemy lines to the city centre in the middle of the night.

Tadeusz Targoński heard the Germans drawing nearer to his building, with a 'growing clatter of caterpillar tracks, hoarse shouts of drunken Germans . . . tanks are approaching and right behind them the fascists with the sleeves of their uniforms rolled up are advancing *en masse*'. The situation was hopeless. 'We were aware that nobody was going to help us anyway. All of Czerniaków was ablaze in front of us.' Lidia Kowałczyk-Strzelecka crawled from her home. 'Outside was terrible, it seemed that everything had been destroyed.' Under German fire she reached the underground passage which led through the houses to the river. 'The cellars were full of people, patients, civilians and soldiers. They were unsettled, there was not enough air. It was physically and psychologically unbearable for a healthy person.'

Jerzy Dudyński from 'Parasol' watched as a friend went to check their connection with the unit. 'He was killed immediately after leaving the staircase. The shot came from the part of the building facing Okrąg Street, and then I understood that we had been cut off. I tried to jump and get out through the basement, but we had no ammunition, so I simply hid in the cellar. Then the Germans came to round up the civilians.'[97] The Germans quickly took control. 'The women were brought to a big corner room; I went in with them, leaving my weapons, jacket and coat with insignia behind. They started to hit me and check for weapons. They took my documents and pictures and after a while ordered us to move the dead Poles and put them onto the fire burning in a room on the first floor.' As he was moving a body he found some civilian clothes, and quickly changed into them.

'The Germans were ordering old people to leave Ludna, so I mingled with them and went to Gazownia. The people were forced to carry the bodies of the dead, which the Germans ordered to be put in the left part of the burning PKO building. The Germans were raping women in the Red House.* We waited about an hour before they ordered us to form a column and to march carrying the bodies of the Germans killed during the fighting.'[98]

Lidia Markiewicz-Ziental of the 'Zośka' Battalion was left in a stifling cellar with a group of wounded who could not be moved. There was no help, no provisions, nothing. 'The next morning I went to the courtyard in search of water and was stunned by the strange, almost eerie silence.' A soldier, Janusz Stolarski, ordered her to leave the wounded and to flee to the wreck of the riverboat *Tale* on the Vistula while she had the chance. 'This saved my life.'[99] The wounded were later killed.

The nurses who chose to stay with their patients were among the unsung heroines of the uprising. In her post-war testimony, Irena Konopacka-Semadeni stated: 'I helped to take off the uniforms and red-and-white armbands of our wounded soldiers and gave out civilian clothes. One guy, Topolnicki, was huge and weighed over 100 kilos.' She tried desperately to rid him of his SS camouflage gear, but he was too heavy. She was wearing her white apron with the red cross when the Germans came in. 'They interrogated a patient, a young man from Silesia . . . he claimed he had been forced to work for the AK. A German officer, a very young blond guy, wrote out his testimony on two pieces of paper. He then put the paper in his pocket, put on his gloves, took his gun and shot this man in the head. Then he executed the rest of the people lying there. He ordered me to check if any were still alive.'[100] The process was repeated in the next basement. 'The first

---

* So called because of its bright red walls.

to be killed was Topolnicki. They kicked him and then they killed him.'[101]

Janina Chmielińska saw many such executions. 'First the victim would be kicked in the face and was then shot. One of the runners was on her knees begging for her life but was also shot.' Janina only survived because she was pulled into a crowd of civilians and was able to mingle with the old people and children.

Stanisław Likiernik was in the cellar of a hospital at Okrąg Street with two other injured AK soldiers. All three of them were dressed in civilian clothes. 'Suddenly, the peace was broken by ear-splitting shouts: "*Raus!* All those capable out . . . out . . . upstairs," accompanied by the loud clatter of steel heel-caps, rifle shots and the screams of the wounded being murdered next door.' A German soldier appeared at the door of their cellar, and one of Likiernik's fellow patients, a Pole called Burkhardt, began to speak to him in German. The Feldwebel demanded to see his papers. 'You have a German name!' he exclaimed. 'This saved our lives.' The soldiers were Dirlewanger men, and came to visit the patients in the cellar for several days. The Feldwebel, a Rhinelander, 'had been assigned to a punishment company for having hit his lieutenant when he had found his French fiancée in bed with the officer. He was sent first to the Russian front and then transferred to the penal unit in Warsaw.' They were a strange group. 'Still another, slightly tipsy, sat on my pallet and said, "*Schade, schade ich bin nicht Pole, ich wäre auch Partisan*" – Pity, pity that I am not a Pole, I would also have been a partisan. Naturally, I protested vigorously: "I am a civilian. I have never been a partisan." He patted me on the shoulder and left.'[102] Nevertheless, the Dirlewanger men were cold-blooded killers: when an injured man was pulled from the ruins next door 'the officer pointed to the creased right sleeve of the man's jacket. "A sniper. Shoot him," he ordered. The same two soldiers who had dragged him out of the burning house took the man to the side and shot him through the head.'[103]

Irena Konopacka-Semadeni was lucky that the SS and SD units which had taken her building were replaced by Wehrmacht soldiers. They quickly made themselves at home. They had with them some Polish women, who seemed to move with the unit and who acted as concubines. 'Each lady got a cup of hot water and each had some silver and expensive jewellery,' she recalled. 'They came to our basement to clean up and wash, and then they went to the soldiers. Music from the gramophone played in the background, the party went on all night.'

After one such evening Janina Chmielińska went to ask the Germans for food and water for the people in her cellar. The Wehrmacht soldiers gave her a cup of sweet coffee, some honey, and a few cans of spinach. She then asked for help to move her patients to the temporary clinic at Okrąg 2. A German from Silesia, a cook for his unit, obliged. 'I knew the house at Okrąg 2,' she said. 'I knew that there was still a lot of food from the Społem warehouse in the basement. There was sugar, marmalade, pasta and even bandages, underwear and medicine.' She set up a kitchen there, and cooked for her patients and for the Germans: 'The soldiers visited every day and we bribed them to leave us alone with bowls of tomato soup with pasta.' One night a group of Jews who had been in Gęsiówka, including a French journalist who had been at Auschwitz and in a *Verbrennungskommando*, came to them. They ate some food, and then moved on.[104]

This surreal life in the ruins was about to end. On 20 September Janina returned to the building to find a Wehrmacht officer and his men waiting for her. He announced that he had orders to shoot all the patients still in the building and then burn it down. 'I tried to explain to them in my very bad German that they should not . . . and finally in a crazy way I simply started to cry, telling them that I was here with my little son trying to protect these people and now they were coming to shoot them. I was embarrassed, but I couldn't stop crying. I was surprised because when they saw me crying they said that they were sorry about the whole mess and walked away.' In the end, she managed to get permission from the Germans to move her patients to Milanówek, thereby saving their lives.

Others were not so lucky. One woman was hiding in her cellar when the Germans entered it. 'They kicked me in the stomach, they took my mother's gold watch. I heard them enter the second room and execute the patients lying there.'[105] Many others died in the warehouse at Społem. The 'Parasol' soldiers there included a number of Jews who had been freed from Gęsiówka: Dr Turek, Soltan Safijew and Peter Forr ('Paweł'). 'Dr Turek spoke German very well, and when it became clear their situation was hopeless he decided that the only way out was to go to the Germans and negotiate. Paweł was in uniform, as was Dr Turek, and when they opened the door we heard Germans outside. "*Banditen!*" they yelled, and a salvo followed; both men fell to the ground. At the same time two gas grenades were thrown in from the other side of the warehouse, filling the cellar with choking smoke. We all started to run out of the entrance used by Turek and Paweł.'[106] There they faced the SS. 'These were Dirlewanger men with their weapons ready to shoot. We were all in civilian clothes.' A group of prisoners stood with raised hands behind an SS cordon. 'I saw an SS man bring in a *Berlingowiec* [Berling soldier]. They told him to get down on his knees. The SS man shot him directly in the face and then in the back of the head. This soldier was executed while wearing the uniform of the Polish army.'

The civilians were told to stand in rows beside a ditch as three machine guns were set up opposite. 'The SS guys took jewellery and valuables. Then I heard a German voice yelling, "They are civilians! Don't shoot!" We were taken to another square, where piles of dead men lay on the ground.'[107] The group was later taken to Pruszków.

The Germans pushed on into Solec Street in a wave of brutal killing. Dirlewanger's men raped and murdered 122 people in the paint factory at Solec 53; twelve of them died by hanging. One victim was the priest Józef Stanek, chaplain of the 'Kryński' Battalion, who was hanged with his own cassock.

For those not fortunate enough to have made it to the sewers, the only possible way out was to get to the river, in the hope that they would be saved by Soviet boats. The Germans were clearing the district street by street, building by building, and squeezing ever more people towards the water's edge. Licia Markiewicz-Ziental desperately tried to get her wounded husband to the river. 'We went on a narrow path between wounded people lying under the roof of a huge hall, then through a hole in the wall, then to the sand of the riverbank,' she recalled, relieved to have got him away from the SS.

But the river was no safe haven. Włodzimierz Rosłoniec was sent to do reconnaissance nearby: 'Germans are everywhere,' he said. 'We hear Germans talking, and retreat' At Czerniaków harbour he saw a small boat drifting in the water. 'A dead man is lying there. He has no hat or helmet but has a machine pistol with ammunition.' They took his thick coat and went back to headquarters. It was the coat of a Soviet soldier, complete with colours and shoulder markings. One of Berling's men.

By 20 September the riverbank was crowded with the desperate residents of Czerniaków who had nowhere else to go. Some tried to swim across, but many of them died under the hail of German bullets; those who made it further often drowned when the current pulled them down. There were scenes of terrible suffering and desperation amongst those huddled along the riverbank, freedom just out of reach across the water. Lidia Markiewicz-Ziental recalled the sheer misery: 'Groups, crowds of people sat there, under the terrible silence of the grave.' Zbigniew Rylski made it to the riverbank late one night, and was horrified by the sight: 'I could see hundreds of wounded people along the bank who had managed to get there, either on their own or they had been carried. Many were calling for help or for water – it was so crowded that some of the badly wounded were stepped on.'[108] A group of around fifty people had made it to the viaduct by the water's edge, but had become trapped there. They were all killed.

More grim still were the scenes aboard the old riverboat *Bajka* ('Fairytale'). The boat had appeared a few days before to take soldiers back to Praga, but had been shot out, and lay half sunk near the shore. People had swum out to it to escape the German bullets, and many were wounded. 'It was like a scene from Dante. The boat was covered in dead bodies, and the wounded were calling for help. The people lying there could not protect themselves. The boat was under German fire, with rockets lighting up the sky.'[109]

The Germans were only kept back by Russian fire from the other side of the river, but sometimes this hit the refugees too. The Germans responded by throwing grenades into the mass of people on the riverbank and shooting at those on the *Bajka*. Dead bodies floated off the deck and into the water. Szymon Nowak recalled people trying to get to the other side of the river any way they could: some tried to use the hulking drowned spans of the Poniatowski Bridge for protection, but the Germans opened fire with machine guns and rocket launchers, killing them too.

On the night of 21 September Jerzy Gawin from 'Zośka' Battalion stood with a torch and a green light to try to direct boats from Praga towards the *Bajka*. Instead of the hoped-for hundred vessels, only a dozen came. Two hundred soldiers were hanging on to the *Bajka*, but only ninety-four were evacuated that night. The boats were shot at, and a number twirled in the current and then sank with their tragic cargo still on board. The next night more boats arrived, but there were far too few to take civilians. Lidia Markiewicz-Ziental tried to get her husband onto one of them: 'They didn't want to take a badly wounded person,' she recalled. She threatened them at gunpoint, and they reluctantly took him. The little group crossed the river, her husband lying on the old toilet seat she had used as a stretcher while she swam alongside, holding onto the little boat. The final rescue attempt came on the night of the 23rd, when twenty-five boats came across; only eight made it back.

Those who were left on the shore knew there was no option but to swim. 'Daybreak was coming. It was now or never,' one 'Parasol' soldier recalled. 'Guys like Jerzy, Długa and Granat were so exhausted that they could not even take off their clothes.' He helped them undress, but it caused them terrible pain, as their wounds were oozing pus. It started to drizzle with rain for the first time in weeks, and their teeth were chattering. 'The three badly injured men grabbed a piece of wood but the current pushed them inexorably towards the Germans.'[110] They were all killed.

Tadeusz Targoński remembered preparing to swim the Vistula: 'When I looked for the last time at burning Czerniaków tears as large as peas ran down my cheeks. Maybe it was because of the smoke all around, or because the great sacrifice and effort had been in vain.'[111]

It was Major Fischer, Chief of Staff of the Reinefarth Group, who took the last house in Czerniaków.[112] The 9th Army was delighted to report that 'after heavy fights lasting the whole night Berling's defence was broken and the southern cauldron was taken, the last house with eighty-two Polish "legionists" and fifty-seven Home Army soldiers, thirty-five killed. Amongst the PoWs was a woman sniper.'[113] Janina Błaszczak, the woman officer, had been wounded and listed as dead by the Soviets. Amazingly, the Germans did not kill her, but sent her to a field hospital, from which the AK managed to arrange her escape. They then hid her until the end of the war. Most of Berling's soldiers and those suspected of being in the AK were shot.

At 6 a.m. on 23 September the Germans finally took over Czerniaków. Anyone unable to move was killed where they lay; Dirlewanger's men tore through the area raping women, even setting up rooms in the 'Red House' for the purpose. Tadeusz Rybowski was in his basement when the Germans came. 'I saw soldiers in *Feldgrau* beside a tank, probably a Tiger. We were marched out. We could see damaged villas and houses, fallen walls revealed pieces of furniture, beds, linen, pictures. It looked indecent, as if we were intruding into people's personal lives.' One group, still hiding in Solec Street, was led by Father Pául Józef Warszawski, a chaplain of the 'Kedyw' Group. When they heard the Germans approaching he gave everyone absolution. The Germans were enraged to find that one young woman had a gun, and she was hanged in front of them. Another young woman from 'Parasol' was taken away with a large group. She was transported to Pruszków, but two of her friends were taken to Gestapo headquarters, where they were executed.[114] Dirlewanger's men shot two hundred people on Wilanowska, while a pile of hundreds of corpses lay on the street outside Solec 53 – men, women and children.

Once again Spilker had his men scour the groups for insurgents and Jews. Mateusz Wrzosek was pulled from the crowd and interrogated by Spilker himself because he was wearing a German army-issue sweater.[115] When Maria Celtys was asked, '*Bist du Banditin?*' she answered that she was a soldier of the Home Army. She was shot. The Berling soldiers were targeted too. One nurse watched as a number who had not managed to change their clothes were taken from her group: 'People tried to help them, but the Berling soldiers were taken to the German leaders at the building at Sokołowksa Street and were executed there.'[116]

German reports of interrogations of the Berling men offer a tragic glimpse into their short lives. Most were from distant villages, and had been forced to serve; one report read that when they were shown a picture of the Führer, three of them did not even know who he was. 'One of them took off his hat and stood up, the other thought he was General Berling, the last recognized the portrait and said that he had a similar picture in his house.'[117] Hitler's surname was recognized by only four of the Berling men who were questioned, and only one knew the terms 'National Socialism' and 'Communism'. Most could not read or write. 'During interrogations the prisoners asked only where and when they were going to be executed.'[118]

When the fires died down the SS set up another Sonder-kommando to deal with the growing piles of bodies. Kazimierz Żeglarek was taken from his home on Szara Street to Litewska 14 and forced to join a group of 120 prisoners. Once a week a handful were chosen at random and executed; the rest were sent to burn or bury the bodies of the dead. Żeglarek was put to work 'burying the bodies in the pharmacy on the corner of Marszałkowska and Oleandrow . . . At the end of September I buried the bodies of those killed at Wilanowska 14 . . . There were around two hundred people in the courtyard of the huge hall, mostly men with AK armbands.' He also helped clear the corpses at Społem. 'We moved the bodies of over two hundred men and a few women and buried them. Some had AK insignia.' In the ruins of the paint factory at Solec 54 'we found a priest in a cassock, he had been hanged. On the other side were four women also hanged . . . we buried them in the square. We buried male civilians in front of the house at Solec 43; they had been robbed. From flats and courtyards in the square between Wilanowska, Zagórna and Czerniaków we buried a few hundred more, including a few dozen soldiers from Berling's Army.[119] During this grim work he saw 'many piles of clothes, mostly men's clothes . . . uniforms of tram workers, railway workers and many men's hats. The fellow prisoners told me they were the clothes of those who had been executed. The belongings were sorted and loaded onto lorries.'[120]

Once the civilians had been moved out, the Germans set about clearing the area of any valuables, looting anything that could be loaded onto lorries and trains. Leutnant Peter Stolten, stationed next to the Powiśle electricity plant, wrote to his parents of his work: 'From these buildings that have not already been completely destroyed we take sculptures, sofas and tapestries – everything will be burned soon. Already most things are demolished. We are stuck up to the knees in equipment, rubbish, pieces of crockery and dirt. There is an unimaginable shocking abandoned feeling of emptiness.'[121] Von dem Bach praised Dirlewanger for a job well done: 'Heavy enemy fire did not hold SS Oberführer Dirlewanger back. Again fighting at the front line, inspiring his men through daredevil acts and bravery towards a fast advance, even though there were heavy losses amongst themselves, the banks of the Vistula were completely clean.'[122]

Czerniaków had fallen, and the losses had been terrible. The 1st Polish Army alone lost 4,939 men in the crossing of the Vistula, with only 1,500 actually reaching the western bank. The civilians who survived were now being herded towards Pruszków, and then on to concentration camps or into slave labour in the Reich. The fall of Czerniaków had other implications too. For a brief moment Stalin had appeared ready to help the AK and the people of Warsaw. Now the AK leadership had to decide if he was going to save them, or abandon them for good. It was a question of the utmost urgency.

Stalin's Game

The battle for Czerniaków had been particularly cruel, not just because of the bitter fighting and the desperate, almost Biblical plight of the helpless civilians gathered on the riverbank. It was cruel, too, because Stalin had sent just enough help to make Warsawians believe that he was going to save them. In a matter of days he had taken Praga, had allowed Berling's soldiers to cross the Vistula, had finally permitted American planes to drop supplies over Warsaw, and had even sent Soviet airdrops to the AK insurgents. Stalin had not suddenly changed his views about the AK and the Poles. The key to his behaviour lay with Churchill alone.

Despite his apparent indifference at times, Churchill really did care about Poland, the country for which Britain had gone to war. It was he who had started the British airlift from Italy to Warsaw at the beginning of August, and he who had become increasingly angry as RAF losses mounted because its planes were not allowed to land on Soviet territory. An open rift began to develop between Churchill and Stalin over the issue of landing rights and the treatment of the AK in Warsaw.

When the post-war Soviet Foreign Minister Andrei Vyshinsky collapsed and died just before making a speech at the United Nations in New York on 22 November 1954, the *New York Times* wrote: 'We do not mourn his death.' Cruel, ruthless and brilliant, Vyshinsky was best-known as the state prosecutor of Stalin's 'purge trials' of the 1930s. But in 1944, while serving as the Soviet Deputy Commissar for Foreign Affairs, it was he who announced to Churchill that the Soviet government objected to British or American aircraft landing on Soviet soil. The reason, he said, was that the Soviet government did not want to be associated 'directly or indirectly' with the 'reckless and terrible adventure in Warsaw'.[123]

Churchill was furious. On 20 August, the day that American B-17 bombers carried out the first of the raids on IG Farben's plant at Monowitz, only a few kilometres east of Auschwitz-Birkenau, he persuaded Roosevelt to send a joint statement to Stalin requesting that the Allies not 'abandon' the Poles, but should work together to 'save as many of the patriots [in Warsaw] as possible'.[124] 'We are most anxious to send American planes from England,' Churchill wrote. 'Why should they not land on the refuelling ground which has been assigned to us behind the Russian lines?' He told Roosevelt he was tempted to send planes to land on Soviet soil without permission, just to see what would happen. Roosevelt replied that he did not want to join in this 'exceptionally provocative move'.[125]

When Churchill wrote to Stalin again, the dictator was extremely insulting about the AK: the Poles who had started the uprising were nothing but a 'gang of criminals', he said. On 4 September Churchill again pushed for joint landing rights.[126] He wrote to Roosevelt, giving him the text written to the Pope by the women of Warsaw: 'Warsaw is in ruins,' they said. 'The Germans are killing the wounded in hospitals. They are making women and children march in front of them in order to protect their tanks.'[127] He also sent Roosevelt a text he proposed to send to Stalin: 'We wish the Soviet government to know that public opinion in this country is deeply moved by the events in Warsaw and by the terrible sufferings of the Poles there,' it read. 'The fact that such help could not be sent on account of your government's refusal to allow United States aircraft to land on aerodromes in Russian hands is now becoming publicly known. If on top of all this the Poles of Warsaw should now be overwhelmed by the Germans, as we are told they must be within two or three days, the shock of public opinion here will be incalculable.'[128]

The problem festered for weeks. On 27 September Major

General Sir Alfred Knox asked Foreign Secretary Anthony Eden why the Soviets had not allowed RAF planes to land, thereby 'rendering the position of the Polish forces tragic'. Hugh Lunghi, a member of the British military mission to Moscow, thought the Soviet decision 'a most terrible betrayal, not only of the Poles but of the Allies'.[129]

On 1 September George Orwell went on the attack, writing in *Tribune*: 'Since, it seems, nobody else will do it I want to protest against the mean and cowardly attitude adopted by the British press towards the recent rising in Warsaw.' He ended with a warning: 'Do remember that dishonesty and cowardice always have to be paid for. Don't imagine that for years on end you can make yourself the boot-licking propagandist of the Soviet regime, or any other regime, and then suddenly return to mental decency . . . There can be no real alliance on the basis of "Stalin is always right". The first step towards a real alliance is the dropping of illusions.'[130] Others began to question Stalin's motives: the *Spectator* contrasted the recent liberation of Paris with the hell in Warsaw.

The American view, too, was undergoing a shift of sorts. Averell Harriman, US Ambassador to the Soviet Union, wrote on 16 August that 'the Soviet government's refusal is not based on operational difficulties, nor on a denial of the conflict, but on ruthless political calculations'. George Kennan wrote that 'This was a gauntlet thrown down, in a spirit of malicious glee, before the Western powers. The Soviets were stating that "We intend to have Poland lock, stock and barrel. We don't care a fig for those Polish underground fighters who have not accepted Communist authority. To us, they are no better than the Germans; and if they and the Germans slaughter each other off, so much the better." ' Kennan concluded that the United States should finally 'stand up' to Stalin.[131] As he put it, the Soviets were going to do what they wanted with Eastern Europe, but 'instead of pushing poor

Mikołajczyk to make what would have been a disgraceful sell-out of his own county . . . we should have gone to the Russians and have said: "Look here, if you people are going to behave this way in Eastern Europe – if you're going to pin foreign-inspired dictatorships on these people, and deprive them, really, of all national and individual freedom – then it is simply not worth it for us to give you assistance to enable you to do that for the remainder of the war . . . We cannot stop you from doing this, but we also will not take responsibility for it." ' Some Americans were talking about stopping Lend-Lease altogether. Kennan wrote: 'If the Russians had said, "Well how do you know we are going to do these things?" well, now after the uprising we had the argument for it. We could have said, "Look at your reaction to the Warsaw Uprising. It is quite clear that you were quite prepared to have these fellows slaughtered off . . . The Poles have been our allies . . . we are not going to support you in these policies." Now, it seems to me that it would have been possible to say this to Stalin.'[132]

Churchill was by now so upset by Stalin's 'strange and sinister' behaviour that he began to threaten to stop all sea convoys with equipment, provisions and arms bound for Russia. This was a real threat which even Stalin could not ignore. He reluctantly decided to make concessions to the West. He would, after all, allow the Americans to drop supplies into Warsaw.

The presence of American planes on Soviet soil was not new. The idea was first introduced in October 1943 in the form of the American Military Mission to the Soviet Union. At first it was known as Operation 'Baseball', but it was then changed to Operation 'Frantic Joe', in reference to Stalin's 'frantic' appeals for help. The Americans had proposed to set up Army Air Force bases on Soviet territory to be used to attack German targets beyond the range of Britain or Italy.[133] Roosevelt brought up the subject again at Tehran the following month, and Stalin allowed the creation of three bases in Ukraine – at Poltava, Mirgorod and Piryatin – which became operational in the summer of 1944. As a concession the Soviet air force was given access to an Allied base in Italy, where two Soviet squadrons came under British command.

The bases were a source of tension from the start. Deploying Air Force units required enormous resources, including over 9,000 personnel and three battalions of anti-aircraft artillery, all of which had to be brought in from the United States via Murmansk and Arkhangelsk (Churchill called this 'the worst journey in the world') and then by train to the airfields. The first American shuttle mission, part of Operation 'Frantic' (the 'Joe' had been tactfully dropped), took place on 2 June 1944, when 127 B-17s and sixty-four Mustangs bombed Debrecen in Hungary; this was followed by missions in Romania and Lower Silesia. There was a serious setback when a Luftwaffe pilot followed the planes back to the Poltava base, resulting in a devastating German bombing attack. The Americans blamed the Soviets for not providing adequate air-base protection, which further soured relations.

The US tried to increase its presence on Soviet territory, but Stalin was growing increasingly hostile. The Soviets had captured virtually all the targets originally proposed in Operation 'Frantic' in the summer of 1944, and he no longer needed American help; on the contrary, he was irritated by the presence of US soldiers in Ukraine, and wanted them out. Tensions increased between the Americans and their obstructionist Soviet minders – equipment was stolen or damaged, pilots were followed, and the Americans were made to feel unwelcome at every turn. Things got worse when some US pilots claimed to have been shot at by the Soviets. Roosevelt and Churchill began to negotiate with Stalin to allow American planes to fly to Warsaw, but in Moscow Averell

Harriman was told point blank that Stalin was opposed to any 'Frantic' operations over the city. And then, on 10 September, he suddenly changed his mind.

The Soviet announcement came as a welcome surprise. The first flight, 'Frantic 7', was postponed at first due to bad weather, but took place on 18 September; it would be the only military contribution that the Americans made to the uprising. As we have seen, the parachutes that drifted slowly into German-held territory did not help the AK, but the drops boosted morale in the stricken city. The West had been appeased. Finally, Stalin was seen to be doing his part.

The second such sop to public opinion came with Berling's river crossing to Czerniaków. Berling was important to Stalin as a political pawn, and the Soviet leader had always planned to use the Berling Army to make it look as if the Poles had liberated their own capital – he had even intended to feature it in a 'victory march' into Warsaw if it had been taken in 1944. In his memoirs, General Sergei Shtemenko recalled the first discussion on the subject: 'Silence falls in the cabinet. Stalin paces by his table with an empty pipe in his hand. Finally he breaks the silence, saying: "Tell *Tovarishch* Zhukov that Rokossovsky and he are to help out with Warsaw . . . Tell them to think about how to bring Berling's soldiers into the city'.[134] Berling never took part in a victory parade. Stalin found another use for his men.

Berling always claimed that he had crossed the Vistula to Czerniaków on his own initiative, but this was impossible, as he could not have mounted such an attack without Stalin's knowledge and approval.[135] The Red Army was organized in such a way that Berling would have been unable to obtain weapons, ammunition, boats, troops or other matériel without Rokossovsky's and therefore Stalin's knowledge; he may have jumped the gun and gone a little earlier than expected, but Stalin must have known about the general plan. It is also highly significant that although Berling was blamed for the failure of the Czerniaków crossings, he was not arrested or put to death. If he had acted alone, against Stalin's wishes, he would not have survived; instead he was simply dismissed, and replaced by the reliable Major General Korczyc, who had been a member of the Red Army since 1917.

It is most likely that Stalin sent Berling's men to Czerniaków with every expectation that they would fail. Many facts point to this. It was the poorly trained and poorly equipped 3rd Division of the 1st Polish Army, rather than the more effective 1st Division, which was sent across the Vistula. There was very little (but, importantly, some) artillery support from the eastern bank, and almost no air support. It was effectively a suicide mission, but one which made Stalin look as if he was trying to help. Stalin even told George Kennan in Moscow that 'some infantry battalions' had been ferried across the Vistula 'to support the resistance groups'. The Americans and the British were relieved that Stalin was actively aiding the uprising, but in reality it was all for show.

Stalin knew exactly what he was doing. He was very well informed about everything that was happening in Warsaw, and his actions there were very carefully considered. When Izolda Kowalska, an AL member and personal friend of many of the 'Lublin Poles', managed to swim across the Vistula on 11 September, she made her way to Berling's headquarters. 'Marshal Rokossovsky appeared and asked who we were'[156] – proof that Rokossovsky was with Berling four days before the crossings. Rokossovsky ordered that Kowalska and her group be fed, given wine and allowed to rest. Later that day she spoke by phone to General Michał Rola-Żymierski, whom she knew personally, and her friend Władysław Gomułka ordered that they be taken to Lublin. She talked to Berling again before she left Praga. He asked how badly Warsaw was damaged, and was particularly interested in the damage on

Żurawia Street, where he had lived. He seemed genuinely moved by the fate of the Polish capital.

On 16 November Kowalska met Stalin in Moscow. He too was very interested in Warsaw's fate. 'Stalin asked who was in the uprising. He was interested in what Warsaw looked like, and wanted to hear about the destruction and the losses.' Kowalska told him that she did not understand why there had been no help for Warsaw, and that she had had 'doubts'. 'What doubts?' he snapped back. 'Why there had been no plane cover over the city, nor did the Soviets bomb bridges or airports, as most of the destruction had been caused by German aircraft and heavy mortars.' Stalin answered that Warsaw could 'only be liberated by a flank pincer movement, but this had been impossible, that the attempt to attack frontally across the river had failed and had ended in serious losses. Any other form of help could not have had a significant effect.'[137] In reality Stalin had had no desire to help the AK, but had been forced by Churchill's dogged criticism to make it look as if he had tried. The rift between Churchill and Stalin was temporarily bridged, but it would soon become a chasm with the onset of the Cold War.

'The First Battle of World War III'

The growing antagonism between Churchill and Stalin might have been cause for concern in the West, but in the Wolfsschanze it was a reason for celebration, and was eagerly watched by Hitler and his entourage. As the tension grew they became more excited, until Hitler began to believe that the Western Allies might actually split from Stalin over the situation in Warsaw. Then, the theory went, the war would end and Britain and the United States would join Germany in a third world war against the Soviets.

The notion was of course preposterous, but by this time Hitler was clutching at straws. His health had declined markedly during the Warsaw Uprising, and he had fallen ever more under the influence of Theodor Morell, the only doctor he now trusted. Morell treated Hitler's stomach cramps with camomile enemas, and for the injuries sustained on 20 July the Führer was given increasingly powerful doses of cocaine, poured into his nose daily by his valet Heinz Linge.[138] He became ever more paranoid, to the point that, as Linge put it, his lack of trust became 'excessive'.[139] Hitler lived in a world of phantom armies and imaginary tank divisions; one day he would declare the need to create a 'suitable peace' for Germany, the next he would be planning a 'knockout blow' in the Ardennes. His secretary Christa Schroeder recalled watching from the Wolfsschanze as Allied bombers headed in bright sunshine towards the Reich. 'Do you believe, *mein Führer*, that we can still win the war?' she asked. 'We have to,' he replied.[140]

For some time Hitler refused to get out of bed: 'The Führer sends his regrets' became a common refrain. His adjutant Otto Günsche complained that Hitler was 'completely apathetic' about events around him. There was also a growing sense of gloom about the war, and an uneasy realization that the terrible crimes committed by the Nazis were about to be discovered. General Warlimont recalled a meeting with Lieutenant General Westphal and Lieutenant General Krebs on 31 August in the Wolfsschanze. 'Things are coming to light which make your hair stand on end,' Hitler said. 'The German people has kept its mouth shut so far but now everybody's talking . . . frightful things are going to come out in the east; they're only just becoming clear.'[141]

Hitler's inner circle had been loyal up until now, but serious doubts had crept in during that fateful summer of 1944. Albert Speer recalled that by the end of August, when the uprising was at its height, 'Hitler's authority in the party was no longer what it had been. His closest paladins simply ignored him or went counter to Hitler's pronouncements . . . These were the first clear signs of disintegration; now the party apparatus and the loyalty of Hitler's leading men had been affected.' Hitler's mood constantly veered between apathetic and highly emotional; when he was agitated, Speer noted 'the lively fluttering of his hands, the way he chewed his fingernails when he was tense'. His face would flush deep red, his eyes become lifeless and fixed.[142] Worst of all, he had become 'totally unpredictable', and talked about ever more far-fetched hopes for victory.[143] 'Hitler began more and more pointedly alluding to future new weapons which would decide the war, arousing hopes among the generals and the political leaders'; Speer wrote to him in mid-September pointing out that the belief in these decisive weapons 'is widespread among the troops'.[144] Most in the inner circle now realized that only a miracle could save them, although 'in those turbulent times in which everyone was eager to find reason for hope, rumours found fertile soil'. It was in this 'fertile soil' that the supposed rift between Churchill and Stalin turned in Hitler's mind to possible salvation for Germany.

By September 1944 Hitler was predicting that 'the enemy coalition will soon come apart'. Goebbels took this seriously, and repeated 'the Führer's prediction'. After discussing the situation far into the night with his friend Hans Schwarz van Berk, Goebbels noted that the political aspects of the situation were 'very promising'.[145]

By now many of Hitler's most trusted underlings were making plans to negotiate for peace either with the Western Allies or with the Soviets. Goebbels favoured the latter. After speaking to his trusted confidant Werner Naumann, he set to work. Naumann had told Goebbels about a conversation he had had with Hiroshi Oshima, Japanese Ambassador in Berlin, who argued that in an effort to attain such an agreement 'Japan would even make concessions that would pave the way for a German–Soviet peace treaty'.[146] Oshima saw no point in talking to the British or the Americans, but called Stalin a 'realist'. British intelligence also knew about this meeting. On 26 September Guy Liddell wrote in his secret diary: 'It was made clear that while peace with England or America was out of the question Germany would not be averse to peace with Russia if a favourable opportunity occurred.'[147]

Unlike Goebbels, Himmler was still contemplating approaching the West. He too had fallen ill in September, and had spent some weeks at Karl Gebhardt's nursing home at Hohenlychen, a hundred kilometres north of Berlin, suffering from crippling spasms; his personal assistant Rudolf Brandt saw him pacing away the night of 10 September in pain which could only be relieved by the attentions of his masseur, the Finnish doctor Felix Kersten.[148] Himmler was breaking down physically and mentally, and fell increasingly under the influence of Walter Schellenberg, the head of SS military intelligence and one-time lover of Coco Chanel, who pressed him to negotiate with the West for a separate peace. Himmler was also swayed by his mistress Hedwig Potthast, or 'Häschen', with whom he had two illegitimate children, Helge and Gertrud; she also favoured peace with the West, and was not afraid to tell him so. The most important role, however, was played by Kersten, who used his influence over Himmler to try to 'humanize' him, and attempted to persuade him to sanction the release of prisoners held throughout the Reich.

Himmler's illness was in part due to mental stress and the dilemma he found himself in. He wanted to remain Hitler's 'Treuer Heinrich', but felt that the Führer was now a liability; he increasingly believed that his only salvation would be to negotiate a peace for Germany, and try to ensure that he played a role in any post-war German government. That Himmler could think in these terms is a measure of his self-delusion and complete lack of understanding of how he was despised in the rest of the world. He genuinely believed that a few gestures of goodwill would be enough to repair his reputation in the West and secure him future power.[149] His sudden glimmer of humanity towards the Jews, the Poles and others can only be explained in this self-serving light.

Himmler's bizarre negotiations had begun in May 1944, when Obersturmbannführer Adolf Eichmann offered Joel Brand, of the Hungarian Aid and Rescue Committee, which helped Jews in Nazi-occupied Europe, the lives of 700,000 condemned Jews in exchange for 10,000 lorries; he followed this with deals to save both Swiss and Romanian Jews.[150] When Hitler heard about these transactions he gave Himmler a dressing down he would never forget, but this did not dissuade him. On 12 September, the day Dirlewanger began his vicious attack on Czerniaków, Kersten petitioned him on behalf of a group of twenty-seven imprisoned priests. Himmler agreed to release them, even telling Kersten that the Nazi attack on the Christian faith had been 'a mistake'. 'When I am dead, will these priests pray for my soul?' he asked.[151]

In the autumn of 1944 Himmler ordered an end to the extermination of the Jews, although the machinery he had put in place could not be stopped so easily – the death marches, beatings, tortures and shootings continued unabated until May 1945. Schellenberg, who was talking to the International Red Cross on Himmler's behalf, believed that he had only entered into negotiations about prisoners because he was looking for ways of getting in touch with the Western Allies to sue for peace.

In mid-September Himmler, now feeling better, returned to Hagewald-Hochwald, close to the Wolfsschanze. He suddenly announced to Kersten that the whole course of the war 'will be affected by the troubles developing between the Americans and the Russians'.[152] He believed that, with the 'enemy coalition broken apart' as a result of the Polish problem, World War Three was on the horizon, and the British and Americans would soon ask the Germans for help in the war against Stalin. On 16 September Himmler met General Andrey Vlasov, who had created the collaborationist Russian Liberation Army in the hope of eventually overthrowing Stalin, and even agreed to raise ten divisions in preparation for this 'inevitable' conflict

Himmler's attempts to open negotiations with the West continued throughout the uprising and beyond. One of his most important envoys was SS Obergruppenführer Dr Wilhelm Harster, who was well connected to important Italian industrialists like Franco Marinotti, who had strong English connections. On 24 October the two men met at Harster's villa near Lake Como; Harster told Marinotti that he spoke 'with the approval of the Reichsführer Himmler'.[153] Then he explained the purpose of the meeting. Hitler had decided to destroy absolutely everything in the Reich with his 'scorched-earth policy'. However, if the Allies were willing to negotiate, Himmler could offer them the twenty-five German divisions which were still in Italy, and take them to the east to fight against Stalin. In return, the Allies would guarantee the inviolability of the Reich and its population.[154]

Himmler had another reason to change his attitude towards the Poles. He detested the nation, but the behaviour of both the civilians and the AK during the uprising had elicited his grudging respect; on 21 September he even told Hitler that 'I wish we had a multitude of men like General Bór.' It would have been unthinkable four years earlier, but Himmler was now using the AK as a kind of role model for a new German 'People's Army'. If the AK and the Polish people could fight so hard in Warsaw, perhaps the Germans could do the same against the advancing Russians. The tenacity and dogged determination of the insurgents in Warsaw was one of the factors which led to the creation of the *Volkssturm* a few days later.

The *Volkssturm* was officially created in a decree issued on 25 September, when the uprising was still raging in Warsaw. Hitler decreed that all German men between the ages of sixteen and sixty who were capable of bearing arms were to be drafted into the new organization. As Commander-in-Chief of the Reserve Army, Himmler would be in charge. Registration centres were to be set up all over the Reich, and Party functionaries put in charge of forming militia groups.[155] Himmler officially announced the creation of the *Volkssturm* to the nation in a speech broadcast from East Prussia on 18 October, a gigantic eagle and swastika flags in the background. He began by invoking the Prussian *Landsturm* of 1813, when the people had banded together to sweep the French from the land; now it was time for Germans to repeat this great victory, he said. Ordinary people were to become the protectors of Germany, which was to be 'defended by men, young lads and greybeards and – if it has to be – by women and girls'.[156] Never and nowhere were members of the *Volkssturm* permitted to capitulate.

'For our Western enemies the war is becoming ever more difficult,' Himmler stated solemnly. And then he did the unthinkable. Warsaw was the capital of a 'betrayed Poland', he yelled, and the 'prudent' General Bór had been 'disgracefully deceived and abandoned by his allies'. The Poles were no longer to be called '*Banditen*', and the AK were to be treated like combatants according to the Geneva Convention. This was an astounding turnaround. It is possible that Hitler and Himmler agreed to give the Poles combatant status, at least in part, because of the creation of the *Volkssturm*. If the Germans treated the AK according to the Geneva Convention, they could expect that the boys and older men of the *Volkssturm*, about to strap their own black, white and red armbands over their threadbare civilian clothes, might be treated as combatants in return. Himmler even checked with the Americans and the British that this would be the case. It was confirmed. The AK had set an extraordinary precedent. Himmler's *volte face* was soon reflected in the treatment of the Poles in Warsaw.

Ernst Kaltenbrunner, the head of the RSHA, the Reich's Security Office, was the only person Himmler was genuinely afraid of at this point. He had used the persecution of the 20 July plotters to work his way into Hitler's favour, and had been active in the persecution of Warsawians since the beginning of the uprising. On 26 August he had informed von dem Bach that all men and women from Warsaw who were taken to the Reich to work would have to live under 'concentration camp conditions',[157] and Polish babies and small children were to be taken from their mothers for forced adoption by childless German couples.[158] Himmler cancelled these orders on 9 September.

According to him, prisoners from Warsaw were no longer to be taken to the camps, but would be treated like all other prisoners. On 29 September he even contemplated cancelling the order that all Poles working in the Reich had to wear the letter 'P' on their uniforms – he thought a sheaf of yellow wheat against a red-and-white background might be more appealing.[159]

The change of attitude towards the AK was reflected in the Nazi press. Most of the coverage of the uprising continued to focus on the bravery of the German troops and the power of the weapons brought in to pound the city, but by September other articles began to appear too. Hans Frank and the OKW were given permission to start Operation 'Berta' in September 1944, which saw nine new Polish newspapers set up under German control. Their main story, repeated *ad nauseam*, was the need for Poles to cooperate with Germany against the Soviet Union; this marked the first time since the beginning of the war that the Germans tried to recruit Poles into the anti-Bolshevik front. It was the first time, too, that Polish national identity was actually celebrated: the names of once-banned national heroes like Batory, Sobieski, Kościuszko and Mickiewicz began to appear. Poland, it was said, was a 'European' country.[160] For the Nazis this was a revolutionary concept.

The RSHA, too, was intent on using the uprising for its own ends. In a report dated 17 August, Otto Ohlendorf pointed out that some of its elements might be useful to German propaganda. Warsaw proved, for example, that the Bolsheviks 'did not want to help the Polish population or give them support', and that their only aim was 'to take power'.[161] In a confidential report written the previous day, entitled 'The Current Mood of the English People', Goebbels noted that an anti-Bolshevik debate had been sparked in England by 'the partisan uprising in Warsaw'. Two days later he wrote: 'With the difficult question of Warsaw we accuse the English and the Bolsheviks equally' in their 'betrayal' of the Poles.[162] At the beginning of September, after reading the text of a speech given by Mikołajczyk, Goebbels wrote in his diary: 'We are about to see a serious English–American–Soviet conflict.'[163]

Three days later, his suspicions were confirmed. In England 'the blind obedience of the British government to the Soviets is being attacked. The magazine *Tribune* published an article [that by George Orwell] against British politics towards Poland which might have been published in the *Völkischer Beobachter*!' One wonders what Orwell would have thought of the endorsement. 'The conflict that started with Katyń,' Goebbels wrote, 'will flare again because of the Warsaw Uprising.' The situation was now 'simmering', and he was 'full of hope' that it would lead to greater things. He then devised a new policy regarding Poland. 'We will keep our distance temporarily, but in my opinion the time will come to get involved.' The British were now in the process of launching a 'massive attack' against the Kremlin, and the resulting split would prompt Stalin to begin negotiations with Hitler which would end the war. Goebbels passed a report summarizing these ideas to the Führer himself on 21 September.[164]

On 3 October Himmler ordered that the propaganda drive towards the Poles be intensified, and two days later he declared that the Polish version of the magazine *Signal* could be distributed to Polish workers in the Reich. The Germans in Warsaw began to be portrayed not as conquerors but as 'liberators' and 'protectors' of the city's population. A number of articles were written praising the 'humane' and 'exemplary' conditions at Pruszków camp. For their part, the Soviets were portrayed as deceitful villains: 'From 2 June,' the *Völkischer Beobachter* wrote, 'radio station Kościuszko systematically appealed to Warsaw civilians to start the uprising.' The Soviets were accused of a double betrayal, because they had encouraged the Poles to fight and had then refused to come to their aid. 'Kremlin promises of weapons were not honoured. The civilians were the ones to suffer. The situation in Warsaw became like another Katyń.'[165]

Since the beginning of August the AK had been depicted in the German press as '*Banditen*', with Bór the '*Herszt*' bandit – chief bandit; now they were portrayed as honourable soldiers who had been 'cheated' by their allies. 'The Soviets, in hypocritical cooperation with the English and American governments, refused permission for the landing of the planes meant to bring provisions for the insurgents. It was easy for London and Washington to avoid responsibility for not giving military help to Poland.'[166] Goebbels' propaganda newspaper *Das Reich*, too, held that the Soviet Union was guilty because it called for the uprising and then did nothing.[167]

This 'pro-Polish' propaganda continued well into October. The last article about the uprising in *Das Reich* called it a 'senseless tragedy'. There was, predictably, no mention of Germany's own role, and its responsibility for the horrific acts of violence perpetrated against the people of Warsaw.

This propaganda made no difference to Warsawians, of course. The Poles were well aware of who was really to blame for the Wola massacres, the rapes in Ochota and the destruction of the Old Town, and no Nazi propaganda would change their views. Governor Fischer was right to warn that 'collaboration in Poland is rare'; if the Poles had not aided the Germans in 1939, why would they now, when they had suffered so much at the hands of the Nazis, and the war was almost over? All attempts to persuade the Poles to join the Germans failed, but Hitler, Himmler and Goebbels persisted for some time in the belief that World War III was coming, and that they might be induced to join in. It was a fantasy, but it would be of enormous importance in the weeks to come. If the AK were to be considered regular soldiers and not 'bandits', peace negotiations between the Germans and the Poles would have to be conducted accordingly. The AK would indeed be treated according to the Geneva Convention, something that would have been unthinkable in the first weeks of August. Hitler's fantasy would save thousands of lives.

12

THE END GAME

———◦◦◦———

Carthage being destroyed Scipio gave the soldiers a certain number of days for plunder, reserving the gold, silver and temple gifts. He also gave numerous prizes to all who had distinguished themselves for bravery. (Chapter XX)

On 21 September General Helmuth Staedke, Chief of Staff of the 9th Army, looked at a map of Warsaw. He was furious. The Soviet guns had fallen silent now, and from time to time Red Army troops could be seen sunbathing on the opposite shore. Staedke wanted to secure the riverbank and take the city once and for all. 'Let's just clear up this pile of shit,' he said angrily.[1]

That was not going to be easy, however. Three large districts remained to be conquered. Worse still, two of them snaked along the Vistula directly across from the Soviet troops, and the Germans could not be certain that Stalin would not move forward again. But it had to be done.

The Germans decided to attack the southern district of Mokotów first. Von Lüttwitz, gambling that the Russians would stay put for a while, authorized the use of regular troops – most notably the 19th Panzer Division – for an entire week. This was important in its own right, but it was also meant as an insult to Himmler, who was again being criticized for his failure to take Warsaw. Lüttwitz was all the more angry when he learned on 16 September that von dem Bach had been confirmed as full Corps Commander of Korpsgruppe von dem Bach, which put even the 19th Panzer Division under his command. Lüttwitz refused to use the new title, spluttering, 'Our Wehrmacht units should no longer be led by a dilettante from the SS.'[2] Whoever was in charge, the use of regular army troops would make an enormous difference to the civilians on the ground. The looting, raping and mass killings that had been such a feature of Bach's SS corps would, at least to some extent, be diminished.

Mokotów

Mokotów has always been a wealthy suburb, resplendent with elegant villas and marble-clad apartment buildings. Even in September 1944 it would not have looked out of place in Paris or Vienna, had it not been for the twenty or so heavily guarded barricades that blocked every major street leading to and from its centre. Its inhabitants had been spared the worst of the uprising so far, but by September they had begun to suffer the sort of deprivations which had become common elsewhere in the city. The bombing had started with the fall of the Old Town, and the hospitals were now filled with the 'twisted and burned' bodies of those caught in *Krowa* attacks and air raids. Food and water were becoming scarce, and there was a sharp increase in cases of typhus and dysentery. The people of Mokotów still prayed that the Allies might somehow reach them before the Germans came. In reality, they were doomed.

The quiet that had reigned in the suburb came to an abrupt, shocking end on 24 September. Stukas suddenly filled the sky, dropping their bombs onto houses and streets, and a massive barrage of mortars blasted in from the south and west. Tanks gathered on Szustra, and rolled towards the centre. Enormous blasts shook the ground, fires raged and entire buildings collapsed under the might of the bombs. People ran for their shelters and basements, stunned by the sheer ferocity of the attack. Thirteen-year-old Barbara Kaczyńska-Januszkiewicz was in her home when the ground started shaking. 'The glass door to our room was demolished by the banging. The glass fell out, shattering throughout the room, the frames were ripped out.'[3] Even Agaton was surprised by the firepower directed at Mokotów, and the 'massive' onslaught of the Stukas. 'I could see German Panzer cars begin to move in along Corazziego,' very close to AK head-quarters.[4] The air was black with smoke, and the streets became hot with the fires. He had seen enough. He knew already that Mokotów would soon fall.

The AK units in Mokotów were led by Lieutenant Colonel Rokicki ('Karol'), who had been joined by the remainder of Radosław's forces and members of the AL. They fought ferociously against the Panzer battalions and German troops now pressing in from all sides. Using everything they had, they managed to hold off the tanks attacking at Niepodleglości Avenue, but their losses were very high, and Rokicki knew he could only hold out against such force for another two days, at the most. The German Army Group Mitte reported that 'the attack from the south came up against isolated insurgents . . . their defence was very fierce. Our forces are not concentrated enough or supported enough by artillery . . . tomorrow there must be a concerted attack on one point – artillery must shoot precisely, this is the only way we will be successful in such street fighting.'

Von dem Bach complained at the lack of progress. '*Sturm* spirit is low,' he wrote. 'The Azeris do not attack.' At 7 o'clock on the evening of the 24th an anxious Bach told Staedke, 'Mokotów will not be successful. The Muslims and such do not attack . . . Rohr has enough soldiers but no artillery.' He feared that Mokotów would not be taken in the required two days, and that he would be blamed yet again. Staedke called Rohr an hour later: 'No matter what, create these points – attack the houses one by one, keep the front of the attack narrow and concentrated.'

Bach was so worried that he begged for one more day to crush Mokotów. At the same time, in keeping with Himmler's new policy of trying to win over the Poles, he decided to allow the trapped civilians to leave the district. He sent two Polish prisoners of war to Rokicki's headquarters to tell him that the Germans intended to destroy Mokotów, but were willing to allow civilians to get out. In his generosity he would call a two-hour ceasefire to enable them to do so. He was doing this, he said, in a spirit of cooperation, because 'in the future Poland and the German army will fight together against the Bolsheviks'.[5]

News of the ceasefire spread quickly, but people did not know what to do. They had not endured the hell of Wola or the Old Town, and their homes were still largely intact. Many were tempted to hang on, as nobody really trusted the Germans, and they feared they might be murdered. Yet it was clear that Mokotów was about to be overrun and smashed to pieces, so some felt it was safer to take their chances rather than wait to be buried under a building or burned alive in a cellar. Eventually over 9,000 people took their lives in their hands and crossed the barricades with their bags and bundles. They were not killed, but were taken to Pruszków camp as von dem Bach had promised.

The departure of so many people led to a collapse of morale in Mokotów. AK losses in the bloody street fighting were rising, and there was only enough food for three more days. German tanks rolled down Puławska Street, and despite vicious battles for the Królikarnia Palace and the school at Woronicza, the Germans simply proved too strong for the AK; even night-time counter-attacks were pushed back. Barbara Januszkiewicz, who had spent the previous week planning her thirteenth birthday party, was appalled to learn that her best friends – young people from the 'Bałtyk' Battalion who had been billeted in her house – had died in the fighting: 'Mach is with us in the basement . . . Three pieces of shrapnel hit him in the jaw and chin. Kuba and Marian are dead. Mach saw it happen with his own eyes. Marian was hit in the temple, and the bullet exited through the back of his head. Kuba was hit in the chest . . . The funeral will be at 10. They are already decomposing. It is terrible to think that the boys – cheerful, healthy, always appearing before our eyes – are now transformed into two rotting corpses.'[6]

By 26 September Rokicki and his troops had been forced to retreat to a small fortified sector in the north of the district; morale was at rock bottom. Seventeen hundred AK soldiers had been killed. Some civilians did the unthinkable, and put out white flags; the AK took them down, but they reappeared at night. Other civilians paid five hundred złoty to 'guides' to take them across German lines.[7]

On 27 September the Germans attacked from all sides. In a hail of shells the tanks of 19th Panzer Division rolled over the last of the barricades protecting the tiny enclave around Rokicki's headquarters. The Poles were completely encircled. 'Panic is spreading in the army,' Rokicki had written at four in the morning on the 26th. 'I am planning gradual evacuation to the sewers. Own losses – 70 per cent. Morale – catastrophic.'

Colonel Monter, who was unaware of the true situation, forbade the retreat, and ordered Rokicki to fight on. Fortunately the order did not reach Mokotów in time, and Rokicki and his men started to leave. The evacuation was chaotic, as hundreds of soldiers jostled with civilians to try to get to the manholes. By now the Germans had booby trapped and damaged the sewers, but there was no other way out. Of the 3,000 AK soldiers who had fought in Mokotów only six hundred managed to escape to safety. One of the worst incidents took place on Dworkowa Street, where filthy and exhausted AK soldiers emerged into the sunshine expecting to be helped out by their colleagues, when in fact they had come up in German-held territory. Each man was pulled out quickly, so that he would have no time to alert those behind him: 140 were shot by the Schutzpolizei. Others got lost underground, and many bodies were recovered after the war: forty-two at Agrykola, thirty-two under Pohorosy, eight under Zagórna. Still more died because of the booby traps, grenades, mines and 'typhoon' rockets. Some reached what they thought was freedom, only to find themselves trapped behind iron grilles and bars from which they could not escape, a terrifying fate immortalized in Andrzej Wajda's classic film *Kanał*, in which two characters lie only centimetres from the Vistula, its water just beyond the grille which holds them prisoner. The audience can see Russian-held Praga in the distance, calm and peaceful.

When Monter heard that Rokicki had made it to the city centre he had him arrested for desertion, an absurd charge which was only dropped when he realized that his order not to evacuate had not reached Mokotów. Monter sent him back to his post, but by then the entire district had been captured.

In keeping with Himmler's new policy towards the Poles, the 5,000 civilians captured in Mokotów were treated leniently. Survivors were called from their cellars with the familiar '*Raus! Hände hoch!*', but for the most part grenades were not thrown in through the windows, nor were men separated out and shot. One witness recalled being forced from her shelter, but her group was not brutalized: 'The Germans told us to leave. We grabbed our suitcases and began a horrible journey in the direction of Jerusalem Avenue . . . We tripped over rubble and unexploded munitions. Our feet fell into potholes. The tanks shot at the city. Shells were flying overhead. Add the screaming of the Germans and the wailing of children to this chaos.'[8] But they were not harassed. Only twenty days before, Father Michał Czatoryski and the eleven badly wounded men for whom he was caring were shot nearby by Dirlewanger's troops; now everyone was spared. The only people in grave danger were Jews; for them, there was still no mercy.

Generalmajor Rohr was in charge of rounding up the AK soldiers, disarming them and sending them to the city's racetrack for 'processing'. For the first time since 1 August AK prisoners were not executed *en masse*, and most were eventually led to Pruszków camp. Many of those who refused to surrender and continued to hide in the rubble were shot. but even then some were lucky. Ilse Gleicka was leading a group of 'Kedyw' soldiers through Mokotów after the surrender when they were stopped by a commandant at one of the inspection posts. 'He did not even want to look at their papers. Miss Ilse tried to calm him down, but he was stubborn and said he could not break the rules and must release the order to execute them. They decided to bribe him, and asked if anyone had any money. They had forty dollars.* She told the group to keep on walking and went up to the Wehrmacht guy. He took the money and let them run away.'[9]

Radio Berlin announced the surrender of Mokotów on 27 September: 'The footsoldier units, SS units and aircraft units which were part of the von dem Bach Corps group led by Generalmajor Rohr have, despite strong defences in street fights and buildings,

---

* A steady supply of US dollars and gold was brought into Warsaw by couriers from London.

taken over the southern suburb of Warsaw – Mokotów.[10] It had been a quick and efficient operation. Bach hoped for the same in the next target: Żoliborz.

Żoliborz

The northern enclave of Żoliborz was a beautiful, leafy green suburb which stretched along the river, running into Marymont and Bielany in the north and bordered by the ghetto ruins in the south. It had been built in the 1920s and 30s to house the civil servants, officers and journalists of the newly created country, and their villas, apartments and cooperative houses were carefully laid out around parks and playgrounds, cafés and shops.

Like Mokotów, the district had been spared the worst of the fighting in the uprising, and in many respects its people had lived relatively normal lives. The sparsely populated northern district of Marymont had been taken over on 14–15 September, and a number of brutal murders of civilians had been committed there, but the Germans had stopped to wait for reinforcements. Food, on the other hand, had been a problem from the beginning. Unlike other areas of Warsaw, there were no huge warehouses filled with grain, tins of butter or lard, or sugar, and although there were some allotment gardens along streets like Promyka, the Germans kept them under fire. By the end of September food shortages had become so acute that people were coming down with scurvy.

In mid-September the Germans began to bomb the area to 'soften it up'. Jan Rossman, who had made it through the sewers to the 'safe haven', remembered that 'everything changed when Stuka attacks, heavy artillery, missiles and the railway gun started pulverizing Żoliborz'. Within a week the large apartment blocks around Plac Wilsona and the houses at the western edge of the

'Journalist Quarter' were reduced to rubble, and the blocks of cheaper housing near the Gdańsk station were destroyed. 'As the planes were not fired upon they could sweep low over the roofs of the apartment houses and one could easily see the huge bombs attached to their fuselages.' From one day to the next the district was filled with victims of bombs and fire: 'One middle-aged women, her legs smashed and twisted, told us just before she lost consciousness that there had been others in the cellar with her. We started to dig . . . Now we noticed a head, a leg or an arm under the debris – a sign that we were coming to more bodies . . . we found a woman holding a baby in her arms. The baby wailed like a wounded bird and its mother, although injured herself, clasped her child tightly. She lay in a very difficult position so it took a long time to free her.'[11] When the fifteen-year-old Julian Kulski went to report to his battalion headquarters at Plac Wilsona he found that there was nothing left: 'Among the ruins of the Warsaw Cooperative Housing Colony, the grotesquely positioned corpses of women and children lay in bomb craters. Other bodies hung from the balconies. Even the once-lush green trees of Żoliborz were now uprooted and entangled with the dead.'[12]

Some of those whose homes had been destroyed found shelter in holes dug in the grounds of Żeromski Park and in the old brick forts that formed the outer ring of the Russian-built Citadel. The conditions were desperate. 'Hunger is written all over their miserable grey faces. Many people have had nothing in their mouths apart from water for several days. The lamentable state of children cries out for help. In these smelly damp holes around 25,000 people live in the open air. The lack of water and medical care spreads illness and death.'[13] They risked their lives creeping into the allotment gardens at night, and many were injured or killed trying to get food.

Żoliborz was defended by Lieutenant Colonel Mieczysław

Niedzielski ('Żywiciel') and his 1,500 troops, bolstered by a handful of Berling's men who had crossed the river, but they were not ready for the scale of the attack being prepared for them. On 28 September the artillery bombardment began in earnest, exploding houses around Krasiński Street and Plac Wilsona. The 19th Panzer Division under General Källner moved into position. By 29 September the battle was raging on all sides. AK Battalion 'Żniwiarz' fought bitterly for the Opel factory at Wólczańska Street, while 'Żyrafa' Battalion held the ruins of the convent at Plac Wilsona; snipers in the high apartment buildings made it deadly for the Germans to move forward. 'No results,' the 9th Army report recorded.[14] The Germans responded by sending fighter planes and a cohort of Goliaths to blow up the buildings: 'Like a crushing blow the first bombs of our fighters wiped out a net of resistance somewhere behind the Citadel. The other weapons were silent for a moment, as if they had to pause while the bombs did their work. But soon it was there again. It screamed and whistled – the unrelenting fire.'[15] Kampfgruppes Reck and Schmidt were sent in for the final push.

The next German attack did not begin with the usual rounds of artillery fire, a change of tactics which surprised the AK soldiers. 'The Germans are now advancing at a terrific speed,' Julian Kulski wrote. 'From a window in our cellar we could easily see the tanks rolling along the boulevard. Then, after taking positions in front of the apartment houses we were holding, they began to destroy it methodically.'[16]

It had become clear to Niedzielski that recent Soviet promises of help had been a lie. He decided that the situation was hopeless, and Bór gave him official permission to surrender at 6.30 p.m. on 30 September. Some of his troops refused to lay down their arms, and members of the AL chose to try to get across the river; but Niedzielski stood firm. The troops came out of their shelters and bunkers and lined up, not yet able to believe what was taking place, as it had all happened so quickly. 'Lieutenant Szeliga stood before our company . . . and began to read aloud the order from Colonel Żywiciel. "Soldiers! An hour ago as ordered by the Supreme Commander of the Armed Forces, General Bór-Komorowski, I signed the surrender document of our group . . . We are surrendering to the Wehrmacht as a regular army and we will be treated according to the Geneva Convention." ' The men fell into formation, and walked slowly towards Plac Wilsona.

To their surprise they were protected by their captors: 'At 10 o'clock in the morning [of the following day], a carload of leather-coated Gestapo men arrived [but they were] unable to touch us as we were under the "guardianship" of the SS Lower Saxon Panzer Division.' The men were treated as PoWs, and taken to Pruszków. Żoliborz was emptied of its inhabitants, and abandoned. 'Burnt-out windows looked down from the wall,' an SS newspaper correspondent reported. 'Everything is blackened by fire.'

Von dem Bach spent the evening preparing a report for Himmler. 'Reichsführer, I report to you today that the 19th Panzer Division strengthened by two units of the von dem Bach Corps after two days of very hard fighting took over 4/5ths of Żoliborz. According to my negotiations with General Bór the Polish Kommandant of Żoliborz capitulated at 7.40 p.m. PoWs 800. Killed 1,000. Evacuated civilians 15,000.'

Von dem Bach was duly rewarded. 'Dirlewanger and I have been awarded the Knight's Cross by Hitler,' he wrote in his diary. 'Reinefarth got Oak Leaves to his Iron Cross.' This was like a dream come true for Bach, who had so often feared that he would be passed over for this most prized decoration. Not all were pleased at the news. Von Lüttwitz had been forced to congratulate von dem Bach on his success in Mokotów, but this was really too much: 'Please take care not to let these [SS] people decorate themselves with too many Iron Crosses and Oak Leaves without consulting us first,' he spluttered.[17] In many ways Lüttwitz was right. The quick victories in Mokotów and Żoliborz had been due to a number of factors – the wide streets, which were accessible to tanks; the realization by many Poles that the Soviets were not going to help them; sheer exhaustion; and the knowledge that surrender was preferable to an unpleasant death in the rubble – but also to the fact that the fighting was done by the 19th Panzer Division, and not by the murderers and thugs who had raped and slaughtered their way through Wola, the Old Town, Ochota and Czerniaków. When faced by the likes of Dirlewanger or Kaminski, Warsaw's civilians had been left little choice but to resist to the bitter end. Now at least they were up against professional soldiers. This is not to say that the Wehrmacht were not very tough, but their main aim was to conquer territory, not to loot, rape, murder and generally terrorize the population as von dem Bach's men had done. Bach of course took credit anyway, but he was now preoccupied with the next problem. One district still remained. And it posed a huge problem for the Germans.

The City Centre

The city centre, Śródmieście, lay at the very heart of Warsaw, a large district covering an area the size of Wola and Ochota combined. Unlike the distant suburbs of Mokotów and Żoliborz, it had been at the very heart of the modern, bustling European capital before the war. Its narrow streets were lined by six- or seven-storey buildings packed with offices and apartments, hotels and shops, cinemas and theatres. The district was now cut in half by the German-held Jerusalem Avenue, but the AK had created a tunnel to allow passage from north to south. Over 250,000 people were crowded into the city centre, many of them refugees from the Old Town, Wola and the rest, and its streets were crammed with well-built barricades and checkpoints. Von dem Bach had no desire to try to fight his way through this nightmare, but he knew that the surrender of the city centre would mean the surrender of the whole of Warsaw. He was not sure that Bór was ready to take that final step.

Like Mokotów and Żoliborz, the city centre had been largely untouched by the worst of the uprising until September, and refugees who fled there from the Old Town or Wola had been amazed to find its inhabitants walking around the streets, going to cafés or the cinema or visiting friends as if nothing was wrong. The district was made up of people from every walk of life – intellectuals and factory workers, civil servants and artists. Cultural life had carried on in the form of concerts and poetry readings, cabaret and plays. There were lectures and performances at the Palladium Theatre, the Capitol and Urania and Apollo cinemas still functioned, there were concerts at the Conservatory and Chopin recitals in a café on Nowy Świat. The postal service, run largely by scouts, functioned into September. An ingenious field power plant installed at Hoża 51 generated electricity for hospitals, the famous 'Blyskawica' and 'Burza' radio stations, and even the pump for a deep-water well. This building was also the home of BIP propaganda, which produced newspapers, handbills, and even films about the AK fights, which were screened to eager audiences. Antonina Mijal and teams of women sappers ran workshops making weapons at Marszałkowska and later Szpitalna Streets; she helped to blast out the crucial passage between the two districts of the city centre under Jerusalem Avenue. Another AK group made hand grenades, and even produced twenty-five howitzers, at an old metal foundry at Wilcza 61; yet another scooped the gunpowder out of a huge unexploded German mortar shell, which had crashed into the wall of the Adria restaurant, to make more bombs. Other workshops created everything from booby traps to false identification papers to maps – one architectural student spent the entire uprising drawing plans of the ever-changing maze of basement passages, which were sent to the workshop on Wilcza Street and turned into maps for the AK.[18]

This semblance of normality was due in part to the abundant supply of water early on, and to the large German stores of food and other supplies captured by the AK at the beginning of August – the mill on Prosta Street; the warehouse at the Haberbusch and Schiele, packed with wheat and barley which residents collected and then ground in their coffee grinders; the storehouse Związek Mleczarski at Hoża 51, with 140 tonnes of sugar, fifty tonnes of artificial honey and twenty tonnes of butter.

Even housing was not a problem at first: refugees who had made it in from Wola or the Old Town were given the keys to properties which had belonged to *Volks* or *Reichsdeutsche*, as long as they signed a statement explaining their situation; the RGO* also organized large shelters for a total of a thousand people. All men between the ages of seventeen and fifty were obliged to work for six hours a day at tasks like digging wells, fighting fires and burying the dead. The RGO set up over eighty soup kitchens, which in August were preparing more than 10,000 meals a day.

The city centre did not wholly escape the violence. Throughout the uprising fierce battles were fought along its outskirts. The Germans tried time and again to push through the barricades, and above all to take control of the entire length of Jerusalem Avenue, but they never succeeded. There were also isolated battles for German strongholds throughout the district, some of which would become the stuff of AK legend. The 'Kiliński' Battalion

---

* The Rada Główna Opiekuńcza, or Central Welfare Council, one of the few civic organizations allowed by the Nazis. It provided food, shelter and clothing for those in need, and was funded by both the German and the Polish authorities.

managed to take a number of German-held posts – the Cristal restaurant on Jerusalem Avenue, the Café Club on Nowy Świat, the 'Small Pasta' building at Piusa 19 – but its most important victory was at the so-called 'Pasta' building (Polska Akcyjna Spółka Telefonów – the central telephone exchange) on Dzielna Street. This ten-storey complex, with its mock medieval tower perched on top, had been used to great effect by German snipers throughout the uprising. It also housed Warsaw's main telephone exchange and communications centre, which made it a vital target. Two hundred German troops were trapped inside, but, convinced that capture meant certain death, they fought viciously against successive AK attacks. One of them, Kurt Heller, a Wehrmacht soldier from Munich, wrote in his notebook a few days before the final battle: 'the Poles have moved in to drive us away with fire and with bottles of benzene'. Some of the Germans had lost their nerve and committed suicide, and 'a terrible stench was rising from the bodies lying on the street. On the last day he wrote that the Poles had surrounded them; he feared that he would end up in the mass grave in the courtyard.[19]

On the night of 19 August the Poles pumped oil and petrol into the basement and set it on fire, forcing the Germans to the upper floors. 'The Germans defended it furiously,' Janusz Hamerlinski of 'Kiliński' Battalion recalled. Zbigniew Dębski fought from room to room: 'From above they threw grenades on us, fired with submachine guns. We conquered, in turn, the second and the third floors.' The Germans hung a yellow distress flag on the side of the building, but no help came. When the Poles reached the top floor they discovered that the Germans had made their way down to the cellars using a small spiral staircase at the back of the building. They were finally trapped in the boiler room, and gave up. 'When we let them put their hands down and we gave them a cigarette some of the old Wehrmacht soldiers cried like children and cursed Hitler and the war. All the German soldiers became PoWs.'[20] The fighting had claimed the lives of about thirty-five AK men, while 115 Wehrmacht and SS soldiers were taken prisoner.

Apart from these isolated battles on the edges of the district and for specific buildings, Śródmieście remained more or less calm until the fall of the Old Town. But then the bombing started, and everything changed. 'Karl' mortars, *Krowas*, Stukas and the rest were turned on the district, shattering the relatively peaceful lives of the civilians in the district: 'They are bombing Złota, Chmielna, Zgoda – the house is shaking . . .' One AK soldier recounted the massive impact of a mortar shell which failed to explode: 'We're sitting in the canteen, quiet and empty. St. R. Dobrowolski comes in, sits down and falls asleep. The light flickers and, above, the sound of crashing floors increases, a thud – I see an enormous slab of wall approach us. It is moving so slowly that I have time to pull "Elä" under the table, push Dobrowolski and duck myself. The tinkle of breaking mirrors, a thick, milky air fills the room, you cannot see anything, silence, shrieks . . . wounded are being carried in, six, two have been killed.'[21] Had it detonated, everyone in the building would have perished. The sudden increase in bombing caused a wave of panic and fear, above all among the 60,000 refugees from Wola, Ochota and the Old Town, who knew exactly what it meant: 'The same thing all over again for the fourth time,' Miron Białoszewski wrote. 'Once again, they would have to face the prospect of a violent and horrible death.'[22]

The Stukas were loathed. Nurse Anna Szatkowska was carrying medical equipment to her hospital when she was spotted by one of the pilots: 'They have noticed me and they will shoot and I will die here alone,' she thought. She curled up as close as she could to a wall: ' "*Dominus illuminatio mea*," I said over and over. "The lord is my light and my salvation." The machine gun sprays bullets all around me and I am buried in dust. Then they fly away.'[23] Zbigniew Dębski was in command of a post based in an ice-cream shop at Nowy Świat 21 when the Germans directed Stukas against his building. 'At that moment aeroplanes arrived and bombarded our positions. All my dear friends died under the debris. I had known them from secondary school . . . I was hurt and buried under the rubble but because I had been further forward the rescue party saw my shoe sticking out and I was saved.' The building was bombed again later in the day, making any further rescues impossible. 'Nobody else got out alive.'

One nurse was sent to care for a wounded girl who had been carrying food for the AK soldiers. 'We pulled out the top of her skull. She is unconscious. It is obvious there is no helping her. A while later she dies.' The nurse recognized the girl as 'sporty young Irena', with whom she had worked only days before. They found a coffin, but it was too small: 'Irena's legs hang out of the end.'[24] Planes were coming over the destroyed houses. 'People who had been queuing for water ran away into a hole or to the basement.' Two bombs fell in the courtyard. 'I am flying through the air and land on people crowded at the bottom of the stairs. The power of the explosion tore my smelly but precious jacket which had gone with me through the Old Town and the sewers.'[25]

As the bombing increased people were forced to move to the basements and shelters. Buildings disappeared 'from the top down, chunk by chunk or blown to smithereens by one direct hit'. Nowhere was safe, as the large mortar shells could smash through an entire building and into the basement. The Speaker of the Sejm (Parliament) and his entire family were buried in the rubble at Hoża 14, as were thirty other people. Their remains were exhumed after the war.[26] The electricity supply was cut off, and the dank underground hiding places were lit only by carbide lamps or candles.

The great warehouses of food were now running out of supplies, and people began to starve. With the recent influx of refugees from Czerniaków there were now nearly 200,000 mouths to feed. Dr Wronowski wrote of Pańska Street that 'the condition of the refugees is terrible, especially as they have no food. The kitchen which used to work has stopped because there is no water. Famine has started.' A civilian remembered being 'shattered when the children in the basement started dying'. Infant mortality rose astronomically, as mothers had no food, water or milk, and disease took its toll. People started to barter along Wilcza and Krucza Streets, trading cigarettes or anything else they had for meagre scraps of food. 'Money was worth as much as garbage. Krucza Street between Hoża and Wilcza was like a bazaar.' The RGO was forced to inform the Regional Delegate at Krucza Street that most of the soup kitchens were now closed. There was simply nothing to eat.[27]

The shortage of water was even worse. The Germans had cut off the mains water supply, and deliberately targeted people lined up at the wells. The desperation that resulted was visible everywhere. When it rained for a short time in September 'people knelt on the ground, spoon in hand, taking rainwater from puddles and poured spoon after spoon into cans and dishes'.[28]

Life in the cellars became unbearable: 'People face the loss of everything – even their lives – in the rubble. They are starving and ill, and add the lack of electricity which means everything is done in the twilight of primitive lamps and candles, in the crowds reading is impossible, people talk constantly, there is no water so people cannot wash.'[29] Many turned to religion for comfort, and Masses were held in cellars and courtyards. Nuns and priests often showed enormous bravery, helping the wounded under fire or hauling people to safety. One priest gave Communion to a group standing against a wall about to be executed.[30]

The heady optimism of August had been replaced by a general sense of gloom: 'We were depressed as we realized it was our turn this time. There was no false bravado. Everyone feared the "*Krowas*" and the air attacks. We felt we just couldn't survive.'[31] Worse still, winter was coming. 'Nights are now very cold. People have lost their belongings, blankets are taken for the wounded patients. The ruins and basements are freezing but they cannot make a fire as people would die of smoke inhalation. Some try to make fires in the courtyards but this is dangerous because of bombs and shells.'[32]

The eight first-aid posts were overwhelmed. Doctors performed operations by the light of an old torch or an oil lamp propped up on a shelf; the floors were slippery with blood, and there were no anaesthetics or medical supplies. Many of those brought in were seriously wounded in the abdomen or the legs, and hundreds died. Graves were hastily dug in parks, public squares or pavements, but when the bombs fell the corpses would be churned up again, leaving them exposed as food for the rats and flies. In the final weeks many bodies were left unburied. The stench was terrible.

Finally, morale broke down, and people started to look for scapegoats. The Allies and Stalin were top of the list, but the AK too came under fire. Newspapers, once so eagerly awaited, were now dismissed for not having any real news. A report written for the information department of BIP quoted a man who said: 'We read in the paper that we have the University of Technology, when we know we have lost it already . . . we are not children to whom you can feed fairy tales.' Conflicts developed between those who were still in their own homes, often with hidden food stores, and those in shelters, who had nothing. Klaudiusz Hrabyk faced starvation: 'We ate sparrows, pigeons and dogs and cats. Dysentery not life-threatening but problematic. Instead of bread, some mush, instead of cigarettes I smoke slightly chopped dry pine needles.'

It was not enough to keep them going: 'During the second half of September we were all actually starving. Money had no value. You could get food in exchange for other food or clothes but we didn't have any of those things – Eva and I were without any clothes, without money or hope that we would ever get back to our house.'[33] He was given a bit of bread by the mother of a shop assistant they had known before the uprising, but most people were 'indifferent or unable to help'. Jan Rosner was depressed about the loss of everything he had worked for, above all his precious bookshop. He escaped into literature: '25th. No bread. No water. Gave a lecture about Huxley.'[34]

Resentment grew, too, about the RGO work programme. 'The atmosphere amongst civilians gets worse every day,' one report read. 'Often we have to push people to participate in the street work and even when building wells there are problems with water. The food portions are very poor and the number of people fainting from the lack of food is growing.' A professor at the University of Technology complained that the RGO programme was unfair, as it exploited the homeless and the vulnerable: 'It is wrong to use people who have been expelled, who have lost their homes, who have no place to live, who do not have food or clothes, who are depressed and tired and bitter.' He continued: 'It reminds me of German methods of recruitment which I have known for five years. The police come between 6.30 and 7.00 in the morning, to flats and attics and bunkers, and start pulling people out of their beds.' He believed that the people should at least be given the same rations as the AK, 'as they have to work very hard under fire in very dangerous conditions with no money, for the public good'.[35] Another official BIP report held: 'There is a group of healthy young men who drink all day and do nothing except try to get vodka. People make themselves out to be house commandants and yet do nothing. They don't participate in building barricades while they make old and ill people do it. Very often the drinking causes fights and very loud behaviour into the middle of the night and also sexual behaviour. They criticize the uprising without shame.'[36]

For almost the first time there was open criticism of the AK. The civilians of Śródmieście had not witnessed the bravery of the soldiers, unlike those of, say, the Old Town. All they saw were people whom they believed had done 'very little', yet had special passes and privileges – above all, access to food and water. Some who had escaped from the Old Town blamed the AK for not having allowed civilians to escape through the sewers on time: 'They left us there, and maybe they are planning to do the same here.' There was talk of people arming themselves in defiance of the AK; there were also increasing reports of civilians trying to leave the city centre through the German lines.[37] 'You hear complaints about drunken AK soldiers and about their unpleasant excesses. The drinking is usually by people in lower positions, but civilians observe it and comment on it. You hear about requisitions at gunpoint. Yesterday at 1 p.m. on Żurawia . . . two AK soldiers walked around in the flats in the neighbourhood showing their pass and demanding wheat and *kasha*, grits and wine.'[38]

By 18 September all the public kitchens had closed down. Five of the hospitals had been bombed out, thousands of people were standing in line for water every day, and many were dying. On 22 September Bór was told: 'Yesterday a tank fired into the line, after a short attack two people were killed and some wounded at Pole Mokotowskie. People usually wait six to eight hours in the queue for water.'[39] Another report said that 'in almost every cellar you find people who only eat once every few days. People are in bunkers all the time. They are very apathetic and dirty and do not go out for air. The famine is spreading and people are in nervous shock because of starvation. The cost of one kilo of flour is 1,200 złoty. People pay with gold or foreign currency for a small amount of rye.'[40]

On 22 September Bór made an official tour of the city centre, greeted at some of the barricades by someone playing a violin or even a piano. The men talked about their preoccupations – the shortage of coats, the cold nights, the lack of cigarettes, the dearth of weapons and ammunition, the increasing problem of lice, but it was the condition of the civilians that concerned him most. It was clear to him that people would not be able to hold out much longer. 'Exhaustion reached such a pitch that even the first-aid service, which hitherto had worked very well indeed, slackened. People became indifferent to everything, even to the cries of those buried in the basements of destroyed houses. All their strength had been used up and there were no more men to clear the rubble.'[41] Again, Bór was contemplating negotiations with the Germans. 'The attacking and bombing of the town, which continues with no retaliation, increases awareness that the enemy is trying to destroy the whole town . . . the ceaseless battle, the increasingly smaller food rations for fire victims and the exhaustion of food for the permanent residents, the high death rate amongst infants, the hostile agitation of unfriendly agents, the lack of water and electricity in all districts . . .'[42] Agaton found the situation of the civilians desperate: 'They were crowded in basements without water, dirty and ill and under constant fire.'[43] By the end of September it was virtually impossible to find a space in the crowded basements, and people were starving. 'We sat around with our beards growing. We didn't wash.' To get water they had to wait until after dark, 'but at twilight the grenades, mortars, Berthas and *Krowas* go wild'. People were being ripped to shreds or buried alive. 'On Krucza between Wspólna and Hoża lay a woman's bloody shoe.' It still had a chunk of heel in it.[44]

Von dem Bach and the Bid for Peace

The increasing sense of despair in the city centre had been reported to von dem Bach on a regular basis, and he had been delighted. He had tried to negotiate a peace settlement weeks before, and had even arranged a ceasefire on 7 and 8 September, during which around 60,000 civilians had left for Pruszków camp, but his plans had been thwarted by the Soviet takeover of Praga and the ensuing American and Russian airdrops, which sent AK morale soaring. Bór had stopped all talks. But now, with the plight of the civilians worsening and with no sign that the Soviets intended to come to their aid, a reluctant Bór decided to resume negotiations. Bach was ready to agree to almost anything to get the deal signed as quickly as possible so the Wehrmacht could not claim victory for themselves. He had laid the groundwork early. Warsaw was to be his prize, and his prize only.

As early as 2 September, Bach had convinced Hitler to give him the right to negotiate as his 'proxy'. The Führer had consented, but strictly on the condition that any agreement with the AK was to be in the form of an 'ultimatum', and not achieved by 'negotiation'. Bach pretended to accept this order, although he disobeyed it later on. He had also told General Staedke, 'I am the only one permitted to oversee this game. Please pass on this information. NO other authority in the government has the right to conduct negotiations.' To his fury, however, the Chief of Staff of Army Group Centre, General Heidkämpfer, gave General Rohr permission to conduct negotiations himself, saying, 'Many things have happened. This has nothing to do with von dem Bach.' Bach had to act quickly if he was to secure the peace himself.

Bór too decided to act. He named Lieutenant Colonel Zygmunt Dobrowolski ('Zyndram') as his official representative, and sent him to meet von dem Bach. At 7.15 in the morning of 28

September Dobrowolski and an interpreter went with white flags flying to the barricade at Żelazna Street, where they were met by five German officers and an interpreter. Major Kurt Fischer was waiting for him at Kozaków 81, and Dobrowolski gave him a letter for von dem Bach requesting a meeting. Bach was thrilled, but made the Polish representatives wait. Finally the answer came back. He agreed to the meeting.

The Poles were taken by von dem Bach's motorcade – with his usual escort of motorcycles and police cars – to his headquarters in the small manor house at Ożarów, twenty kilometres from Warsaw. Again they were made to wait before finally being ushered in. Von dem Bach met them in the drawing room, a huge Dutch chandelier overhead and old Polish portraits on the walls. In keeping with Himmler's new tactic the Poles were not treated like *Banditen* but as honoured guests, and the obsequious Bach was in his element.

His long, flowery opening speech spoke volumes about this master of self-delusion. He began by stressing the lore of the ancient knights and the noble tradition of honour in defeat. He was not modest. 'My family has lived in East Prussia since the fifteenth century,' he said. 'We were there during the time of the Teutonic Knights, and that is why I am perceived in some army and government circles as a specialist on East European affairs.' He paused. 'I am not just a soldier and an SS general. I am also a politician and have even been a deputy of the German parliament for thirteen years. This has helped me to get a broader outlook on the matters we are about to discuss.' He could, even now, not resist a dig at the 9th Army and General Rohr: 'I will be able to treat these questions a little differently, as I am more than a mere soldier.'

Bach did not stop there. In an effort to allay Polish fears about the poor treatment of civilians, he tried to explain away the crimes committed by Dirlewanger and the rest: 'I took over the leadership of the German army in Warsaw on the eighth day of the uprising,' he said. 'There were many different units in the German army at that time. The quality of these units varied and they were brought from different places, which is why the fight was conducted using uncivilized methods. In its fight against the Bolsheviks the German army needed these methods.' He paused again, hoping that he was making himself clear. 'Street fights are some of the most difficult and are exhausting for the soldiers. The abnormally difficult conditions were made worse here because of the specific conditions of the Warsaw Uprising during which civilians participated in fights and problems with uniforms and all these things made it difficult for the German soldier to keep his blood cold and that is why some very unpleasant things took place, things which should not take place between two cultured nations.'[45]

After that, he essentially granted everything the Poles were asking for: the AK would be given combatants' rights, they would be sent to PoW camps, and all evacuations would be conducted under the auspices of the Red Cross. It was clear that Bach wanted a quick end to the uprising. 'I would like to save as many Polish units as possible,' he said, 'because of the heroism which they showed during the fights in Warsaw. The activities of the AK were unique. The AK has passed its own exam in history.'[46] This echoed what he had told Countess Tarnowska of the Polish Red Cross during earlier negotiations: 'I am really sorry about the deaths of the AK soldiers,' he had said. 'They would have been very useful in the future,' as they all knew that 'Soviet Russia is the common enemy of Poles and Germans.'[47]

After this extraordinary encounter with one of the most vile criminals of the Third Reich, Dobrowolski was taken back to Warsaw. He crossed the barricade at 1 p.m. and went to a meeting with the AK leadership, including Bór and Deputy Prime Minister Dr Klonowski. All agreed that the Soviets did not seem willing to help, and that the Western Allies were in no position to do so. Furthermore, Bach had agreed to their conditions. What should they do?

Monter wanted to fight on, and continue to use the civilians of Warsaw as what amounted to little more than a gigantic human shield. Negotiations should be out of the question and civilians should not be allowed to leave: 'Today the soldier knows that by fighting he is also defending the civilians. If the civilians are evacuated the soldier will feel lonely and he will not be able to defend the mountain of rubble which is Warsaw today.'[48]

Fortunately, Monter was overruled by the civil authorities, who argued that to continue the fight was 'insanity'. The task now should be to save as many people as possible, and to prevent the 'human capital' – the elite of Poland – from being further pulverized, buried or burned.

Bór agreed that the fight was 'hopeless' and that the civilians should be spared, but he wanted to keep the door open for a possible last-minute change of heart by Stalin. This led to a two-pronged strategy: talks about civilian evacuation were to come first; talks regarding the capitulation of the AK second.

To that end, on 29 September Bór requested more information from the Germans about the fate of the civilians. There was still a very real fear that they might be massacred, and Bór asked for a group of his representatives to be permitted to visit Pruszków, to see what the camp was like. He agreed that if fears about the camp, medical care, food, transport and help for children, the old and the sick were allayed, the Germans could begin the evacuation of civilians straight away. A delegation was duly sent to Pruszków, and although they reported back that conditions were at best 'adequate', Bór gambled that the civilians would be better off being sent there than enduring a slow death by starvation, injury or illness in the city centre.

The second meeting between Bach and Dobrowolski took place on 29 September. Bach was desperate to show his 'humanitarianism' to the world: 'London Radio has released information that I have been put on the list of war criminals,' he complained in his diary. He considered this to be deeply unfair, given that he had 'saved so many women and children'. If he brokered a peaceful resolution to the Warsaw problem, he thought, perhaps he would salvage his reputation and the Allies would reconsider their verdict.

The first agreement, signed on 30 September, called for a ceasefire between 5 a.m. and 7 p.m. on 1 and 2 October. Civilians were to be allowed to leave, unharmed, for Pruszków camp. Leaflets were dropped showing where they were to gather and emphasizing that they would be escorted by General Rohr's troops or by the Reinefarth *Sturm* group. Sturmbannführer Diehl was to oversee the 'resettlement' in Pruszków. 'The civilians are to get one piece of bread and one portion of liquid.'[49]

Bach was nervous about the reaction of his men. He told Dobrowolski that he would try to protect civilians going to Pruszków, but added: 'I cannot guarantee that some German soldiers might not break the rules. Up until now they had been told they were fighting against bandits and that the civilians were participants as well . . . now the German soldier is expected to be some kind of guardian angel!' In the event people would be harassed, and some shot, but this was no longer the murderous rout from Wola or the Old Town.

For the civilians, news of the evacuations brought a mixture of fear and relief. 'In the morning of 1 October everything grew still. The main front was quiet. The Germans were quiet . . . at once everyone started coming out from all the cellars, vaults, holes . . . It wasn't a day of mourning. Nor was it a holiday . . . It was simply the population crawling out onto the surface.'[50]

For some, after the weeks of fear and bloodshed, and the deafening noise of mortars, bombs and sniper fire, the sheer silence was the most shocking thing of all. People packed their meagre belongings and tentatively made their way towards the barricades. There were mixed reactions in the crowds of onlookers, some of whom regarded the civilians as 'deserting the ship'. One young AK soldier said, 'If I saw my mother in the crowd I would shoot her,' and others jeered at the lines of people with their tired faces and exhausted children, calling them traitors for going. In other cases, however, AK soldiers escorted their families to the barricades and said goodbye in person.[51] The fighting resumed at seven in the evening. Von dem Bach, completely misreading the Polish mentality, put the city centre under a massive bombardment after 8 o'clock, killing and maiming civilians who had dared to leave their shelters. The Poles do not respond well to being bullied, and he very nearly derailed the negotiations by this act.

More civilians left on the second day. 'A lot of people, loaded down for the journey, milled around the departure point. People were sitting on bundles. They were searching for their relatives . . . Suitcases, children . . . the whole departure proceeded slowly. It resembled an assembly for the Last Judgement.'[52] By 7 o'clock in the evening, over 16,000 civilians had left Warsaw.

Bach was pleased, and was now even more impatient to sign an agreement with the AK itself. His greatest fear was that Stalin would play some last-minute trick, pretending to be on his way into Warsaw and thereby prolonging the uprising yet again. He was right to worry, as Bór did in fact delay capitulation as long as he could, stating as late as 28 September that if the Soviets promised to help even in the final hour he would cancel the settlement with the Germans. But no help came. It was time.

The AK delegation, given plenipotentiary powers by Bór, consisted of Dobrowolski and Kazimierz Iranek-Osmecki. At 8 o'clock on the morning of 2 October they crossed the barricade at Śniadecki Street, where Major Fischer and Major Bock were waiting for them. Meanwhile, Bach was nervously pacing around the manor house at Ożarów. 'Today I am going through the most critical day of my fight in Warsaw,' he wrote. 'General Bór is either conducting a vicious game, or he will capitulate.'

Negotiations began promptly, but they were not easy. German interpreter Gerhard von Jordan recalled: 'The Poles were tough and they made von dem Bach compromise over and over again.' Bach had little choice. He needed the document signed.

The 9th Army leadership was nervous too, because failure would mean they would have to mount a full-scale attack on the city centre; nobody wanted 'another Stalingrad', as Himmler had put it. At 12.35 the Chief of Staff of the 9th Army, General Staedke, telephoned Bach to find out what was happening. 'How is it?' he asked. 'Everything is fine,' Bach replied, 'but there are some difficulties, not only on their side, as instructions are not very precise. We have so far settled that 1) all German PoWs are to be released, 2) from tomorrow morning the barricades will be dismantled. I emphasized that if this did not happen I would cancel the cease-fire.' 'Is it possible to start dismantling barricades today?' Staedke asked. 'No, it needs time.'

After a light lunch the negotiations began again, and by the time an equally edgy von Lüttwitz telephoned at 7.25 p.m. Bach was able to report: 'Negotiations are over. Now only translations.' Lüttwitz wanted to know how many AK soldiers were left in Warsaw. 'Rohr is reporting around 15,000.'

At twenty minutes past eight the agreement for the cessation of hostilities in Warsaw was signed, and many promises were made. The Germans agreed to treat the AK soldiers as PoWs, giving them combatants' rights according to the Geneva Convention, not to retaliate against actions that had taken place before the uprising, and to deal 'humanely' with civilians. Objects of artistic, cultural or sacred value were to be evacuated, and such 'public and private property as remains in the city' was to be 'protected'. The Germans estimated that there were as many as 250,000 civilians still in Warsaw. They were to be processed at Pruszków camp. Finally, after sixty-three days of 'some of the most bitter fighting of the war', the uprising was over.

The first thing Bach did was to call Führer headquarters in triumph. To his horror, the agreement was very nearly scuppered by Fegelein, and indeed by Hitler himself. 'When the final conditions were settled, Bach telephoned the Führer to try to get his approval,' Jordan recalled. 'Bach got Fegelein on the phone, who at first was critical of the compromises: "You should not negotiate with these kinds of bandits," he said. Finally Fegelein asked, "Who is this guy Bór anyway?" ' For most of the uprising Bór's true identity had been kept a secret. 'Bach said, "Oh didn't you know? This is the famous showjumper Count Komorowski. You must know him." "Oh, him!" Fegelein answered. "A fantastic guy! That changes everything! Wait a minute please." ' Fegelein must have talked to Hitler and told him that the deal was acceptable. 'After a short while Fegelein passed on Hitler's acceptance for the capitulation conditions.'[53] So the deal that ended the Warsaw Uprising was sealed not because of its merits, but because Bór had competed against Fegelein at the Berlin Olympics.

Bach was relieved, and bursting with pride. 'I am part of history. I am proud and happy that my sons will find out about it one day. I am negotiating based on General Proxy with the Poles who are being advised from London. It is big politics,' he gloated in his diary.[54] He chided the Wehrmacht yet again: 'Staedke was highly sceptical of my negotiations. He regarded them as showing weakness of will on our part, and that from the point of view of the enemy it was only a ploy to gain time until the Russian offensive.'

But there had been no Russian offensive, and Bach had won his prize. He was beside himself when Hitler called to congratulate him personally. 'The Führer is delighted that the situation in Warsaw was handled with such honour,' he said. Now, all that remained was for him to meet Bór in person and try to convince him to join the German side in the 'coming war' with the Bolsheviks.

In the meantime, messages of congratulation poured in – from Guderian, from Himmler, from Staedke, from Lüttwitz and from Reinhard. Bach was riding high. But feelings were much more mixed in Warsaw itself.

The Surrender

When news of the surrender broke, many in the AK were simply devastated. They had lost a valiant fight, their city was in ruins, and they were to be sent into captivity. They were proud of their achievements, but felt betrayed by the Western Allies and let down by the Soviets. It was a bitter moment, but there was nothing for it. They had to decide whether to pretend to be civilians and be sent to Pruszków, or to prepare themselves for an uncertain future as prisoners of war of the Third Reich.

The final days of freedom were spent in a kind of unreal haze. Gloomy officer briefings and soldier gatherings were held in Warsaw for the last time on 2 and 3 October, at which the group commanders officially read out the capitulation agreement, along with a farewell letter from Monter. The first paycheques were given out, and arrangements were made to hide documents and some of the better-quality arms and ammunition for possible future use. It had been agreed that around three hundred soldiers from the 'Kiliński' Battalion and 120 from 'Miłosz' would stay and keep order until the Germans took over; the rest were to prepare to march into captivity. Józef Rybicki told his elite unit:

'All those in "Kedyw" have two options – to return to civilian life or to become PoWs.' Many still did not trust the Germans to treat them under the Geneva Convention. One nurse wrote that her 'Kedyw' pass made her doubly suspect; she escaped capture and hid in the villa colony of Wilanów until the end of the war. Many others felt that they could not let themselves be taken by the Germans, and decided to leave as civilians. Women in particular chose this route, as it was possible to get false papers through local companies like Wedel Chocolates and the Blikle bakery. It turned out to be a wise decision, as the Germans did not treat all of the women as PoWs: many were forced to do physical labour in German munitions factories, in violation of the Geneva Convention, and 1,705 were sent to work at Oberlangen PoW camp in north-western Germany. All official protests were ignored.[55]

Many took the opportunity in those last hours to go back to their homes and try to find out what had happened to their loved ones. Agaton approached the shell that had been his building, to find the old sign with his father's visiting hours – long out of date – still hanging by the door. His family's apartment was all but destroyed, and was filled with things that did not belong to them, which could only mean that strangers had been living there. His father's valuable paintings by Julian Fałat and Aleksander Gierymski were gone, and the dining room had only one wall and no ceiling. He was overwhelmed by memories of a life now gone forever, and took with him some family photographs and an old map of Poland which had hung above his father's desk. Later, at Langwasser PoW camp, he would have to explain to the guards that he was not going to use the map to plan an escape – it was sent to 'deposit', and only given back to him when he was later sent to Colditz Castle* in Saxony.[56]

* The PoW camp used for 'incorrigible' Allied officers who had repeatedly attempted to escape from other camps, and also for 'Prominente' – German for 'celebrity' – prisoners, including Bór and five other Polish generals.

Other men tried to safeguard possessions, bury weapons and hide belongings which they knew would be confiscated at the checkpoints. Kazimierz Iranek-Osmecki, the AK's intelligence chief, ordered a group of soldiers to hide Bór's personal archive, which they put in a large box that had been coated with tar. It was buried along with family photographs and other personal mementos, including the original 1864 manuscript of an aria from Stanisław Moniuszko's *The Haunted Manor*, one of Poland's most beloved operas.[57]

The soldiers from the AK had no intention of looking dejected and cowed when they marched out of the city for the last time, and stood in line for water so they could wash and shave. 'At battalion headquarters much movement. They check and sort weapons. The worst ones will be given away the best are hidden in selected basements.' They tried to make their uniforms look as fresh as possible.

On 4 October the stage was set for the final act. German film crews and photographers had been brought in, and German troops were lined up at the spot where the Śniadecki Street barricade had once stood. 'A crowd of civilians stand to pay their respects, some of them are crying, saying, "Our children are leaving. God bless you, come back to us." But there are also people cursing, saying, "You wanted a war, you stupid brats, you can have it. Do you see what you did?" The boys did not react.'[58]

General Monter appeared in his uniform and placed himself at the entrance to Lwówska Street to take the salute from the AK troops, but just before the parade began three German officers appeared in the middle of the square. Monter sent his people to find out what was going on. Kurt Fischer, chief of Reinefarth's staff, announced that he had been ordered to take General Bór prisoner himself.

Bór moved forward. Fischer gave the Hitler salute and said,

'*Herr General! Ich habe den Befehl und die Ehre Sie in die Gefangenschaft zu übernehmen*' – Herr General! I have been ordered, and have the honour, to escort you into captivity. One of the German war correspondents wrote: '4 October. 11 o'clock. The German officers wait for Bór. He comes, lonely, in a dark-brown coat and a hat of the same colour, a very thin face and dark intelligent eyes, soldier's movement, gentleness and honesty.'[59] One thing was obvious: even in defeat the prisoners were no longer to be seen as the 'bandits' of Goebbels' propaganda.

Bór was taken away for his meeting with von dem Bach. Then, as the cameras rolled, the AK troops lined up solemnly in rows of four with their weapons in hand, red-and-white armbands and Polish eagles proudly on display. They marched defiantly past the Germans, dropping pistols into woven baskets held by Rohr's men and placing larger weapons on the tables provided. The Nazi newsreel *Die Deutsche Wochenschau* showed the scene, explaining how the Poles had been 'betrayed by the Anglo-Americans' and the Russians; words like 'chivalrous' and 'knightly' ran through German press articles in the coming weeks. The German soldier Peter Stolten wrote to his mother: 'I was there when the *Chronicle Wochenschau* was being shot and I saw the drama of the Polish capitulation. Let's not lie to ourselves. Warsaw fell because of the concentration of our heavy weapons and not because of the courage of our units even if some were fighting very well . . . The insurgents really deserve to be treated like soldiers. What could they do as they lost their state and did not have their own army? I would not like to have lived under German administration either. General Bór was taken from Warsaw in a column of cars, some Colonel announced capitulation and then the Poles marched in rows of four . . . without despair, unbreakable in their national pride.'[60]

The columns moved in complete silence. An excited Bach was kept informed by phone. At 10.30 he called Staedke: 'One battalion of 665 people disarmed, the second battalion is coming, the third battalion is crossing the line . . .'[61] Singing the Polish national anthem, the AK soldiers marched out past the German checkpoints and onto the trains that would take them to captivity.

Meanwhile, Bór was taken to meet von dem Bach at Ożarów, his first glimpse of the western part of the city since the beginning of August. 'We went through Wola. We could hardly recognize streets which we had known so well before,' recalled Agaton, who was a member of the party. Bach had been waiting for this meeting for months. He came out of 'his' manor house acting every bit the 'honourable knight', surrounded by his SS guard in their long coats and with machine guns in their hands. Bór got out of the car and Bach ushered him inside with a kind of mock bonhomie, then proceeded to give another of his speeches, astounding in its insensitivity.

The 'repression in Warsaw' had been unnecessarily harsh, even 'stupid and cruel', Bach said. The Germans could not prevent the mobilization of such a large and trained underground army. 'This,' he added, referring to his work in Byelorussia, 'is something I know from my experience in fighting the resistance before Warsaw.' Then he turned to the business at hand.

'The war will finish quickly thanks to new German weapons,' he continued confidently, 'so it is necessary to create an anti-Communist front.'[62] He asked Bór to release an order for all AK units throughout Poland to stop the 'small war' with Germany immediately so that they could cooperate in the 'real war' with the Soviets. Bór answered curtly that it was impossible for him to give such an order.[63]

Bach, somewhat disappointed, invited Bór for a meal to commemorate the momentous day. Bór turned him down flat, also refusing lodging in the palace at Skierniewice: 'I will share the fate of my soldiers,' he said. Bach was deeply offended by this 'snub', and could not understand why the Polish leader did not want to share a meal with him. In fact Bór could not wait to leave.

When he returned to Warsaw he wrote a dejected letter to the Polish Prime Minister in London, which was sent on the evening of 4 October. 'I report that the army that fought in Warsaw is surrendering weapons today and tomorrow and I will be a prisoner of war as well . . . Today I met with Bach with whom I signed the capitulation agreement. I was invited for breakfast . . . I refused to participate.'[64]

Despite his disappointment, at 4.55 p.m. Bach told Lüttwitz, 'I tried to convince him to release an order for the whole army to cease fire.' Leutnant Weller of the 9th Army was more realistic: 'Yes, the Poles are ready to fight Bolshevism, however they also want independence. And the Pole with his strongly developed sense of honour will never take on the role [of cooperating with the Germans].'

Bach did not give up. Two days later Bór was taken to Himmler's headquarters at Kruglanken, where he was again asked to order the capitulation of the AK throughout Poland; again he refused. On 9 October he and a small group of officers were bundled onto a train to Berlin. The Poles were wearing civilian clothes, but with their red-and-white armbands in clear view. People looked at them curiously as they were escorted through the city: 'We could hear the word "*Banditen*",' Agaton recalled. 'Berlin was empty, like a dead city – empty streets and rubble.' They were taken to a beautiful villa used by Himmler's staff. 'We waited for him all day in the garden but the meeting never took place. In the evening we were taken to the SS barracks. Suddenly there was an air-raid warning and we were taken to a bunker, but a fight ensued as the chief of the bunker did not want Polish "*Banditen*" inside. Our SS guards fought with him as they did not want to lose their lives either.' In the end the AK officers spent the night on the staircase leading to the bunker, guarded the whole time by the SS.[65] The next day they were taken to Langwasser, near Nuremberg, and joined their fellow AK officers in captivity.

It was clear that at the time of the capitulation both Himmler and Bach genuinely believed that they could convince Bór and the AK to fight with the Germans against Stalin. This was reflected in the way the Poles were treated as prisoners of war. The Wehrmacht soldier Hasso Krappe was one of their guards as they went into captivity, but admitted that he was confused about how to treat these erstwhile 'bandits'. 'It was completely new . . . we got no information as to how we were to behave. Close to Frankfurt-am-Oder the train stopped on the siding and a group of International Red Cross representatives appeared to carry out an inspection. The prisoners had only dry bread and very poor wagons with no provisions. We asked them to look at our wagons. We, too, had only dry bread; on the other side was a pile of straw on which we slept.' He found the treatment of the captives highly unusual: 'When the 1,800 Poles got off at Altengrabow the highest-ranking Colonel saluted them. "I hope we will see one another in better times and better circumstances," he said. He deliberately showed the Poles who fought in 1944 . . . the highest respect. It was impressive.'[66]

The Germans continued to try to woo the Poles, going so far as to set up 'help units' in October to try to recruit men from Warsaw who had nowhere to go. On 20 November they attempted to recruit Poles under the slogan 'Volunteers in the Fight Against Bolshevism'; both initiatives failed.[67] Also in November 'two high functionaries of the Gestapo appeared in the camp [at Langwasser] to persuade General Bór to participate in an anti-Communist front'.[68] He refused. Bór was even approached later, in Colditz Castle: 'They sent a nice old man who talked about pre-war Polish-German

society. Bór told them they were wasting their time.' He was resolute: there could not and would not ever be cooperation between
the Nazis and the AK.[69] Even so, Himmler's belief that the AK
might be persuaded to fight alongside German troops probably
saved their lives, although they were never entirely out of danger.
In the final days of the war Hitler ordered that all important prisoners of war, including the Poles, were to be shot: '[SS Brigadeführer
Gottlob] Berger was about to leave the meeting when Hitler got
up. His hands and legs were shaking and he said, "You have to
shoot them – all of them." ' Agaton is right to say that if Berger
had obeyed Hitler's order, all of them would have died.[70]

The Civilians Leave

As Bór was being hauled back and forth for phantom meetings
with Himmler, the remaining citizens of Warsaw were being
forced to leave their beloved city. The evacuation was completely
pointless, as almost all those left in the capital would have been
able to find somewhere to live had they been given the chance.
Apart from anything else, it would have spared the need for the
Germans to round up, move, process and feed 200,000 people.
But the Führer had spoken.

Warsaw was silent, and in those last days the people could
finally move around and prepare for the end. Many went to look
for lost relatives or friends; some tried to find winter clothes,
others searched for food. All had to say goodbye to their city and
to the lives they had once known. Many wept as they packed up
their few belongings, others were simply relieved to be getting
out alive. For a few short days food reappeared, as secret stockpiles
were made available. People came together to talk, to confer, to
plan, to mourn. The final editions of the insurgent newspapers
Robotnik and *Biuletyn Informacyjny* appeared on 3 October. Jan

Georgica made the final broadcast over 'Błyskawica', the radio station the Germans had tried for months to find. He played the 'Warszawianka' song as a last farewell before smashing the transmitter with a hammer.

The journalist Klaudiusz Hrabryk remembered his last day in the city. 'After capitulation we had some time. Marszałkowska was ruined, destroyed, burned out. There were still the remains of barricades on the streets with trams and huge bomb craters. There were unexploded artillery shells everywhere. People left their shelters to tend to the final things before they had to leave. This was the end of the uprising. A city of one million had become a ruin.'[71] He buried his typewriter, and left.

Many ordinary civilians were frightened of the prospect of being sent to a camp or to the Reich to work, but for the Jews still in Warsaw the exodus presented a terrible dilemma. They could choose to stay in bunkers and 'melinas' – long-term hiding places – and risk being caught in the coming weeks, or they could leave with the refugees and hope they were not identified. The Germans were still relentless in their search for Jews. A 9th Army report compiled after the 7 September ceasefire noted the 'high number of Jews' amongst the refugees; they were taken out and murdered. One witness remembered crossing the barricade and being surprised at the Germans' vigilance. 'As we approached one of the German officers stared at us attentively. He stared at us one by one. One moment at me. He walked up to me. And quickly frisked me from head to toe.'[72] Several hundred Jews left Warsaw mingling with the refugees, and some of them did escape; it is not known how many.[73]

Between 3 and 7 October over 150,000 civilians walked to collection points around the city, including the hated Zieleniak market and the St Stanisław church. 'People leave Warsaw with children in their arms or held by the hand. They walk with packed suitcases and go in silence . . . this column of expelled people marches on the first, the second, the third day without end.'[74] The Germans organized evacuations for the wounded, who were taken first to Wolski hospital or the clinic at St Stanisław church before being transported to clinics and hospitals outside the city. 'Stretchers passed. Stretcher after stretcher . . . Carts were driving up . . . the sick and wounded were being loaded.'[75] Fourteen thousand patients were evacuated from the city centre, along with medical personnel; even those found badly wounded in cellars and shelters were taken to hospital. 'Young tired starving girls had to carry patients . . . one often saw girls carrying stretchers with wounded in bandages and gypsum with packages of personal stuff, and they were crying from the strain.'[76] St Stanisław's operated until 24 October, when it too was closed.

The silence was now broken by the sound of dynamite as the Germans began to demolish what remained of the city. 'Our march through Ochota goes through destroyed, rubble-filled streets and is slow and tiring. We can see messages written in chalk or coal or paint: "Here lies . . ." or "Here is buried . . ." and everywhere that terrible smell.'[77] Everyone was frightened. 'We went through a dead city. All the exits were guarded by German soldiers with machine guns. We were allowed to rest at St Stanisław church in Wola. The vicarage vegetable garden was in the back and those who ran really fast could go and get food. We were watched by old German soldiers who behaved quite properly.' One group brought a bucket of dog meat with them. 'We walked down Marszałkowska, already destroyed. We crossed the corner of Jerusalem Avenue and saw a huge wall of ruins reaching to the first floor. We were with thousands of people now moving to Dworzec Zachodni [the western railway station] and Pruszków.'[78] Jan Rosner made the long journey to Pruszków with the civilians. 'It was a terrible sight, with huge burned-out blocks . . . in front of me was an unbelievable sight, an endless line of people with luggage and also with strange things like bicycles and prams. The younger generation searches for food and collects potatoes and onions and tomatoes . . . vegetables which they have not seen for two months.'[79] 'We did not know where we were going. The gathering point at Lwówska Street was already crowded . . . people left houses, basements and shelters carrying huge amounts of luggage. They were pulling trolleys and carrying the wounded and old and ill people. There was no solidarity or empathy for others in the crowds.' The people walked in lines down the destroyed streets, the air heavy with the stench of decay. 'The threat of disease was high as myriad flies covered the dead and formed grey-black swirling clouds over the wounded.' Rats fed on the corpses in broad daylight; the Germans took potshots at them.

A tremor of fear ran through the crowd as they finally approached the German lines. Some tried to turn back, but it was no use: Wehrmacht soldiers guarded every entrance and exit. You could leave, but you could not get back in. The only way out was to the west.

Psychologically, it was a terrible moment. Rosner remembered the feeling of leaving 'free' Warsaw, however grim, only to find himself back in German hands after everything he had been through. He boarded a train to Pruszków. 'I feel as if I am in prison. There is no escape. Two months of Polish freedom is over.'

Those herded to Dworzec Zachodni saw evidence of looting: 'The whole station is filled with robbed Polish goods . . . there is also a machine gun on each platform ready to shoot.'[80] 'We wait two hours then we have to get into a wagon. It is open. We go through Wola, full of partly burned houses.'[81] The cattle wagons used to transport them were crammed so full that the people could not move or relieve themselves; they could barely breathe. 'Beside Maria Starzyńska is a mother whose little boy died in her arms. The mother held onto the baby. When the train stopped she hoped to be able to bury the boy, but they were not allowed out. The mother carried the corpse in her arms all the way.'[82]

Pruszków Camp

The little town of Pruszków lies fifteen kilometres to the west of Warsaw, directly on the Vienna–Warsaw line. A huge train repair works surrounded by a wall nearly two kilometres long lay in the centre of town. For Bach it was the ideal place for the collection and 'processing' of the refugees from the city.

Pruszków had been used as a work camp for Jewish prisoners in 1941, so the obligatory guard towers, bunkers and machine-gun nests were already in place. The Jews had long since been murdered and the camp mothballed, but when Hitler demanded that the civilians be removed from Warsaw, Bach reopened it on 6 August 1944 as *Durchgangslager* 121 (Dulag 121).

The idea of a *Durchgangslager*, or transit camp, was just that – prisoners were to be herded together for a short time and quickly selected for one of three fates: work in the Reich, transport to a concentration (or, for AK soldiers, a PoW) camp, or release into local towns and villages. Many prisoners were there for only two or three days, but even so the experience was harrowing.

The various waves of prisoners had mirrored the destruction of each district of Warsaw, and nurses recalled that each group had its own characteristic set of symptoms: Ochota – injuries caused by rape; the Old Town – burns. The biggest wave came after capitulation, when there were so many people that temporary spill-over camps were created in nearby Ursus, in the Kabel factory in Ożarów, the Era warehouses in Włochy and the Tudor factory in Piastów.

Pruszków was officially under three military authorities – the Wehrmacht under Oberst Sieberts, the SS under Sturmbannführer Diehl, and the Civil Administration under Dr Friedrich Gollert; but real power lay with the SS, and Diehl was a cruel master. In typical fashion, the Germans took care of security but the Poles had to pay for their own incarceration. The RGO was made responsible for food and medical care, and gathered funds via its Polish Care organizations: the RGO in Kraków gave around 650,000 złoty, mostly to create shelters for children and the elderly who had been left homeless when they were pushed out of Pruszków; they also created forty-three hospitals to care for the ill who had nowhere else to go after 'processing'. The RGO even obtained permission to go into Warsaw to search for bedlinen, clothes, underwear, shoes and pots, and bring them back to the camp – although they were strictly forbidden to take valuables, and were thoroughly searched on their return. Pruszków also received some help from abroad: Switzerland sent 13,200 cans of condensed milk and clothes in September, Sweden 14,450 kilos of sugar, 22,600 kilos of sardines, and 325 men's winter coats.[83] Lady Sinclair set up the British Fund for Warsaw in London, and the Irish, Swedish and Swiss Red Cross helped too, but for the most part conditions for the shocked and frightened refugees from Warsaw were terrible.

People arrived in Pruszków not knowing what to expect. The whole camp was surrounded by high walls, with just one main gate. Because of the crowds, most new arrivals had to wait in line for hours just to get inside. It made no difference if they were sick or exhausted. One nurse wrote: 'I can risk the statement that all people expelled from Warsaw who came to the camp were in a state of physical and nervous exhaustion and many of them were ill . . . there were recent illnesses contracted during the uprising like dysentery, typhus, digestive problems, respiratory problems like pneumonia and bladder problems, contusions, burns ... the burns were terrifying, particularly burns on the hands and faces. There was a separate category for women who had been raped ... The German order was that only ill people could be released, but they included raped victims.'[84] Count Antoni Plater-Zyberk had volunteered to work at Pruszków; his first glimpse of the camp was shocking: 'I saw, in the garden, the amputation of a person's leg which had been smashed below the knee. I was frightened. Four medical people were keeping the patient down and the surgeon did the operation without anaesthetic using a kitchen knife.'[85]

The camp was huge, and its vast yard was criss-crossed by railway tracks leading to gigantic warehouses or halls. Jan Rosner recalled: 'It is a square full of buildings, halls, tracks, squares surrounded by high walls. I really feel as if I am in a prison. I do not think that this is the idyllic place promised by the Red Cross. This really is a camp.'[86]

At first people were forced into Hall 2 for 'processing', where they were made to stand in front of a table behind which sat German doctors and members of the Gestapo. They would be scrutinized in turn and their fate decided. Everyone was registered on a list; those with papers had to hand them over, and then the Gestapo would decide: young/old/male/female/sick/healthy – which translated into 'work in the Reich', 'to a camp' or 'to be resettled'. There were tragic scenes during the selection as families and friends were split up. One woman recalled 'the shouting, the crying people as the Gestapo yelled at them – they did not want to be separated from one another but this was an everyday thing, part of every day in the camp. I was helpless watching this sad drama, we sisters were not allowed to approach the group then, and those who tried had their passes taken, and they too were moved out.'[87] Healthy people who had been chosen to work were taken under guard to one of the halls further away; the sound of crying and begging for another chance filed the air as fathers were taken to one area, mothers with young children to another, older children to a different place yet again. Maria Stokowska, who volunteered to help in the camp as a nurse, recalled that 'the people who were unloaded were often selected immediately and sent to the different barracks . . . On my first day I walked around like a mad person . . . it was terrifying and I asked how to help and what to do and how to get these starving, spiritually and physically devastated people out of this hell.' Barbara Kaczyńska-Januszkiewicz, aged thirteen remembered the terror of the selection and of ending up on her own: 'They took men, women and teenagers for forced labour in the Reich. Daddy, looking very frail with glasses on, was not picked, although they checked him twice. Mother was afraid for me because I am so tall, but I also was passed over.'[88] Jan Rosner's family was split up: 'Mother was sent to Hall 1 – not for work – and we were sent to Hall 4 – for work.' Generally children up to the age of fourteen could stay with their mothers, but only if she had papers to prove that the child was hers – many women had none, and their children were taken away. There were tragic cases of unclaimed infants, orphans and the elderly with no one to take care of them: 'Five-year-old Hania had lost her hand due to shrapnel, and was orphaned as both parents had died.' It is not known what happened to her.[89]

People lived in constant fear. They had no control over their destiny, and no chance to see their loved ones again once they had been separated. Each hall held different categories of people: Hall 1 'not for work'; Hall 2 'for the sick'; Hall 4 'selected for work'; Hall 5 for citizens of other countries, such as those with Ukrainian, Byelorussian or Lithuanian identity cards, and *Volks* and *Reichsdeutsche*, who were sent by special trains back to Germany. Hall 6 was for work in the Reich: it was heavily guarded, and no

Polish inmates were allowed near it; when Bishop Antoni Szlagowski came to bless the prisoners he had to stand behind the barbed wire. Hall 8 contained wounded members of the AK, and although some of them were very badly hurt, the Polish doctors and nurses were allowed to do no more than change their bandages. But they smuggled in civilian clothes and managed to get some of them into other halls. Antoni Plater-Zyberk was appalled by the treatment of the innocent civilians. On his first day he was talking to an elderly couple, when 'suddenly the conversation is interrupted by police who shout "*Raus! Raus! Schnell! Schnell!*" They take a few hundred people somewhere.' Later, in the main hall he saw 'a few thousand women and children in a terrible crowd. All of them are loaded onto open coal trucks. The cars are all ready and waiting for them.' The train was heading towards Łódź. 'Thank God they are not going to Auschwitz,' he thought.[90]

The halls had no amenities whatsoever. A few people managed to find old mats or bits of wood to lie on, but straw was not allowed because the refugees might infest it with lice. 'The camp looks awful,' one witness reported. 'People are in dreadful shape, many are wounded, they are exhausted and ill and in shock after their experiences. They are located in eight massive halls, although only seven are in use. We can see raw sewage, which is dangerous, and there is a lot of filth and disorder. People lie on the cement floors unless they have a piece of wood or some baggage.'[91] An internal RGO report feared for the lives of civilians, particularly as winter was coming: 'The mortality rate may increase sharply.'

Von dem Bach, sensitive as ever to world opinion, was keen to present the camp in the best possible light. He paid a much-publicised visit on 5 September, but it was stage-managed from the start. Crews had been sent days before to clear up the mess, and there were suddenly even mugs and plates in the kitchen. Bach arrived with his usual fanfare, and was taken on a tour of the camp. He went first to Hall 2, where he met the German doctors and the rest of the commission. Kazimiera Dreszer, a volunteer nurse in the camp, acted as an interpreter. 'When we left the hall the Germans started taking pictures. Von dem Bach had one taken with an old Polish lady holding onto his arm and smiling up at him.' They went on to Halls 3 and 4. 'Suddenly a horse and wagon appeared and started to distribute food from the kitchen. Von dem Bach and the priest Tyszka each had two plates of soup. Tyszka wanted to avoid having his picture taken, but was ordered to pose and smile.'[92] Later, Bach asked the priest if the RGO had any special requests regarding the camp, and Tyszka immediately asked that families no longer be separated. Bach appeared to be shocked to hear that this had been happening, and solemnly declared, 'Upon my word of honour this will no longer take place.' After more photos von dem Bach left. The pictures duly appeared in *Der Adler* a few days later.

Soon after Bach's departure Dreszer heard Diehl dictating to his German secretary: 'According to von dem Bach's order it is not permitted for families to remain together when they are sent to the Reich. Therefore, the instruction about the separation of families remains in force.' Bach's promise had been a lie, and families continued to be cruelly split up until the camp was closed. Many never found out what had happened to those relatives who were sent away.

A visit by members of the International Red Cross on 18 September was also carefully planned. This time Dreszer was ordered to write an announcement in German giving a detailed account of how well the civilians were being treated; she was then told to sign it, together with a statement that she had written it of her own free will and that it was all true. 'All the while, the SD officer, although very polite, was toying with his pistol.'[93] The Germans lied throughout the entire Red Cross visit.

Questioned about the splitting up of families, Sturmbannführer Diehl retorted, 'This does not take place.' When asked why the Germans were continuing the senseless deportation of people from their homes in Warsaw, he answered that the city had to be emptied 'because it is within ten kilometres of the front'. The real reason, that Hitler had ordered the complete destruction of the city and the punishment of its inhabitants, was not mentioned.[94] At the end of the visit the Polish doctors were permitted to talk to the Red Cross officials alone, but Diehl's Polish mistress Jadwiga Kulbaszyńska – a midwife from Milanówek who was pretending to be a doctor – was also present. Dr Oszkielowa bravely told the Red Cross representatives the truth about conditions in the camp, but after they had left she was arrested by the Gestapo. She was later released, but was no longer permitted to work at Pruszków.

Such perfidy was common. At the end of August the Gestapo had ordered that all Polish doctors gather together in Hall 5 so they could be released back to Poland as a group; more than fifty doctors and their families went there, expecting to be freed. It was a hoax. 'We managed to find out that the doctors were all sent to the Reich: "We also need doctors in Germany," they were told.'[95]

For their part, the Poles never stopped trying to get as many people as possible out of the camp under the noses of the Germans. The attempts to beat the system began even before the prisoners arrived, Polish railroad workers having arranged for the train coming from Warsaw and the one returning from Pruszków to stop at the same platform at the same time. They bribed the German guards to allow people from the Pruszków-bound train to jump to the unguarded one returning empty to Warsaw, from which they could then escape into the countryside. Over a thousand people were saved in this way.

The Poles arriving at the camp tried everything to avoid being sent to Germany. Some pretended to be medical personnel so they could work rather than risk deportation: one violinist claimed that she was a gynaecologist, and even helped deliver two babies before being found out – the real medical staff covered for her, and eventually got her out of the camp.[36] Maria Stokowska found herself working with another 'fake doctor'; when the two were sent to bandage patients in one of the halls she realized that he could not carry out the simplest of tasks, although by evening he was doing 'quite well'.

Some prisoners tried to escape by hiding under the straw in wagons bringing food and supplies to the camp, but this was highly risky; others put on white aprons and Red Cross armbands and tried to bluff their way past the guards, but they needed identity papers, so this rarely worked. Some bribed the guards to allow them to move from one hall to another from which they had a better chance of escape. One nurse was saved because 'Sister Maria gave Untersturmführer Witte two beautiful dog collars.'[97]

The real heroes, and the most successful at foiling the Germans, were the Polish doctors and nurses who were allowed to work at Pruszków. At the peak in October there were over two hundred Polish medical volunteers in the camp, most of whom had been sent by the RGO. They worked tirelessly to get people out, and came up with myriad schemes to fool the Germans.

When people first arrived at the camp they were questioned by the Gestapo and the German doctors. Being assigned to Hall 2 gave the best chance for salvation, as anyone who could 'prove' they were sick would not be sent away to work. The prisoners were taken to a small examination room on the right side of the main table at the entrance; if they were judged to be ill they were sent to the very back of the hall, where old people, exhausted children, the injured, the burned and those suffering from typhus or dysentery lay on the bare concrete floor. Guards watched them, and pulled out anyone they thought was faking.

Only a small percentage of Warsawians could speak German, so the Polish personnel who had to translate simply made up conversations. The Polish staff knew that an injury such as the loss of an arm was not enough to prevent transfer to the Reich – 'Poles can still pluck with one hand', the Germans said, referring to the collection of goosedown. 'The Germans did not care if a woman had been trapped in Warsaw by accident and caught in the uprising, or if her children were still in Warsaw – we knew she would not get released for that. But we knew that they would release her if she was pregnant, if she had venereal disease or some illness of the reproductive system. For men the most useful were tuberculosis, dysentery, typhus and stomach inflammation. We claimed many pregnant and raped women, and many TB patients and syphilitics.'[98]

The sheer chaos in Hall 2 worked to the Poles' advantage. Nurses would surreptitiously add names to the official lists of those to be released when the German doctors were not looking; these 'patients' would then be processed in Hall 2 and given legitimate papers. 'Every day the German doctors signed thousands of papers, so it was not difficult to add more without them knowing.' They even faked the signatures of the German doctors: 'The master was Eryk Lipiński,* who was working as a nurse.' Another method was to get blank medical forms and fill in the names of people in the various halls; later, if the guards asked for their identity card 'they were to say it had been burned'.[99]

Another ruse was the 'left-hand release', which was reserved for those who, like Jews who did not have false papers, could not be put in front of the commission in person. The prisoner's name would be added to the list of seriously ill patients who had to be evacuated to hospital quickly; the nurses did this by brazenly

---

* A famous graphic artist who produced false documents for Jews and members of the underground throughout the war.

slipping loose pieces of paper onto the pile on the main table, right under the noses of the Germans. These would be processed along with the rest, and the 'patient' taken to hospital sight unseen. 'The fact that the system was so obvious provided a kind of security; the Germans did not think we would do such a thing.' In September this ruse was improved, when the German doctors started leaving for their lunch break, taking with them the key to the drawer containing the blank release forms. 'They thought it was safe because of the guards. In reality we bribed the guards with sweets and vodka which were provided by the villagers and smuggled into the camp for this purpose; the blank forms were then filled in with the names of patients.'[100]

To keep up the charade, the Polish doctors had to vary the illnesses from which the 'patients' were suffering: 'At times there were too many patients with TB, so we changed some to dysentery.' The Germans became suspicious of that, so they changed the diagnosis to 'kidney stones' or 'inflammation of the stomach lining'. When German doctors wanted to examine a particular 'patient', the Poles had to coach him or her: 'The actor Jerzy Pieczyński simulated the symptoms of appendicitis so well he was immediately taken to a hospital in Pruszków to have it taken out.' Some doctors injected sterilized milk to induce fever; others created symptoms of pregnancy, venereal disease or hepatitis. Because of the fear of typhus, the Germans tended to release people who were badly infested with lice; the Poles immediately started spreading lice on purpose. The German doctors also released rape victims immediately; one nurse overheard a doctor say he was 'disgusted by the *Untermenschen*' who had done these 'terrible things' – as a result, the number of 'rape victims' increased.[101]

Janina Chmielińska avoided being deported to the Reich by simulating the symptoms of tuberculosis, and was sent to the TB barrack. 'The Germans were so terrified of the disease that all the staff forced to work there were Russians.'[102] Another woman, who would later become a doctor herself, was saved by her lice infestation and dysentery. 'I was sent to a hospital in Miechów and stayed on as an assistant, cleaning toilets, changing linen. The patients there had all kinds of infectious diseases: dysentery, typhus, tetanus . . . never in my future medical career would I see all the diseases I saw there.'[103]

The next stage in obtaining an official release was to get the papers signed by the Gestapo office, which was located in a green railway car parked in the centre of the camp's main square. Many schemes were employed to obtain these crucial signatures. One involved giving young men's surnames a feminine 'a' ending. 'The Scharführer checked every surname, but when the nurse explained that the person was a woman he would sign. She always took a sack of fruit and gave it to him, and he liked fruit and pretty girls and she was pretty.' With the signed release form in hand they would have to reverse the process at the main gate. 'Above all we had to convince Captain Langut, the head guard, that the surnames referred to men and not women,' despite the 'a' ending.[104]

If someone heard the magic word 'released', their documents were signed and they were given a legitimate identity card with official papers from the camp. This was crucial, as the Germans continued to round up all Warsawians aggressively for months after the uprising was over. Anyone caught without the correct papers was sent back to Pruszków, to again face possible transport to the Reich. This endless, dogged persecution of Warsawians was Hitler's punishment of the people of a city that had dared to defy him.

Getting healthy people released was dangerous for the doctors and nurses, and if they were caught they would be expelled from the camp or sent to the Reich themselves. One man begged to be smuggled out on a stretcher, but was caught at the checkpoint.

'The nurses were taken away' – he does not know what happened to them.[105] Only very occasionally did the Germans let people out for any reason other than illness. Kazimiera Dreszer remembered the day a group of professors from the University of Technology were brought in. They had been in hiding in a cellar, had been bombed and starved and were clearly in shock. 'They stood in front of the commission. They looked ghastly. They were black with soot, had plaster on their clothes which were torn to pieces, their eyes were bloodshot, they were like a group of old men wearing sackcloth. We were familiar with the appearance of Warsawians, as so many people were starving and run down, but this group was really shattered.' The nurses decided not to pretend the men were ill, but said: 'They are professors . . . they are old and will not organize the next uprising . . . the doctor looked at us as if we were lunatics.' Even so, nine of the professors were allowed to leave the camp: 'When the sister brought confirmation from the Green Wagon that they were to be released we organized a Polish demonstration in the camp.' Normally only one person would go to the gate with a released prisoner, but this time a large group accompanied the men. When the German guards asked who they were, they answered, 'They are Polish professors.'[106]

In the end, however, the best methods were the most basic: bribery and flirtation. 'It must have looked odd that Polish girls would do their hair and make-up and joke with the Germans, giving them fruit and sweets and vodka. We knew that people might think unpleasant things about us, but we didn't care as it helped us to free more people . . . when they were in a sour mood it was much more difficult to save people as they became more suspicious and more ruthless.' People in the villages knew the situation, and 'gave us sweets and alcohol and fruit for the Germans.'[107]

Despite all the efforts of the Polish medical staff, the German quotas had to be filled. Hitler saw Warsaw as a windfall of slave labour, and Albert Speer, Fritz Sauckel and the rest agreed. In total 55,000 people from Pruszków were sent to concentration camps, of whom 13,000 went to Auschwitz; the last transport left on 17 September. Kaltenbrunner conceded to Himmler that no one else from Warsaw would be sent to the concentration camps after that date, but he refused to release those who were already at Pruszków. Many perished either in the camps or in the death marches that came later. On 3 December the RGO complained about the large number of Poles who were still in concentration camps, citing the earlier agreement that Warsaw prisoners would be released from Auschwitz, but they were ignored. Kazimiera Dreszer, the brave thirty-year-old nurse who had saved so many people in Pruszków, was arrested by the Gestapo for having 'illegally released prisoners' and sent to Auschwitz-Birkenau. 'I was arrested on 13 September because of a tip-off to the Gestapo made by Janina Łódziewicz, one of the nurses who worked in the camp.' The Germans called these corrupt nurses 'Goldenenschwestern' – Golden Sisters – because they took money from people who were trying to escape. 'I went to Birkenau. There were two barracks filled with people. There were around three hundred old ladies in one, and in another around two hundred small children from Warsaw. While I was still in Pruszków I learned that around 10,000 men had been sent to Mauthausen; a few thousand men from Pruszków were in Auschwitz. On 17 September another transport of more than 4,200 men went from Włochy to Auschwitz.'

Over 150,000 Warsawians were loaded onto trains and sent to the Reich as forced labourers. For many this sentence came as a terrible shock. These innocent civilians had endured the uprising, lost their loved ones, their homes and possessions, been separated from their families at Pruszków, and now they were to be sent as virtual slaves to do the bidding of the hated enemy in the Reich itself: 'We never believed that we would be sent to work camps in Germany, which is why we didn't take German money or even a map with us, we just took clothes and things for our wives and children.'[108] Jan Rosner was put in a cattle wagon and taken to Lamsdorf transit camp, where he was told to choose between agricultural or factory work. Both were equally harsh. The prisoners lived in primitive barracks and were given a ration of between six and eight hundred calories a day, although towards the end of the war they seldom got even that. They were forced to wear uniforms with the letter 'P' on the back, and were often treated little better than slaves: a typical Polish '*Zwangsarbeiter*', or forced labourer, worked six or seven days a week for ten to twelve hours a day. They were set to work in aircraft and munitions factories, on farms or in construction, on the railroads or in private households, digging anti-tank ditches or clearing rubble, in textile factories or in mines. They were not even allowed in air-raid shelters, and many perished or were injured during bombing raids.

Officially, attitudes towards the foreign workers were changing by the summer of 1944. Hitler had declared his 'war against Bolshevism', and some Germans now saw the workers as potential allies in the war against Stalin. Himmler never managed to introduce his proposed new uniform for Polish labourers, but by the time Warsawians were being sent to the Reich even Fritz Sauckel had started to change his views. Sauckel wrote a lavish book called *Europe Works in Germany*, its pages filled with pictures of happy labourers in well-organized camps working hand in hand with Germans in the fight against the Bolshevik hordes. He claimed he wanted to engage the foreign workers 'for a new Europe and thereby for the German war potential'.

But such changes at the very top of the Nazi hierarchy made

little difference on the ground, and the attitude towards Polish workers in Germany remained hostile. There were exceptions, but most were treated with barely concealed contempt. When the war was over the Warsawians were left stranded far from home with no money and no help, their city a ruin and their country under Soviet rule.

The largest group of released prisoners from Pruszków were to be resettled in other parts of Poland. This was by far the best option, but it was still filled with uncertainty, poverty and discrimination. For most, 'resettlement' meant little more than having to find a bed to sleep in and a little food, but even that was not easy in the winter of 1944. The majority of the Warsawians released from Pruszków were run-down, had no money, no winter clothes or shoes, and nowhere to go. The RGO helped the most desperate cases, but resources were few, and many had to rely on the generosity of others.

Polish cities and towns were asked to rehouse the refugees. The first transport of 37,000 people arrived in Kraków on 5 October, and most of these found shelter, but accommodating the newcomers became more difficult as their numbers increased. 'Currently in Łowicz,' one report read, 'we already have 22,000 refugees . . . most are very poor Warsaw civilians . . . their situation is terrible. They have summer clothes and no warm things, the clothes we got from Kraków have already been distributed, they need above all shoes for women and children, warm coats for children, men and women; if they don't get them most people will begin to suffer from the cold very soon. Blankets are needed as there are quite a lot of children old and sick people.' By 3 November, 100,000 Warsawians were searching for shelter in the central and western districts of Poland, and many of the ill, shocked and starving people simply could not cope. The seventy-five-year-old former President of Poland Professor Stanisław

Wojciechowski was sent from Pruszków to a village near Kraków. He was found leaning against a fence with his luggage by his side, having fainted on the street.[109]

The lucky ones found shelter with friends or relatives, but even then these houses and apartments were often filled with dozens of people. Maria Baranowska, a runner in the AK, moved into her cousin's place, but 'there were already fourteen people there sleeping on the carpet. We were glad for a roof and dinner, but knew we had to leave.' There were official appeals for help, but the response was less than enthusiastic from people who were themselves very poor and had no real understanding of what had happened in the capital city: life was often hard. The refugees were sometimes billeted with locals, but were not always accepted by people themselves struggling to survive the deprivations of the war.[110] It was often very difficult for the sophisticated residents of the capital city to adapt to village life. The new places could be terrible for a person from Warsaw, with animals living in the house and the host family washing by spitting into their hands.[111] There were many examples of immense kindness and generosity, but there were also cases of exploitation. Refugees would sometimes be given a room, but would have to 'pay' for it by doing all the household chores or working as labourers. They were often forced to move on after a few months, and grew tired of 'going from one scruffy place to another'. 'Not many people were that nice,' one woman recalled. 'Many inhabitants of Brwinów and Milanówek treated Warsawians as if we were greedy and were withholding our money and jewels. I have no idea why they thought like that.'[112]

Many tried to earn some money, but this was extremely difficult, as their skills did not translate to small-town or village life. Instead, professionals cooked or cleaned or tended animals. Antonina Mijal learned how to knit sweaters, and Maria Baranowska's mother baked cookies while she herself 'tried to earn money by painting toys; I drew different patterns like ducks. I left at 4 a.m. for Kraków to sell them at 6 a.m . . . one day I was stopped by a German, but thankfully I had my daughter's birth certificate and begged him to leave me alone because of my child. I had to stop going to Kraków.'[113]

In all, over 350,000 destitute Warsawians faced the coming winter in the Polish countryside or in towns and villages, with very little help and very few prospects. Feelings of loneliness, of destitution and of an inability to fit in elsewhere drew many of them back to the city after the Soviets took over in January 1945. They simply had nowhere else to go.

Pruszków camp continued to operate until the Red Army occupied Warsaw. The civilians were gradually moved out in October and November 1944, leaving mostly young male prisoners, who were forced into work details to aid the Germans in the looting and destruction of the city. On 10 January 1945, only seven days before liberation, the Germans began another massive series of round-ups to catch those remaining Warsawians who had not been 'processed'. Many were caught along the rail lines and sent to Pruszków; when the Soviets rolled in there were still seven hundred prisoners being held there.

Predictably, von dem Bach tried to defend himself over the record of Pruszków after the war. In his Nuremberg testimony of 29 January 1946 he claimed: 'I am very surprised that nobody made me aware of the fact that people were dying as a result of neglect . . . [The Polish authorities] could have had the courage to tell me about it personally as they met me on several occasions . . . I can only assume that the Poles even at that time thought that the deaths were the result of difficulties people went through before, and not because of, the camp itself.' He remained silent about the nature of these 'difficulties', which had, after all, been largely caused by him. He appeared to have convinced himself that he had acted in a 'humanitarian' way throughout, and seemed blind to the reality of what he had done. When asked why he had been so offended by Żywiciel's rejection of his peace offer in Żoliborz at the end of September, when Żywiciel had dared to raise the issue of crimes committed against Polish civilians in Marymont, he replied: 'The tone was different from the noble and chivalrous attitude in the city centre and Mokotów. If we talk about German brutality, the Germans could also mention some brutal acts committed by AK soldiers during the uprising.' The notion that German and Polish crimes in Warsaw were in any way comparable was outrageous, but Bach seemed to believe it. 'Further discussion is pointless,' he said.[114] Occasionally the mask slipped. When one of his Polish questioners asked why the nation that had given the world Goethe and Schiller 'had tried to take away our right to freedom and existence through the use of terror', Bach had replied, 'This is war.'[115]

The Destruction of Warsaw

Władysław Szpilman watched in great sadness as the people of Warsaw left the city. It was, he thought, like seeing the life blood flowing from the body of a murdered man, first vigorously and then more and more slowly. 'The last people left on 14 October. Twilight had long fallen when a little company of laggards, their SS escorts urging them to make haste, passed the building where I was still hiding. I leaned out of the window, which was burnt out by the fires, and watched the hurrying figures bowed under the weight of their bundles until darkness had swallowed them up. Now I was alone, with a tiny quantity of rusks at the bottom of the bag and several bathtubs of dirty water as my entire stock of provisions. How much longer could I hold out in these circumstances, in view of the coming autumn, with its shorter days and the threat of approaching winter?' He reflected on his recent past. 'At first I had a home, parents, two sisters and a brother. Then we had no home of our own any more, but we were together. Later I was alone, but surrounded by other people. And now I was lonelier, I supposed, than anyone else in the world. Even Defoe's creation, Robinson Crusoe, the prototype of the ideal solitary, could hope to meet another human being . . . but if any of the people now around me came near I would need to run for it and hide in mortal terror. I had to be alone, entirely alone, if I wanted to live.'[116]

They called themselves 'Robinsons', the ones who stayed behind, and the name fitted. When Robinson Crusoe built his shelter on the desert island he had to conceal all traces of his presence, 'that there might not be the least shadow for discovery'. Crusoe knew that if the 'savages' found him 'naked and unarmed' they would murder him. The Warsawians who chose to hide faced the same fate. All knew that if they were discovered they would be killed. The 'Robinsons' not only had to survive in an extremely harsh environment, with scant food, water, medicines or fuel, they also had to erase all signs of their existence, just as Crusoe had done. It was an extremely difficult thing to do, and many perished.

Nobody knows how many people tried to hide in the ruins and bunkers of Warsaw after the capitulation, but they certainly numbered in the thousands. They included AK soldiers who had been too ill to leave at the beginning of October; nurses like Major Danuta Ślązak, who hid with the patients she had saved from a burning hospital; and others who simply did not trust the Germans, and preferred to take their chances in hiding. But the largest number of 'Robinsons' were Jews who did not want, or could not risk trying, to pass themselves off as Aryans among the columns of refugees. Those who knew from bitter experience what the Germans were capable of – like Chaim Goldstein, who had been in Auschwitz, or Dawid Landau, who had been Jan Karski's bodyguard during his famous journey through the Warsaw ghetto – preferred to take their chances in the capital.

In his book about the hidden Jews of Warsaw, Gunnar Paulsson wrote: 'They had to endure four months of hunger, thirst and winter weather, and were also vulnerable to German patrols and Polish scavengers. A few hundred survived to see liberation on 17 January 1945.'[117] Many had gone into hiding during and after the Ghetto Uprising, and a fortunate few had managed to remain hidden, largely in the ruins and the sewers of the ghetto. They had been forced to spend months, and in some cases years, underground, but they understood that it was their only chance of survival. For the Jews hiding in Warsaw there were two choices: either be captured and killed, or hide. And so they hid.

The ruins of the ghetto were the centre of this clandestine life. When Jan Rossman returned to the Old Town via the sewers at the end of September, just before he left Warsaw, he found evidence of this hidden world: 'The landscape was unbelievable. We could see only ruins, burning ruins. Not one house survived. We spent some hours there, but when we tried to come back using the same sewer we met a man sleeping in the basement. We were shocked. I had my revolver and talked to him in German, but realized he was Polish. He told us that there were still people hiding in the basements and sewers of the New Town, and he belonged to a group hiding under Freta Street. "From time to time a woman brings water, but we have also heard that the Germans are starting to look for people under the houses. They pull them out and shoot them." I saw a light in a distant tunnel. It was probably a group that had been living in the sewers since the ghetto was destroyed. From our walks through the sewers we could see traces of the bridges where

Jews had lived during the Ghetto Uprising. We also found sites under the Jewish cemetery.[118]

The most successful bunkers were ingeniously constructed and cleverly hidden, with ventilation and access to water. Others were little more than holes in the rubble, found in a last-minute panic.[119] There were bunkers all over Warsaw – under Sienna Street, in the rubble of the Gymnasium on Królowa and in an attic at Bagatela 12. A group of seven people lived under the graves in the Jewish cemetery, while others sought refuge in the ruins of Czerniaków 6. Dawid Fogelman hid in a cellar at Szczęśliwa 5. One group hid in Solna Street after the fall of Czerniaków. Chaim Goldstein organized a hiding place for six people in the sewers under Franciszkańska, where they suffered not only from hunger and thirst but also from the torments of confinement in such a dark and dank space.[120]

The deprivations were terrible. Alicja Haskelberg found a garage that had been completely covered by rubble. 'We hid there literally at the last moment because the Germans, shouting and shooting, were again taking over all the houses. We managed to gather a little water in barrels and to take a little food.' She and her group were there for sixteen weeks. 'My little son, with his broken legs in plaster, began to swell up, and on 30 December 1944 he died. Likewise the husband of the woman who had gone down into the bunker with us lay in agony, and my brother, who was little by little reaching the end. The body of my little son lay with us for a long time.'[121]

Very occasionally, 'Robinsons' managed to get out of Warsaw and past the German lines. The most famous of these were Jewish fighters from 'ŻOB' battle group, including Marek Edelman, Cywia Lubetkin and 'Antek' Zuckerman, who had been hiding in Promyka Street in Żoliborz, opposite a large allotment garden. In November an AK courier, Ala Margolis, managed to make contact with them, and in an extraordinary operation mounted by a Polish doctor and two Jewish hospital workers the men were taken through the German lines to Brwinów dressed as doctors and nurses, carrying fake papers made up by Dr Węgrzynowski, director of the AK medical unit.[122] They ended up in Grodzisk Mazowiecki, and worked to help other Jews still in hiding. Testimonies of what they had seen in Warsaw were sent to the Polish government-in-exile in London.

One of the most extraordinary bunkers was organized at Sienna Street by Professor Henryk Beck and Roman Fiszer, who converted the basement of an AK first-aid post into an invisible hiding place. In the days before the capitulation they brought in food, water and medicines. Later, when the water ran out, they managed to dig a well, removing the earth bucket by hidden bucket. Thirty-seven people managed to survive in this bunker. Beck had even brought art supplies with him; the precious collection of drawings and paintings he produced in the bunker is now in the Jewish Historical Institute in Warsaw.

The only hope of survival for most people was to remain completely hidden: 'The entrances were tightly sealed and camouflaged by rubble, rubbish, or even the corpses of their comrades. Mainly in darkness, often suffocating because of lack of fresh air, they had to maintain absolute silence in order not to betray their presence by a suspicious noise. Outside, they could hear the sounds of the Germans all around.'[123] Life in these secret places was extremely stressful. Nobody knew what was happening in the rest of the world, and for some this lack of news was the worst hardship of all. For Szpilman, 'what tormented me most was not knowing what was happening in the battle areas, both on the front and among the rebels . . . Where were the Soviet troops? What progress was the Allied offensive making in the west? My life or death depended on the answers to these questions, and even if the Germans did not discover my hiding place it was soon going to be my death – of cold if not starvation.'[124]

Those who ventured out were in constant danger of being spotted by German patrols, many of which – though not all – tended to shoot anyone they found on sight. One soldier sent to live in the 'German quarter' of Warsaw was ordered to help in the destruction of the city: 'A lot of people lived in the ruins,' he recalled. 'Robinsons from *Robinson Crusoe*. They left their shelters at night. I saw them as we walked around the ruins . . . we watched as they pulled out baked potatoes, there were no orders to shoot them.'[125] Szpilman was plagued by German patrols: he counted thirty 'flying visits' in one hiding place alone, mostly by German soldiers looking for food.[126] On one occasion he was caught by a soldier who agreed to let him go in return for half a litre of spirits, but the encounter shook him deeply. Even the Polish slave labourers forced to work digging fortifications for the Germans were a danger. Szpilman once left the safety of his hiding place and, seeing no Germans around and seized by a longing for human contact, approached one of the work crews. 'What are you doing here?' he asked, finding talking difficult after so many months of silence. 'Digging fortifications. What are you doing here yourself?' 'Hiding.' The men left shortly afterwards. Szpilman was nervous, and pretended to go into a nearby villa. 'When I reached its charred doorway I looked round again: the troop was going on its way, but the leader kept looking back to see where I went . . . Within ten minutes the civilian with the armband was back with two policemen. He pointed out the villa into which he had seen me go. They searched it, and then some of the neighbouring houses, but they never entered my building.'[127]

The lives of the 'Robinsons' were made all the more dangerous as the Germans began going from street to street, from house to house, blowing up everything in their path and flushing out the last survivors with flames and smoke. By November the destruction was reaching virtually every part of the city.

Führer Order: Warsaw Will be Levelled to the Ground

The first order to raze Warsaw to the ground had been given by Hitler on 1 August 1944, when he first heard about the uprising. He had not changed his mind. Despite the 'honourable' peace with the AK there was to be no mercy for the Polish capital, and the order to reduce the once lovely city to rubble was reissued on 9 October. Himmler had wavered in his policy towards the Poles because of his desire to use them in the fight against Russia, but Hitler stayed doggedly on course: Warsawians were to be used as slave labourers, the Jews were to be killed, and the city was to be 'glattraziert' – levelled. It was all very simple.

The new order was given to Guderian at the Wolfsschanze on 9 October, after a discussion about the future of 'Festung Warschau' – Fortress Warsaw. The city had to be emptied of its contents and then destroyed, Hitler said. Only bunkers for use by the Wehrmacht were to be left. Guderian informed Lütwittz, who in turn sent a report to Reinhardt, the head of Army Group Centre. 'Von dem Bach has been informed by Himmler of the Führer Order,' he concluded. Lüttwitz was ordered to 'conduct a full material evacuation of Warsaw'. In reality, this meant looting.

On 11 October Governor Fischer informed Hans Frank in Kraków that 'Obergruppenführer von dem Bach has been given a new order to pacify Warsaw that means to raze . . . Warsaw to the ground as long as it does not interfere with the military need to build a fortress. Before the destruction there are to be removed from Warsaw raw materials, textiles and all furniture. That is for the civilian authorities.'[128] On the same day Guderian told Bach: 'this new Führer Order about the destruction of Warsaw is of the greatest importance for any further policy in Poland'. The next day, Himmler told an SS officers' conference about the plans for the hated capital: 'The city must completely disappear from the surface of the earth and serve only as a transport station for the Wehrmacht. No stone is to remain standing. Every building must be razed to its foundations, the quarters for the army will be set up in basements, there will be no barracks, only technical equipment and the railway buildings will be left.'

The idea, of course, was madness. There was absolutely no military necessity for the utter destruction of Warsaw; on the contrary, it would divert manpower and material to a pointless project when it was in desperately short supply elsewhere. Yet no protests were heard. Even at this late date any *Führerbefehl* – even one as absurd as this – was carried out without question. Nobody – not Goebbels or Speer or Lüttwitz or Guderian – raised an eyebrow. Neither Himmler nor von dem Bach appeared to notice the absurdity of trying to woo the Poles while systematically grinding their capital city into the dust, nor did they seem to care that by doing so they were blatantly contravening the capitulation agreement, which had clearly stated that objects of cultural value were to be preserved by and for the Poles. At Nuremberg, Guderian, Ernst Rode and von dem Bach would get into a dispute over the embarrassing question of the order. Guderian tried to blame the other two, but Rode reminded him of the discussion between himself and Hitler.[129] In reality all of them knew about it, and were keen to be involved for one simple reason: loot.

Thanks to Hitler, an entire city was now ripe for plunder. Looting on this scale was unusual even for the Nazis, and evoked images of Alaric's Visigoths and the sacking of Rome. But with the Soviets refusing to move, the Germans were free to do with Warsaw what they wanted. There followed the unedifying spectacle of various Nazis trying to grab their share of the booty before their rivals muscled in. But one man was forced reluctantly to bow out, despite all he had done to get to this point. After a grim three months in Warsaw, Hitler decided that Erich von dem Bach would be of more use in Budapest, and he was sent there on 11 October. All tasks relating to the evacuation of civilians and the destruction of the city were to pass to his replacement, Paul Otto Geibel. Geibel reported directly to Hitler, and as a result got first pick of the spoils.

The plundering of Warsaw was undertaken with great thoroughness, and the project was given its own name – the '*Auflockerung, Räumung, Ladung und Zerstörung*', or ARLZ, which translates roughly as 'dispersal, clearance, loading and destruction'. These activities were to be coordinated by a specially appointed '*Räumungsstabe*', or 'clearing-up staff', under Colonel Wilhelm Rodewald.

This did not stop the squabbling between the SS, the Wehrmacht, the German administrative authorities, Ludwig Fischer, Gauleiter Artur Greiser, Albert Speer – who from his offices on Wolska Street tried to get equipment and slave labourers – and the rest. At Nuremberg, Guderian would explain that the 'clearing' of Warsaw was supposed to be overseen by the Gauleiter of Wartheland, Artur Greiser, but that Hans Frank had been angry at this, as Warsaw was in the General Government. 'Frank demanded the privilege for himself. He thought that if it was necessary to destroy Warsaw the most valuable things should go to him . . . I discussed the question personally with Bach. Bach said that our transport capacity was too small . . . it was actually true. However, later . . . Gauleiter Koch from East Prussia took over the organization of the transport in the General Government with the Führer's permission.'[130]

By now many Germans had realized that the war was lost and were keen to make preparations for its next phase. Even

Kaltenbrunner was in on the act: shortly after giving the order to murder the remaining Jews of the Łódź ghetto on 10 June 1944 he had held a meeting with a number of Germany's top industrialists in a hotel in Luxembourg to discuss the question of capital flight. For years money, paintings, gold and other valuables had been sent from the countries of Nazi-occupied Europe to Spain, South America, Switzerland and elsewhere; loot from Warsaw would now be added to these secret caches.

Everything, however, had to be done 'correctly', and the *Räumungsstäbe* set its priorities. The official list of who was to take what was written by Herr Weisker, who managed the Economic Office in Poznań.[131] The first priority was to take anything from Warsaw that might be of use to the Wehrmacht; these things were to be sent to the Provisions Department of the 9th Army. The civilian unit, organized by the German authorities of the Warsaw District, took goods and valuables for use in the Reich. The Warsaw police units were sent to steal for Gauleiter Artur Greiser.

The lists of who was to get what were meticulous. All leather goods were to be taken by Greiser. Gum was to go to a factory in Poznań. Soap was to be sent to German workers on construction sites, although 'some small amounts can be given as Christmas gifts to German women whose husbands are at the front'. Paraffin and candles were to be sent to those building barricades; iron and machinery were to go to the Department of Farm Economy; and the rest was to be decided by Himmler, as were coloured metals, wires and cables, electrical equipment, ovens, textiles, rope, paper . . . and on it went.[132]

The organization quickly broke down. Harry von Craushaar, manager of the Main Department of Internal Affairs in the General Government, began his report on the robbing and destruction of Warsaw with the words 'Only the Wehrmacht has the competence to conduct this kind of operation.'[133] This was a forlorn hope, and there were constant conflicts over the spoils. Himmler, Speer, Greiser and Governor Fischer had regular spats; Reinefarth was chided when his units stole '225 pieces of cloth, five metres of velvet, duvets, towels, fifty ball gowns, 102 tuxedos, and sixty bedroom carpets'. Albert Speer even wrote to Hitler on 10 December requesting support in claiming 'his' property from Warsaw.

Ordinary soldiers also looted from apartments, arguing that as everything was to be burned there was no harm in it. In normal circumstances this was frowned upon, as it was seen to lead to a breakdown in discipline and morale. Stealing from vanquished populations was of course the norm, but it had to be done through the correct channels: when the seventeen-year-old Irish-German soldier John Stieber of the Hermann Göring Division took some apples out of a farmhouse which was about to be blown up he was stopped by the military police. 'This is looting!' he was told. 'You will have to face a court martial!' He was only saved by an incoming shell which frightened off his accuser. 'About once a week, during assembly,' he recalled, 'our commanding officer read out a list of men who had been convicted of looting . . . the typical sentence for looting small items was one or two days' detention . . . Any significant looting by German armed forces of which I am aware was usually officially sanctioned and carried out on specific instructions from a higher authority.'[134]

In Warsaw, however, there was a kind of last hurrah before the end, and soldiers took what they could; some were even ordered to empty buildings before they were destroyed, and the goods were delivered to the Wehrmacht.[135] German staff officer Hans Thieme recalled: 'I was in the city a few times with Major Weiss and the city was still covered in thick black smoke and was shattered by explosions and fire . . . Azerbaijanis, SS and police were looting and burning all that was left. According to Hitler's order Warsaw was supposed to be levelled. Lorries were packed full of goods, furniture, provisions from some huge cold rooms. We found an enormous quantity of eggs, we were paddling in eggs . . . my room was equipped with a new typewriter which Major Weiss took. Colonel John fixed for himself a huge new six-lamp Telefunken radio transmitter and he was wearing a gold signet ring and drank together with Feldwebel Oberwacht-meister Mühl along with a few Polish "ladies" who were spending the night.'[136]

By 15 October 23,300 train cars had been loaded with booty, including 1,600 wagons of grain. One woman on her way to Pruszków remembered: 'we passed piles of goods robbed from Warsaw – machines, furniture, carpets, bedding . . .'[137] Major Max Reck's Kampfgruppe broke into the Emisyjny Bank: 'Bombs did not damage the vaults,' he reported. 'Transports around 250 million złoty.'[138]

Art, too, was looted. The Belvedere Palace in Łazienki Park had been earmarked for Hitler's future Warsaw residence; it was also to be Frank's home in the city. As a result it contained a huge collection of very high-quality stolen art.[139] When Frank learned that the paintings had been taken by the SS he was furious, and fired off a telegram to Himmler demanding to know where 'his' things were. Secretary of State Dr Josef Bühler testified at Nuremberg that the art was superb: 'It came from all the Polish museums and all Polish collections, and there were also pieces of art from other countries.'[140]

Another high-profile Nazi joined the fray, in SS Obersturm-bannführer and 'Reich Agent for Fashion' Benno von Arent. He took charge of dealing with the Polish National Museum, and looted the most valuable pieces, including *The Hunt* and other works by Julian Fałat, which were only returned to Poland in

2011. Around 60,000 other works of art which disappeared from Polish collections during World War II are still missing.

Looting went straight to the top. Reinefarth thought it would be nice to give Himmler two sacks of finest-quality Chinese tea from Warsaw. Frau Himmler got two violins and four accordions – Geibel kindly sent a telegram to Himmler on 30 October telling him of the 'gift'. Churches were looted and then put to other uses: one on Nowolipki was used first as a stable, then as a furniture warehouse.[141]

The Poles got almost nothing from their city. An office created under the RGO and run by Marian Drozdowski oversaw five units of one hundred people each from Pruszków, who were allowed to search for clothing and bedding for the refugees; these units were divided into groups of ten people, each of which was escorted by two or three German guards, to search the buildings of Warsaw. Many pocketed tiny objects of value and used them to bribe the guards, but this was risky. This operation lasted from 17 October until 13 November, and 190 tonnes of goods were taken from Warsaw. A collection point was set up at Pruszków to sort the items, which were then distributed to the prisoners and refugees.[142]

By 20 November the city had been picked bare. The Economic Department in Warthegau wrote to the Minister of the Economy in the Reich that the booty taken out of Warsaw by the Reinefarth units was now in safe hands: 'The goods are protected and temporarily kept in appropriate companies in the Warthegau – these firms take care of the goods, sort, clean and keep them. We need to underline that some of these things were in a terrible state, others really good. The Reichsführer SS ordered in a document on 10 October that goods are to be used by those Germans who are now being moved from the east and also for 300,000 workers now working on building the defensive lines.'[143]

With the city emptied of its valuables, it was time to move to the next phase: total destruction. On 1 October Hitler had appointed Generalmajor Helmuth Eisenstück as Commandant of Fortress Warsaw, with responsibility for the mutually exclusive aims of strengthening the 'fortress' while utterly destroying it.[144] At first, he concentrated on the former.

Reinforcements were brought in to Warsaw to get the job done fast. A region of about seventeen square kilometres was to be razed to the ground, and this required battalions of sappers and men from Organization Todt. The sapper units specialized in the burning and demolition of buildings; film footage shows their awful work, with wall after wall, building after building being set on fire, leading to the whole structure crashing down, bringing balconies, railings and ornate plasterwork with it, into a huge cloud of dust. It was a veritable orgy of destruction.

Maria Stokowska, who had been allowed back in to Warsaw from Pruszków to collect supplies, watched them at work. 'A group of German soldiers near Aleje Ujazdowskie walked by shouting and singing. We did not want to see them so we hid at a gate and the unit passed by. There was fire all around us as they put the houses under fire, systematically burning all that was left after the uprising – we had to go very quickly as the district was supposed to be totally destroyed. We went past our old house at Chopina. It was burning, the smoke was coming from the basement. I was waiting impatiently when in front of the next gate I saw a beautifully polished samovar shining beside a silver sugar bowl with cups as if someone was just having tea. Further along, furniture had just been thrown through the window.'

A special Verbrennungskommando unit was formed to burn buildings using flamethrowers. Polish prisoner Kazimierz Żeglarek was forced to work in the city: 'I saw how the police units worked – they systematically burned houses in the section from Mokotowska Street to Plac Zbawiciela to Chopina. They were led by SS Oberleutnant Kruger, whom I knew as he often came to our prison.'

Buildings were dynamited, too. On her way to Pruszków Anna Szatkowska saw German engineers explaining to their crew where the explosives were to be placed.[145] Holes were drilled into the sides of palaces, churches and schools, the dynamite was put in and the structure exploded. Polish crews were brought in from Pruszków camp to help. Żeglarek was a member of one of them: 'I had to drill holes for mines in the church of St Barbara, the Brühl Palace and the Ministry of Foreign Affairs in Alberta Street, in the Belvedere Palace in Łazienki Park, in the stock exchange at Królewska Street . . . in the water tower at Koszykowa and the hospital of St Lazarus.' He worked until January 1945, when he managed to escape.[146]

Eighteen-year-old Wehrmacht soldier 'Erich' was sent to Warsaw on 4 October 1944. He joined a brigade whose only task was to walk around Warsaw for eight hours a day with flamethrowers burning the ruins. The first days of torching things were 'really fun'. But 'After a few days it stopped being so great. We ran out of food, no soup, just bread with dripping and hot tea. We didn't have tinned meat, as it was too old and we were afraid of getting food poisoning.'[147] Someone had marked all the buildings with large numbers in red paint, as the destruction had to be done in a certain order. 'These buildings were already burned out, and the petrol was poor quality, so it was very difficult to get them to burn again.' After a hard day of work they would return to the German quarter in Mokotów: 'We felt safe because the gates to this German part of the city were guarded by fifty German soldiers. We drank raw spirit every day. One of my colleagues was so upset by the work he poured spirit onto himself and burned himself to death . . . We ruined the city,' 'Erich' told his post-war Polish interviewer. 'I am so sorry.'[148]

The looting and destruction of Warsaw was illegal under the terms of the peace treaty signed by von dem Bach, according to which the Poles were to be allowed to save cultural and other treasures. In reality very little was given back to them. The Geibel Commission, led by Professor Lorenz and other Polish scholars, tried to retrieve objects from the churches, libraries and archives of Warsaw, but the harsh reality was that Hitler wanted all traces of Polish culture to disappear, and did not mind if this centuries-old heritage went up in flames. The Poles managed to save some old prints and rare books from the library of the theology department of Warsaw University, while the library of the architecture faculty of the Polytechnic had been sent to Łowicz just after the uprising. The books were hidden in sacks in the basement of a convent, and were so heavy that they broke the coffins on top of which they had been lain.

The list of destroyed treasures is heartbreaking. The Krasiński Library, created in 1844, was first shelled in August, but some books had been saved by being thrown out of its windows. It did not matter: by October they had all been burned. On 20 October the Załuski Library – the oldest public library in Poland, dating from 1747 – was burned along with 400,000 printed items; only around 1,800 manuscripts were saved. The Czetwertyński libraries were burned; only a hundred manuscripts out of tens of thousands were spared. On the same day the National Archives were destroyed, along with the historic records, papers and documents not only of Warsaw but of the whole of Poland: the treaties, the letters, the manuscripts; only 4 per cent of the archives survived. Much was burned only days before the Soviets arrived. In a cruel twist of fate the Polish Library, which had been created in Rapperswil, Switzerland, in 1870, and only brought back to the newly re-created nation in 1927, was deliberately set on fire.[149]

It was not just books: great European landmarks – the Brühl

Palace, the Saski Palace, the National Museum – were wantonly destroyed. Statues, churches, clinics, hospitals, schools, industrial buildings, apartment blocks – everything went. By January 1945 around 85 per cent of all the buildings of Warsaw had been destroyed: 10,455 buildings out of a total of 24,724 had been reduced to rubble; many of the rest were burnt-out shells which could never be repaired. Nine hundred and twenty-three of the city's historical buildings were gone; so too were twenty-five churches and synagogues, fourteen libraries, eighty-one primary schools, sixty-four high schools, the University of Warsaw, the Warsaw University of Technology, monuments, squares, palaces and homes. The treasures lost had represented the height of Polish culture and history, but works by artists, writers and composers from all over Europe had also gone forever. The Germans, too, lost a part of their history in the flames.

The destruction of Warsaw was unique even in the terrible history of the Second World War, and was the only time that Hitler actually put into practice the insane notion of erasing an entire capital city. The fact that this was done at a time when equipment, explosives and personnel were desperately needed elsewhere only highlights the Führer's madness. When the engineers ran out of explosives, Hitler ordered more to be sent to them. Thirty per cent of the destruction of Warsaw took place after the city had capitulated.

The relentless destruction of Warsaw lasted from 1 August 1944 until 17 January 1945, but the city was not yet completely defeated. Some 'Robinsons' still clung to life in the rubble; Władysław Szpilman fought the cold in his attic. And at last the Soviets were coming.

CONCLUSION

———— ⟩⚬⟨ ————

It was not to be expected that . . . you would make further demand
that Carthage itself be destroyed. (Chapter XII)

'The New German City of Warsaw'

In his play *The Fall of Carthage*, the Nazi writer Eberhard
Wolfgang Möller describes a hateful place steeped in cosmo-
politanism and teeming, foetid modernism. His Carthage is a
soulless capitalist state ruled by greedy Jews and unscrupulous
businessmen, a city so void of decency and nobility that its
inhabitants are not even really human. Möller's Carthaginians
have no concept of love, or the soil, or self-sacrifice, and 'gold
not blood ran in their veins'. Carthage was for him the antithesis
of the Roman republic, where the great Consul Marcus Porcius
Cato tended his nation of soldiers and farmers like a benevolent
father. It was Rome which deserved to conquer and colonize and
spread its heritage to the rest of the world, and it was Rome which
took upon itself the duty of erasing Carthage – which might have
been the very model for the Nazi stereotype of the Slavic-Jewish
city of Warsaw – from the map.

Hitler hated 'Banditenstadt Warschau' – Warsaw, City of Bandits – probably more than any other city in the world. It was the capital of the detested Polish nation, and had been home to the world's second-largest Jewish community, which in itself condemned it in his eyes; furthermore, it had been at the epicentre of urban resistance to his rule from 1939. He wanted it to disappear.

Hitler had been thinking about Warsaw's fate long before the 1944 uprising. Under the guise of carrying out 'scientific research', a host of German scholars, architects and historians had descended on the city in the 1930s, ostensibly to document its most important streets and buildings. In reality they were studying which ones could claim German ancestry, and as such would be worthy of preservation should the question ever arise. It arose more quickly than they thought.

Shortly after the German occupation of Poland in 1939, the Nazi engineer and architect Friedrich Pabst published a report, 'Die neue Deutsche Stadt Warschau' (Warsaw, the New German City), which included a section entitled 'Der Abbau der Polenstadt und der Aufbau der Deutschen Stadt' (The Destruction of the Polish City and the Construction of the German City). Based on the earlier research, Pabst concluded that every single one of the capital's beautiful and historic buildings should be ripped down, with the exceptions of those in the Old Town (minus the Warsaw Castle), the Łazienki Palace and the Belvedere Palace, which Hitler would use as his residence when in town.[1] Hitler greatly admired the 'Pabst Plan', which apart from the physical destruction of Warsaw also called for the reduction of the city's population from 1.3 million to just 80,000 Poles, who were to be restricted to the east bank suburb. Warsaw was to be reconstructed to look like a medieval German town, with a proposed population of 130,000 German inhabitants brought in from the Fatherland.

Hitler took this project very seriously, so much so that he

encouraged the Luftwaffe to bomb Warsaw as heavily as possible in 1939, thereby hastening the demolition process. A new version of the Pabst Plan was drawn up by architects Hubert Gross and Otto Nurnberger to take account of the 'progress' brought about by the bombing raids. Their plan came complete with full-colour drawings of the new 'Germanic' city centre, with winding cobbled streets and timber-framed houses. It was presented to Hans Frank on 6 February 1940, and was entitled *'Neue Deutsche Stadt Warschau'* – The New German City of Warsaw.

The clearing of the Warsaw ghetto and the widespread demolition of the city after the uprising meant that by January 1945 the first phase of the Pabst Plan – the *de facto* destruction of Warsaw and the murder or deportation of most of its inhabitants – was almost complete. Hitler had no intention of abandoning the city; on the contrary, he believed that the Soviets were weak, that the Allied coalition would soon disintegrate, and that the front would stay at the Vistula. He simply could not accept that he might lose Warsaw to the Soviets. Its transformation from a Polish to a German city lay at the very core of the concept of *Lebensraum*, and was meant to be the ultimate symbol of German rule in the east. It had to be held at all costs. The problem was, there was nothing to hold it with.

Defeat at the Vistula

On 12 November 1944 Hitler declared that he would never 'repeat the shame of 1918', but would 'fight the Bolshevik monster' until the end. According to him, Germany's First World War leaders had caved in too soon: 'In 1918 Germany laid down its arms at a quarter to twelve . . . I always stop at five past twelve.' In a speech to his generals at Berchtesgaden on 28 December he rambled on about past victories which at the time had seemed impossible: the

Romans after Cannae, or the Seven Years War, when '3,700,000 Prussians were pitched against about 52,000,000 Europeans . . . and won'.[2] The Soviets might have fooled the world, he said, but in reality they were weak. 'Although you may sometimes hear it said that the Russians send over gigantic quantities of ammunition, the fact is that the German expenditure of ammunition is exactly 100 per cent higher than the Russian.'[3] It was pure fiction.

In Hitler's fantasy world the Vistula marked the final westward line of the Soviet advance; they were not to be permitted to go any further. As a result the front was prepared as if for a First World War attack. Prisoners and civilians were press-ganged into building concrete bunkers and tunnels, trenches and tank traps, and laying mines and barbed wire, so that the Warsaw area began to resemble something from the old Hindenburg Line. But, crucially, Hitler's insistence on the complete destruction of Warsaw removed the one defensive position which might actually have been useful. The 9th Army had hoped to be able to use the buildings and barricades of the city for protection as the insurgents had done in August 1944, but by December there was so little left of Warsaw that Lüttwitz estimated he would be able to hold it for a week at best. The situation was so bad that the Wehrmacht tried to intervene to have some of the stronger buildings saved, but Hitler would not hear of it. The head of 46th Panzer Corps, General Eberhard Kinzel, even complained to Himmler personally at the end of December that Geibel was still blowing up structures which were supposed to have been spared.[4] Thanks to Hitler's insane destruction order the Germans had in effect destroyed their own 'fortress'. Hitler was not concerned. He disbelieved intelligence reports pointing to the Soviet build-up of forces in the area. 'It is the biggest bluff since Genghis Khan!' he spat.

The Soviet Offensive

While the Germans were wasting their time and effort blasting away what remained of the Polish capital, the Stavka was preoccupied with more serious matters. The Soviets had debated throughout the late summer and autumn as to where to attack Germany, and many possibilities had been advanced. On 28 and 29 October the Stavka met in Stalin's presence and put forward the outline for the Vistula–Oder Operation. The plan was simple: Soviet forces would continue to fight in Hungary to draw off German reserves, but the main attack was to take Warsaw and then mount a massive thrust towards the German capital. Stalin approved it on 29 October. The stage was set for the invasion.

If preparations for Bagration had been impressive, those for the January 1945 offensive were simply mind-boggling. In the central front alone the Soviet generals controlled 163 divisions, with over two million men and 4,500 tanks. They were up against German Army Group A under Generaloberst Josef Harpe, who had only 400,000 troops, three hundred tanks and six hundred assault guns. The Luftwaffe had just three hundred fighters against 10,500 Russian aircraft. The Soviets had mobilized 6.7 million men along the entire front. As in Bagration half a year before, the Germans were doomed.

On 9 January Guderian, now chief of the General Staff, tried to warn Hitler of the impending danger. He had learned from German intelligence that an overwhelming 225 Soviet infantry divisions and twenty-two armoured corps had been amassed between the Baltic and the Carpathians. Hitler still refused to listen. 'Who is responsible for producing this rubbish?' he asked. Guderian argued that the German front was like a house of cards which could collapse if broken through, but Hitler had retreated to a fantasy world. When shown reconnaissance photographs of Soviet planes concentrated near the Vistula, Göring declared that they were simply decoys. 'Fortress Warsaw' could be held.

On 12 January 1945 the Soviets started their massive offensive from their positions north and south of Warsaw. 'Rolling fire' heralded the creation of a gigantic pincer movement that would cut off the Germans in the city, led by Zhukov at Magnuszew, and by Puławy and Konev at Sandomierz.

The first attack started at 4.30 in the morning with a massive artillery barrage at Sandomierz. Four hours later the attack on the Magnuszew and Puławy bridgeheads began; by the end of the day the Soviet 1st Polish Army, the 61st Polish Army and the 47th Army had encircled Warsaw. Von Lüttwitz recognized immediately that his forces were about to be cut off, and on the morning of 15 January begged for permission for the 46th Panzer Corps to be allowed to retreat. He heard nothing. All of the generals knew that Hitler had ordered Warsaw to be held to the last man, but at that very moment the Führer was on his train heading back to Berlin for the last time.

Hitler's absence gave Guderian a tiny window of opportunity to muddy the waters and act without the Führer's interference. Lüttwitz informed Guderian that the evacuation of 'Fortress Warsaw' had to be now or never, while General Harpe of Army Group A, then responsible for Warsaw, told the OKH that the city would have to be abandoned. On the evening of 15 January Guderian ordered the 46th Panzer Corps to fall back to Sochaczew, and told Lüttwitz to give Colonel Bogislaw von Bonin authorization for the evacuation of the city itself.

Pandemonium broke out when the small German garrison heard the news. To the sound of the Soviet guns which had been audible in the city since 12 January they struggled to move equipment as fast as they could, and scrambled to get out before the Russians came, desperate to avoid being killed or hauled off to a Soviet PoW camp at this late date. The roads to the west were soon clogged with support and service troops trying as best they could to move trucks and trains to safety. The headquarters staff got out at the last minute, abandoning signals equipment in the snow.

Władysław Szpilman heard the bustle of German activity from his hiding place, but did not know what it all meant: 'On 14 January unusual noises in the building and the street outside woke me. Cars drove up and then away again, soldiers ran up and down the stairs, and I heard agitated, nervous voices. Items were being carried out of the building all the time, probably to be loaded into vehicles.'[5] In fact Warsaw was undergoing a replay of the scenes witnessed half a year earlier, when the Germans had very nearly abandoned the city at the end of July 1944. This time, however, they were leaving for good.

Hitler arrived in bleak and bombed-out Berlin on the morning of 16 January after a nineteen-hour journey, and was driven past the snow-covered craters and mountainous ruins of the beleaguered city to the Reich Chancellery. He pulled down the blinds so he would not have to see the destruction of his capital.

When he arrived for the midnight situation conference that night he fully believed that Warsaw was being successfully defended. It fell to Guderian to admit that the 'fortress' was already being evacuated. Enraged, Hitler revoked Guderian's order and commanded that the city be held to the last man, but by then nothing could be done. Radio communication had conveniently broken down, and Lüttwitz could not revoke von Bonin's order. By noon on 17 January the Soviets had taken Warsaw.

It was Guderian who had ultimately given the order to abandon Warsaw, but fearing the Führer's wrath, he put the blame on his operations officer, Colonel von Bonin. Von Bonin, a mild-mannered cavalry officer who counted Claus von Stauffenberg amongst his school friends, was just the sort of officer Hitler now detested. He was the perfect scapegoat. 18 January was von Bonin's birthday, and the OKH had gathered at its headquarters in Zossen, south of Berlin, to toast his health with a glass of *Sekt* when the Gestapo burst in and hauled him away. When Guderian protested about the arrest Hitler screamed that he was 'out for the General Staff's blood!'[6] Von Bonin was taken first to Flossenburg concentration camp and then to Dachau, where he found himself incarcerated along with a number of those accused of involvement in the 20 July plot; he was released only at the end of the war.

The punishments continued. Hitler sacked Generaloberst Harpe and Lüttwitz, along with 36th Panzer Corps commander Walter Fries.[7] He raged for days about the loss of Warsaw, screaming that the German soldiers should regroup and 'throw the Soviets back across the Vistula'. The loss was so unimaginable that it had to be due to 'sabotage' by the OKH. Speer claimed that Guderian 'tried in vain to dissuade Hitler from his mad decision to continue the hopeless battle for Warsaw'. When 'two officers of the chiefs of staff who on their own responsibility had ordered the city to be given up to the Russians, thereby saving the lives of tens of thousands of German soldiers, had been arrested on Hitler's orders and sent to a concentration camp', Speer claimed that the strain on Guderian was so great that he 'had only with difficulty been stopped from killing himself'.[8]

The loss of Warsaw had grave consequences for all the German generals. Hitler was so convinced that he had been the victim of a plot that he ordered that henceforth no commander would be permitted to attack or retreat without first having consulted him, giving him enough time for the order to be cancelled if he saw fit. This attempt to micro-manage every aspect of the fighting further hindered the effectiveness of the generals at the front. Hitler still refused to accept that Warsaw, and Poland, were lost.

General Warlimont wrote that he remained in a mad rage for days after receiving the news.[9]

The fall of Warsaw came as a shock to the German people, too; not because they cared about the Polish capital *per se*, but because they knew it meant that the Soviets had crossed the Vistula and were now moving towards the Reich itself. Important officials began to pack up and leave as quickly as they could. On 17 January Hans Frank gave a farewell meal for thirty-six guests in Kraków, and went for a last walk around 'his' castle. It was an '*ergreifender Abschied*', he recalled – a moving farewell. 'I stood alone in the great halls with the superb views over the wonderful old town and thought of the path that had taken us here,' he mused. The Poles might have been treated a little too harshly, he conceded, although there was not a word of remorse for the Jews and others who had been murdered during his time in command. As he was driven away in his Mercedes, licence-plate number 'Ost 4', he looked back to admire the city in the beautiful winter weather, certain that his career would continue to flourish when he was back in the Reich.

The Bleak Midwinter

The Soviet troops who made their way into Warsaw on 17 January found it a dark and terrible place. The city was in ruins. Shards of buildings pushed up through the snowdrifts; collapsed houses covered the decaying bodies of thousands of men, women and children, and piles of smouldering rubble and rubbish filled the air with acrid smoke. Even in the cold the stench of decay was unbearable. This once imposing capital city had been reduced to a gigantic wasteland. It was eerily quiet.

Ludwik Skokuń was one of the first Berling soldiers to enter Warsaw. 'It was a phantom city. We saw a few civilians. Bodies were everywhere. I saw a German soldier lying there without hands and legs, still alive – he was crying to us, probably calling for us to kill him. I already knew that Warsaw could have been liberated earlier and that we could have prevented this destruction. Nobody wanted to talk about it out loud as it was very easy to be sent to a punishment battalion for such things.'[10] The soldiers went timidly at first, not sure if the Germans were hiding and ready to attack. But it soon became clear that they had left in a hurry. Evidence of panic was everywhere: abandoned equipment and ammunition littered the ground, broken-down vehicles lined the roads to the west, and caches of flamethrowers and mortars lay abandoned in the snow. The *New York Times* banner headline read: 'Russians Take Warsaw', followed by the story that 'Russian and Polish troops yesterday captured devastated Warsaw to free its last survivors of five years of Nazi tyranny.' None were so relieved as those still hiding in the devastated city.

'The Robinsons'

On the eve of liberation Władysław Szpilman had waited in silence, fearful that the Germans were about to begin the battle for the city. To his amazement nothing happened. 'Around one o'clock I heard the remaining Germans leaving the building. Silence fell, a silence such as even Warsaw, a dead city for the last three months, had not known before. I could not even hear the steps of the guards outside the building. I didn't understand it. Was there any fighting going on?'[11]

When the Soviets walked into Warsaw on 17 January 1945 the transfer of power had been so quiet that many hiding in their bunkers did not realize that they had been liberated. Szpilman learned only when 'the silence was broken by a loud and resonant noise, the last sound I had expected. Radio loudspeakers set up somewhere nearby were broadcasting announcements in Polish of the defeat of Germany and the liberation of Warsaw. The Germans had withdrawn without a fight.'[12]

The history of the 'Robinsons' of Warsaw is one of the most extraordinary stories of human endurance and courage to come out of the uprising. Many of the thousands who hid in bunkers, cellars and sewers died of starvation or cold, or where shot upon discovery by the Germans, but several thousand huddled in their cramped hiding places with precious little food or water, in darkness and silence, and with no idea when their ordeal might come to an end. Julianna Wilak-Niewiedziałowa had spent over three months underground with thirty-seven other people in a bunker in Sienna Street. It had been cramped and dark, and they had been forced to whisper the entire time; by the end they were all physically and spiritually exhausted. At first she did not believe the news of liberation: 'I felt dizzy . . . I simply fell on the pillow and the absolute certainty of the past, that in a moment I would be torn to pieces by a grenade, gave way to the information that we are free. It was such a shock that I consider this moment to be the most dramatic of my entire life.'[13] Szpilman was overwhelmed when he heard from his hiding place 'the voices of women and children, sounds I had not heard for months, women and children talking calmly just as if nothing had happened. It was like the old days, when mothers could simply walk down the street with their young ones.'[14]

Helena Midler, who had dubbed Warsaw 'the city of eternal night', as she had not been outside in daylight for months, was surprised to see what her hiding place actually looked like from the street.[15] Alina Winawerowa and nine others had spent 103 days hiding in the ruins of the School of the Merchants' Union in Prosta Street. They heard a muffled announcement about liberation, and crept outside slowly, terrified that it was a trick. Irina Grocher, in hiding at Mariańska Street, wrote in her diary: 'Thursday, 18 January 1945. The Soviet army has been in Warsaw since Wednesday morning. We are free!'

Władysław Szpilman was almost killed in the confusion of those first days. He crept downstairs wearing a German overcoat, and tried to talk to a woman on the street. 'She stared at me, dropped her bundle and took to her heels with a shriek of "A German!" Immediately the guard turned, saw me, aimed and fired her machine pistol.' His building was surrounded, and he feared he was going to be shot by Polish soldiers 'in liberated Warsaw, on the very verge of freedom, as the result of a misunderstanding . . . I began slowly coming down the stairs, shouting as loud as I could, "Don't shoot! I'm Polish!" '[16]

Stalin ordered Nikita Khrushchev, at that time the Premier of Ukraine, to go to Warsaw to help set up the new Soviet administration. Khrushchev recalled: 'It was completely devastated, a vast graveyard for many thousands of inhabitants buried under the ruins. The worst part of the city was the famous ghetto into which the Germans had driven the Jewish population, then bombed and shelled it to ruins. I remember seeing a huge heap of rubble where a house had once stood and then noticing that people were still living in the basement. It was impossible to imagine that people could go on living in such conditions.'[17] The official Military Council report to Stalin read: 'The Fascist barbarians have destroyed Warsaw, capital of Poland. With sadistic cruelty they demolished one block of houses after another . . . Thousands upon thousands of civilians have been annihilated, the rest driven out. It is a dead city.'[18]

Ever more people were rescued as the days went on, many close to death. On 26 January the Żydowska Agencja Prasowa (Jewish News Agency) reported that forty-eight people had been found, while the Soviet writer and journalist Vasily Grossman, who had also been shocked by the sheer destruction he witnessed in Warsaw, himself located four Jewish and six non-Jewish Poles. The survivors were given food and clothing by the Soviets, and exchanged stories of their miraculous survival – where they had managed to get food, and how many had died. One showed Grossman a copy of the bunker 'magazine' they had written to keep their spirits up. An excerpt 'for tourists' read: 'Why go to Egypt to see the pyramids – there are so many more ruins in Warsaw.'

Survivors and soldiers alike were shocked to see what had become of the city. 'I walked down a broad main road, once busy and full of traffic, its whole length now deserted,' Szpilman recalled. 'There was not a single intact building as far as the eye could see. I kept having to walk round mountains of rubble, and was sometimes obliged to climb over them as if they were scree slopes. My feet became entangled in a confused mess of ripped telephone wires and tramlines, and scraps of fabric that had once decorated flats or clothed human beings, long since dead.'[19]

Liberation also brought freedom for those Warsawians living on the outskirts of the city, although the arrival of the Soviets was not necessarily positive. Helena Brodowska-Kubicz ('Mewa'), who had fought in AK Battalion 'Chłopcy', was living in a house near the city when she heard that the Soviets were coming. 'We were ready to welcome them into the house. A young Soviet officer came in and tried to convince me to hide, as terrible things were going to happen. He saved me, because a few hours later it turned out that the soldiers were raping the women and killing the men.'[20] Others recalled the Soviets rounding up suspected insurgents, and 'shooting all the local AK officers'.[21] The NKVD set up its offices in Praga, and began to arrest and imprison anyone suspected of being in the AK. The Cold War had already begun in the Polish capital, and the Soviet noose was beginning to tighten around anyone Stalin deemed a possible enemy of the Soviet Union. This was not unique to Warsaw: on the day the city was freed, Raoul Wallenberg was arrested by the Soviets in Budapest. The Russians even began using Buchenwald and Sachsenhausen concentration camps and other places of terror for the incarceration of their own political prisoners.

Coming Home

The Warsawians who survived had been through a unique and terrible ordeal, and many felt alienated from those who had not experienced the same things. The sculptress Halina Adamska had left Warsaw for Pruszków camp with nothing, and managed afterwards to find refuge in a convent in Jasna Góra. When she tried to describe what had happened to her a woman said, 'Well, if you knew you were going to be expelled and that winter was coming, why didn't you just hire a car and take some bedding and warm clothes with you?' It was hopeless to try to explain.[22] Antoni Plater-Zyberk tried to tell people about the scale of the bombing in Warsaw. 'One Krakowian lady said, "We also had bombs in Kraków." "You are right," I said, "but one small five-kilo bomb which broke a wooden fence is not the same." ' They simply did not understand.

And so Warsawians, destitute and often starving, returned home. In January 1945, 12,000 of them came back; in February, 67,000; in March, 77,000. From the beginning of May those who had been in forced labour camps, concentration camps and PoW camps began to struggle back too. 'Tomorrow I must begin a new life,' Szpilman thought. 'How could I do it, with nothing but death behind me?'[23] Irena Konopacka 'met other people in Czerniaków just wandering around in the rubble like me, not knowing what they were looking for.'[24]

There were very few places to live, and at first people were drawn to the less destroyed Praga district, the former 'German quarter' Mokotów, and Żoliborz. Even so, many could only find refuge in bombed-out or destroyed buildings, and eked out an existence in half rooms with only a few sheets or tarpaulins for the walls. Agaton's mother and sister lived in 'a destroyed apartment which was so cold that the nieces could skate in the middle of the dining room'. His sister sold her ring and her grandmother's ring, and baked biscuits to make some money.[25] He had sent his friend 'Hanka' some winter clothes, but she had been forced to sell them for food.[26] German soldier Matthias Schenk, who had been wounded in his flight west and saved by a Polish family, also returned to the city. 'A temporary Belgian embassy had been set up in Warsaw. I found myself on the steps of a building which I had last seen when I was trying to capture it. People were living in the ruins of cellars.'[27]

As they returned they tried to track down missing friends and family members. Targowa Street in Praga became the main pedestrian street, and people would search the crowd for loved ones. It became the custom to leave messages in chalk or on pieces of paper by destroyed buildings giving information about the former occupants' whereabouts. 'I went to the house on Koszykowa where my mother and sister had lived to find only a single wall standing,' recalled Stefan Bałuk, one of the 'Cichociemni' who had now returned from Grossborn PoW camp. 'On the wall there was a scrap of paper, with the message "Maria and Barbara are in Skarżysko", together with an address.' He was one of the fortunate ones to find his family alive.

Allied Amnesia

Stalin had been delighted by the capture of Warsaw. Khrushchev, who met him shortly after the news had arrived, recalled, 'Stalin was in the highest spirits. He was strutting around like a peacock with his tail spread.'[28] With the front moving inexorably westward, the subject of Warsaw, which had caused such friction between Roosevelt, Churchill and Stalin, was diplomatically pushed from the agenda. When Churchill met Stalin for the Tolstoy Conference in Moscow between 9 and 19 October 1944, the Soviet dictator had tried to make light of the situation in the Polish capital, claiming that he could not possibly be held responsible for what was happening there. Churchill responded: 'There is no serious person in the United Kingdom who credits that the failure has been deliberate. Criticism only referred to the apparent unwilling-ness of the Soviet government to send aeroplanes.'[29] Averell Harriman confirmed that the United States agreed with this assess-ment. All had been forgiven, at least for now.

Stalin seemed to treat the uprising as if he had been little more than a concerned bystander, even offering up an interesting theory as to why it had started 'prematurely'. The Germans, he said, had threatened to deport the entire male population of Warsaw as the Red Army approached the city, leaving the Poles with no option but to fight. 'Either option meant death. This forced the majority of the Warsaw underground to fight the Germans.'[30] Churchill and Stalin had even joked about the Poles: on 9 October Stalin had said, 'If there is only one Pole he will start to quarrel with himself out of sheer boredom.' For his part, Churchill noted that General Bór would no longer trouble the Soviets, as 'the Germans were looking after him'.[31] The thorny question of the Warsaw Uprising had been pushed aside, allowing the statesmen to co-operate in a more or less civil manner until the end of the war.[32] For them, the whole episode would become little more than an uncomfortable footnote in the history of a noble conflict.

The End

By 20 January the Soviets had destroyed Hitler's defensive system and pushed west along a line stretching from East Prussia to the Carpathians. The 4th Panzer Division and the 9th Army were 'reduced to a drifting mass of men and mangled machines, left far to the rear and oozing in a glutinous military mass in the direction of the Oder and hopefully home'.[33] The top Nazis all knew the end was coming, and each had to decide for himself how to face the uncertain future. They had lived in a world of privilege and propaganda for so long that very few of them actually realized how loathed and despised they were in the rest of the world. A number of them had become literally sick on power. On a visit to the Peenemünde weapons factory in October 1944, Göring, dressed in 'bright red, soft Morocco leather riding boots with silver spurs', was so drugged that he could not stand up, and his eyes rolled 'until one could only see their whites'.[34] Others were more practical: the ever more powerful Kaltenbrunner still insisted that Jews be marched to their deaths even in the final days of the Reich, while at the same time sending vast sums of money abroad.

Himmler was still wavering madly, unsure if he should remain loyal to Hitler or redouble his attempts to negotiate for peace with the Western Allies. When Hitler ordered him to take command of Army Group Vistula he was delighted by the longed-for chance to prove himself on the battlefield and to gain a Knight's Cross for himself. He brought von dem Bach to lead the Tenth SS Corps, which was stationed around Deutsch-Krone. Himmler turned out to be a disaster as a military leader, and even Hitler was later forced to admit that he was 'no commander', as he 'totally lacked the divine spark'.[35] When von dem Bach, irritated by Himmler's mishandling of the situation, retreated without permission, Himmler blamed him and their friendship began to unravel.[36]

As the Red Army bore down on Berlin Himmler tried to build up his reputation abroad in preparation for what he saw as his inevitable role as Hitler's successor. The desire to ingratiate himself with the international community, and to try to sue for peace with the West, even induced him to risk Hitler's wrath by secretly meeting with Norbert Masur, the head of the Swedish section of the World Jewish Congress, at a private house near Berlin on 21 April 1945. Masur had risked his life by flying to Berlin's Tempelhof airport in order to ask Himmler to release all the Jews left alive in Germany, and to call for an end to the camp evacuations. It ranks as one of the most bizarre meetings of the entire war.

Himmler behaved with Masur as if the Holocaust had never happened at all. This was the first time he had entertained a Jew as an equal, and he greeted Masur warmly, telling him 'how glad I am that you have come'. He then launched into a long speech explaining that the treatment of the Jews in the concentration camps was nothing like the way it appeared in the propaganda which was now spreading throughout Europe; on the contrary, the camps had been nothing more than 'training centres'. 'Let bygones be bygones,' he said.[37] When Hitler got wind of Himmler's continued attempts to sue for peace he threw his 'Treuer Heinrich' out of the Nazi Party and ordered his arrest.

In the last weeks of April 1945 Hitler still clung to the hope that the relationship between the Allies would break down. He was, he said, 'like a spider at the centre of the web' from which he could watch the divisions grow between them. But Roosevelt's death on 12 April did not produce the desired split, and as the Soviets began to pound Berlin he accepted at last that the war was lost, and became fixated on the idea of Götterdämmerung. In his mind the German people had failed him, and there was no alternative but to bring about the complete destruction of the nation. 'If the war is lost, the people will be lost also. It is not necessary to worry about what the German people will need for elemental survival. On the contrary, it is best for us to destroy even these things. For the nation has proved to be the weaker, and the future belongs solely to the stronger eastern nation. In any case, only those who are inferior will remain after this struggle, for the good have already been killed.'[38]

This might have been seen as some sort of noble end by the likes of Hitler and Goebbels, but none of the other top Nazis had any intention of dying in the Führerbunker. They raced away to try to save their skins.[39] Fegelein slipped out of the bunker and disappeared on 25 April. An SS guard was sent to arrest him; they found him in his mistress's flat wearing civilian clothes, with a bag packed full of money and diamonds on the bed. Hitler had him shot. Himmler shaved off his moustache, donned an eyepatch and the uniform of the Geheime Feldpolizei – not realizing that this 'lowly' organization was on the Allied 'black list', its members subject to automatic arrest. He was caught by the British while trying to get to Bavaria, and committed suicide in captivity; his body was dumped in a secret pit on the Lüneburg Heath. Erich von dem Bach also went into hiding, and was preparing to leave Germany when he was arrested by the US Military Police. He agreed to act as a witness for the prosecution at Nuremberg, and as a result never faced trial for war crimes. Heinz Reinefarth, too, testified at Nuremberg and was never charged with any crime for his activities in Warsaw; he later held high political office in West Germany, and practised as a well-respected lawyer, dying peacefully in his bed, unrepentant to the last about what he had done in the Polish capital. Oskar Dirlewanger fled, and was arrested near the small Swabian town of Altshausen by the French. Although the facts are murky, it seems that he was recognized by two Poles and was beaten to death in a detention centre in early June 1945. Ludwig Hahn changed his identity after the war, evading arrest until 1975. Alfred Spilker disappeared altogether, along with most of his colleagues in the Warsaw SS. With a few exceptions, no leading Nazis were ever prosecuted for the crimes they committed during the Warsaw Uprising.

On the contrary, many were proud of what they had done in subduing the 'nest of bandits'. In his December 1944 report about the uprising, Ludwig Fischer called it an 'undoubted victory of the German army after so many failures . . . holding Warsaw despite it staging the biggest uprising in Polish history is one of the greatest achievements of the German army. It is a military achievement of the highest rank.'[40] The officers and generals congratulated one another on a job well done. A special badge was made depicting a gigantic eagle with a swastika around its neck crushing a twisted serpent in its long talons. 'Warschau 1944' is emblazoned across it.

Living Memory

After the war, evasion, lies and amnesia dominated the collective German, Soviet, British and American memories of the Warsaw Uprising. When Guderian was asked at Nuremberg if the destruction of the city was not more extreme than the military situation demanded, he retorted: 'Those instructions were released by Himmler. He is responsible. He hated Warsaw.'[41] While a prisoner of war in Moscow, Reiner Stahel wrote: 'The responsibility for the suffering which was inflicted on the civilians of Warsaw lies not only with us Germans but also with the Home Army leaders who set off the civilians in a fight which was destined to fail.'[42]

The uprising ranks among the great tragedies of the Second World War. When the Germans invaded Poland in September 1939, Warsaw had a population of 1.3 million people. Four hundred thousand Jews from the city and its surrounding area who were herded into the ghetto were murdered. When the 1944 uprising broke out in August 1944, 720,000 people lived on the west bank of Warsaw, and 920,000 in the city as a whole. Over 150,000 civilians and 18,000 AK soldiers died during the uprising.[43] Of the 520,000 Warsaw refugees processed through Pruszków, around 60,000 were sent to concentration camps, 90,000 to work camps in the Reich, and 18,000 to PoW camps.[44] Many never returned home.

For those who lived through it, the terror remains. One former AK nurse still finds herself waking up screaming in the middle of the night; another cannot read anything related to the uprising for fear of bringing back the memories.[45] The horrors continued long after the uprising itself, and countless thousands died of illness or were weakened for the rest of their lives as a result of their ordeals. Unknown numbers of Warsaw orphans live in Germany with no idea of their true origin, while many families deliberately ripped apart at Pruszków were never reunited. The physical and emotional scars, compounded by the grim realities of life in Stalinist Poland after the war, meant that the cost to Warsawians was very high indeed.

The fate of the AK soldiers was not much better. General Bór was reduced to painting houses for a living in England, while Colonel Monter wrote plaintive letters to Agaton begging for an apartment and a job in Warsaw. Over 100,000 people were arrested by the Soviets between August 1944 and August 1945, many of them AK members. Władysław Bartoszewski was not the only one of them who found himself serving time with ex-Nazi functionaries imprisoned in Warsaw; many others were transported east, and never heard from again. The most notorious of these transports, known as 'the Trial of the Sixteen', occurred when Stalin invited sixteen prominent AK members, including Leopold

Okulicki and Jan Jankowski, to a 'conference' to discuss their entry into the Soviet Provisional Government. Instead they were arrested by the NKVD, and endured a grotesque show trial in Moscow. Their security had been guaranteed by the United States and Britain, but three of them were executed.[46]

Warsaw was a modern-day Carthage. When US General Dwight D. Eisenhower visited the city immediately after the war, he was appalled. 'I have seen many towns destroyed,' he said, 'but nowhere have I been faced with such destruction.' The battered city lay under twenty million cubic metres of rubble, and its people eked out a grim existence in the ruins.

Even so, it soon became clear that Warsaw would live again. On 5 November 1945 the Association of Architects held its first meeting to discuss how the city could be rebuilt. With the help of old photographs, postcards and even Canaletto paintings, and tens of thousands of volunteers, the Old Town, the New Town, Czerniaków and the rest began to rise from the ruins. Hitler had wanted to erase 'Polish Warsaw' from the map, and he and Himmler had murdered hundreds of thousands of its citizens in the process. Today Himmler's skeleton lies mouldering in an unknown grave in northern Germany, and the dusty skull claimed to be Hitler's rolls around its box in a Moscow archive. Their grotesque experiment failed. To be sure, much of Warsaw has been lost forever, not least its once thriving Jewish community, but unlike Carthage, Warsaw rose again. It is a testament to its people that the city has turned itself into one of the most exciting, dynamic and innovative in Europe. Despite everything, the people of Warsaw have persevered, and their city lives on.

Author's Note and Acknowledgements

This book is based primarily on a library given to me by my father-in-law, Władysław Bartoszewski, which contains hundreds of books, pamphlets, underground newspapers, photographs, testimonies, Nazi publications and newspapers and important documents including a copy of Erich von dem Bach-Zelewski's diary, as well as many post-war testimonies given before the Polish War Crimes Tribunal in the mid-1940s. I have talked to and interviewed dozens of people over the eight years it took to write this book; however, I have made a conscious decision to rely primarily on the official post-war testimonies when it came to crimes committed in Warsaw, as they have an immediacy and accuracy that can sometimes fade later in life. Many of these are contained in the collections *Ludność cywilna w powstaniu warszawskim* and *Exodus Warszawy ludzie i miasto po Powstaniu 1944*, which I have drawn on extensively.

This book could not have been written without the help of many extraordinary people. First and foremost I would like to thank my father-in-law Władysław Bartoszewski, not only for giving me access to such a wealth of material, but also for his wit and wisdom and for having so generously spent time discussing this subject. I would like to thank Wioletta Gurdak for her dedication to the project, and for being such a great friend. Thank you to Zofia Bartoszewska, Sergiusz Michalski, Antony Polonsky, Chris Szpilman, Mścisław Lurie, the late Wanda Machuch and

Zygmunt Walkowski for their kind help; and to the late Jan-Nowak Jeziorański, Jan Milewski and the late Leszek Kołakowski for their encouragement. I would like to thank the scores of people who lived through the uprising and who took the time to talk to me about it; the wartorn city was brought to life by these conversations, which helped me to understand what it was like to be in Warsaw both during the uprising and in the months that followed; I hope the book in some way does justice to their experiences.

I would like to thank Sarah Chalfant of the Wylie Agency for her enthusiasm and support throughout. I was very fortunate to have worked with extraordinary teams at both William Collins in London and Farrar, Straus and Giroux in New York. My heartfelt thanks to my fantastic editor in London, Arabella Pike, for her invaluable input and wealth of experience and guidance throughout. I would like to thank Stephen Guise for all his work as senior project editor, Robert Lacey for his exacting line editing, Tara Al Azzawi for the marketing proofs, Sarah Hopper for help with the pictures, John Gilkes for the maps, Helen Ellis for promotion, and Joseph Zigmond for his valuable help. I would also like to thank the magnificent team at Farrar, Straus and Giroux, who did so much to bring the book to fruition. Thank you to my amazing editor in New York, Alex Star, for his many creative ideas and insight and patience throughout. I would like to thank Jonathan Galassi for his support from the beginning, Jeff Seroy and Greg Wazowicz for all they have done to promote the book, and Dan Gerstle for his very able assistance. Thank you, too, to Albert Tang for the innovative book design and Charlotte Strick for help with it. It was a privilege to be able to work with such talented people both in London and in New York.

I would like to thank my family, and in particular Władek for his patience and guidance, for reading the manuscript and helping in so many ways. Finally, this book is dedicated to my beloved Antonia and Caroline, who simply mean the world to me.

Guide to Polish Pronunciation

ą: as in French 'en' in Rouen
c: ts, except in the combinations below
ć: ch
ci: ch
cz: ch
ę: as in French 'in' in voisin
ł: w
ó: u
rz: zh
ś: sh
si: sh
sz: sh
w: v
ż: zh
ź: zh
zi: zh

German Ranks

SS Rank	Wehrmacht Rank	British Equivalent
None	General-Feldmarschall	Field Marshal
SS-Oberstgruppenführer	Generaloberst	General
SS-Obergruppenführer	General der Infanterie, der Artillerie etc.	Lieutenant General
SS-Gruppenführer	Generalleutnant	Major General
SS-Brigadeführer	Generalmajor	Brigadier
SS-Oberführer	None	None
SS-Standartenführer	Oberst	Colonel
SS-Obersturmbannführer	Oberstleutnant	Lieutenant Colonel
SS-Sturmbannführer	Major	Major
SS-Hauptsturmführer	Hauptmann	Captain
SS-Obersturmführer	Oberleutnant	Lieutenant
SS-Untersturmführer	Leutnant	2nd Lieutenant
SS-Sturmscharführer	Stabsfeldwebel	Regimental Sergeant Major
SS-Standarten-Oberjunker	Oberfähnrich	None
SS-Hauptscharführer	Oberfeldwebel	Battalion Sergeant Major
SS-Oberscharführer	Feldwebel	Company Sergeant Major
SS-Standartenjunker	Fähnrich	None

SS Rank	Wehrmacht Rank	British Equivalent
SS-Scharführer	Unterfeldwebel	Platoon Sergeant Major
SS-Unterscharführer	Unteroffizier	Sergeant
SS-Rottenführer	Obergefreiter	Corporal
SS-Sturmmann	Gefreiter	Lance Corporal
SS-Oberschütze	Oberschütze	None
SS-Schütze	Schütze	Private

Notes

Archives

AAN	Archiwum Akt Nowych. Central Archive of Modern Records, Warsaw
BA-B	Bundesarchiv, Berlin Lichterfelde
BA-MA	Bundesarchiv-Militärarchiv, Freiburg im Breisgau
CAMOFR (TsAMO)	Tsentralnyi Arkhiv Ministersva Oborony Rossiiskoi Federatsii. Central Archive of the Ministry of Defence of the Russian Federation. Podolsk
HIA	Hoover Institution Archives, Stanford
IPN	Instytut Pamięci Narodowej. Institute of National Remembrance containing archives of the secret police, Warsaw
IWM	Imperial War Museum Archives, London
LHCMA	Liddell Hart Papers, Liddell Hart Centre for Military Archives, King's College, London
MPW	Muzeum Powstania Warszawskiego. Museum of the Warsaw Uprising
Muzeum Historyczne Miasta Stołecznego Warszawy Archiwum	Archives of the Historical Museum of the City of Warsaw
NARA	National Archives and Records Administration, Washington, D.C., College Park Annex microfilm and documents collections (includes a near-complete collection of Himmler's papers and German 1944 aerial photographs of Warsaw)
USHM	United States Holocaust Memorial Museum Archives
WHI	Wojskowy Instytut Historyczny Institute of Military History, Warsaw
Wiener Library	

NOTES

Introduction

1 Hans Hopf, 'Die Fugger in Warschau', *Das Vorfeld*, 5/6 Folge, Schulungsamt der NSDAPAGG, Krakau, 1942. On Himmler's racial policy towards the Poles HIA Heinrich Himmler Papers 8 XX060-8.36
2 J. Noakes and G. Pridham (eds), *Nazism 1919–1945. A History in Documents and Eyewitness Accounts*, Vol. 2, Schocken, New York, 1988, p. 988
3 Robert Forszyk, *Warsaw 1944. Poland's Bid for Freedom*, Osprey Publishing, Oxford, 2009, p. 26
4 *Exodus Warszawy Ludzie i Miasto Po Powstaniu 1944* (henceforth E.W.), Państwowy Instytut Wydawniczy, Warsaw, 1993, Vol. II, p. 175
5 Heinz Reinefarth, *Kurze Schilderung des Kampfes um Warschau August–Oktober 1944*, statement signed at Nuremberg, 23 September 1946, Archiwum Komitet Centralny, IIIP/828, No. 9
6 Gunnar S. Paulsson, *Secret City*, New Haven, 2002, p. 1

Chapter 1: Byelorussian Prelude

1 Colin Heaton, 'Interview with World War II Luftwaffe Ace Günter Rall Pulled from the Wreckage of his Messerschmitt', *Aviation History*, 12 June 2006 (http://www.historynet.com/worldwar2)
2 Hans von Luck, *Panzer Commander. The Memoirs of Colonel Hans von Luck*, Dell Books, New York, 1989 p. 178
3 Wilhelm Keitel (Walter Gorlitz, ed.), *The Memoirs of Field-Marshal Keitel*, Musterschmidt-Verlag, Göttingen, 1961, p. 229
4 Testimony of Joanna Kryńska in front of the War Crimes Committee, 'Warszawska Komisja Badania Zbrodni Niemieckich o zbrodniach popelnionych przez hitlerowców w rejonie szpitala Św. Stanisława przy ulicy Wolskiej', 14 March 1947, in Marian Marek Drozdowski, Maria Maniakówna and Tomasz Strzembosz (eds), *Ludność Cywilna w Powstaniu Warszawskim*, Vol. I (henceforth L.C.P.W.,

Vol. I), Państwowy Instytut Wydawniczy, Warsaw, 1974, p. 320
5 H.R. Trevor-Roper, *Hitler's Table Talk 1941–1944*, Weidenfeld and Nicolson, London, 1972, p. 229. German figures for planned-for deaths of Byelorussians called for the murder, largely by starvation, of 10,600,000 people. Bundesarchiv-Militärarchiv Freiburg (BA-MA) RW (Wirtschaftsstab Ost) 31/299, p. 72. Timothy Snyder quotes the figures of 300,000 Byelorussians killed in 'reprisals' against 'partisans' and the deaths of around 700,000 Soviet prisoners of war with a total of half the population of Soviet Byelorussia being 'either killed or deported'. See Timothy Snyder, 'Sleepwalking to War', *Times Literary Supplement*, 19 July 2013, p. 10; see also Timothy Snyder, *Bloodlands. Europe Between Hitler and Stalin*, Random House, London, 2010
6 Hans Fritzsch interviewed by Leon Goldensohn at Nuremberg quoted in Robert Gellately, *The Nuremberg Interviews. Conversations with the Defendants and Witnesses*, Random House, London, 2004, p. 66
7 Franz W. Seidler, *Die Kollaboration 1939–1945*, Herbig, Munich, 1995, p. 488
8 Stephen G. Fritz, *Frontsoldaten. The German Soldier in World War II*, Kentucky University Press, Kentucky, 1995, p. 50
9 Erich von dem Bach's testimony, given at Nuremberg on 7 January 1946, Tribunal Day 28, is available at http://Avalon.law.yale.edu/imt/01-07-46.asp
10 Walter Schellenberg interviewed by Leon Goldensohn at Nuremberg quoted in Robert Gellately, *The Nuremberg Interviews*, p. 423
11 Erich von dem Bach-Zelewski, *Kriegstagebuch*, BA R 020/000045b. fol. 1–117, p. 45. For an excellent account of von dem Bach's movements in Byelorussia see Philip W. Blood, *Hitler's Bandit Hunters. The SS and the Nazi Occupation of Europe*, Potomac Books, Dulles, VA, 2006, and Timothy Patrick Mulligan, *The Politics of Chaos. The Attempts to Reform Hitler's Ostpolitik Autumn 1942–Spring*

1943, unpublished Master of Arts Degree, University of Maryland, 1977, HIA Mulligan, Timothy Patrick, 80048-10V

12 Harriet Eder; Thomas Kufus (directors) *Mein Krieg*, Part V, BBC Elstree, 1991

13 Gottlob Herbert Bidermann, *In Deadly Combat. A German Soldier's Memoir of the Eastern Front*, University Press of Kansas, Kansas, 2000, p. 13

14 Catherine Merridale, *Ivan's War. The Red Army 1939–45*, Faber and Faber, London, 2005, p. 124. On the Wehrmacht's role in these crimes see Norbert Müller, *Wehrmacht und okkupation 1942–44. Zur Rolle der Wehrmacht und ihrer Führungsorgane im Okkupationsregime*, Deutsche Militär Verlag, Berlin, 1971. From the Soviet perspective see Iurii V. Arutiunian, *Sovetskoe krest'ianstvo – gody Velikoi Otechestvennoi krest'ianstva okkupirovannykh oblastei RSFSR protiv nemetscko-fashistskoi okkupatisionnoi politiki 1941–1944*, Nauka, Moscow, 1976

15 Erich von dem Bach interviewed by Leon Goldensohn, 14 February 1946, in Robert Gellately, *The Nuremberg Interviews*, p. 271

16 Christian Gerlach, *Kalkulierte Morde. Die deutsche Wirtschafts - und Vernich ungs - politik in Weissrussland 1941 bis 1944*, HIS Verlag, Hamburg, 1999, p. 522

17 Martin Pollack, *Der Tote im Bunker. Bericht über meinen Vater*, Taschenbuch Verlag, Munich, 2004, p. 170

18 Funkspruch HSSUPF Russland Mitte 18/10/1942. NARA Microfilm Publication T175 Roll 18

19 Mark Mazower, *Hitler's Empire. Nazi Rule in Occupied Europe*, Penguin, London, 2008, p. 488

20 HIA Office Files, Personlicher Stab Reichsführer SS, 1936–1945 Box 12, Folder 1–25 (Himmler's Order Banning the Use of the Word Partisan 1942). See also Philip W. Blood, *Hitler's Bandit Hunters*. Blood has written an excellent account of von dem Bach's participation in the Bandenbekämpfung and his post-war attempts to cover up his involvement in mass murder.

21 Erich von dem Bach, *Kriegstagebuch*, pp. 77–78

22 The SS-Befehl was issued on 21 June 1943. See also Andrej Angrick, 'Erich von dem Bach-Zelewski. Himmlers Mann für alle Fälle', in Ronald Smelser and Enrico Syring (eds.) *Die SS Elite unter dem Totenkopf*, Friedrich Schöningh, Paderborn, 2003, p. 42

23 Philip W. Blood, *Hitler's Bandit Hunters*, p. 106

24 Ibid., p. 108. See also Timm C. Richter, 'Die Wehrmacht und der Partisanenkrieg', in Rolf-Dieter Müller and Hans-Erich Volkmann (eds) *Die Wehrmacht. Mythos und Realität*, Oldenbourg Verlag, Munich, 1999, p. 855

25 Stephen G. Fritz, *Frontsoldaten*, p. 51

26 Ibid., p. 51

27 Johannes Hürter, *Ein deutsche General an der Ostfrong. Die Briefe und Tagebücher des Gotthard Heinrici 1941/42*, Sutton Verlag, Erfurt, 2001, p. 107

28 French L. MacLean, *The Cruel Hunters. SS-Sonderkommando Dirlewanger. Hitler's Most Notoricus Anti-Partisan Unit*, Schiffer Publishing, Atglen, PA, 1998, p. 28

29 Ibid., p. 27

30 Ibid., p. 31

31 Ibid., p. 33

32 H.R. Trevor-Roper, *Hitler's Table Talk*, p. 640

33 French L. MacLean, *The Cruel Hunters*, p. 61

34 Stephen G. Fritz, *Frontsoldaten*, p. 58

35 Philip W. Blood, *Hitler's Bandit Hunters*, p. 178

36 Ibid., p. 129

37 Christian Ingrao, *The SS Dirlewanger Brigade. The History of the Black Hunters*, Skyhorse, New York, 2011, p. 127

38 Christian Gerlach, *Kalkulierte Morde*, p. 943

39 Ibid., p. 950

40 Christian Ingrao, *The SS Dirlewanger Brigade*, p. 25

41 Erich von dem Bach, *Kriegstagebuch*, p. 81

42 Christian Ingrao, p. 25

43 Ibid., p. 26

44 Ibid., p. 134

45 Ibid., p. 142

NOTES

Chapter 2: To the Very Gates of Warsaw

1 Willy Peter Reese, *A Stranger to Myself. The Inhumanity of War: Russia, 1941–1944*, Farrar, Straus and Giroux, New York, 2003, p. 53 Reese's extraordinary memoir covers the German retreat into Byelorussia; the scorched-earth policy and partisan war he describes so vividly continue as the Germans are forced west in the summer of 1944.
2 Gottlob Herbert Bidermann, *In Deadly Combat. A German Soldier's Memoir of the Eastern Front*, University Press of Kansas, Kansas, 2000, p. 200
3 Ibid., p. 199
4 Guy Sajer, *The Forgotten Soldier*, Harper and Row, New York, 1967, p. 417. Sajer recounts Germans committing suicide rather than risking falling into the hands of the Soviets as 'Russia inspired such terror'.
5 This was a risky strategy as a wound had to be disabling to remove the soldier from combat duty.
6 On the Soviet weapons build-up see John Erickson, *The Road to Berlin*, Vol. II, Grafton Books, London, 1985, pp. 108–113
7 Gottlob Herbert Bidermann, *In Deadly Combat*, p. 91
8 Stephen G. Fritz, *Frontsoldaten*, p. 204
9 Ibid., p. 205
10 Ibid.
11 Erich Stahl, *Eyewitness to Hell. With the Waffen SS on the Eastern Front in W. W. II*, Ryton Publications, Bellingham, WA, 2009, p. 169
12 Red Army soldiers were shocked by the sight of the towns and villages, such was the scale of the destruction. 'Whatever had been left after two years of Nazi rule was torched, including livestock and harvested grain.' Catherine Merridale, *Ivan's War*, p. 201
13 Willy Peter Reese, *A Stranger to Myself*, p. 149
14 Ibid., p. 135
15 Konstantin Rokossovsky, *A Soldier's Duty*, Progress Publishers, Moscow, 1985,

p. 250
16 Robert Conquest, *The Great Terror. A Reassessment*, Overlook, New York, 2001, p. 253
17 Christopher Duffy, *Red Storm on the Reich. The Soviet March on Germany, 1945*, Routledge, London, 2001, p. 23
18 Georgii Zhukov, *The Memoirs of Marshal Zhukov*, Jonathan Cape, London, 1971, p. 525
19 Sergei Shtemenko, *The Soviet General Staff at War 1941–1945*, Progress Publishers, Moscow, 1981, p. 332
20 John Latimer, *Deception in the War*, Overlook, New York, 2001, p. 253
21 Georgii Zhukov, *The Memoirs of Marshal Zhukov*, p. 527
22 Paul Adair, *Hitler's Greatest Defeat. The Collapse of Army Group Centre, June 1944*, Brockhampton Press, London, 1994, p. 60
23 Ibid., p. 86
24 Ibid., p. 64
25 Gitta Sereny, *Albert Speer. His Battle with Truth*, Macmillan, London, 1995, p. 434
26 Stephen G. Fritz, *Frontsoldaten*, p. 33
27 Vasily Grossman was permitted to join General Batov's 65th Army to observe the offensive. 'A cauldron of death was boiling here, where the revenge was carried out – a ruthless, terrible revenge over those who hadn't surrendered their arms and tried to break out to the west'. Vasily Grossman (Antony Beevor and Luba Vinogradova eds), *A Writer at War. Vasily Grossman with the Red Army 1941–1945*, Random House, London, 2005, p. 273
28 Stephen G. Fritz, *Frontsoldaten*, p. 151
29 Rolf Hinze, *Das Ostfront-Drama 1944. Rückzugskämpfe Heersgruppe Mitte*, Motorbuch-Verlag, Stuttgart, 1988, p. 332
30 Ibid.
31 Ibid., p. 334
32 Grossman wrote of the aftermath at Bobruisk: 'Men are walking over German corpses. Corpses, hundreds and thousands of them, pave the road, lie in ditches, under the pines, in the green barley. In some places, vehicles have to drive over the corpses, so densely they lie upon the ground'. Vasily Grossman, *A Writer at*

War, p. 273

33 Gottlob Herbert Bidermann, *In Deadly Combat*, p. 223

34 Gitta Sereny, *Albert Speer*, p. 434

35 Steve Zaloga, *Bagration 1944. The Destruction of Army Group Centre*, Osprey Publishing, Oxford, 1996, p. 97

36 Georgii Zhukov, *The Memoirs of Marshal Zhukov*, p. 353

37 Albert Speer, *Inside the Third Reich*, Warner Books, London, 1993, p. 488

38 Stephen G. Fritz, *Frontsoldaten*, p. 150

39 Ibid., p. 150

40 Willy Peter Reese, *A Stranger to Myself*, p. 52

41 Włodzimierz Borodziej, *The Warsaw Uprising of 1944*, University of Wisconsin Press, London, 2001, p. 57

42 Tadeusz Piotrowski, *Poland's Holocaust*, McFarland & Company, Jefferson, NC, 1990, p. 99

43 Ibid., p. 100

44 Marcel Stein, *A Flawed Genius. Field Marshal Walter Model. A Critical Biography*, Helion and Compnay, Solihull, 2010, p. 139

45 Christa Schroeder, *He Was My Chief. The Memoirs of Adolf Hitler's Secretary*, Frontline Books, London, 2009, p. 87

46 Ibid., p. 125

47 Ibid., pp. 181–184

48 Albert Speer, *Inside the Third Reich*, p. 534

49 Excerpt from the United States Strategic Bombing Survey Report (European War), 30 September 1945, United States Government Printing Office, Washington, DC, reprinted in *Colliers Magazine*, May 1946

50 Marcel Stein, *A Flawed Genius*, p. 147

51 General Walter Warlimont, *Inside Hitler's Headquarters 1939–1945*, Weidenfeld and Nicolson, London, 1964, p. 442

52 Gottlob Herbert Bidermann, *In Deadly Combat*, p. 228

53 Josef Goebbels (Hugh Trevor-Roper, ed.), *The Goebbels Diaries: The Last Days*, Pan, London, 1978, p. xxxi

54 Georgii Zhukov, *The Memoirs of Marshal Zhukov*, p. 536

55 Lew Bezymenski, 'Radzieckie uderzenie w kierunku Wisły', in Stanisław Lewandowski and Bernd Martin (eds), *Powstanie*

Warszawskie 1944, Wydawnictwo Polska-Niemieckie, Warsaw, 1999, p. 270 (in 1944 Bezymenski was an officer in Unit 1-C of the 1st Byelorussian Front)

56 Norbert Bacyk, *The Tank Battle at Praga July–Sept. 1944. The 4th SS-Panzer-Corps vs the 1st Belorussian Front*, Leandoer & Ekholm Publishing, Stockholm, 2009, p. 28

57 Laurence Rees, *World War II Behind Closed Doors. Stalin, the Nazis, and the West*, BBC Books, London, 2009

58 Norbert Bacyk, *The Tank Battle at Praga*, p. 39

59 Ibid., p. 28

Chapter 3: Ostpolitik

1 Anna Kotańska, Anna Topolska, *Warsaw Past and Present*, Parma Press, Marki, 2005, p. 8

2 Chester Wilmot, 'Notes on interrogation of General Franz Halder', LH 15/15/150/2, Liddell Hart Papers, Liddel Hart Centre for Military Archives, King's College, London (LHCMA)

3 Gunnar S. Paulsson, *Secret City. The Hidden Jews of Warsaw 1940–1945*, Yale University Press, New Haven, CT, 2002, p. 209

4 Peter F. Dembowski, *Christians in the Warsaw Ghetto. An Epitaph for the Unremembered*, University of Notre Dame Press, Notre Dame, IN, 2005, p. 19

5 Wladyslaw Szpilman, *The Pianist*, Phoenix, London, 2002, p. 103

6 Ibid., p. 107

7 Yankel Wiernik, *A Year in Treblinka. An Inmate who Escaped Tells the Day-to-Day Facts of One Year of His Torturous Experiences*, American Representation of the General Jewish Workers' Union of Poland, New York, 1945

8 Stroop planned the destruction of the synagogue in advance, promising to end the clearing of the ghetto 'on 16 May 1943 at dusk, by blowing up the Synagogue'. The Stroop Report is available on http://www.jewishvirtuallibrary.org/jsource/Hol. Himmler wrote to SS Obergruppenführer Krüger applauding the demise of '500,000 Untermenschen'.

HIA Heinrich Himmler Papers XX060-8.36 12-13

9 Stanisław Aronson; Patrycja Bukalska, *Rysiek z Kedywu. Niezwykłe Losy Stanisława Aronsona*, Znak, Kraków, 2009, p. 89

10 Peter F. Dembowski, *Christians in the Warsaw Ghetto*, p. 19

11 Helmut Krausnick, *Hitler's Einstazgruppen. Die Truppen des Weltanschauungskrieges 1938-1942*, Deutsche-Verlags Anhalt, Stuttgart, 1989, p. 77

12 *Man to Man … Destruction of the Polish Intelligentsia in the Years 1939-1945*, Rada Ochrony Pamięci Walk i Męczeństwa, Warsaw, 2009, p. 46

13 Ibid., p. 63

14 Roman Zbigniew Hrabar, *Hitlerowski rabunek dzieci polskich*, Śląsk, Katowice, 1960, p. 28. Himmler's plan to Germanize Polish children HIA Heinrich Himmler Papers XX060-8-36 12-10

15 Richard C. Lukas, *Forgotten Holocaust. The Poles under German Occupation 1939-1944*, University Press of Kentucky, Kentucky, 1986, p. 25

16 Ibid., p. 26. The plans to colonize Poland were taken very seriously. In March 1942 Martin Bormann wrote that the Germans had 'identified one million *Volksdeutsche*' in Poland; this meant that according to Generalplan Ost, thirty-five million more Germans would have to be settled in Poland. He added: 'The number [of Poles] to be evacuated ['*zu Evakuierenden*'] has therefore to be much greater than envisaged in the current plan.' Lew Besymenski, *Die letzten Notizen von Martin Bormann. Ein Dokument und sein Verfasser*, Deutsche Verlags-Anstalt, Stuttgart, 1974, p. 91

17 Ibid.

18 Alceo Valcini, *Golgota Warszawy 1939-1945. Wspomnienia*, Wydawnictwo Literackie, Kraków, 1973, p. 327 Richard C. Lukas, *Forgotten Holocaust*, p. 35. Hitler said to Hermann Rauschning: 'We are obliged to depopulate … as part of our mission of preserving the German population. We shall have to develop a technique of depopulation. If you ask me what I mean by depopulation, I mean the removal of entire racial units. And that is what I intend to carry out – that, roughly, is my task. Nature is cruel, therefore we, too, may be cruel. If I can send the flower of the German nation into the hell of war without the smallest pity for the spilling of precious German blood, then surely I have the right to remove millions of an inferior race that breeds like vermin. And by "remove" I don't necessarily mean destroy; I shall simply take systematic measures to dam their great natural fertility … It will be one of the chief tasks of German statesmanship for all time to prevent, by every means in our power, the further increase of the Slav races.' Hermann Rauschning, *Hitler Speaks*, Thornton Butterworth, London, 1940, p. 141

19 Wojciech Fałkowski, *Straty Warszawy 1939-1945. Raport*, Miasto Stołeczne Warszawa, Warsaw, 2005, p. 301; see also Gunnar S. Paulsson, *The Secret City*, pp. 199-230

20 Gottlob Herbert Bidermann, *In Deadly Combat*, p. 214

21 Rochus Misch, *Der Letzte Zeuge. Ich war Hitlers Telefonist, Kurier und Leibwächter*, Piper, Munich, 2008, p. 165

22 Stanisław Jankowski 'Agaton', *Z fałszywym Ausweisem w prawdziwej Warszawie*, Vol. I, Państwowy Instytut Wydawniczy, Warsaw, 1980, p. 148

23 Włodzimierz Borodziej, *The Warsaw Uprising of 1944*, p. 9

24 Alceo Valcini, *Golgota Warszawy*, p. 276

25 Stanisław Jankowski 'Agaton', *Z fałszywym Ausweisem*, Vol. I, p. 148

26 Stanisław Aronson, *Rysiek z Kedywu*, p. 121

27 Stanisław Jankowski 'Agaton', *Z fałszywym Ausweisem*, Vol. I, p. 149

28 Testimony of Stanisław Ruskowski in L.C.P.W., Vol. I, Part 1, p. 155

29 Alceo Valcini, *Golgota Warszawy* p. 277

30 Heinrich Himmler, order 6 August to SS-Obergruppenführer Wihelm Koppe ordering the arrest of the Landgerichtspräsident who allowed the prisoners to escape in Marek Getter, Andrzej Janowski (eds), *Ludność Cywilna w Powstaniu Warszawskim*, Vol. II (henceforth L.C.P.W., Vol. II), Państwowy

Instytut Wydawniczy, Warsaw 1974, Document 33, p. 68

31 Dr Jerzy Dreyza testimony, March 1967, in L.C.P.W., Vol. I, p. 383

32 Eugeniusz Szermentowski, *Dzienniki z Powstania Warszawskiego*, Wydawnictwo Literackie, Kraków, 2004, p. 101

33 Alceo Valcini, *Golgota Warszawy*, p. 277

34 Maria Teodozja Hoffman, diary fragment written August 1944, L.C.P.W., Vol. I, Part 1, p. 248

35 Stanisław Jankowski 'Agaton', *Z fałszywym Ausweisem*, p. 151

36 The Poles may have misunderstood the sign but as Marcel Stein points out, 'Model's final stabilization of the chaos, and the re-establishment of a coherent front line, must rank among the greatest performances by German commanders during World War II'. Marcel Stein, *A Flawed Genius*, p. 141

Chapter 4: Resistance

1 The AK was first known as the Służba Zwycięstwu Polski (SZP), Polish Victory Service, then the Związek Walki Zbrojnej (ZWZ), Union for Armed Struggle. It was officially named the Armia Krajowa (AK), Home Army, in February 1942. For simplicity I have used the abbreviation AK throughout.

2 Tadeusz 'Bór' Komorowski, *The Secret Army*, The Battery Press, Nashville, TN, 1984, p. 22

3 Ibid., p. 42

4 Stefan Korbonski, *Fighting Warsaw. The Story of the Polish Underground State 1939–1945*, Hippocrene Books, New York, 2004, p. 21

5 Jan Karski, *Story of a Secret State. My Report to the World*, Penguin, London, 2012, p. 71

6 Stanisław Likiernik, *By Devil's Luck. A Tale of Resistance in Wartime Warsaw*, Mainstream, London, 2001, p. 81

7 Stanisław Aronson, *Rysiek z Kedywu*, p. 77

8 Borecki was captured in February 1940. Karski learned that he had been treated with great brutality. 'He was beaten for days on end. Nearly every bone in his body was systematically and scientifically broken. His back was a mass of bloody tatters from an endless succession of blows administered with iron rods. The gaunt, ailing old man never lost control of himself, never divulged a single secret. In the end, he was shot. The Nazis' newspaper later announced that a Polish adventurer and bandit had been sentenced to death by a court-martial because of his disloyalty toward the German Reich.' Jan Karski, *Story of a Secret State*, p. 103

9 Ibid., p. 132

10 J.K. Zawodny, *Nothing but Honour. The Story of the Warsaw Uprising, 1944*, Macmillan, London, 1978, p. 49

11 Richard Lukas, *The Forgotten Holocaust*, p. 104

12 Ibid., p. 103

13 Ibid., p. 106

14 Tadeusz 'Bór' Komorowski, *The Secret Array*, p. 166

15 Andrzej Chwalba, 'Fortepian Schoppinga', *Gazeta Wyborcza*, 13 May 2010

16 Jan Karski, *Story of a Secret State*, p. 331

17 Włodzimierz Borodziej, *The Warsaw Uprising of 1944*, p. 79

18 Jonathan Walker, *Poland Alone. Britain, SOE and the Collapse of the Polish Resistance, 1944*, Spellmount, Stroud, 2010, p. 148

19 Interview with Robert Snowden, headmaster of St Michael's University School, Victoria, BC, July 2012

20 Jan Karski, *Story of a Secret State*, p. 73

21 Ibid., p. 74

22 Generalleutnant Hans Källner, like Fegelein, had been a professional tournament rider and had made friends with General Bór. 'General Källner did his best to assist Bór in a soldierly surrender.' Marcel Stein, *A Flawed Genius*, p. 153

23 Andrzej Krzysztof Kunert (ed.), *General Tadeusz Bór-Komorowski*, Rytm, Warsaw, 2000, p. 138

24 Józef Garlinski, *The Survival of Love. Memoirs of a Resistance Officer*, Basil Blackwell, Oxford, 1991, p. 105

25 Stanisław Likiernik, *By Devil's Luck*, p. 69

26 Stanisław Aronson, *Rysiek z Kedywu*, p. 115

27 Tadeusz Bór Komorowski, *The Secret Army*, p. 156

28 Claude Lanzmann, 'Interview Dr Franz Grassler, Deputy to Dr Auerswald, Nazi Commissioner of the Warsaw Ghetto', http://www.holocaustresearchproject.org/ghett

29 Hanna Rybicka (ed.), *Oddział Kobiecy Warszawskiego Kedywu. Dokumenty z lat 1943–1945*, Wydawnictwa uniwersytetu Warszawskiego, Warsaw, 2002, pp. 7–10

30 Ibid., p. 10

31 Stanisław Aronson, *Rysiek z Kedywu*, p. 81

32 Jonathan Walker, *Poland Alone*, p. 174

33 Ibid., p. 177

34 Tadeusz 'Bór' Komorowski, *The Secret Army*, p. 65

35 Andrzej Krzysztof Kunert, *Generał Tadeusz Bór-Komorowski*, p. 333

36 Stanisław Jankowski 'Agaton', *Z fałszywym Ausweisem*, p. 42

37 Jan M. Ciechanowski, *The Warsaw Rising of 1944*, Cambridge University Press, Cambridge, 1974, p. 216

38 Kazimierz Iranek-Osmieckie, *Powołanie i Przeznaczenie. Wspomnienia Oficera Komeny Głownej AK 1940–1944*, Państwowy Instytut Wydawniczy, Warsaw, 1998, p. 415

39 Ibid., p. 420

40 Ibid.

41 Józef Roman Rybicki, *Notatki szefa Warszawskiego Kedywu*, Wydawnictwa Uniwersytatu Warszawskiego, Warsaw, 2001, p. 184

42 Kazimierz Iranek-Osmieckie, *Powołanie i Przeznaczenie*, p. 419

43 Ibid., p. 420

44 Ibid., p. 421

45 Jan Nowak discusses the uprising in a Radio Free Europe interview with Janusz Bokszczanin, http://www.polskieradio.pl/68/2461/Audio/294878

46 Heinz Reinefarth, *Kurze Schilderung des Kampfes um Warschau August–Oktober 1944*, p. 22; HIA Himmler File XX060–8.36 12–13

47 Jan M. Ciechanowski, *The Warsaw Rising of 1944*, p. 234

48 Władysław Bartoszewski, *Dni walczącej Stolicy. Kronika Powstania Warszarskiego*,

Swiat Książki, Warsaw, 2004, p. 21

49 Tadeusz 'Bór' Komorowski, *The Secret Army*, p. 181

50 Andrew Borowiec, *Destroy Warsaw! Hitler's Punishment, Stalin's Revenge*, Praeger, London, 2001, p. 77

51 Ibid.

52 Stanisław Aronson, *Rysiek z Kedywu*, p. 119

53 Ibid., p. 120

Chapter 5: The Uprising Begins

1 Julian Eugeniusz Kulski, *Dying We Live. The Personal Chronicle of a Young Freedom Fighter in Warsaw 1939–1945*, Holt, Reinhart and Winston, Austin, TX, 1979, p. 208

2 Władysław Szpilman, *The Pianist*, p. 149

3 The generation was named after Roman Bratny's book *Kolumbowie Rocznik 20*

4 Julian Eugeniusz Kulski, *Dying We Live*, p. 308

5 Robert Forczyk, *Warsaw 1944*, p. 38

6 Jan M. Ciechanowski, *The Warsaw Rising of 1944*, p. 240

7 Jan Magdziak – Biblioteka Muzeum Powstania Warszawskiego – Folder Zeznania Świadków Naocznych, p. 4265

8 Włodzimierz Rosłoniec, 'Memoir 1944', *Znak*, 4 October 1989

9 John Ward was a British ex-PoW and a member of the Polish Home Army between 1941 and 1945. His coded radio messages were dispatched from Warsaw to London between 7 August and 29 September 1944, bringing first-hand and reliable news of events in the city. His messages are reprinted in Andrzej Pomian, *The Warsaw Rising. A Selection of Documents*, HIA – The Andrzej Pomian Papers, 2009C45-3

10 For Anders' view on the uprising see: Władysław Anders, *An Army in Exile. The Story of the Second Polish Corps*, The Battery Press, Nashville, TN, 2004

11 Today the Śląsko–Dąbrowski railway lies on the supports of the old Most Kierbedzia. See Andrzej Szwarc, *The Great Book of Warsaw*, Syrenka, Warsaw, 2000, p. 83

12 The bridge that existed for a short time

south of the Royal Castle between 1775 and 1794 was pulled down by supporters of the Kościuszko Uprising to stop the Russians reaching the west bank of Warsaw.

13 Włodzimierz Borodziej, *The Warsaw Uprising of 1944*, p. 85

14 Andrew Borowiec, *Destroy Warsaw!*, p. 275

15 Janusz Brochwicz-Lewiński, 'Interview with Janusz Griff Brochwicz Lewinsky', 18 December 2004, Archiwum Historii Mówionej, Muzeum Powstania Warszawskiego

16 Włodzimierz Rosłoniec, *Grupa „Krybar" Powiśle 1944*, Instytut Wydawniczy PAX, Warsaw, 1989, pp. 36–40

17 Stanisław Aronson, *Rysiek z Kedywu*, p. 131

18 Anna Szatkowska, *Był Dom … Wspomnienia*, Wydawnictwo Literackie, Warsaw, 2006, p. 49

19 Hans Thieme, 'Wspomnienia niemieckiego oficera sztabowego o powstaniu warszawskim', in Stanisław Lewandowski and Bernd Martin (eds), *Powstanie Warszawskie 1944*, p. 270

20 'Zeznania własne sierżanta artylerii przeciwlotniczej Waltera Schrödera. 3/09/1944', in Piotr Mierecki, Wasilij Christoforow (eds), *Powstanie Warszawskie 1944 w dokumentach z archiwów służb specjalnych*, Instytut Pamięci Narodowej, Warsaw, Moscow, 2007, p. 347

21 United States Holocaust Memorial Museum, List of Jewish Casualties, Members of the Polish Home Army (AK) supplied by Willy Glazer, http://www.citinet.net/ak/polska_40_f2.html

22 A. Pinon-Gacka, 'Dni chwały i klęski', in L.C.P.W., Vol. I, Part 1, p. 439

23 Dr Krug quoted in Andrzej Dryszel, 'Zapomniane ofiary', *Przegląd*, April 2010, p. 1

24 Andrew Borowiec, *Destroy Warsaw!*, p. 91

25 Stefan Talikowski testimony in L.C.P.W., Vol. I, Part 1, p. 298

26 Ibid., p. 290

27 Jan Rossmann, Anna Zawadska and Tadeusz Zawadski, *Zóska*, Oficyna Wydawnicza Interim, Warsaw, 1991, p. 211

28 Eulalia Matusiak testimony, 'Wypędzeni z Warszawy 1944. Losy Dzieci. Banwar 1944', 27 June 2007, Muzeum Historyczne m. St. Warszawy

29 Tadeusz Szczęsny testimony, in L.C.P.W, Vol. I, Part 1, p. 290

30 Ibid., p. 290

31 Stanisław Aronson, *Rysiek z Kedywu*, p. 132

32 Ibid., p. 134

33 Stefan Wojciech Talikowski testimony in L.C.P.W., Vol. I, Part 1, p. 298

34 Ibid., p. 298

35 Jadwiga Stasiakowa testimony in L.C.P.W., Vol. I, Part 1, p. 299

36 Ibid., p. 301

37 Ibid., p. 302

38 Tadeusz Rybowski interview, 23 March 2005, Archiwum Historii Mówionej, Muzeum Powstania Warszawskiego

39 Halina Wiśniewska, *Gawędy druhny Babci*, Harcerskie Biuro Wydawnicze Horyzonty, Warsaw, 2001, p. 120

40 Stefania Chmielewska testimony, 'Warszawska Komisja Badania Zbrodni Niemieckick o Zbrodniach popełnionych przez hitlerowców na Starym Mieście oraz w pobliżu Powązek', in L.C.P.W., Vol. I, Part 1, p. 469

41 Sabina Sebyłowa diary extract quoted in Jerzy S Majewski, 'Wojenne dzieje Pragi', *Gazeta Wyborcza*, 6 August 2010

42 Ibid.

43 Testimony of Jadwiga Stasiakowa, in L.C.P.W., Vol. I, p. 214

44 Anna Szatkowska, *Był Dom*, p. 62

45 Larysa Zajączkowska, *Powieść życia. Dzienniki i wspomnienia*, Adam Marszałek, Warsaw, 2008, p. 87

46 Władysław Bartoszewski, *Dni walczącej Stolicy*, p. 38. On the genesis of flights to aid Warsaw see 'Memorandum for Polish Representative with the Combined Chiefs of Staff, "Immediate Assistance to the Polish Home Forces in Warsaw"' 18 August 1944. HIA Mitkiewicz, Leon. 3 3:6 65001–3.M.19

Chapter 6: 'Himmler Has Won'

1 Hans Frank, *Dziennik Hansa Franka*, Vol. 1 (Stanisław Piotrowski, ed.), Wydawnictwo Prawnicze, Warsaw, 1957, entry 12 May 1944, p. 237

2 BA-MA RG 242, T78, roll 562 OKH, Generalstabes des Heeres, Fremde Heere Ost, 1 July 1944

3 Tadeusz Sawicki, *Rozkaz Zdławić powstanie. Niemcy i ich sojusznicy w walce z Powstaniem Warszawskim*, Bellona, Warsaw, 2010, p. 14

4 Ibid., p. 15

5 Tadeusz Kur, *Sprawiedliwość pobłażliwa. Proces kata Warszawy Ludwiga Hahn w Hamburgu*, MON, Warsaw, 1975, p. 274

6 Affidavit of Karl Kaleske at Nuremberg, February 1946, reprinted in French L. MacLean, *The Ghetto Men*, Schiffer Military History, Atglen, PA, 2001, p. 88

7 Władysław Bartoszewski, *Powstanie Warszawski*, Świat Ksiąski, Warsaw, 2009, p. 463

8 Ibid., p. 162

9 Tadeusz Kur, *Sprawiedliwość pobłażliwa*, p. 325

10 Marcel Stein, *A Flawed Genius*, p. 154

11 Heinz Guderian, *Erinnerungen Eines Soldaten*, Motorbuch Verlag, Stuttgart, 2003, p. 359

12 Sabina Sebyłowa diary extract quoted in Jerzy S. Majewski, 'Wojenne dzieje Pragi', *Gazeta Wyborcz*, 6 August 2010

13 Hasso Krappe, 'Powstanie warszawskie we wspomnieniach oficera Wehrmachtu', in Stanisław Lewandowski and Bernd Martin (eds), *Powstanie Warszawskie 1944*, p. 261

14 Wacław Gluth-Nowowiejski, 20 February 2007, Archiwum Historii Mówionej, Muzeum Powstania Warszawskiego

15 M.M. Drozdowski, *Kościoł a Powstanie Warszawskie: wybór i opracowanie*, Znak, Warsaw, 1994

16 French L. MacLean, *The Ghetto Men*, pp. 114–118

17 Jerzy Kirchmayer, *Powstanie Warszawskie*, Książka i Wiedza, Książka i Wiedza, Warsaw, 1959 p. 158, n. 2

18 On Stahel's career see entry in Franz Thomas, *Die Eichenlaubträger 1939–1945*. II: *l–z*, Biblio Verlag, Osnabrück, 1988

19 Joseph Goebbels (Elke Frölich, ed.) *Die Tagebücher von Joseph Goebbels. Im Auftrage des Instituts für Zeitgeschichte*, K.G. Saur, Munich, 1995, entry 28 July 1944, p. 186

20 Walter Warlimont, *Inside Hitler's Headquarters*, p. 468

21 Hans Frank, telephone call 10.15 p.m. with Dr Fischer on night of 1 August 1944. Hans Frank, *Dziennik Hansa Franka*, p. 262

22 Christa Schroeder, *He Was My Chief*, p. 181

23 Walter Warlimont, *Inside Hitler's Headquarters*, p. 462

24 Colin Heaton, 'The Last Interview with Erich Hartmann', *World War II Magazine*, 13 February 2006

25 Heinz Guderian, *Erinnerungen Eines Soldaten*, p. 342

26 Ibid., p. 344

27 See, for example, 'Morgenlage vom 1.9.1944 in der Wolfschanze' in which Hitler, Fegelein and Guderian discuss the uprising and the destruction of Warsaw. HIA Oberkommando der Wehrmacht Führerhauptquartier, Box 11, D757 G374 v.3–5

28 Joseph Goebbels, *Tagebüch*, entry 3 August 1944, p. 195

29 Tadeusz Sawicki, *Rozkaz*, p. 204, n. 10

30 Ernst Rode testimony at Nuremberg, 28 January 1946, http://avalon.law.yale.edu/subject_menus/imt.a

31 Heinz Guderian, *Erinnerungen Eines Soldaten*, p. 355

32 BA-MA, H 12-9/9

33 Heinz Guderian, *Erinnerungen Eines Soldaten*, p. 358

34 Hanns von Krannhals, *Der Warschauer Aufstand 1944*, ars una, Frankfurt am Main, 1962, p. 309

35 Interrogation of Erich von dem Bach-Zelewski, 26 January 1946, *Zburzenie Warszawy. Zeznania generałów niemieckich przed polskim prokuratorem, członkiem polskiej delegacji przy Międzynarodowym Trybunale Wojennym*

w Norymberdze, AWIR, Katowice. 1946, p. 91, Muzeum Powstania Warszawskiego
36 Ibid.
37 Ibid.
38 Marcel Stein, *A Flawed Genius*, p. 166
39 Christian Gerlach, *Kalkulierte Mord*, p. 51
40 J. Noakes and G. Pridham (eds), *Nazism*, Vol. II, p. 996
41 Himmler announced this on 16 February 1943. For an overview of his plans in Poland see Bruno Wasser, *Himmlers Raumplanung im Osten. Der Generalplan Ost in Polen 1940–1945*, Birkhäuser Verlag, Basel, 1993
42 Hitler's Lagebesprechung 1.9.1944, HIA Oberkommando der Wehrmacht Führerhauptquartier, Box 11, D757 G37< v.3–5
43 Ibid.
44 Robert Forczyk, *Warsaw 1944*, p. 26
45 Erich von dem Bach, *Kriegstagebuch*, p. 106
46 Ibid.
47 Ibid., p. 105
48 Interrogation of Erich von dem Bach-Zelewski, p. 91
49 Ibid.
50 Erich von dem Bach, *Kriegstagebuch*, p. 124
51 Philip W. Blood, *The Bandit Hunters*, p. 228
52 Erich von dem Bach, *Kriegstagebuch*, p. 107
53 General Bór recounted that amongst German PoWs who were caught in the first week was 'a German fireman from Köpenick next to Berlin ... Himmler personally sent a huge unit of firemen from Köpenick to Warsaw on the second day of the uprising, but they weren't sent here to put the fires down but to organize fires.' Tadeusz 'Bór' Komorowski, *The Secret Army*, p. 236

Chapter 7: The Massacre in Wola

1 Fernschreiben sent to Dr Lammers at 21.50 on 3 August 1944, HIA Himmlerfile, XX060-8-36, Nr 343
2 Fernschreiben 4 August 1944 to the ACK in which General Krebs outlines the collection of troops now moving towards Warsaw, including Dirlewanger and Kaminski, in preparation for the attack on the city (BA-MA H-12-9/5). See also Kurt Mehner (ed.), *Die Geheimen Tagesberichte der deutschen Wehrmachtführung im Zweiten Weltkrieg 1939–1945*. Vol. X: 1 März 1944–31 August 1944, Biblio Verlag, Osnabrück, 1985
3 BA-MA, H 12-9/9
4 'Kurzberichte des VB', *Völkischer Beobachter*, 19 August 1944
5 Testimony of Joanna Kryńska, 'Warszawską Komisją Badania Zbrodni Niemieckich o zbrodniach popelnionych przez hitlerowców w rejonie szpitala Św. Stanisława przy ulicy Wolskiej', Warsaw, 14 March 1947, in L.C.P.W., Vol. I, p. 320
6 The exchange was heard by a victim who survived under a pile of bodies. Central Commission for Investigation of German Crimes in Poland, Record No. 53, Howard Fertig. New York, 1982
7 'Własnoręczne zeznanie komendanta garnizonu Warszawa gen. Reinera Stahela pt. „Powstanie w Warszawie", Moscow 25.08.1945', in Piotr Mierecki and Wasilij Christoforow, *Powstanie Warszawskie 1944 w dokumentach z archiwów służb specjalnych*, Instytut Pamięci Narodowej, Warsaw and Moscow, 2007, p. 615
8 Hans Umbreit, 'Jednostki i Wehrmachtu i jednostki specjalne w walce przeciwko powstańcom i ludności', in Stanisław Lewandowski and Bernd Martin (eds), *Powstanie Warszawskie 1944*, p. 124
9 Hans Thieme, 'Wspomnienia niemieckiego oficera sztabowego o powstaniu warszawskim', in Stanisław Lewandowski and Bernd Martin (eds), *Powstanie Warszawskie 1944*, p. 269
10 Ibid., p. 272
11 Ibid., p. 270
12 Jerzy Jankowski and his sister Janina Mankowska created the exhibition 'Wola oskarża 1939–1944 r.', opened 10 August 2009, to commemorate the victims of the Wola massacre. Amongst the guests at the opening was Mścisław Lurie, whose mother survived the massacre at the Ursus factory.
13 Interview with Matthias Schenk, in

Michal Nekandy-Trepki (director), *Die Toten die nie gestorben sind*, 2004

14 For a street-by-street description of the Wola massacre see Karol Mórawski, Krzysztof Oktabiński and Lidia Świerczek, *Wola. Warszawskie Termopile 1944. Przewodnik historyczny po miejscach walk i straceń z dni powstania warszawskiego*, Fundacja 'Wystawy Warszawa Walczy 1939–1945', Warsaw, 1994; see also Katarzyna Uttacka, *Powstańcze miejsca pamięci Wola 1944*, Urząd Dzielnicy Wola, Warsaw, 2009

15 Matthias Schenk in Dietrich Schubert (director), *Letzte Reise nach Polen*, ZDF, 2002

16 Jerzy Sawicki, *Zburzenie Warszawy*, p. 76

17 Stanisław Jankowski 'Agaton', *Z fałszywym ausweisem*, p. 230

18 Stefan Talikowski testimony, in L.C.P.W., Vol. I, Part 1, p. 299

19 Irena Jakubowska testimony, http://www.sppw1944.org/index.html?http:/ww

20 Central Commission for Investigation of German Crimes in Poland, Record No. 59

21 Ibid., Record No. 95

22 Wacław Gałka testimony, in L.C.P.W., Vol. I, Part 1, p. 317

23 Karol Mórawski, *Wola*, p. 156

24 Ryszard Piekarek in L.C.P.W., Vol. I, Part 1, p. 272

25 Piotr Dolny testimony, 15 January 1946, in L.C.P.W., Vol. I, Part 1, p. 314

26 French L. MacLean, *The Cruel Hunters*, p. 180

27 Bogdan Duda testimony, 4 January 1946, in L.C.P.W., Vol. I, Part 1, p. 309

28 Jan Grabowski testimony, http://www.sppw1944.org/powstanie/wola

29 Hans Thieme, 'Wspomnienia niemieckiego oficera', p. 269

30 Ibid., p. 230

31 Sebastian Pawlina, 'Czarna sobota' na Woli – 5 Serpnia 1944 r. 5 August 2011', http://historia.org.pl/2011/08/05/czaarna-sobota

32 Szymon Datner and Kazimierz Leszczyński (eds), *Zbronie okupanta w czasie powstania warszawskiego w 1944 roku w dokumentach*, MON, Warsaw, 1962, pp. 62–65

33 Włodzimierz Nowak and Angelika Kuźniak, 'Mój warszawski szał – Druga strona Powstania' (interview with Matthias Schenk), *Gazeta Wyborcza*, 08 July 2004

34 Krzysztof Jóźwiak, 'Miasto rozstrzelane', *Uważam Rze*, 28 July 2013

35 Tadeusz Klimaszewski, *Verbrennungskommando Warschau*, Czytelnik, Warsaw, 1959, p. 80

36 *Trials of the Major War Criminals before the International Military Tribunal Proceedings Volumes (The Blue Set)*, Vol. VIII, p. 18, http://avalon.law.yale.edu/subject_menu/imt.a

37 Włodzimierz Starosolcki testimony, 13 March 1947, in L.C.P.W., Vol. I, Part 1, p. 327

38 Tadeusz Klimaszewski, *Verbrennungskommando Warschau*, p. 51

39 Stefan Talikowski testimony, in L.C.P.W., Vol. I, Part 1, p. 304

40 Telephone call between von Vormann and Reinefarth in M.J. Kwiatkowski, *Tu mówi powstańcza Warszawa – dni powstania w audycjach Polskiego Radia i dokumentach niemieckich*, Państwowy Instytut Wydawniczy, Warsaw, 1994, p. 28

41 Jerzy Kirchmeyer, *Powstanie Warszawskie*, Książka i Wiedza, Warsaw, 1959, p. 243, n.3

42 Hans Thieme, 'Wspomnienia niemieckiego oficera', p. 269

43 Jerzy Kirchmeyer, *Powstanie Warszawski*, p. 243

44 Ibid., p. 244

45 Erich von dem Bach, *Kriegstagebuch*, p. 106

46 French L. MacLean, *The Cruel Hunters*, p. 179

47 Ibid., p. 164

48 Ibid., p. 163

49 Ibid., p. 179

50 Jerzy Kirchmeyer, *Powstanie Warszawskie*, p. 246

51 French L. MacLean, *The Cruel Hunters*, p. 260

52 Ibid., p. 183

53 Matthias Schenk in Włodzimierz Nowak and Angelika Kuźniak, 'Mój warszawski szał'

54 Interview with Matthias Schenk in Michal Nekandy-Trepki (director), *Die Toten die nie gestorben sind*

55 Ibid.

56 Joanna Kryńska testimony, 14 March 1947, in L.C.P.W., Vol. I, Part 1, p. 320

57 Tadeusz Kur, *Sprawiedliwość pobłażliwa*, p. 422. During the trial Hahn's secretary, a *Volksdeutsche* named Irene Chmielewicz, testified that during the uprising around 1,000 Polish civilians had been herded to the Cadet School in Łazienki Park. Three young girls were chosen by members of the SiPo and SD, forced to drink alcohol until they were completely inebriated, then raped. One was raped by Hahn. Another witness, SS-Obersturmführer Ulrich Stern, ordered her immediate execution. When nobody volunteered, Hahn shot her himself.

58 Matthias Schenk in Włodzimierz Nowak and Angelika Kuźniak, 'Mój warszawski szał'

59 Christian Ingrao, *The SS Dirlewanger Brigade*, p. 159

60 Matthias Schenk in Włodzimierz Nowak and Angelika Kuźniak, 'Mój warszawski szał'

61 French L. MacLean, *The Cruel Hunters*, p. 180

62 Ibid.

63 Stanisław Kicman interview in Michał Rogalski (director), *12 Ton. Oni wszyscy tam są*, 2008

64 Karol Mórawski, *Wola*, p. 178

65 Wesław Kępiński interview in *12 Ton. Oni wszyscy tam są*

66 Maria Cyrańska testimony, 4 May 1946, in L.C.P.W., Vol. I, Part 1, p. 312

67 Włodzimierz Nowak and Angelika Kuźniak, 'Mój warszawski szał'

68 Ibid.

69 Peter Stölten, 'Listy niemieckiego porucznika z płonącej Warszawy', in Stanisław Lewandowski and Bernd Martin (eds), *Powstanie Warszawskie 1944*, pp. 266–267

70 Ibid., p. 267

71 Tadeusz Klimaszewski, *Verbrennungskommando Warschau*, p. 67

72 Stefan Talikowska, in L.C.P.W., Vol. I, Part 1, p. 304

73 Władysław Stępien, in L.C.P.W., Vol. I, Part 1, p. 285

74 Włodzimierz Nowak and Angelika Kuźniak 'Mój warszawski szał'

75 Zbigniew Wożniewski, *Książka raporów lekarza dyżurnego. Szpital Wolski w okresie Powstania Warszawskiego*, Panstwowy Instytut Wydowniczy, Warsaw, 1974, p. 32

76 Tadeusz Klimaszewski *Verbrennungskommando Warschau*, p. 78

77 Central Commission for Investigation of German Crimes in Poland, Record No. 80

78 Ibid., Record No. 91

79 Dr Bernard Filipiuk testimony, http://www.sppw1944.org/index.html?http://ww

80 Hans Thieme, 'Wspomnienia niemieckiego oficera', p. 269

81 Jan Becwalek testimony, http://www.sppw1944.org/index.html?http://ww

82 Zbigniew Wożniewski, *Książka raporów lekarza dyżurnego*, p. 31

83 Karol Mórawski, *Wola*, p. 165

84 Central Commission for Investigation of German Crimes in Poland, Record No. 215

85 Wanda Łokietek-Borzęcka testimony, in L.C.P.W., Vol. I, Part 1, p. 251

86 Wiesław Chełmiński testimony, 6 May 1946 in L.C.P.W., Vol. I, Part 1, p. 310

87 Stanisław Rutkowski, *Głowna Komisja Badania Zbrodni Przeciwko Narodowi Polskiemu*, Institut Pamięci Narodowej, Warsaw, 1994, p. 84

88 Władysław Barcikowski testimony, http://www.sppw1944.org/index.html?http://ww

89 Zbigniew Wożniewski, *Książka raporów lekarza dyżurnego*, p. 45, n. 6

90 Stanisław Bayer, *Służba Zdrowia Warszawy w walce z Okupantem 1939–1945*, Wydawnictwo Ministerstwa Obrony Narodowej, Warsaw, 1985, p. 102

91 Joanna Kryńska testimony, 14 March 1947, in L.C.P.W., Vol. I, Part 1, p. 320

92 Zbigniew Wożniewski, *Książka raporów lekarza dyżurnego*, p. 55

93 Joanna Kryńska testimony, in L.C.P.W., Vol. I, Part 1, p. 320

94 Ibid., p. 264

95 Ibid., p. 266

96 Ibid

97 Ibid., p. 320

98 French L. MacLean, *The Cruel Hunters*, p. 129
99 Ibid.
100 Ibid., p. 130
101 He recommended SS-Sturmbahnführer Weiss be awarded the German Cross in Gold on 9 September 1944 for his fine work during the Warsaw Uprising.
102 French L. MacLean, *The Cruel Hunters*, p. 130
103 Włodzimierz Nowak and Angelika Kuźniak, 'Mój warszawski szał'
104 Ibid.
105 Interview with Matthias Schenk in *Die Toten die nie gestorben sind*
106 French L. MacLean, *The Cruel Hunters*, p. 262
107 Ibid., p. 203
108 Ibid., p. 204
109 Ibid., p. 214
110 Ibid., p. 208
111 'Protokół przesłuchania komendanta garnizonu Warszawa generala Reinera Stahela 25.08.1945 Moskwa', in Piotr Mierecki and Wasilij Christoforow, *Powstanie Warszawskie*, p. 615
112 Ibid.
113 Dennis Deletant, *Hitler's Forgotten Ally. Ion Antonescu and His Regime, Romania 1940–1944*, Macmillan, London, 2006, p. 211
114 Antonescu's comment to the Turkish chargé d'affaires is at http://dailytrh.tripod.com/0805.html

Chapter 8: The Fate of Ochota

1 Adrian Weale, *The SS. A New History*, Little, Brown, London, 2010, p. 258; see also Rolf Michaelis, *Russians in the Waffen-SS*, Schiffer Military History, Atglen, PA, 2009, p. 8
2 Philip W. Blood, *Hitler's Bandit Hunters*, p. 206. On 5 August 1944 General Krebs of OKH ordered SS-Sturmbrigade RONA (Brigade Kaminski) to move to Warsaw. BA-MA H-12-9/5
3 Antonio J. Munoz (ed.), *The Kaminski Brigade: A History, 1941–1943*, Axis Europa Books, New York, 2003, p. 10
4 Alexander Dallin, 'The Kaminsky Brigade. A Case-Study of Soviet Disaffection'. Unpublished, 1967. HIA, Dallin, Alexander, 5-53 79093 10.10, p2
5 Erich von dem Bach, *Kriegstagebuch*, p. 70
6 Testimony of Major Iwan Frolow, '1 września 1946, b.m.w. Własnoręczne zeznanie dowódcy zbiorczego pułku brygady RONA mjr. Iwana Frolowa', Doc. No. 256, Muzeum Powstania Warszawskiego, p.5
7 Jürgen Thorwald, *The Illusion. Soviet Soldiers in Hitler's Armies*, Harcourt Brace Jovanovich, New York, 1975, p. 179
8 'Himmler's Order Banning the Use of the Word Partisan', HIA, Heinrich Himmler, Box 12, Folder 1, no. 25
9 Alexander Dallin, *The Kaminski Brigade: A Case-Study of Soviet Disaffection*, 1967, HIA, Dallin, Alexander, 5/5-3 790093 10.10, p. 55
10 Han Bouwmeester, *The Beginning of the End: The Leadership of SS Obersturmbannführer Jochen Peiper*, Fort Leavenworth, Kansas, 2004, p. 26
11 Testimony of Major Iwan Frolow, p. 3
12 Maria Antoniewicz testimony in Lidia Ujazdowska, *Zagłada Ochoty. Zbiór relacji na temat zbrodni hitlerowskiej dokonanej na ludności Ochoty w czasie Powstania Warszawskiego* (henceforth Z.O.), Fronda, Warsaw, 2005, p. 97
13 They were shot and buried at Plac Narutowicza. A dead horse was dumped over their dead bodies. Kazimierz Tomaszewski in Z.O., p. 102
14 Józef K. Wroniszewski, *Ochota 1944*, Wydawnictwo Ministerstwa Obrony Narodowej, Warsaw, 1970, p. 142
15 Protocol from the Interrogation of Alexander Pierchurow, 16 July 1946, Doc. No. 106, Muzeum Powstania Warszawskiego
16 Testimony of Major Iwan Frolow: 1 September 1946, p. 5
17 Protocol from the Interrogation of Alexander Piechurow
18 Ibid. See also interview with former RONA soldier Rudolf von Knüpfer, 27 May 1952. HIA, Dallin, Alexander, 5 5-2 79093 10.10

19 Maria Antoniewicz, in Z.O., p. 98
20 Kazimierz Tomaszewski, in Z.O., p. 102
21 Szymon Datner and Kazimierz Leszscyński, *Zbrodnie okupanta*, p. 92
22 Eugenia Wolczyńska, in Z.O., p. 14
23 Wiesława Chmielewska, in Z.O., p. 35
24 Janina Gałecka, in Z.O., p. 21
25 Halina Jedyńska, in Z.O., p. 27
26 Melania Bischof, in Z.O., p. 89
27 Maria Antoniewicz, in Z.O., p. 101
28 Eugenia Wilczyńska, in Z.O., p 15
29 Halina Jedyńska, in Z.O., p. 27, http:// www.warsawuprising.com/witness/ulank
30 Ibid.
31 Władysław Dziegała, in Z.O., p. 83
32 Barbara Slivnska, in Z.O., p. 49
33 Testimony of Major Iwan Frolow
34 Władysław Szpilman, *The Pianist*, p. 162
35 Ibid., p. 164
36 Ibid., p. 173
37 Erich von dem Bach, *Kriegstagebuch*, p. 107
38 Erich von dem Bach, Nuremberg Testimony. 26 January 1946
39 Von dem Bach's attempts to whitewash his past were astounding. He told Leon Goldensohn at Nuremberg: 'it was for the best that a few decent fellows like myself were influential in the SS and thus staved off bad things'. Leon Goldensohn, *The Nuremberg Interviews*, Pimlico, London, 2006, p. 269
40 Göring's outburst seems to have impressed von dem Bach, who told Goldensohn: 'You know that Göring was punished later on because he loudly called me a traitor and a pig in full view of the court.' Ibid., p. 268
41 Peter Padfield, *Himmler. Reichsführer-SS*, Papermac, London, 1995, p. 545
42 Ibid., p. 745
43 A recording of this speech has survived: HIA sound recording of Himmler speech in Posen 4 October 1943, Reel 25–27
44 Philip W. Blood, *Hitler's Bandit Hunters*, p. 206
45 Tadeusz Sawicki, *Rozkaz*, p 32
46 HIA Heinrich Himmler Papers 7–3 no. 291
47 Peter Padfield, *Himmler*, p. 585
48 Roger Manvell and Heinrich Fraenkel,

Heinrich Himmler, Heinemann, London, 1965, p. 231
49 Niall MacDermot, Chief Counter-Intelligence 21st Army Group HQ, interview in Peter Padfield, *Himmler*, p. 576
50 Wiesława Chmielewska, in Z.O., p. 35
51 The evidence had been collected against Kaminski for some time. On 10 August von dem Bach wrote to OKH that the Kaminski Brigade seemed to be 'more interested in plunder than in fighting'. KT9, BA-MA H-12-9/3
52 Testimony of Major Iwan Frolow. On Kaminski's execution see Alexander Dallin, 'The Kaminsky Brigade'. HIA Dallin, Alexander 5–53 79093 10.10 p. 55
53 The looting continued well after capitulation: on 9 October 1944 Lüttwitz ordered more trains to be provided for the 'clearing' of the city. BA-MA H-12-9/8
54 Heinz Guderian, *Erinnerungen*, p. 325
55 Ibid., p. 326
56 Peter Padfield, *Himmler*, p. 538
57 Nigel West (ed.), *The Guy Liddell Diaries*. II: *1942–1945*, Routledge, London, 2005, entry for 26 September 1944, p. 37
58 HIA Dallin, Alexander, 5–52 79093 10.10 p. 5

Chapter 9: 'Mountains of Corpses'

1 On 4 August 1944 the Abwehr wrote a report outlining areas of danger outside Warsaw, including the 'forest area' and the area around Pruszków, as there was a real fear that the uprising would spread. BA-MA H-12-9/7 Bl. 922 261
2 SSD secret report, 9 August 1944, BA-MA H-12-9/7
3 Piotr Stachiewicz, *Starówka 1944*, Wydawnictwo Ministerstwa Obrony Narodowej, Warsaw, 1983, p. 73
4 Stefan Talikowski, in L.C.P.W., Vol. I, Part 1, p. 301
5 Edmund Baranowski, 'Szlak bojowy zgrupowania „Radosław" w powstaniu warszawskim', in Stanisław Lewandowski and Bernd Martin (eds), *Powstanie Warszawskie 1944*, p. 253
6 Stanisław Jankowski 'Agaton', *Z fałszywym Ausweisem*, p. 240

7 Piotr Stachiewicz, *Parasol. Dzieje oddziału do zadań specjalnych kierownictwa dywersji Komendy Głownej Armii Krajowej*, Instytut Wydawniczy PAX, Warsaw, 1981, p. 512

8 Tadeusz Sawicki, *Rozkaz*, p. 42

9 Janusz 'Gryf' Brochwicz-Lewinski testimony, 18 December 1944, Archiwum mówione w Muzeum Powstania Warszawskiego

10 Anna Szatkowska, *Był Dom*, p. 158

11 The Western Allies attempted to supply Warsaw during the uprising, but the missions were complicated by the fact that Stalin refused to allow Allied planes to land on Soviet airfields. The first drop was on the night of 4 August with flights continuing throughout August and into early September when they were suspended due to bad weather. The Americans, too, attempted to make drops, but again the USAAF 'Frantic' flights destined for Warsaw were blocked by Stalin so that only one drop was made on 18 September. Only 288 of the 1,284 containers reached the Polish forces. The flights came at great cost, particularly to the RAF and SAAF pilots: a total of forty-one allied aircraft were destroyed out of 306 sent to Warsaw.

12 'Własnoręczne zeznanie komendanta garnizonu Warszawa gen. Reinera Stahela pt. „Powstanie w Warszawie", Moscow, 25.08.1945', p. 615

13 Piotr Stachiewicz, *Starówka*, p. 64

14 Karol Mórawski, *Wola*, p. 144

15 Piotr Stachiewicz, *Starówka*, p. 82

16 Anna Szatkowska, *Był Dom*, p. 145

17 L.C.P.W., Vol. II, p. 145

18 L.C.P.W., Vol. II, p. 377

19 Władysław Bartoszewski, *Dni walczącej Stolicy*, p. 66

20 Klaudius Hrabyk testimony, in L.C.P.W., Vol. I, Part 1, p. 400

21 Jan Rossman testimony, in L.C.P.W., Vol. I, Part 1, p. 150

22 The Germans were irritated by Hungarian 'unreliability' born of old ties between the Hungarians and the Poles. Von Vormann said, 'You cannot count on the 12th Hungarian Reserve Division to complete their task of cutting Warsaw off from the north and clearing up the large forest area north west of Warsaw. The Hungarian army was warmly received by the Polish population. There were signs of fraternization. The leaders of the national movement are trying to talk directly to the Hungarian commanders. In the name of the centuries-long friendship between Hungarians and Poles they are appealing to the Hungarians to stop all military activity. The units up till now controlled by the commanders, but we can't give any guarantee that this state of affairs will remain given the small number of officers especially in the 12th. The battle-readiness of the 12th Hungarian Reserve Division is like the head of a hanged man and not worth mentioning.' As for the 5th Hungarian Reserve Division, he spat: 'Should they be attacked by the Polish army they will certainly not fight. You will have to pay special attn to increased danger of espionage and transfer of Bolshevik propaganda to the Poles.' The 9th Army Report confirmed that the Hungarians partly supported the uprising by giving the Poles some weapons and even brought in special provisions for the Hungarians 'to prevent them from revolting'. Von Vormann report to Army Group Centre, 9 August 1944, BA-MA H-12-9/4

23 L.C.P.W., Vol. II, p. 56

24 Lidzki wrote: 'General characteristic – Amongst the civilian population, depression'. L.C.P.W., Vol. II, p. 82

25 Monter's report of 8 August about the behaviour of civilians read: 'the reaction in every district is a bit different. The citizens of Powisle "passed the exam", are braver and manage better with the situation, and are fighting better with the AK, strengthening barricades and building new ones. There is also a good mood in Żoliborz, in Sródmiescie and on the border with Mokotow. The civilians of Wola have calmed down but they brought with them chaos and mental turmoil.' L.C.P.W., Vol. II, Part 1, p. 76

26 Władysław Stępień testimony, in L.C.P.W., Vol. I, Part 1, p. 283
27 Hans Thieme, 'Wspomnienia niemieckiego oficera', p. 281
28 Irena Jankowska testimony, 23 October 2008, MPW Archivum Historii Mówionej
29 Stanisław Jankowski 'Agaton', Z fałszywym Ausweisem, p. 181
30 Tadeusz Klimaszewski, Verbrennungskommando Warschau, p. 48
31 Pogrzeb jakiego nie zna Świat. Sto trumien prochów ludzkich z GISZ-u i Woli', Gazeta Ludowa, no. 207, 31 July 1946
32 Yitzhak Arad, Belzec, Sobibor, Treblinka. Operation Reinhard Death Camps, Indiana University Press, Bloomington, 1987, p. 173
33 Alexander Donati (ed.), The Death Camp Treblinka, Holocaust Library, New York, 1979, p. 211
34 Tadeusz Klimaszewski, Verbrennungskommando Warschau, p. 8
35 Ibid., p. 50
36 Ibid., p. 51
37 Ibid., p. 82
38 Ibid., p. 130
39 Ibid., p. 81
40 Ibid., p. 84
41 Zenon Piasecki testimony, in L.C.P.W., Vol. I, Part 1, p. 324
42 Tadeusz Klimaszewski, Verbrennungskommando Warschau, p. 159
43 Ibid., p. 70
44 Ibid., p 28
45 Ibid., p. 130
46 Ibid., p. 60
47 Ibid., p. 132
48 Ibid.
49 Ibid., p. 80
50 Ibid., p. 87
51 Ibid., p. 149. A similar memoir was written by Leon W. Wells, who was interned in Janowska concentration camp and sent to the 'Death Brigade' that was also ordered to destroy the evidence of mass murder. See Leon W. Wells, The Death Brigade. The Janowska Road, Holocaust Library, New York, 1978
52 Tadeusz Klimaszewski, Verbrennungskommando Warschau, p. 136
53 Ibid., p. 171

Chapter 10: Hitler's War Against the Old Town

1 The term 'Old Town' or Stare Miasto refers both to the medieval core of the city and to the broader surrounding area; by the end of the fighting in the district the Poles held only the small original medieval city – the Old Town proper.
2 Stanisław Jankowski 'Agaton', Z fałszywym Ausweisem, p. 201
3 Wacław Zagórski report, 26 August, in L.C.P.W., Vol. II, p. 469
4 Władysław Bartoszewski, Dni walczącej Stolicy, pp. 102–103
5 Stanisław Likiernik, By Devil's Luck, p. 129
6 Stanisław Jankowski 'Agaton', Z fałszywym Ausweisem, p. 198
7 Aniela Pinon-Gacka testimony, in L.C.P.W., Vol. I, Part 1, p. 434
8 Anna Szatkowska. Był Dom, p. 163
9 Miron Białoszewski (Madeline Levine, ed. and trans.), A Memoir of the Warsaw Uprising, Northwestern University Press, Illinois, 1991, p. 45
10 Ibid., p. 58
11 Aniela Pinon-Gacka, 'Dni chwały i klęski', in L.C.P.W., Vol. I, Part 1, p. 435
12 Grażyna Dąbrowska testimony, in L.C.P.W., Vol. I, Part 1, p. 379
13 Janina Lasocka testimony, in L.C.P.W., Vol. I, Part 1, p. 418
14 Gunnar S. Paulsson, Secret City, p.171
15 L.C.P.W., Vol. I, Part 1, p.384
16 Gunnar S. Paulsson, Secret City, p. 176
17 Ibid. p.183
18 Ibid. p. 185
19 Marek Edelmann, Metro, 30 July 2004, p. 10
20 Gunnar S. Paulsson, Secret City, p. 187
21 Anna Szatowska, Był Dom, p. 167
22 Joanna K.M. Hanson, The Civilian Population and the Warsaw Uprising of 1944, Cambridge University Press, New York, 1982, p. 112
23 Andrzej Krzysztof Kunert and Zygmunt Walkowski, 'Życie w piwnicach', Gazeta Wyborcza, 07 September 2004, p. 7
24 Wacław Bużycka memoir, in L.C.P.W., Vol. I, Part 1, p. 371
25 Piotr Osęka, 'Zabawa pod barykadą', Przekrój, August 2004, p. 34

NOTES

26 Ibid., p. 35
27 Dirlewanger report in which he recommends Schreiner for the German Cross in Gold. Erich von dem Bach warmly endorses the recommendation. French L. MacLean, *The Cruel Hunters*, p. 184
28 Robert Forczyk, *Warsaw 1944*, p. 66
29 Von Vormann to Army Group Centre, 3 a.m., 13 August 1944, in Hanns von Krannhals, *Der Warschauer Aufstand 1944*, p. 375
30 'Własnoręczne zeznanie komendanta garnizonu Warszawa gen. Reinera Stahela pt. „Powstanie w Warszawie", Moscow 25.08.1945', p. 615
31 Himmler to chief of Main Economic Office, WVHA, 31 August 1944
32 Jerzy Dreyza, 'Relacja o Szpitalu Maltańskim', in L.C.P.W., Vol. I, Part 1, p. 386
33 A 21 August 1944 confidential Wehrmacht report admits that German progress is slow and that leaders of units should 'see it as their main duty to encourage men to fight and to do everything to inspire soldiers to fight. The will to fight should be rewarded and particularly for creativity such as finding shelters, secret passages etc'. BA-MA H-12-9/3
34 'Morgenlage vom 1.9.1944 in der Wolfschanze', HIA Oberkommando der Wehrmacht Führerhauptquartier, Box 11, D757 G374 v.3–5
35 Kenneth Warren Chase, *Firearms. A Global History to 1700*, Cambridge University Press, Cambridge, 2003 p. 43
36 As Hitler put it, 'The foundation of St Petersburg by Peter the Great was a fatal event in the history of Europe; and St Petersburg must therefore disappear utterly from the earth's surface. Moscow too. Then the Russians will retire into Siberia ... As for the ridiculous hundred million Slavs, we will mould the best of them to the shape that suits us, and we will isolate the rest of them in their own pig-sties, and anyone who talks about cherishing the local inhabitant and civilising him, goes straight off into a concentration camp!' H.R. Trevor-Roper, *Hitler's Table Talk*, entry 6 August 1942, p. 44

37 Ibid.
38 'Morgenlage vom 1.9.1944 in der Wolfschanze'
39 BA-MA H 12-9/3 K141
40 BA-MA H 12-9/9
41 Anna Szatkowska, *Był Dom*, p. 176
42 1,204 combat sorties were flown over Warsaw during the uprising with a total of 1,580 bombs dropped in 63 days
43 Stanisław Jankowski 'Agaton', *Z fałszywym Ausweisem*, p. 199
44 Janina Lasocka memoir, in L.C.P.W., Vol. I, Part 1, p. 419
45 Miron Białoszewski, *Memoir*, p. 69
46 Ibid., p. 38
47 Władysław Bartoszewski, *Dni walczącej Stolicy*, p. 122
48 Ibid.
49 Anna Szatkowska, *Był Dom*, p. 201
50 Piotr Stachiewicz, *Starówka*, p. 135, n. 72
51 Miron Białoszewski, *Memoir*, p. 31
52 Known as the Sturmpanzer IV (SdKfz166) or 'Brummbär'
53 This footage is at https://www.youtube.com/watch?v=SCbFyIaVC
54 At the time this weapon was known as the Jagdpanzer 38(t); Guderian introduced the name 'Hetzer' to Hitler in 1944, claiming it had been called this by the troops, with whom it was popular. One Hetzer (renamed 'Chwat') was captured by the AK Kiliński Batallion near Plac Napoleon during the uprising. See Hillary Doyle, Tom Jentz, *Jagdpanzer 38 'Hetzer' 1944-45*, Osprey Publishing, Oxford, 2001
55 Peter Stölten, 'Listy niemieckiego porucznika z płonącej Warszawy', in Stanisław Lewandowski and Bernd Martin (eds), *Powstanie Warszawskie 1944*, pp. 266–267
56 Miron Białoszewski, *Memoir*, p. 74
57 Ibid., p. 48
58 Ibid., p. 61
59 Irena Orska, *Silent is the Vistula*, Longmans, London, 1947, p. 81
60 Grażyna Dąbrowska, in L.C.P.W., Vol. I, Part 1, p. 380
61 Ibid.
62 Jerzy Kirchmeyer, *Powstanie Warszawskie*, p. 302
63 Miron Białoszewski, *Memoir*, p. 52

64 Ibid., p. 92
65 Anna Szatkowska, *Był Dom*, p. 203
66 Klaudiusz Hrabyk, in L.C.P.W., Vol. I, Part 1, p. 399
67 Białaszewski, *Memoir*, p. 67
68 Klaudius Hrabyk, in L.C.P.W., Vol. I, Part 1, p. 402
69 Marek Getter, 'Władze cywilne powstania warszawskiego', in Stanisław Lewandowski and Bernd Martin (eds), *Powstarie Warszawskie 1944*, p. 129
70 Anna Szatkowska, *Był Dom*, p. 171
71 Janina Lasocka, in L.C.P.W., Vol. I, Part I, p. 419
72 'Eighth Army Moral Report 1944', in E.J. Phillips, *Psychiatry at Corps Level*, Wellcome Institute for the History of Medicine, London, 1944, 9GC/135/B1/112
73 Irena Orska, *Silent is the Vistula*, p. 64
74 The Nebelwerfer came in five calibres: 130, 210, 280, 300 and 320 mm (the last only incendiary).
75 Miron Białoszewski, *Memoir*, p. 39
76 Stanisław Jankowski, 'Agaton', *Z fałszywym Ausweisem*, p. 204
77 Anna Szatkowska, *Był Dom*, p. 171
78 Władysław Bartoszewski, *Dni walczącej Stolicy*, p. 124
79 Irena Orska, *Silent is the Vistula*, p. 64
80 Miron Białoszewski, *Memoir*, p. 74
81 Ibid., p. 39
82 Jerzy Kirchmeyer, *Powstanie Warszawskie*, p. 288
83 Piotr Stachiewicz, *Starówka*, p. 68
84 The situation was so bad that people sometimes simply had to 'close their eyes to the fact that they were eating noodles cooked in water which had flowed over dead bodies'. Quoted in Joanna K.M. Hanson, *The Civilian Population and the Warsaw Uprising*, p. 110
85 Stanisław Likiernik, *By Devil's Luck*, p. 125
86 Jan Rosner testimony, in L.C.P.W., Vol. I, Part 1, p. 342
87 Ibid., 380
88 Antoni Przygoński, *Stalin i Powstanie Warszawskie*, Grażyna, Warsaw, 1994, p. 388
89 Anna Szatkowska, *Był Dom*, p. 204
90 Jozef Lewandowski, *Wokół Biografii K. K.*

Baczyński, Ex Libris, Uppsala, 1991
91 The piece Klaudiusz Hrabyk heard was 'Etiuda rewolucyjna'. See L.C.P.W., Vol. I, Part 1, p. 402
92 Father Kwiatkowski, in ibid., p. 414
93 Ibid., p. 415
94 Grażyna Dąbrowska, in ibid., p. 379
95 Pictr Stachiewicz, *Parasol*, p. 528
96 Stanisław Jankowski 'Agaton', *Z fałszywym Ausweisem*, p. 242
97 L.C.P.W., Vol. I, Part 1, p. 421
98 Mieczysław Adamczyk and Janusz Gmitruk, *Powstanie Warszawskie w dokumentach i wspomnieniach ludowców*, Muzeum Historii Polskiego Ruchu Ludowego, Kielce, 2011, p. 80
99 L.C.P.W., Vol. I, Part 1, p. 404
100 Ibid., p. 378
101 www.1944.pl/historia/powstancze-biogramy/Grazyna_Dabrowska
102 Miron Białoszewski, *Memoir*, p. 87
103 Ibid.
104 Anna Szatkowska, *Był Dom*, p. 171
105 Piotr Stachiewicz, *Parasol*, p. 528, n. 137
106 See Bożena Urbanek, *Pielęgniarki i sanitariuszki w Powstaniu Warszawskim w 1944r*, Państwowe Wydawnictwo Naukowe, Warsaw, 1988
107 Anna Szatkowska, *Był Dom*, p. 170
108 Piotr Stachiewicz, *Parasol*, p. 540, n. 166
109 Ibid.
110 Ibid., p. 528, n. 138
111 Anna Szatkowska, *Był Dom*, p. 181
112 Ibid., p. 171
113 L.C. P.W., Vol. I, Part 1, p. 438
114 Piotr Stachiewicz, *Parasol*, p. 134
115 Ibid., p. 549
116 Anna Szatkowska, *Był Dom*, p. 186
117 Irena Orska, *Silent is the Vistula*, p. 88
118 Anna Szatkowski, *Był Dom*, p. 189
119 Ibid., p. 190
120 Ibid., p. 191
121 Stanisław Likiernik, *By Devil's Luck*, p. 127
122 L.C.P.W., Vol. I, Part 1, p. 107
123 Stanisław Likiernik, *By Devil's Luck*, p. 107
124 L.C.P.W., Vol. II, p. 233
125 Piotr Osęka, 'Zabawa pod barykadą', p. 64
126 L.C.P.W., Vol. I, Part 1, p. 377
127 Jerzy Kirchmeyer, *Powstania Warszawskie*, p. 301
128 Captain Roman Chmiel testimony,

'Wojenne relacja lotników', http://www. polishairforce.pl_relacja15html

129 Władysław Bartoszewski, *Dni walczącej Stolicy*, p. 105

130 Andrzej Krzysztof Kunert, *Generał Tadeusz Bór-Komorowski*, p. 156

131 Miron Białoszewski, *Memoir*, p. 44

132 Anna Szatkowska, *Był Dom*, p. 166

133 Jerzy Ficowski, 'Moja samotność jest wybredna', *Rzeczpospolita*, 4–5 September 2004

134 Jerzy Kirchmeyer, *Powstanie Warszawskie*, p. 300

135 Tadeusz Sawicki, *Rozkaz*, p. 58

136 Miron Białoszewski, *Memoir*, p. 128

137 Piotr Stachiwicz, *Parasol*, p. 555

138 L.C.P.W., Vol. I, Part 1, p. 394

139 Miron Białoszewski, *Memoir*, p. 69

140 Ibid., p. 116

141 Sub-Colonel E. Rozłubirski, 'Gustaw', 'Sub-Colonel Wachnowski Loses Control', *Walka Młodych*, 27 August 1946. This could be published in 1946 despite general censorship because Rozłubirski had commanded Armia Ludowa – i.e. Communist – units in the Old Town during the uprising.

142 Jerzy Kirchmeyer, *Powstanie Warszawie*, p. 303

143 Miron Białoszewski, *Memoir*, p. 116

144 Ibid., p. 126

145 Stanisław Jankowski, 'Agaton', *Z fałszywym Ausweisem*, p. 231

146 Stanisław Likiernik, *By Devil's Luck*, p. 126

147 Piotr Mszkowski, 'Śladami Powstańczej Warszawy', *Odkrywca Wszystko o Skarbach i przygodzie*, no. 8 (67), August 2004, p. 27

148 Ibid.

149 Stanisław Likiernik, *By Devil's Luck*, p. 133

150 Wacława Buzycka, in L.C.P. W., Vol. I, Part 1, p. 368

151 Ibid., p. 370

152 Despite the people's deep patriotism, and despite their fear of the Germans, there is no doubt that at this point in the Old Town discipline had broken down. See Joanna K.M. Hanson, *The Civilian Population*, p. 117

153 Karol Ziemski 'Wachnowski', quoted in 'Wymordowanie rannych w szpitalu powstańczym na ul. Długiej 7', http:// www.pw44.pl/dluga.htm

154 Ibid.

155 Stanisław Aronson, *Rysiek z Kedywu*, p. 145

156 Jan Rosner, in L.C.P.W., Vol. I, Part 1, p. 350

157 Ibid.

158 Ibid., p. 406

159 Mary Stypułkowska also took part in the assassination of Kutschera. Andrzej Krzysztof Kunert, 'Zamach na Kutscherę', *Gazeta Wyborcza*, 30 January 2004

160 Anna Szatkowska, *Był Dom*, p. 217

161 Stanisław Jankowski 'Agaton', *Z fałszywym Ausweisem*, p. 250

162 Jan Rosner, in L.C.P.W., Vol. I, Part 1, pp. 407–408

163 Anna Szatkowska, *Był Dom*, p. 219

164 Jan Rosner, in L.C.P.W., Vol. I, Part 1, p. 351

165 Miron Białoszewski, *Memoir*, p. 131

166 Karol Mórawski, *Wola*, p. 117. On the agonizing decision faced by Jews as to what to do as the Germans moved in again, see Gunnar S. Paulsson, *The Secret City*, pp. 183–189

167 Ibid., p. 117

168 Jerzy Kirchmeyer, *Powstanie Warszawskie*, p. 325

169 Ibid., p. 326

170 Piotr Stachiewicz, *Parasol*, p. 571, n. 222

171 'Tagesmeldung vom 2. September 1944', in which it was reported that 'In Warschau brach der Aufstand in der Altstadt (N-Kessel) zusammen' (In Warsaw the uprising in the Old Town (N-cauldron) has been defeated). In Kurt Mehner, *Die Geheimen Tagesberichte der Deutschen Wehrmachtführung im Zweiten Weltkrieg 1939–1945*, Vol. X, p. 5

172 For a detailed account of losses in the Old Town, see Wojciech Fałkowski, *Straty Warszawy 1939–1945. Raport*, Miasto Stołeczne, Warsaw, 2000

173 BA-MA Warschau-Akte Film, 21/22 B1786 K279fl02

174 Dr Jerezy Dreyza, in L.C.P.W., Vol. I, Part 1, p. 386

175 To Ujazdowski hospital on 14 August and Wolski hospital 15 August

176 L.C.P.W., Vol. I, Part 1, p. 288

177 Ibid., p. 389

178 Testimony of Leokadia Chołodowska, 8 March 1945, in Piotr Mierecki and Wasilij Christoforow, *Powstanie Warszawskie 1944*, p. 555

179 Adam Borkiewicz, *Powstanie Warszawskie 1944. Zarys działań natury wojskowej,* Instytut Wydawniczy PAX, Warsaw, 1957, p. 302

180 Zbigniew Galperyn 'Antek', from 'Chrobry' Batallion, testimony, http://www.sppw1944.org/index.html?http://wv

181 'Wymordowanie rannych w szpitalu powstańczym na ul. Długiej 7, http://www.pw44.pl/dluga.htm. See also Maria Przyborowska testimony, 2 January 1948, http://pl.wikisource.org/wiki/Zeznanie_Marii_Pr

182 Robert Bielecki, *Długa 7 w Powstaniu Warszawskim*, Naczelna Dyrekcja Archiwów Państwowych, Archiwum Głowne Akt Dawnych, Warsaw, 1994, p. 52

183 Ibid., p. 53

184 Ibid., p. 54

185 Ibid., p. 55

186 Ibid., p. 53

187 Ibid., p. 54

188 Ibid., p. 58

189 Ibid.

190 Ibid., p. 60

191 Ibid., p. 61

192 Ibid.

193 Ibid.

194 Ibid., p. 65

195 Stanisław Aronson, *Rysiek z Kedywu,* p. 160; this story is also recounted in Stanisław Likiernik, *By Devil's Luck,* p. 135

196 For a description of hospitals see L.C.P.W., Vol. II, pp. 419–433

197 Tadeusz Sawicki, *Rozkaz,* p. 79

198 The exhibition 'Wypędzeni z Warszawy 1944' at the Muzeum Historyczne Warszawy charts the fate of some of these dispossessed people trying to find their loved ones.

199 Testimony of Leokadia Chołodowska, 8 March 1945, in L.C.P.W., Vol. I, Part 1, p. 553

200 Ibid., pp. 553–555

201 Ibid., p. 553

202 Zeznanie Zofii Zamsztejn-Kamieniecka, in L.C.P.W., Vol. I, Part 1, p. 475

203 Janina Lasocka, in ibid., p. 424

204 Ibid.

205 Ibid., p. 425

206 Ibid., p. 309

207 Ibid.

208 Karol Mórawski, *Wola,* p. 176

209 Robert Bielecki, *Długa 7 w Powstaniu Warszawskim,* p. 53

210 Stefania Chmielewska, in L.C.P.W., Vol. I, Part 1, p. 307

211 Robert Bielecki, *Długa 7 w Powstaniu Warszawskim,* p. 53

212 Stefania Chmielewska, in L.C.P.W., Vol. I, Part 1, p. 308

213 Ibid., p. 308

214 Protokół Willi Fiedler 29 witnessed by Captain Jan Odrowąz-Pieniążek, 29 November 1945 at Oversache Camp nr. 2228, Belgium. Archiwum Komitet Centralny, III P/5 No. 8 p. 2. The Protocol is also quoted in Jerzy Sawicki, *Zburzenie Warszawy,* p. 198

215 Ibid., p 4

216 Testimony of Oberleutnant Eberhard Schmalz. Schmalz commanded the 2nd Platoon of Panzer-Jäger Abteilung 1101 of the 102nd Infantry Division. www/warsauprising.com/witness.htm

217 Peter Stolten, 'Listy niemieckiego porucznika z płonącej Warszawy', in Stanisław Lewandowski and Bernd Martin (eds), *Powstanie Warszawskie 1944,* p. 267

Chapter 11: The Allies, Hitler and the Battle for Czerniaków

1 Hermann Teske, *Die silbernen Spiegel. Generalstabdienst unter der Lupe,* Vowinkel, Heidelberg, 1952, p. 228

2 Warren F. Kimball (ed.), *Churchill & Roosevelt. The Complete Correspondence. III: Alliance Declining February 1944–April 1945,* Collins, London, 1984. Antony Polonsky discusses the new research on figures for Poles deported by the Soviets in 1939 in Chapter 10 of *The Jews in Poland and Russia Vol. III. 1914–2008,* Oxford, 2012, p. 384

3 David Dilks (ed.), *The Diaries of Sir*

Alexander Cadogan, 1938–1945, Cassell, London, 1971, entry 18 June 1943, p. 537

4 J.K. Zawodny interview with George F. Kennan, 30 May 1972, in J.K. Zawodny, *Nothing but Honour. The Story of the Warsaw Uprising*, Macmillan, London, 1978, p. 227

5 Ibid. The pressure on the Poles to accept Katyń as a German crime was immense. In a letter to Tadeusz Romer, the Polish Foreign Minister, in advance of Mikołajczyk's trip to Moscow, the British Ambassador Sir Archibald Clark-Kerr wrote: 'Some kind of withdrawal from the suggestion that the killing at Katyń was done by the Russians. About this there is very strong feeling here. I am sure that you do not need to be reminded of that. For myself I think that the easiest way out of this difficulty would be the acceptance of the findings of the Soviet Commission that enquired into the crime.' HIA Mikołajczyk, S. 49-44.17 78111-9.01/02

6 Charles E. Bohlen, *Witness to History*, Norton, New York, 1973, p. 146

7 Raymond H. Dawson, *The Decision to Aid Russia 1941*, University of North Carolina Press, Chapel Hill, 1959, p. 152

8 Ibid., p. 104

9 Robert Nisbet (ed.), *Roosevelt and Stalin. The Failed Courtship*, Simon & Schuster, London, 1984, p. 47

10 Ceslovas Lauinacicious, 'The Kaleidoscope of Possibilities Facing Lithuanian Statehood in 1944', *Lithuanian Historical Studies*, no. 9, 2004

11 'Chester-Wilmot Notes on Interrogation of Kurt Zeitzler', Liddell Hart Papers, LH 15/15/150/2

12 Laurence Rees, *World War II Behind Closed Doors*, p. 294

13 Ibid.

14 Eugeniusz Duraczyński, 'Polska 1944r.: między Wschodem a Zachodem', in Stanisław Lewandowski and Bernd Martin (eds), *Powstanie Warszawskie 1944*, p. 50

15 As reported by General Krajniukow, who witnessed this meeting as a member of the Military Council, 1st Ukrainian Front

16 Nikołaj Iwanow, *Powstanie Warszawskie*

widziane z Moskwy, Znak, Kraków, 2012, p. 140

17 Ibid., p. 140, n. 12 (AMSZR folder Molotow 6-550-42,s.1,2). For Molotov's later view of Mikołajczyk see Albert Resis (ed.), *Molotov Remembers. Inside Kremlin Politics*, Ivan R. Dee, Chicago, 1993, p. 55

18 Laurence Rees, *World War II Behind Closed Doors*, p. 283

19 Nikołaj Iwanow, *Powstanie Warszawskie*, p. 142 (I am grateful to Nikołaj Iwanow for the CAMOFR (TsAMU) references)

20 Lech Bezymenski, 'Radzieckie uderzenie w kierunku Wisły', in Stanisław Lewandowski and Bernd Martin (eds), *Powstanie Warszawskie 1944*, p. 78

21 Nikołaj Iwanow, *Powstanie Warszawskie*, p. 143

22 Ibid., p. 144

23 Kalugin's appeal to Stalin HIA Mikołajczyk, S. 49.49.18 78111-9.01.02. On Kalugin's role in the uprising see Iwanow, pp. 176–187

24 Rozmowa Premiera Mikołajczyka z Marszałkiem Stalinem' Moscow 9 August 1944 HIA Mikołajczyk, S 49-49.22 78111-9.01.02.

25 Lech Bezymenski, 'Radzieckie uderzenie', p. 73

26 For an excellent overview of the Battle for Warsaw, see Norbert Bacyk, *The Tank Battle at Praga*, p. 39

27 The 1st Ukrainian and 2nd and 3rd Byelorussian Fronts

28 2nd Guards Tank Army, 8th Armia Gwardii, 27th, 47th, and 69th Armies and the 1st Polish Army – the 2nd Guards Army was to be supported by the 47th Army.

29 Norbert Bacyk, *The Tank Battle at Praga*, p. 159

30 Lech Bezymenski, 'Radzieckie uderzenie', p. 74

31 Ibid., p. 75

32 CAMOFR (TsAMO), 233-2356-159, s. 1-3

33 Nikołaj Ivanow, *Powstanie Warszawskie*, p. 115

34 Lieutenant General Chuikov talked to Stalin and told him that he was ready to move forward immediately; there was no doubt that he would have moved had he

NOTES

been ordered to do so. CAMFOR (TsAMO), 1st Byelorussian Front - 2356, s. 145

35 CAMOFR, 233-2356-178, s. 346
36 Nikołaj Ivanow, *Powstanie Warszawskie*, p. 93
37 CAMOFR 233-2356-178, s. 355-58
38 Nikołaj Ivanow, *Powstanie Warszawskie*, p. 93
39 CAMOFR, 233-2356-171, s. 1
40 CAMOFR, 233-2356-170, s. 4-212
41 Nikołaj Iwanow, *Powstanie Warszawskie*, pp. 126-127
42 Ibid., p. 160
43 John Stieber, *Against the Odds. Survival on the Russian Front 1944-1945*, Poolberg Press, Dublin, 1995, p. 68
44 SS-Unterstürmführer Gösta Borg, a Swedish volunteer in the Waffen SS, 'The Red's Massed Attack', in Norbert Bacyk, *The Tank Battle at Praga*, p. 338
45 Ewald Kaptor, *Viking Panzer. The German 5th SS Tank Regiment in the East in World War II*, Stackpole Books, Mechanicsburg, PA, 2011, p. 338
46 Ibid., p. 339
47 'The IV SS-Pz. Korps versuchte der Gegner mit 4. Div. Nach stärkstem Arilleriefeuer und mit laufender PanzerunterstUtzung den Br. Kopf Warschau von NO her einsudrücken. Nach äusserst harten, wechselvollen Kämpfen geland es dem Feind, in etwa 5 km Breite un 3 km Tiefe in de Front der SS-W einsubrechen'. See Kurt Mehner, *Die Geheimen Tagesberichte der Deutschen Wehrmachtführung im Zweiten Weltkrieg 1939-1945*, Vol. X, p. 488
48 Norbert Bacyk, *The Tank Battle at Praga*, p. 159
49 Nikołaj Iwanow, *Powstanie Warszawskie*, p. 115
50 Antoni Przygoński, *Stalin i Powstanie Warszawskie*, p. 424
51 Ibid., p. 341
52 9th Army Report, 10 September 1944, WIH t 312, roll 346, kl. 7920618-7920619
53 Bartosz T. Wielinski, 'Biała i czerwona spięta agrafką', *Gazeta Wyborcza*, 7 May 2010, p. 18
54 W. Tuszyński, *Kościuszkowcy w walce o*

Pragę (propaganda pamphlet), MON, Warsaw, 1953, p. 11
55 Nikolaj Iwanow, *Stalin i Powstanie*, p. 205
56 Ibid., p 233
57 W. Tuszyński, *Kościuszkowcy*, p. 11
58 Norbert Bacyk, *The Tank Battle at Praga*, p. 198. See also Franz Hack (ed.), *Panzer Grenadaere der Panzerdivision „Wiking" in Bild*, National Europa Verlag, Coburg, 1984, p 227
59 L.C.P.W., Vol. I, Part 1, p. 178
60 Ibid., p. 179
61 Army Group Centre Report, 13 September 1944, WIH t. 312, roll 248, kl. 7804332
62 W. Tuszyński, *Kościuszkaowcy*, p. 46
63 Norbert Bacyk, *The Tank Battle at Praga*, p. 163
64 Nikołaj Iwanow, *Powstanie Warszawskie*, p. 208
65 Cynthia Flohr, 'Pozorna zmiana stanowiska Stalina wobec Powstania Warszawskiego we wrześniu 1944', in Stanisław Lewandowski and Bernd Martin (eds), *Powstanie Warszawskie 1944*, p. 193
66 Ibid., p. 194
67 *Pravda*, 15 October 1944 (fragment of Stalin's order to Marshal Rokossovsky)
68 'Makarenko', *Pravda*, 15 October 1944
69 'The Soviets moved into my house and we had to move to the kitchen, the rooms were taken by the Russians who changed over every three days. In the next house was a Polish unit, Polish uniforms Russian language. They were NKVD looking for Home Army people whom they arrested and put into a camp which they organized at the old ammunition factory in Rembertow. Amongst them our commander Dr Amałowicz and school director Sosnowski were arrested and imprisoned in that camp. Some of these people were murdered.' 'Wspomnienia Barbara Łożczyńska', author interview, Warsaw, 2001
70 Włodzimierz Rosłoniec, *Lato 1944*, ZHAK, Krakow, 1989, p. 159
71 Warlimont, *Inside Hitler's HQ*, p. 453
72 Erich von dem Bach, *Kriegstagebuch*, p. 110; see also Walter Warlimont, *Inside Hitler's Headquarters*, p. 453

679

73 Zbigniew Ścibor-Rylski ('Motyl'), http://www.1944.pl/historia/powstańcze-biogramy

74 Piotr Stachiewicz, *Parasol*, p. 578

75 Stanisław Likiernik, *By Devil's Luck*, p. 142

76 Włodzimierz Rołoniec, *Lato 1944*, p. 138

77 Jan Rosner, in L.C.P.W., Vol. I, Part 1, p. 257

78 14 September, Lüttwitz to Staedke

79 9th Army Report, 14 September 1944, WIH, t. 312, roll. 347, kl. 7922150

80 Stanisław Likiernik, *By Devil's Luck*, p. 140

81 Ibid., p. 141

82 Report of 2 October signed by Rokossovsky, Telegin and the Chief of Staff of the 1st Byelorussian Front General Colonel Malinin, quoted in Cynthia Flohr, 'Pozorna zmiane', p. 183

83 J.K. Zawodny, *Nothing but Honour*, p. 185

84 This was the 1st Battalion, 9th Regiment of the 3rd Infantry Division under Major Mierzyrynski

85 Testimonies: Stanisław Komornicki 'Nałęcz', Maria Stypułkowska-Chojecka 'Kama', Zbigniew Ścibor-Rylski 'Motyl', Tadeusz Targoński, Czesław Zaborowski 'Cesiek', 'Lalka', 'Zabor'. Interviews complied by Szymon Nowak, edited by Maciej Janaszek-Seydlitz, translated by Sabina Decowska in 'The Soldiers of Czerniakow', Warsaw, 2012, http://www/sppw1944.org/index.html?http:ww

86 Cynthia Flohr, 'Pozorna zmiana stanowiska Stalina wobec Powstania Warszawskiego we wrześniu 1944', in Stanisław Lewandowski and Bernd Martin (eds), *Powstanie Warszawskie 1944*, p. 197

87 Ibid.

88 Ibid.

89 Stanisław Likiernik, *By Devil's Luck*, p. 141

90 Ibid., p. 142

91 Piotr Stachiewicz, *Parasol*, p. 591

92 Włodzimierz Wołoszyn, *Na warszawskim kierunku operacyjnu. Czialania 1 Frontu Białoruskiego i 1 Armii WP 18.VII–23.IX 1944*, MON, Warsaw, 1964, p. 286

93 Testimony of M. Nitecki, http://www.1944.pl/historia/powstancze-biogramy

94 Testimony of Lidia Kowałczyk-Strzelecka in Piotr Stachiewicz p 594

95 Ibid.

96 General Vokel, 21 September 1944, in Tadeusz Sawicki, *Rozkaz*, p. 133

97 Piotr Stachiewicz, *Parasol*, p. 584

98 Ibid., p. 585

99 Lidia Markiewicz-Ziental, http://www.sppw1944.org/index.html? http://ww

100 Testimony of Dr Irena Semedeni-Konapocka, Folder P/73, Muzeum Powstania Warszawskiego, p. 12

101 Ibid.

102 Stanisław Likiernik, *By Devil's Luck*, p. 144

103 Ibid., p. 145

104 Testimony of J. Chmielińska-Nina, Folder P/73, Muzeum Powstania Warszawskiego, p. 8

105 Testimony of J. Bem-Dymecka, Folder P/73, Muzeum Powstania Warszawskiego, p. 8

106 Piotr Stachiewicz, *Parasol*, p. 601, n. 288

107 Ibid.

108 Ibid., n. 289

109 Ibid., n. 288

110 Ibid., p. 595

111 Włodzimierz Wołoszyn, *Na warszawskim kierunku*, p. 286

112 Major Fischer, lecture, 23 September 1944, BA-MA BA-MA,R H 12-9/1

113 Profile of Janina Błaszczak in 'Żołnierze Czerniakowa', www.sppw1944.org/index.html?http://www.sppw1944.org/powstanie/czerniakow.html

114 Testimony of Tadeusz Rybowski, Archiwum Historii

115 Piotr Stachiewicz, *Parasol*, p. 599, n. 286

116 Ibid.

117 Photocopy of interrogaticn of 'Parasol' solider, ibid., p. 601, n. 287

118 Ibid.

119 L.C.P.W., Vol. I, Part 1, p. 166

120 Ibid.

121 Peter Stolten, 'Listy niemieckiego', p. 266

122 French L. MacLean, *The Cruel Hunters*, p. 194

123 Warren F. Kimball, *Churchill & Roosevelt*, p. 302, n. 36

124 Ibid., p. 302, n. 37

125 Ibid., p. 295

126 Ibid., p. 296

127 Ibid., p. 297

128 Laurence Rees, *World War II Behind Closed Doors*, p. 289

129 George F. Kennan, *Memoirs 1925–1950*. Atlantic, Little, Brown, Boston, 1967, p.211
130 George Orwell, 'The Recent Rising in Warsaw', *Tribune*, 1 September 1944
131 George F. Kennan, *Memoirs*, p. 211
132 J.K. Zawodny interview with George F. Kennan, 30 May 1972, in J.K. Zawodny, *Nothing but Honour*, p. 227. Harriman wrote to Major General Frederick Anderson as early as 19 August saying: 'At the moment I am absorbed by my indignation and wrath at the Soviets for their stopping our attempts to drop supplies on Warsaw . . .' HIA Frederick Anderson 27-1 75054-8M.07
133 Some Americans, including Major General Frederick Anderson, were in favour of pushing the Soviets. On 23 August he complained: 'Apparently we are not welcome over Poland.' HIA Frederick Anderson 27-3 75054-8M.07. On 26 August he wrote that because of the deadlock with the Russians 'we have missed several opportunities'. HIA Frederick Anderson 27-5 75054 8M.07. See also Mark Conversino, *Fighting with the Soviets. The Failure of Operation Frantic*, University of Kansas Press, Kansas, 1997, p. 211
134 Cynthia Flohr, 'Pozorna zmiana', p. 188
135 The order is quoted in 'SSSR and Polska'. The only existing order on paper regarding Berling's Army and the crossing of the Vistula is from a staff officer of the 1st Byelorussian Front ordering the 1st Polish Army to 'concentrate units on the east bank of the Vistula in preparation for gaining a bridgehead on the west bank in the Warsaw area'. Ibid., p. 198
136 Izolda Kowalska testimony, in Antoni Przygoński, *Stalin i Powstanie Warszawskie*, p. 389
137 Ibid., p. 391
138 Rochus Misch, *Der Letzte Zeuge*, p. 176
139 Heinz Linge, *With Hitler to the End. The Memoirs of Adolf Hitler's Valet*, Frontline Books, London, 2009, p. 173
140 Christa Schroeder, *He Was My Chief*, p. 125
141 Fragment of discussion between Hitler, Lieutenant General Westphal and Lieutenant General Krebs on 31 August 1944 in the Wolfschanze, quoted in Walter Warlimont, *Inside Hitler's Headquarters*, p. 453
142 Albert Speer, *Inside the Third Reich*, p. 547
143 Ibid., p. 544
144 Ibid., p. 549
145 Ralf Georg Reuth, *Goebbels*, Constable, London, 1993, p. 337
146 Ibid.
147 Diary of Guy Liddell, entry 26 September 1944, p. 37
148 Kersten, brought in by Karl Wolff, was a Finnish chiropractor who was so successful at treating Himmler's stomach cramps that he became his personal attendant in the final years of the war. Himmler trusted him and he became a confidant, discussing even normally forbidden subjects such as the murder of Jews with the Reichsführer. Kersten used his position to influence Himmler to think in a more humanitarian way and eventually encouraged him to free some prisoners from the camps. Himmler called him his 'Magic Buddha'.
149 Roger Manvell and Heinrich Fraenkel, *Heinrich Himmler*, p. 198
150 Ibid.
151 Peter Padfield, *Himmler*, p. 538
152 Roger Manvell and Heinrich Fraenkel, *Heinrich Himmler*, p. 191
153 'Of all the extraordinary "summits" in history, an incontestable place must be given to a two-hour wartime meeting on 20 April, 1945, between Heinrich Himmler, the archi-killer of Jews, and Norbert Masur, Swedish representative of the World Jewish Congress.' Frank Fox, 'A Jew Talks to Himmler', *Zwoje (The Scrolls)*, no. 1 (38), 2004, p. 1
154 Peter Padfield, *Himmler*, p. 544
155 HIA Heinrich Himmler Papers 12-9-10-304. See also Ralf Georg Reuth, *Goebbels*, p. 341. The Germans feared that the Allies would consider the Volkssturm an illegal partisan organization. The first step towards legal recognition was to recognize the Polish AK. Other organizations soon followed; in October they also recognized

all members of the French Forces of the Interior as regular soldiers as long as they wore either a uniform or the standard tricolour armband bearing the cross of Lorraine. It worked. Britain and the United States assured the Germans in early November that as long as the milita acted in accordance with international law, they would consider the Volkssturm men legal combatants. See also David K. Yelton, *Hitler's Volkssturm. The Nazi Militia and the Fall of Germany, 1944–1945*. University Press of Kansas, Kansas, 2002, p. 93

156 Peter Padfield, *Himmler*, p. 543

157 Heinrich Schwendemann, 'Kapitulacja: niemiecki odwet i niemiecka agitacja na rzecz frontu antybolszewickiego', in Stanisław Lewandowski and Bernd Martin (eds), *Powstanie Warszawskie 1944*, p. 209

158 Ibid., p. 210

159 Ibid. In a letter to Reichsminister Dr Lammers on 4 August 1944 Frank had already pointed to the Polish pressure on the 'English and Americans' to drop supplies to them in the city, noting that the Poles saw the Russians as '*Todfeinde*' – deadly enemies. HIA Heinrich Himmler Papers, XX060-8.36 12-13

160 Oliver Samson, 'Niemiecka propaganda zagraniczna: starania o zawiązanie antybolszewickiego frontu', in Stanisław Lewandowski and Bernd Martin (eds), *Powstanie Warszawskie 1944*, p. 229

161 Ibid., p. 233

162 Joseph Goebbels, *Die Tagebücher*, entry 28 July 1944, p. 393

163 Ibid., p. 380

164 Ibid., p. 236

165 A glimpse at the headlines of German newspaper articles in autumn 1944 mirrors the interest in the effect of the uprising on the Allied coalition: 'Moskau verhaftet Aufstandpolen. Der bolschewistische "Befreiungsausschuss" tritt gegenüber London und Washington schon als Regierung auf' (*Völkischer Beobachter*, 1 September); 'Der Fall Polen und andere Fälle' (*Völkischer Beobachter*, 5 September); 'Das Drama von Warschau.

Furchtbarer Leidensweg der Zivilbevölkerung der ehemaligen polnischen Hauptstadt' (*Völkischer Beobachter*, 8 September); 'Stalin verbot englishce Hilfe für Warschau' (*Völkischer Beobachter*, 13 September); 'Die Sowjets gefährliche Länderräuber' (*Völkischer Beobachter*, 23 September); 'Warschau – Symbol und Warnung' (*Völkischer Beobachter*, 4 October); 'Warschauer Totentanz' (*Das Reich*, 26 November)

166 Tanja Villinger, 'Powstanie w sprawozdaniach niemieckich środków masowego przekazu', in Stanisław Lewandowski and Bernd Martin (eds), *Powstanie Warszawskie 1944*, p. 244

167 *Völkischer Beobachter*, 1 September 1944

Chapter 12: The End Game

1 Staedke referred to Warsaw as an Augean stable.

2 Tadeusz Sawicki, *Rozkaz*, p. 152

3 Testimony of Barbara Kaczyńska-Januszkiewicz, 'Powrót do Wspomnień', http://www.warsawuprising.com/witness/januszkiewicz

4 Stanisław Jankowski 'Agaton', *Z fałszywym Ausweisem*, p. 262

5 Fragment 'Meldunku sytuacjnego Komendanta Obwodu Mokotów do Ko. Okręgu Warszawskiego AK', 25 September 1944, in L.C.P.W., Vol. II, p. 458. See also Joanna K.M. Hanson, *The Civilian Popluation*, p. 145

6 Testimony of Barbara Kaczyńska-Januszkiewicz

7 Joanna K.M. Hanson, *The Civilian Popluation*, p. 145

8 Testimony Barbara Kaczyńska-Januszkiewicz

9 Stanisław Aronson, *Rysiek z Kedywu*, p. 167

10 The 9th Army report of 27 September 1944 stated that 'Im Südteil des Stadtgebiets von Warschau wurden nach Kapitulation des Kessels von Mokotow etwa 2000 Gefangene eingebracht'. There was no mention of executions. Kurt Mehner, *Die Geheimen Tagesberichte der Deutschen Wehrmachtführung im Zweiten Weltkrieg 1939–1945*, Vol. X, p. 73

11 Julian Eugeniusz Kulski, *Dying We Live*, p. 215

12 Ibid., p. 218

13 Joanna K.M. Hanson, *The Civilian Population*, p. 191

14 Tadeusz Sawicki, *Rozkaz*, p. 152

15 Unnamed SS correspondent quoted in *The Times*, 13 September1944

16 Julian Eugeniusz Kulski, *Dying We Live*, p. 216

17 Tadeusz Sawicki, *Rozkaz*, p. 152

18 Stanisław Jankowski 'Agaton', *Z fałszywym Ausweisem*, p. 282

19 Kurt Heller diary, 'Decydujący bój PASTę', http://www.info.pc.home.pl/Whatfor/baza/kilir

20 Testimony of Jan Magdziak, Battalion 'Kiliński', Archive Muzeum Powstanie Warszawskiego, Testimonies Folder 5

21 Aleksander Maliszewski 'Piotrowski', recounted by Halina Auderska, reporter for the AK Office of Information and Propaganda. Halina Auderska, 'The Dancing Shell', *Stolica*, no. 1, 3 January 1971

22 Miron Białoszewski, *Memoir*, p. 163

23 Anna Szatkowska, *Był Dom*, p. 236

24 Ibid., p. 237

25 Ibid., p. 244

26 Miron Białoszewski, *Memoir*, p. 107

27 L.C.P.W., Vol. II, p. 499

28 Anna Szatkowska, *Był Dom*, p. 248

29 Ibid., p. 244

30 J.K. Zawodny, *Nothing but Honour*, p. 167

31 Testimony of Janusz Hamerliński, 'Żołnierza batalionu AK „Kiliński"', http://sppw1944.org/index_ukr.html

32 Anna Szatkowska, *Był Dom*, p. 248

33 L.C.P.W., Vol. I, Part 1, p. 410

34 Ibid., p. 363

35 L.C.P.W, Vol. II, p. 187

36 Ibid., p. 152

37 Ibid., pp. 288, 301

38 Ibid., p. 215

39 Ibid., p. 435

40 Ibid., p. 450

41 Joanna K.M. Hanson, *The Civilian Population*, p. 173

42 Ibid., p. 155, n. 30

43 Stanisław Jankowski 'Agaton', *Z fałszywym Ausweisem*, p. 262

44 Miron Białoszewski, *Memoir*, p. 173

45 L.C.P.W., Vol. II, p. 502

46 Ibid., p. 504

47 Ibid., p. 315

48 Ibid., p. 511

49 Tadeusz Sawicki, *Rozkaz*, p. 175

50 Miron Białoszewski, *Memoir*, p. 173

51 L.C.P.W., Vol. II, p. 328

52 Białoszewski, *Memoir*, p. 211

53 Testimony of Gerhard von Jordan in Andrzej Krzysztof Kunert, *Generał Tadeusz Bór-Komorowski*, p. 138. Hasso Krappe recalled: 'When after general capitulation General Bór met the leader of my division General Leutnant Kaellner they were both astonished and looked at one another as they knew one another personally from tournaments of pre-war times .. after a while Bór said to Kaellner: "General, if I had known you were on the other side I would have capitulated much earlier to save the civilians suffering and unhappiness."' Hasso Krappe, 'Powstanie warszawskie we wspomnieniach oficera Wehrmachtu', p. 263

54 Tadeusz Sawicki, *Rozkaz*, p. 174

55 E.W., Vol. I, p. 12

56 Stanisław Jankowski 'Agaton', *Z fałszywym Ausweisem*, p. 281

57 Ibid., p. 350

58 Anna Szatkowska, *Był Dom*, p. 254

59 Andrzej Krzysztof Kunert, *Generał Tadeusz Bór-Komorowski*, p. 271

60 Peter Stolten, 'Listy niemieckiego', p. 268

61 Tadeusz Sawicki, *Rozkaz*, p. 185 HIA Werner Martin, 'Im Krieg in Russland', p. 87. 80047-10. V

62 Stanisław Jankowski 'Agaton', *Z fałszywym Ausweisem*, p. 192

63 Tadeusz Sawicki, *Rozkaz*, p. 186

64 L.C.P.W., Vol. I, Part 1, p. 587

65 Stanisław Jankowski 'Agaton', *Z fałszywym Ausweisem*, p. 192

66 Hasso Krappe, 'Powstanie warszawskie we wspomnieniach oficera Wehrmachtu', p. 263

67 Heinrich Schwendemann, 'Kapitulacja: niemiecki odwet i niemiecka agitacja na rzecz frontu antybolszewickiego', in Stanisław Lewandowski and Bernd Martin (eds), *Powstanie Warszawskie 1944*, p. 220

68 Stanisław Jankowski 'Agaton', *Z fałszywym Ausweisem*, p. 238

69 The steadfast refusal to cooperate did not stop the Soviets from accusing Bór and the AK leadership of collaboration. In March 1945, for example, the Soviet-run Polish newspaper *Szpilki* published a 'joke' piece calling the AK 'collaBORators'.

70 Stanisław Jankowski 'Agaton', *Z fałszywym Ausweisem*, p. 304

71 L.C.P.W., Vol. I, Part 1, p. 412

72 Miron Białoszewski, *Memoir*, p. 218

73 Gunnar S. Paulsson, *The Secret City*, p. 236

74 Anna Szatkowska, *Był Dom*, p. 252

75 Miron Białoszewski, *Memoir*, p. 218

76 Stanisław Beyer testimony, in E.W., Vol. I, p. 28

77 Anna Szatkowska, *Był Dom*, p. 257

78 Testimony of Józef Gredowski, in L.C.P.W., Vol. I, Part 1, p. 397

79 L.C.P.W., Vol. I, Part 1, p. 367

80 Testimony of Adam Bień, in Mieczysław Adamczyk and Janusz Gmitruk, *Powstanie Warszwskie w dokumentach i wspomnieniach Ludowców*, p. 107

81 L.C.P.W., Vol. I, Part 1, p. 367

82 Maria Starzyńska, http://107www.1944.pl/historia/powstańcze-biogramy

83 L.C.P.W., Vol. I, Part 1, p. 651

84 E.W., Vol. I, p. 59

85 Ibid., p. 87

86 Jan Rosner, in L.C.P.W., Vol. I, Part 1, p. 367

87 Maria Stokowska, in E.W., Vol. I, Part 1, p. 107

88 Barbara Kaczyńska-Januszkiewicz, 'Warsaw Diary', http://www.warsawuprising.com/witness/janus

89 Jan Rosner, in L.C.P.W., Vol. I, Part 1, p. 359

90 E.W., Vol. I, p. 83

91 Ibid., p. 610

92 Testimony of Kazimiera Drescher, in E.W., Vol. I, p. 77

93 Ibid., p. 77

94 L.C.P.W., Vol. II, p. 612

95 E.W., Vol. I, p. 61

96 Ibid., p. 77

97 Ibid., p. 78

98 Ibid., p. 76

99 Ibid., p. 108

100 Ibid., p. 70

101 Ibid., p. 71

102 Testimony of Janina Chmielińska, 31 August 2005, Archiwum Historii Mówionej, Muzeum Powstania Warszawskiego, p. 14

103 Testimony of Zofia Rusicka-Kreowa, ibid., p. 9

104 E.W., Vol. I, p. 74

105 Testimony of Adam Bień, p. 107

106 E.W., Vol. I, p. 68

107 Ibid., p. 69

108 L.C.P.W., Vol. I, Part 1, p. 368

109 Ibid., p. 626

110 E.W., Vol. I, p. 174

111 Ibid., p. 176

112 Ibid., p. 174

113 Ibid., p. 176

114 Von dem Bach in conversation with AK Major Kazimierz Szternal, in J.K. Zawodny, *Nothing but Honour*, p. 193

115 Ibid.

116 Władysław Szpilman, *The Pianist*, p. 183

117 Gunnar S. Paulsson, *The Secret City*, p. 235 See also the collection of extraordinary testimonies of 'Robinsons' who survived in M.M. Drozdowski *et al.*, *Ludność cywilna w Powstaniu Warszawskim. Pamiętniki. Relacje. Zeznania*, Vol. I, Part 2 (henceforth L.C.P.W., Vol. I, Part 2)

118 L.C.P.W., Vol. I, Part 1, p. 154

119 Barbara Engelking-Boni and Jacek Leociak, *The Warsaw Ghetto. A Guide to the Perished City*, Yale University Press, New Haven, CT, 2009, p. 813

120 Chaim Icel Goldstein, *The Bunker*, Jewish Publication Society of America, New York, 2007

121 Gunnar S. Paulsson, *The Secret City*, p. 190

122 Ibid., p. 189

123 Testimony of Julianna Wilak-Niewiedziałowa, in L.C.P.W., Vol. I, Part 2, p. 560

124 Władysław Szpilman, *The Pianist*, p. 166

125 Romuald Kulik, 'Sześć weekendów z Wehrmachtem', *Gazeta Wyborcza*, 16 January 2008

126 Władysław Szpilman, *The Pianist*, p. 169

127 Ibid., p. 175

128 Letter to Hans Frank from Dr Fischer, 11 October 1944, in Hans von Krannhals, *Der Warschauer Aufstand 1944*, p. 413

NOTES

129 Ernst Rode testimony at Nuremberg, 28 January 1946, http://avalon.law.yale.edu/subject_menus/imt.a

130 Interrogation of Heinz Guderian by Prosecutor Professor Jerzy Sawicki, 29 January 1946, Nuremberg, in *State Department Special Interrogation Mission - Interrogation of Colonel General Heinz Guderian*, Department of State. Washington, D.C., 1945, p. 6 (CD-ROM)

131 L.C.P. W., Vol. II, p. 580

132 Ibid., p. 582

133 Ibid., p. 583

134 John Stieber *Against the Odds*, p. 97

135 'Rüstungskommando in Warschau', 13 July 1944, Okupationspolitik, p. 205, n. 21

136 Hans Thieme, 'Wspomnienia niemieckiego oficera sztabowego o powstaniu warszawskim', p. 273

137 Anna Szatkowska, *Był Dom*, p. 257

138 Jerzy Sawicki, *Zburzenie Warszawy*, p. 145

139 Interrogation of Josef Bühler, n ibid., p. 271

140 Ibid., p. 273

141 Karol Mórawski, *Wola*, p. 147. For a detailed description of goods to be taken from Warsaw see the letter from Hans Frank to Ludwig Fischer, 6 December 1944, BA-MA H-12-9/7. On Frau Himmler's violin se HIA Heinrich Himmler Papers, XX060-8.36 12-13. Himmler ordered that the violin and four accordions be sent to his wife for Christmas. A collection of fur coats was to be sent to Berlin. He would decide what to do with a case of stamps, as well as gold watches and coins, later.

142 Marek Getter, 'Władze cywilne postania warszawskiego', in Stanisław Lewandowski and Bernd Martin (eds) *Powstanie Warszawskie 1944*, p. 137

143 L.C.P.W., Vol. II, p. 638

144 Telegram from Albert Speer to Heinrich Himmler, 9 December 1944, HIA Heinrich Himmler Papers XX060-8.36 12-13. Raumungsstäbe was divided into three groups: the first reported to the Provisions Department of the 9th Army, the second to SS Oberführer Geibel and the head of the Wartheland District Arthur Greiser, and the third to the civilian authorities of the Warsaw District. Marek Getter, 'Władze cywilne postania warszawskiego', in Stanisław Lewandowski and Bernd Martin (eds), *Powstanie Warszawskie 1944*, p. 141

145 Anna Szatkowaska, *Był Dom*, p. 267

146 Romuald Kulik, 'Sześć weekendów z Wehrmachtem', *Gazeta Wyborcza*, 16 January 2008

147 Ibid.

148 Ibid.

149 Janusz S. Morkowski, *Polish Museum, Rapperswil* (trilingual English-Polish-German guidebook), Polish Museum, Rapperswil, 1994

Conclusion

1 In a letter to SS-Obergruppenführer Krüger on 16 February 1943 Himmler explains that the physical destruction of the ghetto is a positive development, as '*die Millionenstadt Warschau, die immer ein gefährlicher Herd der Zersetzung und des Aufstandes ist, verkleinert wird*' (the million-person city Warsaw, which was always a dangerous oven of subversion and rebellion, will be reduced in size). HIA Heinrich Himmler Papers XX060-8.36 12-13. See also Niels Gutschow and Barbara Klain, *Urbanistyka Warszawy w latach 1939-1945*, Deutscher Werkbund, Frankfurt am Main, 1995, p. 68

2 Hitler's speech to generals, 28 December 1944, in Felix Gilbert (ed.), *Hitler Directs his War*, Charter. New York, 1950, p. 223

3 Ibid., p. 226

4 In a report to the A.O.K. Generalleutnant Kinzel wrote on 26 December 1944 that 'SS-Brigadeführer Geibel is blowing up things which might for a time have had political importance, but which are tactically absolutely unimportant objects.' BA-MA H-12-9/8

5 Władyslaw Szpilman, *The Pianist*, p. 183

6 Antony Beevor, *Berlin. The Downfall 1945*, Viking, London, 2002, p. 20

7 Walter Lüdde-Neurath, *Regierung Donitz. Die letzten Tage des Dritten Reiches*, Munsterschmidt Verlag, Berlin, 1964, p. 757

8 Gitta Sereny, *Albert Speer*, p. 483
9 Walter Warlimont, *Inside Hitler's Headquarters*, p. 500
10 Bartosz. T. Wieliński, 'Biała i czerwona spięte agrafką', *Gazeta Wyborcza*, 7 May 2012
11 Władysław Szpilman, *The Pianist*, p. 184
12 Ibid., p. 184
13 L.C.P.W., Vol. II, Part 2, p. 503
14 Władysław Szpilman, *The Pianist*, p. 184
15 L.C.P.W., Vol. II, Part 2, p. 508
16 Władysław Szpilman, *The Pianist*, p. 185
17 Nikita Sergeevich Khrushchev, *Khrushchev Remembers. II: The Last Testament*, Penguin, New York, 1974, p. 209
18 Georgii Zhukov, *The Memoirs of Marshal Zhukov*, p. 585
19 Władysław Szpilman, *The Pianist*, p. 186
20 Testimony of Helena Brodowska-Kubicz, in L.C.P.W., Vol. II, Part 2, p. 115
21 Jonathan Walker, *Poland Alone*, p. 164
22 Halina Adamska, in E.W., Vol. I, p. 152
23 Władysław Szpilman, *The Pianist*, p. 187
24 Testimony of Dr Irena Semedeni-Konapocka, Folder P/73, Muzeum Powstania Warszawskiego
25 Stanisław Jankowski ('Agaton'), *Z fałszywym Ausweisem w Prawdziwej Warszawie*, Państwowy Instytut Wydawniczy, Warsaw, 1980, p. 307
26 Ibid.
27 Włodzimierz Nowak and Angelika Kuźniak, 'Mój warszawski szał', *Gazeta Wyborcza*, 23 August 2004, p. 7
28 Nikita Khrushchev, *Khrushchev Remembers*, Vol. II, p. 209
29 Nikolai Tolstoy, *The Secret Betrayal*, Scribner, New York, 1977, p. 71
30 Warren F. Kimball, *Churchill & Roosevelt*, p. 350
31 Ibid., p. 351
32 Cynthia Flohr, 'Pozorna zmiana', p. 203
33 John Erickson, *The Road to Berlin*, p. 617
34 Anthony Read, *The Devil's Disciples. The Lives and Times of Hitler's Inner Circle*, Pimlico, London, 2003, p. 856
35 Josef Goebbels, *The Goebbels Diaries*, p. 241
36 Philip W. Blood, *Hitler's Bandit Hunters*, p. 280
37 Felix Kersten, *Totenkopf und Treue. Heinrich Himmler ohne Uniform; aus den Tagebuchblättern des finnischen Medizinalrats*, Mölich, Hamburg, 1957, p. 329
38 Albert Speer, *Inside the Third Reich*, p. 588
39 Hugh Trevor-Roper, *The Last Days of Hitler*, Macmillan, London, 1995, p. 152
40 L.C.P.W., Vol. II, p. 701
41 Interrogation of Heinz Guderian by Jerzy Sawicki, 29 January 1946, Nuremberg, in *State Department Special Interrogation Mission – Interrogation of Colonel General Heinz Guderian*, p. 5
42 'Własnoręczne zeznanie komendanta garnizonu Warszawa gen. Reinera Stahela pt. „Powstanie w Warszawie", Moscow 25.08.1945', p. 615
43 Wojciech Fałkowski, *Straty Warszawy 1939–1945. Raport*, p. 301
44 E.W., Vol. I, p. 37
45 Testimonies of Janina Bem-Dymecka and Zofia Rusiecka-Kreowska, Biblioteka Muzeum Powstania Warszawskiego, Folder Zeznania Świadków Naocznych, P/73
46 An overview of the trial and its aftermath was published by Information Division, Executive Committee of Polish Council of National Unity, *A Trial in Moscow: Tenth Anniversary of the Capture of Sixteen Leaders of Underground Poland*, Polish Council of National Unity, London, 1956

Bibliography

135 Pluton AK VII Zgrupowania „Ruczaj" i jego kadeckie korzenie, ed. Dławichowski, Andrzej, Warszawa: Dorota Karaszewska, 1994

Adair, Paul, Hitler's Greatest Defeat. The Collapse of Army Group Centre, June 1944, London: Brockhampton Press, 1994

Adamczyk, Mieczysław, Gmitruk, Janusz, Powstanie Warszawskie w dokumentach i wspomnieniach ludowców, Warszawa: Muzeum Historii Polskiego Ruchu Ludowego, Kielce: Wszechnica Świętokrzyska, 2011

Anders, Władysław, An Army in Exile. The Story of the Second Polish Corps, Nashville: The Battery Press, 2004

Anders, Władysław, Bez ostatniego rozdziału. Wspomnienia z lat 1939–1946, Warszawa: Bellona, 2007

Angrik, Andrej, Besatzungspolitik und Massenmord. Die Einsatzgruppe sudlichen Sowjetunion 1941–1943, Hamburg: Hamburger Edition, 2003

Armia Krajowa w dokumentach 1939–1945, ed. Czarnocka, Halina, Londyn: Studium Polski Podziemnej, 1989

Ascherson, Neal, The Struggles for Poland, London: Michael Joseph, 1987

August, Jochen, SonderaktionKrakau. Die Verhaftung der Krauker Wissenschaftler am 6. November 1939, Hamburg: Hanburger Edition, 1997

Bagration 1944. The Destruction of Army Group Centre, ed. Zaloga, Steven J., New York: Osprey, 2009

Baird, Jay W., Hitler's War Poets. Literature and Politics in the Third Reich, Cambridge: Cambridge University Press, 2008

Baluk, Stefan, Silent and Unseen. I was a Polish WW II Special Ops Commando, Warszawa: Askon, 2009

Bałuk, Stefan, Michałowski, Marian, Polski czyn zbrojny 1939–1945, Warszawa: Polonia, 1989

Bańkowska, Maria K., *Powstańczy dziennik Łączniczki z „K-1"*, Warszawa: Felicja Bańkowska „Wanda" , 1944

Baranowski Edmund, Kulesza, Juliusz, *Bankowe Szańce. Bankowcy polscy w latach wojny i okupacji 1939–1945*, Warszawa: Askon, 2009

Barański, Marek, Sołtan, Andrzej, *Warszawa-Ostatnie spojrzenie. Niemieckie fotografie lotnicze sprzed sierpnia 1944*, Warszawa: Muzeum Historyczne m.st. Warszawy, 2004

Bartelski, Lesław M., Bukowski, Tadeusz, *Warszawa w dniach Powstania 1944*, Warszawa: Krajowa Agencja Wydawnicza, 1980

Bartelski, Lesław M., *Mokotów 1944*, Warszawa: Wydawnictwo Ministerstwa Obrony Narodowej, 1986

Bartoszewski, Władysław, *1859 Dni Warszawy*, Kraków: Znak, 2008

Bartoszewski, Władysław, *Abandoned Heroes of the Warsaw Uprising*, Kraków: Biały Kruk, 2008

Bartoszewski, Władysław, *Dni walczącej Stolicy. Kronika Powstania Warszawskiego*, Warszawa: Świat Książki, 2004

Bartoszewski, Władysław, *Powstanie Warszawskie*, Warszawa: Świat Książki, 2009

Bartoszewski, Władysław, *Prawda o von dem Bachu*, Warszawa, Poznań: Wydawnictwo Zachodnie, 1961

Bartoszewski, Władysław, *Warszawski pierścień śmierci 1939–1944. Terror hitlerowski w okupowanej stolicy*, Warszawa: Świat książki, 2008

Bartov, Omer, *Hitler's Army. Soldiers, Nazis, and War in the Third Reich*, New York, Oxford: Oxford University Press, 1992

Batorski Stanisław, *Czas poza domem*, Warszawa: Młodzieżowa Agencja Wydawnicza, 1984

Bayer, Stanisław, *Służba zdrowia Warszawy w walce z okupantem 1939–1945*, Warszawa: Wydawnictwo Ministerstwa Obrony Narodowej, 1985

Beevor, Antony, *Stalingrad*, London: Penguin, 1998

Bender, Roger J., Petersen, George A., 'Hermann Göring'. *From Regiment to Fallschirmpanzerkorps*, Atglen, PA: Schiffer, 1993

Białous, Ryszard, *Walka w pożodze. Batalion Armii Krajowej „Zośka" w Powstaniu Warszawskim*, Warszawa: Oficyna Wydawnicza Rytm, 2000

Białous, Ryszard, *Walka w pożodze. Harcerski batalion Armii Krajowej „Zośka" w Powstaniu Warszawskim*, Warszawa: Oficyna Wydawnicza Rytm, 2009

Biddiscombe, Perry, *Werwolf! The History of the National Socialist Guerrilla Movement 1944–1946*, Cardiff: University of Wales Press, 1998

Bidermann, Gottlob H., *In Deadly Combat. A German Soldier's Memoir of the Eastern Front*, Kansas: University Press of Kansas, 2000

Bielański, Ryszard, *Prawie życiorys, 1939-1956*, Warszawa: Ryszard Bielański, 1986

Bielecki, Robert, Kulesza, Juliusz, *Przeciw konfidentom i czołgom. Oddział 993/W Kontrwywiadu Komendy Głównej AK i batalionu AK „Pięść" w konspiracji i w Powstaniu Warszawskim 1944 roku*, Warszawa: Radwan-Wano, 1996

Bielecki, Robert, *Żołnierze Powstania Warszawskiego*, Warszawa: Neriton, 1995

Bierut, Bolesław, *Sześcioletni plan odbudowy Warszawy*, Warszawa: Książka i Wiedza, 1950

Bieszanow, Władimir, *Rok 1944. Dziesięć uderzeń Stalina*, Warszawa: Bellona, 2011

Bishop, Chris, *Order of Battle. German Infantry in WW II*, London: Amber Books, 2008

Bishop, Chris, *Order of Battle. German Panzers in WW II*, St Paul, MN: Zenith Press, 2008

Blood, Philip W., *Hitler's Bandit Hunters. The SS and the Nazi Occupation of Europe*, Washington, DC: Potomac Books, 2006

Borecka, Emilia, Sempoliński, Leonard, *Warszawa 1945*, Warszawa: Państwowe Wydawnictwo Naukowe, 1975

Borkiewicz, Adam, *Powstanie Warszawskie 1944. Zarys działań natury wojskowej*, Warszawa: Instytut Wydawniczy PAX, 1957

Borkiewicz, Celińska A., *Batalion „Zośka"*, Warszawa: Państwowy Instytut Wydawniczy, 1990

Bratny, Roman, *Pamiętnik moich książek*, Warszawa: Czytelnik, 1980

Braun, Sylwester, *Reportaże z Powstania Warszawskiego*, Warszawa: Krajowa Agencja Wydawnicza, 1983

Browning, Christopher R., *Ordinary Men. Reserve Police Battalion 101 and the Final Solution in Poland*, London: Penguin Books, 2001

Brzozowska, Helena, *Nasza dziwna Grupa ZWZ-AK*, Kraków: WAM, 1993

Buczkowski, Marian R., *Warszawski dowcip w walce 1939-1944*, Warszawa: Wydawnictwo Gebethnera i Wölffa, 1947

Buhler, Pierre, *Polska droga do wolności 1939-1995*, Warszawa: Wydawnictwo Akademickie Dialog, 1999

Bukalska, Patrycja, *Rysiek z Kedywu. Niezwykłe losy Stanisława Aronsona*, Kraków: Znak, 2009

Burleigh, Michael, *The Third Reich. A New History*, London: Pan Books, 2001

Butler, Rupert, *SS-Wiking. The History of the Fifth SS Division 1941–45*, Havertown, PA: Casemate, 2002

Carius, Otto, *Tigers in the Mud. The Combat Career of German Panzer Commander Otto Carius*, Mechanicsburg, PA: Stackpole Books, 2003

Chiari, Bernhard, *Die polnische Heimatarmee. Geschichte und Mythos der Armia Krajowa seitdem Zweiten Weltkrieg*, Munchen: R. Oldenbourg Verlag, 2003

Churchill & Roosevelt. The Complete Correspondence. III: Alliance Declining February 1944–April 1945, ed. Kimball, Warren F., London: Collins, 1984

Ciechanowski, Jan M., *The Warsaw Rising of 1944*, Cambridge: Cambridge University Press, 1974

Ciechanowski, Jan S., *Wkład polskiego wywiadu w zwycięstwo nad Niemcami w II Wojnie Światowej*, Warszawa: Urząd do spraw Kombatantów i Osób Represjonowanych, 2010

Coutouvidis, John, *Reynolds Jaime, Poland 1939–1947*, Leicester: Leicester University Press, 1986

Crankshaw, Edward, *Gestapo, narzędzie tyranii*, Warszawa: Książka i Wiedza, 1959

Crawford, Steve, *Front wschodni. Dzień po dniu, 1941–45*, Ożarów Mazowiecki: Olesiejuk, 2009

Czajewski, Wiktor, *Ilustrowany przewodnik po Warszawie na rok 1892*, Warszawa: Sowa, 2009

Czajkowski, Zbigniew G., *Warsaw 1944. An Insurgent's Journal of the Uprising*, Barnsley: Pen & Sword Military, 2012

Czajkowski-Dębczyński, Zbigniew, *Dziennik Powstańca*, Kraków: Wydawnictwo Literackie, 1969

Czarski, Andrzej, *Najmłodsi żołnierze walczącej Warszawy*, Warszawa: Instytut Wydawniczy PAX, 1971

Czugajewski, Ryszard, *Na barykadach, w kanałach i gruzach Czerniakowa*, Warszawa: Instytut Wydawniczy PAX, 1970

Dallin, Alexander, *German Rule in Russia 1941–1945. A Study of Occupation Policies*, London: Macmillan Press, 1981

Davies, Norman, *Rising '44. 'The Battle for Warsaw'*, New York: Macmillan, 2003

The Days of Freedom, ed. Kowal, Paweł, Ukielski, Paweł, Warszawa: Muzeum Powstania Warszawskiego, 2009

Deczkowski, Juliusz B., *Wspomnienia żołnierza baonu AK „Zośka"*, Warszawa: Wydawnictwo Instytutu Historii PAN, 1998

Dembowski Peter S., *Christians in the Warsaw Ghetto. An Epitaph for the Unremembered*, Notre Dame, IN: University of Notre Dame Press, 2005

Die Ostfront 1943/44. Der Krieg im Osten und an den Nebenfronten, Vol. VIII, ed. Frieser, Karl-Heinz, Schmider, Klaus, Schonherr, Klaus, Schreiber, Gerhard, Ungvary, Krisztian, Wegner, Bernd, München: Deutsche Verlags-Anstalt, 2007

Die tödliche Utopie, ed. Möller, Horst, Dahm, Volker, Mehringer, Hartmut, München: Institut für Zeitgeschichte, 1999

Dirks, Carl, Janßen, Karl, *Der Krieg der Generale. Hitler als Werkzeug der Wehrmacht*, Berlin: Propyläen, 1999

Dobrosław, Kobielski, *Warszawa z lotu Ptaka*, Warszawa: Interpress, 1971

Drabienko, Edward, *Jedno życie. Wspomnienia z lat 1942–1951*, Londyn: Polska Fundacja Kulturalna, 1987

Drozdowski, Marian M., *Marceli Porowski. Prezydent Powstańczej Warszawy*, Warszawa: Vipart, 2010

Dunin-Wąsowicz, Krzysztof, *Warszawa w latach 1939–1945*, Vol. V, Warszawa: Państwowe Wydawnictwo Naukowe, 1984

Dyakov, Yuri, Bushuyeva, Tatyana, *Red Army and the Wehrmacht. How the Soviets Militarized Germany, 1922–33, and Paved the Way for Fascism*, New York: Prometheus Books, 1995

Dzieci i młodzież w latach drugiej Wojny Światowej, ed. Pilichowski, Czesław, Warszawa: Państwowe Wydawnictwo Naukowe, 1982

Dzieciństwo i wojna, ed. Mazurczyk, Joanna, Zawanowska, Krystyna, Warszawa: Czytelnik, 1983

Dzięciołowski, Stanisław *Parlament Polski podziemnej 1939–1945*, Warszawa: Wydawnictwo Sejmowe, 2004

Dzienniki z Powstania Warszawskiego, ed. Pasiewicz, Zuzanna, Łomianki: LTW, 2004

Dzier, Tadeusz, *Myśmy tu zawsze byli … Dziennik z Powstania Warszawskiego 27 VII 1944–3 x 1944*, Warszawa: Państwowy Instytut Wydawniczy, 1982

Dzikiewicz, Lech, *Zbrodnia Stalina na Warszawie*, Warszawa: Bellona, 1996

Edelman-Margolis, Alina, *Ala z Elementarza*, Londyn: Aneks, 1994

Eksterminacja ludności w Polsce, w czasie okupacji Niemieckiej 1939–1945, Poznań, Warszawa: Wydawnictwo Zachodnie, 1962

Engelking, Barbara, Libionka, Dariusz, *Żydzi w Powstańczej Warszawie,* Warszawa: Stowarzyszenie Centrum badań nad Zagładą Żydów, 2009

Englert, Juliusz L., *Generał Bór-Komorowski,* Londyn: Polska Fundacja Kulturalna, 1994

Erickson, John, *The Road to Berlin. Stalin's War with Germany,* Vol. II, London: Grafton Books, 1985

Exodus Warszawy. Ludzie i miasto po Powstaniu 1944. I: Pamiętniki. Relacje, ed. Berezowska, Małgorzata, Borecka, Emilia, Dunin-Wąsowicz, Krzysztof, Korpetta, Jacek, Szwankowska, Hanna, Warszawa: Państwowy Instytut Wydawniczy, 1992

Exodus Warszawy. Ludzie i miasto po Powstaniu 1944. II: Pamiętniki. Relacje, ed. Berezowska, Małgorzata, Borecka, Emilia, Dunin-Wąsowicz, Krzysztof, Korpetta, Jacek, Szwankowska, Hanna, Warszawa: Państwowy Instytut Wydawniczy, 1993

Exodus Warszawy. Ludzie i miasto po Powstaniu Warszawskim 1944. III: Archiwalia, ed. Kazimierski, Józef, Skorwider, Danuta, Śreniawa-Szypiowski, Romuald, Warszawa: Państwowy Instytut Wydawniczy, 1994

Exodus Warszawy. Ludzie i miasto po Powstaniu Warszawskim 1944. IV: Archiwalia, ed. Kazimierski, Józef, Skorwider, Danuta, Śreniawa-Szypiowski, Romuald, Warszawa: Państwowy Instytut Wydawniczy, 1994

Exodus Warszawy. Ludzie i miasto po Powstaniu Warszawskim 1944. V: Prasa, ed. Górski, Jan, Kersten, Krystyna, Szapiro, Paweł, Wiśniewska, Maria, Warszawa: Państwowy Instytut Wydawniczy, 1995

Fenby, Jonathan, *Alliance. The Inside Story of how Roosevelt, Stalin and Churchill Won One War and Began Another,* London, Sydney: Pocket Books, 2008

Fritz, Stephen G., *Frontsoldaten. The German Soldier in World War II,* Kentucky: University Press of Kentucky, 1995

Garliński, Józef, *Poland in the Second World War,* New York: Macmillan, 1985

Garliński, Józef, *The Survival of Love. Memoirs of a Resistance Officer,* Oxford: Basil Blackwell, 1991

Gdy zaczniemy walczyć miłością. Portrety kapelanów Powstania Warszawskiego, ed. Górny, Grzegorz, Kopiński, Aleksander, Warszawa: Muzeum Powstania Warszawskiego, 2004

Gellately, Robert, *Stalin's Curse. Battling for Communism in War and Cold War*, Oxford: Oxford University Press, 2013

Generał Tadeusz Bór-Komorowski w relacjach i dokumentach, ed. Kunert, Andrzej Krzysztof, Warszawa: Oficyna Wydawnicza Rytm, 2000

German Army Elite Units 1939–45, ed. Williamson, Gordon, New York: Osprey Publishing, 2002

German Places of Extermination in Poland, ed. Lachendro, Jacek, Marki: Parma & Press, 2007

Gilbert, Gustav M., *Nuremberg Diary*, New York: Da Capo Press, 1995

Giziowski, Richard, *The Enigma of General Blaskowitz*, London: Leo Cooper; New York: Hippocrene Books, 1997

Goldensohn, Leon, *The Nuremberg Interviews*, London: Pimlico, 2006

Górecki, Ryszard, *Przemoczone pod plecakiem osiemnaście lat*, Warszawa: Książka i Wiedza, 1974

Górski, Jan, *Warszawa w latach 1944–1949* VI: *Odbudowa*, Warszawa: Państwowe Wydawnictwo Naukowe, 1988

Gozdawa-Gołębiowski, Jan, *Obszar Warszawski Armii Krajowej*, Lublin: Redakcja Wydawnictw Katolickiego Uniwersytetu Lubelskiego, 1992

Grünberg, Karol, *SS-czarna gwardia Hitlera*, Warszawa: Książka i Wiedza, 1975

Grunwald, Zdzisław, *Żubry na Żoliborzu. Wspomnienia żołnierzy Powstania Warszawskiego*, Warszawa: Stowarzyszenie Środowiska Żołnierzy AK „Żywiciel", 1993

Grupa Bojowa 'Krybar' w walce o Powiśle i Uniwersytet Warszawski, ed. Boruń, Krzysztof, Warszawa: Wydawnictwa Uniwersytetu Warszawskiego, 1995

Grynberg, Mikołaj, *Ocaleni z XX wieku: po nas nikt już nie opowie, najwyżej ktoś przeczyta . . .* , Warszawa: Świat Książki, 2012

Gryżewski, Tadeusz, *Harcerska poczta polowa Powstania Warszawskiego 1944*, Warszawa: Agencja Wydawnicza Ruch, 1966

Guderian, Heinz, *Panzer Leader*, London: Penguin Books, 2000

Hałko, Lech, *Kotwica Herbem wybranym*, Warszawa: Askon, 1999

Hanfstaengl, Ernst, *Hitler. The Missing Years*, London: Eyre & Spottiswoode, 1957

Hanson, Joanna K.M., *The Civilian Population and the Warsaw Uprising of 1944*, New York: Cambridge University Press, 1982

Hempel, Andrew, *Poland in World War II. An Illustrated Military History*, New York: Hippocrene Books, 2000

The 'Hermann Göring' Division, ed. Williamson, Gordon, New York: Osprey Publishing, 2003

Heydecker, Joe J., Leeb, Johannes, *Der Nurnberger Prozess. Bilanz der Tausend Jahre*, Köln: Kiepenheuer & Witsch, 1959

Hinze, Rolf, *East Front Drama 1944. The Withdrawal Battle of Army Center*, Winnipeg: J.J. Fedorowicz, 1996

Hinze, Rolf, *To the Bitter End. The Final Battles of Army Groups North Ukraine, A, Centre, Eastern Front 1944-45*, Solihull: Helion & Company, 2005

Historia Polski w liczbach. Ludność. Terytorium, ed. Jezierskiego Andrzeja, Warszawa: Główny Urząd Statystyczny, 1993

Hitler and his Generals. Military Conferences 1942-1945, ed. Heiber, Helmut, Glantz, David M., New York: Enigma Books, 2004

Hitlerowski Terror na wsi Polskiej 1939-1945. Zestawienie większych akcji represyjnych, ed. Madajczyk, Czesław, Warszawa: Państwowe Wydawnictwo Naukowe, 1965

Hoffman, Joachim, *Die Geschichte der Wlassow-Armee*, Freiburg: Verlag Rombach, 1984

Honkisz, Władysław, *Trudna Historia. Polemiki i repliki*, Warszawa: Instytut Naukowy im. generała dywizji Edwina Rozłubirskiego, 2000

Inferno of Choices. Poles and the Holocaust, ed. Rejak, Sebastian, Frister, Elżbieta, Warszawa: Oficyna Wydawnicza Rytm, 2011

Ingaro, Christian, *Czarni Myśliwi. Brygada Dirlewangera*, Wołowiec: Czarne, 2011

Ingrao, Christian, *The SS Dirlewanger Brigade. The History of the Black Hunters*, New York: Skyhorse, 2011

Invitation to Moscow. Trial of the 16 Leaders of the Polish Underground State, ed. Kunert, Andrzej K., Walkowski, Zygmunt, Warszawa: Urząd Miasta Stołecznego Warszawy, 2005

Iranek-Osmecki, Kazimierz, *Powołanie i przeznaczenie. Wspomnienia oficera Komendy Głównej AK 1940-1944*, Warszawa: Państwowy Instytut Wydawniczy, 1998

Iwanow, Nikołaj, *Powstanie Warszawskie widziane z Moskwy*, Kraków: Znak, 2012

Jagielski, Jan, *Niezatarte ślady Getta Warszawskiego*, Warszawa: Oficyna Wydawnicza Mówią Wieki, 2008

Jankowski, Stanisław, *Z fałszywym Ausweisem w prawdziwej Warszawie. Wspomnienia 1939–1946*, Vol. I, Warszawa: Państwowy Instytut Wydawniczy, 1980

Jankowski, Stanisław, *Z fałszywym Ausweisem w prawdziwej Warszawie. Wspomnienia 1939–1946*, Vol. II, Warszawa: Państwowy Instytut Wydawniczy, 1988

Jasiński, Grzegorz, *Żoliborz 1944. Dzieje militarne II obwodu okręgu Warszawa AK w Powstaniu Warszawskim*, Pruszków: Oficyna Wydawnicza Ajaks, 2008

Jastrzębski, Stanisław, *Zaczęło się pod Arsenałem*, Warszawa: Czytelnik, 1981

Jeffrey, Ron, *Wisła jak krew czerwona. Wspomnienia Anglika-Żołnierza Armii Krajowej*, Warszawa: Bellona, 2008

Jewsiewicki, Władysław, *Poezja i film Powstania Warszawskiego 1944*, Toruń: Adam Marszałek, 2004

Jewsiewicki, Władysław, *Powstanie Warszawskie 1944. Okiem Polskiej kamery*, Warszawa: Interpress, 1989

Kamiński, Aleksander, *Kamienie na Szaniec*, Katowice: Wydawnictwo Śląsk, 1958

Kamiński, Aleksander, *„Zośka" i „Parasol". Opowieść o niektórych ludziach i niektórych akcjach dwóch batalionów harcerskich*, Warszawa: Iskry, 1970

The Kaminski Brigade. A History, 1941–1945, ed. Munoz, Antonio J., New York: Axis Europa Books, 2003

Karski, Jan, *Wielkie Mocarstwa wobec Polski 1919–1945. Od Wersalu do Jałty*, Lublin: Wydawnictwo Uniwersytetu Marii Curii-Skłodowskiej, 1998

Kaska, Adam, *Nadwiślańskie Reduty. Czerniaków, Powiśle, Żoliborz*, Warszawa: Książka i Wiedza, 1971

Kasprzak, Jerzy, *Tropami powstańczej przesyłki. Zapiski Zawiszaka*, Warszawa: Czytelnik, 1969

Katalog Muzeum Powstania Warszawskiego, ed. Dąbkowska-Cichocka, Lena, Gawin, Dariusz, Kowal, Paweł, Ołdakowski, Jan, Warszawa: Muzeum Powstania Warszawskiego, 2006

Kempka, Erich, *I Was Hitler's Chauffeur. The Memoirs of Erich Kempka*, London: Frontline Books, 2010

Kępińska-Bazylewicz, Halina, *Łączniczka Kora*, Warszawa: Burchard Edition, 1994

Khrushchev, Nikita Sergeevich, *Khrushchev Remembers. II: The Last Testament*, New York: Penguin Books, 1974

Kirchmayer, Jerzy, *Powstanie Warszawskie*, Warszawa: Książka i Wiedza, 1959

Klapdor, Ewald, *Viking Panzers. The German 5th SS Tank Regiment in the East in World War II*, Mechanicsburg, PA: Stackpole Books, 2011

Kledzik, Maciej, *62 dni bez porucznika 'Rygla'. Reportaż z walk w Śródmieściu*, Hove: Caldra House, 1993

Kledzik, Maciej, *Królewska 16*, Warszawa: Instytut Wydawniczy PAX, 1984

Kledzik, Maciej, *Między Marszałkowską i Żelazną, Al. Sikorskiego i Pańską. IV Zgrupowanie AK „Gurt" w Powstaniu Warszawskim*, Warszawa: BICO, 1994

Klimaszewski, Tadeusz, *Verbrennungskommando Warschau*, Warszawa: Czytelnik, 1959

Klisze Pamięci. Z fotokroniki Powstania Warszawskiego, ed. Rogalska, Barbara, Sołtan, Andrzej, Warszawa: Agencja Omnipress, 1984

Kliszko, Zenon, *Powstanie Warszawskie. Wspomnienia i refleksje*, Warszawa: Książka i Wiedza, 1968

Kochanski, Halik, *The Eagle Unbowed. Poland and the Poles in the Second World War*, London: Penguin Books, 2012

Koehl, Robert L., *The SS. A History 1919–45*, Stroud: Tempus, 2004

Kołodziejczyk, Edward, *Tryptyk Warszawski. Wypędzenie. Dulag 121. Tułaczka*, Warszawa: Wydawnictwo Ministerstwa Obrony Narodowej, 1984

Komornicki, Stanisław, *Na barykadach Warszawy. Pamiętnik podchorążego „Nałęcza"*, Warszawa: Oficyna Wydawnicza Rytm, 2003

Komorowski, Tadeusz 'Bór', *Powstanie Warszawskie*, Warszawa: Oficyna Wydawnicza Rytm, 2008

Komorowski, Tadeusz 'Bór', *Armia Podziemna*, Szczecin: Suplement, 1981

Kopf, Stanisław, *Lata Okupacji. Kronika Fotograficzna walczącej Warszawy*, Warszawa: Instytut Wydawniczy PAX, 1989

Kopf, Stanisław, *Muzy tamtych dni*, Warszawa: Askon, 2002

Kopf, Stanisław, *Powiśle. Warszawskie Termopile 1944. Przewodnik historyczny po miejscach walk i pamięci czasu okupacji i Powstania Warszawskiego*, Warszawa: Fundacja 'Wystawa Warszawa walczy 1939–1945', 1999

Kopf, Stanisław, *Wyrok na miasto. Wypędzenie, rabunek, zagłada. Warszawskie Termopile 1944–1945*, Warszawa: Fundacja 'Wystawa Warszawa walczy 1939–1945', 2001

Korbonski, Stefan, *Fighting Warsaw. The Story of the Polish Underground State 1939–1945*, New York: Hippocrene Books, 2004

Korboński, Stefan, *Polskie Państwo Podziemne. Przewodnik po Podziemiu z lat 1939–1945*, Bydgoszcz: Nasza Przyszłość, 1989

Korboński, Stefan, *W imieniu Rzeczypospolitej …*, Warszawa: Bellona, 1991

Korwin, Marta, *In Spite of Everything*, Kilmarnock: Standard Printing Works, 1942

Koschorrek, Gunter K., *Blood Red Snow*, Yorkshire: Frontline Books, 2011

Koskodan, Kenneth K., *No Greater Ally. The Untold Story of Poland's Forces in World War II*, Oxford: Osprey Publishing, 2011

Kosuń, Jadwiga, Kwaśnik, Badmajew, *Pamiętnik Jagody*, Warszawa: Bellona, 2003

Kotańska, Anna, Topolska, Anna, *Warsaw. Past and Present*, Marki: Parma Press, 2005

Kotarba, Ryszard, *Niemiecki w Płaszowie 1942–1945*, Warszawa, Kraków: Instytut Pamięci Narodowej, 2009

Kowalewski, Lech, *W Hitlerowskim obozie pracy Wspomnienia z Kędzierzyna 1941–1945*, Opole: Wydawnictwa Instytutu Śląskiego, 1973

Krause, Werner H., Dieter-Karl, Albert, *Aż wszystko legnie w gruzach …*, Warszawa: Książka i Wiedza, 1960

Krawczyńska, Jadwiga, *Zapiski Dziennikarki Warszawskiej 1939–1947*, Warszawa: Państwowy Instytut Wydawniczy, 1971

Krężel, Janusz, *Szare Szeregi na terenie południowo- wschodniej Polski. I: Konspiracja harcerek 1939–1945*, Tarnów: CNC, 1996

Krutol, Edward J., *Bez Munduru. Wspomnienia z Powstania Warszawskiego*, Warszawa: Wydawnictwo Spółdzielcze, 1990

Kubalski, Tadeusz, *W szeregach „BASZTY"*, Warszawa: Wydawnictwo Ministerstwa Obrony Narodowej, 1969

Kubalski, Tadeusz, *Żołnierze walczącej Warszawy*, Warszawa: Instytut Prasy i Wydawnictw 'Novum', 1988

Kulesza, Juliusz, *Sierpień przez całe życie*, Warszawa: Anta, 1994

Kulesza, Juliusz, *Z tasiemką na czołgi. Wspomnienia z walk na Starym Mieście w sierpniu 1944 roku*, Warszawa: Czytelnik, 1979

Kulski, Eugeniusz J., *Umierając żyjemy*, Warszawa: Czytelnik, 1984

Kunert, Andrzej K., *Rzeczpospolita Walcząca. Powstanie Warszawskie 1944. Kalendarium*, Warszawa: Wydawnictwo Sejmowe, 1994

Kurdwanowski, Jan, *Mrówka na Szachownicy*, Warszawa: Educator, 1993

Kwiatkowski, Maciej J., *Tu mówi Powstańcza Warszawa … Dni Powstania w audycjach Polskiego Radia i dokumentach niemieckich*, Warszawa: Państwowy Instytut Wydawniczy, 1994

Leksykon Militariów Powstania Warszawskiego, ed. Komudy. Michała, Warszawa: Instytut Pamięci Narodowej, Muzeum Powstania Warszawskiego, 2012

Leszczyński. Kazimierz, *Heinz Reinefarth*, Warszawa, Poznań: Wydawnictwo Zachodnie, 1961

Linge. Heinz, *With Hitler to the End. The Memoirs of Adolf Hitler's Valet*, London: Frontline Books, 2009

Lokajski. Eugeniusz, *Fotografie z Powstania Warszawskiego*, Warszawa: Gebethner i Ska, 1994

Lubicz-Nycz. Bronisław, *Batalion „Kiliński" AK 1940–1944*, ed. Strzembosz, Tomasz, Warszawa: Państwowe Wydawnictwo Naukowe, 1986 ,

Lubomirska, Wanda, *Karmazynowy Reportaż*, London: Wydawnictwa Polskiej Biblioteki w Londynie, 1946

Ludność cywilna w Powstaniu Warszawskim. I: Pamiętniki. Relacje. Zeznania, ed. Drozdowski, Marian M., Maniakówna, Maria, Strzembosz, Tomasz, Warszawa: Państwowy Instytut Wydawniczy, 1974

Ludność cywilna w Powstaniu Warszawskim. II: Archiwalia, ed. Getter, Marek, Jankowski, Andrzej, Warszawa: Państwowy Instytut Wydawniczy, 1974

Ludność cywilna w Powstaniu Warszawskim. III: Prasa, druki ulotne i inne publikacje powstańcze, ed. Bartoszewski, Władysław, Warszawa, Państwowy Instytut Wydawniczy, 1974

MacLean, French, *The Cruel Hunters. SS-Sonderkommando, Dirlewanger. Hitler's Most Notorious Anti-Partisan Unit*, Atglen, PA: Schiffer Military History, 1998

MacLean, French L., *The Ghetto Men. The SS Destruction of the Jewish Warsaw Ghetto April–May 1943*, Atglen, PA: Schiffer Military History, 2001

Mącior-Majka, Beata, *Generalny Plan Wschodni. Aspekty ideologiczny, polityczny i ekonomiczny*, Kraków: Avalon, 2007

Madajczyk, Czesław, *Generalna Gubernia w planach hitlerowskich*, Warsaw: Państwowe Wydawnictwo Naukowe, 1961

Madajczyk, Czesław, *Polityka III Rzeszy w okupowanej Polsce*, Vols. I & II, Warszawa: Państwowe Wydawnictwo Naukowe, 1970

Mallmann, Klaus M., Paul, Gerhard, *Karrieren der Gewalt. Nationalsozialistische Taterbiographien*, Darmstadt: Wissenschaftliche Buchgesellschaft, 2004

Man to Man … Destruction of the Polish Intelligentsia in the Years 1939–1945, Warszawa: Rada Ochrony Pamięci Walk i Męczeństwa, 2009

Manstein, Erich von, *Lost Victories*, ed. Powell, Anthony G., St Paul, MN: Zenith Press, 2004

Manvell, Roger, Fraenkel, Heinrich, *Heinrich Himmler*, London: Heinemann, 1965

Mańkowski, Zygmunt, *Między Wisłą a Bugiem 1939–1944. Studium o polityce i postawach społeczeństwa*, Lublin: Wydawnictwo Lubelskie, 1978

Margules, Józef, *Przyczółki warszawskie*, Warszawa: Wydawnictwo Ministerstwa Obrony Narodowej, 1962

Marszałek Polski Michał Żymierski, ed. Kosiorek-Dulian, Barbary, Warszawa: Wydawnictwo Ministerstwa Obrony Narodowej, 1983

Masakra w Klasztorze, ed. Paluszkiewicz, Felicjan, Warszawa: Rhetos, 2003

Materiały do Słownika Biograficznego kobiet uczestniczek walk o Niepodległość Polski 1939–1945. I: Poległe i zmarłe w II Wojnie Światowej, nazwiska od A do J, ed. Turkawska, Wanda, Warszawa: Towarzystwo Miłośników Historii, 1978

Matłachowski, Jan, *Kulisy genezy Powstania Warszawskiego*, Warszawa: Ojczyzna, 1994

Mazur, Grzegorz, *Biuro Informacji i Propagandy SZP-ZWZ-AK 1939–1945*, Warszawa: Instytut Wydawniczy PAX, 1987

Miasto na szklanych negatywach. Warszawa 1916 w fotografiach Willy'ego Römera, ed. Kubaczyk, Ewa, Warszawa: Dom Spotkań z Historią, 2010

Michaelis, Rolf, *Russians in the Waffen-SS*, Atglen, PA: Schiffer Military History, 2009

Miejsca pamięci gminy Rembertów, ed. Pasternak, Jan, Warszawa, Rembertów: Wydawnictwo Sióstr Loretanek, 1995

Mikorska, Maria, *Spring Held no Hope. The Facts of the German Occupation of Poland*, Edinburgh: The Riverside Press, 1941

Misch, Rochus, *Der letzte Zeuge. Ich war Hitlers Telefonist, Kurier und Leibwachter*, München: Piper Verlag GmbH, 2008

Mistecka, Maria L., *Zgromadzenie sióstr Zmartwychwstania Pańskiego w czasie Powstania Warszawskiego*, Lublin: Katolicki Uniwersytet Lubelski, 1980

Mitcham, Samuel W., *The Panzer Legions. A Guide to the German Army Tank Divisions of World War II and Their Commanders*, Mechanicsburg, PA: Stackpole Books, 2000

Molotov Remembers. Inside Kremlin Politics, ed. Resis, Albert, Chicago: Ivan R. Dee, 1993

Müller, Klaus J., *The Army, Politics and Society in Germany 1933–45. Studies in the Army's Relation to Nazism*, Manchester: Manchester University Press, 1987

Munoz, Antonio J., Romanko, Oleg V., *Hitler's White Russians: Collaboration, Extermination and Anti-Partisan Warfare in Byelorussia, 1941–1944*, New York: Europa Books, 2003

Na oczach Kremla. Tragedia walczącej Warszawy w świetle dokumentów Rosyjskich, ed. Knecka, Krystyna, Warszawa: Agencja Wydawnicza 'Egros', Wojskowy Instytut Historyczny, 1994

Nawrocka, Barbara, *Powszedni dzień dramatu*, Warszawa: Czytelnik, 1961

Nawrocka, Barbara, *Przed godziną „W"*, Warszawa: Nasza Księgarnia, 1969

Nazarewicz, Ryszard, *Z problematyki politycznej Powstania Warszawskiego 1944*, Warszawa: Wydawnictwo Ministerstwa Obrony Narodowej, 1980

Nazism 1919–1945. A History in Documents and Eyewitness Accounts. Vols I–II: *Foreign Policy, War and Racial Extermination*, ed. Noakes, Jeremy, Pridham, Geoffrey, New York: Schocken Books, 1990

Nazism 1919–1945. Vol. II: *Foreign Policy, War and Racial Extermination. A Document Reader*, ed. Noakes, Jeremy, Pridham, Geoffrey, New York: Schocken Books, 1988

Neitzel, Sonke, Welzer, Harald, *Soldaten. On Fighting, Killing, and Dying. The Secret World War II Tapes of Germany's PoWs*, London, New York: Simon & Schuster, 2012

Niemcy o zbrodniach Wehrmachtu. Fakty, analizy, dyskusje, ed. Lulińscy, Barbara, Lulińscy, Daniel, Warszawa: Bellona, 1997

Nir, Yehuda, *The Lost Childhood. A Memoir*, San Diego, CA: Harcourt Brace Jovanovich, 1989

Niżyński, Leszek, *Batalion Miotła*, Warszawa: Instytut Wydawniczy PAX, 1992

Nowak, Szymon, *Przyczółek Czerniakowski 1944*, Zabrze: Inforteditions, 2011

Oddziały Powstania Warszawskiego, ed. Kowalik, Alicja, Warszawa: Instytut Wydawniczy Związków Zawodowych, 1988

Odział Kobiecy Warszawskiego Kedywu. Dokumenty z lat 1943–1945, ed. Rybicka, Hanna, Warszawa: Wydawnictwa Uniwersytetu Warszawskiego, 2002

Odziemkowski, Janusz, *Warszawa w wojnie obronnej 1939 roku*, Warszawa: Państwowe Wydawnictwo Naukowe, 1989

Okolski, Tadeusz, *Batalion „Dzik" w Powstaniu Warszawskim*, Warszawa: Wydawnictwo Fundacji 'Historia pro Futuro', 1994

Olszewski, Andrzej, *Pierwsi w mieście*, Warszawa: Krajowa Agencja Wydawnicza, 1975

Oosreling, Paul, *SS-Standartenfuhrer Johannes Mühlenkampund seine Manner*, Vol. II, Erpe: De Krijger, 2005

Osiem misji Kuriera z Warszawy, ed. Kunert, Andrzej, K., Kunert, Zofia, Warszawa: Edipresse Książki, 2005

Ostrowska, Elżbieta, *Kanały: Z tajemnic Powstańczej Warszawy. Łączność dowodzenia i ewakuacje na trasach południowych*, Warszawa: Askon, 2003

Owen, James, *Nuremberg. Evil on Trial*, London: Headline Review, 2006

Padfield, Peter, *Himmler. Reichsfuhrer-SS*, London: Papermac, 1995

Pamiętniki żołnierzy baonu „Zośka". Powstanie Warszawskie, ed. Szumiński Tadeusz, Warszawa: Nasza Księgarnia, 1970

Pamiętniki żołnierzy baonu AK „Zośka". I: *Wola*, ed Sikorski, Piotr, Wyganowski, Stanisław, Warszawa: Społeczny Komitet Opieki nad Grobami Poległych Żołnierzy Batalionu 'Zośka', 2013*Pamiętniki żołnierzy baonu AK „Zośka".* II: *Starówka*, ed. Sikorski, Piotr, Wyganowski, Stanisław, Warszawa: Społeczny Komitet Opieki nad Grobami Poległych Żołnierzy Batalionu 'Zośka', 2013*Pamiętniki żołnierzy baonu AK „Zośka".* III: *Czerniaków*, ed. Sikorski, Piotr, Wyganowski, Stanisław, Warszawa: Społeczny Komitet Opieki nad Grobami Poległych Żołnierzy Batalionu 'Zośka', 2013*Panzer Grenadiere. Der Panzerdivision "Wiking" im Bild*, ed. Hack, Franz, Hahl, Fritz, Coburg: National Europa Verlag GmbH, 1984

Patzwall, Klaus D., *Das Bandenkampfabzeichen 1944–1945*, Norderstedt: Verlag Klaus D. Patzwall, 2003

Paulsson, Gunnar S., *Secret City. The Hidden Jews of Warsaw 1940–1945*, London: Yale University Press, 2002

Paulsson, Gunnar S., *Utajone miasto. Żydzi po aryjskiej stronie Warszawy (1940–1945)*, Kraków: Znak, Centrum Badań nad Zagładą Żydów IFiS PAN, 2009

Pełczyński, Tadeusz, *Armia krajowa i Powstanie Warszawskie*, Kraków: Muzeum Armii Krajowej, 2003

Pełczyński, Zbigniew, *A Life Remembered*, Guildford: Grosvenor House, 2012

Pełnić służbę ... Z pamiętników i wspomnień harcerek Warszawy 1939–1945, ed. Zawadzka, Anna, Zawadzka, Zofia, Warszawa: Państwowy Instytut Wydawniczy, 1983

Pietras, Stanisław, Zgrupowanie „Sosna", batalion „Chrobry I", Warszawa: Warsgraf, 1993

Pietrzykowski, Jan, Tajemnice archiwum gestapo. Przyczynki do historii niemieckiej okupacji w Polsce, Katowice: Śląski Instytut Naukowy, 1989

Pinkus, Oscar, The War Aims and Strategies of Adolf Hitler, Jefferson, NC: McFarland & Company, 2005

Piotrowski, Jan, Jak zdobyć Kościół św. Krzyża i Komendę Policji?, Warszawa: MEDIArt, 1994

Piotrowski, Stanisław, Proces Hansa Franka i dowody Polskie przeciw SS, Warszawa: Wydawnictwo Prawnicze, 1970

Piotrowski, Stanisław, Dziennik Hansa Franka, Warszawa: Wydawnictwo Prawnicze, 1956

Podgórska-Klawe, Zofia, Szpitale Warszawskie 1388–1945, Warszawa: Państwowe Wydawnictwo Naukowe, 1975

Podlewski, Stanisław, Rapsodia Żoliborska, Vols. I & II, Warszawa: Instytut Wydawniczy PAX, 1979

Podlewski, Stanisław, Wolność krzyżami się znaczy, Warszawa: Ośrodek Dokumentacji i Studiów Społecznych, 1989

Pohanka, Reinhard, Pflichterfüller. Hitlers Helfer in der Ostmark, Wien: Picus Verlag, 1997

Polak, Tadeusz, 63 dni Powstania Warszawskiego. Dziennik przeżyć cywila, Kraków: Instytut Wydawniczy IW, 1946

Poległym chwała, wolność żywym. Oddziały walczącej Warszawy, ed. Panecka, Agnieszka, Warszawa: Muzeum Powstania Warszawskiego, 2005

Pollack, Martin, The Dead Man in the Bunker. Discovering My Father, London: Faber & Faber, 2006Polonia wobec Powstania Warszawskiego. Studia i dokumenty, ed. Drozdowski, Marian M., Warszawa: Oficyna Wydawnicza, 2001

Polonsky, Antony, The Jews in Poland and Russia, Vol. III: 1914–2008, Oxford, 2012

Polska 1939–1945. Straty osobowe i ofiary represji pod dwoma okupacjami, ed. Marterski, Wojciech, Szarota, Tomasz, Warszawa: Instytut Pamięci Narodowej, 2009

Polsko-Brytyjska współpraca wywiadowcza podczas II Wojny Światowej. II: Wybór dokumentów, ed. Ciechanowski, Jan S., Warszawa: Naczelna Dyrekcja Archiwów Państwowych, 2005

Potulicka-Łatyńska, Teresa, *Dziennik Powstańczy 1944*, Warszawa: Kwadryga, 1998

Powstanie w Ich pamięci, ed. Panecka, Agnieszka, Warszawa: Muzeum Powstania Warszawskiego, 2008

Powstanie Warszawskie 1944, ed. Lewandowska, Stanisława, Martina, Bernda, Warszawa: Wydawnictwo Polsko-Niemieckie, 1999

Powstanie Warszawskie 1944. Wybór dokumentów. I: *Preliminaria operacyjne. Natarcie powstańców i opanowanie miasta 31 V–4 VIII 1944*, ed. Matusak, Piotr, Warszawa: Agencja Wydawnicza Egross, 1997

Powstanie Warszawskie 1944. Wybór dokumentów. II, Part 1: *Okres przejściowy 8–10 VIII 1944*, ed. Matusak, Piotr, Warszawa: Agencja Wydawnicza Egross, 2002

Powstanie Warszawskie. Antologia Tekstów nieobecnych, ed. Sawicki, Jacek Z., Toruń: Wydawnictwo Adam Marszałek, 2004

Powstanie Warszawskie. Studia i materiały z konferencji naukowej, ed. Koseski, Adam, Pułtusk: Wyższa Szkoła Humanistyczna im. Aleksandra Gieysztora, 2005

Powstanie Warszawskie. The Warsaw Uprising, ed. Kamińska, Elżbieta, Kamiński, Marek, Mark.: Parma Press, 2004

Prasa Powstania Warszawskiego w zbiorach Biblioteki Publicznej m. st. Warszawy. I: *Katalog*, ed. Lewandowska, Grażyna M., Warszawa: Biblioteka Publiczna m. st. Warszawy, 2004

Przewłocka, Irena, *Miasto w ogniu*, Warszawa: Spółdzielnia Wydawniczo-Oświatowa, 1949

Przewodnik po upamiętnionych miejscach walk i męczeństwa. Lata wojny 1939–1945, Warszawa: Sport i Turystyka, 1964

Przewoźnik, Andrzej, Strzembosz, Adam, *Generał „Nil"*, Warszawa: Światowy Związek Żołnierzy Armii Krajowej, Oficyna Wydawnicza Rytm, 1999

Przygoński, Antoni, *Udział PPR i AL w Powstaniu Warszawskim*, Warszawa: Książka i Wiedza, 1970

Przygoński, Antoni, *Z problematyki Powstania Warszawskiego*, Warszawa: Wydawnictwo Ministerstwa Obrony Narodowej, 1964

Raczyński, Edward, *W sojuszniczym Londynie. Dziennik Ambasadora Edwarda Raczyńskiego 1939–1945*, Londyn: Instytut Polski i Muzeum im. gen. Sikorskiego, 1974 Raczyński, Edward, Żenczykowski, Tadeusz, *Od Genewy do Jałty. Rozmowy radiowe*, Londyn: Puls, 1988

Radzymińska, Józefa, *Zawsze niepodlegli*, Wrocław: Toporzeł, 1991

Raus, Erhard, *Panzer Operations. The Eastern Front Memoir of General Raus, 1941–1945*, New York: Da Capo Press, 2003

Read, Anthony, Fisher, David, *The Fall of Berlin*, London: Pimlico, 1993

Read, Anthony, *The Devil's Disciples. The Lives and Times of Hitler's Inner Circle*, London: Pimlico, 2004

Reese, Willy P., *Obcy samemu sobie. Nieludzka wojna. Rosja 1941–1944*, Gdańsk: Wydawnictwo, 2006

Reese, Willy Peter, *A Stranger to Myself. The Inhumanity of War. Russia, 1941–1944*, New York: Farrar, Straus & Giroux, 2005

Refleksje z Powstania 1944. Zofia Korbońska świadek historii, ed. Gogut, Anna, Waszyngton-Warszawa: Fundacja im. Stefana Korbońskiego, 2004

Reuth, Ralf G., *Goebbels*, London: Constable, 1993

Rhodes, Richard, *Masters of Death. The SS-Einsatzgruppen and the Invention of the Holocaust*, New York: Alfred A. Knopf, 2002

Rocki, Jan, *Dziewiąta Dywersyjna*, Warszawa: Wydawnictwo Ministerstwa Obrony Narodowej, 1973

Roosevelt and Stalin. The Failed Courtship, ed. Nisbet, Robert, London: Simon & Schuster, 1984

Rosłoniec, Włodzimierz, *Grupa „Krybar" Powiśle 1944*, Warszawa: Instytut Wydawniczy PAX, 1989

Rosłoniec, Włodzimierz, *Lato 1944*, Kraków: Znak, 1989

Rossino, Alexander B., *Hitler Strikes Poland. Blitzkrieg, Ideology, and Atrocity*, Kansas: University Press of Kansas, 2003

Rowecki, Stefan, *Walki uliczne*, Warszawa: ZP, 2013Rozłubirski, Edwin, *Ludzie z innego Świata*, Warszawa: Wydawnictwo Ministerstwa Obrony Narodowej, 1959Rudniewska, Alicja, Michelis, Adam de, *Pod rozkazami „Konrada". Pierwsza monografia III Zgrupowania obwodu Warszawskiego AK*, Warszawa: Oficyna Wydawnicza Volumen, 1993

Russell of Liverpool, Lord, *The Trial of Adolf Eichmann*, ed. Overy, Richard, London: Pimlico, 2002

Rutherford, Philip T., *Prelude to the Final Solution. The Nazi Program for Deporting Ethnic Poles, 1939–1941*, Kansas: University Press of Kansas, 2007

Rybicka, Hanna, *Oddział kobiecy warszawskiego Kedywu. Dokumenty z lat 1943–1945*, Warszawa: Wydawnictwa Uniwersytetu Warszawskiego, 2002

Rybicki, Józef R., *Notatki szefa Warszawskiego Kedywu*, Warszawa: Wydawnictwa Uniwersytetu Warszawskiego, 2001

Rzepecki, Jan, *Wspomnienia i przyczynki Historyczne*, Warszawa: Kraj, 1957

Sawicki, Tadeusz, *Front wschodni a Powstanie Warszawskie*, Warszawa: Państwowe Wydawnictwo Naukowe, 1989

Sawicki, Tadeusz, *Rozkaz zdławić powstanie. Niemcy I ich sojusznicy w walce z Powstaniem Warszawskim*, Warszawa: Bellona, 2010

Sawicki, Tadeusz, *Wyrok na miasto*, Warszawa: Bellona, 1993–2011

Scheiderbauer, Armin, *Adventures in My Youth. A German Soldier on the Eastern Front 1941–1945*, Solihull: Helion & Company, 2003

Schenk, Dieter, *KrakuerBurg Wawel jako ośrodek władzy generalnego gubernatora Hansa Franka w latach 1939–1945*, Kraków: Wysoki Zamek, 2013

Schroeder, Christa, *He Was My Chief. The Memoirs of Adolf Hitler's Secretary*, London: Frontline Books, 2009

Sęk-Małecki, Józef, *Armia Ludowa w Powstaniu Warszawskim. Wspomnienia*, Warszawa: Iskry, 1962

Siedem dróg do wolności, ed. Zawadzka, Mirosława, Zawadzki, Andrzej, Warszawa, Detroit, MI: Amerykańsko-Polskie Centrum Kulturalne, 2000

Sierakowska, Aniela, *Cały naród walczył*, Londyn: Oficyna Poetów i Malarzy, 1977

Skarżyński, Aleksander, *Polityczne Przyczyny Powstania Warszawskiego*, Warszawa: Państwowe Wydawnictwo Naukowe, 1964

Skoczek, Marian, *„Gurt"–„Kedyw" 1939–1945 w konspiracji i w Powstaniu*, Londyn: Veritas Foundation Publication Centre, 1987

Skrawek Wolnej Warszawy. Codzienność powstańczej Starówki w fotografii Jerzego Chojnackiego, ed. Maliszewska, Izabella, Walkowski, Zygmunt, Mikulski, Maciej, Warszawa: Muzeum Historyczne m. st. Warszawy, 2008

Śląski, Jerzy, *Polska Walcząca*, Warszawa: Instytut Wydawniczy PAX, 1990

Słomczyński, Adam, *W Warszawskim Arsenale. Wspomnienia archiwisty miejskiego 1939–1951*, Warszawa: Czytelnik, 1971

Słownik biograficzny kobiet odznaczonych orderem wojennym Virtuti Militari, Vol. I, ed. Zawacka, Elżbieta, Toruń: Fundacja 'Archiwum i Muzeum Pomorskie Armii Krajowej oraz Wojskowej Służby Polek', 2004

Smelser, Ronald, Syring, Enrico, *Die SS. Elite unter Dem Totenkopf. 30 Lebensläufe*, Paderborn: Ferdinand Schöningh, 2003

Snyder, Timothy, *Bloodlands. Europe Between Hitler and Stalin*, London: Random House, 2010

Sosabowski, Stanisław, *Freely I Served*, Nashville, TN: The Battery Press, 1982

Speer, Albert, *Inside the Third Reich*, London: Warner Books, 1993

The Spoils of War. World War II and its Aftermath. The Loss, Reappearance, and Recovery of Cultural Property, ed. Simpson, Elizabeth, New York: Harry N. Abrams, 1997

Spór o Powstanie. Powstanie Warszawskie w powojennej publicystyce polskiej 1945–1981, ed. Gawin, Dariusz, Warszawa: Muzeum Powstania Warszawskiego, 2004

Stachewicz, Piotr, *PARASOL. Dzieje oddziału do zadań specjalnych kierownictwa Dywersji Komendy Głównej Armii Krajowej*, Warszawa: Instytut Wydawniczy PAX, 1981

Stachewicz, Piotr, *Starówka 1944*, Warszawa: Wydawnictwo Ministerstwa Obrony Narodowej, 1983

Stahl, Erich, *Eyewitness to Hell. With the Waffen SS on the Eastern Front in W.W. II*, Bellingham, WA: Ryton Publications, 2009

Stawiński, Jerzy S., *Godzina „W". Węgrzy. Kanał*, Warszawa: Państwowy Instytut Wydawniczy, 1957

Stawiński, Jerzy S., *Kanał i inne opowiadania*, Warszawa: Czytelnik, 1981

Stawiński, Jerzy S., *Młodego Warszawiaka zapiski z urodzin*, Warszawa: Czytelnik, 1980

Stawiński, Jerzy S., *Opowieści powstańcze*, Warszawa: Trio, 2004

Steiner, Jean F., *Varsovie 44. L'Insurrection*, Paris: Flammarion, 1975

Stompor, Józef, *Płonące Lazarety. Powieść powstańcza*, Warszawa: Ludowa Spółdzielnia Wydawnicza, 1979

Straty Warszawy 1939–1945. Raport, ed. Fałkowski, Wojciech, Warszawa: Miasto Stołeczne Warszawa, 2005

Streit, Christian, *Keine Kameraden. Die Wehrmacht und die sowjetischen Kriegsgefangenen 1941–1945*, Bonn: Verlag J.H.W. Dietz Nachf., 1997

Stromenger, Aleksander, *Człowiek z zakalcem. Notatki wspomnieniowe z lat 1939–1945*, Warszawa: Instytut Wydawniczy PAX, 1970

Strzembosz, Tomasz, *Odbijanie i uwalnianie więźniów w Warszawie 1939–1944*, Warszawa: Państwowe Wydawnictwo Naukowe, 1972

Świadectwa Powstania Warszawskiego 1944, ed. Brożyna, Piotr, Wiśniewska-Tomczyszyn, Teresa, Warszawa: Kuria Metropolitalna Warszawska Wydział Duszpasterstwa, 1998

Świrszczyńska, Anna, *Budowałam barykadę*, Warszawa: Czytelnik, 1974

Szarota, Tomasz, *Okupowanej Warszawy Dzień Powszedni. Studium Historyczne*, Warszawa: Czytelnik, 1988

Tak rodziła się wolność. Wspomnienia uczestników walk o wyzwolenie Ojczyzny, ed. Czeszko, Bohdan, Dobrowolski, Stanisław R.. Warszawa: Wydawnictwo Ministerstwa Obrony Narodowej, 1954

Tarczyński, Jan, *Pojazdy Powstańców Warszawskich 1944*, Warszawa: Wydawnictwa Komunikacji i Łączności, 2009

Teka Podobizn. Prasa Powstania Warszawskiego, ed. Lewandowska, Małgorzata G., Warszawa: Biblioteka Publiczna m. st. Warszawy, 2004

Temkin-Bermanowa, Basia, *Dziennik z Podziemia*, ed. Grupińska, Anka, Szapiro, Paweł, Warszawa: Wydawnictwo Książkowe Twój Styl, Żydowski Instytut Historyczny, 2000

Toborek, Tomasz, *Edward Pfeiffer "RADWAN"*, Łódź: Instytut Pamięci Narodowej, Komisja ścigania Zbrodni przeciwko Narodowi Polskiemu, 2009

Tokarski, Stefan J., *"Wichrzyciel" z AK-owskim rodowodem*, Warszawa: Polska Oficyna Wydawnicza, 1996.

Tomaszewski, Jerzy, *Epizody Powstania Warszawskiego*, Warszawa: Krajowa Agencja Wydawnicza, 1979

Tomaszewski, Jerzy, Berus, Elżbieta, *Powstanie Warszawskie w reportażach Jerzego Tomaszewskiego*, Warszawa: Polonia, 1994

Trevor-Roper, Hugh, *The Last Days of Hitler*, London: Macmillan, 1995

Troński, Bronisław, *Tędy przeszła śmierć. Zapiski z Powstania Warszawskiego*, Warszawa: Czytelnik, 1970

Tuszyński, Witold, *Kościuszkowcy w walce o Pragę*, Warszawa: Wydawnictwo Ministerstwa Obrony Narodowej, 1953

Ujazdowska, Lidia, *Zagłada Ochoty. Zbiór relacji na temat zbrodni hitlerowskiej dokonanej na ludności Ochoty w czasie Powstania Warszawskiego*, Warszawa: Fronda, 2005

Umiński, Zdzisław, *Kanoniczki 1944*, Warszawa: Instytut Wydawniczy PAX, 1988

Uniwersalność Polskości. I: Tragizm Powstania Warszawskiego, ed. Kuczyński, Janusz, Krakowiak, Józefa K., Warszawa: Wydawnictwo Akademickie Dialog, 2006

Urbanek, Bożena, *Pielęgniarki i sanitariuszki w Powstaniu Warszawskim 1944 r.*, Warszawa: Państwowe Wydawnictwo Naukowe, 1988

Valcini, Alceo, *Golgota Warszawy 1939-1945. Wspomnienia*, Kraków: Wydawnictwo Literackie, 1973

Viatteau, Alexandra, *L'Insurrection de Varsovie la Bataille de 1944*, Paris: Presses de l'Université de Paris-Sorbonne, 2003

Voss, Johann, *Black Edelweiss. A Memoir of Combat and Conscience by a Soldier of the Waffen-SS*, Bedford, PA: The Aberjona Press, 2002

W imię czego ta ofiara. Obóz Narodowy wobec Powstania Warszawskiego, ed. Engelgard, Jan, Motas, Maciej, Warszawa: Biblioteczka Myśli Polskiej, 2009

The Waffen-SS 24 to 38 Divisions, and Volunteer Legions, ed. Williamson, Gordon, New York: Osprey Publishing, 2004

Walker, Jonathan, *Poland Alone. Britain, SOE, and the Collapse of the Polish Resistance, 1944*, Stroud: Spellmount, 2010

Warsaw Concerto. Powstanie Warszawskie w poezji, ed. Kunert, Andrzej K., Warszawa: Muzeum Powstania Warszawskiego, 2004

Warszawa. Zburzona i odbudowana, ed. Zieliński, Jarosław, Warszawa: Festina, 1997

Warszawa '44, ed. Kalinowska, Bożena, Kędryna, Marcin, Warszawa: Edipresse, Zysk i Ska, 2004

Warszawski przewodnik literacki, ed. Cieliczka, Paweł, Warszawa: Fundacja na rzecz Badań Literackich, 2005

Warszawskie Konfrontacje, ed. Budrewicz, Olgierd, Warszawa: Sport i Turystyka, 1968

Wasser, Bruno, *Himmlers Raumplanungim Osten. Der General Plan Ost in Polen 1940–1944*, Berlin: Birkhäuser Verlag, 1993

Weale, Adrian, *The SS. A New History*, London: Little, Brown, 2010

Wegner, Bernd, *The Waffen-SS. Organization, Ideology and Function*, Oxford: Basil Blackwell, 1990

Weitz, John, *Hitler's Diplomat. The Life and Times of Joachim von Ribbentrop*, New York: Ticknor & Fields, 1992

Wielka Ilustrowana Encyklopedia Powstania Warszawskieg. I: Działania zbrojne, ed. Rozwadowski, Piotr, Warszawa: Bellona, Fundacja 'Warszawa Walczy 1939–1945', 2005

Willenberg, Samuel, *Surviving Treblinka*, Oxford: Basil Blackwell, 1989

Wiśniewska, Maria, Sikora, Małgorzata, *Szpitale Powstańczej Warszawy*, Warszawa: Oficyna Wydawnicza Rytm, 1991

Wiśniewski, Wojciech, *Rzymianin z AK. Rzecz o dr Józefie Rybickim ps. „Andrzej", „Maciej"*, Warszawa: Oficyna Wydawnicza Volumen, Marabut, 2001

Witkowski, Henryk, *„KEDYW" Okręgu Warszawskiego Armii Krajowej w latach 1943–1944*, Warszawa: Instytut Wydawniczy Związków Zawodowych, 1984

Witkowscy, Henryk, Witkowscy, Ludwik, *Kedyw-iacy*, Warszawa: Instytut Wydawniczy PAX, 1973

Wohnout Wiesław, *Opowiadania Warszawskie*, Nowy Jork: Pion, 1946

Wojciechowski, Bronisław, *W Powstaniu na Mokotowie*, ed. Bartelski, Lesław M., Warszawa: Instytut Wydawniczy PAX, 1989

Wojna Wyzwoleńcza Narodu Polskiego w latach 1939-1945. Szkice i schematy, ed. Rawski, Tadeusz, Stąpor, Zdzisław, Zamojski, Jan, Warszawa: Wydawnictwo Ministerstwa Obrony Narodowej, 1966

Wojsko Polskie 1939-1945. Barwa i broń, ed. Komornicki, Stanisław, Warszawa: Interpress, 1984

Wola. Warszawskie Termopile 1944. Przewodnik historyczny po miejscach walk i straceń z dni Powstania Warszawskiego, ed. Mórawski, Karol, Warszawa: Fundacja 'Wystawa Warszawa Walczy 1939-1945', 2000

Wolfgang, Paul, *Panzer-General Walther K. Nehring. EineBiographie*, Stuttgart: Motorbuch Verlag, 2002

Wołoszyn, Włodzimierz, *Na warszawskim kierunku operacyjnym. Działania I Frontu Białoruskiego i I Armii WP 18 VII-23.IX.1944r.*, Warszawa: Wydawnictwo Ministerstwa Obrony Narodowej, 1964

A Woman in Berlin, ed. Ceram, Curt W., London: Secker & Warburg, 1955

Woźniewski, Zbigniew, *Książka raportów lekarza dyżurnego. Szpital Wolski w okresie Powstania Warszawskiego*, Warszawa: Państwowy Instytut Wydawniczy, 1974

A Writer at War. Vasily Grossman with the Red Army 1941-1945, ed. Beevor, Antony, Vinogradova, Luba, London: Random House, 2005

Wróblewski, Zbigniew, *Pod komendą „Gozdawy" 1 VIII-4 X 1944*, Warszawa: Instytut Wydawniczy Związków Zawodowych, 1989

Wroniszewski, Józef K., *Ochota 1939-1945*, Warszawa: Wydawnictwo Ministerstwa Obrony Narodowej, 1976

Wroniszewski, Józef K., *Ochota 1944*, Warszawa: Wydawnictwo Ministerstwa Obrony Narodowej, 1970

Wyganowska-Eriksson, Anna, *Pluton pancerny w Powstaniu Warszawskim*, Warszawa: First Business College, 1994

Wypędzeni z Warszawy 1944-losy dzieci, ed. Bartoszewski, Władysław, Warszawa: Muzeum Historyczne m.st. Warszawy, 2004

Wysokiński, Eugeniusz, *Wyzwolenie Warszawy*, Warszawa: Wydawnictwo Ministerstwa Obrony Narodowej, 1955

Yelton, David K., *Hitler's Volkssturm. The Nazi Militia and the Fall of Germany,* *1944–1945*, Kansas: University Press of Kansas, 2002

Z powstańczych przeżyć 1944 roku, ed. Baranowska, Konstantyna. Ledóchowska, Teresa, Hoffman, Teodozja, Lublin: Redakcja Wydawnictw Katolickiego Uniwersytetu Lubelskiego, 1994

Zabłocki, Jerzy, *„Jerzyki" z „Miotłą" w tarczy,* Warszawa: Efekt, 1944

Zaborski, Zdzisław, *Tędy przeszła Warszawa. Epilog Powstania Warszawskiego.* *Pruszków Durchgangslager 121 6VIII–10X 1944,* Warszawa: Askon, 2004

Zagórski, Wacław, *Wicher wolności,* Londyn: Nakładem Czytelników-Przedpłacicieli, 1957

Załęski, Grzegorz, *Satyra w konspiracji 1939–1944,* Warszawa: Wydawnictwo Ministerstwa Obrony Narodowej, 1958

Zarzycki, Tadeusz, *Pierwszy i ostatni dzień,* Londyn: Veritas Foundation, 1974

Zawodny, Janusz K., *Nothing but Honour. The Story of the Warsaw Uprising,* *1944,* London: Macmillan, 1978

Zawodny, Janusz K., *Uczestnicy i świadkowie Powstania Warszawskiego.* *Wywiady,* Warszawa: Instytut Pamięci Narodowej, 2004

Zayas, Alfred-Maurice de, *The Wehrmacht War Crimes Bureau, 1939–1945,* London: University of Nebraska Press, 1989

Zbrodnia niemiecka w Warszawie 1944 R., ed. Serwanski, Edward, Trawińska, Irena, Poznań, Wydawnictwo Instytutu Zachodniego, 1946

Żenczykowski, Tadeusz, *Samotny bój Warszawy,* Dziekanów Leśny: LTW, 2005

Zhukov, Georgii Konstantinovich, *The Memoirs of Marshal Zhukov,* London: Jonathan Cape, 1971

Żołnierz, Poeta, Czasu kurz . . . Wspomnienia o Krzysztofie Kamilu Baczyńskim, ed. Wasilewski, Zbigniew, Kraków: Wydawnictwo Literackie, 1970

Zürn–Zahorski, Zbigniew, *Pseudonim „Jacek",* Bydgoszcz: Instytut Wydawniczy Świadectwo, 1993

Żwirska, Joanna, *Ogień i druty. Wspomnienia z powstania i obozu kobiet–jeńców* *wojennych,* Warszawa: Iskry, 1958

Życie w Powstańczej Warszawie. Sierpień-Wrzesień 1944. Relacje-dokumenty, ed. Serwański, Edward, Warszawa: Instytut Wydawniczy PAX, 1965

Żydzi w Walce. I: Opór i walka z Faszyzmem w latach 1939–1945, ed. Diatłowicki, Jerzy, Warszawa: Stowarzyszenie Żydów Kombatantów i Poszkodowanych w II Wojnie Światowej, 2009

Select Press Sources

Bończa-Szabłowski, Jan, 'Moja samotność jest wybredna'; interview with Jerzy Ficowski, *Rzeczpospolita*, 4 August 2004 p. 13

Bugajski, Ryszard, 'List. Ryszard Bugajski do Marii Fieldorf-Czarskiej', *Nasz Dziennik*, 24 April 2009, p 2

Ciechanowski, Jan M., 'Nie tylko głupota, ale zbrodnia. Generał Władysław Anders a Powstanie Warszawskie', *Przegląd*, 2 August 2010, pp. 16–21

Ciechanowski, Jan M., 'Zryw przed Burzą', *Polityka*, 31 July 2004, p. 60

Daszczyński, Roman, 'Powstanie nie powinno było wybuchnąć' [interview with Jan Ciechanowski], *Gazeta Wyborcza*, 31 July 2009, pp. 18–19

Dryszel, Andrzej, 'Masakra Woli', *Przegląd*, 7 August 2011, p. 12

Edelman, Marek, 'Warszawskie Dzieci', *Metro*, 1 August 2004, p. 10

Fried, Nico, 'Schröder gedenkt in Warscau des Aufstands vor 60 Jahren. "Versohnung mit Polen wirkt wie ein Wunder" ', *Süddeutsche Zeitung*, 2 August 2004, p. 1

Gańczak, Filip, 'Legiony hańby', *Newsweek* , 2 August 2009, pp. 18–19

Gil, Radosław, 'Czas fantastycznej wolności', *Rzeczpospolita*, 2 August 2004, p. 5

Heffer, Simon, 'It's Time to Move On. Britain has no Reason to Apologise to Poland', *Spectator*, 7 August 2004, p. 16

Kalicki, Włodzimierz, 'Bor-Komorowski. Skok w przepaść', *Gazeta Wyborcza*, 3 September 2009, pp 16–17

Kalicki, Włodzimierz, 'Byliśmy żołnierzami', *Gazeta Wyborcza*, 1 August 2007, p. 2

Kalicki, Włodzimierz, 'Ten cholerny zachód' [interview with Norman Davies], *Gazeta Wyborcza*, 26 July 2004, pp. 2–7

Krasnodębski, Zdzisław, 'Powstanie bez bożej gwarancji', *Plus Minus*, 10–11 January 2009, pp. 18–20

Leszczyński, Adam, 'Jak można było żyć poza gettem', *Gazeta Wyborcza*, 26 June 2009, p. 1

Leszczyński, Adam, 'Obalam uprzedzenia Polskie i Żydowskie' [interview with Gunnar S. Paulsson], *Gazeta Wyborcza*, 26 June 2009, p. 22

Majewski, Jerzy S., 'Spalony rękopis słownika', *Gazeta Wyborcza*, 24 April 2009, p. 12

Majewski, Jerzy S., 'Stolarze i patrioci', *Gazeta Wyborcza*, 28 May 2010, p. 13

Nowak, Włodzimierz, Kuźniak, Angelika, 'Mój Warszawski Szał', *Gazeta Wyborcza*, 23 August 2004, pp. 4–7

Osęka, Piotr, '*Zabawa pod barykadą*', *Przekrój*, 1 August 2004, p. 64

Rolińska, Joanna, 'Czułem radość, że mogłem walczyc'; interview with Stanisław Krupa, *Dziennik*, 19 August 2007, p. 4

Rzeczpospolita, 29–30 May 2004, no. 1

St Oswald, Lord, 'Former Polish Allies in Great Britain', House of Lords, Thursday, 27 October 1966, Her Majesty's Stationery Office, St Stephen's Parliamentary Press

Schroder, Christa, 'What Hitler's Secretary Saw', *The Week*, 9 May 2009, pp. 44–5

Sroczyński, Grzegorz, 'Boję się wymówić słowo „bezsens" ', *Gazeta Wyborcza*, 2 August 2011, p. 2

Stach, Andrzej, 'Romantyczni straceńcy. Powstanie Warszawskie w świadomości Niemców', *Rzeczpospolita*, 30 July 2004, p. 6

Stempin, Arkadiusz, 'Szczerość oficera', *Newsweek*, 2 August 2009, pp. 16–17

Stölten, Peter, 'Walczyli, na Boga lepiej niż my', *Newsweek*, 2 August 2009, pp. 12–15

Torańska, Teresa, 'Hamlecik' [interview with Peter P. Lachmann], *Gazeta Wyborcza*, 31 August 2004, pp. 6–9

Urzykowski, Tomasz, 'Były tam tłumy wesołe' [interview with Tomasz Szarota], *Gazeta Wyborcza*, 24 April 2009, p. 8

Urzykowski, Tomasz, 'Dzień 11 sierpnia 1944 r.' [interview with Stanisław Sieradzki], *Gazeta Wyborcza*, 20 February 2009, p. 10

Das Vorfeld, 1942, nos. 5/6

Wieliński, Bartosz T., 'Biała i czerwona spięte agrafką', *Gazeta Wyborcza*, 7 May 2010, pp. 18–19

Wieliński, Bartosz T., 'Starzy przyjaciele i młodzi awanturnicy' [interview with Władysław Bartoszewski], *Gazeta Wyborcza*, 13 August 2009, pp. 14–15

Wodecka, Dorota, 'Kiedy życie się liczy na dni', *Gazeta Wyborcza*, 31 July 2009, pp. 16–17

Wróbel, Jan, 'Nie próbujmy wygrać Powstania po 63 latach', *Dziennik*, 1 August 2007, p. 16

Wroński, Paweł, 'Fortepian Schoppinga' [interview with Andrzej Chwalba], *Gazeta Wyborcza*, 13 May 2010, pp. 9–11

Wronski, Pawel, 'Monter wraca', *Gazeta Wyborcza*, 28 July 2004, p. 2

Contemporary Underground Publications

The following is a selection of titles from the author's collection of underground newspapers, handbills and other documents written, printed and distributed in different districts of Warsaw between 1 August and 5 October 1944. Some consist of just a sheet or two of typed and copied information about urgent local matters such as the collection of water; others are well-produced newspapers of several pages, and include general news about the war in addition to specific information about life in the city. The names of the writers were not given, for obvious reasons of secrecy.

Barykada (City Centre)
Barykada Powiśla (Powiśle)
Barykada Wolności
Biuletyn Informacyjny
Biuletyn Podokręgu Nr. 2 (Żoliborz)
Czerniaków w Walce (Czerniaków)
Dzień Warszawy
Dziennik Radowy (Żoliborz)
Głos Demokracji
Głos Starego Miasta (Old Town)
Kobieta na Barykadzie
Komunikat Informacyjny (Mokotow)
Kronika Polska (Old Town)
Nowiny Żoliborskie (Żoliborz)
Nowy Dzień (City Centre)
Nowy Świat (City Centre – Northern Sector)
Robotnik
Rzeczpospolita Polska
Sprawa
Syndykalista
W walce (Old Town)
Warszawa Walczy! (Wola)
Wolsko Polskie (City Centre)
Z pierwszej linii frontu... (City Centre – Northern Sector)

Pamphlets

Broniewski, Stanisław, 'Szare Szeregi', Oficyna Księgarska, Warsaw, 1947
Komitet Redakcyjny, 'Posterunek na Czerniakowskieje', Wydawnictwo Pamiątkowe, Warsaw, 3 October 1947
Lityński, Zygmunt, *Warsaw, A Warning* London, 25 August 1944
Nagórski Jr, Z., 'Warsaw Fights Alone. Warsaw Needs Your Help NOW', London, 1 September 1944
Noel-Baker, P.J., (Foreword), 'Underground Poland Speaks', Victoria House, London, August 1941
Nowak, Jan, '63 Days', Speech delivered at Caxton Hall to the British League for European Freedom, 16 February 1945
Parker, John, MP (Forward), 'Democratic Poland Answers', Polish Brains Trust 22 January 1944
Polish Labour Group, 'Poland Fights' New York, November 1945
'Wir und die Polen', Sonderausgabe des Führerdienstes Gebiet Wartheland (38), Posen, 1943

Selected Newspaper Articles

Christoph Frhr. V. Imhoff, *Warschauer Totentanz. Das Trümmerfeld der 120 Quadratkilometer, Das Reich* 26 November 1944
Hermann Albrecht, *Die Zweite Kapitulation. Politische Randbemerkungen zu Warschau* 15 October 1944
Völkischer Beobachter:
Ein satanisches Spiel. London und Moskau hetzten Warschau zum Aufstand auf und liessen es im Stich 18 August 1944
Der Aufstand in Warschau. Heer, Waffen-SS und Ostsoldaten bekämpfen die Erhebung der 'unterirdischen Polen' 19 August 1944
Nachspiel zu Warschau. Zynische Erklarungen in Moskau und London, 22 August 1944
Neue Hilfeschrei der Warschauer Untergrundbewegung 23 August 1944
Warschau bereitet Roosevelt Wahlsorgen 25 August 1944
Dr. Th. B. *Moskau verhaftet Aufstandspolen. Der bolschewistische 'Befreiungsausschuss' tritt gegenüber London und Washington schon als Regierung auf* 1 September 1944

Moskau lässt nicht mit sich diskutieren. So wurden die Warschau-Polen im Stich gelassen 5 September 1944

Londoner 'Spectator' stellt fest: 'Warschaus Schicksal eroffnet dunkle Aussichten für die Zukunft' 6 September 1944

Das Drama von Warschau. Furchtbarer Leidensweg der Zivilbevölkerung der ehemaligen polnischen Hauptstadt 8 September 1944

Stalin verbot englische Hilfer für Warschau 13 September 1944

General Bór: 'Die Sowjets gefährliche Länderräuber'. Der Warschauer Aufständischenführer wusste Bescheid 23 September 1944

Warschau – Symbol und Warnung 4 October 1944

Die Kapitulation der Warschau-Polen 6 October 1944

Krejci: Hacha wählte den richtigen Weg (article in which Dr Krejci of the Protectorate says: 'We have learned from the fate of Poland. We do not want Prague to share Warsaw's fate.') 3 November 1944

Himmler beim 'Tag der Freiheit' in Posen: Die Grenzmark wird das Reich schützen. Generaloberst Guderian: Neue schwere und gute Waffen unzahlreiche Armeen 7 November 1944

715

Index